PEOPLE OF INDIA

JAMMU & KASHMIR

VOLUME XXV

PEOPLE OF INDIA

NATIONAL SERIES

VOL. I.	PEOPLE OF INDIA	AN INTRODUCTION
VOL. II	PEOPLE OF INDIA	THE SCHEDULED CASTES
VOL. III	PEOPLE OF INDIA	THE SCHEDULED TRIBES
VOL. IV	PEOPLE OF INDIA	INDIA'S COMMUNITIES (A-G)
VOL. V	PEOPLE OF INDIA	INDIA'S COMMUNITIES (H-M)
VOL. VI	PEOPLE OF INDIA	INDIA'S COMMUNITIES (N-Z)
VOL. VII	PEOPLE OF INDIA	IDENTITY, ECOLOGY, SOCIAL ORGANIZATION, ECONOMY, DEVELOPMENT, PROCESS AND LINKAGES: A QUANTITATIVE PROFILE
VOL. VIII	PEOPLE OF INDIA	COMMUNITIES, SEGMENTS, SYNONYMS SURNAMES AND TITLES
VOL. IX	PEOPLE OF INDA	LANGUAGES AND SCRIPTS
VOL. X	PEOPLE OF INDIA	THE BIOLOGICAL VARIATION IN INDIAN POPULATIONS
VOL. XI	PEOPLE OF INDIA	AN ANTHROPOLOGICAL ATLAS

STATE SERIES

VOL. XII	ANDAMAN AND NICOBAR ISLANDS
VOL. XIII	ANDHRA PRADESH
VOL. XIV	ARUNACHAL PRADESH
VOL. XV	ASSAM
VOL. XVI	BIHAR
VOL. XVII	CHANDIGARH
VOL. XVIII	DADRA AND NAGAR HAVELI
VOL. XIX	DAMAN AND DIU
VOL. XX	DELHI
VOL. XXI	GOA
VOL. XXII	GUJARAT
VOL. XXIII	HARYANA
VOL. XXIV	HIMACHAL PRADESH
VOL. XXV	JAMMU AND KASHMIR
VOL. XXVI	KARNATAKA
VOL. XXVII	KERALA
VOL. XXVIII	LAKSHADWEEP
VOL. XXIX	MADHYA PRADESH
VOL. XXX	MAHARASHTRA
VOL. XXXI	MANIPUR
VOL. XXXII	MEGHALAYA
VOL. XXXIII	MIZORAM
VOL. XXXIV	NAGALAND
VOL. XXXV	ORISSA
VOL. XXXVI	PONDICHERRY
VOL. XXXVII	PUNJAB
VOL. XXXVIII	RAJASTHAN
VOL. XXXIX	SIKKIM
VOL. XL	TAMIL NADU
VOL. XLI	TRIPURA
VOL. XLII	UTTAR PRADESH
VOL. XLIII	WEST BENGAL

PEOPLE OF INDIA

JAMMU & KASHMIR

VOLUME XXV

General Editor
K.S. SINGH

Editors
K.N. PANDITA
S.D.S. CHARAK
B.R. RIZVI

ANTHROPOLOGICAL SURVEY OF INDIA

MANOHAR
2003

ISBN 81-7304-118-0

Published on behalf of ASI by Ajay Kumar Jain
Manohar Publishers & Distributors, 4753/23 Ansari Road, Daryaganj, New Delhi-110 002

Typeset by AJ Software Publishing Co. Pvt. Ltd, New Delhi-110 005

Printed at Lordson Publishers Pvt. Ltd., Delhi-110007

CONTENTS

ILLUSTRATIONS

A NOTE ON THE SERIES

There exists an information gap on a very large number of communities in India, and whatever information exists on them is scanty or needs to be updated. The Anthropological Survey of India (ASI) launched a project on the People of India on 2 October 1985. The objective of the project was to generate a brief, descriptive anthropological profile of all the communities of India, the impact on them of change and development processes and the links that bring them together. This was in accordance with the objectives of the ASI, established forty-five years ago in December 1945. The ASI has been pursuing bio-cultural research among different population groups from its eight regional centres. Its objectives have been redefined in the policy resolution, adopted in 1985, which commits this organization to the survey of the human surface of India.

The identification of the communities and their listing have had a long history which started from the early period of our history, with Manu. Regional lists of communities figured in Sanskrit works. Medieval chronicles contained a description of communities located in various parts of the country. Listings in the colonial period were undertaken on an extensive scale after 1806. The process gathered momentum in course of the censuses from 1881 to 1941. In our compilation of the lists of the communities of India under the People of India project, we drew upon ethnographic surveys, the lists of Scheduled Castes and Scheduled Tribes drawn up by the Government of India, the lists of backward classes prepared by Backward Classes Commissions set up by various state governments, and the list that exists in the Mandal Commission Report. We were able to put together about 6,748 communities at the start. This list was taken to the field, tested and checked, and finally 4,635 communities were identified and studied.

Unlike surveys in the colonial period, which covered British India and a few princely states, our project covers the whole country, bringing within its ambit such areas that had not been ethnographically surveyed earlier or where the survey had been done in a perfunctory manner. Each state and union territory was treated as a unit of study. It was decided to start with the investigation of the least known communities, and then move on to a field study of the lesser-known and better-known ones. Investigators for the survey were identified for each area on the basis of their experience and expertise. Teams of investigators of the Survey, as well as local scholars, were set up for each state and union territory to plan the surveys, seek the co-operation of local scholars, generate and evaluate findings, etc. Later, editorial boards consisting of local scholars—one or more of these were nominated as co-editors for each local volume—were set up for each state and union territory. We sought the cooperation of the state governments in implementing the project, and this we received in ample measure, particularly from the welfare and backward classes departments of the state governments, local officers of the Census of India, tribal research institutes, university departments of anthropology, other departments of local universities, etc. Local scholars participated enthusiastically in our project as well as in the seminars held by us.

The progress in the investigation and coverage of communities from 2 October 1985 to 31 March 1992 was steady and impressive. We were able to identify, locate and study 4,635 communities in all the states and union territories of India, out of the 6,748 listed initially. As many as 600 scholars participated in this project, including 197 from 26 institutions. About 100 workshops and rounds of discussions were held in all the states and union territories, and in these about 3,000 scholars participated. The investigators spent 26,510 days in the field, which works out to 5.5 days per community studied in the various states and Union Territories of India. Our scholars interviewed a large number of people, out of whom we have recorded only the key informants, i.e. 24,951. This works out to about 5 'informed' informants per community. Of the informants, 4981 were women. Our instruction to the investigators was to study a community at two or three places, and in at least two or three cultural regions into which the larger states of India ware divided. Interviews were conducted in connection with the study of the communities in 3,581 villages, mostly multi-community villages, and in 1,011 towns and cities spread over almost all the districts of India, i.e. 421 districts and 91 cultural regions. We were able, thus, to study on an average a community at about two places. It should be noted that most of the smaller communities could be studied at only one place since they are not located in more than one area.

A major achievement of this project was the preparation of

cartographic maps showing the distribution of the communities and the location where they were studied. About 4,000 maps were prepared. Yet another achievement was the visual documentation of the people of India as part of the field operations. About 21,362 photographs were generated, most of them in black & white, and a substantial number in colour, by amateur photographers.

An early stage of our project in March 1985 we decided to transfer the data to a computer. We were subsequently able to develop probably the first software in the country—and one of the first in the world—in ethnography, in close collaboration with the National Informatics Centre. From 28 May 1988 we started transferring the quantitative data collected in computer format to floppies. Simultaneously, the transfer of descriptive data (abstracts, etc.) on to the computer also started at almost all the regional centres. We succeeded in computerizing an enormous mass of data, and also in producing the first results of univariate analysis, by March 1990.

The descriptive material, running into 120 manuscript volumes, and the quantitative data contained in 157 diskettes, were released on 1 October 1990 by Sri Chimanbhai Mehta, Minister of State for Human Resource Development, in the presence of a distinguished audience in Delhi, for use by scholars at the Nehru Memorial Museum & Library, and at eight regional centres of the ASI.

The phase of more elaborate analysis started in July 1991, in collaboration with the Centre for Ecological Sciences, Indian Institute of Science, Bangalore. This resulted in a voluminous output of analysed data, which have been presented in a comprehensive matrix consisting of the four categories of populations, the constitutional, religious, occupational and locational. These sets of data, together with a map, were released by Shri Arjun Singh, Minister of Human Resource Development, on 24 December 1991. The last workshop on the People of India project was held at the Indian Institute of Social and Economic Change in Bangalore, where the preliminary results of the analysis presented by the ASI were discussed by distinguished scholars.

It should be noted that the study of communities has been conducted in 3,581 villages and 1,011 towns situated in 421 districts of the states and union territories of India. The information was collected from about 25,000 of the 'learned' informants by our scholars, 500 of them, over the period 1985 to 1992.

Therefore, the observations relate to this limited time frame and to the universe of the ethnographic project titled People of India. The percentages relate strictly to the responses made by the informants to the questionnaire contained in the schedule guideline and computer format, and to the queries made by the investigators at the places of investigation. The responses have been supplemented with the observations of the investigators, the secondary material has been checked and cross-checked at many levels with other sources of information by scholars, particularly local scholars.

We are presenting the material published under the People of India project in two parts which are interrelated. The first consists of the ten-volume national series, five of which contain an abstract on all communities across the length and breadth of the country. The data generated in this respect has been strengthened by the addition of information from census and other secondary sources. These volume include two on the Scheduled Castes and Scheduled Tribes, prepared as part of the celebration of Dr. B.R. Ambedkar's birth centenary; three on all the communities of India, and two containing data on the languages and biological structures of Indian population. The remaining volumes contain description of the quantitative profile, communities and their segments, community-specific languages and the biological structure of Indian populations.

The second part comprises the state/union territory volumes based on a detailed write-up on each community of India. The contributors of the national volumes on the SC, ST and all communities are listed in the last volume, Volume VI. The Glossary given in Volume VI is common to all the national volumes. At the end of each account we have given references to the texts from which we have quoted, or references for further reading. This is only illustrative. An exhaustive bibliography appears at the end of the national volumes, in Volume VI.

Oxford University Press are publishing the national volumes. A consortium of publishers has been set up to publish the material on states and union territories. Seven volumes each for the northern states, southern states and the islands, the central and western states are being published respectively by M/s Manohar Publishers & Distributors (New Delhi), M/s Affiliated East-West Press Private Limited (Madras) and M/s Popular Prakashan Pvt. Ltd. (Bombay). The eleven volumes on the north-eastern and eastern states are being published by M/s Seagull Books Private Limited

(Calcutta), which has already published the introductoıy national volume. This is bring republished as a revised edition by Oxford University Press.

I trust the series on the People of India, which is based on a comprehensive anthropological survey of the country, will be found useful by all sections of our people, including students, researchers, teachers, social activists, administrators and political leaders. I hope we have laid the groundwork for a more comprehensive ethnography of the people of India which needs to be continually updated and built upon by successive generations of researchers and scholars.

K.S. SINGH

FOREWORD

> Learning, lofty houses, saffron, icy water and grapes. Things that even in heaven are difficult to find are common here.
>
> KALHANA, *Rajatarangini*

> Shiva abides in all that is, everywhere / Then do not discriminate between a Hindu and a Musalman./ If thou art wise, know thyself / That is true knowledge of the Lord.
>
> Lal Ded, JAYALAL KAUL, *Lal Ded*, 1973

> Mohammad—radiates light all around / Pujari lost his wits / while offering flowers/Iswara showered rain/Come, let us blow the sankh around Sankara/ Mohammad—radiates light all around.
>
> A Sufi poet, Ahad Zarger, cited in Riyaz Punjabi, 1990

The state of Jammu & Kashmir described as the crown of India emerged in three phases as highlighted by Dogra histriography. The nucleus was provided by the Jammu raj established by the Dogras in the tenth century which alongside the main kingdom mushroomed into lineage based petty estates. As the Dogra chief wanted to control the trade in *pashmina*, he annexed Ladakh—and then Baltistan—by conquest in 1834-41, surrounding the Valley. Last of all, the Valley of Kashmir was added to the kingdom. Under the treaty signed at Amritsar on 16 March 1846, Kashmir was given to the Dogra chief. Thus the princely state of Kashmir as popularly called came into existence, which consisted of the five distinct regions defined by language, culture, ecology, religion and ethos. The Dogra rulers who called themselves the rulers of the kingdom named 'Jammu and Kashmir and Tibet etc.' maintained the autonomy of each region by granting them freedom in cultural and religious matters. After Independence, the Indian state of Jammu and Kashmir emerged which was left with the former three regions, the Valley, Jammu and Ladakh. Jammu & Kashmir remains the most diverse region of the country. The two other regions, went to Pakistan where they are now known as Azad Kashmir and the Northern Territory (Gilgit-Baltistan). However, throughout history, the Kashmir Valley was the most important of these territories. It was the pivot, the centre of civilization, culture, power, politics and movements which influenced and was influenced by developments, migration, trade and politics in adjoining regions.

Kashmiri is one of the few regions in the country with an identity and autonomy of its own crafted by a long and uninterrupted tradition of scholarship in Sanskrit and Persian which produced a plethora of literature on various subjects. The Kashmiris wrote about their kings, rulers and queens with all their eccentricities, nobility and perversity, and about themselves. However, no systematic ethnographic survey of the state as it exists to day was undertaken in the colonial period under the aegis of the ethnographic survey in British India and like in some princely states of the south. A thin ethnography existed in the *Provincial Gazetteer of Jammu and Kashmir* territories written by W.R. Lawrence in 1875. He mentions female infanticide, *sati* and hypergamy across the Rajputs and other castes. The traders and merchants from Kashmir and Central Asia and Dogra soldiers married local Ladakhi women and bred Arghun and *ghulamzadas*, that is, slave born, respectively.

There were ethnographic materials in Persian compiled during the nineteenth and twentieth centuries. A comprehensive ethnography in Urdu was compiled in 1930 by Muhammad Din Fouq, *Tarikh-i-Aqwam-i-Kashmir* (Lahore, 1934) but it was not available to us in print or in translation.

The Anthropological Survey of India under the People of India project undertook the first ever ethnographic survey of the communities of this state in collaboration with local scholars and local institutions during the period 1985-9, before disturbances in the Valley occurred.

Kashmir was the abode of the Naga people who according to myth had sought refuge against Garud, their step brother and enemy. Their father Prajapati Kashyap and his wife Kadru, the daughter of Daksa, fathered not only the Nagas but also the Devas, Daityas, Khasas and Bhadras, etc. Kashmir swarmed with the Naga lineages, the important ones being, Takshak (from which Takshila has been derived), Kashyapa and Korkota.

Kashmir was a major seat of Naga cult associated with the historical Nagas who gave it identity. According to the latest researches being conducted all over South-East Asia the Nagas lived off water. Close relationship of the Nagas with water resources in the Kashmir Valley is suggested by the name *naga*, a common name for the Naga people, serpent and water springs. The original Naga myth about the reclamation of Kashmir Valley deserves to be re-examined. It seems that Nagas had two branches, the earlier one represented by Jalodbhava who lived in the lake. The water demon Jalodbhava probably represented the early wave of Nagas who developed differences with the Nagas who came in later, ready to reclaim land from water in order to switch over to agriculture. This transition from water to land or fishing to agriculture was mediated by Balaram, a Naga himself who carried his plough as a weapon. Invited by Kashyap to drain the water of the lake Satisar, Balaram bored a hole with his plough through Varahmullah (Baramulla) hill. The geologists tell us that some 80,000 years ago due to tectonic developments the water from the lake did drain out from a gorge in Varahmullah (Arun Kaul, 2002). The lake was transformed into land for agriculture. The stage was set for the neolithic revolution later, as suggested by Burzahom rock art site. This completed the transition of the Nagas from a water based people to agriculture, the beginning of settlement and the rise of Kashmir as a kingdom. The Nagas were thus associated with all major events in myth and history, the draining of Satisar lake, the birth of Vetasta (Jhelum), the cultivation of *kesar*, the worship of Naga deities, from Nagar in Gilgit to the Valley, Buddhism and Nagarjuna.

There are many versions of the etymology of Kashmir. It seems to derive from its ecology, the mythical reclamation from a lake of the river basin that today forms the Kashmir Valley (*ka*-water, *shimir*, reclamation, Ved Kumari, *Nilamata Purana*, vol. 1, p. 22). A semitic tribe, Kash is said to have founded the cities of Kash, Kashan and Kashgar. Local people call their land 'Kasheer' not Kashmir. The Himalayan tribe Khasa inhabited south-west Kashmir in the ancient period but now there are no Khasas as such in Kashmir which are distributed along the lower reaches of the Himalayas in Himachal Pradesh, Uttaranchal and Nepal. However the first historian, Herodotus identified Kashmir with Kashyap Muni; Kashyap *mir* is the mountain of Kashyap. According to another version Kashmir is derived from Kashyap *mar*, the abode of Kashyap. It seems that the draining of water of the lake by Balaram invited by Kashyap was considered such a great feat that it identified Kashyap with the reclaimed territory.

After draining came the settlement of peoples. The *Nilamata Purana* composed by the King Nil in the sixth-seventh centuries AD discusses this process and describes the Naga lineages, about three hundred of them who lived in Kashmir and adjoining territories of Darva (Dard territory), etc. Kashyap is said to have invited Pishachas, Manavas, Darvas (or Dardas), Abhisaras, Gandharas, etc. The Dardic people probably represented the earliest wave of speakers of the Dardric language group which is said to be anterior to later Indo-Iranian and Indo-Aryan language families. The Pishachas were probably sheep herders who introduced mutton-eating or cattle breeders who outnumbered other groups (Riyaz Punjabi, 1990). There were conflicts between Pishachas and Manavas who were favoured by the Nagas. A group of Nagas was expelled from the Valley, who set up a Naga kingdom in the new territory Jammu. The *Nilamata Purana* described 14 communities, the most important of them being Nagas and some occupational groups such as Aurabhrikas (shepherds), Mallas (wrestler), etc.

Kalhana describes Kashmir not only as a seat of Nagas ruling lineages but also a place guided by great Naga spirits such as Nilnaga, Sankhnaga and Padmanaga. Sheshnag is spring of life. Kalhana describes the annual festival held in honour of the great Nagraja Takshaka on the twelfth day the waining moon of *Jyeshtha* and Kashmiri Pandits continue with the remeberence and worship of snakes, observation of many practices mentioned in the ancient texts including *Nilamata Purana*, such as *khechri amyabas* (offering *khechri* to Yaksha), *vyth-e-truvih*, i.e. floating down earthen lamps in the river Vitasta (Jhelam) and worship of Naga deities (Riyaz Punjabi, 1990). A part of the Naga heritage of Kashmir as mentioned above also merged with Mahayan Buddhism which flowered in the Valley, a Kashmiri version of Buddhism.

The earliest reference to Kashmir, occurs in Panini and the *Mahabharat* which also refers to Kashmirah as a people. The *Mahabharat* mentioned Kashmirah as a distinct community along with Dard, Khasa, Pisacha, etc.

Kalhana's *Rajatarangini* deals with a larger number of communities and describes Kashmir as a multiethnic land. In fact, *Rajatarangini* and other sources suggest that the population of Kashmir in the ancient times was heterogenous; it is more so today. Thus there are references to the Mlechhas (Huna), Vankala Pamaras, a land owning community, Tantrins, Ekangas, Dar or Dangar, Lavanyas or Lon. Kalhana mentions Mlechhas and Magas in the reign of Ashoka and his son Jaluka. Another tribe Khasa is also mentioned at this juncture and they find frequent mention in Kashmir chronicle after this date. It was a powerful tribe which frequently interfered in the Kashmir politics. A section of this tribe inhabiting the Valley of Jhelum down to Kishan Ganga were converted to Islam and afterwards came to be called Khakha. Another tribe Vankala is mentioned during the early ninth century events but nothing is known about this community. However, evolution of a new community of Damaras into an important landowning and warlike community of Kashmir Valley presents an interesting phenomenon. The Damaras exalted their status by marrying their daughters in the royal family. Kalhana says that the Damaras are more like cultivators, though they carry arms. The Damaras seem to have arisen from local population. Nothing much is known about Tantrins and Ekangas. They are usually held to be local communities which came into prominence during the eleventh and twelfth centuries. Tantrins embraced Islam and their survivors are still known by the *kram* 'Tantre'. Ekangas have disappeared. The Lavanyas were another community of political influence in Kashmir in the early middle centuries and the community, survives with the modern *kram* name Lon. The name Magre seems to have been derived from the Sanskrit word '*mirgasa*', meaning the 'lord of the gate or pass'. There were the chiefs who guarded the paths or passes (gates) letting into the Valley. The term became applicable to the offspring of the Margesas and it acquired the commonly spoken from of Magra. Similarly, 'Raina' seems to be a corrupt form of 'Rajanaka', a chief, a petty local leader who in the hills of Jammu and Kangra is known as 'Rana' (personal communication from Charak).

The Introduction mentions the pre-Islamic social hierarchy in *Rajatarangini* with Brahmans at the top, Rajputra (Tantrins, Ekangas, and Lavanaya) in the second place followed by Domara (landed aristocracy), Kayastha, Shudra, Nishad, tribal groups such as Khasa (Khakha), Bomba, Dard, Bhatta, Kirat and others. It is interesting to note that the Rajputs in the north-west which are later mentioned probably included not only the ruling elite (Mian) but also soldiers, the cavalry, the cultivators, the labour and the workers who generally are placed at the bottom. In fact even today Rajput and Brahmans were divided into two groups, viz., *swaran* or superior, unsoiled by soil, and the *hal-bah* or 'plough-drivers'. The original function of Brahman is learning, knowledge of scriptures and performance of religious rites. For them other professions were considered inferior and those who took to them, lost superior status and became relegated in rank in their own community and in estimation of other communities. In the hills, more especially those of Himachal Brahmans have taken to shopkeeping and petty local trade. They are usually called *shah*; and are considered of inferior status. However, those poor Brahmans who have taken to the plough, and till their own land, have been considered the lowest in Brahman communities so that the upper class Brahmans do not enter into any matrimonial alliance and formally did not share *pangat* with them.

Kashmir emerged early in history as one of the important centres of Indian culture and civilization, of interaction of streams of heterodoxy and orthodoxy, of extraordinary creativity in spirituality, philosophy and crafts. Kashmir was the subcontinent's window on Persia and Central Asia, which absorbed influences from all over the subcontinent, the Central Asian regions and Western Asia. The immigrants were assimilated into Kashmir society. In the early medieval period Kashmir became a haven and refuge for the communities such as traders, artisans, mercenaries, *sufis* and others coming from Central Asia. They facilitated the acceptance of Muslim rule, brought in the technology of carpet weaving, *shawl* embroidery, wood-carving, etc. In the wake of Mongol invasions the pace of migration went up. During the rule of the sultans of Kashmir in the Valley new warrior communities come to the forefront, some of which were indigenous, while others came from outside and made Kashmir their home. Among these may be counted Saiyid, Dar, Magre, Chak, Raina who attained eminence in the fourteenth and fifteenth centuries. Later the Mughal and Pathan communities who came from outside Kashmir, settled in the Valley. In the fourteenth-eighteenth centuries, the Chaks and Rainas were prominent. The Chaks were a powerful, turbulent and ruthless people and finally the Chak chiefs succeeded in establishing the last Kashmiri dynasty which was overthrown by Akbar. The last ruler lies buried at Kashmir Chak in Bihar alongside the grave of Habiba (could it be the legendary Habba Khatun, the beloved wife of last Chak ruler Yusuf Shah Chak?). Afterwards Chaks merged with the rural agricultural population. The Kashmiris consider the 400 years of the Mughal, Afghan, Sikh and Dogra rules in the Valley as the rule by the aliens.

It appears that the advent of Islam in its early phases was a peaceful affair. For example, Sanskrit continued as the official language till the reign of Zainul Abedin (1420-70) who replaced Kashmiri and Prakrit with Persian. His father Sultan Sikandar (1389-1413), called *butshikan* (breaker of idols) desecrated temples, converted Hindus to Islam and forced all Brahmans except 11 families to leave the Valley. A later day apologia says that the large scale destruction of temples and desceration of images was abetted by a Hindu convert Suha Bhatta and there was evidence that a Shiva temple with the golden *linga* was constructed by the sultan's Hindu wife (Ishaq Khan, 1997, p. 80). His son Zainul Abedin set a remarkable example of tolerance by not only allowing the Brahmans to return to the Valley but also to reconvert even though reconversion was not permitted by Hinduism then or later, on any significant scale. He repaired temples and restored religious rights, abolished the poll tax, got translated the Sanskrit classics into Persian and vice-a-verca. He carried forward the public works started by *rishis*, and introduced the art of the weaving and papier mâché. It was the golden age of Kashmiriyat. Jahangir noted the similarities that existed between Hindus and Muslims in the Valley in matter of customs including inter marriages. Most of the Kashmiri Muslims till today follow the customary law in the succession of paternal properties in certain cases against the Islamic Law of inheritance. For instance in the case of Dukhtar-i-Khama Nishin, i.e. a daughter who prefers to live with her parents even after marriage (Jamal Ahmad Khan, 2001). Aurangzeb found the situation discomfortable and described Kashmiri Muslims as *be pir*.

Kashmir developed its own variant of Islam within the framework of world Islamic society, borrowing many elements from its pre-Islamic Hindu and Buddhist heritage. Thus as in Buddhism the relics of the holy men would be preserved and exhibited. There was a network of *dargahs* and the architecture of the mosques had multiple designs ranging from spires to domes. The faithful would visit mosque in the morning to offer prayers and chant the names of the Allah together (composed *a la* Sanskrit texts in honour of Shiva or Vishnu), observe vegetarianism occasionally. This was due to the influence of the three outstanding personalities of Kashmir history who were almost contemporaries, Lal Ded, Shaikh Nooruddin Rishi and Zainul Abedin. Lal Ded in her *vaak* composed in Kashmiri language criticized orthodoxy, and preached *advait* in the idioms of Kashmiri Shaivism. There existed a large number of Brahman ascetics. Nooruddin Rishi was the founder of Indigenous Rishi Order to which a number of Brahman ascetics were converted. After their conversion they introduced austerity, simplicity, vegetarianism during the days of *urs*, non-violence, tolerance, etc., in the Kashmir variant of Islam. Nooruddin Rishi enjoined the dignity of manual work and encouraged extension of cultivation, plantation of fruit bearing trees, environmental conservation including non killing of some wild life as part of religious duties. The ruler Zainul Abedin, popularly known as Badshah, translated these lofty ideas into state policy which has been described above. Abul Fazal has this to say about the *rishis*

> The most respectable class in this country is that of the *Rishis* who, notwithstanding their need of freedom from the bonds of tradition and custom, are true worshippers of God. They do not loosen the tongue of calumny against those not of their faith nor beg, nor importune. They employ themselves in planting fruit trees and are generally a source of benefit to the people. They abstain themselves from flesh and meat, and do not marry.
>
> (Riyaz Punjabi, 1990)

The Emperor Jahangir mentions that there were 2,000 *rishis* in the Valley at that time. There were women *sufis* also. The Rishi Order came to end during the seventeenth and eighteenth centuries as the *ziyarats* (the shrines of *sufis*) 'turned into breeding grounds for superstition and social exploitation, [which] sounded the death-knell of Rishi movement (Khan, Ishaq, 1997, p. 229). The Rishi-Sufi tradition ended, but its impact is still felt among the *sufis* and others.

The Muslims emerged as a dominant community in the medieval period in the Valley and adjoining regions. There were conversions of all Hindu castes except Brahmans in the Valley. In the mountains the ancient tribes such as Dards were converted to Shia sect. The large scale conversions were as a result of a combination of factors, use of force, offer of allurements, prospect of share in power, extension of cultivation, personal motivation and conviction. There were conversions from all communities in the Valley, but not to the same extent. The 1931 data shows that the Kashmiri Brahaman remained a sizable community while all other Hindu communities had almost ceased to exist. There was almost enbloc conversion of a community following the conversion of the chief.

There were many other factors in conversion. According to current popular belief Islam spread in the Valley mainly owing to the supernatural feats of the *rishis* against the Brahman *rahibs* (ascetis) and various dieties (Ishaq Khan, p. 82). In fact it was the syncretic character of Kashmir ethos that led to the acceptance of Islam while retaining as mentioned above local, cultural characteristics (occasional vegetarianism, preservation and display of relics of *rishis*) post-*namaz* collective recitation of compositions in Kashmiri languages, in honour of the Allah, the Prophet and the local saints, called *aurad* (invocatory prayer). This was made possible by the role of Muslim *rishis* whose *ziyarats* became the centre of the diffusion of Islam. As mentioned above these *rishis* took over the entire gamut of pre-Islamic traditions such as non-violence, tolerance, spirituality and added to it personal care of tamed animals, extension of land and cultivation, planting trees, conservation of forest, prohibiting the hunting of *hangul* (the Kashmiri stag), the prize possession of the Valley forest, which are still relevant.

Outside the Valley, in Jammu the Rajputs converted in larger numbers. The Rajput chiefs to embrace Islam first of all were those of the Khokhar tribe. One of their chief Khokhar Rai called Kokar Sanka in the *Tabakat-i-Nasiri*, had embraced Islam in the time of Muhammad Ghori. The Rajput population was the thickest around the Mughal road leading from the plain of western Punjab into Kashmir through the Bhimbar–Rajouri–Shupian route across the Pir Panchal. Manhas and Salehria Rajputs became Muslims in large numbers on the borders of Jammu in the region called Salahr-tappa and Manhas-tappa of Baramanga. The communities like Jaral, Salehria and Manhas have a considerable number of converts. The Rajputs in Jammu, particularly the Chib in the land of Chibal situated between the rivers Tawi and Jhelum converted to Islam in a big way. In pre-Independence period the number of Muslim Rajputs was even more than double of that of Hindu Rajputs in Jammu province. Most of the Muslim Rajputs migrated to Pakistan in 1947. Gujars of this tract are wholly Muslims, and so are the Khokhar who have only a few Hindu families.

In early stages the converted Rajputs continued with preconversion practices. Charak tells us

> a Musalman, entertained the services of a *Purohit*, i.e. family priest, and even issued a grant of land of him; and it is probable that this custom had continued unbroken in the family in the time of his predecessors, who took Hindu names also along with the official Muslim names, the latter being less pronounced. Most of the Muslim Rajputs liked to keep closer social contacts with Hindu Rajputs. Both participated in the social functions of each other. Some Muslim Rajput families had kept alive the sort of *Bartan-vihar* (social intercourse) which had existed with other Hindu families before their conversion to Islam. Muslims invited Hindu 'relatives' to their social functions like birth of a son, *mundan*, betrothal, marriage, etc. The Muslim Rajput hosts would provide dry ration for the Hindu invitees to be cooked at their camp by Hindu cooks or at the house of mother Hindu family of the village. The Hindu Rajputs also reciprocated. Their old tradition of offering *tambol* and exchange of gifts was continued till recently, that is till a decade before independence. (personal correspondence from Charak)

A question often asked is what happened to the people mentioned in the chronicles. The Nagas survived as Thaka. The Khasas who occupied south-west of Kashmir, moved out and dispersed around the Himalayan ranges. As mentioned earlier, the Chaks after they lost power took to breeding cattle and sheep and became known as Galwans (breeder of cattle). Many communities after conversion to Islam survived with their *krams* (*gotar*/family affiliate) and followed the rule of endogamy before giving it up. Muslims of Pandit, Kol, Butt, Aitu, Rishi, Mantu, Ganai are supposed to be descendants of Brahmans, while Magres, Tantreys, Dars, Rahtors, Rainas, Dangars and Naiks are supposed to be descendants of Kshatriyas. A *kram* Lone is of Vaishya origin and the Damaras are descendants of Shudras (personal communication from Charak). It appears that after the conversion to Islam many Hindu communities retained their family affiliation (*kram*), which indicated the Hindu community from which conversion had taken place and its high and low status. So strong was this institution as an exogamous division that even Pathans flaunted Khan as their *kram*. The *kram* could be easily manufactured, particularly by the lower order who were eager to claim a higher status. However, it is not *kram* but wealth and power that determine status now. (correspondence with Charak)

We may briefly discuss the historical ethnography of the two other regions, Jammu and Ladakh.

The ancient name of Jammu was Duggar which derived from ecology marked by a difficult terrain. The earlier inhabitants were the predecessors of the present day Domb (Dum), Megh, Koli, Batwlas, the dark-skinned people of the early Sanskrit texts, the Australoid. Later texts mentioned Madars, Salvas and Audambars around seventh century BC and the Sakas who gave the name Sialkot. Madradesha included Jammu. They were followed by foreign tribes such as Indo-Parthian, Saka-Palhavas and Hunas and autochthones like Darvas, Abhisaras, Khasas, Dards, Gurjaras, and Durgars. The Khasa controlled Kishtwar, Rajouri, Lohara. They are also known as Khakha community. A section of the Naga was exiled by Naga ruler Nila to the land of Darva (Jammu). An inscription of the fifth/sixth century mentioned Naga ruler Vibhunaga as one of the nine Naga kings conqured by Samundragupta. The cult of Vasuki and Pehar Naga has been popular in Jammu region. Takshak segment of the Naga survive as Tak and as Takka Rajput. Kashmir was also called Takkadesha. The Takka settled down in western part of Jammu and converted to Islam. In the course of the People of India project, we came across a community of Nagvanshis called the Thakkar Nag (derived from Takshak lineage) in the Reasi region of Jammu which could be a remnant of the old Naga people. Later the Gurjara tribe dominated north-western Punjab and also controlled the part of Jammu and Kashmir. However it was the Durgaras who emerged as the dominant community around the first half of the tenth century as Durgareshwara or the lord of the Durgar. This ecological identity was also lent to the other communities that came in later. Jammu is derived from Jammumarg of the *Mahabharata* or from Jamvant one of the warriors of Rama's army. The Jamwal lineage is derived from Jammu, Jambulochan of this lineage was the founder of Dogra dynasty. It appears that the ruling lineage, Jamwal derives its identity from Jammu rather than the other way about. Other Dogra lineages such as Baloria, Lakhanpuria, Bahuwals, Charak, Manhas, etc., who branched off the main line and some of them took the name of the places where they set-up the kingdom. Other Rajput lineages were Pathanias, Salahrias, Jarals, etc.

Jammu is a meeting ground of many languages, i.e. Dogri, Punjabi, Gujjari, Pahari, etc. It was a autonomous region dominated by the Dogra who derive their identity from Durgardesha and shared elements of its culture. In the course of time many communties migrated from Punjab, making it in a partial sense an extension of Punjabi ethnographic universe. The Punjabi communities are Arain, Bafanda, Teli, Mirasi with Muslim segments which have also emerged among Hajjam, Tarkhan, Kumhar, Lohar, Mochi and others, Chuhras, Jhiwars, who have taken new caste names of Masalli and Mashki. The Hindu segments of Chamars called themselves Arya and Dums prefer to be called Arya Mahasha. There are some additions to minor communities like Gorkha, Cargar, Arora and Kayeth. The Brahmans came with their Rajput patrons. They are a heterogeneous group. The Khatris were an important trading class members of which rose to be *diwans*, generals and administrator. By the close of the nineteenth century their influx from Punjab has increased and their number stood at 50,000. In 1927 when the Dogra ruler, Pratap Singh introduced the domicile conditions and reserved state services for bonafide state subjects, the outsiders were removed from all officers and a majority of Khatris had to leave the state. The Sikhs came in as mercenaries who were paid in grain (*jins*) and called Jinsi Sikhs in parts of the Valley. The Punchi Sikhs were Brahmans converted to Sikhism who retained the Brahman surnames such as Soodan, Raina, Reena, Ishar, Khajuria, etc.

Before 1947 Jammu was the most populous region. The Line of Control divided the Jammu from its western parts which shared ethnic and linguistic linkages, while the Kashmiri speaking region remained intact. However, the identity of Jammu as a region has developed with the recognition of Dogri and Pahari paintings.

Ladakh, in Tibetan, is called *la-tags* which means lowland or redland. It is also called *mar-yul* and *kha-chan-oa*, which refers to the snow-land. Both of these names were used by the old Chinese travellers. Ladakh is the meeting ground of two language families, Tibeto-Burman and Indo-Iranian/Indo-Aryan (Dardic) and of the two morphological types, the Mongoloid (Champa, Ladakhi, Balti) and Europoid (Dard/Broqpa). There are folklores about the purest type of the Europoids. Routes of migration and trade lay through this bleak terrain. The Indo-Aryans took these routes among others. Their staple cereal was barley which is still the main cereal of Ladakh. Eleven communities inhabit the Ladakh region. Champas are an ancient nomadic community engaged in trade. The Ladakhis are most numerous divided into thirteen occupational groups including the former raja, high officials, carpenters, goldsmith, blacksmith (Gara), shoemakers, musicians and singers (Mon and Beda). Muslims from Kashmir Valley and Yarkand settled down and inter married with Ladakhis and there is a mixed community known as Argon. A section of the Bedas/Mon converted to Islam. The Dard known as a Broqpa some times pronounced Dokhpa which means a highlander, migrated from Gilgit in the remote past. The Baltis converted to Shia cult and gave up polyandry. The Moravian Christians called Mashikpa by Ladakhis are a land owning, stratified community of Leh converted from the original Buddhist faith.

There existed a large kingdom of Ladakh which included, besides the present Ladakh division of Jammu & Kashmir state, Lahul and Spiti and adjoining Tibetan district called Naris lying to the east of Ladakh upto to the Maum pass. This kingdom disintegrated by the middle of the nineteenth century.

The closing of the international border with China and cessation of border trade and cultural links with Tibet in the 1950s had disastrous results. The nomads ceased to nomandise, and economic stagnation had social consequences, which will be discussed later.

II

The All India Anthropometric Survey suggests that the people of Jammu & Kashmir are generally short or below medium in stature, have long and narrow head, nose and face. The Ladakhi populations, which bear Mongoloid features, show greater incidence of whorls (56.0 per cent) than loops (42 per cent) but in populations of Valley and Jammu, loops (48-52 per cent) preponderate over whorls (45-51 per cent). Among the Muslims the incidence of loops and whorls range from 43-52 per cent and 45-54 per cent respectively. Pattern intensity index varies from 14 per cent recorded in Muslims to 16 per cent found in Mongoloid communities. Colour blindness has been reported in 7 per cent of individuals. Incidence of A gene is high among Muslims (15-51 per cent) than other communities (14-25 per cent). Non-taster gene (PTC) shows high frequency in Indo-Aryan speakers and Muslims (51-63 per cent) than Ladakhi population (24 per cent). Incidence of G6PD is low (4-6 per cent).

The frequency of M gene is relatively low in Muslims (58 per cent) than other communities or Scheduled Tribes (70-86 per cent). Incidence of d (Rh) is low in Mongoloid populations (9 per cent) as compared to other communities (18 per cent) or Muslims (22-30 per cent). Biochemical traits have been mostly studied in Muslims are as follows: P^{C} (1-20 per cent), PGM^{1} (63 per cent), ESD^{2} (25.60 per cent), AK^{1} (93.80 per cent), ADA^{1} (88.80 per cent) and GLO^{1} (29.70 per cent).

III

It is paradoxical that a rich and living language like Kashmiri has never become the language of the state and administration. A reason could be that Kashmiri was never spoken in all the regions of the state, past and present. Kashmiri was and still is mainly the language of the people of the Valley, of the mystics and poets, with a six hundred year old uninterrupted literary tradition.We earlier described Kashmiri as a language belonging to the Dardic branch of the Indo-Aryan sub-family of the Indo-European language family. It is also mentioned as the Pisacha branch of the Indo-European family of languages. The Dardic branch has two sub-groups, viz., Khowar group consisting of Khowar and Chitrali or Chatrari or Arnia languages and Dard group consiting of Kashmiri, Shina, Dardi and Koshistani languages. According to another view, the Dardic group of languages belong to the Indian branch of the Indo-Iranian sub-family. There is little doubt that Kashmiri is not like any other language of the Indo-Aryan family such as Punjabi or Hindi. Those who relate Kashmiri identity to Kashmiri language stress the views of those linguists who believe that Kashmiri stands midway between the Indo-Iranian and Indo-Aryan language families. There are however other linguists who believe that the claim to separate Kashmiri from the Indo-European languages on the basis of purely syntactic arguments is not very strong. There is also a view that Kashmiri and Shina—which share some features with Indo-Aryan languages and also have features that separate Shina from Kashmiri—belong to the Dardic group. This however does not answer the question whether the Dardic group is a branch of the Indo-Aryan or a branch of the Indo-Iranian family of languages. Therefore, a good deal of research is still required to settle the issue (personal communication from Prof. Anjani Kumar Sinha, Department of Linguistics, Delhi University).

Persian was the official language of the state from the Mughal period to the period of the Dogra rulers. The Sikh ruler Maharaja

Ranjeet Singh introduced Urdu as the medium of administration in various parts of the kingdom. The Dogra ruler Ranbir Singh introduced Urdu in his state. The last Dogra ruler introduced compulsory schooling through Urdu medium. After independence Urdu continued as the official language and as lingua franca.

In all, nineteen languages were returned in the state of Jammu & Kashmir under the People of India project as follows:

> Balti, Changpa, Dogri, Droskhat, Gujarati, Gujjari, Haryanvi, Hindi, Kashmiri, Ladakhi, Nagari, Punchi, Punjabi, Pahari, Parimu, Pasto, Shina, Sikligari, Urdu.

Kashmiri is spoken by the largest number of communities (48) followed by Dogri (34), Punjabi (6) and Ladakhi (5). The four Scheduled Tribes: Beda, Bodh, Gara and Mon speak Ladakhi. The other Scheduled Tribes, six in all, speak Kashmiri. The four languages (Balti, Changpa, Droskhat and Ladakhi) belong to Tibeto-Burman language family. The Pasto spoken by Afghan is a language of the Indo-Iranian sub-family. Parimu spoken by Gujjars is unclassified. Kashmiri and Shina (spoken by Broqpa) are a language of Indo-Aryan sub-family (Dardic branch) of either Indo-Aryan or Indo-Iranian language family, till the matter is settled.

The people of Kashmir called Kashmiri Kasheer. Kashmiri speaking communities did not constitute an absolute majority in the state before or after 1947.

According to 1981 census, Kashmiri is spoken by the largest number of persons (31,30,870) followed by Dogri (14,60,279), Hindi (10,37,116), Punjabi (1,69,965) Ladakhi (72,593), Balti (48,498), Lahnda/Multani (13,360), Shina (15,344), Urdu (6,315) and Tibetan (4,699). The persons speaking the scheduled languages including Dogri speakers are mostly bilingual in Kashmiri, Urdu, English and Hindi. Among the Balti, Ladakhi, Shina and Tibetan speakers, more speakers are bilingual in Urdu. Among speakers of Lahnda and Gorkhali/Nepali more people are bilingual in Hindi.

The post-Gupta Siddhmatrika script developed into the Sharada script in Kashmir from the eighth century onward. Kashmiri language was written in Sharada script which was thus the script in which the earliest literary works and other documents were written. But, Sharada script fell into desuetude following political changes and was replaced by Nagari from the eighth century onward. Later Perso-Arabic script was introduced. The standardized Kashimri orthography follows the conventions of Urdu, since Urdu is the mainly written and official language of Jammu & Kashmir. The Perso-Arabic script is widely used in the state of Jammu & Kashmir. The Bodhi and Balti are the other minor scripts used, the first by Bodh, Champa, Gara and Mon and the second by Broqpa. At present Sharada script is restricted to the religious and ritual purposes only.

IV

Jammu and Kashmir is endowed with abundant natural resources including forest water and land which grows a variety of crops, cereals, pulses, vegetables and fruits.

In the Valley *kesar* is the most visible symbol of the cultural geography of Kashmir (Arun Kaul, 2001). No other object so vividly symbolizes the cultural dynamics of a region, be it religion, customs, traditions, condiments, spices, medicines or trades, so interwoven role in the fabric of Kashmiri society. Like everything else the cultivation of saffron flowers are traced to Naga or the holi string. There is a popular myth that during the reign of Lalitaditya (699-735) a Naga chieftain who fell sick with an eye complaint was cured by the *vaidya*. The Naga chief in gratitude gave pulp of *kesar* and a cultivation of *kesar* as a wonderful flower began. *Kesar* has many uses in rituals, in religious ceremonies, in curing, in toiletry and beautification. *Kesar* was exported for a value. The Mughals introduced the state monopoly of *kesar* cultivation.

V

When I first visited Srinagar to organize the project for the state I was told after discussions with local scholars at the Centre for Central Asia Studies, that there is only one Muslim community in the Valley. I reminded the audience that the world Islam is a multilingual and multiethnic community. After a good deal of discussions about 50 communities were initially identified in the Valley according to the traditional accupations.

(*a*) *Agriculture/Wage Labour:* Afghan, Baba, Bomba, Bhat Muslim, Botraja (migrant), Dander, Rather, Saiyid, Tantrey.

(*b*) *Cattle rearing/Pastoralism:* Bakarwal, Chopan, Gujjar, Pohul.

(*c*) *Artisan:* Banduk Khar, Beg, Chhan, Dhobi, Kraal, Lohar, Lone, Nalband, Namdagur, Naqqash, Navid, Para, Sangtrash, Sanur, Setch/Ses, Shaksaz, Sofi.

(*d*) *Cultural worker or entertainers:* Bhand, Dhamali Faqir.

(*e*) *Labour:* Cheintz.
(*f*) *Fisherfolk:* Dar.
(*g*) *Business:* Ganz, Malik, Manjygur.
(*h*) *Miscellneous/service castes:* Gorkan (grave digger), Kavoj (cremators), Panyach (performers of death rituals), Watal, Waza.
(*i*) *Service:* Kashmiri Pandit.

Prof. Bashir Ahmad Dabla has contributed a paper on castes in the Valley in which he has listed 700 entries including the surnames, titles, family affiliates (*kram*), etc., which both Hindu & Muslim share. (Appendix I)

For Jammu region the following communities were listed according to the traditional occupations:

(*a*) *Agriculture/Labour:* Barwala, Basith, Batwal, Bazigar, Bhagat, Charak, Chib, Chibali, Chhimba, Dhyar, Dogra, Dogra Muslim, Domal, Dosali, Jaral, Jat, Katoch, Manhas, Megh, Mughal, Mohyal Brahman, Punchi Sikh, Sen, Nagvanshi.
(*b*) *Business/Service:* Charji, Dholwala, Jain, Jangam, Khatri, Mahajan, Salaria, Sansi.
(*c*) *Labour & Other work:* Chuhra.
(*d*) *Miscellanious:* Dogra Brahman, Dogra Jheer, Dum, Gujarati Brahman (migrant com.), Perne, Rattal, Bhojru.
(e) Pastoral/Cattle dairy: Gaddi, Pohul, Gujjar, Chopan, Bakarwal.
(*f*) *Culture workers/entertainers*: Gardi, Jogi, Bhand, Dhamali Faqir
(*g*) *Artisan:* Gumar, Mochi, Sansi, Sikligar, Sochi, Tarkhan, Teli, Barwala.

In Ladakh we identified 11 communities engaged in traditional occupations.

(*a*) *Agriculture*: Argon, Balti, Bodh, Broqpa, Dokhpa, Mon, Moravian.
(*b*) *Trade/Business:* Argon, Balti, Mon.
(*c*) *Cultural workers:* Beda, Mon.
(*d*) *Cattle rearing:* Champa.
(*e*) *Artisan:* Gara.

We initially studied 111 communities in the state to which we added two more, Nagbanshi and Punjabi linguistic group. However, for the purpose of the analysis of data we kept intact the original figure. We did not generally study floating populations, refugees, dispersed groups which still have to aquire the characterstics of a community.

Of the total of 44 communities constituting 39.6 per cent inhabit rural settings and only 8 communities reported to have been dwelling in urban settings while as many as 53 communities corresponding to 47.7 per cent live in rural/urban settings.

The major communities of Jammu & Kashmir and their population according to 1931 census are as follows: Gujjar Muslim (3,99,122), Rajput (2,56,020), Brahman (2,53,529), Sheikh (1,55,613), Jat (1,49,037), Lohar (1,12,021), Saiyid (72,376). According to 1981 census the major Scheduled Castes are Megh or Kabirpanthi (1,99,242), Chamar or Ramdasia (1,22,292), and so on.

According to POI data out of the total 111 communities studied in Jammu & Kashmir 53.2 per cent are Muslims, 36.9 per cent Hindus, 4.5 per cent Sikhs, 5.4 per cent Buddhists, 1.8 per cent Christians and the rest follow other religions. According to 1981 census 64.19 per cent are Muslims, 32.24 per cent Hindus, 2.23 per cent Sikhs, 1.17 per cent Buddhists, 0.14 per cent Christians, 0.03 per cent Jains and the rest follow other religions. The state has a rich tradition and contemporary scenario of syncretism, Muslim-Buddhist (Shia/Muslim and Buddhist), Muslim-Hindu, Hindu-Buddhist and followers of Buddhism-Bon shamanism. The communities professing Islam are 53.15 per cent as against national average of 12.60 per cent.

The Valley population is marked by homogeneity of religion and language, about 94 per cent of the population is Muslim and 89 per cent speak Kashmiri language (1981 census). The Muslims are the dominant community in the Valley. The Introduction mentions the social hierarchy that emerged in Kashmir, with Saiyid at the top followed by Sheikh who included converts from Brahmans and Rajputs in the second place followed by others almost in the same order as in pre Islamic Kashmir. The Saiyid are descended from the high ranking foreigners who played an important role in the history of Kashmir from thirteenth century onward. They affix Mir as their *kram* and are agriculturists. The Sheikh are stratified into various groups such as Pirzada, Babas, the Rishis, Mullas. The local warrior groups consisted of Chak, Mughals who came during Muslim rule, Bomba, Khakha. The Pathans came during the Afghan rule and many families were settled by Dogra rulers in the hills to guard frontiers. The agricultural castes were divided into the *zamindars* who were superior and *taifadars* who were considered inferior and consisted of gardeners, herdsmen, shepherds (Chopans/Pohul), horsemen (Galwan/Guliwan), boatsmen (Hangi), leather workers, ministrels (Bhagat/Bhand), scavengers (Watal), artisans (Nangars), cremators (Kavoj) and others.

The Hindus who remained in the Valley consisted of Kashmiri Brahmans and a few others. The Brahmans considered the Valley as their universe complete with all symbolisms such as the Ganga, Ayodhya, etc., within the broad frame of Bharat. The Kashmiri Brahmans described as a branch of Saraswat Brahmans of north and western India, use the prefix or suffix of Pandit which is said to have been bestowed on them as a title by Mughal ruler Muhammad Shah. The Pandits today are very conscious of their role in history. They have contributed enormously to development of culture and civilization of the Valley and beyond, to the growth of Kashmiri, Sanskrit and Persian languages and literatures. They are the custodians of the sacred texts. Their ancestors were the founders of the school of Kashmiri Shaivism which is distinguished for its concept of *advaita*, gender equality and unique and multiple techniques of Yoga. The traditional festivals celebrated by Pandits are Shivratri, Janmashtami, and Navaratra, Navreh (New Year). Deepawali and Holi are recent additions. The Kashmir Brahmans are heterogeneous, as suggested by their various components including segments and *gotra*. Among the leading *krams* of Pandits may be mentioned the following names: Bhan, Dar, Duku, Fotedar, Tikku, Kachru, Kak, Munshi, Mattoo, Madan, Muju, Pandit, Razdan, Raina, Tikku, Thusu, Sipru, Wangu, Zitshu. Of these the members of the Dar family have probably been the most influential. A Deccan connection is suspected. They have contributed to the development of the composite notion of the Kashmiriyat and being one of its components, they have participated in struggles. In 1928 the Kashmiri Pandits led the agitation, 'Kashmiri for Kashmiris and compelled the state authority to pass the state subject law under which non-Kashmiris were debarred from purchasing non-movable property in the state. After independence the Kashmiri Pandits lost their pre-eminent position in administration and professions, and their land was declared surplus, acquired without compensation and re-distributed among other communities. The exodus from the Valley started. Going by the 1931 census population of Pandits the Kashmiri diaspora is now estimated to be 4,00,000 strong. Since 1948 Kashmiri Pandits who once constituted sizeable part of the population have started leaving the Valley where the population now stands at 9,000, which is 4 per cent of their 1931 population.

The J&K communities differentiate themselves into the indigenous and immigrant categories based on self perception and perceptions by others. Some of the indigenous communities of Jammu and Kashmir are Gujjar Muslim, Bakarwal, Bhaba, Balti Sheikh, Saiyid, Rajput, and

Brahman. Immigrant communities in the state are Afghan, Pathan, Moravian, Christians and others.

According to the *Census of India*, 1981, there are 13 Scheduled Castes in the state with a population of 6,27,440. The Scheduled Castes include Barwala, Basith, Batwal, Chamar/Mochi, Chuhra, Dhyar, Dum or Mahasha, Gardi, Megh or Kabirpanthi, Rattal, Sariyara, Watal.

For many years there were no Scheduled Tribes in the state. In 1989 eight communities in Ladakh were notified as Scheduled Tribes which included Balti, Beda, Bodh, Broqpa, Champa/Chamgpa, Gara, Mon, Dokhpa. Later, two were added—Bakarwal and Gujjar in Jammu and the Valley.

There is an extraordinary range of heterogeneity among J&K communities in terms of segments and exogamous divisions locally called *aal/al*, *gotra*, *khandan*, the family surnames (*kram*). As mentioned earlier a local scholar has a list of about 700 divisions. The social divisions go with hierarchies (22/19.8 per cent) among Muslims (5), Buddhists (2) and Hindus (13) may be earlier. Differentation within a communities exists at many levels, social (33), economic (51), religious (10), occupational (50), territorial (2), educational (33). There is no differentiation at religious level among Muslims, but differentiation at other levels suggests growing disparities. Most communities perceive themselves as occupying its middle position, mostly Muslim (39), followed by those who perceive themeselves as occupying the low position (34). This self perception matches others' perceptions at the middle level (42) and at the low level (58).

A larger Dogra identity is being reconstructed with the inclusion of 5 communities in the generic Dogra category, identifying themselves with ecology and history. The large complex stratified communities are the Rajputs, Brahmans, Moravian Christians, Ladakhis, etc.

There are miscegenated groups like Argaon, Dond, Domal, etc.

Many of the Backward Castes invoke the Rajputization model and consider themselves to be degraded Rajputs such as Dosali, Dhyar.

There are communities divided into religious segments such as Hindu (Rajput)-Muslim, Muslim-Buddhist, and Buddhist-Hindu. A good deal of preconversion practices survives in the segments and dividing line in some cases is very thin and fluid.

Jammu & Kashmir shares with many parts of western India surnames that suggest linkages with environment, plants and animals (Dand, Chopan, Khar, Panj) and local birds (Kaw/crow, Braer/cat, Barkhoo and Gagaroo/rat), physical features (Teng/mound, Nehru/

nahar), high post (Raina/Rana, Razdan). There is a plethora of *kram* names shared by Pandit and Muslims. A feature of some surnames is the last two alphabets of suffix with the ending *oo*, such as in Mattoo, Handoo, etc., to facilitate writing in Devenagari and Perso-Arabic scripts.

A distinguished feature of Kashmiri surnames which is an identity marker is their relationship with environment. Used by both Hindus and Muslims as mentioned earlier they indicate their relationship with animals, plants and features of environment. The Nehrus derived their identity from *nahar*, the canal. The Kashmiri Pandits in the Valley continue with their delightful way of adopting, discarding and changing surnames, after physical features:

> A Pandit named Vasudev had a mulberry tree in his courtyard and was therefore named Vasudev *tul*—that being the Kashmiri word for mulberry. Vasudev had the tree cut down leaving only its trunk. His name was changed to Vasudev *mond*—that being the Kashmiri word for a tree trunk. So the Pandit had the trunk dug out from its roots. His name was changed to Vasudev *khoud*—that being the Kashmiri word for a pit. Pandit had the pit filled up. His name underwent a corresponding change. He became Vasudev *teng*—that being the Kashmiri word for a small mound. By then, poor Vasudev had enough of changing suffixes added to his name by nosy neighbours and resumed the name *teng* which stayed and went down to his descendants in the male line. (Quoted in Khushwant Singh, 'Malice', What's in a nick name?, *Afternoon on Sunday*, 8 June 1997)

The minorities in the state comprise Moravian Christians and Jains.

The communities which extend specialized services are Kavoj, Panyach, Dokhpa/Drokpa and Gujarati Brahman.

The environment explains the presence of tailors and stitchers of cloth and cloth patches (Sochi/Sofi)

There are some occupations which was strictly related to ecology and resource endowments such as cattle breeding and pastoralism, basketry, horticulture, fishing (Dar), boating (Hanji). The pastoral nomads include communities Gujri/Goor, Pohul, Batti, Champa/ Chamgpa, Gaddi, Gujjar Muslim to mention a few. There is a higher incidence of shifting cultivation, terrace cultivation, animal husbandry, pastoralism, bee-keeping, horticulture, which have been expanded as have business and trade. A sharp rise in skilled and non-skilled labourers is reported.

There are again some occupations unique to Kashmir Valley such as grave digging, cremation, cooking, begging, etc. More and more communities are showing business and trade, service and professions as subsidiary occupations.

The analysis of the occupations pursued by various communities in the POI show that as many as 60 communities corresponding to 54.1 per cent pursue agriculture, 32 communities (28.8 per cent) are engaged in animal husbandry and only 3 communities (2.7 per cent) are engaged in fishing and an equal number of communities in hunting and gathering. The communities engaged in fishing are Dogra Jheer, Dar/Dhar and Hanji. A large number of communities—52 (36.8 per cent) are engaged in unskilled labour; 43 communities (38.7 per cent) are in unorganized services. Majority of the communities i.e. 90 (81.1 per cent) are engaged in organized services. Members in 77 communities (69.4 per cent) are self employed in trade and industry. The communities pursuing business and trade are Jain, Banduk Khar, Wani, Khatri and Mahajan.

Kashmir has a large population of artisans, 46 communities (41.4 per cent). The artisans include Ganz, Namdagur, Chhimba, Gumar/ Kumhar, Kraal, Basith, Cheintz, Sonar/ Sanur, Sangtarash, Lohar and Sikligar.

There is a strong Persian component among artisans such as Bafandar, Namdagur (weaver of warm cloths), Naqqash (designer), Para (maker of mill stone), Setch/Ses (tailors), Sofi (making garments out of patches). The presence of so many tailoring groups suggests the ecology induced need for different types of clothing. There are also artisan groups unique to the state such as Watal (skinning), Saryara (working labour). Wani (grocer), Waza (cook). There are artisan groups from neighbouring states like Sikligar, Tarkhan, etc. The three artisan groups, Waza, Kavoj, Wani, serve all groups including Pandits.

There have been occupational shifts and diversification. The Lone who once traded in rock salt brought from Peshawar have now taken up carpet weaving, *shawl* embroidery, business and service in police and military departments, fruit orchard, etc. The Bazigar, finding the traditional occupation of acrobat not remunerative enough have become peddlers, daily wages labours, drivers, motor mechanics. The Bafanda are no longer engaged in cotton dressing and have moved into other fields. The Sofi are no longer cultivators but subsist on making and sale of bakery products. The Galwan have given up housekeeping and taken up agriculture, fruit business and selling of timber. The Nalband are moving out of their traditional occupation of shoeing the horses and taking up wood carving and weaving. The larger and more influencial groups have gone into services and business in a big way.

VI

We will now discuss the traits that stand out in the three regions of Kashmir, Jammu and Ladakh.

According to 1981 census Kashmir region comprises 52.36 per cent of the total population of the state, with Kashmiri Muslims forming 96 per cent of population. The Gujjars and Paharis who constitute 10 per cent of the population, living on the periphery of the Valley are closer to Jammu. Sixty-one communities are living in Kashmir Valley. As many as 82.69 per cent of the communities inhabit the Valley as against national average of 5.09 per cent. They are distinguished by the attire of long coat (*pheran*) of both male and female. Another identifying marker is the headgear used by males 19.23 per cent communities as against national average of 5.52 per cent and by females in 17.31 per cent communities as against national average of 1.32 per cent. Skull coat or turban is used as headgear by men while a cotton or silk scarf is used by the women to cover their head. The ear pendant (*dehjore*) is marriage symbol and typical identity marker of Kashmiri Pandit women. The portable earthen brazier (*kangri*) is a unique component of Kashmiri need. They are also distinguished by their *shawl*. Male *shawl* is used by 7.69 per cent of communities as against national average of 2.25 per cent communities and female *shawl* is used by 5.77 per cent of communities as against the national average of 1.70 per cent. Non-vegetarianism is high 73.08 per cent as against national average of 49.77 per cent. Almost all the communities of the Valley are non-vegetarian, with or without beef. Intake of mustard oil as the cooking medium is high (92.31 per cent as against national average of 48.89 per cent). Consanguinity in the form of parellel cousin marriage FBD (92.31 per cent) and MSD (9.38 per cent) and cross cousin marriage FSD (92.31 per cent) and MBD (92.31 per cent) exists in almost equal proportion among the Muslims. Junior sororate is practised by 76.92 per cent of communities (as against national average of 58 per cent); junior liverate is also practised by 61.54 per cent communities (as against national average of 30.33 per cent). Rishi cult and Sufism, which were once part of the tradition of syncretic relationship across communities in the Valley, still exist in parts among the followers of different faiths.

Out of 57 Muslim communities as many as 50 communities live in the Valley while the remaining 4 are in Jammu and 3 in Ladakh. We studied four Hindu communities in the Valley including Kashmiri Pandit, Panyach, etc.

The Jammu population forms 45.40 per cent of the total population of the state, which consists of 66.33 per cent Hindus, 29.60 per cent of Muslims and 3.68 per cent of Sikhs. Three out of six districts adjoining Kashmir Valley, Rajouri, Poonch and Doda have a Muslim majority. Like in Punjab the Scheduled Castes form a major chunk of the population, 16.17 per cent and 31 per cent of Hindu population.

In Jammu historical account exists for 60 per cent of the communities as against national average of 38.43 per cent. Non-vegetarianism is high among them (62.5 per cent as against national average of 37 per cent). Presence of phratry and moiety organization is reported in 2.08 per cent communities against national average of 1.32 per cent and 0.73 per cent respectively. Hypergamy is high (12.5 per cent as against national average of 4.44 per cent). Junior sororate is in vogue among 70 per cent of the communities as against national average of 58.04 per cent. Junior levirate exists (54.17 per cent against national average of 30.33 per cent) and senior levirate is reported (10.42 per cent against national average of 4.21 per cent), which is quite high. Dowry is given in cash and kind in as many as 66.67 per cent of communities as against national average of 40.04 per cent. Equigeniture rule of inheritance is followed by members in 31.25 per cent of communities. Of crafts, weaving is practised widely (28.83 per cent against national average of 12.15 per cent), and embroidery on cloth (35.42 per cent as against national average of 9.23 per cent).

Ladakh has a population of 1,34,372 out of which the Buddhists account for 50.88 per cent, Muslims 46.05 per cent and others 3 per cent. In Leh the Muslims comprise 15 per cent of the population and Kargil has a Muslim majority. Most of the communities live in hilly terrain (81.82 per cent against national average of 2.39 per cent) and experience heavy snowfall (90.19 per cent against national average 2.22 per cent). The typical Ladakhi dress comprises woollen cloak (*guncha*), girdle (*sherak*) and woollen trouser. The decorated cap (*khoi*) and gorgeous ornamental attire of silver and precious stone are distinctive of Ladakhi women. Distinct dress pattern for males exists (45.45 per cent of communities against national average of 12.25 per cent). Distinct dress for females is noticed among members of 72.73 per cent of the communities. Members in 45.45 per cent of the communities wear headgear for males (against 5.52 per cent of national average) and 54.55 per cent of communities have headgear for females (against national average of 1.32 per cent).

In 1989 eight communities of Ladakh as mentione above were notified as Scheduled Tribe constituting 69 per cent of the population and 63.64 per cent of communities (against national average of 8 per cent). Non-vegetarianism is high (72.73 per cent against national average of 49.77 per cent). All communities of Ladakh are non-vegetarian with beef (Yak meat). The Dokhpa abstain from consuming cow-milk, egg and chicken as per their tribal usage. The practice of hypergamy is reported among 27.27 per cent of communities as against national average of 4.44 per cent. Levirate in the form of junior (54.55 per cent against national average of 30.33 per cent) and senior (18.18 per cent against national average of 4.21 per cent) is high. Remarriage of widow, widower and divorcee is allowed. Cross-cousin marriage, prevalence of bride price and dowry, levirate and sororate, marriage by exchange of sisters (*shabdeb*), marriage by service (*maqpa*), marriage by elopment, marriage by temporary contract (*muta*), practice of inviting man other than the husband to stay with the woman (*pharsak*) and fraternal polyandry to a limited extent are the salient features of the communities of Ladakh. Fraternal polyandry is reported among Bodh, Changpa, Dokhpa/Drokpa (27.27 per cent of communities against national average of 0.60 per cent. Bride price is given in cash and kind among 27.27 per cent of communities as against the national average of 14.99 per cent. Male primogeniture is the rule in 45.45 per cent of communities. Half of the communities (45.45 per cent) are landowners as against the national average of 30.64 per cent and half are landless. Both the Muslims and a section of Bodh mutually accept water and food and at the same time share the funerary expenses of the common kin. The Dokhpa who claim to be Buddhist also worship Sun, deities, demons, animals and sacrifice animals.

VII

While each of the three regions Jammu and Kashmir is unique in the traits they share, the three regions, put together, have been part of the larger identity called Jammu and Kashmir, which ecologically, historically and culturally has been unique, and there are traits that stand out in the state as a cultural and ecological region as a whole in comparison with the country. We will therefore discuss the features of Jammu & Kashmir which stand out in relation to national average

There is a sharp awareness of identity as suggested by historical accounts which exist for 46.85 per cent communities as against the national average of 38.43 per cent.

About 49 per cent of the communities reside in cold region and

18 per cent in extreme cold region as against the national average of 14.95 per cent and 2.39 respectively. Seventy per cent of communities inhabit the hilly terrain as against 25.83 per cent of national average. The Valley region is inhabitated by 42 per cent communities as against national average of 5.09 per cent.

Traditional dresses are worn by members among males in 25 per cent of communities and among females in 24 per cent of communities (as against national average of 12 per cent and 13 per cent respectively). Male headgear and female headgear are used by members in 21.6 per cent and 18.02 per cent communities respectively as against national average of 5.52 per cent and 1.32 per cent. They use silver ornaments which are of varied designs.

During winter Kashmiri women—Hindu and Muslim—dress in ornamental *pheran* and Kashmiri Pandit women also sport headgear (*tarang*) while the male wear *pheran*, and *safa* loosely tied on special occasions.

It is interesting that the traditional or ethnic marriage symbol for Kashmir among Pandits is not vermilion but *dehjore* worn in each ear with a long string made of gold or cotton or gold. Other marriage symbols include vermilion (34 communities/30.6 per cent against national average of 52.1 per cent), bangles, finger rings, toe ring, *bindi* is the most popular (34 communities/30.6 per cent against national average of 18 per cent) followed by nose ring, ear ring, nose stud. The symbols are not strictly observed (29.7 per cent against national average of 69 per cent). Bedecking a bride with flowers and garlands is a noteable Kashmiri practice.

Rice is the staple cereal (100 communities/90.09 per cent). There are also a larger number of consumers of wheat (84.64 per cent against national average of 59.70 per cent). The intake of maize is high (55.86 per cent as against 24.79 per cent national average). Of the oil seeds, mustard is most popular as medium of cooking (92.79 per cent as against national average of 48.89 per cent). Of the pulses the popular ones are *moong* (95 communities/85.59 per cent) and *masur* (87 communities/78.38 per cent) followed by *urad* (67) and gram (63). Maize is occasionally taken with mustard leaves. Wheat cakes moistened with water (*grin*) is the staple food among the people of Ladakh. The consumption of fruit, vegetables and milk are relatively high. They take all types of vegetables (80). Mutton is consumed by the middle and upper class people. Milk and Milk products are taken by the people (89). Roots and tubers are also widely taken.

Kashmiri cuisine consists of traditional mutton delicacies marked by the use of special Kashmiri *mirch*, special Kashmiri onion (*praau*), ginger, aniseed (*saunf*) and *hing* (astofaedica). It is followed by *kahwa*, in which tea leaves, sugar, saffron, almonds and cardimum are used. The other tea (*noon-chai*) has tea leaves, salt, almond and milk. There are also vegetarian dishes.

Considering the ecology of Jammu and Kashmir, the number of vegetarian communities is one of the lowest (5/4.5 against the national average of 16.1 per cent); they include the Jains, Gujarati Brahmans, Tarkhan and Jangama while some other Brahman groups are non-vegetarian. There is a shift from non-vegetarianism to vegetarianism among the Scheduled Castes, Khatris and Bhagats under the influence of Arya Samaj and Radha Swami cult. The non-vegeterians are most numerous (61/55.0 per cent against the national average of 49.4 per cent) which include Muslims (43), Hindus (12), Buddhists (4) and Sikhs (3). Beef of cow is eaten more often than the beef of ox by Muslims (27) and Buddhists (4), and it is generally confined to rural and hilly areas. We were told that the Badshah had prohibited cow slaughter and Jammu & Kashmir is one of the few states to have banned cow slaughter, and made it a penal offence and that the spurt in consumption of beef is due to the influence of the extremists. Pork is consumed by Hindu (24). There are non-vegetarian women (72) belonging to Muslim (45), Hindu (22) and other communities which are on a lower scale than the national average, due probably to the impact of Rishi tradition. Among some communities the women cook non-vegetarian food for men but do not take it. Consumption of alcoholic drinks among men is lower than the national average 42.3 per cent against 53.3 per cent it is much lower among the Muslim men (10/16.9 against the national average of 39.6 per cent). Consumption of drinks by women is almost neglible, nil among Muslim women. Consumption of milk is a little lower than the national average. Smoking *bidi*/cigarette and chewing loose tobacco, a concession to ecology, is higher than the national average.

The communities are mostly endogamous (107), but inter community marriage is also reported. The communities generally are monogamous (109) and prefer adult marriage (103).

Consanguinity in the form of parallel cousin and cross cousin marriages is in vogue. Consanguinous marriage in the form of parallel cousin exists among 36.04 per cent of communities (as against national average of 6.97 per cent.)

Traditional preferential forms of marriage are reported, sororate junior (79 communities/71.17 per cent against national average of

58.04 per cent) and levirate junior (64/57.66 per cent against national average of 30.33 per cent).

The spouse is selected either through negotiation (103) and by mutual consent 48 (43.24 per cent against national average of 25.83 per cent). Polyandry (fraternal) exists in 4 communities (3.6 per cent against national average 0.60 per cent) and non-fraternal polyandry in one.

Marriage by exchange or reciprocal marriage is widely reported among communities in the state (34/36.6 per cent against national average of 16.7 per cent). The communities include Muslims (17), Hindu (12), Buddhist (4).

They follow the rule of patrilocal residence.

Nuclear family is common (93) though vertically extended (56) and mixed extended family (47/42.3 per cent against national average of 32.75 per cent) are also numerous.

The inheritance of property is either in terms of equigeniture in 26 communities (22.5 per cent against national average of 10.97 per cent) or in terms of male equigeniture (62). The eldest son succeeds to the position of authority in the family (110).

Though the status of women is considered either low (66) or equal (42), they play an important role in economy, bringing of water, collection of fuel, social and ritual function, etc. A reason for better status of women in the Valley could be their right in property, recognized as *streedhan* under Mitakshra which also governs the customary law among Muslims and provides for equal rights of an unmarried daughter in the family property. Similarly customary law in Valley is recognized in the right of the adopted son.

Awareness of Varna order and its recognition is mostly reported from Hindus (37) followed by Sikhs (4) and Muslims (3). Nine communities are recognized as Brahmans including one Sikh (Punchi Sikh), 17 as Kshatriyas who include 4 Sikh and 1 Muslim communities, 5 as Vaishyas including 1 Jain and 17 as Shudras which include Muslim and Christian groups.

Folk traditions particularly folk tales and folk songs mostly recreated in literature are alive but at a lower level because of the growing influence of institutional religion. Folk dances are performed mostly by women and men only and separately and less frequently together. Pahari paintings have received well deserved recognition. Santoor is the best recognized instrument of Kashmiri music.

Syncretism in the Valley is attested by many living examples. The *samagri* (items used in performing *puja*) is sold by Muslims inside the compound of Kheer Bhawani temple. The Amarnath cave is managed by a Muslim family which gets one third of the offering as share for managing the temple. There is interdependence between Pandits and the artisans groups like the potters (Kraal), cooks (Waza) and cremators (Kavoj). The interdependence of Buddhist and Shia Muslims in spite of rise of communalism and undermining of Ladakhi identity is close and there are instances of conversion from one religion to another, even from Muslim to Buddhist, of inter-marriages, and of participation in life cycle ceremonies and festivals. The consolidated religious community has a larger network of affiliation to *pir* at individual and family levels and of *silsila*. The sacred specialists from the same communities and the other communities perform rituals, are supposed to cure ailments and exorcise evil spirits. Change of religion is reported on a larger scale than the national average but conversion is in communities, in which young boys and girls in love change religion to facilitate marriage (personal correspondence from Balraj Puri).

VIII

The communities depend on such resources as land (72), forest (11) and water (7). Landlessness is widely reported by members of 42 communities as mentioned above. Most of the individuals are engaged in terrace cultivation (15/13.5 per cent) against national average 4.75 per cent and in settled cultivation (29). Agriculture is the mainstay of the economy. Excessive dependence on agriculture and lack of diversified economic activities are the characteristic features of the region.

The extraordinary creativity of the artisans and craftsmen shows through their products particularly in weaving and embroidery which is at a level higher than the national average, besides carving, pottery, basketry, etc. In the Kashmir Valley tourism and small cottage industries such as *shawls* and wood carving are the subsidiary sources of income. The people are well versed in the art of weaving basketry and embroidery on cloth, and have evolved refinement in the pattern and techniques of *shawl* making, carpet weaving, chain stitch, etc. Development of agriculture in Ladakh is hindered by physical and climatic conditions, and the subsidiary sources of income are wage labour, service and self-employment.

The communities are directly linked with the market (103) through the daily market (100/90.09 per cent) against national average 76.29 per cent. A few communities (21) are linked with the market through middlemen barter as a medium of exchange exists in eight communities. Barter both in cash and kind is on a larger scale than elsewhere in the country.

Traditional caste council and village council exist. They exercise social control and initiate welfare measures. Because of the impact of religious institutions and rules and regulation, role of the caste council and village council is some what restricted. Statutary panchayats are yet to make a mark.

Jammu & Kashmir had a headstart in development particularly in education and health. Redistribution of land substantially helped a large number of communities, boosted their income and raised their status. However with the fragmentation of holdings and other factors the tempo of development slowed down. In terms of Human Development Index the state seems to have slid down from 19th rank to 21st during the period 1981-91 and in Gender Disparity Index from 19 to 25. However in terms of Human Poverty Index its ranking is 16 among states and per capita consumption expenditure is Rs. 746.74 against the national average of Rs. 590.98 which suggests a fair level of living (Planning Commission, Government of India, *National Human Development Report-2001*, Oxford, March 2002).

According to 1981 census, 26.67 per cent of the population in Jammu & Kashmir are literate, the male literacy being 36.29 per cent and female literacy rate is 15.88 per cent compared to 46.89 per cent males and 14.82 per cent females at all-India level. According to POI data 82.9 per cent communities prefer education for boys and 56.8 per cent for girls. Religion-wise break up shows that 87.8 per cent Hindus, 79.7 per cent Muslims, 100.0 per cent Christians, 80.0 per cent Sikhs and 66.7 per cent Buddhists prefer education for girls. In 2001 census there has been a marked improvement with female literacy at 41.82 per cent and male literacy at 55.75 per cent against the national average of 75.85 per cent and 54.16 per cent respectively, despite disturbed conditions which also explain the lower rate of female literacy.

Family welfare is accepted by members in 57.7 per cent communities. Religion-wise break up shows that 92.7 per cent Hindus, 37.3 per cent Muslims and 60.0 per cent Sikhs accept family welfare. The modern methods of family welfare programmes are adopted by members in 42 communities (37.8 per cent). Sterilization for men is adopted by members in 12 communities (10.8 per cent) and sterilization for women by members in 29 communities (26.1 per cent). Members in 28 communities (25.2 per cent) are benefited by employment through IRDP. Coverage by radio is reported by members in 109 communities (98.2 per cent), television by members in 81 communities (73.0 per cent) and by cinema by members in 89 communities (80.2 per cent).

The child labour population in J&K was 2,58,437 (1981 census) drawn according to POI from the ranks of 31 communities including Scheduled Castes (8), Scheduled Tribes (1) and others (22).

Owing to economic conditions a significant number of people go out to seek work for a period of two weeks to 5 months within the Valley (35.4 per cent), outside the Valley (20.3 per cent), and outside the state (34.3 per cent).

According to 1981 census the sex ratio in the state is adverse with 892 female per 1,000 males which is lower than 934 at all-India level. It has slightly improved to 900 against national average of 933 in 2001 census. However while the sex ratio of girl child population in the age group of 0-6 years is favourable, 937 against national average of 927, it is adverse, 894 against national average of 955 in the age group of 7 years and above.

Status of women as mentioned above is mostly perceived as low among communities (66) comprising Muslims (32), Hindus (28), Sikhs (4), Buddhists (3). The women's status is reportedly equal among 42 communities mostly Muslims (27) followed by Hindus (12). Women's status is reported by high among 4 communities including Buddhist (2), Christan (1), Hindu (1). Women have a considerable role in economy (agriculture, animal husbandry, fishing), in maintaining household (collection of fuel, fetching water), social and religious functions. Muslim women participate in religious functions have been open. However, they have a small role in politics (17.1 per cent), the Muslim women having a lesser role (5.1 per cent against Hindus 31.7 per cent). They have little social control (13.5 per cent). They have a lesser role in decision-making (35.1 per cent). However they control a higher percentage of expenditure (52.3 per cent) which is more than national average for both Hindu and Muslim women. They are mostly involved in household jobs (41.4 per cent against the national average of 22.6 per cent).

There is a higher incidence of *mahr* (dower) being demanded or promised for future than *mahr* instantly paid or promised but not paid. There is similarly a higher incidence of divorce being permitted and wife compensated. Remarriage is allowed for widow and widower in equal proportion. Female get a less share in property than male. Women have almost an equal role in economy, maintaining household, social and religious functions, but have lesser role in politics. They contribute to income and make decisions.

These findings of our project are broadly supported by the findings of a project on gender discrimination in the Kashmir Valley (1996). Though there has been a remarkable progress in women's education, there has been no corresponding occupational advantage for women. Gender discrimination in the lower order persists, the women participate in dairy activities, sheep rearing, production of handicrafts items, *shawl* embroidery in rural areas. They also participate in processing, drying, winnowing, seed management, transplantation, weeding and applying fertilizers in agriculture. The traditional belief that the women do not work outside home does not hold. However according to 1991 census only 9 per cent women fall in the categories of main workers. While the women favour men controlling agricultural land and animal wealth, they favour joint control of cash and jewellery, joint decision regarding education and marriage of children, sale and purchase of property. There is awareness of development programmes and availing of health facilities. Dower ranges from Rs. 50,000 to 1,00,000 depending on the status of the groups. There are different responses to whether the payment of *mahr* to the girl by the boys at the time of marriage is considered adequate, whether the *mahr* is paid in full or in parts and whether it is deferred and not paid except in the case of divorce. Divorce is permitted; a majority are remarried. There are differing perceptions about inheritance laws.

The recommendations made at the National Seminar on Gender Discrimation in the Kashmir Valley, 1997, drew attention to the rising incidence of atrocities against women, and the possibility of a rise in the trafficking in women, 'not as yet rampant in the Valley' with the onset of consumerism.

Consumption of fuel resources has important implications for environment and gender relations. The state being the coldest regions has returned one of the highest rates of consumption of fire wood, straw leaves (106 communities/95.5 per cent, against the national average 92.4 per cent), cow-dung cake (81/73 per cent), coal (37/33.3 per cent), saw dust (22/19.8 per cent), kerosene (98/88.3 per cent), electricty (100/19.1 per cent) all above national averages. However the consumption of *gobar* gas, solar energy is low.

J&K has reported a higher level of sharing and linkages among communities across religions. There is a higher level of acceptance and exchange of water and food, inter-community marriages, putative kinship, mitual visits to religious shrines and participation in festivals.

Besides the traditional linkages, J&K because of its progress in education also report a higher rise of entrepreneurs, businessmen and higher turn out of scholars, engineers, doctors, members in defence services. However political leadership is emerging slowly at regional and local levels. Because of the effective implimentation of land reforms and direct ownership of land, there is less incidence of inquitous relationship as landlord-cultivators, etc.

IX

Kashmiriyat (we may also add Ladakhiyat and Jammuriyat) is a recent concept but an old idea nurtured by ecology, culture, history and the traditions of living together as perceived by people. Kashmir was always considered a universe in itself with its unique schools of Kashmir Shaivism, Kashmiri Islam and the Rishi-Sufi school, its language and literary traditions in Sanskrit and Persian, etc. This composite culture which is the essence of Kashmiriyat has been much written about and is in evidence. However like composite culture and syncretism elsewhere Kashmiriyat is under attack by forces unleashed by fundamentalism, like in other parts of the world. Instead of a pluralistic view of history and culture of people or communities, a uni-dimensional view is sought to be developed, which strikes at the very root of the notion of people living together.

We saw evidence of this during our field study in the state. History was being reinterpreted, new constructions were being put on historical events and historical personages. Places were being renamed. Kashmiri language was being Persianized, complained the Pandits, or Sanskritized, complained others. *Shikar* was being replaced by domes. On the other hand we also saw evidence of very serious and sincere efforts being made to preserve and promote elements of the composite heritage symbolized by Kashmiriyat. We were told that the Pandits and Muslims of the Valley were like twins, inseparable.

After we concluded our field work the Valley exploded in unprecedented violence. Destruction of properties, distruption of economy and traditional way of life, occurred causing distress to people. The second largest migration of the Kashmiri Pandits from the Valley, occurred in 1989-90. About 2,75,000 of them moved out of which 33,000 families are registered in Jammu and 22,000 families are registered outside the state. They were followed by a number of Muslim families. Kashmir students migrated to Jammu and other parts of the country. Kashmiri marriages are reported as far as Chennai and

Guwahati. Matters became worse when the foreign mercenaries who had little feeling for Kashmiriyat arrived. All symbols of Kashmiriyat including the shrine of Nooruddin Rishi, Charar-i-Sharif, were burnt down.

There were suggestions to trifurcate the state. The sub-regions within each region were identified on the basis of history and ethnicity. The Committee on Regional Autonomy within Jammu & Kashmir (1997) headed by Balraj Puri recommended political, administrative, financial and cultural measures for autonomy of the three regions. Another committee identified additional autonomous regions of Rajouri, Poonch and Doda on the basis of history and ethnicity. Leh and Kargil were identified as autonomous regions according to the same criteria. Though Doda and Rajouri–Poonch are Muslim majority areas, they want to maintain their separate identity and stay with Jammu. Earlier the Ladakh Autonomous Hill Development Council was set up in 1994. Recently a Hill Council has been announced for Kargil to be set-up on 30 June 2003. The status of the reports of the two committees is not clear; a Hill Council for Doda is proposed. There is another suggestion that a Muslim state should be formed by uniting the Valley with the Muslim majority areas of adjoining Jammu and Ladakh regions. However the common view within Jammu and Ladakh is that these regions should not be broken up along the communal lines, and that the composite character of Kashmir as a state as also the existing character of the three regions should be maintained while granting substantial autonomy to each of them. This will be in consonance with the ethos of Kashmiriyat of which many touching demonstrations are available during the bloodiest period of violence and mayhem. The Valley people remain one of the gentlest peoples on earth. The Muslims would spontaneously join hand to celebrate the marriage in a lone Brahman family or arrange funeral of the Hindus who were killed. A recent survey suggests that 67 per cent of people in the Valley support Kashmiriyat, almost all of them eagerly wait for return of the Kashmiri Pandits and others and that 61 per cent of the people of the state want to remain in India for its democracy and economy (Manoj Joshi, June 2002). The results of the recent assembly elections also show that apart from 25 per cent people in the Valley, the rest want peace and therefore have participated in elections, risking their lives (Manoj Joshi, October 2002).

Similarly, the collective ethos of Ladakh and Jammu, is under stress with the rise of religious antagonism, misunderstanding and mutal suspicion. There is fear of losing one's identity. There is reaction against overcentralization of power and demand for regional autonomy which has been supported by all leaders of the state in the past and the present. The answer lies in genuine autonomy being given to the three units rather than trifurcation of the state or the reorganization of its various units as identified now along religious lines. Here also there are examples of communal harmony; there has been no communal flare up in Jammu or Ladakh. In fact there is coming together of religious groups in matters concerning autonomy for this region.

No matter what structure of political autonomy at regional and state levels may emerge, the elements of composite culture shared by people of all communities must continue to be preserved, developed and recreated.

K.S. SINGH

ACKNOWLEDGEMENTS

The People of India project for Jammu & Kashmir witnessed the involvement of the largest number of scholars, and organization of many rounds of discussions held in Srinagar, Jammu and Leh. Sri Mohd. Yusuf Taing, Director General and Secretary, Jammu and Kashmir Academy of Art, Culture and Languages, and his colleagues, extended all help when this project was in progress in Jammu & Kashmir. Special thanks are due to Prof. A.C. Bose, Head of History Department, Jammu University and his colleague Dr. Y.B. Singh, who, not only introduced us to a number of local scholars but also extended their full co-operation in arranging a workshop in Jammu University. Director, Centre for Central Asian Studies, Kashmir University, Srinagar, alongwith his colleagues Sri Riyaz Rufai of Documentation Office and Dr. Mohd. Iqbal Nazki cooperated with us. Sri Nawang Tsering, Reserch Officer, Jammu and Kashmir Academy of Art, Culture and Languages, Leh, also introduced us to the local scholars and provided valuable information on the communities of Ladakh. An informal discussion was held on Ladakh material in Leh.

The people of Kargil especially Sheikh Hassan and Agha Mahdi of Hardas not only made our stay comfortable in Kargil but also furnished information on the communities living in Kargil. Special thanks are due to Smt. Mehar Banu, a former K.C.S. officer, Mr. S.A.S. Rizvi, I.A.S., former Additional Chief Secretary, Jammu & Kashmir, and his wife Mrs. Janet Rizvi, a scholar of repute.

Prof. S.D.S. Charak made valuable contributions on the communities of Jammu. Dr. K.N. Pandita, Fellow Emeritus, Fotedar House, Jawahar Nagar, Jammu Tawi, not only contributed scholarly write ups on a number of communities of Kashmir but also edited the manuscripts and offered comments. Other scholars from outside who helped us included Dr. Ashok Aima, Reader, Department of Management Studies, Jammu University, Jammu, Dr. (Mrs.) A.K. Billawaria, Lecturer, Department of History, Jammu University, Jammu, and Dr. (Mrs.) Archana Kesar, Lecturer, Department of Dogri, Jammu University, Jammu.

Our scholars who contributed to the volume are Dr. B.R. Rizvi, Dr. A.C. Srivastava, Dr. P.N. Lal, Dr. B. Joardar, Shri B.K. Basu, Shri

B. Singh, Shri Anand Saran, Dr. D.K. Chakraborty, Shri Mukul Hazra, Smt. Indu Bala Aima Dhar, Fellow, all of the Anthropological Survey of India, North-Western Regional Centre, Dehradun. The General Editor acknowledges the excellent assistance extended by Sri Badal Kumar Basu in finalizing the volume. The General Editor also acknowledges the excellent note on historical ethnography prepared by Prof. S.D.S. Charak which was very useful in writing a part of the Foreword. The supporting technical and administrative staff which included Smt. S. Naswa (Librarian II), Shri B.B. Das (Photographer), Shri R.S. Jambulkar (Photo-Artist) and Shri Mahendra Singh (Sound Technician) are also thanked.

The General Editor thanks Prof. Riyaz Punjabi, Prof. Bashir Ahmad Dabla and Sri Balraj Puri for offering their comments on the Foreword.

The views and opinions expressed in this project are those of the scholars and researchers involved in it, as in all such projects and do not reflect the authorized views and opinions of the Anthropological Survey of India.

INTRODUCTION

ECOLOGICAL FEATURES

The Indian state of Jammu & Kashmir is bounded by China in the north and east, Afghanistan in the north-west and Pakistan in the west. In the south it is linked with the rest of the country. Here the state boundaries of Himachal Pradesh (south) and Punjab (south-west) touch the southern boundaries of Jammu & Kashmir. With a total geographical area of 2,22,870 sq. km., the state lies between 32° 17° N to 37° 5° N longitudes and 72° 40° E to 80° 30° E latitude. The declaration of a cease-fire line on 1 January 1949 left an area of 83,809 sq. km. under the illegal occupation of Pakistan. Thus about one-third territory of the state is under illegal occupation of Pakistan alone (Chib, 1977: 29-52). In October 1962, China captured an area measuring about 41,500 sq. km.

The physiography of Jammu & Kashmir presents a picture of a three storeyed house with three distinct physiographic divisions (Raina, 1972: 1). The first storey is formed by the piedmont plain bordered by the Shivalik Hills in Jammu. The second storey constitutes the Middle Himalaya which borders Kashmir Valley on the south; Pir Panjal is a significant mountain of this group. Beyond the Kashmir Valley are located the Greater or Inner Himalayas running north-west to south-east, in many parallel ranges. These ranges constitute the third storey. In fact two huge mountain masses of the world, viz., Karakoram and the Himalayas dominate the landscape of Jammu & Kashmir, with the Indus entrenched between them.

The state consists of many river valleys. The valleys of Kashmir, Gilgit, Hunza, Sind, Shigar, Zanskar, Shyok and Nubra are notable among a large number of valleys found in the length and breadth of the state.

The drainage pattern as found in the state too has a peculiarity which, in geological parlance, is known as 'antecedent drainage pattern' which denotes that the rivers of this region are older than the mountains. They have a special geographical significance for the state of Jammu & Kashmir. The entire landscape of the state has been eroded by the rivers resulting in a divergence in topographical features. The Indus, the Jhelum, the Chenab and the Ravi are the famous rivers of the state and some of their tributaries are the rivers

Poonch, Tavi, Ujh, Lidder, Kishenganga, Sind, Dras, Shyok, Nubra, Shigar Hunza, Gilgit and Astore. The state is studded with a number of lakes: Maansar, Surinsar and Sonsar lie in Jammu region. Majority of the lakes in Kashmir region such as Dal, the Wular, the Manasbal and the Achchabal, are some of the loveliest glacier-fed lakes. Among the salt water lakes, viz., Pangong Tso, Tsomoriri and Lingzithang, all situated in the arid deserts of Ladakh plateau.

The varied topography determines the varied climate of the state. The plains and the lower reaches of the valley have hot and tropical moist climate but it becomes cool temperate beyond 2,000 metres above the mean sea level. At an elevation of 3,000 metres and above the climate is pleasantly cool until it embraces the perennial snow-line where it is arctic. The amount of rainfall goes on increasing progressively up to an altitude of 2,500 metres above sea level before it starts decreasing. There is scant rainfall in the mid-Himalayan region and no rainfall in the trans-Himalayan region of the state. The precipitation is greatly affected by the direction and intensity of winds. South-west monsoon causes minimal rainfall beyond Punch and Uri whereas the western disurbances affect this state to the maximum resulting in heavy rainfall and snowfall. Mean monthly temperature in the state varies between 14° C to -17° C. An exceptionally high temperature was recorded at Jammu (47.2° C) on 12 June 1953 whereas exceptionally low temperature was recorded at Dras (-45° C) on 28 December 1910.

The Jammu region exeriences humid subtropical or monsoon type climate. The temperature ranges between 42° C in summer to 13° C during winter. Proximity of hills saves this region from the devastating hot winds blowing in the plains of north India. The region experiences rainfall both during summer and winters.

> One of the most powerful expressions of Kashmir's personality is observable in its weather.... Besides altitude, the surrounding mountains with their snow-clad peaks exert an overriding influence on the local weather making processes. They protect the valley from the blasting cold of the north as well as the scorching heat of the south and contribute significantly to its notable temperate character . . . a mild summer, a not too vigrous winter and an absence of regular rainy season are three distinctive features of the climatic regions of the Kashmir Valley:
>
> Heat there is, but hot 'tis not
> Cold there is, but cold 'tis not . . . Sufi (Raza et al. 1978: 61)

It is under this magic spell of Kashmir that Jahangir, the Mughal emperor exclaimed:

Gar Firdaus bar roo-e-zameen ast,
Hameen ast-o, hameen ast-o, hameen ast-o.

(If there is a paradise on Earth; it is here, it is here, it is here.)

Nowhere his ears revelled with such a sumptuous feast of sounds played by a harmonious symphony of its numerous springs, streams, rivulets and rivers; nowhere his eyes met with such a brilliant combination of colours: the sapphire-blue sky, the azure glassy sheet of water, the thick green mountainous surroundings casting their waivering shadows in sprawling lakes, the majestic arms of vast glaciers nursing the delicate water streams into the roaring torrents; its salubrious climate, the innumerable *margs* (meadows) and *nargs* (springs), the verdant gardens bedecked with flowers of hues that decorate a rainbow and the stately Chenars (*Cheh* = what; *naar* = flame). The beautiful nature has endowed the Valley with the best of beauty, richness and colours. Jehangir was doubtlessly enthralled by the valley's lush greenery but he could, not possibly have been thinking of that arid region in eastern Kashmir which is known as Ladakh. . . . If Ladakh cannot boast of nature's bounty, its high desert plateaus and granite peaks have a rugged charm of their own. (Ahluwalia, 1987: 10)

How did Ladakh become arid and desolate? The local traditions attribute this to the curse of Zoji-Lha-Mo, the goddess of the four seasons, who was the wife of Naropa. When the latter went to Ladakh, he wished her to be left behind. She was displeased at that, and turned her back towards Ladakh and her face towards Kashmir. This caused Ladakh to dry up and Kashmir to become fertile (Francke, 1972: 7). Its isolated, ancient culture endows it with a mystery; its borders touch Tibet, Chinese Turkistan, Baltistan, Pakistan and Afghanistan. It experiences temperature below freezing point for about five months in a year. There is an acute paucity of rainfall and lack of humus in the soil. Ladakh is one of the most elevated regions of the world, and very barren. The air is extremely rare and devoid of oxygen. The climate is rigorous: burning heat in the day succeeded by biting cold at night.

Thus the climate in the state changes from humid tropical to temperate and finally to Arctic and Tundra type near the perennial snowline. The slope, altitude, and lithology also change from place to place. These factors in combination have resulted in a unique type of vegetal cover in this mountainous state. Deciduous, conifer, shrubs, and scrubs are all found within the confines of the state (Chib, 1977: 47).

HISTORY

Jammu

Though inhabited by numerous communities, the political history of Jammu is mainly the story of its rise and expansion under the Dogra rule. Their recorded family traditions take the line back to hoary past and trace their descent from the divine Brahma himself through Ikshvaku, Ram Chandra and Jambulochan, who is said to have founded the city of Jambu or Jammu. But this legendary event evades all research. The early history of the state is shrouded in mystery. According to Vanshavali, the first raja, Angigir is said to have been a brother or kinsman of the Agni-born, the Raja of Ayodhya; his son, Vayusravar, added to his territory as far west as Jammu Tawi. The fifth ruler after him was Agnigarbha, who had eighteen sons, of whom the eldest two were Bahulochan and Jambulochan. Bahulochan succeeded his father and founded Bahu fort. He was succeeded by his brother Jambulochan who founded Jambu or Jammu on a spot atop a hill and made it his capital (Charak, 1971: 30). The state of Jammu was ruled by several dynasties of kings such as Takshila, Rai, Dhar, Dev, Sikhs and Dogras, till the state merged with the unified state of Jammu & Kashmir. It will not be out of place to mention here that the tenth successor of Gandharva Rai, named Jagrai, had a son Malhan Hans, also called Manharas, who became the ancestor of Manhas Rajputs. The city emerged as a *darul amaan* or 'the abode of safety' during the long reign of King Ranjit Dev when refugees, political sufferers, chiefs and princes sought shelter in Jammu. Many chiefs of renown repatriated their families and wealth to Jammu under Ranjit Dev because of upheavals caused by the Durrani invasions. Thus Jammu became a safe haven for rulers and commoners alike. Ranjit Dev also provided patronage to spiritual thinkers, poets and artists. Pahari paintings evolved as a distinct Jammu school under his patronage. The formation of a Sikh kingdom was to be laid in the once affluent city of Jammu under Maharaja Ranjit Dev. By 1808, Jammu came under the absolute sway of the Sikh rulers of Punjab but the Dogra resistance somehow continued during the next decade till Jammu Raj was reconsolidated under Gulab Singh, a military commander in Ranjit's army, who distinguished himself during an expedition to Kashmir in AD 1813 . Thus the scattered units of the former Jammu kingdom began to reconsolidate and the future shape of the emerging state of Jammu & Kashmir became crystal clear. His illustrious general Wazir Zorawar Singh Kahkuria marched into the Ladakhi territory through Kishtwar in 1834. His incursions continued till he finally conquered Leh in 1840. Because of his conquests, the state of Jammu & Kashmir was formed by tagging together three regions of Jammu, Kashmir and Ladakh which had existed as separate countries for centuries before their integration into one unit and Maharaja Gulab Singh was crowned as a ruler of the newly found state. Gulab Singh sent regiments to subdue the local chiefs of Kashmir, including Sheikh Imamuddin, but he failed to subjugate them. The British however intervened on behalf of Raja Gulab Singh. Srinagar was occupied without spilling of blood. Maharaja Gulab Singh of Jammu thus became ruler of Kashmir including Gilgit. He died in August 1857 and was succeeded by his son Maharaja Ranbir Singh who tried to provide a measure of stability to his kingdom by annexing Gilgit, Yasin and Darel Valley. Maharaja Ranbir Singh was succeeded by his son Pratap Singh who allowed the British to retain their Resident in Kashmir, a move that his father resisted till he breathed his last. He was succeded by his nephew Hari Singh as he did not have a son of his own. Hari Singh showed a considerable aptitude for administration. Hence, on becoming the ruler he initiated several schemes aimed at public welfare. He showed keen interest in starting schools, dispensaries, etc. He also took some steps for the upliftment of the rural masses. But in his time, political consciousness dawned through the length and breadth of the subcontinent. At this juncture Sheikh Mohammad Abdullah, a junior school teacher at Srinagar came into the limelight. Sheikh Abdullah worked on the lines of turning his party into a secular party embracing members from all faiths and shades. Under his leadership the National Conference raised a voice against the autocratic Dogra rule. On 20 May 1946 he was put behind bars for launching Quit Kashmir Movement. He was sentenced to three years imprisonment. After the Partition of India, the state of Jammu & Kashmir ceded to India and signed the Instrument of Accession with India while the Pakistani raiders were desecrating the land of Kashmir. Then followed the immediate military assistance by India to drive away the intruders. On 5 March 1940, the Maharaja appointed Sheikh Abdullah as his Prime Minister. In 1951, Sheikh Abdullah prevailed upon Maharaja Hari Singh to abdicate in favour of his son Yuvraj Karan Singh. On 31 October 1951 the Yuvraj was elected as Sadr-e-Riyasat for a period of four years. Thus the curtain was drawn finally on the Dogra dynasty.

Kashmir

The history of Jammu is inextricably woven with the history of Kashmir. It is the land adorned by the Vedas with their six *angas*, the *Vedantas*, the well arranged *Siddhantas*, by logic and grammar, by the Puranas, by the *mantras* and by the school of philosophy; by the followers of Shiva and Vishnu, by the worshippers of the sun, by the Buddhists and *viharas* and *mathas*, by the vine and saffron, the grains and the *shali*, and by fragrant flowers, by the *Shruties* and the *Tarkshastra*, by the Brahman worshipper of fire and the Brahmans devoted to contemplation, austerities, prayers, and anxious for ablution and worship; by the *kotis* of Nagas, by Hari and Hara, and by Gandharvas and Vidyadharas. Here the water is cool like *amrita* of heaven. In this country there are forty-five images of Mahadeva, sixty of Vishnu, three of Brahma and twenty-five of Shakti which are all well known; they have neither a beginning nor an end; and there are Nila and other serpents seven hundred in number, and fourteen *kotis* of good men who live in shrine (Dutt, 1986: 430). *Nilmatpurana*, to which Kalhan refers in his chronicle *Rajatarangini*, claims to furnish sacred legends regarding the origin of the country, and special regulations which Nila, the Lord of Kashmir Nagas, had revealed for his worship, and the rites to be observed by the people to ward off the evil intentions of the *pishachas.* The description and the legends of various *tirthas* furnished in this ancient text, help us to reconstruct an early history of Kashmir. Professor Buhler holds that the *Nilmatpurana* in its present form could not be older than the sixth or seventh century AD. Another source of Kalhana's narratives are *Mahatmyas*—some fifty in number—on their importance, their significance and legends attached therewith (*Bamzai*, 1962: 31). The earliest of the works dealing with the socio-economic life of Kashmir Valley may be mentioned as being *Kuttanimata Kavya* (eighth century AD). *Nrapavali* by Kshemendra (eleventh century AD) is considered as lost but his other work *Desopdesh* gives a vivid account of the daily life of different sections of the people inhabiting the valley such as cheats, misers, prostitutes, bawds, ostentatious pleasure seekers, degraded *saivagurus* and so on. One of the Kshemendra's poem *Samya-matrika* also throws considerable light on the prevailing socio-economic conditions in the valley through the medium of a courtesan, the description of places she visits and the people she comes across. To those poems we owe the earliest reference of the Pir Panjal pass. Finally, the most prestigious place among all the earlier reference to Kashmir, is occupied by Kalhan's *Rajatarangini*, a line of works continued further by Jonaraja and Sriara. The work was compiled during the years AD 1048-9. A Brahman by descent, Kalhan was a Shaiva by faith. But throughout his narrative he shows a reverent attitude towards other faiths.

> History, according to him, was not to learn but something to make people live and understand life. He points out the faults as well as virtues of kings and other characters whom he describes. His observations show that the achievements of the great are merely answers to certain deeds in society and success was only possible because time was ripe. Hence he does not cover up the faults of the state, an individual ruler or group of men. In his history there are no heroes or heroines and the few persons who might be so described are only functionaries of certain groups and have not been over emphasized; indeed whether we love them or not for their virtues it is their vices which make them unforgettable. Another trait in Kalhana is his freedom from narrow nationalism. (Pandit: xxvii)

Though for nearly two centuries after the advent of the Muslim rule Sanskrit continued to be the language for transacting official business, yet with the increasing patronage bestowed on the Persian language and literature by the Muslim rulers, the recording of events in Sanskrit ceased to be in practice. We have thereafter histories written in Persian by eminent Kashmiri scholars. Some of the earliest available works in Persian are by Malik Haider, Narain Kaul Ajiz, Khwaja Mohammad Azam Diddamari, and son Khwaja Mohammad Aslam, Pandit Birbal Kachru and Moulvi Ghulam Hasan.

With the adoption of Urdu and English as the court languages in the state towards the middle of the last century, some valuable contributions to the history of Kashmir were made by Pandit Anand Kaul, Ghulam Mohiuddin Sufi and Mohammad Dini Fouq, who, in 1934, published an exhaustive survey of the origin and history of various communities and well known families of Kashmir which is of considerable interest from an anthropological point of view.

Besides Kashmiri chroniclers, many other authors too have furnished varying descriptions of Kashmir. It has been mentioned as Kashmir in Panini's *obiter-dicta*. The *Mahabharat* also refers to Kashmir and its rulers. *Brihatsamhita* (AD 500) enumerates the tribes living in Kashmir. Some of them are the Abhisars, Darads, Darvas, Khasas and Kirats. A detailed account of Kashmir, its people, agriculture, religion, arts and crafts are given by Mirza Haidar Dughlat, a cousin of Babar, in his magnum opus *Tarikh-i-Rashidi*. Besides, some other important works where Kashmir finds a mention are *Tabqat-i-Akbari, Tarikh-i-Ferishta, Ain-i-Akbari*, Badauni's *Muntakhab-ut-Twarikh, Tuzuk-i-Jahangiri* and *Akbarnama*, etc.

Herodotus' description of Kaspapyros closely resembles Kashmir. Hiuen Tsang reached Kashmir Valley via Urusha (Hazara) in AD 631 and stayed there for two years to study Sanskrit and Buddhist lore. His account of viharas, stupas, of the climate and soil of the valley and of the people are accurate. Hieun Tsang's narrative throws a flood of light on the early history of Kashmir. Alberuni, though he never visited Kashmir, describes in details about the routes, the mountains, rivers, lakes and fortresses. Bernier, who accompanied Aurangzeb to Kashmir in 1665 gives an authentic portrayal of the economic and social life of Kashmir under the Mughals. Father Desidari, who reached Kashmir in 1714, has left an account of various handicrafts notably shawls. Other Europeans who made a detailed mention of Kashmir are Vigne, Moorcraft, Fredrick Drew, Walter Lawrence and Alexander Cunningham.

Geological evidence and mythological traditions are unanimous that the Valley of Kashmir was originally a lake formed of waters from the melting of ice and snow on the high mountain peaks surrounding it. In *Nilmatpurana* the lake has been referred to as Satisaras. In the period of seventh Manu, the demon Jalodbhava, who resided in this lake, caused great distress by his devastations. The Rishi Kashyap, the father of all Nagas, determined to punish the demon, sought help from Brahma and other gods. Brahma commanded all gods to proceed to Satisaras and take up their positions on the lofty peaks. The demon refused to come out of the lake when challenged. Thereupon Vishnu requested his brother Balbhadra to drain the lake which he did by piercing the mountains with his ploughshare. The lake was dried up and the demon was killed by Vishnu after a fierce combat. Rishi Kashyap then settled on the land of Kashmir which had thus been produced. Drew recognized the relation between the legend and those physical facts which seem to support the belief that Kashmir was occupied by a great lake.

Archaeological evidence of Burzahom dates the earliest settlers to 3000 BC, a settlement of early pit dwellers. Who were these people? Where did they come from? How identical artifacts excavated from Burzahom bear a striking resemblance with those excavated from the extreme south India are some riddles for which no scientific explanations are available. *Nilmatpurana* however, provides a clue mentioning settling of human groups from south India in Kashmir by Rishi Kashyapa. Subsequently a group of Aryans branched off from the parent Iranian body and settled in what is now known as Dardistan, which according to the Romans was the entire mountainous tract between the Hindukush and the frontiers of India proper. The Aryan language spoken in this region are, therefore, known as Dardic. They are Kafir, Chitrali, Shina, Kashmiri, and Kohistani. Besides Aryans from the north-west, there also came groups of Sanskrit-speaking Aryans from Punjab and other parts of India in addition to later immigrants of the Persian, Greek and Turkish descent. Tibetans too came in considerable numbers. Subsequently Kashmir absorbed colonies of Mughals, Pathans, Punjabis, and Paharis.

Rajatarangini gives an insight into the ethnic composition of the present state of Jammu & Kashmir. In the south and west the adjacent hill regions were occupied by the Khasas. Their settlements extended from Kishtwar in the south-east to the Jhelum Valley in the west besides the hill states of Rajouri and Punch. North of the Jhelum Valley upto Muzaffarabad was occupied by the Bombas. In the north and north-west, the Dards had their settlement that extended upto Chitral, Yash and Gilgit and the intervening regions towards Kashmir. The regions immediately to the north-east of Kashmir were held by Bhuttas or the modern Bhots or Bodhs of Dras, Kargil and Ladakh.

The history of Kashmir begins with the name Gonanda I whose initial year of reign coincides with the date of coronation of Yudhishtir, the Pandava king. According to Kalhana, this king and his successors were the relations of Jarasanda, the king of Magadh. Gonanda I fought a battle with Krishna and was killed. His son succeeded him. He too was killed in a battle by Krishna when the former wanted to avenge his father's death. On his death his minor son was declared his successor as his queen made a request for the young king. The next thirty-five kings, according to Kalhana, were lost to oblivion. It is, however, surmised that in the intervening period, Kashmir was ruled by kings of the Pandava dynasty. The first of these kings was Haranadeva, the son of Parikshit, the grandson of Arjuna, the third of the Pandava brothers. The recorded history of Kashmir genuinely begins with Ashoka. There is a consensus among the historians that the Ashoka of Kashmir was the Emperor Ashoka of Magadh whose dominion extended eastward to Bengal and westward to Hindukush. The most important event connected with Ashoka's reign was the introduction of Buddhism in Kashmir. Some five thousand monks were settled by Ashoka for turning the valley into a centre of study and propagation of Buddhist religious texts. After Ashoka's demise in 232 BC, his son Jatuka became an independent king of Kashmir. Being a worshipper of Shiva, Jatuka did not take keen interest in further expansion of Buddhism in Kashmir. During his reign the hordes of Indo-Greek Mlecchas tried to establish their colonies near Kashmir borders and Jatuka waged a ruthless war against them. This contact culminated into the emergence of Gandhara art style, new style of temple architecture with infusion of Greek characteristics. After Kashmir came under Kushan rulers, viz., Hushka, Jushka and Kanishka; the latter called the third Buddhist Council in Kashmir making the influence of Kashmir very marked in the development of Mahayana and its propagation by Kashmiri monks beyond India. From Kashmir it penetrated to Kandahar and Kabul and onward to Bactria. Tibetan Buddhism too was essentially of Kashmiri origin. Kanishka's Council gave a fresh impetus to the faith. Besides Tibet, South Central Asia and China came under the sway of Mahayanist or Northern Buddhism; the Kirgiz are said to have carried Buddhism to settlements as far as the Caspian. Buddhism, however suffered a reverse in Kashmir after the reign of Kanishka and his immediate successors. The old Shaivite faith was restored and the traditional Brahmanic learning was also revived under the King Jushka. The drive against Buddhism continued during the reign of his successor Gonanda III. Passing through the hands of Huns, Kashmir came under the rule of Harsh kings of Ujjain. This was followed by the revival of Gonanda dynasty which too came to an end with the death of Durlabhvardhana (AD 625-61) or Durlabhdeva, heralding the era of Baladitya and of Karkota dynasty that lasted till Muslim rulers established their rule in Kashmir.

By the beginning of the thirteenth century AD, Kashmir was being gradually influenced by the preachings of numerous Islamic teachers and a fair proportion of the people had already embraced Islam. The name associated with the earliest propagation of Islam is that of Saiyed Sharaf-ud-Din alias Bulbul Shah, a Moosavi Saiyed from Turkistan who first visited the valley in the reign of Sahadeva. He enjoyed enormous influence among the people; he worked and lived a life of complete abnegation. It is because of him that Kashmir came under the rule of the first Muslim king Rinchin (AD 1320-3) who embraced Islam in the hands of Bulbul Shah. The two became great friends. Bulbul Shah conferred the title of Sadruddin on Rinchin. Francke (1926: 227) notes the following praise of Rinchin:

Yar-eman bahr-e-mahfil aarai
Shud tamashai, har tamashai
Rooe-ookard daaw-e-Islam
Moo-e-ookard Kufr aarai

Kufr-o-Islam rabachang arad
Khud mar-an-changra tamashai

My friend has become the ornament of assemblies, the observed of all observers. His face claims Islam and his hair adorns paganism. He holds both paganism and Islam in his fist and his fist too is the cynosure of beholders.

Rinchin too had a great regard for Bulbul Shah and constructed a building in the name of his spiritual guide and named it Bulbul Lankar; he endowed a hospice and free kitchen (*langar*) for the poor. Rinchin's brief rule lasting for three years heralded the Muslim rule in Kashmir with timespan of 480 years which can be further broken into 247 years of Sultanat, 167 years of Mughals and 66 years of Afghan rule followed by 27 years of Sikh rule and 101 years of Dogra rule. A mere chronology of events or a portrayal of the train of various kings and rulers is beyond the scope of this study. It will, however, be interesting to know about the changing ethnic profile of the Kashmir Valley from Kalhan to the present day.

SOCIAL STRUCTURE

The social structure of Jammu & Kashmir has undergone many changes since first described in Kalhan's *Rajatarangini*. The following picture emerges from the *Rajatarangini*:

Brahmans	:	Custodians of scriptures, priests, teachers and warriors.
Rajputras	:	Tantrins, Ekangas, and Lavania.
Damara	:	Landed aristocracy.
Kayastha	:	Officials.
Shudra	:	Menials (Dombas), Chandal.
Nishad	:	Boatmen.
Miscelleneous tribal groups	:	Khasa (Khakha), Bomba, Dard, Bhatta, Kirat.

(Forest dwelling hunters and possibly the descendants of Burzahom pit-dwellers)

The distribution of various communities as described by Kalhan have been furnished in the following illustration.

The ethnic composition of Jammu & Kashmir underwent a radical change after the advent of Islam early in the fourteenth century AD With the influx of Muslim saints and philisophers from Persia and Central Asia, with the exception of Brahmans, most of the people belonging to other castes embraced Islam. Some of the Brahmans were, in due course of time, converted to Islam. They were divided into Katkuns and Bhashya Bhatts.

Now a new social structure emerged which could be visualized in the following diagram: All converts to Islam from the *dwij* category of the then existing varna order formed the rank of Sheikhs; Shudras formed the rank of Taifadarans and the autochthonous nomadic tribal groups which never identified themselves with peasantry formed the ranks of Adna-Agwam/Nangar. The new social structure which emerged after Islam took roots in Kashmir may be depicted as follows:

Hindu	*Muslim*
Brahmans	Saiyid
Kshatriyas	Sheikh
Vaishya	Mughal
	Pathan
Shudra	Taifadaran
Miscellaneous nomadic tribal groups	Adna-Agwam/Nangar

It is apparent from the above presentation that excepting Brahmans who were partially successful in retaining their Hindu identity all other castes merged into the fold of Islam. The next phase of social metamorphosis may be depicted in the following presentation:

Brahmans	Saiyid
	Sheikh
	Mughal
	Pathan
	Taifadaran
	Adna-Agwam

In Kalhan's scheme of social stratification of Hindu Kashmir: Brahmans occupy the highest place followed by Rajputras, Damaras, Kayasthas, Shudras, Nishads and miscelleneous tribal groups such as Kirats, Khasas, Bombas, Dardsad Bhatta, the present day Ladakhi Buddhist.

Hassan (1896) is first after Kalhan to present a post-Islamic ethnic profile of the Kashmir state. During his period the socio cultural profile of Kashmir has undergone a drastic change. The traditional varna order was replaced by an Islamic system of values based on equality and egalitarianism and sans differentiations. Consequent to unprecedented large scale conversions, a new ethnic profile of Jammu & Kashmir emerged. Brahmans too were converted to Islam partially but the groups below Brahmans were converted as a whole and the occupational nature of castes got translated to the newly converted societies.

Brahmans (partially), Rajputras, Damaras and Kayasthas after conversion swelled the rank of Sheikhs and were reconciled to a status lower to that of Saiyids who were immigrants and held prime position by virtue of their consanguineal proximity to Prophet Muhammad. After Sheikhs were placed Mughals and Pathans. The Shudras and Nishads joined the ranks of Taifadarans (occupational groups). Miscellaneous tribals were also placed by Hassan in the same category.

Lawrence (1895) placed Brahmans on top of the hierarchy to be followed by Rajputs, Chattri, Thakur, Dogra Rajputs in Jammu whereas in Kashmir Saiyids held the prime position in the hierarchy followed by Sheikhs, Mughals, Pathans, Faqirs, Taifadaran/Nangars. Fouq (1934) enlarged the scheme of social stratification further. According to his scheme Sadaat (Saiyids) held the topmost rung of the hierarchical ladder followed by Sheikhs, Mughals, Afghans, Oadeem Rajput, descendants of Vaishyas, miscelleneous groups and Adna-Agwam.

No continuous ethnic history of Jammu is available except that of Fouq's *Tarikh-e-Aqwam-e-Poonch* which is now out of print. But the ethnic composition of Jammu remained stable through the ages. Conversion took place on a restricted scale. Some members of the Rajput clans like Chib and Manhas got converted. The lower castes were largely influenced by Kabir's Bhakti movement and a majority of them identify themselves as Kabirpanthi. Sikhism too reached Jammu in the twelfth century. Many Brahman and Khatri groups got converted to this faith specially in Punch and Rajouri district. The emergence of Christianity too is a recent phenomenon. The conversion to Christianity, however, took place among the Chuhras of Jammu and Bodhs of Ladakh who now call themselves Moravian Christians.

Ladakh

As mentioned earlier Ladakh was first inhabited by the north Indian Mons followed by Dards who were later displaced by Tibetans. Islam reached Ladakh from Baltistan and a new community, viz., Argon emerged as a result of marital unions between Muslim traders and Buddhist women of Ladakh who were converted to Islam. Buddhism still holds sway in and around Leh, Nubra and Zanskar valleys. Kargil is predominantly inhabited by the Shia Muslim.

FAIRS AND FESTIVITIES

Jammu is predominantly populated by the followers of Hinduism followed by the Sikhs and a negligible number of Muslim, Christian and Jain populations. The Valley of Kashmir is predominantly populated by the Muslims, whereas Ladakh is the bastion of Buddhism. Another segment of Ladakh region is Kargil which is the stronghold of Shiite muslims. Hence the nature and scale of festivals and festivities differ considerably in the three regions. It will be, therefore appropriate to describe Jammu region first to be followed by Kashmir and Ladakh.

The Hindu population of Jammu region celebrate Ramnavami, Krishna Janmashtami, Dussehra, Diwali, Basant Panchami, Rakshabandhan, Devi Poojan, Makar Sankrant, Nag Panchami, Sitla Saptami, Ganesh Chaudash, Anant Chaudash, Deothan Ekadashi, Lohri, Tamden, Basor (Baisakhi), Karka Chaudash, Bachchda, Drubbadi, Holi, Bhugga, and Karva Chauth. The Khatri, in addition to the above festivals also celebrate Guruparb and *urs* of Baba Farid, the famous Sufi saint of Punjab whose couplets find a place in the *Guru Granth Sahib*. The backward communities attend the birth anniversaries of various Muslim saints lying buried in the region. The Christian Chuhra observe Christmas and Easter. The Jains observe Panjsanas, Chhamachari, and Das Lakshmi. The Gujrati (Nagar) Brahman celebrate the worship of *kul-devi* Ambika. They also worship their presiding deity Hatkeshwar during Chait Purnima and observe Panchyatna Puja wherein Lord Ganesh, Vishnu, Surya, Shiva and Shakti are worshipped. The Muslim celebrate Id-ul-Fitr, Id-ul-Zuha, Urs-e-Nabi (Prophet Muhammad's birth and death anniversaries), Meraj-e-Alam, Shab-e-Qadr and Shab-e-Barat.

The Kashmiri Muslim celebrate all the above mentioned festivals observed by the Muslims of Jammu region in addition to keeping alive 'Rishi' and Sufi tradition of celebrating *urs* of various saints. To start with, Hazratbal is the centre of religious and political activities for an average Kashmiri. The shrine and the mosque on the western side of Hazratbal lake is the repository of a sacred hair of the Prophet Muhammad. The holy relic passed on from the descendants of the Prophet to Saiyid Abdullah, the trustee of the Prophet's shrine at Madina. In the year 1634, he left for India with his family and settled at Bijapur. He handed over the said relic to his son Saiyid Hamid. After Aurangzeb annexed Bijapur, the *jagir* of Saiyid Hamid was also confiscated and the latter migrated to Jehanabad where he came in contact with a Kashmiri trader Khawaja Nuruddin Ashwari and sought his help in distress. The Khwaja gave him money readily and requested him to part with the sacred relic. The request was turned down but the same night the Saiyid was directed by the Holy Prophet to hand over the hair relic to the Khwaja who was detained by Aurangzeb at Lahore who wanted to keep the relic at Ajmer. The Khwaja was deeply shocked at being relieved of the relic and died at Lahore, expressing the last wish to a friend, Khwaja Medanish, that should he succeed in getting back the relic, it should be taken to Kashmir and lodged there at a suitable place. Aurangzeb too was directed by the Prophet in a dream to hand over the relic to Khwaja Madenish who carried it to Kashmir. After being kept for some time in the Khanqah of Naqshband, it was finally lodged in the mosque built already by Shahjahan (Bamzai 1962: 537-8). The disappearance of the holy relic during the reign of Bakhshi Ghulam Mohammed engulfed the valley in a turmoil of vast magnitude. The relic was, however, recovered due to the untiring efforts of the Government of India and was restored to its original place. The public display of the relic on the occasion of Barawafat (Prophet Muhammad's birth anniversary) and Shab-e-Meraj are two great events in the life of the Kashmiri Muslims who seek to have a glimpse of the relic. There are numerous other shrines where birth and death anniversaries are celebrated with an elan. These include Urs-e-Shah Hamdan, Urs-e-Pir Dastgir, Urs-e-Rafimal, Urs-e-Baba Rishi, and Urs-e-Naqshband, etc. The Shiite Muslims observe Moharram, Id-e-Ghadir, Nauroz, a festival of harvesting, and birth and death anniversaries of the immediate descendants of the Prophet Muhammad (Ahl-e-Bait).

The Bodhs and Muslims of Ladakh celebrate Losar festival alike but in different ways. The Muslims abstain from dances and music, which are the major activities performed by the Buddhists on this occasion. The birth anniversaries of prominent lamas are celebrated with mask dances performed by the monks at Lamayuru, Liker, Thiksey, Spitook, Matho, Hemis, and Chimry monasteries. The Dards, both Buddhists and Muslims, have a tradition of observing harvesting festival. The Broqpa (Shin) call it *fasal ka sadga* and the Buddhist section of Dards (Dokhpa) know it by the term *chopo stripula*. The Shin Broqpa sacrifice a goat on this occasion and offer *Chabarda Masoomeen* (Fourteen Innocents). The meat is distributed among the kin and neighbours.

LANGUAGES AND DIALECTS

According to Grierson, the languages that were prevalent were Kashmiri, Dogri, Ladakhi, Punjabi, Pahari, Gujri, Balti, Nagari (of Hunza and Nagar), Shina Chang-Khat, Droskhat, Gaddi, Gujrati, Punchi, Sikligari and Pushto. There are some minor languages and dialects which do not find a place in Grierson's *Linguistic Survey* (1927, 1967 reprint), viz., Gaddi, Changskhat (spoken by Champa of Ladakh), Nagri (spoken by a group of settlers from Hunza and Nagar and now settled in Srinagar) and Gujri (spoken by the Gujjars and Bakerwals). All languages and dialects have been superimposed on the existing model evolved by Grierson for the state of Jammu & Kashmir. Under the People of India project, nineteen languages were identified, which are as follows: Balti, Changpa, Dogri, Drokshat, Gujrati, Gujjari, Haryanvi, Hindi, Kashmiri, Ladakhi, Nagari, Punchi, Punjabi, Pahari, Parimu, Pashto, Shina, Sikligari and Urdu.

When the people talk with others they either use Urdu or English. The Ladakhis also talk in Kashmiri.

As many as 62 communities use Arabic script, 32 Devanagari, 7 Ladakhi, and 2 communities use Gurmukhi scripts. The wide usage of Arabic script is due to the fact that Kashmiri, Balti and Punjabi to a limited extent have adopted Arabic script whereas other languages use Devanagari, Bodhi and Gurumukhi scripts.

SETTLEMENT PATTERN

The topography of Jammu, which is of unsystematic rise and fall and steep plateaus, is responsible for the scattered location of the houses. Houses are mostly old in design and are often enclosed by a tank, wastelands, gorges and wells. Temples and graveyards are also attached. The distance between two huts or two groups of houses is variable. The residential pattern in Kashmir consists of a linear cluster of houses with regular open space and with a street lined, except for a few sporadic cases, on either side of houses. An open space generally intervenes between two houses. Almost every house has a separate wooden godown built in the premises and at a short distance from the main building. No compound is enclosed within a wall, making it difficult to determine the boundaries of the premises. Villages in Ladakh are divided into a number of *mohallas* (localities). The distance between the two hamlets varies and depends on the topgraphical features of a village. As most part of the year the weather remains dry with little snow, the houses unlike Kashmir valley, have flat mud roof. The houses, mostly *kachcha* huts, donot form any clusters but are built in tiers, up the side of steep cliffe-like hill. The houses have not been built according to any hygenic plan. One also comes across huts built near land holdings which necessitates the dwellings to be far away from the rest. Compounds attached with the dwellings are neither fenced nor demarcated.

HOUSE TYPES

In rural Jammu both *kachcha* and *pukka* houses coexist though the latter type is lesser in number. *Pukka* houses are usually double-storeyed constructions whereas the *kachcha* houses are mostly single-storeyed constructions. The dimension of a house, on the whole, are 20' x 25' with an average capacity of two rooms. The *kachcha* houses have slanting and flat roofs. *Pukka* houses are constructed with cement, lime, stucco, burnt bricks and stones, and have reasonably good accommodation. *Kachcha* houses, on the other hand, are mud constructions, some are of sun-baked bricks plastered from within and outside with a thick layer of clay and hay. People with low income generally have an insignificant base plinth below the building while the rich raise *pukka* plinths about 2' above the ground with stone or bricks. The *chat* (roofs) in majority of the houses are flat while in the rest the houses are huts with double sloped roofs covered from above with thatch grass, bamboo, mats and branches of trees. Open *chats* are used for sleeping purposes during summer nights. In all the *pukka* houses and in some of the *kachcha* ones, stairs are attached in the compound for having an access to the roof. In some cases, movable bamboo or wooden stairs are used for this purpose. *Pukka* houses are covered with timber, tiles and cement. In the rest of the houses, logs of regular or irregular wood are placed over the opposite walls one and a half feet apart. The intervening distance is covered with branches of trees, bamboo matting, thatch and small wooden planks. Such roofs are further covered with a thick layer of clay and hay and is finally besmeared with an emulsion of cow-dung and clay from above which saves the plaster from breaking when it becomes dry.

Pukka buildings are well constructed with facilities of ventilation and resemble the houses constructed in the towns of Punjab. Most of these dwellings have been constructed with small tiles or bricks depicting old architecture dating to the reign of Maharaja Pratap Singh.

Kachcha buildings consisting of medium-sized rooms attain an average height of 8' and are poorly ventilated with hardly a window for each room. All buildings, except huts, have separate kitchens and cattlesheds. In the huts food is cooked either in a corner or in the attached open compound. An outlet for emission of smoke is made in the roof. Most of these huts neither contain a lavotary nor a bathroom. The inhabitants of such houses therefore defecate in the sprawling fields and bathe in the nearby streams and rivulets.

Majority of houses have a provision for a compound, fenced or unfenced, which are used for storing cow-dung or hay. People sleep in the open in these compounds during searing summers.

In emulating the urban ways of living, the people now construct a latrine and bathroom in a corner of the *pukka* house. Hindus generally like the new houses to face east-south but the people of other faiths have no such reservations. The family priest is invariably consulted before laying the foundation of new houses. The ceremony is called *nee-rakhna*. Friends and relatives assembled on the occasion to felicitate the builder of the house. When the house is ready for occupation, another ceremony, *greh parvesh*, is celebrated. A priest is called to perform *nav-grah pujan* attributed to the nine stars which are supposed to affect human life. Sweets are distributed among the invited guests and close relatives.

Construction of houses in Kashmir are not regulated by any plan. Some of the buildings are closely knitted together while many others are dispersed over comparatively long distances. By and large, most of the house are double storeyed. The soil being rocky, it is not necessary to lay deep foundations. Stone available in plenty are invariably used for the construction of plinths. The wall material consists of wood and both baked and unbaked bricks. The walls are plastered either by mud in the rural areas or by cement in urban areas. The roofs are covered with wood, thatch and in some cases by shingle. The roofs are built in a slanting manner in order to facilitate the clearance of water and snow. The dimensions of rooms vary according to the size of the building, but do not generally exceed 10' x 12'. The height of the rooms on the ground floor are lower than those of the upper floors because of severe cold in winter when the occupants live on the ground floor for being low, warmer and more comfortable. Rooms on the first and second floor are occupied during summer. The ground floor usually consists of two rooms separated by a gallery which gives an access to the first floor. One of the rooms which is unventilated is used as a cowshed. The other is a multipurpose apartment serving simultaneously as a kitchen, a dining, sleeping and living room. Except for a very small window behind the hearth there is no device to exhaust the smoke. In summer, the kitchen is shifted to a corner of one of the large-sized rooms in the upper floor. The staircase is either provided inside the house or is constructed against the outer wall. Though the dimensions of houses vary, the average size in a majority of the houses does not exceed 30' x 25'. The front of the houses faces east. In more spacious buildings, a large number of rooms are provided on each floor. Fodder for animals is generally stored in the upper storey which generally consists of only one room of a fairly large size. The inmates of a single-storeyed building store their stocks of hay on the trees growing in their premises. Windows are provided in the front side of the building facing the compound. Small ventilators are provided in the front to let in light. Houses in urban areas consist of three storeys with glazed windows. The doors are made in two parts supported by hinges. The walls are made of baked bricks and stones. The roofs are usually covered with shingle. Some of these buildings also have verandahs projected from the first and second floors. Bathrooms and lavatories are usually not built within the dwelling in rural areas. An open compound is generally attached to every dwelling. The compounds of the houses built in a row are neither fenced nor demarcated; though the boundaries of each compound are well known to the people concerned. The months of Moharram and Safar are avoided to start the construction of new houses. The third, eighth, thirteenth, twenty-third, and twenty-eighth days of the lunar months are also considered inauspicious to start constructions. Spring and autumn, when the people remain relatively free from agriculture, are the seasons when new constructions are usually started. Family priests are invited to lay the foundation of a new house and recite verses from the Holy Koran. Economically well-off families make an offering of a sheep or goat to mark the occasion and the meat of the slaughtered animal is distributed among the relatives and neighbours. People with limited means serve tea to the guests assembled on the occasion. The head mason is presented with a nine-yard piece of muslin cloth to be used by him as a turban. All the skilled as well as unskilled labourers are served with dinner atleast on two occasions while the construction is in progress. When the building is complete and ready for occupation for the first time, priests, relatives, friends, neighbours and the labourers involved in its construction are invited and served with a sumptuous dinner. On this occasion the priest recites verses from the Holy Koran. On crossing Zoji-La, the whole aspect of the country changes once more. The tall wooden, double-sloped houses of Kashmir Valley give way to low, mud-constructed, flat-roofed dwellings found in other sub-montane areas of the state. In Ladakh, the houses are double-storeyed *kachcha* dwellings. Plinths and foundations are raised with stones. The material of walls consists of either unbaked bricks or stones plastered with clay. The elevation of a storey ranges from 6' to 8'. Owing to intense cold during nights when the temperature falls as low as -23° C and fierce winds blow, the sizes of the doors and windows are kept comparatively smaller, i.e. 2.5' to 5' and 2' to 2.5' respectively. The roofs are flat and are built of poplar beams, peeled about 4" to 5" in diameter and placed on the opposite walls with an intervening distance of 5' to 6'. The gap between the logs is covered with twigs of willow or poplar trees. The house tops are finally plastered with a thick layer of mud mixed with dry grass. Since there is hardly any rain, the house structures last a very long time. No arrangements are noticeable for escape of water from the roofs. An average dwelling measuring 20' x 15' contains six rooms. The ground floor contains two rooms, one of which is used for keeping cows and *zomos* (a mixed breed of cow and yak) while the other is used for accommodating sheep. The first floor consists of the remaining four rooms. These are used as bedroom, kitchen and storeroom. The bedroom is bigger in size than the rest. Kitchens also serve as dining and sleeping rooms in several households due to scarcity of space. The kitchen has an opening in the centre of the *ogun* (room) which serves as an outlet for smoke. Bathrooms and lavatories are built within the residential complex. A small corner of the compound houses the lavatory in a double-storeyed construction. The night soil gets accumulated in the basement from the first floor. The absence of bathrooms may be attributed to the fact that people in Ladakh do not take bath regularly due to the rigours of the climate. Uttensils and clothes are washed either by the side of a *kuhl* or the storage tank. For bathing people go to the adjoining streams. In the house of the headman of a village one room is kept reserved for a little private temple, used chiefly by the head of the house for reading his holy book and repeating his prayers. The visiting lamas invited for worship are also accommodated in this room. Where a whole room can not be set apart a small corner in the best room will be arranged as an altar with all necessary paraphernalia of ritual. Among the Muslims the best room is always used by the head of the household where he performs his ablutions and says his prayers. Most of the houses have a large bright room upstairs for use in summers. For laying foundation the village priest is consulted. The Muslim populace consider the months of Moharram and Safar, and the third, fifth, thirteenth, sixteenth, twenty-first, twenty-fourth and twenty-fifth days of other *Hijri* months inauspicious for starting new constructions. The autumn months are most suitable for starting new constructions. On the foundation-laying day, some elderly respected person of the household or the village is invited to lay the foundation stone. When the function is over, breads smeared with butter are distributed among the guests. No other function is held till wooden beams are laid on the walls and the building is ready. It is not occupied by the members unless they observe another ceremony concluded with a normal dinner in honour of all the guests who are invited to participate in the function.

DRESS

The traditional dress in Jammu region is *pyjama* and *kameez* for men and *kurta* and *lehnga* for women. Men customarily wear a turban as a headgear. Elderly female dress consists of loose *salwar* and *kameez.* The newly-wed wear coloured *sari* and blouse. They also use *dupatta* as their headgear invariably dyed in some colour to add gaiety. The younger generation do not like clumsy traditional dress of their elders. They rather covet the latest designed garments current in towns and cities. Most of them can be seen clad in shirts, bush shirts, ready-made T-shirts, shorts and pants. Children attending school wear smart school uniform. They dispense with the headgear and prefer to keep combed hair. The young school girls too are not favourably disposed to old traditional dresses of their elders but they like a smart outfit of *salwar* and *kameez* of printed mill made cloth with a matching *chunni* or *dupatta.* During winter warm clothings made of wool such as coats, pullovers, and shawls, etc., are used in addition to the above dresses.

Younger people of both sexes in Kashmir usually put on a cotton shirt and trousers during summer. The women wear a *pheran* which covers the body and arms and falls below the calf of the leg. During winters, men too put on *pherans* made of woollen cloth. The sleeves of the *pheran* remain folded not to obstruct in work. The women wear slightly shorter *pherans* than those worn by men. Female *pherans* are embroidered with gold (*tilla*), silk and cotton thread around the neck, sleeves, and lower broad portion covering the knee. The *pheran* consists of two garments of equal size. The inner garment called *pochh* is invariabley made of thin cotton cloth. The outer one is fairly expensive, the cloth used being cotton print, rayon-silk, wool or poplin. Men wear a locally made skull cap on their heads. Respectable people, priests and economically well-off people put on a *karakuli* cap or a turban. Women cover their head with a piece of white cloth or a silk scarf of grey colour. At home, during winters school-going children also put on *pheran.* Women in villages move about freely without observing *purdah*. In cities, however women from respectable families cover their faces with a *naqab* (veil). Saiyids, Mirs and Shahs observe *purdah* strictly but highly educated women among them have given it up completely.

In Ladakh the climatic conditions, scarcity of modern amenities, and backwardness of the area have influenced the inhabitants to wear the traditional dress. It consists of a woollen cloak (*guncha*) made of *pattu* and usually white, brown and black in colour. A *skerak* (girdle) is tied around the waist. Trousers made of *dorma* (wool) and *nating* (woollen caps) are also part of the male dress. The *paposh* (footwear) are made of *pattu* and buffalo hide. The women wear a tunic and trouser made of wool. Unmarried girls put on white trousers whereas the married wear black trousers. While carrying loads in a conical wicker basket, a *sakpa* which is usually made of yak skin, covers their back. It also helps to keep their body warm specially during winters. Usually no shirt is worn under the tunic. The Broqpa women wear a *khoi* (cap) which is tastefully decorated with silver flowers grown in their kitchen gardens and semi-precious stones. The girdle worn around the waist by men contains a variety of items such as a pouch containing fire making apparatus; a *chakmak* (piece of flint), a small iron ball to strike and produce fire and a variety of knives of various shapes and sizes, a metallic or wooden box containing toothpicks, a porceline cup for drinking tea and *khachi* to be consumed on the way on a journey. School-going children wear shirt and shorts as their uniforms during the summers and replace these garments during winters by woollen pants and coats, etc.

ORNAMENTS

The state of Jammu & Kashmir shows a predominent use of silver ornaments by all communities excepting among the Brahmans, Dogra rulers, Kashmiri Pandits and members of the ruling class in Ladakh.

The range of ornaments current in Jammu region consist of *punjaba* (anklet) made of silver, silver made *kaday* (bracelets), silver made *sera* (necklace), silver made *mundri* (finger rings), silver made *jhumka* (earrings), and *kantha* (a long circular ring of silver worn around the neck particularly by old women). Other ornaments used by the women of this region are multi-coloured glass bangles, imitation jewellery and cheap cosmetics. *Bindi* made of red oxide of a red deep colour is invariably applied by married women in the centre of the forehead. *Sindoor* applied on the hair-parting is a symbol of married women. Some of the men folk also wear earrings made of gold which may be attributed to the legacy inherited from their Dogra ancestors and which was popular among the Hindu inhabitants of the state for a long time but has since been discarded. A few of them, however, wear finger rings of gold, *ashtadhatu* and stainless steel.

Only a few in Kashmir wear gold ornaments. Some of the ornaments currently used in Kashmir are: *khilamel* and *halkaband* (necklaces), *korr*, *bavet bungar* and *hachh-band* (bangles), *waij* (rings), *akapawn* (ornaments fastened to hair plaits), *nalasuchen* (pin fastened in *pheran*). These are all made of silver. Among the gold ornaments: *guloband* (necklace), *patri* (bangles), and *waij* (rings) are the common items. The women of Kashmiri Pandits wear *dehjore* (ear pendant) as a symbol of marriage. *Hang taiviz* (amulets) encased in a tiny silver casket are also worn round the neck or forearm by the men and women. Men wear finger rings made of silver.

The ornaments used in Ladakh are *tumar* (head pendant), *hojring* and *kunzum* (necklaces), *allong* and *kanvaij* (earrings), *bazoo-band* (armband), *kabu* (necklace pendant), *phrah* (necklace), *shisha tumar* (head pendant), *pandap* (pendants worn in front by married women), *branshrik* (silver pendant), *nacha* (necklace made of tiny beads of silver), *chapkali* (silver necklace), *urdingu* (bangles made of silver or glass), *khinchan* (amulets encased in a silver casket). These are worn by all irrespective of sex and age. Some people wear small stone discs around their neck and forearm inscribed with *Naad-e-Ali* or *Ayatul Kursi*, the sacred verses.

The ornaments worn in Jammu region show a similarity with the ornaments used in the adjoining states of Punjab and Himachal Pradesh whereas those current in Kashmir and Ladakh regions do not only portray a similarity amongst themselves but are very close to those current in other parts of Central Asia such as Caucasia and Sinkiang.

HOUSEHOLD ARTICLES

Dislocation, poverty and low standard of living characterise villages of Jammu region. They possess bare minimum items of furniture not for themselves but for guests and visitors. A few wooden benches and chairs with hard bottom and cots made of bamboo or wooden frames and woven either with *newar* (canvas strips) or with ropes are usually used for sitting by family elders. Cots are known as *manji*. The items of furniture depend on the economic capacity of a family. Affluent people irrespective of their social status keep sofa sets and wooden cane or fancy aluminium framed chairs.

Kashmir region shows a different picture so far as furniture items are concerned. In villages, items of furniture are rarely used. The cold climate necessitates sitting arrangement with carpet and large mats made of *waggu* (weeds). The sitting room contains besides *waggu* mats, *dari* and carpets made of wool. Affluent family lay a *gallen* (carpet made of wool and a silk) over woolen *dari*. Pillows of various sizes and shapes are kept to provide back rest. The upper class keep fancy sofa sets around the carpet for visitors. Willow, being abundantly grown in Kashmir Valley, is extensively used for making sofa sets, chairs and swings. Similar pattern and type of furniture is used in Ladakh too.

Household utensils used in Jammu region are *patela* (cauldron for cooking rice, mutton and vegetables, etc.), *dhakna* (lids for covering *patela*), *kadchi* (ladle for pouring curry, etc.), *thali* (big plates in which food is served), *chimcha* (spoons), *kaulis* (cups in which cooked vegetable and soups, etc., are served), glass tumblers, *trambi* (a vessel for kneading flour, etc.), and *garvi* (a vessel for pouring water). The above utensils are made of brass. The earthen utensils of Jammu region are: *ghada* (pitcher), *kuni* (used for boiling milk or rice, etc.), *matt* (for storing grains), *kool* (a big box made of wooden planks, bricks and mud for storing grains) and *pandole* (drum-like storage vessel made from bamboo, sticks and mud). Other articles of domestic use are *tawa* (an iron frying pan for baking leavened breads), *kadai* (an iron vessel used for frying and cooking vegetables, etc.), *chakla* and *belna* (round shaped disc made of wood and a wooden roller for flattening and shaping *chapati* (leavened breads), *kundi*, *danda*, or *sil-batta* (mortar and pestle made of stone and used for grinding spices, etc.), and *chakki* (stone mill). *Charkha* (spinning wheels) was also one of the household articles especially among the weavers of Jammu and it used to be given to daughters as an item of dowry in the past but now it has fallen to disuse. Earthen pots are being swiftly replaced by more durable and less heat-consuming aluminium and stainless steel vessels. Pressure cookers are also becoming popular kitchen items.

In Kashmir copper utensils are more in use as brass does not find favour especially with the Muslim population. Earthen utensils, however are still used in Kashmiri villages. The utensils made of copper with tin or lead polishing from inside are: *degchi* (cooking pot for rice, mutton and vegetables, etc.), *patela* (for boiling water), *samawar* (for preparing tea), *toore* (vessel for taking meals), *kenz* (cups used by females for taking meals), *traem* (a big plate from which four persons share meals simultaneously especially during *wazwan* feasts), *lavari* (oil container), *chai chooncha* (a spoon for pouring tea or drawing water), *naer* (a jug used for pouring water), *tash* (a vessel used for washing hands before taking meals), *sarposh* (a lid placed over *traem* while serving *wazwan*), *dul* (container used for storing water or churning tea mixed with butter), *bushqab* (a bowl used for eating rice by male members), *isbandoz* (incense burner), and *kashwa* (a small spoon used for vegetables). The brass utensils are tastefully decorated with engraving of floral and at times calligraphic motifs which reflect the economic status of their users. Plain copper utensils, on the other hand, are cheaper than those adorned with engravings and are used by the middle class people. Spoons and ladles of various shapes and sizes are honed out of blocks of wood also. *Qahwa* and *sheer-chai* (tea) are served in *piala* (ceramic cups). It is interesting to note that *samawar* and *pialas* are widely used by the people of Central Asia also. Earthen utensils are widely used by the people living in villages. These consist of *nott* (pitcher used for storing water), *leij* (pot used for cooking vegetables and other dishes), *khos* (vessel for taking meals), *bushqab* (vessel for taking meals), *matt* (huge pitchers used for storing food grains meant for day to day consumption), *tagair* (wash-basin used for cleaning feet and clothes), *tabachh* (a pot used by females for taking meals), *piala* (a cup used for drinking tea). Other household articles are *kruchh* (an iron ladle for drawing fire from the hearth), *wokhul* and *kajwath* (morter and pestle made of stone for grinding spices), and *gortt* (stone mill for grinding corn, etc.). Sugar, salt, tea and other spices are stored in small tin cans or earthen containers. *Kangri*, an exclusive component of Kashmiri culture is a portable earthen brazier enclosed in wicker work.

Utensils made of copper are also used in Ladakh. The copper

utensils are *samawar*, *tabaq* (plates), *karis* (a pot for taking ablutions), *mongur* (a cup used for serving side dishes), *ketli* (kettle for pouring tea). The items made of Chinese porcelain are used for taking tea and *finjan* (tiny cups) for drinking tea and *qahwa*. *Rezm* (box made of wood) is used for storing *sattu*. Of late copper utensils are being replaced by aluminium and stainless steel. 'Yera' (tumblers) and pressure cookers are fast replacing the traditional utensils. *Gurgur* is yet another contraption exclusive to Greater Himalayas especially to Ladakh and Spiti (Himachal Pradesh). It is a piston-like instrument that churns Ladakhi tea.

AGRICULTURAL IMPLEMENTS

Agricultural implements used in Jammu region are *hal* (plough), *punjali* or *jungla* (yoke), *dandal* and *dhurat* (sickles), *gaintee* and *khurpa* (pickaxe), *kaie* (spade), *gudnoo* (clod-breaker). The agricultural implements used in Kashmir area are more or less the same as those found in Jammu but their nomenclature differs. They are: *albine* (plough), *yepeth* (yoke), *drot* (sickle), *ramb* and *khon* (pickaxe), *belcha* (spade), *yeth phour* (clod-breaker), *maj* (leveller). The agricultural implements used in Ladakh are *hal* (plough), *athar* (yoke), *pheonli* (spade), and *tokche* (pickaxe).

FOOD HABITS

The food habits in the state differ as widely as the altitude, topography and the climate. In Jammu, the staple food is wheat, corn and rice which is also consumed but in a lesser quantity. The people take two main meals in a day besides *nahari* (breakfast) and some refreshments in the evening. In *nahari*, the leftover *chapatis* from the previous night are served with pickles and fried vegetables. Fresh ones may also be prepared in case there is a guest around. The items for lunch and dinner do not show much difference and they consist of *chapatis* made of wheat or maize eaten with gravy of vegetables and pulses. The pulses consumed are *mash*, *mungi*, *rajmah*, *rongi*, *channe*, etc., and the vegetables consumed are *bhindi*, *karela*, *tinda*, *sag*, onion, potato, carrot, turnip, brinjal, tomato, etc. Beans are highly relished. Poor people who cannot afford to buy pulses and vegetables eat *chapatis* with jaggery, pickle or *chutney*. Very few people are purely vegetarian. They relish chicken, mutton, pork and eat them occasionally as most of them cannot afford to treat them as regular items of diet. Milk products such as curds, *lassi* and buttermilk are used regularly. In villages, domestic cattle are the main source of milk supply but families that do not own any cattle purchase milk and milk products from the market. There is no change in staple food because of seasonal variation except that tea is replaced by cold drinks such as *lassi* and soda or *shikanjee* (fresh lime mixed with water and syrup). Inhabitants of towns enjoy ice-cream and *kulfi* in hot months. Tobacco is smoked in the form of cigarattes, *bidi*, and also *hookah* (hubble-bubble). Adult males drink alcohol and drinking of alcohol is reportedly on the increase. Alcoholic drinks are mostly purchased from the market but in villages some families often brew and distil *desi sharab* for their own consumption. Rice is the staple food in Kashmir which is eaten both at lunch as well as at dinner. Breads made out of wheat or maize flour baked hard on slow fire are eaten with salted tea at breakfast. People in the urban areas take *chachru*, *kulcha* or *bakarkhani* which are purchased from the *kandur* (bakers). Besides pulses like *moth* and *rongi*, a variety of vegetable such as potato, tomato, carrot, turnip, pumpkin, *hak*, *karam hak* and *karam mundi*, etc., are eaten with rice. Mutton is consumed by almost everybody of the middle and upper classes. Fowls and fish are also consumed occasionally. On special occasions such as marriage or festivals a variety of dishes are prepared from mutton. Some of these dishes are: *goshtaba*, *rista*, *tabaqmaz*, *kababa* and *yakhni*, etc. During Id guests and visitors are entertained with a variety of cakes. Sweets are not relished much in Kashmir owing to some local inhibitions. Milk is also not a favourite item of the Kashmiri diet but *zamid dudh* (curd) is taken by all sections of the people. Tea, both *noon chai* (salted tea) and *lipton chai*, is highly relished. The latter is more frequently served to outsiders. *Qahwa* too is the drink exclusively for special occasions. The elite like to take black tea garnished with raw lemon juice and call it lemon tea. Mustard oil is used in large quantities for cooking mutton and vegetables. During a marriage or a dinner party, the services of professional cooks, *waza*, are utilized for cooking for a large gathering. On such occasions *dalda* or fat is used as cooking medium. The young people smoke cigarettes whereas the elderly people relax with *jajeer* (hubble-bubble). Elderly women in villages too may be occasionally seen taking puffs from a *jajeer*. Rubbing of snuff on teeth is a common phenomenon with women.

Grim (raw barley) is the staple food of the people of Ladakh region. Wheat too is consumed but occasionally. The meals here usually consists of steamed flour of roasted *grim* (*sampa/khulaq*) eaten with *skiu* (butter) or *mog-mog* which are dumplings made of wheat flour stuffed with minced meat taken along with mutton, beef or vegetables such as *mulag* (turnip), *shinum* (green peas), *gobhi* (cabbage and cauliflower), *aaloo* (potato), *hak* and *karam hak* and *kram-mundi.* Mutton is consumed occasionally as majority of the people cannot afford to include it in their daily menu. Heber (1976) discusses the Ladakhi meals in the following passages.

The better class Ladakhi always washes his face and hands before eating. The Buddhist also performs his particular kind of grace before meals. First he takes a little of his flour which he throws away for the gods. Then he dips his ring finger and thumb into tea or chang , and flips a taste of that away for their benefit, too. He uses the ring finger as he considers this the cleanest of his fingers if he wishes to stir anything, he uses this same member. If for his meals he has killed a sheep, he is supposed to offer up a bit of its heart, liver, kidney and every part of its flesh to his god. But meat is rather a luxury for the normal household, yet they have many ways of cooking it which are really delicious. When a dron or feast is made, the meat, of course, is prepared as a very tasty curry to be eaten with rice, the meat being first fried with plenty of cooking-butter and onions, and stirred for hours till it becomes really tender in a well flavoured sauce with a plenty of vegetables. The rice is served piled up on enormous plates, each of which two or three guests will attack, unless they have brought their own normal sized plates. The grander ones then eat with small spoons, the man's being a different shape from the women's as the latter is double, the second tiny receptacle at one end being for a child. It is not etiquette to finish what is on the plate, in most cases it would be impossible; the mother must take a large portion home for the rest of family. The feast usually is begun with butter tea, and, if so, when the plates of rice and meat have been removed, it is quite good in manners in some circle to clean out the cup with one's tongue, ready to have it filled with stewed dry apricots. After this course, the same cleaning process will prepare the cup for more filling of butter tea. 'Chupattis' are generally served too, and dipped into the apricot juice or the tea. At a very grand feast, proceeding may begin with gyatug; a dish of long vermicelli-like strips of flour paste over which mince meat in a nicely flavoured sauce is poured. Meat is also minced and made into delicious little dumplings called mo-mok or well flavoured and rolled up into sausages, which are eaten with rice; in fact in a rich house, after the plate of rice have been served, many kinds of subsidiary dishes are handed round with meat done up in different ways, sauces and vegetables, the last often soured. For a dron an experienced cook is hired to take charge of all the culinary operations, usually a Musalman, otherwise one of the women of the house superintends the kitchen. But in the villages where there are no butcher shops, and a sheep is killed only occasionally, the staple food is butter-tea and barley-flour, varied with all sorts of vegetables prepared in several ways. The poorest people mix the flour in water just as it is, eating it out of cheap wooden cups with their fingers.

An ordinary middle class family will breakfast on butter tea and small breads called kambir; at midday they will have more tea, and perhaps with chupattis with a sauce of vegetables, mixed with buttermilk, while in the evening, tea may or may not be served again with flour kneaded into a paste in some form or other and mixed with meat well stewed in a broth.

More usually as the hot tea is drunk, the butter floating on the top is blown to one side, and after many cups a nice little residue is left with which to mix up the raw flour with the aid of a finger.

In summer when milk is more plentiful, its various products are much used as a food. The milk is collected in a large pot and warmed, some sour buttermilk is being added to make it curdle. The pot is then covered with garments and blankets so as to maintain the blood-heat for proper fermentation . . . an experienced housewife separates out a fine cone of yellow butter, while in the pot the sour buttermilk is left, the remainder of which, after having retained enough for the households needs is taken to the bazar to be sold . . . . The milk curds when set are also hung up in a bag, and after all the whey has dripped out and the curd is dried, it is well pressed cut into strips, perhaps fried in butter and used in soup. (pp. 117-18)

Non-vegetarianism is common in the state excepting among the Dogra Brahmans, Gujratis, Bhojrus and some other Brahmanic communities of Jammu region. The Kashmiri Pandits, though mostly non-vegetarian, avoid meat during sacred performances and certain festivals. The same holds good about most of the Hindu non-vegetarian communities of Jammu region too. High Buddhist priests in Ladakh region too take resort to vegetarianism owing to their strong but personal adherence to the concept of *ahimsa.* The Kashmiri Pandit and Ladakhi Buddhists have struck an intricate balance so far as the food habits are concerned between Shaivism and Vaishnavism on the one hand and between Buddhism and Islam on the other. The cultural plurality of Kashmir is noticeable in the eating habits of the people. The mutton consumed by the Kashmiri Muslims comes from the shop of Muslim butchers and at times the services of Muslim *waza* (cooks) are employed to cook it. Similarly, the Buddhists too remain dependent on Muslim butchers for their supplies of mutton. The major *gompas* in Ladakh during their annual feasts utilize the services of Muslim butchers for slaughtering animals and supplying mutton to the Muslim guests and other invitees.

DEMOGRAPHY OF JAMMU & KASHMIR

The *Census of India*, 1981, provided a detailed demographic profile of Jammu & Kashmir as one of the sparsely populated areas in the country. In terms of the area it is the sixth largest state occupying

TABLE 1: DECENNIAL VARIATION IN POPULATION OF JAMMU & KASHMIR

Year	Population	Percentage of Variation
1901	21,39,362	—
1911	22,92,535	7.16
1921	24,25,359	5.75
1931	26,70,208	10.14
1941	29,46,728	10.36
1951	32,53,852	10.42
1961	35,60,976	9.44
1971	46,16,632	29.65
1981	59,87,389	29.69

SOURCE: *Census of India*, 1981.

6.76 per cent of the country's total area. But in respect of population its position is sixteenth with its population of 46,16,632 (*Census of India*, 1971). It constitutes 0.84 per cent of the total population of the country.

The population of Jammu & Kashmir state shows a continuous increase since 1951. The decennial of population since 1901 has been furnished in Table 1.

The males dominate females numerically and exceed the latter by 3,00,000 in the state according to *Census of India*, 1971. The density of population according to the 1961 census stands at 26 persons per sq. km. The state presents a predominantly rural profile with 78.95 per cent of its population living in the villages. The cities, however have grown three folds since 1901. In 1901, the urban population was 7.42 per cent of the total popultion of the state which grew to 21.05 per cent in 1981. The sex ratio stands at 858 females per thousand males for the whole state of Jammu & Kashmir. More or less the same picture prevails in all the three constituent regions of the state.

LIFE-CYCLE RITUALS IN KASHMIR

Birth

Married women tie a piece of thread to the tomb of a saint pledging thereby that if they conceive and bear a child they would make suitable offering at the shrine. If the woman is blessed with a child she calls again at the shrine and presents a cow or goat, the sale proceeds of which are either credited to the funds of the shrine or appropriated by the priest on duty. Some people slaughter a goat and feast the priest who organizes special thanksgiving prayers. This belief is shared by the Muslims, Hindus and Sikhs and there is hardly a day in summer when women belonging to these communities are not seen attending shrines.

Women are not allowed to carry heavy loads during the period of pregnancy due to the apprehension of miscarriage. Further, visitors or even members of the family returning home late in the night after performing long journeys are not permitted to meet pregnant women immediately on their arrival. It is believed that such persons carry with them the malevolent influence of evil spirits. During moonlit nights, pregnant women are required to confine themselves indoors as it is believed that moonlight might harm the eyesight of the child to be born. Women who are pregnant for the first time do not live with their husbands and spend the remaining period at their parental house.

The delivery generally takes place at the hands of a *dai* or *warin* (midwife) who does not usually have any formal training but is only a practical hand. She is paid remuneration in cash and kind.

Immediately after birth the newborn baby is given a bath in lukewarm water. It is then initiated by whispering of *azaan* in its ears irrespective of its sex. This is done by a senior male member of the family. A message is also simultaneously sent to the in-laws of the parturient mother announcing the new birth.

In the event of the first birth, breads with sugar balls are distributed among the relatives, friends and neighbours. The largest share goes to the house of the father of the baby. In return, the woman's mother-in-law makes a personal call and offers her felicitations. She also presents three pairs of new clothes for the baby, a large-sized plate full of breads and sugar balls and some money. The ceremony is called *piaw.* The mother-in-law and the guests who accompany her are served a sumptuous dinner. On the seventh day of the delivery, the mother takes her first bath with lukewarm water mixed with juices of some indigenous herbs. Tea is served to the neighbours and close relatives. Some well-to-do families organize prayers on this occasion and the serving priest is served with a dinner and paid in cash. The child is given a name on this day in cosultation with the priest or in his absence on the advice of some learned man. *Sonder* is observed in some households on the seventh day. The child is given a bath and is clad in new clothes. Relatives are invited to dinner and women sing in chorus. On completing forty days the mother of the newborn child is given another bath. From this day no restrictions are placed on the conjugal ties of the parents of the newborn baby. First hair cutting of the child is *zerakasi* celebrated on an elaborate scale. It takes place after a child attains the age of six months. The ceremony is performed by the family *navid* (barber). Relatives and neighbours are invited and served with a dinner cooked by the *waza* or professional cook. While the haircutting is in progress, the women sing in chorus praising the child, the barber and even his razor and other implements. After hair cutting the child is given a bath and clothed in a new dress. The barber is paid in cash and kind. The hair is buried underground along with some walnuts in the belief that the tree which will eventually grow would bear superior variety of fruits. The child is then handed over to the women present on the occasion who shower small sugar balls, almonds and dates on the child. The invited guests make gifts of money to the child which is duly recorded by one of the literate relatives persent at that time. A copper bowl belonging to the barber is circulated around the guests who put some cash in it which is given to the barber along with the bowl.

Khatnahal (Circumcision)

The circumcision ceremony of the male child is obligatory on all Muslims according to their religious doctorine. It is performed when the child is more than two years old. The circumcision is carried out by the village barber or by a qualified surgeon in cities. In villages, a large fowl is kept in a wicker basket and the child is made to sit on its inverted base. His arms and legs are held firmly by one or two persons so that he does not make any movement when the barber applies the razor. After the circumcision the fowl is given to the barber alongwith some money sugar and cereals. During the course of operation the female relatives keep singing in chorus.

Marriage

Youngsters of marriageable age do not enjoy the freedom of selecting the spouses of their own choice. The selection is the exclusive privilege of the parents or guardians as it is believed that the children, however grown-up they may be, would not, because of lack of experience be able to make correct choice. The unmarried persons do not even participate in the discussions about offers received from various parties as it is regarded an act of misbehaviour.

Early marriages which were once very common have been

discontinued partly because of the Infant Marriage Prevention Act, 1928 and partly for the reason that the people have come to realize the bad consequences of such marriages which generally result in divorce besides damaging the health of the married persons.

Services of a *manzymyor*, an intermediary, are invariably utilized for initiating the preliminary negotiations. The *manzymyor* is paid a fee for his services. In villages, a common friend starts marriage negotiations on the intitiative of one of the parties. The intermediary is not paid any fee for his services in villages but he remains present in all ceremonies of the marriage.

After having received the consent of the two parties, a convenient date is fixed for a formal announcement. On this day the bridegroom's father accompanied by close relatives visits the house of the bride where he is served tea. He then deposits some money in a cup which is collected by the host or a senior member of the family signifying the acceptance of the relationship. At times the guests are served dinner also. This ceremony is called *gandum*.

This is followed by *doon-leij* ceremony. On this occasion the bride's father, accompanied by his close relatives visits the house of the bride-groom where he is entertained in the same manner as on the occasion of engagement. He also places an equivalent amount in the cup in which he had tea and supplements it with a full pot of dry fruits. As he returns the host returns the amount he has received from the guests by adding some more money but he retains the dry fruits.

The period intervening between *doon-leij* and the actual marriage varies according convenience of the concerned parties. If during this interval any of the four religious festivals, namely, Id-ul-Fitr, Id-ul-Zuha, Shab-e-Meraj or annual *urs* of a local saint takes place, the bridegroom's father sends some gift for the bride such as silver bangles, sugar candy, etc. In return, the bride's father also reciprocates the gift adding some money. Immediately after a fixed date is announced for the marriage, necessary preparations for the event starts. New garments are ordered for both the bride and the bride-groom. Silversmiths supply necessary ornaments for the bride. Victuals are made ready. Members of the two families visit the houses of their respective relatives and extend an invitation for the marriage. In return they are entertained by their relatives with lunch or dinner. This ceremony is known as *dapanbata*.

As the date of marriage approaches nearer, several ceremonies are performed in succession. Beginning with *malasbehoun* wherein the bride is not permitted to take bath or attend any domestic chore and is kept on solid diet. She is not allowed to drink soup, juices or milk. This lasts for three days after which the second function, *massmechravoun* (loosening of hair plaits), is performed. On this occasion, close relatives and women from the neighbourhood assemble and one of them combs the hair of the bride, others keep on singing in chorus.

On the penultimate day of marriage, a ceremony known as *mala-menz*, is performed in which female neighbours are invited and served dinner. The hands and feet of the bride are dyed in *henna* or *mehndi* (myrtle paste) late in the night while the women keep on singing. They are served tea after mid-night.

The first day of marriage called, *menziraat*, starts with the arrival of invited guests from early morning. They stay in the house until the marriage is over. The neighbours are invited in the night and are served with dinner. Cooking is done by a professional *waza* (cook). The second day of marriage, called *yenevoul*, starts with the bride-groom's father send off with a number of copper plates containing sweets, dry fruits, clothes and ornaments for the bride. The bridegroom is made to sit on a specially laid seat in the centre of the room. The barber gives him a haircut before he takes bath. After bathing the bridegroom is made to wear a new dress, a turban and a new pair of shoes. He then walks into a seraglio where another set of ritual is performed. Then he sits amidst relatives and guests who offer him money which is duly recorded by a family member.

The bridegroom is then taken in a procession being accompanied by his close relatives and friends to the house of the bride. As the procession starts a group of singing women escort the procession for some distance. The procession is welcomed first by a group of women singing in praise of the bridegroom. Senior member of the bride-groom's house receive him and escort him to a seat reserved for him. Sugar balls are showered on the entire marriage procession from the women of the bride's side. The guests are entertained with *qahwa* and specially made cakes. This is followed by *nikah* ceremony which is presided by a priest. The date of wedding is in no way coterminous with the *nikah*. In some cases wedding takes place well after the performance of *nikah*. Usually, however, *nikah* and wedding ceremonies are performed in quick succession. When the bridegroom is personally present at the *nikah* ceremony he is not represented by any attorney. He answers all the questions put forward by the priest. The bride, however, does not make a personal appearance and she is repressented by her close relations who function as attorney and witnesses. No marriage is permissible under the Islamic law unless the amount of *mahr* is fixed in advance. One third of the *mahr* is paid on the spot. The husband, during his life-time does not pay the remaining amount. Usually, however, it is paid only in case of dissolution of marriage at the instance of the bridegroom. The priest prepares the *nikah-nama* (marriage document) in duplicate giving full details about the bride, bridegroom, witnesses and attorneys and also the amount of *mahr* agreed upon by the two parties. Both copies of the document are signed by the two parties in presence of witnesses. After *nikah*, dinner is served in copper *traem* (plates) from which four persons are served simultaneously. The *waza* makes several rounds appearing each time with a new dish which he serves on copper plates. The guests then leave if their houses are nearby but close relatives of the bridegroom stay on until all preparations of *rukhsati* (departure) of the bride are completed. When the departure is announced the bridegroom follows the palanquin in which the bride is made to sit. The bride's female relatives escorts her for some distance singing songs of farewell. After bidding farewell to the bride, they return home. The male relatives, however, accompany the bride to her in-law's house. There she is carried by her uncle to the seat reserved for her. The female members of the bridegroom's side shower sugar balls on the bride and keep on singing until she is seated. The bride remains sitting in a kneeling posture until her mother-in-law raises her head. The women present on the occasion make offering of cash to the bride which is duly recorded on a piece of paper. The bride stays with her husband for seven days. During this period she is invited by her relatives who present her *khabar* (gifts in kind). On the seventh day the bride's mother sends a message inviting five to seven persons for dinner. They attend the bride's house with the presentation of cooked meat and breads. The bride returns to her parental house after dinner. On the following day, called *wathal*, relatives and friends are again invited by the bridegroom's father for a dinner. A few close relatives of the bride also attend this feast. The bridegroom, in return, is invited by his in-laws where he stays for three days. This is called *phirsal.* Before returning on the third day he is presented with some gift known as *bakhshish.*

Death

When a person is about to die, he is asked to utter 'Allah' as it is likely to bring *sawaab* (credit) to the departing soul. The dead body is surrounded by *lahriwadan* (crying of female relatives). A number of male relatives carry the corpse and place it on a wooden platform.

The bath is given by a professional called *snanagor.* The dead body is wrapped in a *kafan* (shroud). The body, then is kept in a *taboot* (wooden coffin) which is carried to the burial ground on the shoulders of relatives, friends and neighbours. The *taboot* is first kept outside a nearby mosque for funeral prayers. A priest leads *namaz-e-janaza* and all those who accompany the funeral procession also participate in the prayer. The grave is dug by a *malla* or *gorkun.* After the corpse is placed in the *lahad* (grave) it is filled with earth and each person accompanying the funeral procession feels duty-bound to throw a handful of earth in the grave as the last gesture to the departed soul uttering '*Inna Lillah-e-wa-inna Alaihe Rajaoon*'. After the *lahad* is filled upto the level of the ground it is further raised up above the ground into a small mound. A memorial stone is placed for identification. Candles and incense are continuously burnt until the next Friday on which relatives, friends and acquaintances from near and far come to offer their condolences to the bereaved family. During the intervening days between burial and the ensuing Friday the near kith and kin pay a daily homage to the departed soul by visiting the grave and reciting the *fateha* in order to bring credit to the departed soul. On Friday morning, female relatives and guests indulge in *lahriwadan* till late in the day. The mourners are served tea and breads. In the afternoon male relatives, friends and neighbours assemble at the grave and pray *fateha.* After that they reassemble at the house of the deceased and pay their condolences to the bereaved family. On the fourth day after death, the priests, relatives and neighbours recite Koran Sharif in honour of the deceased. The ceremony is repeated on the fortieth day. The two functions are called *chaharum* and *chehllum* respectively.

LIFE-CYCLE RITUALS IN JAMMU

Birth

A woman in child birth is attended by a *dai* (midwife) or elderly family member or an experienced woman of her own caste. Now people prefer hospitals, if available in the vicinity. No ceremony is observed at the time of child birth. Nevertheless, the birth of a male child calls for celebrations. Name is given to the neonate by a Brahman priest invited for this purpose and also to prepare a horoscope for the child. He is paid for his services. At times parents also give a name to the newborn.

Sune is observed around the seventh month of pregnancy wherein the father sends fruits, nuts and clothes to his daughter. *Athwan* is the eighth auspicious day falling in the eighth month of pregnancy. Small *laddoos* (balls) made of sugar and rice flour and *sungi* (dry grapes) are distributed among relatives, friends and neighbours. Germinated grams are also distributed and eaten on this occasion. The postnatal rituals are *mundan-sanskar* and *janeu.* In *mundan-sanskar* the hair of the child is shaved within a year of birth. The barber does this job. Economically well-off families celebrate the occasion with great fanfare. A feast is thrown for the relations. The ceremony is performed at Mansar lake. Wearing of sacred thread ceremony is now performed one day before *lagan* (marriage).

Marriage

Marriages usually take place after attaining adulthood. Cross-cousin marriages are not practised. It is a general rule that the age of the bride should not be more than that of the bridegroom. Marriage by exchange is a common practice. In backward areas of the region, hypergamy is also prevalent.

Negotiations for a marriage are initiated on behalf of the girl's parents by a close common friend or a relative who is supposed to be impartial and capable of bringing the two parties together for an agreement. At times this job is done by Brahman priests for a fee. The intermediary fixes a date for marriage according to the convenience of the two parties entering into the marriage alliance. Some of the important ceremonies connected with marriage are as follows.

Sant or *shanti havan* is performed by both the parties at their respective house. This is done in order to seek blessings from the spirits of the departed ancestors. The *havan* or *yajna* is performed under the supervision of the family priests. Thereafter *butna* ceremony is performed in which the prospective bride and bridegroom are annointed with a paste of flour, turmeric and *samagri* (herbs) at their respective places. After a bath and a shave the bride-groom puts on his wedding dress which consists of a new pair of clothes, a turban, a new pair of shoes and socks and a dagger. The turban, pink in colour, is called *sehra.* Hence this ceremony is also referred by the same name. The assembled relatives offer money in cash to the prospective spouse. This ceremony is known as *tamol.* A record of the payments made is retained by the heads of the two households. *Barat* (marriage procession) follows *tamol*. The bridegroom, along with his relatives and friends proceeds in a procession to the bride's house which is received by the close relatives of the bride and they are affectionately welcomed by the father, maternal uncles (father's brother); the ceremony is called *milni*. The guests are entertained with sweets. *Lagan* marks the conclusion of main marriage ceremonies wherein the bride and the bridegroom circumambulate the holy fire after exchanging *varmal* (garlands). The ceremony is performed under the supervision of a priest.

Death

The Hindus burn their dead. The pyre is lit by the son or nearest male relative of the deceased. Bodies of renowned saints are buried. In the past the burning of Rajput women alive on the pyre of their husbands gave rise to a number of sati temples. All such places are called *dehries*. Muslims bury their dead in accordance with the provisions of *shara*. Mourning among the Hindus lasts for thirteen days. Ashes are collected from the cremation ground on the third day for their immersion in the sacred water of the Ganga or Basantar river. The nearest male relative of the deceased who performs funeral rituals pours water on the ground near a *peepal* tree for all the thirteen days of mourning early in the morning. The widow of the deceased also sprinkles water near the door for all the thirteen days. On the tenth day of mourning all relatives of the deceased assemble near a tank to take bath and wash their clothes. The *purohit* is given a bed and a pair of clothes on this day. He is also given dry rations equivalent to thirteen days for his consumption (*rah kharchi*). Six months after the death *adh-barkhi* is performed. The priest is offered *chaji* on this occasion too. *Barkhi* is a *shradh* ceremony performed after one year of death. *Chaubarkhi* is held after four years of death.

LIFE-CYCLE RITUALS IN LADAKH

Birth

Life-cycle rituals among the Muslims of Ladakh is more or less similar to those performed among the Kashmiri Muslims with the variation in the terminology of various ceremonies. The Muslims of Kargil which consist mostly of Shite Balti and Broqpa present a slightly different picture of life-cycle rituals. Recitation of *azaan* into the ears of the child by an *akhun* or *sheikh*, *nosh yoni*, seventh-day ritual when the mother takes her first bath and a feast is served to the guests, *nom-*

chonru (name-giving), *ghusl-e-nifaas*, which is to mark the bath taken by the mother on the fortieth day, *aqeeqa* (tonsure) and circumcision are some of the rituals performed before marriage.

Marriage

The Broqpa marry later than the Baltis. Cross cousin and inter *gatti* marriages are allowed but marriages are avoided with mother's sister's children among the Broqpa. *Muta* or *nikah-e-ingatai* (temporary marriage contract terminable at the will of the husband) is predominantly prevalent. Now there seems to be a growing tendency towards *nikah-e-daimi* (permanant marriage contract). *Muta* may be *bakhstan* (through negotiation) or *khuftan* (secret). *Mahr* is payable to the wife on demand but such cases are unheard of since the incidence of divorce is absent among the Balti and Broqpa. The termination of *muta* marriages is theoretically automatic after the expiry of the stipulated and mutually agreed period but in fact the duration of *muta* unions vary between forty to hundred years making termination of marriage almost an impossibility during the lifetime of the two spouses. Widow remarriages are common. Rich families without male issues prefer to marry off their daughter with such person who agree to live with their *maqpa* (in-laws). Negotiation are initiated by a *hapla* (mediator) who neither demands nor is paid any remuneration for his service as the act of match making is considered as *sawab* (an act of merit). The parents of the bridegroom seek a date for marriage from the parents of the bride by sending a token amount of money through the *halpa* who also negotiates the amount of *mahr* with the Sheikh. In the afternoon the *baqpa* (bridegroom) is given a bath by his *chasis pa* (close friends) who receive the clothes discarded by the bridegroom before putting on wedding clothes. The *baqpa* enters the the sitting room where the *agha*, *sheikh* and *akhun* are already sitting. The *agha* or *sheikh* recites some verses over a cup filled with water which is sprinkled on the dress of the bridegroom. Thereafter *qasida* in praise of *Chaharda Masoomeen* (the Fourteen Incantations) are recited. The bridegroom then, is taken in a procession to the bride's house. Bridegroom's parents do not participate in marriage procession. On reaching the house of the bride the members of the procession seek permission from the village elders to enter the bride's house and fetch the bride. The permission is readily granted. The guests are served with *qahwa* and dry apricots. A feast follows immediately. The *nikah* ceremony is performed in the night at the bride's place and the *segha* (statement) of *nikah* is read by a *mujtahid* or *sheikh* or *akhun* in order of their availability. Attorneys and witnesses from both the parties remain present and ratify the marriage contract. After *nikah* the bride is taken to the bridegroom's house. The guests are served sweet tea and *ishnan mizan* (feast) is given in the night. The guests from the bride's side return after the feast and after two days the bride and the bridegroom go to the bride's house where a ceremonial *shum* feast is given to them. Thereafter the parents of the bridegroom go to the bride's house where a ceremonial *shum* feast is also given to them. The parents of the bridegroom are invited to *khangso* feast by the bride's parents and the bride's kin make offerings of sheep, goats and clothes to the *kin*. The bridegroom, along with his parents return to their village leaving behind the bride who stays with her parents for a couple of months and then returns to her husband's house to live there permanantly.

Death

Death is considered a natural phenomenon. On news of a person's demise the people recite: '*Inna Lillah-e-wa-inna Alaihe Rajaoon*' (one who cometh from Allah returneth to Him) and organize themselves for making funeral preparations. One group starts digging the grave whereas the other makes preparations for *ghusl-e-janaza* (funerary bath) administered to the corpse. A *sheikh* or *akhun*, holding *Mufatehul Jinan* or *Tohfatul Awaam*, the books that contain the procedures and steps of various rituals, supervises the funerary bath. The body, thereafter is wrapped in a black shroud and brought inside the *matamsara*. The *akhun* covers the corpse in yet another shroud which consists of a *kurtani* (shirt) covering the body from shoulders to knee, *sando*, a piece of loin cloth that covers the body from the abdomen to the feet, and a scarf around the head and finally a white piece of cloth covering the body from the head to the feet. Now the coffin is brought outside and the *sheikh* leads the *namaz-e-janaza* (the namaz said in honour of the departed soul). *Marsia khani* (recitation of dirges that narrate various kinds of travails faced in the battlefield of Karbala by Imam Husain and his associates and kin) is performed. The people assembled give vent to their pent up feelings by crying in unison. The face of the corpse is uncovered to pay the final homage to the departed soul. The father of the deceased, if alive, leads the mourners in paying their respects to the dead. Thereafter the body is lowered into the grave and all those assembled at the occasion feel duty bound to throw a handful of earth into the grave repeating '*Inna Lillah-e-wa-inna Alaihe Rajaoon*' over and over again. As the day draws to a close the mourners return to their houses. Those who have come in physical contact with the corpse take a bath known as *ghusl-e-maiyat* and the mourners assemble again for *namaz* prayers dedicated to the departed soul. The deceased's kin slaughter a goat and the mutton is distributed among the villagers. On the third day an assembly is held to recite the Holy Koran to bring peace to the departed soul. The guests extend a helping hand to the bereaved family by bringing some flour of parched barley and a little quantity of butter which, in return, is distributed by the head of the bereaved family among the widows, orphans and other needy persons of the village. In the evening all mourners assemble in the house of the bereaved family and are served a meal. On the fortieth day after death, a similar ceremony is repeated with a wider participation of kins of the deceased. Similar ceremonies are also observed by the Broqpa (Shia).

BUDDHISTS AND MORAVIAN CHRISTIANS

On birth of a child the lama is called to perform *sang* (purificatory ceremony). This ceremony is repeated after forty days which marks the end of pollution caused by birth. Naming ceremony is performed by a *kushak* (reincarnate) lama. Marriage is performed amidst prayers to protect the couple from the malevolent effects of evil spirits. Exchange of *khatak* (silken scarves) complete the marriage ceremony. On death the lama is invited to perform *phoa* ceremony. The body is cremated after three days if the death has occurred during winters. The ashes are collected and are kept in a *chorten*. The *zitsik* feast is given to the mourners. Periodic death rituals are performed after a month and a year of death in which a lama of the local *gompa* is invited for incantation of *mantras*. Other Buddhist communities of Ladakh like Beda, Champa, Dokhpa, Gara and Mon also observe similar ceremonies with slight variations. The Moravians, who belonged to Buddhism until the last one hundred years ago, have adopted the Christian life-cycle rituals after their conversion to Christianity. Childbirth takes place either in a maternity hospital or at home. *Baptisma* (baptism) is carried out in the church when the child attains the age of seven months. The child's name is either given by the priest or by the parents themselves. No ceremonies are performed for naming of the child. When a child attains the age of thirteen years he or she is initiated to the church and is imparted theological teachings. A child at this age is expected to participate regularly in the Holy Communion held once in a month and also attend the Last Supper. Marriages take place at the church during the day time and the pastor confirms marital union by making the couple exchange wedding rings. This is followed by an elaborate feast in which almost all members of the community participate at the bridegroom's house. When a person dies the body is kept in state for twenty-four hours in order to ascertain that death has actually occurred. The corpse is given a ceremonial bath, wrapped in a shroud and is carried to the cemetary in a coffin for burial.

ECONOMIC TRENDS AND DEVELOPMENT PROCESS

Agriculture remains the mainstay of the economy of Jammu & Kashmir as nearly 82 per cent of the state's population lives in villages with agriculture being the primary source of income. Nearly 37 per cent of the state income is generated in this sector (N.S. Gupta and N.C. Prabhakar, 1988: 50). The economy of the state is deep-rooted in agriculture. Excessive dependence on agriculture and lack of diversified economic structure are the characteristic features of the economy of Jammu & Kashmir. Even the development of agriculture is hindered by the diverse physical and climatic conditions prevailing in major parts of the state.

The pressure of population on land is relatively high. The average per capita size of cultivable landholding in the state stands at a meagre 0.78 acre. The relative absence of large scale industries which could otherwise decrease the pressure on land also accounts for economic backwardness of the state. Small scale cottage industries, however, provide some succour to the people.

The economic profile of the people of Jammu & Kashmir is furnished in Table 2.

TABLE 2: ECONOMIC PROFILE OF THE PEOPLE OF JAMMU & KASHMIR

Traditional Occupation	No. of families	Percentage
Agriculture	40	38.83
Horticulture	05	04.85
Business and trade	07	06.80
Artisans and workers	24	23.30
Landless and labourers	18	17.48
Pastoralists	09	08.74
Total	103	100.00

SOURCE: People of India Survey.

None of the above professions, are generally community specific. Artisans practise agriculture in rural areas whereas some of agricultural communities in the periphary of urban areas are also engaged in a variety of handicrafts.

The main crops sown in the state are rice, wheat, maize, cereals, millets, oilseeds, gram, pulses, sugar cane, vegetables and fodder. Rice accounts for 27 per cent of the sown area and 32 per cent area under food grains and is the most important crop in the state. Ladakh and Kargil have no area under rice because of their short crop season. The average yield of rice is 27 quintals per hectare in Kashmir region and over 20 quintals in Jammu region. Improvement in the yeild is noticed marginally in both the regions but only a single paddy crop is possible. Maize occupies 27 per cent of the sown area and 32 per cent area under food grains. The crop is grown throughout the state except in Leh and Kargil district of Ladakh region. Wheat accounts for nearly 21 per cent of the sown area. The crop is mostly grown in Jammu region. Other cereals such as barley, *jowar*, *bajra* and millets are grown on marginal areas where the principal crops do not have a good prospect. All food grains account for 86 per cent of the shown area. The state, however, continues to be deficient in food production. The deficiency is met by import of food grains and pulses. The climatic situation in the state causes a low cropping intensity and 62 per cent of the net area sown yeild a single crop only. Double cropping, however, is practised in Kathua, Jammu, Udhampur and Rajouri districts.

Kashmir has been known for its fruits. According to the 1971 census, 64 per cent of the total working population in the state is engaged in agriculture. A separate department of horticulture was opened in 1962 for economic development of fruit crops. The production of apples in Jammu & Kashmir increased from 27,036 tonnes in 1964-5 onwards to 1,28,000 metric tonnes in 1974-5. The area under fruit cultivation also shows a gradual increase. Apple covers nearly 75 per cent of the total area under horticulture. Another significant crop of the Valley is *kong* (saffron) which is extensively cultivated on the plains around Pempur and Kishtwar. The annual production of saffron (*crocus sativus*) varies from 10 to 12 tonnes. The growers earn about Rs. 120 per 10 gm of saffron. Mushrooms and hops are other important horticulture products accruing handsome benefits to the growers. Walnut is the next important fruit after apple covering 18,000 hectares of land in Jammu & Kashmir.

Kashmir occupies a focal point in the tourist map of the world. The fame of Kashmir as a beautiful land with a rich cultural heritage reached distant corners of the world and travellers, scholars, conquerors, traders, missionaries, saints and sufis from east to west thronged the state. The construction of Pathankot–Jammu–Srinagar–Ladakh road and opening of an air strip in Srinagar and subsequently at Leh gave further boost to the tourist traffic to the state. The temple of Vaishno Devi in Jammu region emerged as one of the major Hindu pilgrimage centres in north India. Thousands of pilgrims attend the annual fair at Amarnath in Anantnag district of Kashmir. Ladakh attracted the attention of many a western and eastern scholars and tourists from all parts of the world throng the 'hermit kingdom'. The tourist traffic from India and abroad rose from 1,95,846 in 1973 to 2,29,140 in 1986. The effect of tourism on state economy can be measured in terms of its contribution to the state's income. The tourist influx in 1978 was estimated to be 5,02,665 which generated an income of Rs. 26,29,60,179. Since the tourist traffic generated 3.2 and 3.6 times the actual amount spent in the state's economy in a period of one year, the income impact of tourists expenditure would be about Rs. 84,14,72,563 to Rs. 94,66,56,633. Besides tourism, food, beverages, woodworks, textiles account for 50 per cent of the registered factories; non-mineral products account for 14 per cent factories. Five per cent are engaged in basic mineral and alloy products and 5 per cent are engaged in machines and machine tools and parts (ibid.) The state's mineral resources generated an income of Rs. 2,91,78,000 in 1983-4 in the state. Every year about 165 lakh cubic feet of timber and about 24.5 lakh cubic feet of firewood are extracted. Besides, about 2,500 quintals of medicinal herbs are obtained from the forests every year. At present the Forest Department earns an annual revenue of Rs. 9.25 crore as compared to Rs. 25 lakh in 1947. From the medicinal herbs available in the forests of Jammu & Kashmir 2,000 quintals of drugs are manufactured every year. Forests cover an area of 20,891 sq. km. including 718.15 sq. km. of sanctuaries and reserves.

Jammu & Kashmir state is the home of small cows, yaks, dzhos (the offspring of yak and common cow), sheep and goats. Nubra Valley of Ladakh is the home of double-humped camels. Asses, horses, ponies and numerous types of fish are also abundantly found and provide necessary capital to the people. The Champa of Changthang, for example, not only sell *pasham* wool but also the heads of sheep and goats in order to get instant cash. Other communities which depend largely on animal husbandry are Gujjars, Bakerwals, Pohul, Chopan and Galwan. The peasants too carry out various agricultural operations by domesticated animals. In Kargil and Ladakh, goats and sheep are an important source of food supply specially during winters. The beasts of burden such as yaks, dzhos, *dzbomso*, ponies and *khotta* (asses) generate considerable income for their masters by way of transportation. The Gad Hanz make a living by catching fish and selling them in the market or vending them from door to door. Supply of high quality wool and an assured mutton supply are the two main benefits of sheep rearing. The size of live stock has grown considerably from 40.79 lakh in 1966 to 58.17 lakh in 1982. Poultry bird too increased from 5.35 lakh to 24.06 lakh during the same period (ibid. 272). Khadi and village industry board takes care of village oil industry, leather industry, pottery, lime industry, soap industry, willow wicker, fibres, bee keeping, papier mâché, fruit preservation and match industry. The total employment in the industrial sector is roughly estimated at 1.46 lakh workers with 96,000 in the household sector and 50,000 in the non-household sector. Handicrafts has witnessed considerable development in the post fourth plan period. It is estimated that this sector alone provides a livelihood of 1.65 lakh persons (both full time and part time). The total production of various handicrafts items is estimated to have been Rs. 81.37 crore in the period ending 1982-8 which was only Rs. 20 crore eight years back. Correspondingly exports rose to Rs. 39.92 crore in 1981-2 from Rs. 7.5 crore in 1973-5.

The banking institutions have spread a network of their branches throughout the state and the number of branch offices has multiplied nearly four-fold from 159 in 1974 to 601 in 1983. An important development during the recent years has been quick expansion of banking facilities in rural areas. Out of 601 bank offices in March 1983 in the state, 417 were located in rural areas and 54 in semi-urban areas. Thus 471 branches (78 per cent) of them were functioning in the rural areas and semi-rural areas. There were also 162 offices of Regional Rural Banks in the state. The involvement of rural banks in Integrated Rural Development has enhanced their role in rural development. Other financial agencies involved in broadening the scope of expansions of small and medium-sized industries are Jammu & Kashmir State Financial Corporation (JKSFC), Industrial Development Bank of India (IDBI), and Life Insurance Corporation of India. The JKSFC was established in 1959 for meeting the requirements of small and medium scale industries engaged or to be engaged in manufacture, preservation, processing, mining, hotel industry, transport of goods and passengers by road or by water, maintenence, repairs, testing and servicing of machinery, vehicles, vessels, motor boats, trailors or tractors; assembling, repairing or packaging of any article with the aid of machinery or power. The IDBI was established in 1964 as a wholly owned subsidiary of the Reserve Bank of India with the assigned role of the principal financial institution for coordinating the institution engaged in financing, promoting or developing industry. Life Insurance Corporation of India is the single largest company doing insurance business in the state. During 1982-3 the total number of policies issued was 11,000. The sum assured has shown great improvement from Rs. 10.92 crore to Rs. 23.48 crore during the period under discussion. The average sum assured per policy has also shown marked improvement from Rs. 12.1 to Rs. 21.44 thousand. The first year premium has moved up from Rs. 56.55 lakh to Rs. 65.17 lakh.

The Government of Jammu & Kashmir has made strenuous efforts in providing social services to the people but much is left to be done. Provision of potable water supply for both rural and urban people unfortunately could not be made available to the whole population so far. To meet the minimum basic need of the people in Srinagar urban areas 11 tube wells have been installed. Similarily, effective steps have been taken to cope up with chronic water shortage in Jammu city. According to *Census of India*, 1971, there are 6,583 villages in the state excluding Ladakh with a population of 38.16 lakh. People living in rural areas face acute water shortage because of depletion of discharge in the springs and the drying up of the rivulets in case of deficient rains. Water has to be carried in a number of such villages by lorries and tankers from various places. In *kandi* areas of Jammu region, the main source of drinking water are ponds which get filled up with rainwater during monsoons. During the summer season, therefore, people have to go on foot for miles to fetch water.

Medical facilities have been considerably increased with the opening of hospitals and dispensaries both in urban as well as in rural areas. The Sher-e-Kashmir Institute of Medical Sciences, the Bone and Joint Surgery Hospital and Lal Ded Hospital, all situated in Srinagar are some of the most important medical institutions in addition to primary health centres, allopathic and ayurvedic dispensaries, family planning centres, leprosy centres, trichoma and amchi centres. Almost all districts are provided with 100-bed hospitals equipped with services of specialists in all major disciplines. The total bed strength in government hospitals and dispensaries has shown remarkable increase from 4,939 in 1973-4 to 6,153 in 1982-3. The number of doctors has gone up from 1,177 in 1973-4 to 2,230 in 1982-3. There are also 447 *vaids* and *hakims*. The doctor/*hakim*/*vaid* ratio has also come down from 3,001 to 2,350 during the same period. The number of nurses has considerably gone up from 433 to 952, the basic health workers from 420 to 600 and of Auxiliary Nurse-cum-Midwife (ANM) and *dais* from 788 to 1,218. There are 164 lady health visitors against none previously (ibid. 353). Rehbar-e-Sehat scheme, launched in 1976, is aimed at educating the community about personal hygiene, nutrition, family welfare, environmental sanitations, control of communicable diseases, mother and childcare, prevention of accidents, and use of available health services by school teachers both male and female. Under the scheme 237 teachers have received training as Rehbar-e-Sehat with the assigned duties of rendering general health education to the public about common health problems, referring various cases to appropriate health institutions, assisting in National Health Programme, participating in Village Health Working Group, supervising birth and death records maintained by the panchayat secretaries, and rendering preliminary first-aid as well as treatment of common diseases. The teachers involved in this programme are given small medical kits containing common medicines effective enough to cure minor ailments, till the case is referred to the nearest available health unit. This scheme has evoked national and international interest owing to its novelty and practicality. It has evoked positive response from the people as well and it is hoped that in the near future the entire state will be covered under this novel experiment.

Family welfare programmes have been extended to all the eligible couples at the family welfare planning centres and sub centres free of charge. Conventional contraceptive device are advanced for newly married couples, intra-uterine device for those having two or more children and are desirious of spacing for subsequent births, and sterlization for those who already have two or more children and do not desire to have more children. Innovative ways have been adapted by the Jammu & Kashmir Government to make this programme a success in the state under the able guidance of the chief minister who has been laying stress on integration of all the services and their easy availability as near as possible to the needy population. He has repeatedly stressed the need for individual education and motivation in this regard.

The scheme of housing development aims at providing house sites to the rural houseless or landless and to assist them to raise huts and tenements on the same. Integrated housing scheme have been taken up for industrial employees, housing boards and cooperatives of industrial workers of economically weaker sections of the society run on contingency basis. The scheme has evoked a good response and more employees are being benifitted by it. Under the low income group housing scheme advances for construction of houses are made to government employees as well as to private individuals. For the middle-income group the scheme was started in 1959-60. Under this scheme too, loans are advanced for construction of houses. Maximum demand for loans is made by this category. The amount spent on the above three schemes since 1982 is Rs. 130.31 lakh for low-income group Rs. 224.68 lakh for middle income group and Rs. 189.60 lakh for house building advance.

Education has always been accorded a high priority in the state. In 1950-1 there were 1,115 primary schools, 139 middle schools, 55 higher secondary schools and 14 colleges which rose to 7,630, 2,102, 909 and 43 respectively in the year 1983-4. The strength of students was 64,000, 19,000, 21,000 and 2,000 respectively which rose to 3,18,000, 21,000, 3,13,000 and 25,000 respectively by the end of 1983 (ibid. 362).

On the development front, the state is making swift strides. The people appear better fed and dressed than what they appeared twenty-five years ago. High rise structures have sprung up in the city of Srinagar and Jammu. Ladakh too has caught up with the trends of development sweeping the state. Kargil, a sleeping township, has emerged as a bustling tourist resort with the opening of more and more areas to the Indian and foreign tourists. The oil boom in the Middle East has absorbed many Kashmiri artisans and medical experts generating a good income for the state in the form of foreign exchange on the one hand and giving a boost to Kashmiri fruits and handicrafts on the other.

RELIGION AND SECTS

The state of Jammu & Kashmir represents almost all the major faiths of India, i.e. Hinduism, Buddhism, Jainism, Christianity, Islam, and Sikhism. A study of 111 communities of the state show the predominance of Islam which is followed by 57 communities, Hinduism comes next with the following rate of 43 communities. Buddhism is the faith of 5 communities, 2 communities follow Christianity and a single community follow Jainism. Sikhism is followed by 3 communities.

Hinduism has its bastion in Jammu region whereas Buddhism is confined to Ladakh. Jainism too has been confined to Jammu excepting a few families which have migrated to Kashmir in connection with their business. Christianity finds a place in Jammu and Ladakh regions. Sikhism too is confined to Jammu though a sizeable number of Kashmiri Sikhs live in and around Baramula district of Kashmir. Our investigations suggest that they are not different from their brethren living in Punch district of Jammu region. Islam as a common faith is present in all three regions though with a varying numerical strength. The Muslims of Jammu region are mostly the converted Rajputs, the nomadic Gujjars and those Kashmiris who have migrated to Jammu region and inhabit the adjacent Doda district. The size of Muslim population saw a considerable change after the formation of Pakistan and the subsequent forced and illegal dismemberment of the region. That was certainly the beginning of undermining the secular character of the state of Jammu & Kashmir which had earned a name for mutual amity, tolerance, and co-existence of various faiths stressed by the Rishi and Sufi traditions. Once this binding force got weakened, which had bound the state into a single politico-cultural entity during the last five centuries, the three regions started drifting apart in different directions. The only way to stem this chasm is to strengthen the glorious tradition of secularism in the state. Political opportunism has caused a havoc with the secular fabric of the state. The common masses of the state are still willing to live as brothers but they are not allowed to have their own natural way of living by the forces alien to the traditional politico-cultural fabric of the state.

The sects present in Jammu region are Arya Samajis, Shaivites and Vaishnoists among the Hindus, Shwetamber and Pitamber among the Jains, Wahhabi and Hanafi among the Muslims. Most of the Christians belong to the Protestant Church though Roman Catholics also exist in limited pockets. Coming to the Kashmir scenario the Hindu population of the Valley is a solid entity which follows a blend of both Shaivism and Vaishnavism and do not show any sect demarcations but the followers of Islam are divided into three visible sects, viz., the Sunni, the Wahhabi and the Shia (Ethna-e-Ashri). The Buddhists in Ladakh are the followers of Gelukpa and Drokpa sects which are of Mahayani order.

The People of India Project which was launched on 2 October

1985 covered 111 communities spread over three cultural zones, 11 districts, 49 cities and towns, and 30 villages. As mentioned earlier, we fielded the largest team of investigators (23) of which 12 were from outside the survey. They spent 785 days in the field, interviewing 414 informants of which 66 were women. The findings were discussed at the seminars held in Srinagar and Jammu. The written reports were scrutnized by team of editors in Dehradun.

AFGHAN

The Afghans came to the Valley of Kashmir 200 to 250 years ago. A sizeable number of them came to India before and during the Mughal rule, and entered Kashmir during the time of Ahmad Shah Durrani, around AD 1753. They belong to various clans and had settled in different parts of the Valley. The prominent Afghan clans of the present day Kashmir are Yousufzai, Khankhal, Afridi, Swati, Malik, Durrani and Qais. They are popularly known as Khans by the local population, but they prefer to be known as Pakhtoons. Over a period of time various batches of immigrant Afghans settled in the upper reaches of the Valley of Kashmir with a view to occupy the virgin lands with abundance of water. Now the Afghan settlements have grown in size and have become full-fledged state subjects since 1947. The Afghans, especially in rural areas, still maintain their indigenous identity.

The Afghans initially came to Kashmir during the time of Ahmad Shah Durrani, and thereafter in batches due to the inter-tribal feuds in their homeland creating insecure conditions. Later on it was Maharaja Gulab Singh, the ruler of Kashmir, who offered them employment opportunities, especially, for guarding the frontiers and, granted them land and *jagirs* and allowed them to settle in colonies of their choice.

The Afghans are stated to have entered Kashmir via Baramula, where they camped for quite some time. Some batches moved to the west of Baramula and settled in Uri. Others moved upwards in the north-west to south-east of Kashmir in search of suitable green pastures and arable land. This is how they came to Pattan, Ganderabal (Gutlibagh), Mattan, and other places in the valley.

The Kashmiri Afghans claim Aryan ancestry though there is no consensus among historians on their ethnic origin. Some consider them to be of Israeli origin while others consider them of Turko-Iranian stock. Though ethnographic and historical accounts about the Afghans in general exist in abundance, the historical account about their migration to Kashmir is sketchy. The Afghans of the Valley perceive their concentration mostly in the settlements at the local level though they are aware of the Afghan population in other parts of India as well.

The Afghans in Kashmir live in cold hilly terrains and plateaus with abundance of forests and low humidity. Kashmir records medium rainfall accompained by heavy to very heavy snowfall. The Afghans speak Pakhto (Pashto) within the family and kingroups. In fact, young children and women speak in their own language and cannot comprehend or speak Kashmiri. However, the adult male Afghans speak in Kashmiri with the other local groups and often use the Arabic script for communication. The traditional male and female dress is quite distinctive compared to the dresses worn by the local Kashmiris. The male Afghans wear turbans and support a big shawl, usually white, over their shoulders with very large shirts and *salwars*. The Afghan females wear a different type of dress which is similar to the Gujjars rather than to the Kashmiri Muslim women. Although living in Kashmir for more than 150 years, even now the Afghans do not wear the *pheran* (a loose body-gown) worn by a majority of the local population. Though wearing ornaments is fast catching up among the Afghan women, but gold ornaments are very rare.

Yusufzai Afghan's dermatoglyphic features reflect predominant Mediterranean affinity. In terms of finger and palmar features, the Afghan immigrants to the Valley are characterized by a higher frequency of whorls (males: 49.4 per cent, females: 43.1 per cent) and ulnar loops (males: 43.1 per cent, females: 49.1 per cent); and a lower frequency of radial loops (males: 2.3 per cent, females: 1.1 per cent) a higher frequency of 11.97 (males: 46.0 per cent, females: 52.5 per cent) and a lower frequencies of 7.55 and 9.75 (males: 10.0 per cent, females: 7.5 per cent); and relatively lower frequencies of true patterns in hypothenar, thenar/I and interdigital II areas, and relatively higher frequencies of true patterns in interdigital areas III and IV in both sexes.

The Kashmiri Afghans are non-vegetarians and consume both beef and mutton. They also take eggs, fish and fowl, but pork is strictly prohibited as per the Islamic tenets. Their staple food comprises of rice and maize. They eat all varieties of pulses and use mustard oil for cooking. A fair amount of *ghee* is also consumed. With rich flora around, roots and tubers are also consumed moderately. The majority of the Afghans are teetotallers and fruit is consumed in plenty. A marked increase has been observed in consumption of vegetables, fruit, pulses and rice. Most Afghans smoke cigarettes and loose tobacco. Snuff is also used by both the sexes. Milk and milk products are regularly consumed. Salt tea or *noon-chai* is a popular beverage among the Afghans.

The Afghans are socially divided into various clans. Individual clans have socio-political affiliations to their clanhead. Besides, a broader stratification has been observed with regard to occupational status. In the hierarchichal differentiation between the Kashghars (carpenters, blacksmiths, barbers, etc.) and the general Afghans the former are considered a low caste group. This differentiation may be a legacy of the *varna* system. Considering themselves as Aryans, the Afghans exhibit a very high sense of pride. Most of the Afghans use Khan as the surname and may also add to it the name of their respective clans, as in Sonaullah Khan Yusufzai (belonging to Yusufzai clan).

The Afghans are exogamous at the clan level and consanguinity is practised. Adult marriage is given precedence over child marriage, although child marriage was common in the past. Marriages are solemnized under the Islamic law and are arranged through negotiation. Monogamy is the common feature, yet there is no social or religious restriction in having more than one wife. There is no bride-price, but *mahr* is negotiated at the time of marriage. It may not be paid immediately and may be promised for future payment. At times, *mahr* may not be paid at all even when promised. The groom leaves at dawn, i.e. with the first ray of the sun, to solemnize the wedding at the bride's parents' house. The dowry of the bride usually comprises of a cow, a bullock, a good number of goats or sheep, etc., besides a few dresses for the bride and the bridegroom, but cash is mostly not given. Divorce may be due to adultery and maladjustment, is granted under the religious sacrament. Divorce compensation is given to the wife by the husband. Either party can divorce. The children are the responsibility of the father in case of a divorce. Remarriage is permissible for either sex, be it of a widow, widower or a divorcee. The average age of marriage has gone up but the Islamic marriage rules are followed strictly. The marriage symbols are observed with flexibility. They follow patrilocal rule of residence after the marriage.

The most common form is the nuclear family. Joint families are breaking up for economic reasons. Interpersonal relations are cordial among the household members. Conflicts and confrontations in the family exist, to some extent. The Afghans follow the Islamic law of inheritance but, in practice, usually male equigeniture is followed. Females may inherit ancestral property, but it is less than that of the males. The eldest son succeeds as the head of the family, though it is not insisted upon in the Afghan families. Interfamily linkages are cordial. In case of a dispute, the local *jirgah* (tribal court comprising of clan heads) may resolve it, and the *jirgah's* decision is binding.

The Afghan women, in comparison to men, enjoy a secondary

status in every sphere of life. They participate in the economic operations (agriculture, animal husbandry, fuel collection, carrying water, etc.), social and religious functions but play no role in political spheres of the region. Women do not have any effective role in decision-making. The entire household chores are performed by the wife. There is no direct contribution of women to the family income, but they do have a say in the management of the family expenditure.

They do not observe any pre-delivery rituals for the pregnant woman, but restrictions on lifting heavy load or speaking to strangers at night are observed. Circumcision is performed on the male children. When the child is able to stand on his legs for the first time, *ghee* and local bread are distributed among the poor. Young girls support a clipped lock on their foreheads to symbolize that they are unmarried. Marriage rituals are performed at the bride's residence but a feast is given by both the parties. Marriage celebrations are now usually a one-day affair and is observed without much fanfare.

The dead is given a bath, put in a *taboot (*coffin*)* and carried on a wooden bier to the *qabristan* (burial ground). The coffin is carried by four to six persons—usually by the near and dear ones. At the *qabristan*, after *the janaza* prayer, the dead body is placed in the centre around which people sit in a circle. Everybody accompanying the dead for burial offers some money to the eldest surviving member of the bereaved family. Money thus collected is partly distributed among the poor and partly given to the *maulvi* (priest). This practice is not found among any other Muslim community of Kashmir Valley. A copy of the Koran, some amount of money and grain are placed by the side of the dead body before it is lowered into the grave. On the Friday that follows, *jumma chai* (community tea) is served after the *fateha* (prayers for the dead). The *chehallum* rite is observed on the fortieth day of death.

The major economic resource for the community is land. Right from the days of their migration, they always tried to settle down on virgin upland, which over a period of time was put to use for culvitation of paddy and maize. Besides, dryland was developed into horticultural belts and most of the upland was retained for pastoral activities. Local forests also supplement their economic activities by providing timber for constructing houses and firewood for cooking and heating. Medicinal roots are also extracted from the local forests. With major land reforms throughout the state, the Afghans have become individual proprietors of the land they have in their possession. Lineage proprietorship also exists. Their traditional occupation has been horticulture, terrace-cum-settled cultivation, animal husbandry, government service, and trade. However, transport business, woodwork, carpet weaving and embroidery are fast catching up as supplementary economic activities. Horticultural activities predominate all other activities in most of the Afghan settlements in Kashmir.

Link with the market exists directly and through middlemen. The mode of buying and selling is both in barter and cash. Land reforms have totally abolished landlessness. Domestic use of child labour is quite common but it is not marketed at a wage. Wages are paid to other types of labourers in cash and kind, or both. Sharing of labour is extensively popular. Under this system, all male or female workers of a village may collectively work on individual plots of farm land in turn so as to expedite the sowing operation, keeping in view the short duration of agricultural season in the Valley.

The local *jirgahs* comprising of a representative from each household within a clan decides about the daily affairs of the community *vis-a-vis* social, political and religious affairs. A dispute among the Afghans is always referred to the *jirgah* which decides the case. Rarely a dispute is taken to the local law courts. In case of a dispute between an Afghan and a non-Afghan, the local panchayat tries to act as the arbitrator. The village panchayats are heterogenous in nature, and assist in the implementation of the welfare and developmental plan activities of the government. However, within an Afghan *jirgah* where chieftainship exists, disputes are not resolved by declaring one party as offender and the other as aggrieved, but instead the defaulter is asked to part with some cash or kind to offer it to the other party as a gift rather than as compensation. Crimes or offences are usually committed over land and water disputes, disrespect for traditional norms, and theft.

The Afghans profess Islam as their religion. They belong predominantly to the Sunni sect. They follow and practise Koranic injunctions devoutly. Within the village, most of the Afghans offer *namaz* five times a day. Individual affiliation to a *pir* is prevalent among the Afghans with affiliation to Sufi *silsila*. *Maulvis*, who may not necessarily be from the same community, perform birth, marriage, and death rites. The people approach a *pir* or a revered *maulvi* for seeking protection from, or removal of, evil spirits, and for confirmation of theft and guilt. They celebrate festivals mostly of religious significance with less emphasis on social festivities.

The Afghans are well-versed in the art of carving and wall painting, but weaving, canework and cloth embroidery are pursued on a commercial basis. Handicrafts are picking up fast as a source of employment and income. Refinements and specialization in the pattern and techniques of shawl making, carpet-weaving, chain-stitching have been gradually evolved. The Afghans are fairly rich in oral tradition of songs, folklore and folk tales. Some of these oral traditions are typically Aryan and are pre-Islamic like sun and water worship. Musical instruments are essentially string instruments like rabab and valve instruments, with light music being the most popular form. The Afghans of either sex participate in dances but females do not perform dances in public.

The Afghans accept both cooked and uncooked food from the local Kashmiri Muslims in particular and also from other communities. They participate and attend all the Muslim religious festivals besides being actively involved in local politics. They share the well and water sources, roads, schools, and panchayats with other communities. Likewise, they share the burial place with the other Kashmiri Muslims. They visit the local Muslim shrines. However, they essentially maintain a business-like relationship with the other local communities since they do not easily invite strangers and unknown people to their homes. Free mixing and socializing is not encouraged by the Afghans to ensure that no exogenous influence or exposure has any adverse impact on their traditional cultural heritage.

A majority of the Afghans have taken well to horticulture turning their settlements into fruit bowls. Correspondingly, trade and commerce has also picked up while increasing numbers among them are seeking government jobs. Employment pattern as such has witnessed a gradual shift. A small number of the Afghans are employed as teachers in primary and secondary schools in the state.

The student population of the Afghans has increased over a period of time. In the case of male education, the increase has been quite fast. They are taking full benefit of the state's free educational policy by sending their children to nearby schools. Girls are not encouraged to study beyond the primary level, but for boys there is no such restriction, although economic constraints may hinder the process of seeking formal or higher education.

Their attitude towards modern medicare is positive. They still use indigenous traditional medicare methods. Of late, they have started to react favourably to family planning and are increasingly using new methods for limiting the size of the family, instead of having six to eight children; as in the past. The Afghans are trying to limit the number to three or four children. It is generally the women who get sterilized. They have drinking water facilities available within their vicinity. Their water sources are rivulets, springs, canals and piped water.

They have actively employed themselves in agriculture, animal husbandry, small-scale industry, transport and handicrafts. They are availing themselves of the media and other communication facilities, some through the community facilities but mostly with their own means. Practically all the Afghan settlements are electrified. They mainly use firewood and cow-dung cakes as fuel for cooking. Most of them are landowners and avail themselves of the irrigational facilities. They have not made use of the midday meal scheme for their children and Integrated Community Development Scheme (ICDS). A majority of them avail themselves of the public distribution system, especially the cooperative stores. They usually do not borrow money from the moneylenders as the use of banking facilities is gradually becoming popular. Their propensity to save and invest is quite high.

The Afghans of the Kashmir Valley have been able to maintain a separate socio-cultural identity despite being settled in the region for more than 150 years. A visit to any Afghan settlement is reminiscent of the Afghans in Afghanistan. They have not allowed any dilution in their native language, or in their customs and traditions. They feel proud of their Aryan heritage and carry it till date. They are proud for being able to attain a reasonable amount of affluence through sheer hard work. They have exploited nature to their advantage to usher in a period of overall prosperity. The noticeable transformation among the Afghans of Kashmir is that they seem to have lost the ferocity, warrior-like qualities and violent temper as exhibited by their compatriots in the North-West Frontier Province (NWFP). They have given up some of the inflexibilities and conservatism of their indigenous ways of life.

INDU AIMA
ASHOK AIMA

ARGON

The Argons are reported to be the offspring of Ladakhi women married to non-Ladakhis of different ethnic groups and communities such as Turks, Pathans, Muslims, Rajputs, Kishtwaris, etc., who thronged the bazaars of Ladakh for trading ventures in the bygone days. They are generally distinguished by their physical prowess and extraodinarily well-developed muscular structure. The Argons identify themselves with the same name and are the inhabitants of Leh mostly concentrated in urban areas.

Ladakh is situated on a high altitude plateau between 3,000 and 4,000 metres above sea level. The Argon speak in Balti among themselves or *nangpa* but speak and write Urdu in Arbric script while communicating with others, who they call *cheepa*.

The Argons are non-vegetarians eating mutton and yak-flesh, but they abhor pork. Fish is relished. Mutton and eggs are consumed in plenty in all seasons. *Tsampa* flour made of barley is their staple diet. When taken wet, it makes *nampey*; prepared with mutton it makes *chutai*; when stuffed with minced meat and cooked under pressure, it makes *mog-mog*. *Thuppa*, which is steamed noodles seasoned with mutton and vegetables is also a favourite dish. The varieties of tuberous vegetables in use are *sarak turmas* (carrot), *miungma* (turnip) and *aaloo* (potatoes); green vegetables consumed are *band-gobhi* (cabbage) and *phool-gobhi* (cauliflower). Apples, apricots, grapes and walnuts are the main fruits. Occasionally, they consume banana also which is brought from the plains of India. Their drinks are usually non-alcoholic. *Gurgur cha*, prepared with butter and salt, is the most popular drink in all seasons. *Qahwa*, or green tea without milk but garnished with saffron and almonds, is prepared on special occasions. Consumption of alcoholic drinks is disapproved due to religious restrictions. *Dahi* (yogurt) and boiled *chumkoo* (buttermilk) are consumed during summer. *Korma*, *yakhni*, *gushtaba* and *roganjosh*, borrowed from the Kashmiri culinary art, are prepared and served in marriages. Consumption of rice was minimal till recently but has now shown an increase in the Argon dietary. In the past, people used to take boiled food but now the situation has changed due to the easy availability of mustard oil as the cooking medium.

Social divisions on the basis of ethnic identity of ancestors do exist. Each group born of Kashmiri, Turkish, Afghan or other groups of

Central Asia has different surnames such as Khuda Birdi (Turkish), Beg (Mongol), Khan (Pathan), Sheikh (Kashmiri), Syed (Kashmiri), Gnai Gun (Kashmiri), Dar (Kashmiri) and Joo (Kashmiri). There is no perceptible hierarchy among these groups. Differentiation is based on profession and economic status. These groupings have no function other than that of maintaining ethnic boundaries. Intermarriages with other groups are common. Being an ethnic minority, they perceive their status at the middle level conceding the upper status to Ladakhi aristocracy and ruling classes. Nevertheless, they do not maintain any commensal ties with the Ladakhi Buddhists. The *cheepa* (others), especially the landed aristocracy, deem Argons of lesser status.

Marriage with non-Muslims is forbidden but a Buddhist can always be considered for marriage after conversion to Islam. The girls generally marry at the age of 20 years and boys at 25 years. Marriage by negotiation (*bakhstan*) is the most prevalent mode of acquiring mates, followed by marriage by service (*maqpa*). Marriage by exchange (*baqship*) is permissible but is rare. Young married girls wear the usual Ladakhi dress consisting of a sleeveless blouse, skirt and scarf but they make it a point to cover their heads with a scarf. After marriage, the Argon ladies wear a *sulma* tunic with pleats around the groin. The amount of *mahr* is decided according to mode of payment. In case of instant payment (*mahr-e-muajjil*) a sum of Rs. 5,000 is fixed whereas, in case of part or deferred payment (*mahr-e-muwajjal*), the amount fixed varies between Rs. 15,000 and Rs. 20,000. Dowry is not given on demand. The girl's parents, however, make gifts of ornaments, clothes and utensils according to their capacity. The Argons are patrilocal and the bride goes to live with her husband after marriage. Women are not given the right of divorce. Divorce is invariably initiated by the husband in two ways: *zabani* (verbal) and *tahriri* (in writing). Uttering *talaq* three times by the husband in the presence of two witnesses completes the divorce proceeding, whereas in the latter case the husband prepares a chargesheet listing the complaints against the wife and submits it to the priest. The latter issues the decree of divorce in the presence of the representatives of the husband and wife. Adultery and mutual incompatibility are the main reasons behind divorce. The husband is bound to pay the amount of *mahr* and return personal belongings of the divorced wife such as ornaments, articles of dowry and cloth, etc. The wife can also seek *khula* (separation) from her husband but then she is liable to return all the ornaments she received from her husband besides exempting him from payment of the *mahr* amount. A woman divorced during pregnancy can marry after the delivery takes place or after the *iddat* period (four months ten days) if she is not carrying a child. A divorcee or a widower can also remarry. With the changing social perspectives, girls have become more assertive in choosing their life partners. If they are married against their will in a rural area, they may fail to adjust and return to their parents.

Choksik dukches (joint families) predominate other forms of family organization. Extension runs both vertically and laterally. The *khanq* (nuclear family), now given preference, is a recent phenomenon surfacing from increasing job opportunities. Further, the eldest male member of the family is the pivot of authority and the custodian of family assets. He is respected and feared by all other family members. Sibling relations are characterized by comaraderie and affection. A distance is duly maintained with the family elders and joking in their presence is avoided. Conflicts and confrontations have now become quite frequent and result in fission of joint families. Succession runs from father to son. The right to inheritance has been bestowed on both the male and the female offspring. A surviving but issue-less widow is entitled to receive the amount of *mahr* from her deceased husband's property. If she has children, she receives only one-eighth of her deceased husband's property. A widower is entitled to one-fourth of his deceased wife's property, the other quarter goes to the daughter and the remaining half portion of property goes to the sons. An adopted son has no right to his foster-father's property except in case of a will, in which case he is entitled to receive one-third portion of property if there is a balance left after the division of assets among the next of the kin, the defraying of burial expenses and dissolution of the deceased's liabilities, if any. Families as constituents of one particular lineage interact more closely in various socio-economic situations than with the families of other lineages. They help each other in a situation of crisis and participate in important family events such as life-cycle rituals.

The status of the Argon women is at par with other Ladakhi women. A woman can inherit her father's property or establish a *maqpa* (uxorilocal) household. Though a majority of the Argons live in urban Leh, a few families live in surrounding villages and own landed property. In such households, women participate in most of the agricultural activities except ploughing. Women play a dominant role in ushering in reforms, especially for curtailing expenses in funeral rites. Three Argon girls have been sent to Malegaon (Maharashtra) for taking religious education. In the field of literacy, Argon girls have made substantial progress. They seek education up to higher secondary level at Government Girls Higher Secondary School, Leh, Islamia School, Leh and Central School, Leh. They are encouraged for higher education and some of them are studying in various educational institutions of Srinagar and Jammu. Their participation in political affairs as also in family finances is minimal.

A parturient mother is assisted by other elderly ladies of the family in delivery. The child is given a bath. *Azaan* is whispered softly in the right ear and *aqamat* in left ear of the neonate. The parturient mother is served *khichri* (semi-solid rice cooked with pulses) and garnished with butter. She is given the first post-delivery bath after two days (during summer) or three days (during winter). Tea is served to all the visitors. The child is given a name on the seventh day. *Aqeeqa* (*shra dakches*) is performed on the seventh day. No age is prescribed for circumcision of male children but the rite must be performed before the child is fifteen. The parturient mother is exempted from offering prayer until the *nifaas* (last purificatory bath) which is administered on the fortieth day after birth. From this day she is allowed to resume normal household duties.

Marriage negotiations are initiated by the groom's side. When a girl is selected for marriage, a delegation consisting of close relatives of the boy's parents visits the bride's house and furnishes necessary details regarding the credentials of the would-be bridegroom. The girl's side asks for time for necessary consultations amongst themselves. On the appointed time the groom's party carries gifts of clothes and engagement ring, etc., for the bride. After the engagement, a day is fixed for marriage. On this day the bridegroom goes in a procession consisting of close relatives. The *nikah* is performed after the sum of *mahr* is fixed. All marriage conditions are written on *nikah-nama*. The *nikah* is recited first in Arabic, then the Ladakhi version of *nikah* verses known as *segha* are also rendered for the convenience of those who cannot understand Arabic. After the *nikah*, dates and dry fruits are distributed to guests. It is followed by a feast given by the bride's side. The bride leaves her parents' house on the same day (*rukhsati*) along-with the bridegroom to the latter's house. Having passed three days at her husband's residence during which a *walima* feast is given by the bridegroom's parents, she goes back to her parent's house and returns again to her in-laws after a couple of days.

Skuth-kherches (clandestine marriages) are also common. In such an event, the engaged girl goes to her maternal uncle's house where the would-be groom is also invited and the *nikah* is performed in the manner described earlier. The ceremony enjoys the tacit approval of the parents of both sides but they stay away from participating in the event. The next day, the bridegroom with his maternal uncle and the bride's uncle go to seek formal permission for marriage from the parents of the bride which, in most cases, is granted. The bride's mother makes a gift of Rs. 50 to the bridegroom which the latter returns to the former after adding an equal amount. The bridegroom then seeks permission of the bride's parents to take her with them. On a fixed date, the bride's mother presents new clothes to the bride-groom and sends the bride to her in-laws' house with dowry.

When there is a death, the dead body is given a bath and *namaz-e-janaza* (funerary prayers) are performed. The close kins send cooked food to the bereaved family for three days. Verses from the Holy Koran are recited on the third and on the fortieth day (*chehallum* or *jibchoo*).

The traditional economy of the Argons was based on trade. Some of the Argons like Mohammad Isa who accompanied Swen Hedin on his adventures in Tibet (Swen Hedin: 1913) and Ghulam Rasool Galwan (Galwan: 1923) became famous caravan *bashis* for the Western travellers and adventurers. Baba Kalam Rasul and Shukur Ali were also famous guides who rendered their valuable services to *sahibs* who made Central Asia known to the outside world (Joldan 1985: 38).

Others among them emerged as leading traders who traversed the entire Central Asia from Mongolia to the eastern shores of the Caspian sea. All trade activities ceased after the annexation of Tibet by China and the emergence of Pakistan. Now their major economic resources are land, self-employment and employment in government and semi-government organizations. Land-owning Argons are few and they reside in the rural areas around Leh whereas those who are in the urban areas eke out their livelihood by service and through running petty shops in the Leh Bazaar. Trade is no more a major economic resource. They depended on fully regulated markets of Leh. During fair weather, they go to Kashmir for marketing.

Significant changes have occurred in Argon economy in the last forty years. The dependence on agriculture, service and self-employment opportunity has increased whereas traditional trade practices have ceased to exist because of sealing of international borders and concentration of the more enterprising Tibetan refugees in Leh.

The Argons are a well-knit community with a high degree of social cohesiveness and close interaction. Anjuman Moinul Islam is the collective forum responsible for ushering in socio-cultural reforms within the community. Modern statutory panchayats have made no inroads due to vast distances and scattered villages. The influence of clergy has shown a marked increase after Independence.

The Argons are Hanafi Muslims and adhere to Sunni faith. The sacred centres are Ajmer and Shey mosque built by Shah Hamdan. Some of the more significant religious festivals are: Id-ul-Fitr, Id-ul-Zuha, Moharram, Milad-ul-Nabi, and Shab-e-Qadr. *Maulvis* play a prominent role in spreading religious education and in life-cycle rituals. Conversion from Buddhism to Islam and *vice-versa* is a simple process, but very few Argons have changed to Buddhism in recent times. The deciding factor responsible for conversions are love marriages.

Folk songs and dances, however, exist. Boys and girls perform marriage dances separately. The boys dance donning a Turkish cap. Archery and polo are the most popular forms of recreation for the Argon youth.

The Sunni Argons interdine with the Buddhists, provided the food is clean. They, however, do not eat carrion and meat of an animal which has not been slaughtered according to the Islamic way, *zabiha* or *shulmet*. The Argons do not interdine ceremonially in a Buddhist house unless the hosts get an animal slaughtered by a Muslim butcher. Similarly the Lamas in the leading Buddhist monasteries employ Muslim butchers, as food is served to Muslim visitors too. Intermarriage between the Argons and Buddhists is permissible provided the latter gets converted to Islam before the marriage is solemnized. The Argons share water sources, places of worship, schools and other public buildings with other communities. Bedas, both Buddhist as well as Muslim, are invited by an Argon family to play music on festive occasions. *Longdeh* or corporate labour system exists. The system consists of exchange of labour on a voluntary basis on demand. The people participating in corporate labour are taken good care of by the client by supplying tea, food and refreshment, etc. The gesture is often reciprocated.

The Argons are moderately literate though some of them have risen to scholarly heights. They possess a positive disposition towards raising the level of female literacy. Children, both male and female, are sent to Srinagar and Jammu for higher education. They also have a progressive orientation towards modern practices of medicare. Though somewhat sceptical about family planning, they still prefer to adopt the small family norm. Leh town is supplied with potable tap water, but the Indus meets all water requirement in the villages. The community has been considerably benefited by various employment and self-employment schemes. A low power transmitter caters to the needs of local television viewers and the Leh station of All India Radio broadcasts in local languages and dialects. Newspapers are flown in from Delhi, Chandigarh and Srinagar.

Irrigation facilities are available to the people living near the banks of Indus. Chemical fertilizers and insecticides are liberally used besides organic manures. Public distribution system is effectively channelized to supply sugar, kerosene, wheat flour and rice to the people. Consumer goods are stored for winter when Ladakh remains cut off from Srinagar by road. Banking facilities are available to the city dwellers and they make use of it. They do not depend on moneylenders and shopkeepers for loans.

BAQAR R. RIZVI

BABA

The Baba trace their descent from Sheikh Abdul Qadir Jilani of Baghdad. They usually serve the *pirs* and are known as *khidmatgars* of *pirs*. Their surnames are Baba and Shah, although Shahs are treated as priests.

The community is identified at the regional level. They speak Kashmiri and use the Arabic script within and outside the family.

Staple foods consumed by them include *gandum* (wheat), *batta* (rice) and pulses such as *moong*, *masur* and *rajmah*. They are non-vegetarians, and consume meat. Leafy vegetables and fruits are consumed moderately by them. They supplement their diet by taking milk and milk products. Alcoholic drinks are a taboo. Special foods consumed are *vopal haak* and meat after child delivery and *saat salona*, *gushtaba*, *pulao*, and *firni* during marriage.

They place themselves in the non-Sayyid category in the middle order of the Muslim hierarchy. The other Muslim communities also place them below the Sayyids. They usually marry with the Mirs and the Shahs. Since there are *biradari* marriages, they practise consanguinity both at parallel and cross-cousin levels. The sororate and levirate (junior) forms of marriages are also present. The usual age of marriage is 17 to 18 years for males and 14 to 15 years for females and the usual form of marriage is monogamy. Marriages are settled through negotiation. Polygyny is also practised, but only rarely. Dowry is prevalent, and usually includes jewellery, clothes and household articles like copper utensils. The parties give and take according to their status. The *mahr* money is fixed according to the status of the bridegroom. These days it is fixed at a minimum of Rs. 900 and a maximum of Rs. 21,000. One-third of the *mahr* money is condoned at the time of marriage. The remaining part of the *mahr* is promised but not demanded by the wife. The rule of residence is patrilocal.

Divorce is permissible on grounds of adultery, barrenness, and maladjustment. The family elders usually decide the divorce cases among themselves. It has social approval. The *maulvi* issues the decree of *talaq* (*talaq-nama*). No divorce compensation is given to the wife but, during *iddat* (99 days), the wife is given maintenance at the rate of Rs. 100 per month. In case of divorce, the articles given at the time of marriage are returned. Only the husband has the prerogative to divorce. Children become the responsibility of the father and only small babies, if any, remain with the mother. The remarriage of a divorcee, widow and widower takes place at some sacred Muslim shrine. Friends and relatives are given a feast on this occasion. *Khatna* (circumcision) of the child is performed within the age of three to four years. Earlier this was done by a barber, but now a qualified surgeon performs the operation and gets his fee. The *oapsoap* (first feeding of cereals) is observed between six and nine months. In this ceremony, *lawas*, biscuit or bread mixed in milk, is given to the infant. *Aqeeqa* ceremony is also performed in certain families of the Baba. In this ceremony, they weigh the child with rice and wheat which is distributed among the beggars. A goat is sacrificed on this occasion and its skin, bones and legs are buried in the ground. Mutton is distributed among the guests, but the immediate consanguineous kin abstain from eating mutton of the sacrificed goat.

Marriages are settled through a *manzymyor (*go-between) who may be a relative or any other person belonging to a different community. The eunuch *laants* also do the job of *manzymyor* and receive some cash from both the parties for the settlement of marriage. In the marriage rituals, *mangnee* or *korimangeh gantha* (betrothal*)* is the first ceremony performed. In this ceremony, the groom's parents and relatives visit the bride's place and offer presents, namely jewellery, clothes, etc., to the bride. They are entertained at the bride's place. This ceremony is followed by *nishani* in which the bride is again given jewellery, sweets and cash by the groom's relatives. This is also held at the bride's place. *Nishani* is followed by *hazri*, in which the bride's relatives (10-12 persons) come to the groom's place and present jewellery and gifts to the persons who visited them in the *nishani* ceremony. Between the *shadi* and the *hazri*, the bride is given clothes and presents on all festive occasions.

In *shadi* (*khandar*), *nikah* ceremony is performed by a *maulvi* or *kazi*. He gets some money for conducting the ceremony and issues the *nikah-nama*. *Mahr* money is also fixed through him before the *nikah* ceremony. At the time of marriage, *vanvun* (singing) is performed by the womenfolk. They sing in praise of the bridegroom. A grand feast is given by the bride's parents in *shadi*. *Bidai* or *rukhsati* is done after marriage. The bride then accompanies the groom and comes to stay at her in-laws' place. The *wathal* feast or *walima* is given on the next day of the marriage at the bridegroom's place. This is attended by the bride's relatives also.

Dadmoj, who is a woman belonging to the same or a different community, or is a relative, accompanies the bride during *bidai* and stays with her for few days at the groom's place. She gets clothes, presents and cash, etc.

After seven days of marriage, both the bride and the bridegroom visit the bride's parents. The bridegroom offers *salami* to elders and gets some presents. A feast is also given on this occasion. This ceremony is called *firsal*.

At the time of death, the *kalma* and some other verses from the Holy Koran are recited in the ears of the dying man. The dead body is given a bath by a *snangor* and wrapped in a *kafan* (cotton cloth). *Namaz-e-janaza* is performed in a mosque and the corpse is kept outside. A *gorkan* digs the grave and gets Rs. 50 to 60 for the job. The dead body is placed in a *lahad* (grave) which is closed from the left side. *Fateha* is recited on this occasion. On the following Friday (*jumma*) *fateha* is recited four times at the *kabristan* (graveyard) and a *pyur* (stone) indicating the name, birth and death dates of the deceased is placed on the grave. *Satijihum* is performed on the fortieth day in which a *maulvi* reads *kalma* and is offered food and other articles.

Land is their main natural resource and is controlled by individual proprietorship. They are also engaged in business, trade, industry, government and private services. They also work as skilled and unskilled labourers. Their link with market exists and the local market is daily and fully regulated.

There is statutory/formal panchayat. It is homogeneous in composition. Its role is mainly to plan and implement welfare and developmental activities in the village.

The Babas profess Islam, are *silsila*-affiliated and mainly *dastgirs*. The sacred specialists are from other communities. They are engaged in religious teachings and perform birth, marriage and death rites in the community.

The Babas observe *bod-doh* (Id) and the festivals of Charar-e-Sharif, Ramzan and Dastgir Sahib. All Muslims in the Valley also observe Sheikh Nooruddin Rishi's day. They visit Sayyed Meeraq Shah Sahib's *takia* at Shalimar. Their festivals are of socio-religious significance.

As for the crafts, the community members weave shawls and do embroidery on cloth. This work is mainly done by the women folk.

Although there is no traditional dance form in the community, yet *vanvun* is performed at the time of marriage. They also sing Kashmiri songs. In the traditional inter-community linkages, they accept and exchange water, *kachcha* and *pukka* (cooked and uncooked) food from the other Muslim communities excepting some occupational groups, namely Watal, Goor, Ganai, Chopan, etc. The community members also share water resources, burial ground and religious shrines, *pirs*, etc., with other communities of the Valley. Modern linkages are established through businessmen, scholars, creative artists, teachers and persons in white-collar jobs. Political leadership has also emerged at the regional level. Formal education is favoured for the boys and partly for the girls. The boys study up to secondary level and drop out from studies owing to economic reasons. Their attitude towards modern medicare is positive. They make full use of it. Their attitude towards family planning is also positive. The couples prefer three children. Generally, men get sterilized.

Drinking water facility is available within the locality. They drink piped water. They are self-employed in agriculture and contractorship. Media and communication facilities are available in the area and they make use of it. They have electricity in their houses. Fuel resources used by them are generally firewood and kerosene oil.

Irrigation facilities of canal water are availed of by them. There is greater dependence on rain water. The community members use chemical fertilizers and insecticides in their fields.

Under the nutrition programme of the government, they avail themselves of the facility of midday meal scheme for children. Integrated Child Development Scheme is also taken advantage of by them. They get the babies immunized by getting vaccines, etc., from the hospitals and health centres. They also make use of the facility of ration from the fair price shops in their locality. Their attitude towards saving is positive and they generally do not depend on moneylenders and shopkeepers.

A.C. SRIVASTAVA

BAFANDA

Bafanda is derived from the Persian term *baftan* which means cotton dresser. In Kashmiri, the term for a Bafanda is *dhoon.* But Bafanda has been accepted as a more respectable name than *dhoon,* just as in Kashmiri the term *navid* (barber) is replaced by the Persian term *hajjam.* The common name in Kashmir for this community is *nadaf,* which is a Persian term meaning cotton dresser. They are the original inhabitants of the Valley and, at the most, have moved from rural areas to the urban centres. The community has popular surnames such as Shah, Bhat and Bazaz. However, they do not have any subtitles and are known by their ancestral profession.

In the census enumerations, they are grouped with the broad Kashmiri Muslim population. They perceive their distribution at the local level. They live in the plains as well as in the hilly regions of the Valley. The region records low humidity and a dense forest cover. The population figure of them as a separate group is not available. They speak Kashmiri among themselves as well as with others. Some of them can speak Urdu and English as well. They mostly correspond in the Arabic script, with a very small number of them in Roman as well.

They wear typical Kashmiri dresses. However, those who still carry on with their traditional professions can be identified with the equipment they carry with them.

The Bafandas are essentially non-vegetarian. They eat all meat varieties, eggs and fish but abstain from eating pork. Their staple food is rice and wheat. They consume all varieties of pulses and use mustard oil for cooking purposes. They eat potatoes and all types of vegetables along with locally available roots and tubers. They consume fruits in large quantities. Milk and milk products are less used, but they drink a lot of salted tea with or without milk, known as *noon-chai.* Alcoholic consumption is very uncommon among them. They smoke cigarettes and loose tobacco by using *hookah* (hubble bubble). A few of them also chew tobacco and use snuff.

The Bafandas do not have any formal social stratification on the basis of religion or social division. The basis of differentation is their economic status. They consider themselves low in status in comparison to other Muslim communities.

The Bafandas practise endogamy at the community level. They

marry within their relatives, irrespective of their status, except with own sisters and brothers. Marriages with father's sister's daughter and mother's brother's daughter are quite common. Sororal polygyny is not reported among them.

Pre-puberty marriages are not common. Nowadays, boys and girls marry after attaining puberty. The age for marriage of males and females varies from 18 and 14 years onwards, respectively. Marital alliances are negotiated by the middlemen, known as *manzymyor* and also by friends and relatives. Monogamy is the most prevalent form of marriage, though under the Islamic laws men can have more than one wife. *Mahr* is prevalent among them, which may be paid in cash or promised to be paid in future. Instant payment is very rarely insisted upon. Divorce is permissible as per the Muslim laws. It may be sought due to maladjustment, cruelty and adultery. Divorce compensation is given to the wife, and children are the responsibility of the father. Rules regarding remarriage are quite flexible. Divorced and widowed persons can remarry without any socio-religious restrictions.

The popular form of family is the nuclear type. Joint families still exist in the rural areas. The joint family system is breaking up owing to the urge of leading an independent life. Interpersonal relations are cordial and informal. Conflicts and disputes are not common, except when there is a clash of economic interests. The Bafanda follow the Muslim law of inheritance. All male children have the right of equal share in the ancestral property while females receive less than the male. As a matter of tradition, most of the women forgo the share of property in favour of their brothers. The eldest son succeeds as the head of the family. Interfamily linkages are quite cordial. In cases of disputes, mutual settlements are sought through friends and relations, failing which legal measures are taken. Crimes and offences of a legal nature are dealt with by the state's judicial system.

The Bafanda women have a secondary position in comparison to their menfolk. They have an unequal share in the ancestral property and decision-making is mostly the domain of their menfolk. Even in socio-religious spheres of life, the women are relegated to the background and cannot participate actively and openly. They attend to all domestic chores, i.e. cooking, drawing water, collecting firewood and looking after the cattle, etc. In their leisure time, especially in rural areas, they take to weaving wool. They participate in most of the farm-related activities. Women's participation in politics is restricted to casting their votes only and that too on the advice of the family elders. Women appear to be quite submissive, docile and willing to accept a secondary position *vis-a-vis* their menfolk. However, as and when possible, they contribute to the family income.

The birth of a child can take place either at the parental or the in-laws' house. Delivery is usually attended by a *dai* (midwife), where hospital or nursing homes are not available. The male children have to undergo circumcision besides performing *aqeeqa*. The first feeding of cereals, known as *oapsoap*, is not a ceremonial occasion among them. *Zerakasi*, i.e. shaving off of the first crop of hair of the children, is also performed. In some cases, the boys who would get circumcised are taken out in a procession on a horse, known as *konthalgur*.

Marital alliances are fixed by negotiations through family friends and relatives. The *manzymyor* (broker) also arranges matrimonial alliances. Marriage rituals are elaborate lasting over two days, i.e. *mehndi-raat* (*menziraat*) and *yenevoul* (wedding day). Customarily, the marriage ceremony is held at the bride's place. The bridegroom, along with a few guests arrives late at night, usually after 10 p.m. at the bride's residence to perform *nikah*. The girl's parents serve a lavish dinner known as *wazwan*. After spending the nuptial night at the groom's house, the bride returns to her parents house the next morning for a minimum of seven days. A messenger, along with gifts and sweets, calls on the bride's father to make a formal request for the return of the bride. Afterwards the bridegroom returns the call by hosting a *wathal* (feast)with a few selected friends at the wife's parental house.

When a person dies the dead body is given a ceremonial bath, wrapped in white cloth (*kafan*) and is carried in a wooden-box called *taboot* to the *kabristan* or *mazar* (burial ground), where the body is buried in a grave as per the Islamic rites; *fateha-khani* or prayers for the dead are offered. On the ensuing Friday (*jumma*) *fateha* is offered to the dead. Close relatives provide food to the bereaved family till then. On the day of *jumma-fateha*, tea, bread and cakes are served to all those who come to join the congregation. On the fortieth day *chehallum* is performed for the dead, and again tea, bread and cakes are served to the mourners. Except the death rites, no other ceremony is observed for the dead.

Life-cycle rituals have become more expensive and elaborate for those who are economically prosperous. Those who are economically weak have curtailed such functions but have not discarded them.

The traditional occupation has been that of cotton dressing coupled with agriculture in the rural areas. However, over a period of time, due to the technological advancement and competition from the outsiders, this occupation has become non-remunerative. As a consequence, they have sought alternative sources of income resulting in occupational diversification and giving up their age-old occupation.

In rural areas, they have become farmers by owning and buying land along with developing fruit orchards.

In the urban centres, some of them have retained their traditional occupation by modernizing the techniques of cotton dressing and selling cloth, cotton made products like pillows, matresses, quilts, etc. Many of them have gone into private business and sought employment in both government and private organizations.

Their women also contribute to the family income by working in the farms and in others spheres where they are allowed to work. Besides this, they attend to the domestic chores and do some handicraft in their spare time. Child labour is frequently used for domestic, farm and non-farm activities but is not commercially marketed. They receive their wages in cash and kind since barter system still operates in the hinterlands. Of late, horticultural practices have increased, especially in *kandi* areas. Broadly speaking, their economic activities have diversified into areas which are occupationally and economically remunerative.

Panchayats exist at the village level. Since such councils comprise members of various communities matters of mutual interests, conflicts, quarrels and divorce cases are decided in these panchayats. Adultery, rape and theft cases are decided under the state's judicial system. These panchayats do not have any power to punish or give awards, though excommunication can be imposed by them on the guilty living in the village. Most of the panchayats participate in the village and block's welfare-cum-developmental works and also act in an advisory capacity to the state official agency operating in the region.

The Bafanda belong to the Sunni sect. They visit the shrines of Hazratbal, Makhdum Sahib, Pir Dastgir Sahib, Shah Hamdan and Rishi Pir, etc. At the village level individual affiliation or family *pir* is reported among them. Fasting during Ramzan and pilgrimage to Mecca to perform *haj* are their main religious obligations. They observe and participate in all the regional religious festivals such as Nauroz, Shab-e-Meraj, Shab-e-Qadr, Jumat-ul-Vida, the Friday following Shab-e-Meraj, Urs-e-Shah Hamdan, Urs-e-Sheikh Nooruddin Sahib, etc.

Some of their youth are now undergoing apprenticeship training in weaving, especially in the rural areas. The oral traditions in terms of folklore and folk tales are all based on religious, historical and cultural events. Some of them are involved in the designing of cotton dresses.

They accept both cooked and uncooked food from other Muslim communities. Some of them do not interdine with non-Muslims. They maintain marital relations with all Muslim groups. They share burial grounds with other Muslims, and schools, wells, panchayat ghar and other public places with Muslims as well as non-Muslim communities. They visit *pirs*, *faqirs* (saints) and Muslim religious shrines of common heritage. They also maintain cordial relations with non-Muslims at socio-economic level. A majority of them in rural areas practice settled agriculture while, in urban areas, they are involved in business, trade and commerce, manufacturing, industry, and administrative services. They are involved in cultivator-labour relations and receive services of skilled artisans such as barber, carpenter, masons, etc.

The Bafanda have become a part of the commercialized market economy. Political awareness among them has grown significantly. They have only a small number of entrepreneurs, doctors, engineers, etc., although quite a few of them are in white-collar jobs. Some of their females are also employed as teachers in public schools.

Formal education is fast catching up with the people, especially among the younger generation of the post-Independence era. Boys are still given preference over girls in pursuing formal education. They study up to school and college levels, depending upon the economic condition of the family. Only those girls who belong to economically sound families study beyond the high school level.

Though their attitude is positive towards modern medicare, the constraint is the non-availability of this facility. Response to family planning programme has been only marginal. It is usually their women who get sterilized. Family size usually varies from five to eight persons. Drinking water facilities are available within their settlements. Other water sources are wells, springs, streams and lakes.

In the rural areas, cooperative societies provide essential goods and various agricultural inputs. Almost all their houses are electrified. They use firewood, cow-dung, kerosene oil, etc., as fuel for cooking, though some of them also make use of cooking gas. Those who own land make use of irrigational facilities, chemical fertilizers and improved seeds. They make use of the public distribution system. Some of them procure consumer goods from shop keepers on credit. Very few of them avail themselves of the facilities of midday meals or other nutritional programmes like Integrated Child Development Scheme (ICDS), Anganwadi and SNP centres. They do not, as a class, exhibit a very strong propensity to save and invest.

The Bafanda have become part of the broad socio-cultural milieu of the Valley. Their traditional occupation of cotton-dressing is in sharp decline and only a few of them have held on to it. They have now got absorbed in the wider Kashmiri socio-cultural environment and their identity is fast eroding.

INDU BALA DHAR

BAJIGAR/BAZIGAR/MADARI

Bazigar is derived from the term '*baji*' meaning rope-dance and acrobatics. In Jammu & Kashmir, they are also known as Madaris. In other areas the Madaris and Bazigars are different ethnic groups. The Bazigars trace their origin back to the Rajputs of Mewar. According to them, emperor Aurangzeb tried hard to convert their ancestors to Islam. So they left Mewar for fear of conversion and went deep into the forests. There they adopted a nomadic life and reared goats and sheep for their subsistence. In course of time, they learnt the art of rope-dancing and acrobatics and soon mastered it. They say that they spread out all over the north-west India during the last two centuries. Though they were nomads, a large number of them started settling in Punjab, mainly in Sheikhupura, Gujranwala and Sialkot districts (now in Pakistan) during the early part of this century. After 1947, most of them migrated from the Pakistan-Punjab to Indian-Punjab and other adjoining areas. Nowadays they are mostly living in Ludhiana, Patiala, Hoshiarpur, Gurdaspur and Sangrur districts of Punjab and Jammu district of Jammu & Kashmir. In Jammu, they are concentrated mainly in Akhnur, Bajipur, Mirsiwala, Bag-e-Bahu and other such places. They used to wander with their families, staying for a few days or weeks at a time in the vicinity of a large village or city in temporary shelters made of grass and reeds. In addition, Ibetson mentioned, 'practising acrobatics feats and conjuring of a low class, they make articles of grass, straw and reeds for sale. They often 'practise sorcery in a small way' (Ibetson, 1881). Regarding their origin, Risley considers them as a group of the Barias of Bengal and states that they are closely akin to the Nats and Kanjars of Hindustan. It is said that the grand-sons of Maharana Pratap (Jai and Vijay), while fighting with the Mughals, lost two major battles to Emperor Akbar, one at Sargoda and another at Gwalior. After the defeat, they fled to the hills and deserts to escape the clutches of the Mughals and spent a nomadic life. Jai's sons adopted blacksmithy as a means of subsistence and became known as Bagri Lohars. Vijay's sons took to rope-dancing and gymnastics to earn their livelihood and came to be known as Bazigars (*baji* means acrobatics). Among themselves, they speak in their own dialect which is called Bazigar *bhasa*. It is a mixture of Dogri and Punjabi. With outsiders, they speak in Dogri and Hindi. The educated Bazigars use Devanagari script.

The men of older generation wear *dhotis*, *kurtas* and put on turbans. The women wear *salwar* and *kameez*. The school going children wear *kurta-pyjama*, or trousers and shirts. Men often wear *lacha/lungi* in place of *pyjama*. The Bazigars are non-vegetarians, but beef is a taboo. They are very fond of meat and prepare non-vegetarian dishes with mutton, pork and poultry as often as they can afford. Those who are the worshippers of the goddess Kali Mata and god Shankar Bhagwan abstain from drinking liquor and eating non-vegetarian food. Wheat is their staple food. Maize comes next. They consume pulses of all kinds available to them, as well as vegetables specially *sarson ka sag* (mustard leaves). Milk and milk-products are also used. But fruit is a luxury for them. They take alcoholic drinks, both men as well as women. Most of them prepare liquor at their homes. They smoke *hookah*, *bidi* and cigarette.

The Bazigars are endogamous and maintain clan exogamy. *Gotra* is the term used to denote the division analogous to clan. It is said that there are twenty-three *gotras*. Some of the older informants claim that there are only seventeen *gotras*. But none could enumerated all the *gotras*. Some of these are as follows: Gaianeke, Ghanwat, Lalka, Khiwaka, Lohat, Manhne, Miane, Dharamshawat, Narshawat, Namshawat, Machhal, Varita, Valjawat, Bhamika, Vanjrawat, Sahoke and Sherike. *Sagotra* marriage is taboo. Similarly the *gotra* or clans of father's sister's husband, maternal uncle and mother's sister's husband are avoided. Monogamy is the general norm and polygyny is rare. Marriages are usually settled by negotiations. Junior-sororate and junior-levirate marriages are permitted and practised among them. *Sindoor* (vermilion) is the symbol of marriage. Residence after marriage is patrilocal. Three other types of marriage are found among them, viz., marriage by purchase, marriage by exchange *vatta* and *punn*. In the bygone days, marriages by purchase were the most common types prevalent among them. *Vatta*, though permitted traditionally, is rarely practised now. In a *punn* marriage, the bride-price is not involved. On the other hand the bride brings dowry from her parents, according to their economic condition. In marriage by purchase, the boy has to pay an amount of ten to twelve thousand rupees to the girl's parents. In such marriages the girl's parents may usually encourage her to desert her husband and come back to them so that they could sell her to another client for a higher amount.

Divorce, though permitted, rarely takes place. A man can divorce his wife in case of her proven barrenness. If a woman is not satisfied with, or is ill-treated by her husband she is free to desert him and look for another mate. Divorces are settled and finalized by the caste panchayat which mediates and fixes the compensation to be given by one party to the other. In case of divorce, the grown up children stay with the father who takes care of them. If the children are very young they would go with their mother. Widows and divorcees without encumbrance are permitted to remarry. At present, there is a considerable increase in the age of marriage, which usually takes place between 18 and 20 years in case of girls, and 20 and 22 years for boys. Child marriage is now rare. The Bazigar families, as a rule, are patriarchal. Extended families are falling into a decline. Nuclear families are becoming more common. They maintain a distance between mother-in-law and son-in-law; daughter-in-law and father-in-law; and husband's elder brother and younger brother's wife. Joking relationship is permitted between elder brother's wife and husband's younger brother; elder sister's husband and wife's sister; elder sister's husband and wife's younger brother. Sometimes conflict and confrontation arise after the death of the father or after the marriage of a son mainly on the division of property. Male equigeniture is the rule of inheritance. But, in the case of death of father, a spinster gets her share of the property. Succession is by the eldest son.

The Bazigar women do domestic as well as outside work and help their husbands in rearing cattle, collecting fodder, firewood and agricultural operations except ploughing. They participate in socio-religious rituals but have no role in politics and the institutions of social control. Previously they used to perform dancing and singing in bazaars to earn money, but now they are being prevented by the younger generation who have formed an All Jammu & Kashmir Bazigar Youth Forum.

Antenatal restrictions are observed. They take special care of the pregnant woman and is not allowed to go to lonely places for fear of the ghosts and other evil spirits. In the advanced stage of pregnancy, she is given only light household duties and is restricted from doing heavy work. About a month before delivery, she is forbidden from taking vegetables and allowed to take only *chapatis* with *dal* of *masur* or *moong* with a little *desi ghee*. During pregnancy, she is not allowed to attend any religious ceremony. After the birth of a child they observe forty days confinement for *sutak* (pollution). On the fourth day, the mother with her newly born child goes to the well, spring or river (or nowadays even to a tap) to conduct *puja* and offer prayers known as *matha tikana*. During this ceremony the child is given its first bath. Then they distribute *bhangur* (a kind of sweet made of *gur* or jaggery) and *ghee* to the neighbours. Generally the mother takes her purificatory bath between eight to ten days after the delivery. On the third day, the child is made to taste *gurti* made of *ajwain* and *gur*. Usually the grandfather or grandmother or any pious person administers *gurti* to the child. After the *matha tikana* ceremony, the child is named. The name is given either by an elder or by any religious person. This is celebrated by distributing *gur* or any other sweets.

Marriage rituals such as *vatna malna* (rubbing paste made of turmeric, wheat flour and oil) and *gharoli* (filling the pitcher) are observed at the bridegroom's house while *vatna malna* and *phera* (circumambulation) are observed at the bride's house. The marriage is completed with a feast in which the womenfolk of both sides eat together.

They cremate the dead and death pollution is observed for ten days. But, the dead bodies of children are buried. The bier is made by the *biradari*. All the rituals current among the Hindus are carried out. Three days after the death, the ashes are collected and carried to holy places such as Hardwar or Kurukshetra for immersion into the sacred water. Mourning is observed for twelve days. Kith and kin gather to perform the closing of mourning ritual in which the son breaks four pitchers full of water. They do not take the services of a Brahman for performing the death rituals.

Most of the Bazigars are landless and only a few of them have land of their own. In rural areas, they are mostly sharecroppers and get one-fourth of the production. They do all types of work except that of the Bhangi, Chamar and similar castes. They mainly subsist on manual work. Most of them are peddlers, rickshaw pullers and day labourers. The traditional profession of acrobatics did not provide them with sufficient income to maintain their families. Hence, they had to switch over to some other occupation. Some of them now work as motor drivers, motor mechanics, etc., and a few have started businesses of their own. But bulk of them are still day labourers and live from hand to mouth. In the present generation, hardly anyone knows the art of *baji*.

They have the traditional caste panchayat to settle the intra-community disputes through their elders who act as judges. Ten per cent of the fines collected are distributed among the leaders who give judgement. Rest of the money goes for the developmental activities within the community. The panchayat looks after the interests and rights of members of the community. Traditional village level panchayat has a greater power than the statutory panchayat. Generally five heads of families who are wise and respected by other members of the community constitute a panchayat. The disputes referred to it are mainly related to marriage, dowry, divorce and sex crimes. The person who wants to lodge a complaint against someone gives a rupee to the judge for justice. He names his opponents and stakes his claim. Then the date of hearing is fixed by the panchayat. The panchayat cross-examines the parties and gives its verdict. Punishment is given in the form of fines. The role of the modern statutory panchayat in the implementation of the developmental activities of the government is not satisfactory so far as the Bazigar community is concerned.

They are Hindus and believe in the Hindu gods and goddesses. They mainly worship Kali and Shankar Bhagwan whose images are consecrated in every household. They are religious minded and take special interest in *satsang* (teachings of Radhaswami sect). They celebrate Baisakhi with zeal and believe that it would guarantee them two square meals a day. They also celebrate other Hindu festivals and worship their ancestors on such occasions. Women, however, do not attend this ceremony. After the worship, the children are given sweets. They celebrate the Maharana Pratap day with great pomp. They believe that they are the descendants of the Rajput hero. They believe in evil sprits and take special care not to visit the haunting grounds of those spirits. They have traditional crafts of grass and reed work. They are good rope dancers and gymnasts. They have a rich tradition of folk songs and folk dance. In the folk dance, colourful dresses of a great variety are used. *Summi* dance is a breathtaking and colourful dance mixed with gymnastics. It seems that the Bajigar women have learnt these dances during their movement from place to place for generations in different parts of the country.

They traditionally accept water and *sidha* food from all communities except the Gorkun, Chamar, Sariyara, Chir, Mase and the like. The Brahmans, Rajputs and other higher castes do not accept water or *sidha* from them. Intercommunity marital alliance is strictly prohibited. Transgression is heavily punished by them. In urban areas they share sources of water, public places and cremation grounds with other communities but in villages they are denied this privilege.

The boys and girls drop out at school level. Girls are usually not sent for higher education as educated girls will not find husbands in their community. They make use of modern medical facilities available in the region. Attitude towards indigenous medicare is most favourable. They are aware of the family welfare schemes and have positive attitude towards family planning. Drinking water through taps is made available to them within their locality. They enjoy the benefits of media like cinema and radio. Those who can afford enjoy television programmes. They avail of the road, railway, postoffice and other such communication facilities. Though there is electricity, only a few of them can make use of it. Most of them cannot afford it either for lighting or for fuel purposes, for which they use wood and kerosene. They make use of public distribution system in the urban areas. They have positive attitude towards savings and hardly depend on the moneylenders. But since they live from hand to mouth they cannot save money.

B. JOARDAR

BAKARWAL

The Bakarwal, one of the pastoral communities of Jammu & Kashmir state, are identified as goat and sheep herders. The name is derived from the word *bakriwale*, meaning goat herders or goat and sheep rearers. Swat region is considered and claimed to be the original homeland of the Bakarwal who started coming to Kashmir in search of green pastures. The community is considered an ethnic group of nomadic herdsmen from the central and eastern part of Asia who actually entered India through Punjab at different points of time and gradually spread over the north-western part. The migration began around the second century BC. In the late nineteenth century, the community migrated to the Kashmir Valley. They are pre-dominantly concentrated in the districts of Rajouri, Punch, Udhampur, Kathua, Jammu and Doda, though they are spread over almost all the districts of the state. Despite the fact that they have permanent homes, they still move to different parts in search of green pastures in order to graze their flock of goats and sheep. The area where they live and move is highly mountainous situated in the extreme north-western part of the country. The temperature in the state varies from place to place: it rises above 30^0 C in summer and goes much below 0^0 C in the winter. Rainfall is medium.

The region is surrounded by the Pir Panjal and Himalayan ranges with thick and thin forests.Though they speak Kashmiri language and use Arabic script yet their dialect is identified as Gujri which is the main dialect of the Gujjars. They speak Urdu, Hindi and Punjabi while communicating with others. The identification mark for male is a turban known as *dastar* and for female a *tupi* (special cap). All the adult male members have long beard. In the state of Jammu & Kashmir, they have been categorized by the government as a Scheduled Tribe.

The Bakarwals are non-vegetarians and their staple food consists of maize, rice, wheat and pulses such as *moong* (green gram), black gram, *urad*, brown gram, *musur* and *moth*. They consume mutton, egg, chicken and occasionally fish. Beef is not consumed, being restricted in the state; likewise pork is also not consumed as it is prohibited religiously. Seasonally available vegetables and fruits are moderately consumed by them. They do not consume any alcoholic drinks. Salted tea is, however, taken several times a day. The consumption of milk and milk products is high among them as they have a number of sheep and goat. They are fond of smoking and almost all men smoke hubble-bubble or *hookah*, *bidi* and cigarettes.

There is no social division in the community but a slight differentiation on the basis of economic status, educational qualification and the size of sheep flock can be noticed among them. They perceive themselves of the middle rank of the regional social hierarchy but others place them in the lower rank. There is no change in their surnames. Endogamy at the community level is always maintained. First preference is given to the cousins, both parallel and cross, in the selection of the bride. Child marriages were prevalent in the past but nowadays they perform their son's marriage between the age of 18 and 25 years and the daughters are married between 16 and 21 years of age. The selection of the spouse is exclusively reserved for the parents and both the boys and the girls do not have any liberty in this regard. Negotiations for marriage are generally initiated by the parents but some times the assistance of some middleman is taken. Monogamy is the general practice though polygyny is also permissible in the community. There is no symbol of marriage. Bride-price and dowry are not prevalent among the Bakarwal. A big feast is arranged on this occasion and ceremonies start with the ritual of *gandum* (engagement). The bridegroom first visits the bride's place and offers some money to the bride and her father. In return, the bride's father presents an earthen pot full of nuts and cash to him. This is called *doon-leij*. After the engagement, marriage invitations are sent to the relatives and friends. As the date of marriage draws nearer, several rituals are performed in succession. In *malasbehoun* the bride is restricted from taking bath and doing household jobs for at least three days before marriage. This is followed by *massmechravoun* or loosening of hair plaits of the bride. This is done by the female relatives. The first day of marriage is known as *menziraat* when the hands and feet of the bride are dyed with *mehndi* (myrtle-paste) at night. *Yenevoul* is the second day of marriage and on this occasion the father of the bridegroom sends sweets, dry fruits, clothes and ornaments for the bride. The *barat* procession is followed by women singing in chorus. Marriage ceremony is performed during day time. The bridegroom is received at the bride's house by the seniormost female member and others are also welcomed. Tea and snacks are offered to the party. The *Nikah* is presided over by the priest (*maulvi*) and the *mahr* money is also fixed at the time of *nikah*. The bride and bridegroom both give their consent for the marriage and a contract is written in the presence of witnesses. The amount of *mahr* fixed varies from Rs. 9,000 to 21,000, promised for future payment. It is generally demanded by the bride at the time of divorce. A big feast is arranged after the *nikah*. The bride goes to live with her husband and in-laws and her female relatives follow her for some distance, singing in chorus. The bride stays with her husband for ten days. On the fourth day a feast is hosted where most of the relatives and neighbours participate and give presents to the new couple. This is known as *wathal*.

The rules of residence are patrilocal. The bride lives with her husband and in-laws after marriage. Divorce is permissible but is rare. A man enjoys better rights and privileges than the woman in the matter of divorce. A husband can divorce his wife on grounds of barrenness, adultery, maladjustment, insanity, etc. The wife can also seek separation if the husband is absconding, or does not bear the expenses of the wife and children or abstains from any sexual contact for more than three years. Divorce may be given either orally or by *talaq-nama* (written document). In case of divorce the woman is prohibited from remarrying within a specified time called *iddat*. If consummation of the marriage had taken place, the *iddat* is for three months and ten days and is enforced till delivery if the woman is pregnant at the time of divorce. It is the duty of the father to maintain the minor children after divorce. Widow, widower and divorcee remarriages are permissible but a widow and a divorced woman are allowed to remarry only after the completion of the period of *iddat*. Nuclear and vertically extended families are the common family types in the community. In most cases the newly married couples establish a new household after marriage. Interpersonal relationship is amicably established among the family members and due love and respect is paid to the youngsters and elders alike. The eldest member of the family is considered as the head and takes the responsibility to control the activities of the family. Avoidance is maintained between the daughter-in-law and father-in-law and between the younger brother's wife and husband's elder brother (*jeth*). Both of them are not allowed to touch each other and even talk directly. Joking is permitted between sister's husband and wife's brothers or sisters. After the father's death, the property is divided among the sons, daughters and widows but the daughters get a lesser share than their brothers. The succession pattern is followed in the male line, from the father to the eldest son. The breaking up of the joint family system and the emergence of the nuclear families are the only change noticed in recent years.

Women have equal status with men and play an important role in all spheres of life. They assist in the household work, milking of animals, collecton of fuel, collection of fodder, bringing potable water, purchase of essential commodities and looking after the wounded cattle. They fully participate in all the social and religious functions and contribute to the family income besides controlling the family expenditure.

The birth of a child is considered a gift of Allah. The pregnant woman is not allowed to carry heavy loads and do strenuous work after five months of pregnancy. Delivery takes place in the tents and no special tent is allotted for such purpose. An old experienced and knowledgeable woman is asked to assist the parturient mother. She may be from the same community or an outsider and she is paid for her service in cash and kind. A senior male member recites *azaan* in the ears of the baby just after birth. Sweets are distributed among relatives and friends. On the third day, all the friends and relatives are invited to take a meal as the day is considered auspicious. On the seventh day *sunder* ritual is celebrated. On that day the mother is given her first bath and the child is named either by the *maulvi* (family priest) or any senior member of the family. Purification and final bath to the mother is given on the fortieth day and after that she is allowed to do all kinds of work. *Zerakasi* is observed after the child attains the age of six months when the head of the male child is shaved by a barber who gets new clothes and cash in return. Sometimes a feast is arranged to mark the occasion. *Khatnahal* (circumcision) is done by the family barber when the child is more than two years of age.

The Bakarwal bury their dead. Members of the deceased's family inform all the neighbours, relatives and friends about the death. When they assemble, a bath is given to the dead by the *snangor*, a professional man, and the body is placed in a *taboot* (coffin) wrapped in a *kafan* (shroud). The body is laid on the ground facing west and the priest recites a prayer. Thereafter the *taboot* is carried to the graveyard where a *lahad* (grave) is dug by the *malkhos* (sexton) or *gorkun* and he is paid money and served tea with bread. The dead body is then buried in the *lahad*. The Koran is recited on the fourth day for peace of the departed soul. The ceremony is repeated on the fortieth day also. These rituals are called *chaharum* and *chehallum*. Mourning is observed for forty days.

The economy of the Bakarwal depends on their livestock. Though they possess agricultural land and are in different allied occupations, those are considered secondary occupations. Each family has at least forty to fifty sheep and goats which they rear for earning their livelihood. Horses are also kept by them to carry their luggage for shifting the camp from one place to another. Their main earning comes from selling the goat and sheep milk and milk products. Besides they rear horses, goats and sheep on a yearly contract for the Gujjar community. They normally sell their goat and sheep in the market especially at the time of their summer pasturage. The *ganai* (meat sellers) are their main customers. Skin, wool, horns, etc., are their main sources of income. They earn an additional amount by way of selling wool. The trimming of wool is done three or four times a year. They sell milk occasionally, specially when they camp near the cities. They are involved in agriculture too but it is done only during winters when they return to their homes. They possess only small plots of land which they often give for sharecropping. The resources are controlled either individually or by family. Bonded labour is not in existence, though sometimes they employ child labourers for paddy and maize cultivation. The payment of wages is made both in cash and kind. Though the Bakarwals are still involved in their age-old occupation of pastoralism, only a few members are now working in different government and private jobs. They also earn money from the tourists by carrying their luggage to the valley of Sonemarg, Gulmarg, Pahalgam, Bhadarwa, etc. In these areas ponies and horses are the only means of conveyance for transportation.

The Bakarwals have their own *biradari* panchayat to settle the disputes within the community. The head of the panchayat is known as the *nambardar*(headman) and is selected by voice vote. The person who generally has knowledge and some academic background is selected as headman of the concerned group. He settles various disputes and gives his verdict in consultation with other senior members of the group. When they live in their original habitat, village statutory panchayats also intervene in inter-ethnic or land disputes. These panchayats work for the development and welfare of the village.

They are followers of Islam and follow the *shariat* and its dictum. They visit several sacred shrines and mosques on different occasions. They have their own *pir*. Sometimes sacred specialists are called from the Gujjar community to perform the birth, marriage and death rites. Different Muslim festivals are observed by them in different months. Urs-e-Nabi or Id-ul-Milad is celebrated on twelfth of Rabi-ul-Awwal. Meraj-e-Alam is celebrated on twenty-sixth of Rajab and the hair relic is also displayed on this day. Id-ul-Zuha, Id-ul-Fitr, Shab-e-Qadr, etc., are other festivals observed by the community. They go for *ziarat* (pilgrimage) to various places in Kashmir and participate in their *urs*.

They attend an *urs* every year along with the Gujjars which is celebrated in the month of July at Wangat village of Srinagar district on the fifth day of Rajab on account of the death anniversary of the father of a Gujjar leader named Mian Bashir. On this occasion Bakarwals from various parts come to join the ceremony. All the festivals are of socio-religious significance. A few members of the community have the skill of embroidering on shawls and weaving of *namdas* and other woolen articles from sheep wool. Folk songs are sung by women on different social functions.

Being nomadic, the Barkarwals establish relations with all the Muslim and non-Muslim communities of the region wherever they move in search of pasturage for their flocks of sheep and goat. Traditional intercommunity linkages, to a great extent, are established with the Gujjar community as they believe that they have originated from the same stock. The Gujjars too maintain economic relations with the Bakarwals. Business linkages are mainly established with the Ganai who purchase goats and sheep from the Bakarwal and sell their meat. They take the services of the Najjar, Shaksaz, Sangtarash, etc., and accept *kachcha* and *pukka* food from all the communities of the region except the watals. Other intercommunity linkages are established through interchange of food, sharing of water sources, burial grounds and sacred religious shrines. The landlord-tenant and patron-client relationship is in existence. Members of the community now hold different government and private jobs and mix with the communities of different states and regions.

Only a few boys have studied up to the primary level. The girls do not study due to social reasons. Though a few mobile primary schools had been introduced by the government they could not attract the Bakarwal children due to lack of adequate motivation, incentives and their continuous movements in the hills and other difficult areas. They still favour their indigenous traditional medicare system because in certain areas where they camp, the facilities of modern medicare are not available. They require more and more hands to assist in the arduous nomadic life. Though the facilities of electricity and drinking water have been provided in their permanent settlements, they complain about the short and irregular supply during winter season. Piped water, springs and streams are the sources of drinking water for them. Most of them are self-employed and involved in their age-old occupation of goat and sheep rearing. Radio is the medium of communication for them. Firewood, cow-dung cakes and kerosene oil are the main fuel resources for them. Irrigation facilities are not available in their area and they have to depend on rain water for agriculture. To get good crop-production, they use both organic and chemical fertilizers. The facilities of public distribution system through fair price shops are available to them. However, they can avail of them only for a few months in their original homeland. They are not dependent on moneylenders or shopkeepers and have a positive attitude towards saving nowadays.

ANAND SARAN

BALTI

The Balti form a majority group among the Muslims of Ladakh. Individuals affix titles like Sheikh, Hajji, Akhun, etc., which are more of an achieved status than an ascribed ethnic identity marker.

The Baltis have been referred to as the remnants of the Scythians or Sakas. Apparently they are the immigrants from Baltistan (Tibet Minor), a neighbouring territory having its capital at Skardo. The Dards refer to them as Palo and Tibetans as Mangkhod. Ptolemy refers to them as Byltae. They perceive their distribution all over Baltistan, Kargil and Ladakh. They inhabit a mountainous region above 11,000 feet from sea level.

The people speak in Balti and write in Arabic script amongst themselves and speak in Urdu with the outsiders. The community has been categorized as a Scheduled Tribe.

Their staple food is the flour of *khulaq* (parched gram) seasoned with butter and eaten with mutton, vegetables and/or chicken, etc., as side dishes. They are non-vegetarians. Millets such as *kangani* and *turumba* are also staple diet. Mustard oil is the main cooking medium. Turnips grown in the area are distinct in size and taste and are used as a sweetening agent for the coarse millet bread. Onions and potatoes are consumed in plenty. Other vegetables consumed are *durpo* (radishes), *gobhi* (cabbage), *shanti* (spinach) and *shanma* (peas). Typical to the western Himalayas, brackish *cha* (tea) is the sweetened favourite drink of the Baltis. *Qahwa* and tea are also in use. Alcoholic drinks fall under a blanket taboo. *Chang*, the home made beer, is also prohibited among the Baltis. Tobacco is smoked in cigarettes or through hubble-bubble. The Baltis, being Shia Muslims, desist from accepting any wet food item from non-Muslims. Dry ration is, however, acceptable from them. *Halwa* and *biryani* are consumed on festive occasions.

The Baltis are divided on the basis of achieved social identities. The apparent divisions based on achieved social status are as follows: Sheikh: is a *mujtahid* (learned priest) who wears *amama* (a white turban) to signify his non-*Saiyid* status. He receives his training in *fiqah* (jurisprudence) and theology from a few selected *madrasas* functioning at Qum, Shiraz, Karbala and Najaf Ashraf in the Middle East. Akhun: is a priest who has received his training in the local *madrasas*. Some of them go to Lucknow and Varanasi for the same purpose. Haji: is one who returns from pilgrimage from Iran, Iraq and Syria after paying his obeisance at the graves of Imams and other martyrs of Karbala. Saget: the remaining Baltis fall under the Saget category which consists of farmers and artisans. Specialization in certain crafts gives rise to the following groups of artisans, irrespective of the status enjoyed by the various status-oriented groups stated earlier: ironsmiths (Garba), cobblers (Lamkhan), carpenters (Shinkhan), mason (Shipkun), tailors (Ghempo-pa), miller (Ranthoq-pa) and weavers (Taqskan).

The Baltis are divided into a number of *quams*, members of which either trace their descent from a common male ancestor or from the place of their origin such as Majan-Pa (the descendants of Mohammad Jan), Hussain Mir-Pa or Karpochuli-Pa (descendants of the land where white apricots are grown). The *quam* division is simply an identity marker, having no function in marriage regulation, social control, or in religious affairs. Nevertheless this differentiation is significantly important in corporate ownership of property and water management. Another aspect of *quam* differentiation is the sharing of mutual obligations and extending necessary help and assistance in crisis. No changes were noticed in surnames, status orientation of various groups and the meanings of their names and functions. They consider themselves superior to Ladakhi Bodhs and Purgis (the inhabitants of Pot-riksha, i.e. the area lying between Photu-La and Zoji-La) but concede a higher status to an Agha Saiyid. The people are not cognizant of the varna order as envisaged in other parts of India. They also do not believe in any concept indicating inequality arising out of caste stratification. Other communities too concede their superiority as the latter came and settled in Kargil as victorious invaders from Skardo. By and large, marriage rules are governed by *Fiqah-e-Jafaria*, i.e. the code of conduct laid down by the eighth Imam, Imam Jafar-es-Sadiq.

Endogamy as a rule of marriage is not observed effectively either at community level or at village level. Ethnic boundaries too are not a serious impediment in matchmaking. The only consideration in the matter of marriage is religion. Whosoever is a Shia Muslim, irrespective of his past background, can marry a Balti girl. Marriage alliances were made with Khache-Pa (Kashmiris), with erstwhile Bodhs converted to Islam before marriage and with the Purig-Pa or Purgis. Marriages are permissible with cousins—both cross and parallel. The prohibited category of kin for the purpose of marriage are: (i) mother sister's children, (ii) siblings of a common parents and (iii) progeny of a woman who has acted as a wet nurse. Levirate and sororate are permissible. Generally the age at marriage for the boys is 20 years and for the girls 17 years.

The general form of marriage is monogamy. The seal of marriage is put by *nikah* which is of two types: *nikah-e-inqatai* (breakeable marriage contract) and *nikah-e-daimi* (permanent marriage contract). The former is known as *muta* which is a recognized form of marriage among the Shia Muslims in general and among the Baltis in particular.

The amount of *mahr* (*rinthe*) negotiable through the services of a *halpa* (mediator) is payable on demand or on the termination of marriage contract after the expiry of the stipulated time limit. The bride goes to stay at her husband's residence after marriage. Owing to temporary marriage contract *muta*, the marriage automatically stands terminated. Hence the concept of divorce is lacking among the people. A husband is entitled to release his wife from conjugal bondage even before the expiry of the mutually agreed time limit. Children are the responsibility of the father. Women are not granted the right to divorce. Balti men and women can remarry—women after completing the specified period of *iddat*. If a pregnant woman becomes a widow she can not remarry till the birth of the child. The most predominant type of family among the Balti is the extended one, mostly vertically extended. Since people live close to border areas, the number of broken families is also high. The head of the family is invariably a male member who enjoys absolute powers on the allocation and distribution of the economic resources of the family. He represents the family in the interfamilial social interaction, commands respect from youngsters and showers affection on them. He is a strong personality whose orders are a command for the rest of the family members. The younger family members neither indulge in loose talks nor smoke in his presence. An elder brother also receives due respect from the younger brothers as head of the family. Conflicts within the family are few. Joking relationships are absent but the degree of frankness is higher in a specific kin category. No marked avoidance was noticed within the different kin categories. Son's wife and husband's father work together in the fields without any inhibition. The degree of familiarity between a young wife and her father-in-law is similar to that between a daughter and her father. Teknonomy, however, is strictly observed.

The laws of inheritance are governed by the *Fiqah-e-Jafaria* (Islamic jurisprudence) according to which a son is entitled to inherit two-thirds of the father's property or in equal shares thereof if the number of sons is more than one. A daughter is entitled to inherit one-third of the deceased father's property or in equal shares thereof if the number of daughters is more than one. In the absence of a male issue, the daughter is entitled to inherit her father's property in full or in equal parts if their number is more than one. If a person dies issueless, the deceased person's property goes to his brother, father's brother, or father's brother's son in order of priority. In case the deceased leaves behind no potential heir, then the property comes under the ownership of the *quam* to which the deceased belonged. Daughters do not claim their share in the parental property. Succession transmits rights from father to the eldest male issue.

Interfamilial linkages are strong both in the sphere of *quam*, locality and the village. Various families of a *quam* pool their resources together for undertaking a social or humanitarian work in the locality. Parents, however, feel a steady erosion in their parental authority.

The Balti woman leads a life full of activities not only within the confines of the house but even beyond. She is entitled to inherit her father's property in absence of male siblings, adopt *maqpa* (uxorilocal residence) and administer her husband's activities, who does not claim a right in her property as the property belongs to her children. In such a situation, she controls household accounts and family resources. She is an active worker in the fields and carries out all agricultural activities except ploughing. She walks 5 to 7 km. a day for collection of juniper bushes that keep her home and hearth warm during long arctic winters. While Kargil eases out a substantial number of its male population for labour in the hills and plains of north India, the Balti men too leave their homes during the winter months and women run their houses in their absence. Like men, their, participation is encouraged in religious spheres. They offer their ornaments to the village *matamsara* and repurchase them on a higher bid. The money thus raised is spent on the maintenance of the sacred centre. Politics, of course, is not their cup of tea. Women's participation in performance of rituals, however, is at par with their male counterparts.

A woman in labour is confined to a separate room and is assisted by elderly and experienced ladies in delivery. She is served salted tea mixed with butter immediately after birth of the baby. The neonate is administered a bath in lukewarm water. Thereafter, the Sheikh or Akhun is called to whisper *azaan* in the ears of the child. The mother takes a bath after seven days known as *bosh-yoni*, and the father throws a feast to all members of *quam* and one member each from the remaining families of the village. The mother's parents and other members of her *quam* offer seven leavened breads of barley to the nursing mother. *Aqeeqa* is performed on the same day; a goat or a ram is sacrificed but the parents of consanguineous kin of the newborn desist from eating the mutton of the sacrificed animal. The Sheikh is again called upon to suggest the name for the newborn. On the fortieth day after birth, the parturient mother is given another bath called *ghusl-e-niffas* which removes all the pollutants from her body and she resumes normal household activities. Circumcision of male children is performed preferrably on the same day the child is born or before the child attains the age of six months. There are no rites pertaining to adolescence for either sex.

Matchmaking, an act of merit, is negotiated by a *halpa* (well-wisher). Through him and with the consent of the Sheikh, a date is fixed for marriage. If the bride's father is in a hurry, he may perform only *nikah* and defer other customary marriage rituals for a later date.

The bridegroom accompanied by his kith and kin and other village elders goes to the house of the bride in a *barat* (procession). *Nikah* is solemnized by the Sheikh who first receives the consent from the bride and thereafter from the bridegroom. After *nikah*, the guests are entertained to a *thazan* (feast) in which *khachi*, butter, mutton, vegetables, apricots and tea, are served. Thereafter, the bride is handed over to the ladies of the bridegroom's party and is brought to the groom's house where she is received by the latter's kin. The guests are served sweet tea and a *ishnen mizaan* (feast) is arranged in the night in honour of the bride's relation. *Khachi*, boiled eggs, pudding, butter, mutton, boiled rice and tea are served on the occasion. The bride is left behind with her *mome* (close friends). After two days the *baqpa* (bridegroom), the *baqmo* (bride) and her *mome* return to the bride's house and the bridegroom is honoured with another feast (*slum*) by his in-laws. Thereafter, the bridegroom's parents come to the bride's parents to take her back to their own village and they are given yet another *khangso* (feast) and gifts of clothes, sheep and goats. The bridegroom returns to his village along with his parents leaving behind his bride who continues to stay with her parents for another month. Thereafter, she returns to her busband's house and stays there permanently.

When somebody dies, his or her near kin and villagers form two groups. One group starts making preparation for digging a grave and the other group gets busy in preparing the body for the last journey. The body is kept in the village *matamsara* for giving a *ghusl-e-maiyat.* The Sheikh and Akhun supervise the rituals associated with the bath.

After the bath, the body is wrapped in a cotton sheet. The body is lowered down in the grave and funerary prayers; *namaz-e-janaza*, are performed. The hearth in the house where death has occurred remains unlit for the day. It is the duty of the near kin to supply cooked food to the bereaved family. At night a sheep is sacrificed by the head of the bereaved family and mutton is distributed in the village. On the third day, all the mourners assemble in the house of the grieved family for recitation of one *surah* from the Holy Koran. Each family of the deceased's *quam* sends 3 kg of *sattoo* (parched barley flour) and 250 gm of butter to the bereaved family. Other families of the village contribute 1 to 5 kg of *sattoo* and a little butter. The offerings are made on the grave of the deceased. The items thus collected are redistributed among the orphans, neèdy widows and other deserving persons of the village. On the fortieth day a similar ceremony is repeated in which each head of the family of the fathers's and mother's *quam* is invited. After recitations from the Holy Koran, a *majlis* is held and food is served to all the participants. In the evening, all the kin go to the site of the grave to offer *fateha* to the departed soul and alms are distributed among the needy.

The traditional economy of the Balti consisted of trade and agriculture. Trade came to a sudden halt after Partition and agriculture emerged as the primary source of livelihood supplemented by labour. Natural resources consist of land and forests. The *quam* exercises ownership of land and reallocates its portions among the constituent households. The canal water is also allocated to the *quams* which, in return, distribute it among the constituent households according to their respective sizes. The Baltis are a land-owning community. Only a few families of recent settlers are landless. The shortfall caused by stoppage of trade was, however, duly compensated by the presence of the armed forces who engaged a bulk of Baltis as labourer to keep the supply line open.

For settlement of all sorts of disputes they look at the Holy Koran, Sunnat and the clergy. *Ahaadis* (traditions) too help them to resolve ticklish issues. Most of the issues that cause conflict and controversies pertain to land. The issues which cannot be resolved by the elders and the clergy are settled at law courts. But such an eventuality is rare. The statutory village panchayats take up the collective issues related to village upliftment in terms of implementation of various schemes initiated by the Government of Jammu & Kashmir from time to time.

The Baltis are Muslims of Ethna-e-Ashari sect (twelvers). Each village has a mosque for prayers and a *matamsara* (*imambara*) for the performance of public and personal rituals. The major sacred centres of pilgrimage are Karbala, Najaf Ashraf, Jannatul Baqi, Kaazmain, Saamra, Meshhad and Qum. Those who return after visiting the above pilgrimages are reverently addressed as Hajji. Sheikh (*mujtahid*) and Akhun are very close to the day to day activities of the Balti from birth to death. No life-cycle rituals can be performed without their supervision and assistance. In the past when people were comparatively less well-off economically and seldom sent their children to Iraq and Iran for priestly education, they used to invite a Sayyid or an Agha from other places and provide them with necessary livelihood by way of contributing (*mal-e-sadaat* portion of khums levy), and offer their daughters in marriage. The Sayyid takes care of serious religious matters and the Akhun conducts life-cycle rituals. He also cures ailments by giving *taaviz* (amulets) or by reciting verses.

Id-ul-Fitr, Id-ul-Qurban, Id-e-Ghadir, Id-e-Shaban, Thirteenth of Rajab, the birthday of Prophet Muhammad and his daughter Fatima-al-Zehra and Moharram are the major festivals.

The Baltis were Buddhists until Mir Shamsuddin Iraqui converted them to Shiism. However, the effects of Buddhism tinged with the animistic Bon traits could not be wiped away completely. They evolved an intricate balance between polytheistic Buddhism and monotheistic Islam in their religion and world views.

Any art form beyond floral and geometric designing and calligraphy is prohibited in Islam. Hence the Baltis possess none. There are no group-oriented crafts excepting specialization in carpentry and masonry. The community has no records of folk tales folk songs, or folklore excepting dirges allowed by Shia religion. Music and dance are totally prohibited.

In eastern Kargil, Muslims and Buddhists live in the same villages but in different localities. In some villages at the western periphery they live with Broq-Pa (Muslim Dard) and Khache-Pa (Kashmiris). In the religious sphere the Dards and the Balti stand together: the Balti maintain cordial relations with the Khache-Pa who settled down in the former's village at the time when Zorwar Singh attacked Ladakh and left behind a few Kashmiri soldiers who decided to settle down in the Balti villages. They embraced Shiism and married the Balti girls. They have now been fully assimilated with the Balti population. The Bodhs who agree to embrace Islam of the Shia sect have also been included in the Balti fold. Hence intercommunity connubial norms are simple and flexible. There is no ceremonial norm of putative kinship. The Baltis share schools, water resources, road facilities and panchayat *ghar* with the Buddhists without any objection but do not accept cooked food from them. At times when they are invited to attend the Buddhist festivities they desist to dine with the Buddhists but accept dry rations. There is no semblance of the *jajmani* system among the Baltis. However, they enter into economic transactions with Yarkandi traders who have their shops at Kargil. Since the Baltis have specialized in most of the artisan crafts such as masonary, carpentry, milling, shoemaking and tailoring they are not only self-sufficient but provide their services to the Broq-pa on a prescribed fee. However, they feel unhappy about how the Kashmiris of Srinagar treat them.

Their relations with the Buddhists are, by and large, smooth and pleasant. Landless families among them eke out their livelihood through labour by working in the fields of relatively well-off zamindars. In case they are found hardworking and reliable, a zamindar feels no hesitation in offering his household as a *maqpa*. Share-cropping has not developed in this part of the country where cultivation was mainly done by absentee landlords during the *shakhsi* (autocratic) rule. After the accession of the state to the Indian Republic, the cultivators were made owners of the land which they had been cultivating for their masters.

Kargil has a higher secondary school for boys as well as for girls, a college and a state run vocational-cum-training centre that imparts training in various crafts such as weaving shawls and *pattoo* cloth. Ladakhi blankets and *razais* have captured the Indian market in a big way. The rate of literacy which was negligible in 1947 has gone up. Modern medicare is available and made use of IRDP and REP have not made any substantial headway. Baltis listen to transistor sets for news. Newspapers do not reach the villages. There are no drinking water facilities other than *kuhl* water which is used for both irrigation as well as drinking purposes. During winter when the *kuhl* is frozen, people dig a hole in the river Dras for fetching water. Like all other villages of Jammu & Kashmir where rural electrification is 100 per cent, Balti villages too are electrified but receive restricted power supply to light their houses.

The Balti are conservationists of energy *par excellance*. People are sceptical about the use of chemical fertilizers in their apricot and apple orchards and in the fields suspecting a lower yeild and a threat to immunity against various plant diseases prevalent in the area. Midday meal programme lacks thrust and serious follow-up measures. Public distribution facilities have not been so far brought to the doorsteps of the Balti and they have to walk all the way to Kargil in order to collect consumer items from fair price shops, which, none the less remain well stocked. People's disposition towards banking facilities is positive. Many Baltis have availed loan facilities to start their own establishments like street corner tea-stalls, grocery shops, etc.

BAQAR R. RIZVI

BANDUK KHAR

The Banduk Khar is an occupational name meaning maker of guns. It is a section of ironsmiths living in the Kashmir Valley. There are different occupational groups among the ironsmiths. Those who make copper utensils and polish them are called Thanthur or Thatehar. There are others who make iron gates and grills, called *Ahangar.* The section of ironsmiths specialized in making guns live in Rainawari and Khanyar areas in the city of Srinagar. The community has no synonym or title. The members of this community own shops or work in sheds in the market areas of the city. Their locality is known as Banduk Khar Mohalla or Hazari Bazaar. There are about 300 households of them in Rainawari. A few families of them are also found in Anantnag district but they are engaged in agricultural pursuits and services. They speak Kashmiri and dress themsleves like other Muslims of Kashmir Valley. They are listed under the economically and educationally backward class in the state. They are non-vegetarian and rice is their staple food. They smoke *bidi*, cigarettes and hubble-bubble. Alcoholic drinks are forbidden. A change has been observed in their food habit as they have started taking *chapati* (bread) made of wheat flour.

Differentiation within the community, if any, is due to education, occupation and economic status. They marry with any Muslim belonging to equal status and occupation. They call themselves *Ahangars* or ironsmiths and are equal to other occupational castes of Kashmir such as Tarkhan (carpenter), Gilkar or Desil (mason), etc. Sayyids are considered a higher caste while the Watal, Dum and Hanji are considered lower by them. Other communities consider them of the middle rank. They are endogamous but this is not followed strictly. Marriages are settled within close relatives. Marriages with cousins, both cross and parallel, are preferred. Sororate and levirate marriages are also permitted. Marriages are arranged after attaining adulthood and are settled by negotiations initiated by either of the parties. When a girl comes of age, her father seeks suitable match for her through a *manzymyor* (mediator). *Nishani* (betrothal) is the first step in the process. On this occasion *nikah* or marriage contract is written and commitment is made regarding the amount of *mahr* and the *than* or cloth which the groom's father has to give at the time of marriage. After marriage, the girl goes to live with her husband and her in-laws.

In case of death of either of the spouse, the survivor is free to remarry. Both sororate and levirate marriages are permitted within the prescribed limits provided they are of matching age. However, a widow's subsequent marriage is possible only after four months and ten days after the death of her husband. The marriage is simple and the expenses are decided by an *alim*, one well versed in religious knowledge. Divorce can be resorted to by either party. Relatives and friends first try to persuade them for reconciliation. After that the matter is referred to the *maulvi* or *alim*. In case the wife seeks a divorce she has to observe *iddat* for a period of three months and ten days. This is to ensure that she is not carrying a baby. After the judicial separation is made the woman is free to go to her parents. She has to condone the *mahr* and return the clothes and ornaments to her husband. When the husband seeks divorce, he has to pay *mahr* to his wife but the ornaments are not returned to him. Children are the responsibility of the father in case of divorce. The mother, however, can keep them till he or she is seven years old. The common causes of divorce are adultery, barrenness, maladjustment, impotency, cruelty, inability to meet the expenses of the wife, etc. The incidence of divorce has considerably decreased due to the huge amount of *mahr* to be paid to the wife by the husband. Other social factors are also the reason for decrease in divorce.

Joint family in its traditional form really does not exist. A son occupies a separate room and kitchen in the same house after marriage. Some times members have to move out to different places for business or service. The eldest male member in the family is given due respect and is consulted on all important issues. Women of the household do not observe *purdah* in the presence of their father-in-law and husband's elder brother. Joking relations exist among the members of the same generation, specially between husband's younger brothers and wife's younger brothers and sisters.

Property is divided equally among all the sons but daughters and the widow also get a share as per the provisions of the *shariat* (Islamic law). In the absence of a male issue, property can be transferred to the daughter if the father so desires. A son who looks after the aged parents is liable to get more. Succession follows the patriarchal line only. A woman of the community does not enjoy equal status with a man. They do most of the domestic chores, a few of them also work in offices and in private organizations.

When the child is born, it is given a bath in warm water and thereafter indoctrinated by the recitation of *azaan* as well as the verses from the

Holy Koran. On the seventh day after delivery the woman takes her first bath with warm water. On this occasion tea is served to the neighbours and close relatives. A priest is invited to recite prayer and is served with dinner. The child is also given a name in consultation with the priest. On completing forty days the woman is given a second bath. *Zerakasi* or the first head shaving of the child is performed when six months old. The hair of the child is buried underground along with some walnuts in the belief that the tree which will eventually sprout will bear superior quality nuts called *kagazi*. The child is then presented to the womenfolk who shower *shirini* (small candy), almonds and dates on him. This is followed by payments made to the host of which a complete record is maintained by one of the literate relatives. A copper bowl belonging to the barber is also circulated among the guests who put in it varying amounts ranging from twenty-five paise to one rupee. The amount thus collected is given to the barber alongwith the copper bowl. *Khatnahal* (circumcision) is performed on the male child when he is more than two years old. Earlier, this was performed by a barber. The child was made to sit on an inverted basket under which a fowl was kept. The operation was performed with a razor. The barber was given the fowl, some money, sugar balls and rice. Nowadays the operation is done in the hospital soon after the childbirth. Important marriage rituals are *gandum* (betrothal) which is followed by presentation of *doon-leij* (earthen pot full of nuts) to the father of the bridegroom by the bride's parents. It is performed about a month after *gandum*. On this occasion the bride's father accompanied by two or three near relatives visits the house of the bridegroom where they are entertained to a feast. The intervening period between these functions and the actual marriage varies according to the circumstances depending on the convenience of the parties to the marriage. If during this interval any of the four principal religious festivals, namely Id-ul-Zuha, Id-ul-Fitr, Shab-e-Miraj and the anniversary of some saints falls, the would-be bridegroom's father sends some gifts such as silver bangles for the would-be bride together with sugar candy and fruits on a *matter*. This is responded by the party with the addition of an amount ranging between Rs. 11 and Rs. 101. A mutually agreed upon date is announced. The announcement calls close relatives for a treat or *dapanbata*. As the date of marriage draws near, several ceremonies are performed in quick succession. These begin with *malasbehoun*. The bride is not permitted to take bath and is kept on solid diet. It continues for three days. The second ritual is called *massmechravoun,* i.e. loosening of the bride's hair plaits, starts on the penultimate day of the marriage and *mala menz* when the female neighbours are invited and served dinner. The hands and feet of the bride are dyed in *henna* (myrtle paste) late in the night while the women keep on singing. The first day of marriage is called *menziraat*. This takes place on the day following *malamenz*. Relatives and neighbours join the function and are served with dinner. The second day of the marriage called *yenevoul* starts with the despatch of a number of copper plates, containing sugar candy, *shirini*, almonds, clothes and ornaments by the bridegroom's father for the bride. Arrangements are made for the feast to be served in the evening to the groom's party at the bride's house where the procession is received by singing women. The groom is escorted to the invitation hall and made to sit on a decorated seat reserved for him. The guests are entertained with *qahwa* (green tea) and cakes of special variety. This is followed by the *nikah* (betrothal) ceremony presided over by the village priest.

Nikah may precede wedding by several weeks or months. It can be held only a day before or in the afternoon of the day of wedding. On such occasions, the bridegroom grants his consent for marriage. Similarly the bride is also represented by an attorney and two witnesses. The priest seeks the consent of the two attorneys and announces the condition before the audience. *Mahr* is settled as also the mode of payment. The *nikah* through an attorney is called *wakalatan*, and if done personally it is called *altan*. The bride's maiden stay at her husband's house is for seven days during which she receives her close relatives making some presents called *khabar*. The bride's return visit to her father's house after the seventh day is celebrated by *Wathal* (feast) when the bridegroom visit his in-laws called *phirsal*.

The dead body is given a bath by a professional called *snangoru*. After the bath, the body is wrapped in *kafan* (white shroud) and is carried to the grave dug by the *malkhosh* (sexton). Mourning continues till the following Friday. Recitation of the Holy Koran takes place on the fourth and fortieth day called *chaharum* and *chehallum*, respectively.

The community is landless. Their traditional occupation was making and repairing single and double-barrel guns.

Influential elders of the community decide disputes of minor nature. But nowadays people prefer to settle civil and criminal cases in a court of law.

The community is Muslim by religion and of Sunni sect. They visit Muslim shrines such as Hazratbal, Dastgir Sahib, Khanqah-e-Maulla,

Charar-e-Sharif and Shaikh-Zain-ud-Din, etc. They celebrate all the Muslim festivals such as, Urs-e-Nabi, Miraj-e-Alam, Id-ul-Fitr and Id-ul-Zuha, etc. A *mulla* serves the religious needs of the community. He officiates at the birth, marriage and death ceremonies.

Ladies are fond of stitching designs on woollen shawls specially for their personal use and not for sale. Folk songs are the same as sung by other Muslims of the Kashmir Valley, namely, *wanawun, wayun* and *rouf* sung on the occasions of marriage, betrothal, circumcision and other festivals.

All economic relations are strictly in *quid pro quo* basis and all terms are generally in cash. Though they belong to Ahangar or ironsmith community, yet they consider their own occupation of making guns superior to the work done by the ordinary smiths. They rank themselves above Tarkhan (carpenter), Gilkar (potter), Hajjam (barber) and Dosil (mason). They consider Watal (scavenger) inferior and refrain from taking food and water in their house. Connubial relations are maintained with any Muslim of equal status and of clean occupation. In their work of making guns, they depend on Ahangar and Tarkhans for making barrels and wooden butts, respectively. The wages to them are paid in cash. They share sources of water, road, school, graveyard with other Muslims.

The basic facilities of primary education, drinking water, electricity, health and transport are available to those who are living in the urban centres. They send their boys and girls to cities and towns for higher education. The primary health centres are available in the villages. They are unable to procure loan under the Integrated Rural Development Programme due to the complex banking procedures. Only a few of them are able to run manufacturing units. They avail of the facilities of the fair price shops.

PARMANAND LAL

BARWALA

The Barwala of Jammu are an agricultural community. They were agricultural labourers and skin-hide removers in the recent past and so they have been grouped with the other lowly placed communities of the region. In fact, the Barwala are a subgroup of the broader ethnic group called Doom.

The Barwala are a community of ex-bonded labourers engaged in skinning of dead animals for the selling hides. Barwala are also called Batwal by many other communities. They are, therefore, recognized and treated as a part of low-caste groups in the Jammu region. With the agrarian reforms in the state of Jammu & Kashmir, they have shifted to agricultural occupations, giving up their traditional occupation. But their social status has not changed significantly. They are spread over many places in the Jammu region, especially in the rural areas of Reasi, Chinari, Naoshera, Jammu, R.S. Pura, Samba, etc. They perceive their distribution at the regional level. In undivided India, it was deemed to be at the trans-regional level. The historical accounts has been forgotten over a period of time. Most of the Barwala are permanent settlers in their present place of habitat while some of them had migrated from Pakistan at the time of Partition. The Barwala settlements record extreme warm climate for better part of the year in the plains of Jammu province. The region is mostly semi arid with high humidity and thin forest cover with medium rainfall during the monsoons. They speak Dogri within the family and kin group and communicate with others in Hindi and Dogri. The script used is Devanagari. They follow the common and most prevalent dress pattern of the local population. They are a Scheduled Caste of the state. Their total population was 18,882 in the state according to 1981 census.

The Barwalas are occasional non-vegetarians with high vegetable consumption. They do not eat beef but consume pork, fish, eggs, fowls, ducks and chicken. Their staple food is wheat, rice and maize. Usually all types of pulses including beans are consumed. They consume all varieties of vegetables which are either available locally or brought from outside. They make regular use of milk and milk-products. Tea is a popular beverage and is taken often with milk. Fruit consumption is occasional to moderate. The menfolk take alcoholic drinks occasionally, while the women abstain from it.

Alcoholic drinks are purchased from the market. Cigarette smoking is quite common among males with frequent use of cheroot. Betel and tobacco chewing is common.

The Barwala do not have any significant social division though differentiation is made at the occupational and educational levels. They identify themselves more closely with the other Scheduled Castes like the Mahasha, Dum, etc. Various subcastes among them are: Narwalia, Mandla, Dalwatiya, Sanjwal, Soniyal, Payaliya, Radha, Bangiyee, Radathiya, Paba, etc. They have a low self-perception and other communities also consider them as such.

The Barwala practise exogamy at surname level but marry within their own community. They seek marriage alliances with upper Hindu castes as well. No restriction is there for sororate (junior) marriage. Pre-puberty marriage was the earlier practice but now a days girls are married usually after puberty. The age for marriage is 16 years onwards for the girls, while for the boys it is above 22 years. The marriage is arranged through mutual consent of the parents and to a much lesser extent that of the boys and girls. Monogamy is the prevalent form of marriage. Sororate (junior) is permissible in case of demise of the wife. Symbols of marriage are vermilion, *mangalsutra* and *bindi*. These symbols are observed as a matter of tradition. *Kanyadan* exists and the dowry is mainly paid in kind, comprising utensils, bedding items and elementry items of furniture. Very little cash is involved in the marriage ceremonies. Cash is not insisted upon. The rules of residence are patrilocal but in cases where there is no male heir, the husband lives with the wife's family. There has been a gradual shift to the neolocal type of residence.

Divorce is permissible for either sex under social and judicial approval and proceedings can be initiated by any one of them. The divorce rate is quite low. The main reasons for divorce are adultery and maladjustment besides cruelty. Usually it is the husband who seeks divorce as socio-cultural conditions do not encourage women to do so. Consequently, divorce compensation is paid to the wife and children become the responsibility of either the mother or father as settled by mutual negotiations or as directed by the court. The rules regarding remarriage are quite flexible. The widows and the widowers can remarry without any restrictions. Likewise a divorcee can also remarry. Increase in the age at marriage is reported.

The family is of extended type, both vertically and horizontally. Daughter-in-law and father-in-law relationship is usually of avoidance because of social taboo and joking relationship is maintained with equals. Conflicts and confrontations are mainly on account of property and to a lesser extent, due to the authority of the elders being challenged. The rules of inheritance are male-equigeniture and females do not claim their share nor are they given it by the relatives. The eldest son normally succeeds as the family head after the father's demise. There has been a rise in the formation of nuclear families resulting in the partial decline of extended family system.

The Barwala women play an active role in most of the farm and non-farm activities which include agriculture, tending of cattle, husking of rice and collecting grass and fodder besides collecting firewood, fetching potable water and carrying out domestic chores. They do not substantially supplement the family income. Women, in general, have a low status and are confined to household jobs. They do not have any control over the household expenditure. Women generally have a secondary position to their menfolk. They are quite docile and submissive and do not seem to be concerned with the overall changes occuring in the society.

Lifting of heavy objects, travelling or meeting strangers during late night hours or looking at the moon during an eclipse are some of the restrictions imposed on an expectant mother during the pre-delivery period. A majority of the babies are delivered at home, with the help of an experienced midwife. Wherever medical facilities in the shape of sub-health centres, district hospitals or main city hospital are available, people go there for the delivery. They observe five days' post-delivery pollution. No postnatal restrictions on mothers are observed. The *mundan* ceremony is performed for the male children. *Annaprashan* (first feeding of cereals) ceremony is not observed.

Marriages are arranged through family friends, relatives and elders. The ceremony is not an elaborate affair but the festivity of the occasion is quite entertaining. The day before the wedding the traditional *mehndi-raat* is performed. The next day the groom accompanied by guests (number varies from 50 onwards) comes to the bride's house after sunset. The marriage ceremony is performed along with the ritual of *jaimala*. Customarily wedding ceremony is solemnized at the bride's residence. The bridegroom comes to the bride's place on a mare carrying a sword. The *sehra* ceremony, i.e. recitation of couplets in praise of the couple is done by a hired person or a close friend. The *lagan* ceremony is performed. The bride's parents offer a feast to the guests accompanying the bridegroom. Vegetarian food is served on this occasion. The bridegroom's side also offers a feast to friends and relatives after the marriage is over. Friends and relatives normally offer gifts or cash to the bridegroom.

The body of a dead person is given a bath and is wrapped in a white cloth and carried on a bier to the cremation ground on the shoulders by four persons. Thereafter, *puja* is performed and the body is cremated. The dead bodies of children below the age of five years are buried. They observe ten days' death pollution. *Rasam-pagri* or *uthala* is performed, after the pollution days are over, for installing the next male member in the hierarchy as the head of the family.

Land is the main source of their livelihood. It is owned individually. A number of the Barwalas are also landless and work as farm and casual workers. Settled cultivation coupled with farm labour has been a traditional occupation. Landlessness among them is a significant feature despite major land reforms enacted by the government which dissolved proprietory rights on land of absentee landlords as 'land to the tiller' policy was introduced. Despite this, agriculture is still their mainstay. Besides, they are engaged in trade, government and private service, self-employment and as un-skilled workers. The Barwala women participate in most of the farm-related and animal husbandry activities or work as casual labourers on farm, construction or road building works. Even marginal and small-scale farmers among them try to work as casual labourers for additional earning. Though there is no child labour, some of their children do work as domestic help. They receive their wages both in cash and in kind. Link with the market is weekly to monthly in rural areas whereas it is daily in urban centres. The mode of payment is both in cash and barter in rural areas but mostly cash transactions are involved in the urban areas. Bonded labour does not exist among them. However, there has been a rise in the number of daily, casual and agricultural workers mainly due to the subdivision and fragmentation of land rendering it economically non-viable.

Heterogenous panchayats exist at the village level. These panchayats are of statutory nature and monitor developmental and various other welfare programmes launched by the governmental agencies. Panchayat may also render services for solving disputes arising out of social or economic frictions by adopting reconciliatory role between the warring parties. Panchayats may also issue edicts for excommunication against offenders or against an individual household. Adultery, dispute over land and water, and theft are some of the crimes reported among these people.

The Barwalas are a lower caste among the Hindus. They are aware of the *varna* system. They are covered under reservation policy. They worship village and regional deities. Religious specialists are drawn from the Brahman community to perform the birth, marriage and death rites. They visit the pilgrimage centres of Vaishno Devi, Raghunath temple, Bahu Fort and Amarnath. Major Hindu festivals celebrated by them are Shivratri, Janmashtami, Diwali, Rakshabandhan, Navratra and Lohri.

Crafts are confined to household and as non-commercialized ventures. Oral traditions, music and dances conform to the Dogri-cum-Punjabi style. Men and women participate in dances occasionally on some joyous occasion. Songs based on local religious and romantic contents besides popular film songs are sung by these people.

They traditionally accept cooked and uncooked food from Hindus placed not only above them but also from other communities which are socially placed and grouped along with them. They accept food and exchange it with Doom, Masha, Megh and many other communities. They share wells and water sources with the other communities. There is no restriction on accepting uncooked food items from the non-Hindus. They maintain marital ties within their own community but there is no rigidity in seeking ties with the high caste Hindus. They share the cremation grounds with the other co-religionists. The Barwalas also share schools, panchayat ghar, water sources with other people of the region. They visit the religious shrines of *pirs* and fakirs. They maintain a cordial patron-client relationship with others. The cultivator-labour relationship exists among them. They receive the services of the village barber, carpenter, masons, etc.

This community is in socio-economic transition. They have white-collar job holders and teachers. Political leadership has emerged from among them both at village and sub-regional level. Some of them are in the police and defence services. A number of them are also directly or indirectly involved in business and entrepreneurial ventures.

Formal education is yet to become mass-based among them. It is considered favourable mainly for boys and partly for the girls. Boys study up to college level and girls up to secondary level. Boys dropout because of economic constraints. For girls both economic and social inhibitions are the restraining factors. However, an awareness in this regard is growing fast among them. Attitude towards health and medicare is still based on indigenous pattern though, of late, they have become favourably disposed to modern medicare.

Their attitude towards family planning is lukewarm. Though they understand the necessity and desirability of a small family, majority of them do not seem to make any concerted effort to keep their family small. The couples prefer four or more children even now. Use of modern methods of family planning is reported in a small segment of this community and it is the women who get sterilized.

Drinking water facilities are available in almost all the Barwala settlements. They get piped water mainly but may as well get it from the wells and tubewells or ponds. Some of them have been covered under Integrated Rural Development Programme (IRDP) but self-employment is mainly in agriculture and petty business. They listen to the radio and watch television individually or at the community centre. People also go to the cinema. Roads and post offices exist within the vicinity while the nearest railhead is in Jammu city, which is not far off. They make use of electricity mainly for lighting purposes. Firewood, cow-dung cakes and kerosene are used as fuel for cooking purposes. Irrigation facilities are available in the villages of the plains. The community uses organic manure, chemical fertilizers and insecticides for their farm operations. However, local manure is still a popular source and extensively used. They avail of the facilities of public distribution of food articles through fair price shops. Their attitude towards savings is favourable but they are still dependent on moneylenders and shopkeepers for cash to meet the social and unforeseen contingencies.

The Barwalas are undergoing a socio-economic change though the pace of transition is slow. With the agrarian reforms in the state, the Barwalas have acquired proprietorship of land. Diversification in occupation has occurred both vertically and horizontally.

INDU AIMA

BASITH

The Basith claim a Rajput descent. They reportedly migrated from Chamba, where they were called Arya, to the present habitat about two hundred years ago. They are also known as Basithe. During the 1965 Indo-Pak war the community took an active role in defending the area against the invader and many members of the community were awarded for their courage, bravery and valour. After the war, the then chief minister, Jammu & Kashmir, visited their villages and awarded them the title of Vashishth Rajput. Since then many of them use the suffix Vashishth or Bashishth after their names. The Basith live in Jammu, mainly in the Punch district of the state. Their population was 9,962 according to the 1981 census.

The people inhabit the hilly terrains amidst thin forests and medium rainfall. They speak Pahari amongst themselves and use Urdu and Hindi when conversing with others. They dress themselves in Dogra apparel. The men invariably wear a turban. They are one of the Scheduled Castes of the state. According to 1981 census their population was 9,961.

The Basiths are non-vegetarians and take pork. Forest game such as hare, porcupine and fowls are also consumed occasionally. Fish and eggs are consumed moderately. The staple food consists of wheat, rice, *jowar* and maize. Among the pulses gram, *masoor*, peas and *rajmah* beans make a regular item in their food. Mustard oil and *ghee* are the media of cooking. Seasonal vegetables and fruits such as pears, plums and apricots are used in good quantity. Alcoholic drink are consumed regularly by men. The variety of items in their diet have, however, been substantially increased due to their easy availability in the market. Bananas, oranges and grapes which were rare in the past are now consumed by all sections of the community due to their easy availability in the market.

They are divided into a number of exogamous *zaat* group such as Pandhal, Chatriyal, Chimal, Raine, Slotre, etc. These groups portray no hierarchy and are treated almost at par with one another socially. However, each *zaat* belongs to a particular *gotra*. Chatriyal belong to Changin *gotra*, Chirnal to Pardwari *gotra* and Raine to Dev *gotra*. *Gotras* do not regulate marriages. Various *zaats* falling in the same *gotra* also categorize themselves into an exogamous group. There is no local term for the latter grouping. Members of one *zaat* live closer to the other in terms of social interaction. They also worship the *kul-devta* collectively. There is no change in the title of sub-groups, but the community as a whole, however, likes to call itself as Vashisht Rajput. They fix their position as Kshatriya in the *varna* order and claim a status below the Brahman but above the Vaishyas. Other communities too concede a Rajput status to them.

The Basiths marry within their own group but observe exogamy at *zaat* and *gotra* level. Cross-cousin marriages have lately been allowed but parallel cousin marriages are not permissible. Sororal marriages are considered inauspicious but junior levirate is permissible. The age of marriage for boys is 18 years and for girls 16 years. *Duathi*, or marriage by exchange is prevalent. Other modes of acquiring mates are by negotiation and by courtship. A sororate polygyny is prevalent; symbols of marriage for women are vermilion, toe rings and *mehndi*. The Basith practise patrilocal residence after marriage. Divorce is allowed only with the consent of both the spouses. Either of the two can initiate divorce proceedings. The husband pays maintenance to his wife and children, if any. In case a woman seeks divorce, she will have to return all the ornaments and other marriage expenses to her husband. Children, even in the latter case, are the responsibility of the father. The motives of divorce are adultery, maladjustment and cruelty. Remarriages in case of widows, widowers and male or female divorcee is allowed. In case of a remarriage, elaborate marriage rituals according to the shastras are not performed. In case of a junior levirate, *chadar dalna*, offering a shawl to the deceased husband's younger brother, is considered sufficient to get married.

The Basiths feel that marriage expenses have gone up. Now one has to sell out a part of land for meeting the dowry requirements. In the past, *charkha* (spinning wheel) used to be the only item of dowry. It was given with a view to make the girl self-sufficient in the event of an exigency. Age at marriage has also come down. Dowry, though not demanded, is usually given to the daughters and has increased considerably.

Extended families, both horizontal and vertical, are the usual family type among them but now intra-family conflicts on account of property and increasing challenge of the youngsters against the authority of the senior family members have contributed to the emergence of nuclear families. Relations between the father, who is invariably the head of the family, and sons remain cordial as long as the latter remain bachelors. Very few persons among them feel happy in a vertically extended family set-up after their marriage. Hence, vertically extended family set-up faces tremendous strains. Conflicts and frictions occur mainly due to the issues pertaining to property. Joking relations prevail between elder brother's wife and husband's younger brother and with wife's younger sister. Avoidance is maintained with wife's mother and son's wife. A woman avoids her husband's elder brother and a man avoids his wife's elder sister. All children of the deceased including girls receive an equal share in the property. The girls who forego their share from the parental property give a written statement in this respect. The line of succession runs from father to son.

Inter-family linkages in the rural set-up are very effective and close whereas in urban set-up the families live in a scattered manner. Various families enter into a number of socio-economic and cultural interactional situations. This close linkage becomes more manifested during extraordinary and festive situation. In the life-cycle rituals, all the families in a village interact with the concerned family in a collective manner. The families enter into economic transactions like taking loans from one another, carrying out collective labour activities on exchange basis. Gifts and visits are exchanged during festivals.

Extended family continues to be the dominant type. Women have been given a share in parental property but very few of them demand or get their share in property.

Unlike the high Rajput clans, the Basith women participate actively in farm activities. They tend cattle, collect fuel for the family and fetch potable water. They participate fully in marriage and other life-cycle rituals. They observe *vrats* (fasts) for the welfare of family members, visit temples and participate in political activities. Decisions in a family are taken with their consent. At times they contribute to family income by doing embroidery, tailoring and other self-employed jobs. If the husband is away from home the woman of the house controls the family expenditure also. Unlike other high Rajputs clan, she is not kept in seclusion.

When signs of pregnancy appear, a woman has to observe a number of restrictions. She does not go out of the house alone, nor does she do heavy manual work. Soon after a child is born, a pandit or *purohit* is called. The horoscope of the child is made, the good news is conveyed to the parents and other relatives of the parturient mother. Women from the neighbouring families help the parturiating mother in delivery. The umblical cord is severed by a knife and the placenta is buried deep in the corner of the house or disposed off in a nearby river. After twenty-two days of birth, the pandit comes and performs *havan* (oblation fire). He gives a name to the child on the same day. The period of pollution lasts for forty days during which the parturient mother does not perform any household work nor is she allowed to venture out of the house till the days of pollution are over. On this day the mother takes the purificatory bath and resumes her normal household duties.

Mundan (tonsuring) is peformed on male children within three or five years of birth. The child is given solid food *in* the *annaprashan* ceremony one year after performing *havan.* The boys undergo the thread-wearing ceremony at the age of 12 years with due celebrations. Nowadays most of the families postpone this ceremony till the penultimate day of marriage. Girls, on coming of age, are required to observe certain restrictions. They are secluded in a corner of the house and keep the company of elder women and companions. They are given a pair of new clothes on the onset of menses.

Their marriage rituals consist of *kurmai*, *tika*, *lagan* and *phera* or *maklawa.* The initiative for marriage is invariably taken by the girl's father, who sends a go-between to the parents of the prospective bridegroom. If the bridegroom's parents agree to the proposal a date is fixed for the engagement (*kurmai*) by the two concerned families. On that day, the bride's parents visit the bridegroom's house along with the family priest who applies *tika* on the forehead of the bridegroom and is presented some items of clothes and money in cash. A day is fixed for the marriage (*biah*) by the family pandit according to the favourable constellation of stars. On the day of marriage, the bridegroom is taken in a procession to the bride's house. The family priest conducts the marriage rituals according to the shastras. Marriage is solemnized when the bride and groom circumambulate the holy fire and exchange garlands. Members of the marriage procession are given a feast and the bride is brought by the bridegroom to his father's house. Consummation of marriage takes place thereafter. After a few days the bride returns with the bridegroom to her parents where she is visited by all her relatives and she too visits them. This custom is called as *phera* or *maklawa.*

When a person is about to die, the family priest is called and he recites hymns and pours a few drops of the Holy Ganga water into the mouth of the dying person and extracts a promise to give some alms (*daan*) for his or her salvation. After death the body is put on the floor where incense sticks are burnt and Vedic hymns are recited by the pandit. The news of the demise is conveyed to all the members of the clan. The body, in the meantime, is given a bath and wrapped in a shroud. Vermilion is applied on the forehead and face. Thereafter, it is taken to the cremation ground. The eldest son lights the fire. The remains are collected after three days and put in an earthen pot for immersion in the Ganga at Hardwar. *Shradh* is performed on the thirteenth day and the eldest male issue is offered a turban. Yet another *shradh* is observed on the first death anniversary. Childrens dead body below seven years are, however, buried. Marriage rituals have become shorter. A change has been introduced in the death rituals by general consensus. Previously, death rites used to be prolonged and all expenses incurred on rituals were borne by the deceased's next of the kin. Now they have decided that it is the responsibility of the concerned *zaat* to bear the expenses of death rituals collectively. Hence, all members of the clan contribute towards the death rituals, feasting, etc.

The Basiths are basically a land owning community. There are very few landless families who resort to either share cropping or farm labour. Land is owned by individual families. Agriculture is their main occupation. Some of them have taken up government jobs in PWD and the State Transport Corporation. Others have acquired new occupations like masonry, carpentry, etc. Their dependence on market is absolute. They purchase items of daily use from Rajouri town where the market is fully regulated. Stray cases of bonded labour have also been reported; child labour also exists though mostly in the farming sector.

The Basith economy has improved due to land reforms initiated by the Government of Jammu & Kashmir. Absentee landlordism has been abolished and tillers have been granted proprietary rights. Thus the extent of landlessness has come down. Now another shift from agriculture to white-collar jobs looks apparent in the community. The educated youth have developed a distaste for agriculture and seek the avenues of employment elsewhere. However, they have not severed their ties completely with the traditional occupation of agriculture but they try to supplement their earning by doing odd jobs. Strict forest laws aiming at wildlife conservation have deprived them of forest games.

The *biradari* panchayat, i.e. traditional caste council, is an effective and forceful forum to decide the customary issues raised by the members of the community. The nature of disputes which are brought before the said forum usually pertain to property, dissolution of marriage and other issues arising thereof. The forum also tries to decide about the political party the community should support in the elections. Senior members of the *biradari* panchayat represent the community in case any member of their community is involved in a dispute with another member of a different community of the village or of another village. The decisions taken by the members of *biradari* panchayat are binding. In case someone disagrees with the judgement of the said body, he may go to the court of law but he does so at the risk of annoying the community and such persons are looked down upon by the rest of the community. The village panchayat consists of the *sarpanch*, *nambardar*, *chowkidar* and village elders. Members are elected by a general consensus. This body takes up general issues concerning the welfare of the village. Statutory panchayats have not made much inroads in alleviating the sufferings of the community members. Cases of inflicting physical injuries and other criminal acts are reported to the police. The offenders violating the verdict of the *biradari* panchayat are excommunicated. The nature of crimes committed in and around the community pertaining land disputes, theft, disrespect to the normative setup of the community and causing insult to any member of the *biradari* panchayat or to the *biradari* panchayat *per se* are dealt with by the *biradari* panchayat. The traditional authority structure has been considerably weakened by the newly emerged process of democratization through adult franchise. The village bodies, have lost much of their sanctity due to political interference in their day to day functioning.

The Basith are Hindus of the Sanatani order. They worship all deities of the Hindu pantheon besides some of their own family deities, *kul-devtas* and *kul devis.* Baba Narsingh is worshipped as a *kul-devta* during Tamden festival which is celebrated after harvesting a new crop. Vaishno Devi, a regional deity of north India, too is visited and worshipped by them. The Basith pay obeisance to the local *pirs* also. Besides Vaishno Devi temple, Hardwar is considered as an important place of pilgrimage where the economically well-off families go to immerse the ashes of the dead.

The pandits or Acharaj Brahmans are the sacred specialists for the Basith who prepare horoscopes for the neonates, perform all life-cycle rituals such as name-giving, thread-wearing, marriage and funeral. They also perform *shradh* and *pitr-paksha* ceremonies for their patrons. Lohri, Diwali, Dussehra, Baisakhi and Tamden are their major festivals. While Dussehra, Diwali and Holi are basically post-harvest festivals, Lohri is celebrated to welcome the onset of summer and spring after a prolonged winter. Tamden is a festival of thanksgiving celebrated in honour of the *kul-devta.* The new crop is not consumed before offerings are made to the *kul-devta* in the form of dishes prepared from the new grain. Hence this particular festival is held after harvesting of each new crop. The Basiths did not report any case of conversion unlike the Rajputs of higher order like Chib, Manhas, Jaral, Domal, etc. There is an increasing awareness among them to introduce certain reforms in the community, especially in the realm of customary laws, abolition of dowry and giving a better place to their women in the society.

The Basiths have resorted to decorating floors of their houses with paintings. The craft of weaving has been forgotten but young women still do a little amount of embroidery on clothes showing motifs such as landscape, wild-life and floral designs on bed covers, pillow, table covers, etc. The Basiths have rich oral traditions of folk songs in Pahari language eulogising the charisma of Vaishno Devi and the acts of bravery of Banda Bahadur. Both men and women sing these folk songs. The musical instruments used by them are harmonium, *dholki*, *shahnai* and *chimta*. Dances are performed on festive occasions, but men and women dance separately.

The Basiths share their habitat with Brahmans, Rajputs, Sikhs, Muslims and Harijans. Water is acceptable only from Brahmans and Rajputs. *Kachcha* food too is acceptable from these two groups. *Pukka* food is acceptable from the Sikhs but not from the Muslims and some Scheduled Castes. Even dry ration, *siddha* food article, is not accepted from the Muslims and some Scheduled Castes though they accept *kachcha* food in principle, they don't give it to others. They attend the Muslim marriages, if invited but they neither interdine with them nor accept cooked food from them unless it is being cooked by a Hindu cook and served in a separate row. Marriages with other communities are not performed but they feel no hesitation in giving their daughters in marriage to the Brahmans in accordance with *anuloma* system of marriage. Putative kinship is not ritual-based but calling people of different ages and sex with the kinship terms used to address one's own kin is prevalent. Sharing of wells with the Brahmans and Rajputs is allowed but not with the Muslims and some Scheduled Castes. Stagnant water, according to them, cannot be shared with lower castes but a flowing stream of water breeds no pollution and, therefore, can be shared with all. Extending collective labour on reciprocal basis to other communities is common. Self-cultivation is the general rule with the landowning families but, at times, they employ farm labourers from within their own as well as from other communities and pay them in cash as per the wages fixed by the government from time to time.

They take a keen interest in all socio-political activities, namely: attending political meetings, casting of votes for parliament, state legislature or local bodies and in social forestry initiated by the Forest Department of Jammu & Kashmir Government. The Basith boys and girls attend schools regularly. They feel that education is the medium through which they can improve upon their standard of living and occupy a better place in the society. Most of the boys and girls study up to matric level, for which facilities are available around their villages, but sending their children for higher education is possible only for a few resourceful parents who seldom send their daughters away for the purpose. Hence, almost all the girls, inspite of their inclination for higher education, drop out due to non-availability of educational institutions whereas very few boys seek higher education due to limited financial resources.

The Basiths show a positive attitude towards both traditional as well as modern systems of medicare but the latter is not available in villages. If someone falls seriously ill, he has to be carried all the way to Rajouri on a cot covering a distance of as much as 20 to 30 km. It is a common scene on Rajouri–Punch road to see serious patients being carried on a cot by a small group. The Rajouri Government Hospital does not possess an ambulance to carry the serious patients.

People appear fully convinced of the need of having a small family with three children, preferably two sons and a daughter. Women usually get sterilized but contraceptives are used by both.

People suffer from acute drinking water shortage during the rainy season when the streams and springs get polluted, compelling the people to walk long distances to fetch potable water. A few are employed in the PWD and Transport Corporation. Radio remains the only medium of communication. Television has yet to make an appearance in their villages. The youngsters go to Rajouri to watch movies. Some of the villages are connected by road. The nearest railway station is Jammu Tawi, which is almost a day's road journey from Rajouri. Villages have been electrified and people use electricity for lighting purposes alone; other sources of energy being firewood and kerosene oil. The irrigation canals supply water to their fields. People use organic manure along with chemical fertilizers and insecticides. The nutrition programmes for children, pregnant and nursing mothers have been started with some measure of success. The midday meal scheme and integrated child development programmes are fully availed of. The facility of supplying consumer items through fair price shops does not exist. People's reaction to banking is highly critical due to malpractices in the banks.

BAQAR R. RIZVI

BATWAL

The Batwal, a landless community of Jammu & Kashmir, is known by this name only. There are different versions of the origin of the word. According to one narration, they were the landless agricultural labourers or ploughmen of the landowning Rajputs. The Rajputs kept them tied. The bond in Dogri language is called *bat.* Hence they are known as Batwal. They were for generations tied to the landowning families like bonded labourers. Another narration says that they are the Bat Rajputs and due to some historical events they lost their lands to others. Only the name Batwal remained. It is not a large group and they mostly live in Jammu, Udhampur and Kathua districts of Jammu & Kashmir. In Jammu they live in New Bahu Fort Colony, village Channibija (Tirkuta Nagar), Bishna and Samba tahsil of Jammu district. The climate of the region is warm and temperate, the terrain is hilly and plain with low humidity. Rainfall is medium and the area is thinly forested. Total population of the Batwal is 26,693 in Jammu & Kashmir according to the 1981 census.

They speak Dogri among themselves and Hindi or Punjabi with the non-Dogras. Their script is Devanagari. Earlier they used to wear *dhoti*, *kurta*, *pagri*, *sadri* and *chadar* but now they wear *kurta*, *dhoti*, *pyjama*, pants and shirts. They are included in the list of Scheduled Castes in Jammu & Kashmir state.

They are non-vegetarian and take eggs, mutton and fish but not beef. Some families are vegetarian. Their staple food is wheat, rice and pulses like *urad* (black gram), *moong* (green gram) and *masur*. Roots, tubers and seasonal vegetables according to their availability are also consumed. They can hardly afford fruits. There is no restriction on taking alcoholic drinks. The use of milk and milk products is moderate. They smoke *bidi*, cigarettes and *hookah*. Normally alcoholic drinks are purchased from the market, but in villages sometimes they themselves brew it.

There are no hierarchical stratification among the Batwals but they are divided into many exogamous *gotras* or *jatis,* namely, Nakodar, Kasim and Moten, which are considered equal. The main function of these *gotras* is to regulate marriage alliances. No change in their surnames or clan names is reported. They are perceived as low by other communities of the region and they too perceive themselves as low in the hierarchy, being Scheduled Castes. They are considered equal to the Chamars. They are aware about the varna system and recognize themselves as Shudras in the *varna* order.

The Batwals are endogamous at the community level and exogamous at the *jati* or *gotra* level. In earlier days, child marriages were common among them but now a days marriages are performed when the boys and girls attain adulthood. Age at marriage for the boys is between 18 and 25 years and for girls between 16 and 21 years. Marriages are usually arranged by the parents or relatives though some sporadic cases of love marriages have also occurred. Sometimes there is a mediator or matchmaker who negotiates between the families. Marriage by exchange in order to curtail expenses was a common practice till a few years back but nowadays it is not observed. Monogamy is the usual form of marriage and only in case of barrenness can a man remarry with the consent of the first wife.

The symbols of a married woman are *sindoor*, bangles, toe-ring and nose-pin. *Kanyadan* has been the practice and is still prevalent. In the past there was a symbolic custom of bride price but that is not in existence now and is being replaced by dowry which includes cash, utensils, ornaments and clothing. Divorce is permissible and can be sought by either of the partners. It is effected with the consent of the *biradari* panchayat on grounds of impotency, adultery, maladjustment, insanity, etc. Sometimes cases of divorce are taken to the *biradari* panchayat or court of law. Widow, widower, male and female divorcee remarriages are permissible in the community. Divorce compensation is given to the wife. In case of divorce, children are the responsibility of the father. Junior levirate and junior sororate is a common practice in case of remarriages. In case of widow or divorcee remarriage, no ceremony is performed, only *sindoor* and bangles are offered to the woman. It is called *ghar baithana*. Emergence of dowry system and decrease in divorce cases are the recent changes taken place due to contacts with the other neighbouring communities. Mostly two types of families, namely nuclear and vertically extended, are common among them. Nuclear families are generally found in urban areas while extended families are found in rural areas. After marriage, in most cases, the newly married couples establish a separate household. Interpersonal relationship is amicably established among the family members. Love and respect are shown to elders. Avoidance exists between the daughter-in-law and in-laws and between the younger brother's wife and husband's elder brother. Likewise joking exists between the elder brother's wife (*bhabhi*) and *devar* (husband's younger brother) and between brother-in-law and wife's sister. Property is equally divided among all the sons. If the father divides his property during his lifetime, the unmarried daughters also get a share. After the father's death, it is the duty of the brothers to marry off their sisters. The succession pattern is followed in the male line, from father to the eldest son. Extended families are declining rapidly due to the impact of urbanization and industrialization. Women have equal status with that of men and play an important role in all the spheres of life. Widows have the right to inherit a share in the property of the deceased husband. Women are engaged in various economic activities like agricultural operations, animal husbandry, collection of fuel, bringing potable water, etc. They play a pivotal role in the social and religious functions. Except for casting of votes they do not have any other role in the political field. They participate in the mechanism of social control only when they are called to do so.

Pre-delivery rituals and restrictions are observed in the community and *reetan*, is performed in the eighth month of pregnancy in which the father of the bride sends sweets, dry fruits, fruits and clothing for his daughter and son-in-law. In most cases delivery takes place at home and a *dai* from the Batwal community or sometimes a female relative who has specialized in the job assists in the delivery. For this the *dai* is paid in cash and kind. The first bath to the child is given on the third day and the next on the fifth day. On this day the mother also takes a bath. This ritual is called *punjap*. A Brahman is asked to prepare a horoscope and sometimes also asked to name the child. But naming ceremony as such is not performed. The period of birth pollution lasts for 21 days. Thereafter the mother and the child take a final purificatory bath and the former is free to enter the kitchen for daily routine. This is called *chautra charhna*. At the age of one, three or five years, tonsuring is done on the male child only. The first ritual of marriage is called *theka* which is followed by *kurmai* or *mundri* and is performed at the bride's place. The father of the bridegroom presents a gold ring, sweets and clothings to the bride. This ceremony is not performed in all the families. The next ceremony is called *sagai* or *sagun* in which the father of the bride proposes a date for marriage and sends sweets, clothings, cash and other articles to the prospective bridegroom's father. Before the actual date of marriage, *sandh* or *shanti yajna* is performed. On this day a feast is given to the relatives and neighbours. On the next day the marriage party goes to the bride's place where most of the marriage rituals are performed. The departure of the *barat* (*bidai*) takes place on the following day of marriage. The *gauna* ceremony is observed.

The dead are cremated but a child is buried who dies before attaining the age of ten years. The dead body is carried to the cremation ground where the eldest or the youngest son or a close relative, in absence of sons, kindles the pyre. On the tenth day *dham* or *daswan* is observed. All the blood and close relatives of the deceased get their heads shaved. On either the thirteenth, fourteenth, fifteenth or seventeenth day the relatives of the deceased assemble for the *biradari khana* called *jag. Adh-barkhi* and *barkhi* rituals are performed in the sixth and twelfth month. The ashes of the dead are collected on the third day and immersed either in the Tawi or Ganga at Haridwar. A new trend of curtailment of the rituals has been observed in the community.

The primary occupation of the community in the past was ploughing, rearing cattle, making winnowing trays, skinning dead animals and performing other farm work of their masters who invariably belonged to higher castes. In return they used to get a part of the produce as wages. They were a type of bonded labour and were not permitted to work for other zamindars. After Independence and abolition of the Zamindari Act they were liberated and set free to do any work of their choice. Now they have started cultivation for themselves and also work as labourers in plantations, road construction and other public works. Some of the families possess small pieces of land. Share-cropping is done by most of them who are landless. They receive wages in cash. The new generation has taken to different jobs as wage labourers, industrial labourers, business, government service, etc.

The Batwals have their own *biradari* panchayat to decide the disputes within the community. Usually disputes pertaining to land and matrimonial discord are solved. There are the *sarpanch* and *panch* in the panchayat who are selected by voice votes. In cities they have their associations (*jati sabhas*) to look after the grievences of the members. Social boycott, excommunication or fine in cash is imposed on the offenders. Excommunicated persons are readmitted only after serving a feast to the community and *panchs*. They have their representatives in the statutory village panchayats too which looks after the implementation of development activities of the village.

They profess Hindu religion and have their own deities and specific shrines for worship. Nagdevta, Babasurgal, Kalibir, Buababa, Babamansa and Muganum are worshipped on different occasions. Members of a particular clan sometimes have their own deity. They sacrifice goats and offer sweets on the occasions such as marriage, curing of diseases, etc., to propitiate their deities. An important fair of the Batwal is held in the month of November called Jhiri ka Mela at

Jhiri village in Jammu, where all the community members come from distant places and worship their ancestral deities (*kul-devta*). Besides, there are the temples and sacred places such as Raghunath Mandir, Vaishno Devi, etc., which are visited on certain occasions. The Brahmans are called to perform the birth, marriage and death rituals. The festivals and fairs are of socio-religious and socio-economic significance, and are celebrated with great zeal and enthusiasm. They also believe in *bhut pret* (ghosts). Making winnowing trays is the traditional craft of the community. A few families are involved also in basket-making. They have oral traditions and folk songs common in the region which are sung by the womenfolk on social and religious functions.

Being Shudras, the Batwals are still avoided by the higher castes though they try to maintain good relations with all their neighbouring communities by offering their services on certain occasions. In earlier days they used to serve the Brahmans and Rajputs only but nowadays, due to their involvement in agriculture, business and labour, they maintain their relations with all the communities of the region. In villages they still serve their patrons and get their share at the time of harvest. They interact directly with the Brahman, Rajput, Dhobi, Kahar, Mali, Lohar, Bharai, etc. In urban areas they are economically better off and social distance with others is not maintained to that extent. They sit, eat and chat together freely with others because of their business and other work. Higher castes still abstain from taking *kachcha* and *pukka* food and water from the Batwal. But the Batwals accept *kachcha* and *pukka* food from all other castes except the Bhangis. Intercommunity marriages normally do not take place, but stray cases have been reported. They share wells, temples, crematoria and other important places with other communities but it is a recent phenomenon which has occured after Independence. In villages patron-client relationship and landlord-tenant relationship exist and the members of the community are employed as labourers to work in the fields. Sharecropping is also done and a sharecropper keeps half of the total production. Putative kinship also exists among them. At present the community is able to establish more contact with other castes of the region as they are engaged in various economic pursuits such as hotel business, cloth merchandise, etc. Some of them are in the government and private organizations and freely mix with all the higher castes of the area. They participate in political activities and public functions at large.

The development programmes of the government adopted for the betterment and upliftment of the Scheduled Castes have not benefited the Batwals and they always complain about it. The attitude of the community towards education of their boys and girls though favourable, they are not able to follow it for their poor economic conditions and non-availability of schools. They study up to primary or secondary level and only a few of them could reach up to the graduate or post-graduate level. Though the attitude of the community towards modern medicare is positive, due to non-availability of government dispensaries and short supply of medicines, they are unable to utilize it. Their indigenous system of medicare still prevails, particularly in rural areas. Family planning programmes have left a good impact on them and now the couples prefer only two or three children. Generally men get sterilized or use other family planning methods. Drinking water and electricity facilities though are available in their locality but they are not adequate. Piped water, well and hand pumps are the sources of drinking water. Cow-dung cakes, wood and kerosene are the main fuels used by them. The government programmes regarding employment have not benefited them. Bulk of the population works as labourers and only a few of them are self-employed. Media of communication is radio but only few of them have it. Roads, postal and railway facilities are available. They have to depend on rainwater to irrigate their fields. They use chemical fertilizers, insecticides and organic manures in their fields. Though the facilities of food distribution system through fair price shops are available in the locality, supply of the articles was reported to be unsatisfactory. They are still dependent on the moneylenders and shopkeepers due to their poor economic conditions.

ANAND SARAN

BEDA

The Beda is a community of musicians of Ladakh who play on flutes and drums. A section of them are nomads who earn their livelihood by begging and giving musical performances. Being a landless community, some of them also work as labourers. The origin and migration of the Bedas is connected with the settlement of Ladakh with various racial groups in ancient times. The predominant Ladakhi or Bhoto consider the Beda inferior because of their profession of musicians. Their major concentration is in the Leh district but they live also settled in the Kargil district. In the Leh district they live along the Indus and Nubra valleys. The Bedas of Indus Valley are Buddhist while those in Nubra Valley are Muslim who are sedentary, not nomadic. The natural environment is characterized as a high altitude cold desert. The Beda speak Ladakhi within the family and kin group. Bodhi is their written script which is a mixture of Tibetan and Ladakhi. They speak Hindi with others. The script used for communicating with other communities is Arabic. Their dress is similar to the other Ladakhis. Men wear *goncha* (long coat), *shakten* (trousers), *sherak* (belt around the waist) and leather or felt shoes. Women dress themselves in *perak*, *goncha firoza* (scarf) on the head and *charton* or leather boots. The community is listed as a Scheduled Tribe in the state.

The Bedas have prominent cheek bones and broad and flat faces. Some obliquity is marked in the eyes having an epicanthic fold. The mouth is large with prominent lips. The nostrils are quite wide and the nose is broad as well as flat. They have scanty hair growth. The head hair are straight to slightly wavy. Women are short statured but men have medium height.

The Bedas are non-vegetarians. They eat mutton and beef (yak). Their staple food consists of wheat, *grim* (baked barley) and barley. Pulses taken are peas, beans, *rajmah*, gram, etc. *Sattoo* made by grinding the roasted wheat and baked barley is the main item of their daily diet. It is mixed with water, kneeded and made into balls. *Sattoo* is taken with *lassi* (curd), vegetables, salted tea and with meat also. *Roti* or thick bread made from wheat flour is also taken. Rice is now becoming popular as a food item. Mustard oil is the cooking medium used by them. Roots and tubers consumed by them are potatoes, radishes, turnips, onions, etc. Both men and women are fond of *chang*, a mild intoxicating drink brewed from baked barley. It is prepared in every home and also purchased from the market. *Gurgur* (brackish tea) is taken a number of times in a day. They smoke *bidi* and cigarettes. Seasonal fruits such as cherry, apricot and pears are taken occasionally. The change observed in their food habit is they now prefer rice to bread.

They are divided into exogamous *gyuts* or *rigs* which refers to a group of people who trace descent from a common ancestor or ancestress. As the group is based on blood ties, the entry of an outsider into the group is not permitted. The *gyuts* have no specific names, but villagers know their respective *gyuts* or *rigs*. In the absence of *gyut* names and in the absence of the existence of clan, there is lack of association between such social groups and the surnames of the individuals. In fact, the Bedas, like the other Ladakhis, do not have surnames. It was reported that among the Gyalpo (Rajas), Gara, Mon and Bedas marriage alliances are not possible without breaking the *gyut* or *rig* for four generations.

The Bedas have their own brotherhood like the other Ladakhis. The members of the *phasphun* worship the same gods or goddesses kept in the Hemis gompa. A Ladakhi, or Gara or Mon cannot become a member of the Beda's *phasphun*. At times it becomes very difficult for the Bedas to carry the dead body to the cremation ground because of non-availability of the *phasphun* members. The other Ladakhis do not participate when death occurs in a Beda family. As a result, sometime only one person carries the dead body to the cremation ground. The *phasphun* group in Ladakh cannot be equated to a clan group. The members of the *phasphun* are not necessarily connected through common descent. They can even marry each other when they are not lineally related through kinship.

Differentiation among the Bedas exists on the basis of education, occupation, territory, religion and other socio-economic conditions. The Beda boys and girls are averse to their ancestral profession. They are responsive to education. Majority of the Bedas are illiterate. Besides their traditional occupation, they find employment as labourers. Many have discarded the occupation of playing flutes and drums and instead adopted ironsmithy. Marriage in other community does not necessitate change of religion. The Bedas have no titles. Surnames used by them are the common Ladakhi surnames such as Tsering, Namgyal, etc. The identification of a particular family in the village is done by the name of the house.

A Beda is not allowed to enter the house of a Ladakhi. He cannot sit on the chair in front of a Bhoto (Ladakhi) even in a hotel or restaurant in Leh. The Bedas are given inferior position by the Bhotos on the occasion of marriage feast or on social and religious gatherings. A Beda male or female cannot become a *lama* or *chomo*, which is the proud privilege of the Ladakhis only. A Beda rising to a high position is not tolerated by the Bhotos. They cannot hold any position in the village council. The Bedas cannot wear new clothes, speak loudly or participate in conversation with the Ladakhis. The Ladakhis treat the Beda, Mon and Gara equal in status. But according to the Beda, the Mon and Gara command higher status than them.

When a boy attains marriageable age (which varies from 18 to 25 years) his father with a few close relatives and *hamsaya* (neighbours) approaches the parents of a particular girl and offers *chang* (local drink) and *khatak* (scarf) with the proposal for marriage. If the father accepts the *chang* and *khatak* it is understood that the proposal is accepted. The bride-price is settled and then a date is fixed for the payment of the bride-price. Some presents are made to the bride. This is called *bakhtum* or acceptance of marriage. The bride-price depends on the health and general appearance of the girl. To start with the value of the bride-price is kept high but it is lowered to Rs. 300 to Rs. 400 on request. At times the amount of the bride-price touches Rs. 1,000. Agreement regarding the bride-price and *chang* is written in the presence of a *goba* (village headman). Marriage by negotiation is thus the most popular mode of acquiring mates.

Marriage by elopement is another way of acquiring mates. After successful negotiations the marriage is settled and the bride-price paid but in the meantime if the girl developes intimacy with another boy living in some other village and elopes with him to an unknown place. After the expiry of a few months, ranging from six months to one year, the parents of the girl are informed. The father of the boy with close relatives and friends pays a visit to the parents of the girl and offers *chang* and *khatak*, and a formal marriage is performed. In such cases, the bridegroom has to pay double of the amount of bride-price which she has received from the earlier boy. *Shabdeb* (marriage by exchange) is also prevalent in the community. Normally the sisters are exchanged between families involved in marriage. Another form of acquiring mates is *maqpa* system. In the *maqpa* system, the boy after marriage leaves his parental residence and goes to stay with the family of his wife.

The Bedas are generally monogamous. A Beda woman may invite

a male other than her husband to live with her. He is called *pharsak*. Junior sororate is allowed only after the death of the first wife. A married woman wears *goncha* (long gown) and *firoza* (scarf) on the head. Bride-price and dowry are both prevalent in the community. The bride-price is paid by the father of the bridegroom to the father of the bride immediately after the settlement of marriage. But the dowry is paid by the father of the girl at the time of marriage. The dowry consists of *goncha*, utensils, cooking oven, ornaments, beddings, etc.

Members of both the sexes are free to divorce. A change of religion by either of the spouse, abusing and beating, laziness, extra marital relations, stealing, infidelity, adultery, impotency, barrenness and inadequate provisions to the wife, especially for food and dress can lead to divorce. In case a couple has children, the wife is given a nominal compensation if she is divorced.

Widow, widower and divorcee remarriage is permitted in the community. An issueless widow usually goes back to live with her parents. The *raktak* given in her marriage is also carried along. Among the Bedas a touching ritual is performed in case of an issueless widow. The ritual is known as *ronang kudpa chhas*. A black thread is tied between the living widow and the body of the deceased husband. The *lama* asks the widow whether to cut the thread or not. If the widow gives her consent then the *lama* cuts the thread. Immediately she is divorced from the deceased husband and departs from the house of her husband and goes to her own parents. She is free to marry anyone after three years. A widow can go for *maqpa* as well as *baqpa* forms of remarriage. But in most cases it is the *maqpa* form. The new husband joins and takes charge of her deceased husband's inherited property. This kind of widow marriage is called *ganzum*. But when a widow goes for *baqpa* marriage, she discontinues her claim to the property of her deceased husband.

The Bedas have vertically and horizontally extended families. The Beda couples generally have large number of children. The flour of fried wheat, *sattoo* (barley) or other edibles collected by begging are distributed first among the children and then among elders. Women do not observe *purdah*. Joking relationship is prevalent between sister-in-law and brother-in-law, and between wife's elder sister and wife's younger sisters and brothers. Conflict and quarrels may arise in the family after excessive drinking of *chang*, or when a check on the freedom of youngsters is imposed. Youngsters sometimes challenge the authority of the elders. The rule of succession is in the male line. Daughters also enjoy the right to their father's property.

The Beda women enjoy a great deal of freedom; they observe no *purdah* and freely consume *chang* and *gurgur chai* (salty tea) in the company of menfolk. Men and women dance together. A woman is free to marry outside her own community. In the family, a woman enjoys a privileged position. Though she is overworked and does all the household jobs from collection of fuel, bringing potable water, cleaning utensils, clothes and preparing *chang* and *gurgur chai* as and when required, she enjoys equal status with men. She is consulted on all matters of the household. Since the girl fetches a bride-price, she is brought up with more care and affection than the boys.

Life-cycle rituals observed among the Bedas are common to the other Buddhist populations of Ladakh. A pregnant woman is not allowed to carry heavy load, cross a river, stream or canal. She is advised not to go out of the house after sunset, etc. In the seventh month of successful pregnancy the *dhunuche* ceremony is observed. The *lama* reads the sacred books and forecasts the fortune of the expected child. When the woman starts having labour pain she is given sufficient quantity of *gurgur chai* and is taken to a corner of the room to deliver the child on a piece of cloth spread out on the floor. The nomadic Beda pitch a small tent beside some river or stream where the child is delivered. After delivery, the baby is given a bath with warm water and is wrapped in warm clothing. The husband and wife both are confined in the room for seven days. During this period the *phasphun* members arrange food for them. On the seventh day, the *lama* performs *laf-tsang* for the purification of the house. *Da-tsang* is the next ritual observed after a month of delivery. The relatives and *phasphun* members bring dresses, *chang* and food. The *onpo* (soothsayer) is invited to read the future of the child. He prepares the horoscope for the infant. Name giving is an important ritual. Among the Bedas the father cuts a few locks of the child's hair and takes it to the *lama*. The *lama* recites hymns and gives a name to the child. Before the male child attains the age of two years *ralchang* (hair shaving) ritual is observed. The shaving of the hair of the child is done either by the mother or father or any person whose parents are alive and himself unmarried. The members of the *phasphun* offer money and *khatak* to the child.

The peculiarity of marriage among the Beda is that the bridegroom does not accompany the *barat*. Besides, the actual marriage ritual is performed at the house of the bridegroom. On the day of marriage, the *nyopa* (a representative of the bridegroom) dresses himself like a groom and accompanies the marriage party to the house of the bride.

The bridegroom's dress consist of *sirtop* (a long cap) made from *shanil* (*koshin*), Ladakhi *goncha* and a *gurga* (gown) which is generally worn by the Ladakhi Buddhists. The marriage party is given a customary feast at the house of the bride. The bride is then taken on a pony or taxi to the house of the bridegroom. The bride is accompanied by her own elder sisters or the sisters of her father. On the way the members of the marriage party sing and dance and drink a lot of *chang*. The bride enters the house of the groom when *mantra* or hymns are being recited by the *lama*. She sits close to the family kitchen and is later joined by the bridegroom. The *lamas* read sacred books and shower blessings on the couple. The *nyopa* who escorts the bride places a silken scarf around the head of the bridegroom which is the culmination of the marriage ritual. A feast is given at the house of the bridegroom after marriage which is called *bakhtun*. The bride stays in the house of the groom for three days.

The Bedas cremate their dead; the body of a child below five years is buried. In case of death of an adult, *phasphuns* are first informed to make various arrangements for the disposal of the dead body and for conducting other rituals. The Ladakhis do not participate in the death rituals of the Beda. The dead body is kept in the house from three to twelve days depending on the economic status of the family. On all these days, the *lamas* recite hymns from religious books and eat food and take *gurgur chai* a number of times in front of the dead body. The members of the bereaved family weep and express sorrow. The members of the *phasphun* carry the dead body to the cremation ground in a sitting position tied on wooden beams and carried by four persons. If four *phasphuns* are not available only one may carry the dead body on his back. At the cremation ground a pyre is prepared on which the dead body is kept. Fire is lit from below the body. Within four days after the cremation the remains and ashes of the dead person are collected and thrown either into the river or left on the hill-top. The *lamas* continue their worship even after the cremation is over. One month after cremation, a rite is observed called *langanj* which involves performance of worship by the *lamas* and a feast organized for the invitees. The *phasphun* members carry food and other eatables. *Zarju* is observed on the forty-ninth day of death. *Lamas* read the sacred scriptures from morning till evening.

The Bedas are a landless community. Even in villages they are not allowed to own land. It is reported that if a Beda is able to purchase land then it will not be tolerated by the Ladakhis. In the village the Beda is given land for homestead only by some *kalhon* (big landowner) or by a *gompa*. In return he has to serve the village community by his musical performances. The Bedas are professional musicians and play on *daman* and *dhap* drums and *surna* flute. They sit at the entrance of a house and say *zu-zu*, i.e. 'we have come for your blessings, give us some food'. Mutton sellers at Leh employ the Beda in their shops on daily wage. They dress and clean the slaughtered sheep and goats. During the Losar festival, the Bedas are engaged for musical performances in the village. A few Bedas are employed in the army. Spinning of wool is quite popular among the Beda women. Women spin the thread by *jutpang* (spinning wheel). A section of the nomadic Bedas consisting of about twenty households with 400 heads have been settled in a colony at the outskirt of Leh town by the state government under the 20-Point Programme in 1984.

Bedas do not have any traditional caste council or *sabha*. The members selected after 1947 got normally registered with the National Congress Office in Leh. Thus, through them the village council is connected to wider political party at the national level.

The Bedas are Buddhists by religion. Only a small section of the Beda living in Nubra Valley have taken to Islam. Almost every Beda family has its own *chotkang*, the family worship room generally in the kitchen where an oil lamp always burns. At the village level there is a *gompa* (vihara) where worship is arranged. The Bedas have easy access to all the *gompas*. The services of *lamas*, *onpo* and *kushak* are available to them on the occasion of birth, marriage and death. The Bedas are the followers of both the yellow and red sects of Buddhism.

Intercommunity relations in the villages are based on interdependence among the communities. The community avails the facilities of formal education for their boys and girls. But only the settled section of the Bedas have been able to enjoy its benefits. The nomadic Bedas are not in a position to avail themselves of the benefits of education. Under the 20-Point Programme of development, about twenty Beda households have been rehabilitated on the outskirts of Leh. For health and medical care they avail the facilities of the hospital at Leh. The nomadic Bedas, however, depend on traditional medicare system and consult an *amchi* (medicine man). Potable water is available in the villages but the nomadic Bedas meet their water requirements from streams and rivulets. There is no self-employed youth among the Bedas. The Bedas living near Leh town listen to the radio, visit cinema shows organized by the defence services and watch the television on a shop window but in the rural areas these facilities are not available. The villages are electrified but not a single Beda house has electric connection. The fuel resources available are cow-dung cakes, firewood and kerosene but these resources are so costly that it is not possible for an average Beda family to purchase fuel from the market. Integrated Child Development Scheme for the infant and feeding mother is available at the block level but the Beda women are rarely the beneficiaries of this scheme. The settled Bedas have ration cards and avail the facility but the same is not available to the nomadic Bedas and those living in the far-flung villages. The Bedas depend on the *gompa*, village shopkeeper and the Bhotos for lending them money.

The community is struggling for its rightful position in the Ladakhi society. In spite of the fact that the Bedas form an integral part of the village community, they are not given any position in the traditional or statutory political set-up. Their say in matters of socio-political control of the village is minimum.

PARMANAND LAL

BEG

The Beg are believed to be Mughals who were the custodians of *khazana* (treasury) during the Mughal period. They were granted state subjecthood by Maharaja Hari Singh in 1939.

The Begs are concentrated in the cities in Anantnag, Baramula and Badgam in the Kashmir Valley. The community is identified at the local level. They speak Kashmiri language and use Arabic script, within and outside the family.

Their staple food consists of *gandum* (wheat), *batta* (rice), *moong*, *masur* and *rajmah* pulses. They are non-vegetarians and consume mutton. Leafy vegetables and fruits are eaten in plenty. They supplement their food with milk and milk products. Alcoholic drinks are taboo.

They place themselves at a high level, whereas others put them in the middle order of the local Muslim hierarchy. Marriages are usually performed within the group, although there is no bar in marrying outside the community. They do not marry among the Mirs (*Pardaposh*), Watal, Doom, Hanji, Nanbai (Sofi), Goor and Bakarwal communities of the valley. Since there are *biradari* marriages, they practise consanguinity both at parallel and cross-cousin levels. The sororate and levirate forms of marriage are also prevalent. Marriages are settled through negotiations. The usual age of marriage for males is 18 to 20 years and for females 15 to 17 years. The form of marriage is usually monogamy.

The dowry usually includes jewellery, clothes and household articles including copper utensils. The parties give and take according to their status, but the expenditure incurred by the bride's parents is lesser than that of the groom's side. The *mahr* money is also fixed acording to the status of the groom. However, it ranges between Rs. 900 and Rs. 9,000. One third of the *mahr* money is instantly condoned by the wife. The remaining portion is either condoned in lieu of land, son, etc., or paid on demand. In case of divorce, the *mahr* money is demanded. The rule of residence is patrilocal. In some cases it is *gharpet* (uxorilocal).

Divorce is permitted on grounds of adultery and maladjustment. The family elders usually decide about the divorce cases amongst themselves. It has a social approval and a *maulvi* issues the *talaq-*

nama or *fatwa*. In a divorce case the articles given at the time of marriage are exchanged. No divorce compensation is given to the wife. Only the husband can divorce. The children become the responsibility of the father in the case of a divorce. The remarriages of divorcee, widow and widower are permissible in the community. The sororate and levirate (junior) are also prevalent.

The family is usually the extended one. But these days separate households within the family are formed. Conflict and confrontations in a family are mainly on property matters. The inheritance in the family runs both along male and female lines. The female get less than the males. Usually, two-third portion of the property is equally divided among the sons. The succession is to the eldest son. In the absence of an adult son, the wife succeeds.

Women in the community have restricted decision-making powers. They participate in the economic activity and supplement the family income. Women share the burden in agricultural operations, bringing potable water, collection of fuel, etc. They participate in the social and religious activities. They also perform rituals and take part in politics.

At birth the infant is given a bath and the *mullah* or *maulvi* whispers the *azaan* in the child's left ear. On the seventh or ninth day both the woman and infant are given a bath; this is called *sonder*. After seven days, the naming ceremony is performed by a *maulvi*, who gets some cash and clothes as reward. The *warin* (midwife) is also given money on this occasion.

The head is shaved (*zerakasi*) after one year at some sacred place. A feast is given on this occasion to the relatives and friends. A goat is sacrificed and its meat is consumed by the family members other than the consanguineous relations. *Khatna* (circumcision) is usually performed within three years of age. Earlier this was done by the *navid* (barber), but these days a qualified doctor does it and gets his fees. On this occasion also a feast is given. *Oapsoap*, the first feeding of cereals, is performed after nine months and in this ritual rice is cooked and offered to the infant.

Marriages are settled through a *manzymyor* (go-between) who may be a relative or a person belonging to different community. The *manzymyor* gets some cash from both the parties for the settlement. In marriage rituals, *mangtee* (first betrothal) or *kori mangeh gantha* is done. In this ceremony, the boy's parents accompanied by friends and relatives visit the bride's place and give jewellery and other presents. They are entertained to a feast. This ceremony is followed by *nishani* in which the bride is again given jewellery, sweets and cash by the groom's relatives. *Nishani* is followed by *hazri* in which the bride's relatives come to the bridegroom's place and present jewellery and other gifts to the persons who attended the *nishani* ceremony. Between *hazri* and *shadi* (*khandar*) the bride is given clothes, etc., on all the festivals. In *shadi* the *nikah* ceremony is performed by a *maulvi* or *kazi*. He gets some money for the performance of the ceremony and issues a *nikah-nama*. *Mahr* money is also fixed through him before the *nikah*. A grand feast is given by the bride's parents on the occasion of the marriage. At the time of marriage, *vanvun* (singing) is performed by the womenfolk. *Rukhsati* is done after the marriage ceremony. The bride then accompanies the groom and comes to stay with her in-laws. Nuptial ceremony is performed at the groom's residence. *Wathal* feast is given on the next day of marriage at the groom's place in which the bride's relatives are also invited. After seven days of the marriage, both the bride and the bridegroom with some relatives and friends visit the bride's place. The bridegroom offers *salami* to the elders and gets some cash and presents. This ceremony is known as *firsal*. A feast is also given on this occasion. Earlier *firsal* ceremony was performed after six months of the marriage.

At the time of death, *kalma* and some verses from the Holy Koran are recited in the ear of the dying person. The dead body is given a *gusal* (bath) by the *snangor* and wrapped in 16 yards (for males) or 18 yards (for females) of white *kafan* (cotton sheet). *Namaz-e-janaza* is performed in a mosque as the dead body is kept outside. The *malkhosh* digs the grave and gets Rs. 50 to 60 for the job. The dead body is kept in a *lahad* (grave) which is closed from the left side. *Fateha* is read on this occasion. On the fourth day *fateha* is read on the burial ground by the *pir*. A stone, with the name of the person, birth and death dates inscribed on it is also placed on this day. On *pachhwar* (the 15th day) and on *satijihum* (fortieth day) after death, the *pir* comes and recites *fateha* and verses from the Holy Koran. He is offered food and other articles on both the occasions. There have been no changes in the observance of rituals. However, life-cycle rituals have become more expensive.

Land, the main resource, is controlled by individual proprietorship. The members of the community possess land which they cultivate. They are engaged in business too. They also join government service or work as industrial workers. They have an active link with the local market. They purchase their day-to-day articles from the market by making cash payments.

Child labour exists and the wages are paid in cash. They do embroidery and weaving of shawl, etc.

Statutory or formal panchayat which is heterogeneous appeared after Independence. Its role is to plan and implement the welfare and developmental activities in the village.

The Begs belong to the Sunni sect of Islam. They have *silsila* affiliation too and most of them are Dastgiri. Makdoomis are very rare among them. The religious personages of the Begs are from other communities. They perform birth, marriage and death rites for them. Besides, they also give religious preachingss to their community members.

The Begs observe Id, Charar-e-Sharif, Ramzan and Dastgir Sahib festivities. These festivals are of socio-religious significance.

The community members weave shawls and do embroidery on cloth. This work is mainly done by their womenfolk and children.

A chorus singing called *vanvun* is performed by the females at the time of marriage. They sing the local Kashmiri songs.

They accept and exchange water, *kachcha* and *pukka* food from the other Muslim communities excepting the Watal (Shaikh). They also share water-resources, burial ground and religious shrines with other Muslim communities. It is found that they have businessmen, scholars, persons in white-collar jobs, teachers, engineers, doctors and members in defence services among them. Political leadership has emerged at the regional level and they have some of their members in the state assembly.

Formal education is considered favourable for both boys and girls. They generally study up to college level. The boys drop out from studies due to economic reasons. Community members have a positive attitude towards modern medicare and make full use of it. They prefer a maximum of three children and their attitude towards family planning is favourable. Generally the men get sterilized.

Drinking water is available within the locality through pipes. The Begs are self-employed and are engaged mainly in agriculture and weaving. Community members make use of the media and communication facilities available in the area. They have electricity in their houses. Fuel resources are mainly firewood, cow-dung cakes and kerosene.

Irrigation facilities are availble to them but they depend a lot on rain-water. They use chemical fertilizers and insecticides.

Under the nutrition programme of the government the children get midday meals. They also make use of Integrated Child Development Scheme (ICDS) (feeding/mother infant care/immunization) programmes. The facility of public distribution through fair price shops is availed of by them. Their attitude towards saving is positive.

A.C. SRIVASTAVA

BHAGAT/KABIRPANTHI

The Bhagat is one of the important communities of the Jammu region. The etymology of the word 'Bhagat is the legacy of the Bhakti movement when the community acquired its present name. As they themselves claim and as other also support their claim, they became devoted to Bhagat Kabir and adopted his occupation of weaving, hence they came to be known as Bhagat after their preceptor Bhagat Kabir. Because of this they are alternatively addressed as Kabirpanthis also. It is said that before they were given the name of Bhagat, they were part of the larger community called Megh in this region. Some of them deny this fact and claim a separate and different origin. The Kabirpanthis are a Scheduled Caste in the state. According to the 1981 census the population of the Kabirpanthis was 1,30,800.

Several interesting theories exist regarding their origin and growth in this state. According to one theory, the Bhagats were originally Kshatriyas but their forefathers adopted the occupation of weaving in order to disguise themselves to escape persecution at the hands of Parashu Ram Brahman who was under a vow to exterminate the Kshatriya race during the *Ramayana* period. The earliest settlers in the state claim to have migrated from Varanasi. Another theory to this effec is that their progenitors were originally Brahmans, but it so happened that a cow died in the house of one of them and, unable to secure the services of a menial to remove the caracass, he had to do the odious work himself whereupon he was declared an outcaste by the Brahman *biradari*. He still followed the Brahmanic traditions and customs in his domestic life but, forced by sheer necessity of livelihood, he had to adopt other means and the profession of weaving seemed to him the most convenient under the circumstances. Subsequent accretions to the caste are also reported from the Hindu Thakurs, and the Bhagats of Panjgrain in Ramnagar tahsil are supposed to be the descendants of Thakurs who had joined their ranks. The title of Kabirpanthi which is associated with the member of this community is attributed to the fact that the ostracized ancestor of the present day Bhagats was contemporary of the renowned Bhagat Kabir, and the preference for the profession of weaving should in that case be also due to this contact with Kabir who himself was a weaver by profession. The Bhagats of Kathua region while taking pride in the designation of Kabirpanthis, trace their descent from some local ruling families.

They also claim that they were the original owners of agricultural lands in Jammu province. Some local histories narrate that when other tribes arrived in Jammu they subjugated them and dispossessed them of their lands. They claim to be the original inhabitants of Jammu region since the known historical ages. This is probably the reason that they inhabit the wet and fertile plain and hill areas. Although they have adopted the profession of weaving yet most of them are agriculturists and agricultural labourers. The tracts of their habitation have three types of terrain: First, the higher hills of north Jammu which abound in water and are hence very productive, with severe winter with blizzards of snow now and then. Second, the arid low highlands, stony and thirsting for water. These areas receive rainfall during summer and grow *makki* and beans in abundance. The population of the Bhagats in this area is sparse. Third, the fertile and canal-irrigated plains in the south has their largest concentration. Here the winters and summers are mild. In the plain strip from Akhnur to Kathua, they are found in large numbers. They numbered about 10,000 each in seven tahsils, their maximum number being in the tahsils of Jammu and Ranbirsingh about 32,000 to 34,000, respectively. The census of 1981 records their number at 1,30,800, constituting 16 per cent of the total population of the Jammu province.

The literate among them usually put on Western dress whereas the unlettered one put on *pyjama* or *dhoti* made of *khadi*. The elderly wear *safa* or *pagri* (turban) as headdress. Most of the working class village people used to go barefooted, but now most of them can afford either boots or country made shoes. Men wear rings and chain around the neck but their females put on the usual ornaments worn in the Hindu communities, if they can afford. They speak Dogri in their homes and also with others. The literate among them converse in Hindi also. The medium of writing is Devanagari at present. Previously the community was almost illiterate. Now they are getting education and training in vocational and professional spheres. They have been included among the Scheduled Castes and are enjoying all the privileges and reservations assured to them by the Constitution of our country. Consequently, their economic and social status has improved much.

The Bhagats are non-vegetarian. They eat flesh of all types and even revelled in consuming meat of dead animals which they were required to remove from the villages. Under the impact of Bhakti movement and that of their religious preceptor, Bhagat Kabir, they have given up the habit of eating dead animals, though they are still non-vegetarian so far as their menfolk are concerned. Their womenfolk do not generally take meat, though they have no prejudice against preparing meat dishes for their families. On religious days, they abstain from taking meat. It seems that ostracism from their original *biradari* had imposed such disabilities upon them that they became impoverished and, in the absence of any means of livelihood, they took to eating flesh of dead animals. Now when their economic condition and social status have improved they have developed an abhorrence towards carrying of carcasses and eating them.

Wheat and rice form their staple food. They use pulses of all types, particularly *mash* (black beans), *masoor*, gram and *moong* (green beans). Among vegetables, potatoes and onions are popular though they also consume other green and leafy vegetables whenever available. Some of them can afford to occasionally consume fruits. The locally grown mangoes, berries, guavas, etc., are eaten during the season. *Sattoo*-water, milk, *lassi* and the usual cold drinks are freely used by them.

Alcoholic drink is a luxury for most of them which is indulged on festive occasions like marriage or birthday celebrations and fairs. Country-made, home-made (*rurhi*) as well as good quality liquor is used according to the occasion. The improvement in the economic condition of the community is also responsible for growing alcoholism in the community. Their food habits have thus undergone much change in recent years insofar as they have discarded taking flesh of dead animals, and taken to frequent use of wine and other non-alcoholic drinks, in fashion among other communities of the state.

There is no stratification or division of the community into high and low, superior and inferior. But the community has been relegated to the fourth or the Shudra *varna* inspite of the fact that they claim Kshatriya or Brahman descent. They themselves now accept this relegation and are treated such by the other communities. In the past they were considered untouchables, but under the impact of the recent reformist trend in the society and the legislation, this stigma is on the decrease and for all social and political purposes they are being considered at par with the Hindu communities except in the field of marital relationship. They have been divided into a number of *gotras* some of which are in common with the Brahman and Rajput communities which lends some support to their claim of descent from the Brahman community later joined by some fallen Kshatriya communities like the Thakur and others. Their *gotras* which are common with the Brahman and other Hindu communities are: Bhardwaj, Magotre, Kaship, Changotre, Sangotre, Kushal, Kalre and Bhadu. These *gotras* are exogamous and their main purpose is only to regulate marital relations. The origin of these *gotras* has been forgotten, though their similarity with those of the Brahman and Rajput communities leaves little doubt that these gotras were brought by the families when they joined the Bhagat fold.

The Bhagats are monogamous. They are endogamous as far as their own caste is concerned, but they are exogamous in matters of *gotra*. The recent trend is towards adult marriages. However, marriages before adulthood still take place in villages. The usual age for marriage is 18 to 20 years in the case of girls and 20 to 25 in the case of boys. Mates are acquired through negotiations which usually start through a *ravara* (mediator) who is a man or woman known to both the families. These negotiations can involve two, three or even more families resulting in the forms of marriage known as *ekahari*, *dohari* and *trehari*. The former form matured directly between two families, one giving away the daughter and the other receiving her as a bride. In case of *dohari*, both the families exchange daughters. The *dohari* form was common in this community. Sometimes three families became involved in the exchange of partners: A giving daughter to B, B to C and C in turn to A. Sometimes even more families could be involved in the process. Even in this complicated exchange system consanguinity and Father's Sister's Daughter and Mother's Brother's Daughter relationships were avoided. But at present this rule is sometimes transgressed. Although the community was economically backward yet dowry in kind was common and was settled at the time of negotiating the marriage. It is practised even now. Previously wives were sometimes purchased, a custom which has now died out. *Sindoor*, *bindi*, *tika*, *nath*, *balakru* (the last two being nose ornaments) and a set of red bangles on both arms are the symbols of a married woman, and a *kantha* or a chain around the neck are symbols of a married male. They follow patrilocal residence after marriage.

Divorce and remarriage are permitted in the community. Both men and women can divorce, which takes place usually in the gathering of the *biradari*. The *biradari* also makes provision for the maintenance of the divorced woman at the cost of the husband. Sometimes the village panchayat is involved. Now legal divorces are also obtained and the maintenance is fixed by a court. Proceedings for a divorce may be initiated by either of the parties. A male acts as if he is still married in the usual way even after divorce. Similarly the divorced woman is free to remarry a man of her choice. In the past cases of divorce and remarriage were comparatively frequent. Now such cases are rare.

The composition of the Bhagat family is nuclear, extended and mixed, sometimes even members of four generations live under the same roof. Usually, the seniormost member of the family is the head. Formerly the community was resourceless with very limited property so the headship of the family did not involve ownership. Now the trend is towards extended formations. Whatever the form of the family or the nature of their economic conditions, proper relationship is observed by all members towards one another according to their age and status. The elders are feared and respected. Of course, there are some occasions for confrontation in the family on matters of undesirable habits such as addiction to wine or drugs and illicit relationships but seldom on the question of property. The eldest son succeeds the father after the latter's demise but, in case of division of the property, all living sons inherit equally. The divisions when disputed are decided by the elders of the community or by the village panchayat. Recent changes noticed are that most of them who were landless have received few acres of land per family which has led to disputed inheritance involving recourse to legal courts for adjudication.

Women of the Bhagat did not have right of inheritance but a woman has the right of maintenance in case of demise of her husband if she chose not to remarry. Bhagat women do not live in seclusion, but go out to work. They do all type of domestic work, such as removal of cow-dung, cleansing of stables, etc. in their own houses as well as of the landowners of the village for which they receive monthly or annual wages in kind. They also collect fuel, fodder for cattle and help their men in various economic activities of the family. They are therefore an economic asset to the family. They contribute to the family income and also manage the household affairs while their menfolk usually remain out side the whole day, busy performing menial jobs for the village landowners or at their own petty fields. Women take part in all social and religious functions of the community equally with men. They move freely to fairs and festivals, participate in the village folk songs and ritual dance. They also take part in the local political activities and particularly those of the village panchayat. Nowadays some of their girls are receiving education up to matriculation and even higher levels. They have got petty government services. Previously they were discriminated against by the women of higher classes. They are now freely allowed to share public places, festivals and fairs and several religious rituals and performances with men and women of all other communities. They have been enjoying and still enjoy the position of honour and respect in their own community and family.

The Bhagats perform almost all the rituals of the life cycle current among the other Hindu communities of the region. The birth of a child involves a short confinement in the house. On the fifth day, the mother and the newborn baby are given a purificatory bath (*punjap*). On the eleventh day, the mother is given another bath of purification accompanied by some simple ritual after which she is free to go out on her usual work. On the twenty-first day, the child undergoes another ritual called *sootre* marking the end of the confinement period. The birth of a son is celebrated with great festivity but that of the girl is not welcomed. The *mundan-sanskar* of boys is performed after the age of four years, usually at six or seven. The recent development in their ritual pattern is the rise of a priestly class among them who now conduct all their religious and social ceremonies. These persons, the *purohit* or pandit among them have taken the place of a Brahman; they wear the *yajnopavita* themselves and make the other Bhagats also wear the same. The thread wearing ceremony is usually carried out at the time of marriage.

Marriage involves searching out the match through a mediator, *thaks* or *mall*, i.e. reservation of the boy, then betrothal which is attended with *shagun* ritual, and finally the marriage itself. In a boy's marriage they do not perform any ceremony at their own house, but a group of elders of the *biradari*, accompanied by the bridegroom, visit the house of the girl's father, where they perform some preliminary ceremonies and then on the following day they return to their own house with the bride. In the following morning, the bridegroom and the bride are taken to a mullberry bush and the new couple is made to sit before it. Then a *mauli* (red cotton thread) is wrapped around the bush, and all present, together with the couple, go round the tree seven times. These *pheras*, as they are called, and other rituals are performed in accordance with the Hindu custom with the help of a Panda Brahman, or their *purohit* from their own community whom they pay offerings.

The *antasanskara* or death rituals corespond to those of all other Hindu communities. The dead body is cremated with all the Shastric rituals. On the fourth day, burnt bones, called *phool*, are collected and kept in an urn and later immersed in the Ganga or any other local river. Mourning is observed for thirteen days. On the tenth day after death the *shradh* is performed and on the thirteenth day the *pugg* ceremony is performed when the *biradari* is served with a feast to mark the end of the mourning period. Then the death anniversary known as *barkhi* is observed, and four years after the death *chaubarsi* or *chaubarkhi* is performed. Afterwards *shradh* is annually performed during the *pitra-paksh*. Recent trend in observation of these rituals is towards simplification and even less important stages are skipped over.

The Bhagats are traditionally associated with agriculture, both as land owners and as farm labourers in the Jammu region. They claim that they were the exclusive owners of land in this region but when the ruling dynasties migrated to this hilly tract they usurped both their lands and political power, with the result that they were reduced to serfdom. Only a minor section of the community was left with the ownership of agricutlural lands. They are now only petty landholders. Some of them, however, have received small areas of agricultural land under the new agrarian reforms in the state. Under the impact of Bhagat Kabir, they adopted weaving as their alternative occupation. In every village there were few Bhagat families which move coarse khadi cloth for the villagers on their domestic handlooms. But this system has now gone out of practice due to the progress of textile industry against which their fabric has no place. They have therefore mostly taken to farm and industrial labour, petty trade and government jobs. The land, if possessed by any family, is owned by the elder member of the family and is equally shared by all male members after the demise of the father. They work mostly in their own or nearby villages as tillers of land and farm labourers on periodical or daily wages, as the case may be, receiving wages both in cash or kind. There is very little mobility among them. Some of them go to Punjab during the sowing and harvesting season to earn wages. Children of 14 or 15 years of age and above are sent out to earn wages. Previously the Bhagat men and women rendered a few days *begar* to the village zamindars and in the houses of the moneylenders to clear their own or their ancestral debts. A limited type of bonded labour system was in practice in this region. Conditions have undergone a great change since Independence and the evil of bonded labour has disappeared from this region. Their traditional occupation of weaving suffered considerably and they have therefore become agriculturist and serving community now. The weaving craft is being revived now under the improved conditions depending on power-driven handlooms. Most of them are reverting to their old occupation. In view of new opportunities available they are getting several economic benefits and, hence, their economic condition has improved considerably. They are directly concerned with the labour market as well as with business for the supply of raw material and sale of their finished products. Agricutlure was their traditional occupation whereas weaving has become their primary, and service labour are the subsidiary occupation at present.

The Bhagats have their own *biradari* panchayat which effect social control on the community. These institutions used to lay down rules of conduct in social ceremonies and rituals to some extent. There are a few religious leaders among them whom they call *gurus*. In most of their domestic and social problems, they approach the *gurus* for decisions. Even the common village panchayat was some time approached in the disputes with members of their own or other communities, particularly pertaining to land and criminal incidents. Now the gram panchayats usually regulate their social and inter-community relations. But in their socio-religious problems they still refer to their community elders and seldom take the case to the legal courts. The accused persons have to pay some sort of fine in cash or kind, or any other compensation mutually agreed upon by the parties. The modern statutory panchayats exercise control over them to the extent to which they are involved with other communities, and do not inerfere with their socio-religious problems unless called upon to do so by the parties concerned.

The Bhagats are Hindu by religion and profess the Vedic and Puranic creed. They follow the teachings of the Vedas as reformed and recast by the preachers of the Bhagati movement during the Middle Ages. Hence they derive their title and the sect from the famous Bhagat Kabir after whom they are called Kabirpanthis and Bhagats. They hold faith in the three gods of the Hindu Trinity and other gods and goddesses revered by all other Hindu communities of the region. However, they have their own *gram-* and *kul-devtas* to whom they turn either for the performance of socio-religious rituals or for help in overcoming evils, disease and other hinderances of life. On festive occasions they propitiate and worship these godlings. The *gram-devtas* such as Sitala, Kali Bir and the regional gods like the Paihr, as well as some local martyrs are worshipped by them. They visit all major Hindu shrines all over India including the cave shrine of Vaishno Devi and local shrines such as Bawa Jitto, Purmandal, Chintpurni, Buddha Amarnath, Vasuki and Sudh Mahadev. They used to take the services of the Brahmans for the performance of their socio-religious rites and customs, but now they have created a class of religious priests of their own community who perform their religious and social customs. Some of the Bhagats are priests at a few Hindu shrines whose services are also utilized by the community. The community has some *chelas* who are supposed to possess occult and supernatural powers and their services are hired for the cure of disease, solution of socio-economic problems and the like. They celebrate and participate in all the Hindu festivals and fairs held in this region, such as Holi, Diwali, Dussehra, Shivratri, Ramnavami, Janmashtami, Navaratra and others. In the present century the Bhagat are influenced by the Arya Samaj and under its impact some socio-religious reforms were introduced. They are strongly against untouchability and social discrimination to which they were previously subjected.

However, they have been fine craftsmen in the field of cotton fabrics and produced not only fine type of village khadi but very artistic bedsheets, called *khesh*, of charming colours and designs. They participate in those cultural activities of the localities which are common to all other communities. Their womenfolk indulge in song and dnace in social ceremonies and participate in the finer side of the social life of the village. Men participate in folk dance like *bhangra* in common with other communities to mark some festive and seasonal occasions.

The community has close linkages with other communities at professional and socila levels though, at the social level, this intercourse has been to a limited level unlike equal participation in festivals and fairs, in agricultural and other occupational levels. But in commensal norms there are limitations. Other Hindu communities do not accept water and food from their hands, though the other fourth *varna* communities and even the Muslim exchange water and all kinds of *kachcha-pukka* food with them. But for the last two centuries the Bhagat stopped such exchanges with the Muslim. Nowadays the Bhagats are invited to participate in the community dinners though they are provided with a separate sitting cloth. Although connubial relations with other Hindu communities were not normally practised, ties of friendship could be established with the Bhagats on certain occasions like marriage or *mundan*. For instance, when a Bhagat couple happens to confront a newly married high caste couple on the way, the tie of friendship between them is accepted then and there. The Bhagats were prohibited from sharing water from the wells because of they ate flesh of dead animals. But later when they gave up this habit, they were allowed to fetch water from all wells and tanks. They were, like the all other Shudra castes, denied entry in temples and the Hindu shrines. But in 1930, Maharaja Hari Singh of Jammu & Kashmir opened all temples and shrines for them, as he did for all other Shudra communities. This was a great step towards the upliftment of Untouchables in this state under the impact of the Arya Samaj reform movement.

A substantial change has taken place in their linkages with others communities and socio-political activities since Independence. They usually participate in all types of political activities at local, regional as well as national levels. They have MLAs, MLCs among them. They have seats reserved for them in the local bodies and village panchayats.

Even their women have become members of the local and village bodies. They have their share in the political movements of the state. Some of them are land-owners whereas the rest of them are farm and industrial labourers. Hence production and landlord-tenant and cultivator-labour relationship exists in the community. They now get jobs in the government and private concerns and a few of them, who have established small industries, employ workers themselves; thus the employer-worker relationship exists in the community.

The community is highly responsive to the modern development programmes and participates in, and benefits from, these at all levels. Their boys and girls are receiving education at matric and higher levels in large numbers. But their older generation is still steeped in illiteracy. They are becoming conscious of health and medicare facilities available in the villages. They use both allopathic and *desi* medicine. They are responsive to the family planning programmes. Drinking water facilities have reached their doors through the government's public health and drinking water schemes which make arrangement for pipewater or tube wells. They get some benefit under the self-employment schemes. They are availing of the media and communication facilities lke radio and television; telephone and telegraph facilities and newspapers are also available to them. Their houses and factories, whether in rural areas or in towns, have been electrified. Most of them still depend on fire-wood or cow-dung as the sources of fuel. Only a small fraction of them enjoy the benefits of cooking gas. They also enjoy irrigation facilities in canal-irrigated tracts. But in most of the *kandi* and mountain regions, they have to depend on rain water. Bhagats, being petty tillers, cannot afford to use much of modern manures, insecticides and fertilizers. They mostly depend on organic manure or cow-dung manure. Public distribution facilities are available to them, both in rural and urban areas, in the form of ration shops. Banking and saving facilities are available even in rural areas these days, but most of them cannot afford to make use of these facilities because of their petty income. However, being a Scheduled Caste community, they are getting the benefits of reservation in services, representation in democratic bodies, scholarships and poverty eradiction programmes undertaken by the government in this state.

ANITA K. BILLAWARIA

BHAND

Bhagat is a corrupt form of Sanskrit word '*bhakt*' meaning devotee. In *Rajatarangini* of Kalhana and also in Lawrence's *Valley of Kashmir*, Bhagats are referred to as devotees singing and dancing in temples in a state of ecstacy. Whether the present-day Bhagat community of Kashmir has had any connection with the spiritual Bhakti movement of fifteenth-sixteenth century in India is not confirmed. Since dancing in the temples was attributed by the ancient Kashmiri Brahmans as an act of pleasing Shiva, it is most probable that acting and performing in temple premises developed with the passage of time. According to the oral tradition among the Bhagats of Akingam in district Anantnag of Kashmir, the Bhagats continued to have great veneration for various Hindu shrines where they still sing and dance on special days in the course of a year. Bhand and Kanil are two synonyms of the Bhagats but with specific difference. The Bhagats traditionally used to give theatrical performances, whereas the Bhands performed farce and lampoon accompanied by music, and the Kanil presented only music. In order to supplement their income, the Kanil do wicker work and hence the title. Abhinav Gupta, the famous Kashmiri dramatist, is reported to have originated the Bhand-natya and Bhand-nritya (drama and dance, respectively). From Bhand-nritya developed what is called Dammaleh Bhand today (jogging Bhands).

The Bhands are distributed in the Valley though their most prominent habitation is Akingam in district Anantnag which has won fame and popularity for the contribution the Bhands have made to the revival and popularization of folk-theatre in Kashmir.

The community is scattered over the rural areas of the Valley and its members are born and brought up in the natural surroundings which abound in mountains: streams of fresh water, green paddy fields, etc. As such there is natural candour and frankness in their way of life. The Bhands speak their mother tongue, i.e. Kashmiri though of course they can express themselves in Urdu also. For all practical purposes only Kashmiri language is used. However, for correspondence, they use Arabic script.

The Bhand is economically a very weak community and lives a hand to mouth existence. Cooked rice called *bhatta* and green vegetables called *hak* is their staple food. They are non-vegetarians but owing to high price of meat, they mostly subsist on vegetables and pulses. Fruits do not form a part of their diet though occasionally apples, abundantly available in Kashmir, are consumed. Salt-tea is very common. They are teetotallers and alcoholic drinks are unknown to them. *Hookah* is very common among the menfolk. Common food items are *sesrih gogjih* (boiled turnips), *seveh hak* (boiled vegetables) and *achar* (pickle). Bread is consumed with tea only. As non-vegetarians they eat mutton if they can afford it. There is general abhorence for beef and the Kanils in particular consider beef repugnant. Eggs are frequently consumed. Among the food grains consumed are rice and cereals. Mustard oil is the medium of cooking. Milk is generally taken with salt-tea but curd may be taken very often. Most of them like to keep milch cows for fresh milk.

As Bhands are scattered all over Kashmir there is no sharp grouping on account of social status. The Kanils (wicker makers) are, however, one marked group which has adopted wicker making to supplement their income. Their profession as dramatists, musicians and entertainers does not allow division of their community into groups. The difference between the Bhagats and Bhands is that the former perform on stage and have nothing to do with music, and the latter play on musical instruments and entertain at marriage and other festive occasions. The Bhand and Kanil go about collecting paddy during the threshing season in the barns. They provide entertainment to the people, enact skits, drawing the theme mostly from commonplace events and occurrences in life with a view to criticizing the evils of the society. By words, by gestures, by quips, repartees, lampoons and lyrics and sometimes even by the use of abusive and obscene language, they manage to uncover the hidden aspects of the society which are harmful to its progress. In doing so they become the mouthpiece of a vast majority of underdogs who have much to grumble about but are without a proper forum to do so.

They are looked down upon due to their traditional profession of singing and dancing. Though nursing a sense of inferiority complex, the community does not feel it necessary to betray undue signs of subordination to any person or group which is economically superior to their own because they subject the economically stronger sections of the society to their scathing ridicule. They even feel pride in being the inheritors of an ancient cultural tradition of song, dance and stage acting. In the changed times, their art—the purest of folk song, folk-theatre and folklore—is receiving wide acclamation in the state and in other parts of the country. It may be noted that prior to Independence or just a decade after Independence, there were a few Hindu Bhand families in Akingam and elsewhere in the neighbourhood who would perform as a troupe with their Muslim coprofessionals. Some of the Hindu Bhands have been playing a key role in some of the most popular folk dramas.

Monogamy is the common type of marriage which is arranged by the parents. Eighteen and above is the normal age for marriage which is performed at the bride's house on an appointed day during the night. A day preceding the nuptials is observed as *mehndi-raat*. Earrings with pendants called *dooreh-hor* is the symbol of marriage for the bride. She does not wear veil, neither before her marriage nor after it. Their marriage ceremony is a small and austere function. There is no dowry system among them, except for some cash gifts called *bhog*. The amount of *mahr* ranges in the neighbourhood of Rs. 500 which becomes threefold after the marriage is solemnized. Out of this amount, one-third may be exempted but two-thirds has to be paid either in cash or in kind (a cow, ox or a goat). Residence after marriages is patrilocal and the bride has to perform all household duties and help her in-laws in agricultural activities as well.

Divorce is uncommon but is resorted to when necessary in accordance with the Islamic law. It can be initiated by either party but a woman may lose the right to *mahr* in case she initiates it. The husband is to bear the expenses incurred on the maintenance of his divorced wife. Infants would not be separated from the divorced mother though grown-ups may choose to live as agreed upon by the parties concerned. Divorce is not looked down upon as an unhealthy practice.

They maintain joint family system as far as possible because of professional needs and economic necessities. Though elders receive due veneration yet their professional habit of cutting jokes does not spare even family members.

The sons are the inheritors of a deceased person's land in equal share. The daughter is entitled to a portion of her dead father's property called *koreh-har* which she has the option of not accepting in case she is economically well off. A father may give his daughters their respective share even when he is alive to avoid any dispute which might arise after his death. The eldest son succeeds his father as head of the family. They maintain interfamily relations as cordial as they can because of the fact that for a means of livelihood, all of them must act together.

Their profession has a very low potential as a dependable means of subsistence. Since illiteracy continues in the community, any diversification in their profession has not been possible. A few folk-theatres have been started by some active members of the community and they perform at various places. But it also does not assure them of a dependable source of income.

In the absence of male issues, daughters inherit the property of their deceased father. A woman does not, normally, inherit the property, particularly the moveable property of her dead husband if she has male or female issues from him. But if there is no issue, she has the right to inherit the property.

A woman performs the daily chores in the household and also works outside which is confined to doing menial jobs. She must attend to her children. The community is politically alive to what is happening around but in an election its womenfolk cast their vote in favour of a candidate recommended by the head of the family or other members of the community.

A woman of this community appears a very subjugated person who has no say in major decisions of the family unless she is gifted by nature with extraordinary intelligence to counsel on vital matters. The Bhand woman presents a dismal picture in contemporary Kashmiri society. However, her role in maintaining good social relations with the kith and kin and the neighbours and friends cannot be underestimated. No female takes part in a *jashn* and all female roles in the theatre are performed by men only.

When a baby is born, one of the elderly persons present on the occasion whispers *azaan* into its ears. Round about five to seven years of age, he is circumcised as per the Islamic tenets. The next ritual pertains to the marriage ceremony. The *nikah* is performed by a priest who first recites from the Holy Koran and then formally asks the bride and the bridegroom to declare their consent for entering into a matrimonial relationship. The ritual is accompanied by a feast from the side of the bride's father. There is also the ritual of sending some milk to the house of the in-laws by her parents when the first conception is announced. The usual death rituals laid down by the *shariat* are followed and the dead body is buried after *namaz-e-janaza.* On the fourth day, the condolence period ends with the offering of a light refreshment to the condolers. On festivals like Id, the womenfolk of the bereaved family cry out wails of agony as a mark to remember the dead. Male members may sometimes visit the grave of the dead.

The Bhands living in rural areas have small holdings and as such land, water and agriculture are the mainstay of their economic activities.

In the distant past, the community had been subsisting on their dramatic art, music and folk-theatre. In return for their cultural services rendered, they collected paddy in autumn by going from barn to barn while paddy was being thrashed. Folk-theatre and music have been their main profession along with their agricultural activities. They provide entertainment to people by their antics called *Bhand-pether* (farce) aimed at criticizing the dark sides of society and highlighting its prevalent ills. In historical terms, the community has a long tradition of folk-theatre and folk-music. The community has also taken up secondary occupations as well in order to supplement their income. The Kanils are mostly busy in making wicker baskets, *kangris*, etc. The community depends on local market to a large extent. Trade by barter is out of question in their present structure. There are no bonded labourers in the community nor are children put to work as labourers. They occasionally take up short term engagements in villages like looking after the orchards, helping in cutting grass and reaping harvests, etc. Increase in landed as well as landless population has been observed.

They have their professional clubs which enlist local calls for recreational programmes and coordinate efforts for the improvement of the recreational programmes. As cultural forums, the clubs are eligible for financial assistance from the Department of Culture. There is no traditional village panchayat or any other organization of the Bhands. It is only the elders of the community who intervene in case there is some dispute among the members of the community. The elders do not take upon themselves the duty of suggesting a punishment for a defaulter. Gram panchayat, wherever it exists, exercises powerful influence on the local inhabitants and the Bhands are no exception to it. They have their professional clubs and councils but these have nothing to do with social affairs.

The community professes Islam and belongs to the Suni sect. In matters of religion, its members are faithful. The Bhands of Akingam worship Shiva Bhagwati or Parvati, the consort of Shiva. By virtue of their history, the Bhands pay their homage at a number of shrines of both the religions, Hindu and Muslim. They also observe particular days for visiting these shrines and staging *jashn* (performance). Ramnavami and Hardoi (the latter means the second day of the lunar fortnight in the month of *Ashadh*/June) are the days on which these are organized to the accompaniment of music at Shiva Bhagwati *asthapan* at Akingam. This is a mixed festival for the Hindus and the Muslims. The other sacred centres are: (*a*) Baba Daud Gowhari's *ziarat* at Gowhari, Wayulu in Anantnag; (*b*) Manak Shah Sahib's *ziarat* at Bidar Hayatpore near Kokarnag where the Bhands perform the *jashn* and the Kanils play music; (*c*) Baba Nasib-ud-Din Ghazi's *ziarat* at Sofshali near Kokarnag. Here *jashn* is performed on four days, i.e. twelfth to fifteenth, of the lunar fortnight in the month of May every year; (*d*) Said Sahib's *ziarat* at Birigama via Kazigund; (*e*) Tekiya Imam Sahib's *ziarat* at Imam Sahib in Anantnag; (*f*) In the month of April each year, Damaleh Bhand dance at Ashmuqam; (*g*) At the *ziarat* of Baba Zain-ud-Din Wali in Seer Kanligund, music is offered by the Bhands; and (*h*) In Kupwara, performance is given at Shardapetha *asthapan*.

The community's theatrical performance amounts to ritualistic offerings to these shrines and *ziarats*. Thereby they also entertain a large number of people gathered there. It has a normal and spiritual aspect and has a powerful secularizing influence. There has not been any conversion of the Bhands to any other religion. By and large, the community has developed a healthy secular approach to life.

The Bhands are the custodians of Kashmir's traditional folklore, folk music and performing arts. They have organized their folk-theatrical clubs and have been receiving small financial assistance from the cultural department and other similar agencies to keep their tradition alive. The instruments they use are *dhol* (drum), *dulij* (one sided drum) and *surnay* (long flute). The drums are slung down the neck. Some Bhand parties carry with them a male dancer clad in a female dress—*jameh* and *kameez*. In olden days, female dancers were inducted into performance and they were called *hafiza*. Now the Bhands have organized theatrical clubs in which others who do not belong to this community but evince interest in the art also join. This has helped them to systematize and standardize their skills and the television media is a strong patron of their art. Cultural troupes include the Bhands and they are deputed to various parts of the country by the state cultural academy. In special programmes like the current festival of India, the Bhands find an opportunity of entertaining the audience.

Most of the members of this community have been forced to find an alternative occupation or at least some means of making both ends meet. Common people think of them as jesting beggars who go from barn to barn to collect paddy and offer good wishes called Bhand-*daekher* in Kashmiri, meaning an insincere blessing.

By and large, this community has very cordial relations with other communities in the area. They have very cordial relations with the

Hindus. However, it has been found that they do not mix freely with the Shia community because of some historical reasons. They sometimes go to the Shia peasants to collect paddy for themselves during the harvesting and threshing seasons. They do not marry in the Shia community at all. Generally a mate is found from among their own community and occasionally outside it, though not outside the Muslim community.

The Bhands accept food and water from other communities. They draw water from the same source as do the members of other communities. Putative kinship ties exist among them, even with Hindus. They make use of the municipal and health facilities as do the rest of the people. They do not have a separate burial ground and share the one with the rest of the Muslims of their locality. Modern life has made only nominal impact as far as intercommunity linkages are concerned. They are politically alive and very much interested in the day-to-day politics.

They do not have large and extensive holdings. The Bhands are considered by the people as blessed with some sort of spiritual guidance since their art originated as a devotional endeavour. As such, people often come to the elderly Bhands and seek their blessings. In particular, Shri Subhan Bhand of Akingam is approached by people for his blessings. They kiss his hands, carry his baggage and show him reverence. In this sense, it may be presumed that the Bhands have a spiritual link with people of all faiths.

The community mostly consists of illiterate members. Illiteracy among its female members is widespread. However, boys and girls have now begun to attend school in villages but the drop-out rate among them is very high. They are ignorant of the basic principles of health. For medicare, they depend entirely on the health facilities provided by government organizations. A few persons have been able to acquire some education up to the middle standard.

The Bhands make use of public transport. There is not a single family which owns any sort of private vehicle even like a horse driven cart. Electricity has been provided by the government and almost all the villages are now electrified. Wood, coal, sawdust, cow-dung and kerosene are the sources of fuel they use. For irrigation of land wherever needed, water from the running streams and brooks is used. Chemical fertilizers along with natural fertilizers and insecticides are frequently used in producing paddy, vegetables, etc. They benefit from the public distribution systems and receive their monthly quota of ration of sugar, kerosene, *atta* and rice at the ration depots opened by the government. The Jammu & Kashmir Bank has opened its branches in far-flung areas also. They are fully aware of the various saving schemes now in force and are free and even encouraged to make use of these. But they are hardly in a position to save something and make deposits in the bank.

K.N. PANDITA

BHAT (MUSLIM)

The Bhat Muslims were converted to Islam from Hinduism. The community is identified at regional level. They speak Kashmiri language and use Arabic script within and outside the family.

Their staple food includes wheat, rice and maize. The pulses they consume are *moong*, *masur* and *rajmah*. They are non-vegetarian and eat mutton. Women are also non-vegetarian. Leafy vegetables are consumed moderately and the fruit consumption is in plenty. They supplement their diet with milk and milk products. Alcoholic drinks are taboo. On the occasion of a marriage feast, various dishes of meat are prepared. A nursing mother is given a special dish of *vopalhak* and meat.

Social divisions exist among the Bhat. These are on the basis of religious sects, i.e. Shia and Sunni. Inter-marriages between the two sects are very rare. They place themselves in the higher order of Muslim hierarchy but are recognized by others in the middle order.

Marriages are performed generally within the community although there is no bar in marrying outside the community. They marry with the Dar, Mir, Malik, Bhat, Wani, Lone and Sheikh communities. Since there are *biradari* marriages, they practice consanguinity both at parallel and cross-cousin levels. The sororate and levirate (junior) forms of marriage are also prevalent. Marriages are settled through negotiations. The usual age for marriage for males is 15 to 25 years and for females 15 to 23 years. The usual form of marriage is monogamy though polygamy is also practised in the community. As marriage symbols, they wear *dur*, *kandu*, and *bangri* at the time of marriage and after twelve days these are taken out and glass bangles are worn. There is no permanent marriage symbol in the community.

Dowry is prevalent and it usually includes jewellery, clothes and household articles including copper utensils. The parties give and take dowry according to their status. The *mahr* money is also fixed as per the status of the groom. These days it ranges between Rs. 5,000 and Rs. 40,000. Some part of the *mahr* money is condoned by the wife after marriage. The remaining part of the *mahr* is payable on demand or at the time of divorce. The rule of residence is patrilocal.

Divorce is permissible and it is given on grounds of adultery and maladjustment. Family elders usually decide about a divorce case among themselves. It has social approval. A *maulvi* issues the *talaqnama* or *fatwa* for the Sunni Bhat. The Shia Bhats consult their priest Maulana Aga Sayed Mustafa of Badgam for divorce cases and the *fatwa* is issued by him. In divorce cases, the articles given at the time of marriage are exchanged. No divorce compensation is given to the wife. But during the period of *iddat*, some maintenance is given to the wife. Only the husbands can divorce. Among the Shia Bhats, if the wife seeks separation known as *khula*, the *mahr* money is to be paid by her which is usually condoned. Children become the responsibility of the father in divorce cases. Remarriages of divorcee, widow and widower are permissible among the Bhats. The sororate and levirate (junior) forms of union are also prevalent.

It is observed that marriage age has increased, divorce matters relating to marriages show a declining trend, and remarriages of divorcees, widows and widowers have been liberally approved in the community.

The family type is usually the extended one. But nowadays separate households within the family are found. The conflict and confrontation in the family are mainly on property matters. Both males and females inherit the property. Females get less than the males. Usually two-thirds of the property is divided equally among the males (sons). The succession generally goes to the eldest son. In case the eldest son is a minor then the wife succeeds after the death of her husband. An adopted son can also succeed.

Women in the community do not enjoy the same status as men and have limited decision-making powers. They participate in economic activities to supplement the family income. The women share the burden of agricultural operations, bringing potable water and collection of fuel, etc. They perform the rituals and participate in the social and religious festivities.

After birth, the infant is first given a bath and the *mullah* or *maulvi* whispers the *azaan* in the child's left ear. On the seventh day, both the mother and infant are given a bath, and this ceremony is known as *sonder*. On the same day, name is given to the infant by a *maulvi*. He is rewarded with some cash and clothes. The midwife (*warin*) is also given some money.

Zerakasi is usually done within one year at some Muslim sacred place. Friends and relatives get a grand feast on this occasion. Skin, head and leg of the goat sacrificed on this occasion are buried. The flesh is given to the *maulvi* and village people. This is known as *sadaka*. *Khatna* (circumcision) is usually performed within three years of age. Earlier this was done by a *navid* but, now a qualified surgeon does it and gets his fees. No first feeding of cereals is observed in this community.

Marriages are settled through a *manzymyor* who is a go-between. A *manzymyor* can be a relative or a person belonging to a different community. Among the Muslims usually *lants* (eunuchs) do the job of go-between and get Rs. 500 to Rs. 2,000 from both the parties. In the first marriage rituals, *mangni* (first betrothal) the boy's parents and relatives visit the bride's place and offer presents of jewellery, clothes, etc., to the bride. They are entertained to a feast. This ceremony is followed by *nishani* in which the bride is again given jewellery, sweets and cash by the groom's relatives. This is also held at the bride's place. *Nishani* is followed by *hazri* in which the bride's relatives come to the groom's place and reciprocate presentations to the persons who visited them in the *nishani* ceremony. Between *shadi* and *hazri* the bride is given clothes, etc., on all the festive occasions.

In *shadi* (*khandar*), the *nikah* ceremony is performed by a *qazi* or *pir* against some money and issues the *nikah-nama*. The *mahr* money is also fixed through him before the *nikah* ceremony. At the time of marriage, *vanvun* singing is performed by womenfolk. They sing Kashmiri songs in praise of the bridegroom. A grand feast is given by the bride's parents. *Bidai* or *rukhsati* ritual is done after the marriage ceremony. The bride then accompanies the groom and stays at her in-laws' house. A sheep is sacrificed before the couple enters the house. This is known as *rathehaap*. The nuptial ceremony is performed at the groom's place. *Wathal* or *walima* (feast) is hosted the following day after marriage at the groom's place in which the bride's relatives are also invited.

Dadmoj, a middle-aged woman, accompanies the bride at the time of *bidai* and stays for some days at the groom's place. She gets clothings, presents, cash, etc.

After seven days of marriage, both the bride and bridegroom visit the bride's parents. The groom gives *salami* to the elders and gets some cash and presents. This ceremony is known as *firsal*. A feast is also given on this occasions.

The *kalma* and some verses from the Holy Koran are whispered into the ears of a dying man. The dead body is given bath by a *snangor* and is wrapped in a white cotton sheet, i.e. *kafan*. *Namaz-e-janaza* is performed in a mosque and the dead body is kept outside. A professional gravedigger (*malkhos*) digs the grave for a sum of Rs. 50 to 60 for the job. The dead body is lowered into the *lahad* (grave) and the grave is now closed from the left side. *Fateha* is recited on this occasion. On the fourth day, the *fateha* is again recited on the burial ground by a *pir*. A stone tablet known as *pyur* indicating the name of the person and dates of birth and death is placed on the grave on this day. Food is not cooked in the bereaved family after the death for about three days. Relatives and friends bring the food for thc family for those three days. *Koran-khani* is done on the tenth and fortieth day.

Land is the main natural resource which is controlled by individual proprietorship. The Bhats are engaged in cultivation, horticulture, business, trade, government service, private service, self-employment and textile-weaving and work as skilled labourers. Their link with the market is very active and the local market is fully regulated. They purchase their day-to-day articles from the market in cash. There is no bonded labour among the Bhats. Child labour is prevalent and the payment of wages is made in cash. They do embroidery and weaving of shawls, etc. The Bhats do not have traditional caste councils or panchayats. Statutory formal panchayats that exist came into being after Independence. Their primary role is to plan and implement the welfare and developmental activities in the villages. The Bhats are both Shia and Sunni. The Sunni section follows the *silsila* affiliation. The practising preachers are from the communities other than the Bhats. Besides, giving discourses on religious matters they perform the birth, marriage and death rites. The Shia Bhats observe Bakr-Id, Id-ul-Ghadir, Id-ul-Fitr, Muharram, Sattara Rabi-ul-Awwal, 13 Rajab and 3 Shaban festivals. The Bhats belonging to the Sunni sect observe Id-ul-Fitr, Id-ul-Zuha, Id-ul-Milad and Miraj-e-Alam festivals. All the Muslims in the valley observe Sheikh Nooruddin Rishi's day. The other saints are Sayed Wali (Pulwama), Zain-ud-Din Wali (Pahalgam) and Mir Shamsuddin Iraqi (Zaddibal). The festivities among the Bhats have socio-religious significance. This work is mainly attended to by the womenfolk. There is no traditional dance in the community; however *vanvun* (chorus) is performed by the females at the time of marriage. They sing the local Kashmiri songs.

They accept and exchange water, *kachcha* and *pukka* food from the other Muslim communities excepting some occupational groups, for example the Watal, Goor, Ganai, etc. They are invited by their pandit counterparts to functions and have a separate place of dinning. The community members also share water resources and religious shrines with other communities of the valley. Intermarriages with other communities are also not rare. In modern linkages it is found that its members are businessmen, scholars, creative artists, teachers, administrators, doctors, engineers, and persons in white-collar jobs and defence services. Political leadership has emerged at the regional level.

Formal education is considered favourable for both boys and girls. They study up to the postgraduate level. Their attitude towards modern medicare is favourable and they make moderate use of it. Their attitude towards family welfare programme is also favourable. Couples prefer four children and use modern methods of family planning. It is generally women who get sterilized.

Drinking water facility is available within the locality. They get piped water. The opportunities for employment are open to them. However, for self-employment, they are engaged in agricultural activities. Media and communication facilities are available in the area and are used by them. They have electricity in their houses. Fuel resources are firewood, cow-dung cakes, coal and liquid petroleum gas.

Irrigation facilities are available to them. The source is usually a canal. The Bhats use chemical fertilizers and insecticides in the fields. They purchase it from the market.

The Integrated Child Development Scheme (feeding/mother infant care/immunization) programmes is availed by them. They avail themselves of the public distribution system and get their food rations from the fair price shops. Their attitude towards saving is favourable and they do not depend on moneylenders and shopkeepers.

A.C. SRIVASTAVA

BHOJRU

The Bhojru are a community of Brahmans who live on alms and fortune telling. The word 'bhojru' is derived from the Hindi term '*boojh*' (to tell). This epithet may be attributed directly to their traditional profession of fortune telling, astrological predictions based on palmistry, numerology or through picking up of a random fortune slip by a parrot. Another popularly used synonym for the community is Dugduge or Dubdube. Opinions differ about the correct usage of the two terms, as both these terms are used commonly. People, however, prefer the term Dugduge as they play on a *dak* (drum) while singing ecstatic songs in praise of Lord Shiva and Shani Devta; another synonym for them is Dakaut. In Jammu they came to be known as Dugduge which later got transformed into Dubdube. They claim to belong to the Panch Dravid category of Brahmans and are Saraswat Brahmans. Most of them affix the title Sharma with their names. They claim their descent from Samanja Rishi. The community perceives its identity at regional level and is found, besides Jammu, in Noorpur, Talwara and Kangra (Himachal Pradesh). They have reportedly migrated from Maharashtra to their present habitat. They face searing summers, medium rainfall and high humidity. The entire area of their habitation is dotted with low hillocks and undulating plains. The forest cover is thin. They speak in a dialect which is a blend of Dogri and Punjabi. Their script is Devanagari. The identity marker is a begging bowl filled with mustard oil and fitted with a small photo frame of Shani Devta in whose name they beg on Saturdays only. Men usually wear a white turban and *dhoti* and put on *tilak* markings on their foreheads. The Bhojru are included among the Backward Classes in Jammu & Kashmir.

They are non-vegetarians and eat pork occasionally. Wheat and maize are their staple diet and *rajmah*, *chana* and *moong* are the pulses commonly consumed by them. Most of their food items are cooked in mustard oil. *Kachalu*, *piaz* (onion), and *aaloo* (potatoes) are some of the tuberous vegetables they consume. Men drink alcoholic beverages occasionally which they purchase from the market but women do not drink. Milk and milk products, if available are consumed in plenty. Men smoke cigarettes and hubble-bubble and the elderly women may be seen smoking *bidis*. Fruit consumption is moderate.

The Bhojrus are divided into a number of exogamous *gotras* which regulate marriage alliances. The basis of differentiation is social. No changes have taken place in surnames and titles. The self-perception of the community is of medium level. Other communities too treat them accordingly. They are fully aware of the *varna* system and recognize their place among the Brahmans.

Endogamy prevails at the community level but at the *gotra* level they are exogamous. Their daughters may be married into higher castes but the latter desist from offering their own daughters to the Bhojrus. Consanguinity is not prevalent. Marriages are arranged in adulthood through negotiation and exchange. Dowry is paid both in cash and kind. *Sindoor* and *mangalsutra* are the marriage symbols. Rule of residence is patrilocal. Divorce is permissible but only men can divorce through judical approval. The wife is paid divorce compensation. Children are the responsibility of the father. Junior levirate and junior sororate are permissible.

Both avoidance and joking relationship exist within a specific kin category. Property disputes and challenging the authority of the elders are the main points of conflict in the family. Equigeniture exists though daughters do not claim their share in property. The eldest male issue succeeds his father. Formation of nuclear families is on the increase.

Women remain confined to the four walls of the house but they tend cattle, collect fuel and fodder, fetch water and play a role in the social functions and rituals. Their status in the society is low. They do not participate in any economic activity that contributes to the family income. Pre-delivery restrictions are observed and the post-delivery pollution (*sutak*) continues for 21 days. *Mundan (jad)* of the male child is performed on or before he attains 5 years of age and a *bali* (sacrifice) is offered to the Devi. The *purohit* is called on the fifth day to name the child and prepare a *janampatri* (horoscope). The wearing of the *janjoore* (sacred thread) is performed at 15 years of age, which is now performed a day before the marriage. Marriage rituals consist of *kurmai, lagan, kanyadan, varmal* and circumambulations around the holy fire. Previously a marriage ceremony used to be a prolonged affair as the *baratis* would come on foot from a long distance but now the rituals have been curtailed due to an effective means of communication network and also due to rising prices. The dead are cremated and the rituals are performed by the *charjis*. *Terahi* is performed on the thirteenth day and death pollution ceases thereafter.

They depend largely on begging of alms in the name of Shani Devta on Saturdays. They are mainly landless and earn through astrological forecasting. The new generation is weaning away from their traditional profession and is getting engaged in self-employment activities such as contractorship of *anardana* (pomegranate seed), collection and construction activities. Their links with the daily market are direct and markets are well regulated. All transactions are in cash. Bonded and child labour is not prevalent. They do not have any traditional *jati* panchayat. The elders resolve the disputes, if any. They have no representation in the statutory panchayats which are responsible for planning and implementing the schemes of rural development.

They are Hindus and worship all gods of the Hindu pantheon, besides worshipping *kul-devi* Sitla Mata. They celebrate all the Hindu festivals of religious significance. Their priests are the *charjis* who perform all their lifecycle rituals. They celebrate all major Hindu festivals such as Holi, Diwali, Navratras, Ramnavami, Janmashtami, etc. Their sacred pilgrimage centres are Hardwar, Rishikesh and Vaishno Devi. Oral traditions possessed by them are of regional nature. They neither sing nor dance but recite the *Ramayana* and *Bhagavata Gita*.

They traditionally do not accept water and cooked food from the Sansis, Perna and Chuhra but accept the same from the higher castes. Other Brahmans do not accept water and food from them. Patron-client relationship exists in the community. The community has businessmen but no scholars and creative artists. Some of them are engaged in white-collar jobs, working in offices and defence services.

Education is favoured for both boys and girls. The former study up to the higher secondary level and then drop out due to economic reasons. The girls too study up to the secondary level and drop out due to social reasons. They consider both traditional and modern medicare useful and avail themselves of the facilities thereof. They are favourably disposed to a small family norm and use modern methods of family planning. Water supply is available in their localities through water taps. They listen to radio and see television in the community centres. Roads, railways and post offices are situated nearby. They use electricity for lighting purposes. Firewood, kerosene and cow-dung cakes are the major fuels used. Nutrition programmes are not available to them. The attitude towards saving is favourable but, due to non-availability of credit facilities, they depend on the moneylenders and shopkeepers.

BAQAR R. RIZVI

BODH

The Ladakhi Bodh, Ladakhspa or Botriksha are basically the inhabitants of Tibet and it is from this territory that they have derived their identity as Pot/Bot/Bhotta. After embracing Buddhism, they were known as Bodh but their ethnic identity remains as the Bhot or Bhatta, a name by which they are known in the Kashmir Valley even today. Ladakh, in its hoary past was inhabited by the Mons, a people of north India before the Aryan Dards started their immigration to Ladakh. The Mons were subjugated and were subsequently given a very low status in the Ladakhi society. The Dard settlers and the present Ladakhi population are a product of miscegenation of the above groups. The people are divided into a number of subgroups such as Gyalpo (rulers), Kahlon (ministers), Mangriks (farmers) and Ringan (lower occupation groups) in the order of hierarchy which is well defined and is mainfested in the seating arrangements made during public functions. They live in Zanskar (the land of white copper), Nubra, Ladakh and Lahaul and Spiti (Himachal Pradesh), an area characterized by high mountains, scanty rainfall, heavy snowfall, a bare brown landscape capped by perenniel snow on hill tops devoid of any vegetation. They speak Bodhi amongst themselves or *nangpa* but switch to Hindustani while conversing with the *cheepa* (others). The Bodh is a Scheduled Tribe of the state.

Primogeniture was a rule in the past but now equigeniture is in practice. Even the *chomos* are given a share in the family estates. The eldest male issue inherits and succeeds.

Women enjoy the right of inheritance and participate in all the socio-economic pursuits of the family, control family finances, indulge in self-employment activities and perform white-collar jobs. They enjoy a high status in the society. One of them, Ms Dolma, is the head of the ladies wing of the National Conference.

On the birth of a child, the lama is called to perform *sangs* rituals (purificatory ceremony) twice: once immediately after the birth and, the second time after a month. The name is given by a *kushak* or reincarnate lama. Puberty rituals are not observed. Marriage is performed at the bridegroom's house amidst *storma* prayers that protect the couple from evil spirits. Exchange of *khatak* (scarves) by the couple and a plethora of rituals complete the formalities of marriage.

A lama is invited to perform the *phoa* ceremony. On death, the body is cremated after seven days in winter and three days in summer. Thereafter the ashes are collected and preserved in a *chorten*. *Zitsik* feast is given to the mourners. Periodic rituals are performed after a month and one year after death.

Land, owned by individuals, is the primary economic resource. There are a few landless among them. The subsidiary economic resources are handicrafts, horticulture, small-scale industries, grinding, wood carving, transportation, etc. Dependence on the regulated daily market is absolute. There is no existence of bonded and child labour in the community. Payment of wages is made both in cash and kind. The economy of the people has thrived recently owing to the consistent effort of the state and central governemnts.

The *goba* heads the committee of the village elders also known as *goba* to exercise social control by settling family disputes, issues relating to divorce, sharing of water, collection of livestock tax and intercommunity disputes. Penalties imposed are paid in cash; previously they were realized in the form of food grains. No rewards are given. The members of the *goba* are given a place next to the nobility in public seating arrangements and are invited in all marriage ceremonies, irrespective of faith and kinship. They are the main agency of labour supply to the armed forces and monasteries.

The Bodhs of Ladakh belong to the Mahayana sect of Buddhism with the Gelukpa (Yellow Shirts), Drokpa (Red Shirts) and Neima subsects. The family deities are Chaskur and Shingmala. Hemis, Rangdum, Shey, Thiksey, Staqna, Likir, Lamayuru, Rizhong gompas, and other centres of Buddhism, such as Dharamshala are their sacred pilgrimage centres. The lamas pray and meditate for the welfare of the community, perform the life-cycle rituals, impart religious training to children, participate in the mask dances, and perform therapeutic rituals. Losar marks the Buddhist new year. On this day, mask dances of the lamas at Hemis, Thiksey, Spituk and Pheyong monasteries honour the illustrious monks. The birth anniversary of Shakapa is celebrated by illuminating houses. Other festivals are Buddha Purnima and Dosmoche. Bonism still survives with the *mudra* running in clockwise direction. Conversions are common. Reverend Kushak Bakula led this community to bring about a number of reforms: curbing alcoholism, banning animal sacrifice and making all efforts to raise literacy levels. Polyandry too was declared an undesirable practice. Elders, however, feel that adherence to faith is on the decline and at the same time they feel that they are being culturally engulfed by the surrounding majority communities. Of late, they have become very sensitive to the activities of the Christian missionaries operating in the state. Lamas are proficient in drawing, painting, carving and engraving. Each Buddhist gompa presents a feast of visual art. They are also adept in the miniature *tankha* paintings and in modelling. The *Kesar* epic and *Jatak* songs keep their oral traditions alive.

The Ladakhi Bodhs and Muslims are interlocked into a number of socio-economic interactional situations. The Muslim butchers ensure mutton supply to the Bodhs as the latter desist from killing animals. The two meet funerary expenses of the common kin, irrespective of their different faiths. Buddhists accept water and food both cooked and raw, from the Muslims, and the Muslim Argons too accept the same from the Buddhist; but Baltis, being Shia Muslims, do not accept water and food from the Buddhists. There is, however, no restriction on accepting dry rations from the Bodhs. Connubial norms necessitate the conversion from one faith to another. *Chuspur* (religious brotherhood) exists between monasteries such as Shey and Hemis. King Jameya Namgyal appointed a number of Muslim occupational groups for rendering services to his subjects. The Muslim Mons still play music at the monasteries. Access to water resources, places of public importance, houses and roads is unrestricted. *Lasna*, a form of *jajmani* system, existed in the past. They participate actively in the political processes. In games, archery contests and polo are organized by the state. Relations between tenants and landholders in sharecropping are free from mutual bickering.

The Bodhs have attained a high level of literacy and they go to the universities of Jammu & Kashmir for higher education. Their attitude is positive towards family welfare measures and they believe in small family. Potable water is available in Leh. *Kuhls*, streams and rivers are the sources of drinking water. People have taken full advantage of the various employment and self-employment programmes. Radio, television and newspapers are available to them. Lower Staqna Hydel Project ensures an uninterrupted electric supply. Ladakhis have created a national record in greenhouse cultivation of vegetables. Fuels used are liquid petroleum gas and kerosene for cooking, and wood to burn *bukharis* for heating the living room during winters. *Kuhls* and the Indus supply enough water for irrigation. They make full use of chemical fertilizers, insecticides and pesticides. Banking services are well developed and are fully availed of. Very few of them are dependent on moneylenders and shopkeepers.

BAQAR R. RIZVI

BOMBA

The Bomba are the Brahmans of lower category in Kashmir being converted to Islam. At present most of them live around the Hapatnar region in district Anantnag of Kashmir Valley. The history of the Bombas is shrouded in mystery as no authentic evidence is available about their original place or habitat. Popular belief has it that they emigrated to Muzaffarabad (Pakistan occupied Kashmir) and Uri district in Jammu & Kashmir. They settled in Kishanganga Valley region before they moved upland to other parts of Kashmir. *Rajatarangini* traces the Bomba settlements to Karnav now known as Karnava where the Khasas lived. These people were restless and warlike, living independently till the Sikh's conquest of Kashmir. However, whenever the Sikh rulers tightened their hold over Jhelum Valley, the Bomba retained certain privileges. Over a period of time they moved out of Kishanganga Valley to other parts of Kashmir, where they settled down peacefully. The community has one popular synonym, i.e. Khan Bombas. However, they do not have any sub-titles and are identified only at the local level as an ethnic community. Their place of settlements record low humidity with dense forest cover. They mainly speak Pahari among themselves, but correspond and communicate with other people in Urdu using Arabic script. The community over a period of time got assimilated into the Kashmiri Muslim culture; thus, they do not have special dress for either sexes as identification markers. They are covered under the Backward category of the state government.

The Bombas are non-vegetarians. They eat eggs, fish, fowl, beef and mutton but not pork. Their staple food is rice and maize. They also consume other cereals and all types of pulses. They mainly use mustard oil as a cooking medium. They take potato, all types of vegetables, locally available roots and tubers. They also consume a fair amount of fruit. They use less quantities of milk and milk products. They drink *noonchai* (salted black tea). Drinking alcohol is almost non-existent among the Bomba. People smoke cigarettes and loose tobacco in *hookah*. Some people chew tobacco and use snuff. There has not been any significant change in their food habits although there has been a marked improvement in the quality of food consumed.

The Bombas do not have any social divisions on the basis of their religion or caste. However, they are stratified on the basis of occupation and more so on economic levels. Surname assumed are Khan or Khanbumb. They do not have a high self-perception. People of other communities also do not have a high perception of the Bombas at the regional level.

The Bombas practise community endogamy. They marry their cousins irrespective of the status of their bloodrelation. Consanguinity or cross-cousin marriage is common. However, sororal polygyny was not reported. The marriageable age for girls varies between 14 and 18 years, and for boys between 20 and 32 years. Marital alliances are negotiated by a middle-man or by their elders. Monogamy is the common norm of marriage. Polygyny permitted under the Islamic Law is rarely practised. There is no marriage symbol. Dowry and bride-price do not exist but, being Muslims, *mahr* is prevalent among them. There is no rigidity about the amount or mode of payment of *mahr*. It can be deferred or paid on demand. In addition to *mahr*. Predominently, rule of residence is patrilocal and divorce is permissible for reasons of maladjustment, cruelty, etc. Divorce compensation is given to the wife and it is usually the husband who can divorce. Children are the responsibility of the father in case of divorce. Divorcee and widow can remarry after observing the *iddat*.

Joint families are gradually breaking up because of the desire to lead an independent life. Agrarian reforms in the Valley have enabled majority of the peasants to become landowners. Interpersonal relations are cordial among the household members though joking relations are not permitted between consanguinous and affinal relatives. Conflicts and confrontations exist to a lesser extent. The Bombas follow the Muslim law of inheritance. All male children have the right to their ancestral property and females inherit a little less than the males. Interfamily linkages are reported to be cordial. Offences of criminal nature are dealt with under the provisions of the state laws whereas social disputes are usually resolved through mutual reconciliations.

The Bomba women enjoy a secondary status as compared to the men in all walks of life. Though they have unequal rights over the ancestral property yet they participate in social activites along with their menfolk. A majority of the women participate in most of the agricultural operations and other related farm activites. They procure water and fuel for their households. Many women have taken to weaving of wool for making blankets. Their participation in politics is minimal though they enjoy voting rights.

When a child is born,the delivery mostly takes place at home, with the help of an experienced midwife. Hospital facilities are also utilized. There are no postnatal restrictions. They do not observe any christening ceremony but the male children have to undergo circumcision according the Islamic practice. The *aqeeqa* ceremony is performed by them.

Marriages are fixed by negotiations through the family heads or marriage-broker or *manzymyor*. The entire marriage ceremony is brief. The bridegroom and his party proceed to the bride's house on the wedding day. *Nikah* is performed and a feast served. The newly-weds proceed to the place of the groom for nuptial. The bride returns to her parents' house for a minimum period of seven days. Thereafter, a messenger formally calls on the bride's parental house bringing with him some gifts, and a request to send the bride to her in-laws' house. A feast is organized by both the sides in the marriage. *Wathal*, a return social call by the groom at his in-laws' place accompanied by some selected guests, is a post-marriage ceremony.

A dead person is given a bath and wrapped in a white shroud. Thereafter, *namaz-e-janaza* (religious prayer) is performed and the body is carried in a *taboot* (coffin) to the *mazar* or the family's private burial ground and is buried in a grave. A forty-day mourning known as *chehallum* is observed by these people. *Jumma-fateha*, i.e. Friday prayer is performed after the death of a person. Customarily, till the day of *jumma-fateha* relatives of the deceased provide food for the family . On the day of *jumma-fateha*, tea and bread are served to all the community members who gather near the grave of the dead person and the same is repeated on *chehallum*. Except for these death rites no other ritual is observed, not even related to the pollution period.

The major economic resource of the community is land and land-related activities. It is mainly a landowning community having a negligible number of landless or farm labourers. Landownership is predominently under individual proprietorship. Their subsidiary occupation is working as casual labourers in the forest and road construction work. A negligible number of them are also engaged in business and government services. They are not directly linked to the regulate market as their dependence on it is very little. On an average, 70 to 80 per cent of their consumption comprises self-grown and produced goods and services. Child labour is not hired or marketed though it is used on domestic farms and other operations. Wages are received in cash and kind and barter system is still prevalent among them. Of late, horticulture has gained precedence over traditional farm practices as most of the land is in dry-belt area where agricultual pursuits are not very remunerative.

The village panchayat system exists among the Bombas. Elderly persons of the village normally sit in the panchayat and decide about the conflicts, quarrels and divorce cases. Cases of adultery, rape and theft are decided under the state's legal system. Village panchayats are of heterogeneous nature as they comprise members belonging to other communities as well. However, these panchayats do not have the power to punish or give awards but social boycott or excommunication can be imposed by them. These panchayats also participate in the welfare and developmental activities of the village in an advisory capacity.

The Bombas profess Islam and are predominently Sunnis. They visit a number of religious places such as the Hazratbal shrine, Makhdum Sahib, Rishi Peer, Pir Dastgir Sahib, Shah Hamdan, etc. Affiliation to a *pir* is also reported. Fasting during the Ramzan and pilgrimage to Mecca to perform *haj* are their main religious obligations. They observe all the Muslim festivals like Id-ul-Fitr, Id-ul-Zuha and Ramzan, Nauroz, Shab-e-Meraj, Friday following Shab-e-Meraj, Shab-e-Qadr, Jumat-ul-Vida.

They are not professional craftsmen but with government assistance, young boys are now being trained as apprentice-cum-trainees at the local carpet weaving centres. Oral traditions pertaining to religious texts are based on local events and hisotry. Some of the folk songs and folklores are also of pre-Islamic era. Fine arts are not practised. A few of their versifiers write mostly religious verses in Sufi tradition. They are good in blanket and straw-mat weaving.

The Bombas participate in all socio-religious festivals of the co-religionists. They normally refrain from eating food offered by the non-Muslims. Marital relations are maintained with almost all sects of the Muslims. They share well and water sources, road, school, panchayat ghars with other communities and also with the non-Muslims. Burial grounds are shared with other Muslim communities. Visits to the shrines of *pirs* and *faqirs* are permissible. They maintain cordial and informal relationship with other members of the community. Services of the artisans are utilized.

The community is gradually becoming more participatory in the market-oriented trade and commerce. Political awareness is also fast developing. They do not have entrepreneurs, creative artists, administrators, engineers and doctors among them. Some of them are employed in the state police service.

Formal education is becoming popular gradually but the boys are encouraged and favoured for education more than the girls. Boys study up to the college level and girls usually up to the secondary level.

Children drop out from schools and colleges due to socio-economic compulsions.

Though their attitude is favourable towards modern medicare, they are not making full use of it. They are receptive to family planning and generally women get sterilized. Their water sources are streams and springs though piped water is now being made available by the government.

The community has not, by and large, benefited under the self-employment and other welfare schemes launched by the government. Cooperative societies help in the distribution of essential commodities and other farm-related requirements. Almost all the households are utilizing electricity for lighting their houses. They use firewood and cow-dung cakes as fuel; chemical fertilizers and insecticides are used but mostly depend on organic manure for their fields. Very few of them have availed of the nutrition programmes through ICDS, Anganwadi and SNP centres. Majority of them are getting rations through the public distribution system. They are not used to seeking loans from the traditional moneylenders but borrow from the shop-keepers to meet their unforeseen contingencies. Only a few avail of the banking facilities. They do not seem to have propensity to save and invest.

The impact of socio-economic transitions has still not made any perceptible dent on the community. The Bombas have integrated into the Kashmiri culture and traditions. They neither preceive themselves as an exclusive ethnic community nor do they aspire for an independent identity.

INDU AIMA

BOTRAJA

Botraja is the name given by the Kashmiris to a small community of migrants whose ancestors originated in Nagar principality of Gilgit Agency of the undivided northern India. The word 'Botraja' is a compound term; Bot being the Kashmiri version of Bhautta (in *Rajatarangini*) and Raja meaning the ruler. The reason for the suffixed title 'raja' will be explained shortly.

Bota is usually the name given by the Kashmiris to the people of Baltistan (Ladakh, Tibet, Zanskar, etc.) on the eastern course of the river Indus. They are of Mongol and Turko-Mongol stock. But the people inhabiting the mountainous regions along the north and north-western course of the Indus in the Pamirs (Gilgit, Hunza, Nagar, Ponyal, Darel, Chitral, etc.) or historically known as Dardistan are called Darads (in *Rajatarangini*). They are distinct from the Baltis because of their Aryan origin and clear surviving Aryan traits. The earliest and somewhat dependable information about the Darads (to which stock the Botrajas belong) is to be found in the early thirteenth century celebrated Sanskrit chronicle of Kashmir, namely *Rajatarangini* of Kalhana. Darad lands of Dardistan (Darada + *sthana*) were integral to the ancient Kashmir kingdom and the Darads played a significant role in the early political history of Kashmir. Sturdy and recalcitrant, Darads have always been the vanguard of the ancient Kashmiri army when proceeding on expeditions. However, they invariably turned rebellious whenever they found that the centre of power in Kashmir had grown weak. In broad general geographical terms, Hunza, Nagar and the Pamirs are situated to the north of Gilgit. Nagar had been one of the several chieftainships comprising Gilgit Agency in the nineteenth century. In the latter part of the 1880s, the chiefs of Hunza and Nagar combined to rise against the government of the state of Jammu and Kashmir of which they had become a part through the annexation process begun by the Sikh rule in about 1840s. Kashmiri troops were attacked and a number of Kashmiri soldiers were taken captive by the Hunza and Nagar rebels who, in turn, sold them to the Kirghiz on the northern slopes of the Pamirs in Central Asia.

In 1886, Uzr Khan, the chief of Nagar was captured by the Dogra troops for his rebellious activities and was interned in the fort of Skardu for about a year. He was then brought to Kashmir along with his small entourage, mostly his closest family members, and was kept a prisoner in the fort of Hari Parbat in Srinagar. Since these people were of the ruling house in Nagar, the Kashmiris misinterpreting them as Botas added the suffix 'raja' to their name to distinguish them from the ordinary Botas. Thus was coined the specific name Botraja for the members of the community coming from Nagar. The Botrajas themselves do not use the term but invariably prefix their names by the term 'raja' such as Raja Ayyub Khan or Raja Safdar Ali.

There are about twenty homesteads of the Botrajas in the Mumeh Khan Mohalla, Andaron-i-Kathi Darwaza in Hari Parbat locality in Srinagar. The story of their imprisonment during the rule of Maharaj Ranbir Singh of Kashmir is confirmed by the fact that these homesteads are settled just below the ramparts of the fort on the declivity of the hillock overlooking the expansive grasslands below and the waters of the placid Nagin lake in the distant background. It is reported that only about five homesteads of the Botrajas are settled outside this locality-in Bemina on the western periphery of Srinagar town. They are all concentrated in the Hari Parbat locality indicated above. In all there are about 350 persons belonging to this community with a near 50-50 ratio between males and females. These figures have been recorded as a result of a recent field survey.

They speak Nagari among themselves, which is a branch of the Dardic language. But they correspond with their people in Urdu using the Arabic script though for confidential communications they use Arabic script for Nagari dialect (which does not have its own script) if and when exigency arises. In dealings with the local population, Kashmiri is extensively spoken and they have now adopted the Kashmiri dialect with perfect intonation. They wear *kameez* and *salwar* indoors like the Kashmiris and wear coat and trousers outdoors. But before Independence or even later, they used to wear the special Chitral cap called *manakfarchin* and a gown called *choga* as an overdress. Chitral robes have now fallen out of use and the distinction of the Botrajas from the local population in terms of dress has almost vanished.

No special constitutional status has been granted to them except that they have been brought within the purview of state subjecthood, and privileges and facilities accruing thereby are enjoyed by them without any discrimination. When their chief, Raja Uzr Khan was made a captive in Kashmir, he was paid a monthly maintenance allowance of Rs. 200 by the state government besides a stipend by the resident. Whereas the latter privilege ceased with the quitting of the British from India, the former privilege continues till date.

The Botraja is a community of non-vegetarians. They generally eat mutton and chicken, and if it is available, they are not averse to eating beef. They have no specific philosophical reason for being non-vegetarians. As the descendants of highlanders, they, by tradition, subsisted upon their flocks of sheep and herds of cattle and, therefore, inherited the total non-vegetarian culture. But now owing to high cost of mutton in Kashmir, the community has adapted itself to the habit of eating vegetables. Rice is their staple food but maize is not at all consumed. Wheat, pulses, *ghee*, and lately, mustard oil are consumed. In olden days, they persisted for some time with the habit of cutting meat into big slices and roasting it on flames and burning charcoal and eating without using condiments. In indigenous culture, only one preparation of meat was made but this has given way to the influences of local culture of preparing several dishes of meat. One of the original special dish in their culture was the bread called *diramfiti*. The Botrajas have a liking for milk and therefore keep their own milch cows. This, however, has become an exceedingly difficult practice to continue. They are fond of apricots in particular of which, according to their own statement, several varieties are grown in their ancient homeland of Nagar. The like of those varieties are not to be found in Kashmir or at any other place. They claim that one of the reasons why their people in Nagar are cancer-free is their excessive consumption of apricot, both fresh and dried. This statement, however, must be verified by medical tests. There is a custom with the indigenous people of Nagar that anybody can consume as much ripe apricot as he likes; the only condition is that the kernel is to be dropped under the apricot tree.

The Botrajas abhor all kinds of alcoholic drinks. Tea with sugar or with salt is commonly drunk and no *sharbats* or soft drinks are used. Bread bought from the baker is consumed with tea twice a day, for breakfast and for afternoon snack. Four persons partake of food from one platter. Condiments are used. Their food habits have undergone a considerable change after Independence and have come closer to those of the Kashmiris. Pure home-produced milk is now substituted by market product of powdered skimmed and unskimmed milk; total non-vegetarian diet has been replaced by partial consumption of vegetables; joint sharing of a food platter by four persons as prevalent among the Kashmiri Muslims is replaced by individual plates, and consumption of superior quality rice has been replaced by coarse rice provided by the consumer shops.

Botraja is a small community of just 350 people whose ancestors had been brought as captives about a century back. Being the offshoot of a ruling family, they had no social divisions nor any hierarchical order except that they, in a body, submitted to the wishes, desires and directions of the eldest member of the group. This was necessitated by the peculiar circumstances in which history had placed them. The elders certainly enjoy the regard and respect of the juniors. It is a single group which, while adapting to the new circumstances, has never ceased to take their eyes away from the pages of their past history. The only significant change which has appeared in their names after settling in Kashmir is the adoption of Arabicized names in greater measure than the ancient Iranian (to be precise, Zoroastrian) names; for instance, Raja Zulfiqar Ali and Raja Safdar Ali instead of Behruz Khan, Roshandil Khan, etc. The community has a lurking sense of superiority being the descendants of a ruling house. But this has not hindered their partial and unavoidable assimilation into the local mainstream. With the local people they seem to have developed cordial relations and have avoided harbouring antagonism.

The community performs marriages according to the Muslim (Shia) customs and rules. Polygyny is extremely rare. Usually 20 is the age for marriage of boys and girls. Marriages are arranged by the parents or elders and there is no specific symbol of marriage either for the boy or for the girl except that the bride, during the first few weeks of her marriage, can be identified by her bright dress and ornaments. In matters of dowry, the local Shia traditions are followed. In olden days, the terms of bride-price (*mahr*), among their ancestors were extremely impossible; for instance, 2 kg of the wings of mosquito. This was just to eliminate even the remotest chance of divorcing a wife. For the first five days following the solemnization of marriage, the bride stays in the house of her husband, i.e. her in-laws, then returns to her parents to stay with them for a couple of weeks. But finally she resides with her in-laws. Though divorces are extremely rare, yet if at all this must take place, divorce can be given either by the husband or the wife. A divorced woman must wait for three months and ten days (called the period of *iddat*) before she remarries. If she has conceived of her divorced husband, the newborn baby is to be provided for by his or her actual father. The care of the older children of the couple is left to mutual arrangement. Sometimes an arrangement of compromise is made. Divorce and after-divorce maintenance of the woman are complex questions and are decided on the basis of the merits of each case keeping injunctions of religion in mind. The community carefully kept track of the Shah Bano case which had been brought before the Supreme Court of India. However, the decree of the *mulla* (priest) ultimately carries weight with the parties. They marry their boys and girls outside their group now, though this is rare. In such cases, the martrimonial alliance is contracted with the local Shia only and not with the Sunnis. Generally speaking, fanfare in marriages is avoided because the economic conditions of the community do not permit it.

Joint family is the common form but the constraints of modern life tend to force a shift to nuclear form. In interfamily relationship, respect and regard are uppermost. They have a very strong sense of interfamily ties because of the special circumstances of the group. The eldest son assumes the patriarchical role in case of his father's death. All the sons become equal shareholders of their deceased father's property as well as debts, if any. The daughters also receive their portion of share which is not equal to the share of the son. The property of a person survived by four sons and one daughter will be divided into nine equal shares; each son receives two shares and the ninth share goes to the daughter. No change has occurred in this system so far. There has been no serious and cognizable demand from the womenfolk for equal rights with men in this matter.

Compared to men, women have a secondary status. Their right over the ancestral property has already been explained. In case of her husband's death, a widow has a right to her deceased husband's property if there is no male issue and as long as she does not remarry. Their womenfolk do no manual work outside their house. Women are generally confined to the four walls of the house, where they do the daily chores. In accordance with the lifestyle in Kashmir, it is the woman who manages and regulates the family, cooks food, renders internal service to the family, brings up chidren and contributes to the maintenance and planning of the homestead. Children of both sexes attend schools regularly and illiteracy is being wiped out. The younger generation is steadily being exposed to the pulls and pressures of the modern life and conservatism and backwardness are gradually yielding place to progress and enlightenment. Women take active part in polling and try to understand everyday politics without claiming to be politicians. Outside their homes, women observe *purdah* (veil) and retire to private rooms when a guest calls upon the elder person of the house.

No specific pre-delivery rituals are observed except for certain taboos. For example, a pregnant woman does not come out to receive a guest, does not go out after dusk, does not work during eclipse, does not carry heavy burden and avoids shopping. Usually delivery (particularly the first delivery) takes place in the house of the woman's parents. Deliveries are conducted in hospitals and the midwifery practice is fast vanishing. Birth pollution is observed for seven to eight days, after which the mother and the child are given a hot bath. When a baby is born, a senior person whispers *azaan* into its ears; a name is given within a few days. For an attractive name, sometimes the holy book is opened to help find a name. The major ritual during the childhood in case of male child is that of circumcision. Usually a trained surgeon does the operation. There are clinics where experts do it under the modern facilities. The child to be circumcised is given new clothes and sometimes his maternal uncles make a small present of money also. Birthdays are not celebrated. Betrothal ceremony takes place when a couple becomes engaged. New clothes, some gold ornaments, platterfuls of cakes and sweets may be exchanged on the occasion. Marriages are solemnized according to the Muslim (Shia) custom in the house of the bride. A *mulla* performs the marriage rites, viz., seeking the consent of the bride and the groom in the presence of a few persons.

They bury the dead in the Muslim (Shia) tradition. Death rites are performed by a *mulla*. There is no *mulla* among the group but the services of one from another community are requisitioned. On the fourth day of the death, the persons who had come to condole the bereaved family are given a farewell. On this day, tea and *halwa*, or just *halwa* and one loaf of bread is offered to each person as a token of the bereaved family's gratitude for sharing grief. The fortieth day is observed as the final farewell day. After burying the dead, a slab is placed on the grave, occasionally with an inscription giving the name and the date of death. They do not have any exclusive graveyard and can make use of the community graveyard. But some portion of the graveyard is identified where their ancestors and other members lie buried.

Land is the main economic resource. Historically, the Botrajas are a landless community but, with the passage of time, they acquired some land though agriculture never became the mainstay of their economic life. They have taken up government, military and police services as their main economic activity though a small number of them carry out a very modest business. The community's households are clustered in one locality with small terraced patches on which they have built their modest houses from stone, brick and mud overlooking the fields and pasture along the foothill. No member of the community has adopted any craft or handicraft as occupation. Their womenfolk do not assist their male partners in earning a livelihood or in supplementing the income of the family. The women remain at home to perform housework. People below the age of 25 are generally literate. The community has no labour orientation and the question of child labour does not arise. Some of the patches of land acquired by them either through purchase or through allotment have almost slipped out of their hands as a result of new agrarian reforms and also because they are incapable of tilling the land themselves. Some well-educated members are holding gazetted posts in the state government.

Disputes are resolved through the intervention of elderly persons of the community. They do not move to any court of law to settle a dispute that might have arisen within the group. They meet at the residence of the eldest member (at present Raja Ayyub Khan) to discuss the problems and deliberate upon the ways and means of resolving the issues of vital communal importance. The advice of the elders carries much weight and is not ignored or violated. The women have only a passive role to play in the deliberations over social issues. Corrective, not punitive, measures are taken against a defaulter. This policy has always had good results. While taking decisions on vital social issues, the local conditions, reactions and viewpoints are not overlooked. This shows that there is a healthy understanding of the local environment and adaptability for assimilation in the mainstream without, of course, loosing their identity entirely. In broader matters, they are guided by the local sectarian decisions which means the decisions of the Shia community of Kashmir.

The Botrajas profess the Islamic religion of Shia faith and the Ithna Ashra (Sect of Twelve). In religious matters, they have identified themselves with the Shia community of Kashmir. They participate in the Muharram *tazias* (mournings), birth and death functions of the holy *imams*. Id-ul-Fitr and Id-e-Ghadir are the two festivals observed in a year beside Nauroz, the New Year's day corresponding to 21 March, the day of the vernal equinox. The sacred specialists or the *mulla* (*mujtahid*) who performs religious rites is from among the Shia *ulema* of Kashmir. The community has been showing deep veneration for the late Agha Sahib of Badgam, as the pontiff of the Shia community in Kashmir. Senior members of the community closely follow the development in the Islamic Republic of Iran, the homeland of Shiism. The late Ayotollah Khomeini, was considered to be the chief Shia figurehead of the time. The community has been feeling somewhat cut off from various socio-religious movement the Subcontinent or the Muslim world during the past one century. The community attaches great importance to a decree issued on important religious matters by the chief Shia ecclesiastical authority—the *mujtahid*. For instance, in the case of family planning, the decree of a *mujtahid* is the final word. But with all this, the community is not insular and is open to interaction with other communities. Nor does it ferment aggrandizement against any other community. It is difficult to comment on the possible changes in their religious behaviour because it is a migratory group having lost all contact with the indigenous people of Nagar from where they came.

Perhaps political and religious considerations could be the reason for that phenomenon. They have not adopted any craft either as a hobby or as a profession. They have the folk songs and oral tradition but these refer to their indigenous group and homeland far away from Kashmir.

They accept both cooked and uncooked food from other Muslim communities including the Sunnis. They participate and attend all social functions and festivals of the Muslim communities if invited. They even lend a helping hand in various social functions, marriage, death, etc. The question of not accepting water from the same tap does not arise. However, they would refrain from eating with the Chamars (sweepers, cobblers, and scavengers). In the matter of matrimonial alliances, they remain confined to the Shia community only. They share the civic facilities like water, electricity, education, medicare, means of communication and burial places, etc., with the local Muslims and the community as a whole. They receive the services of the barber, washerman, cobbler, waterman, electrician, etc., from the local Muslim community.

Economic necessities have helped develop a sense of corporate living among this group. Cooperation in business matters, in alleviating social problems, securing more civic facilities and improving environmental ecology is readily forthcoming from the members of the community They do not look at the common problems from any subjective or sectarian and factional angle but identify their own interests with the interests of the entire population in the locality.

Literacy in the younger generation (below 24) is almost 100 per cent. There is absolutely no discrimination in admission to educational, professional or technical institutions. For healthcare, they benefit from the government health service as all other citizens do. Discrimination in this regard does not exist. In family planning, they are not hardliners. Employment under the rural programme is not relevant to them and self-employment is on a very limited scale. The community benefits from the works of public utility like water, electricity, communication, roads, etc. They are provided ration from the food and supplies department as are other people provided in the town. They make use of the banking facilities as they like. However, they are not too enterprising to come out of their shells and roam about in the wide world to widen the circle of their activity. Their attitude towards the development programmes is very positive and the level of their economic strength has slightly risen. The standard of living has also improved slightly and more and more amenities and gadgets find way into their houses. It is a landless community depending entirely on service, whether with the government or private sector.

The community is fast assimilating in the major cultural mainstream of Kashmir. It is possible that they may lose their identity except their dialect in the next fifty years or so because of the deep and rapid inroads made by the modern lifestyles. The Botrajas are getting exposed to the new pressures of scientific and technological age, literacy is on the increase and younger people are aspiring, and rightly so, for lucrative and respectable professions—doctors, engineers, professors, etc. However, they pay scant attention to literary tastes and tradition. Likewise, they are not interested in arts, crafts and aesthetics which go in the making of wholesome life. They are dragged by the imperatives of modern life but do not try to ride the tide to mould it to their own requirements. Some of the older people still hold on tenaciously to their conservatism but not without marvelling at the new horizons which modern science and technology unfolds.

K.N. Pandita

BROQPA

The Broqpa are the Muslim Dards who trace their ancestory from the Aryans. Broqpa is a compound of two terms *broq* (hills) and *pa* (people), hence 'the hill dwellers'. They call themselves Shin while neighbours call them Broqpa.

The Broqpas perceive their distribution in the villages in Kargil and Suru vallies. Their habitat Kargil (*kar* = white, *geil* = curves) suggests a chain of mountains completely devoid of all forms of vegetation excepting sparsely scattered bushes of juniper. The rainfall is accompanied by heavy snowfall. The climate is generally dry in summer but arctic in winter when mercury touches -17^0 C at Dras. They speak Shina amongst themselves but converse in Balti or Bodhi or Urdu with others. They use Balti script for writing. Educated Broqpas have attained a good knowledge of Arabic and Persian. Men do not show any symbol of identity but women can be distinguished by the traditional Dard caps adorned with typical ornaments and flowers grown in their own kitchen gardens.

The Broqpa are included among the Scheduled Tribes in Jammu & Kashmir. They are non-vegetarians and eat yak meet. Fish is not consumed but eggs are consumed moderately. *Grim* (baked barley) and *kachi* (flour of parched *grim*) is the staple diet and mutton and leafy vegetables constitute side dishes. Rice is consumed only occasionally. Millets like *gangni* and *turumba* are cultivated. Turnips grow abundantly. The tuber is peeled, cut into pieces, boiled, dried and powdered, and the powder is mixed with millet flour to sweaten the bread. Locally available fruits such as apricots and apples are consumed in plenty. Alcoholic drinks including the home-made *chang* fall under a blanket ban. Cha (tea) is their main drink. Lipton *cha* (sweetened tea) is offered to the guests. *Qahwa* (black tea, garnished with saffron and almonds) is a very special drink prepared on festive occasions.

A liking for rice is a recent phenomenon and milk and milk products are consumed. Smoking of cigarettes and use of snuff are common among them.

The people are divided into a number of *gatti* (lineages) such as Aibakeh (the descendants of Aibak), Koleh (the descendants of Quli), Jalalbekeh (Jalal Beg), Adule, Shatusingye, Dusre, Goreh, Nurialeh, etc. Each *gatti* is composed of various *khandan* (families). There is no hierarchy among the various *gattis*. It is traditionally an endogamous unit but, due to non-availability of suitable matches, intra-*gatti* marriages often take place. The members of a *gatti* live closer and cooperate in the socio-economic pursuits. A *gatti* owns agricultural land and parcels it out to the constituent households.

The people are stratified into a number of groups in order of hierarchy such as Sheikh (priestly class), Raj Rom (ruling class), Shin (peasantry) and Dom (artisan class). Another dimension of their division is the sect denomination. The Broqpa belong to both Shia (*Ethna-e-Ashari*) and Sunni and refuse to enter into matrimonial alliances with one another.

Consanguinity is allowed but a marital alliance with mother's sister's daughter is not allowed. Other prohibited categories of kin for the purposes of matrimonial alliances are: (a) siblings of a common parent, (b) children of a wet nurse and (c) non-Muslims.

The marriageable age for boys is 20 to 25 years and for girls 17 to 19 years. Early marriages are not practised. The amount of *mahr* (dower), usually between Rs. 5,000 and Rs.10,000, is payable by the bridegroom to the bride on demand.

Mutah, or temporary marriage contract, is the predominant form of marriage. The other prevalent form of marriage is *nikah-e-daimi* (permanent marriage contract) which comprises a fixed amount of *mahr* and bestowes the right to inherit one another's property. Marriages are accompanied by elaborate formalities of hosting feasts alternately by both the parties.

The Broqpa are patrilocal and the bride goes to live in her husband's house. Only men have the right to divorce. In the event of the wife being the complainant, the husband is bound to pay the amount of *mahr* in cash. In case a woman wishes to seek *khula* (separation), she is supposed to exempt her husband from payment of *mahr* and responsibility of her maintenance. Remarriage of widow, widower or divorcee is governed by the Islamic (Shia) rules. Economic resurgence in post-Independence period has discredited some of the old practices.

Broqpa is a male dominated patrilineal community in which the majority of families are extended, more vertically than laterally. Nuclear families too are noticeable but their formation is a recent phenomenon.

All activities within family are controlled by its head who allots specific duties to the members. The children show their parents due respect, obedience and love, and the old are treated with sympathy. No semblence of joking or avoidance can be noticed in their kinship behaviour. Teknonymy, however, is observed rigidly.

Male equigeniture is the rule of inheritance. Sons inherit two-thirds of the property of the deceased father and daughters inherit one-third. If the number of sons or daughters is more than one, the property is equally divided amongst them in the ratio stated earlier. Girls, however, do not claim their share in the property. In the absence of a male issue, the female issue inherits her deceased father's property. Succession runs in the male line from father to son.

A *gatti* owns agricultural land and divide the produce amongst the constituent families. Before the harvesting of the first millet crop, a festival known as Nazari, in which each family in the village used to sacrifice sheep in the past, is still observed. This practice has been shortened now. Nuclear families are replacing joint families; interpersonal relations, rules of inheritance and succession remain unchanged, and interfamilial linkages continue to be strong.

Women participate actively in fuel collection, agricultural operations and ritual performance. The high status of women is reflected in the high amount of *mahr* that they demand. In marriage, the bride goes in a procession to marry her spouse. Of late, girls are showing a keen interest in going to primary schools.

A newborn child is given a bath in lukewarm water. The *sheikh* or *akhun* recites *azaan* in both the ears of the neonate. The parturient mother receives a bath on the seventh day which is also a day of feasting. Naming ceremony is followed by a final purification bath for the mother on the fortieth day of delivery whereafter she resumes normal activites of life.

The dead receives burial in accordance with the Muslim practice of *ghusl-e-maiyat* (bath), *namaz-e-janaza* (prayers) and recitations from the Holy Koran.

The traditional economy having received a setback, land emerged as the main economic resource. The Broqpa by and large own lands which remain under the proprietorsip of the *gatti*. The *kuhl* (canals) supply water for irrigation. Wage labour is the subsidiary means of their livelihood. The nearby market at Kargil is fully regulated. All purchases are made in cash. There is no child and bonded labour in the community.

The ending of trade and poor agricultural yield in a hostile climate has compelled the Broqpa to come out seeking job avenues in the plains as the succour provided by army was of a temporary nature and the job avenues with the army dried up soon. There has, however, been an increase in self-employment activities like running small shops, hotels or plying taxis.

The *bari adalat* (court of elders) or the village council is responsible for maintaing social control. It is headed by a village chief called *nambardar* who is assisted by the *wazirs*, *motbars* and *kotwars*. Statutory village panchayats have not been able to make any breakthrough or involve people in decision making processes. The people have participated in a number of elections since Independence and show a high level of political awareness.

The Broqpa are Shiites who observe religious duties. The main sacred centres are Karbala, Najaf-Ashraf, Jannat-ul-Baqi, Samra, Kazmain, Mecca, Madina, Qum and Mashhad.

The sacred specialists are *sheikhs* and *akhuns* who undertake performance of religious rites of the community members. Some of them give *taviz* (charms) to cure ailments. Id-ul-Fitr, Id-ul-Zuha, Moharram, birth and death anniversaries of Prophet Muhammad, members of his family known as *ahl-e-bait* and descendants are the main festivals.

Converted from Buddhism to Islam, the Broqpa have retained some cultural traits of the pre-conversion period. The Broqpa *gattis* such as Tseringialeh (descendants of Tsering Ali) Doodeh (of Doodu), etc., show a transitional phase standing at the crossroads of Buddhism and Islam. Likewise, the presentation of leavened breads in birth, marriage and death ceremonies is reminiscent of the Bont fertility cult.

The Broqpas had a rich oral tradition of folk songs in the past depicting their migration from Chillas and Gilgit to their present habitat.

They live in proximity to the Baltis, Doms and Ladakhi Bodhs. They do not accept cooked (wet) food from the Bodhs but the latter accept it from them. Sharing of food with the Doms, who are also Shia Muslims, and Baltis is permissible. The Broqpa have matrimonial alliances with the Doms and Baltis but not with the Bodhs unless the latter are converted to Islam. In places where the Muslim Broqpas are outnumbered by the Buddhists, the spouses stick to their respective faiths. The sons follow their father's faith and the daughters their mother's. Interdining in such cases is also allowed between the Broqpas and the Bodhs in a peculiar manner. The Muslims opt for the *halal* meat whereas the Buddhist, averse to bloodshed, prefer to consume the meat of an asphyxiated sheep or yak. The *halal* pieces of meat are tied with a thread for identification and are cooked with the meat of an asphyxiated yak sheep. While sharing, the followers of both the faiths separate the meat chunks of their preference. Putative kinship terms like *mulai* (daughter), *dado* (father's father), *momo* (mother's brother) are used only in the classificatory sense.

Water for drinking is obtained from flowing canals and this is shared by all. Supply of water for irrigational purpose is regularized. Graveyards are *gatti*-oriented. There is no restriction in sharing the places of worship with other Muslim communities. The community benefits from the medicare facility extended by the military organizations in the area. Interaction with the army is carried on harmoniously. People are getting interested in politics.

The Broqpa attitude towards the various development programmes initiated by the state government is positive and their response is quite enthusiastic. They take full advantage of the medical facilities being provided by the primary health centres located in their villages. Very few of them have been able to make use of the self-employment programmes mainly for geo-climatic reasons. Some of them, however, are engaged in self-employment schemes such as running petty shops for consumer items or tailoring shops. Radio is the only source of communication. Electricity is not available in the Broqpa villages. They use bushes, wood and kerosene oil as fuel. Chemical fertilizers are not used and nutrition programmes are absent. The public distribution system is availed of and the people get rations and fuel from the fair price shops.

BAQAR R. RIZVI

CHAMPA

The Champa or Changpa inhabit the frozen northern plains and deserts that separate Ladakh from Tibet. Their past is shrouded in mystery. They used to operate between Lhasa and Nyoma with their herds and *reboos* (conical yak-skin tents). Now they move from Hanley to the farthest Lato village. Hanley Valley in which their six habitats are situated is extremly cold and ravaged by snowstorms. No population figures are available. They speak Changskhat amongst themselves but converse in Bodhi with others. Their script is Bodhi. They are distinguishable by their *reboos* and self-tailored dresses of hide and wool. They are categorized as a Scheduled Tribe. They are non-vegetarians and eat yak, *kiang* (wild assess) and beef. The staple food is *tsampa* (powdered barley), meat of yak and *kiang*. Dried cheese (*chura*) and meat are consumed by them. *Chang* is the main beverege but the daily drink is salted tea (*cha*).

The Champas are divided into two subgroups: the Fangpa (sedentary) and the Phalpa (nomadic). The ruling aristocracy among them is known as Nono. The stratification is based purely on the level of economy and achieved status. Intermarriages among the three segments do take place without any reservations. The community's self-perception of its status is low.

The rules do not allow cross-cousin marriages. Parallel cousin marriages, however, are allowed after a lapse of five generations. Sororate, both senior and junior, are practised but levirate has not been reported. Polyandry is permissible but has fallen out of practice and tendency is towards monogamy. Boys marry at the age of 18 years and girls at 16. No marriage symbols were reported. *Bakhstan* (negotiated form of marriage) is the main mode, though marriage by exchange is not absent. No bride-price is given by the husband barring the items of jewellery. Residence is patrilocal after marriage. Divorce may be sought by either party on grounds of wife's incompetence and her sour relations with the in-laws. Remarriage of male and female divorcees, widows and widowers is allowed.

Relations within the family members are characterized by informality and an amount of ease though, at times, disputes on reallocation of family resources give rise to tension and conflicts culminating in the breakup of a joint family. Mutual borrowings, assistance and corporate labour characterize interfamilial ties. The occurrence of joking relationships among the family members and avoidance among some specified relations like father-in-law and daughter-in-law are non-existent. Women have the right to inherit parent's property to the extent of one-third portion. They are actively engaged in the economic pursuits of the family.

A parturient mother is helped in delivery by elderly ladies besides her own mother. The lama performs the purificatory worship after a week and a *zataq* (horoscope) for the child is prepared. The *radaq* (tonsuring ceremony) is performed after three years. Marriage is preceded by *taq-kuk* (engagement). The lama performs the marriage rituals at the bridegroom's residence. After the birth of the first child, the couple erect their own *reboo.* The wife's parents present to the couple the former's share of property once they start living independently. When a Champa dies, the lama and close relatives are summoned to give the dead a bath and wrap the dead body in a shroud. The body is interred for a week before final disposal, enabling kith and kin of the deceased to come and pay their last homage to the departed soul. Thereafter the lama prescribes the appropriate mode of disposal of the dead body. The personal belongings of the deceased are given to the lama. Last death rites take place after three months and the lama performs them.

The Champas' major economic resources are their herds of yaks and goats. The former is the beast of burden and the latter is the sole suppliers of the earnings in terms of the world-famous pashm or *pashmina* wool which they sell to the government-run cooperative societies. The people do not have their own landholdings but live on lands owned by the Hemis Gompa. There are no markets in the vicinity. They, therefore, depend for their economic transactions on the vendors or visitors from Changthang Nyoma, where markets are fully regulated. There are neither bonded labourers nor child labourers among them. The people feel economically better off with the opening of a network of cooperative societies which pay them a handsome amount for the *pashmina* wool. Often, they sell goats to the butchers or visitors to their settlements against cash payments.

Goba is the traditional forum for dispute management. The statutory gram panchayats have not been able to penetrate in this inhospitable tract. *Goba* is slowly losing its hold over the people in the process of emergence of regulated courts of law.

They belong to the Drokpa sect of Buddhism. Religion occupies a central place in their cultural matrix. Each *reboo* invariably accommodates the family deity Donaq, and a picture of their spiritual head, His Holiness the Dalai Lama. The family deity is worshipped on the fifteenth day of the seventh Buddhist month. Hemis and Dharamshala are their places of pilgrimage. Chakman Paldon Lhamo is worshipped for protection against epidemics ravaging human and animal populations. Losar and Kunchyut Gastor are the other major festivals. Yebro folk dances are performed by the girls during Losar and other festivals. These songs are sung in honour of the pre-Buddhist Bon deity Keysar Gyalpon Gyalshung. Bon heritage, therefore, is quite visible in the Champa religion. No changes were reported in religious practices. The Champas possess no faculty either for arts or crafts. Folk dances and songs are, however, a part of the culture.

There is hardly any concept of commensal taboos as there is no other community in the Champa's neighbourhood. Even marriages are performed with the other Buddhists in case no suitable spouse is found in their own community. Putative kinship unions were not reported. They are the sole users of drinking water from the Shashil glaciers. They are not in contact with any other community in terms of jajmani relations. Their participation in political activities is minimal. Of late, the sedentary Champas have come in contact with the Tibetan settlers and some of their children attend the schools run by the Tibetan missionaries at Changthang Nyoma.

The Champas' attitude towards education is positive. No sources of drinking water have been developed and no schemes for their employment have been taken up. They live in absolute isolation so far as media of communication are concerned. Electricity is a remote dream for them. Yak dung, *kiang* (wild horses) droppings and bushes grown along the banks of Indus are the only source of fuel they use. Schools are lacking and so are nutritional programmes for their women and children. Ration supply through fair price shops and banking facilities are a far-fetched dream for them. The Champas live in absolute isolation and time seems to have frozen in this vast tract. They live far away from the developmental activities. The diseased are left to die a slow and painful but natural death due to want of medical facilities. Many bright young girls pass the rest of their lives in squalid nunneries as *chomos*. In short, the Champas live far away from the horizon of modernity and development.

BAQAR R. RIZVI

CHARAK

The word Charak is derived from the Hindi word '*charhava*', i.e. offering male to the deity. Legend has it that a Rajput ruler named Gangadhar who ruled around the eighth-ninth century was childless. Consequently, he visited a number of religious places, *pirs* and *faqirs* craving for a child. He was visited by the goddess Kalika Devi in a dream, who granted him the wish of being blessed with sons, the eldest of whom he would have to offer as a sacrifice to her. The dream came true as the king was blessed with two sons. The king brought his eldest son named Sozaldhar to the temple of the goddess Kalika Devi for sacrifice. However, the temple priest prevented the king from sacrificing his eldest son by quoting verses from *Manusmriti* wherein it was stated that the human sacrifice could be avoided by offering the child to a priest. It implied that a human sacrifice could be substituted by donating the child to the priest without actually sacrificing it. Thus, Sozaldhar was offered to the temple priest and came to be known as Charak or Chadak, i.e. the 'offered one'. Subsequently, Sozaldhar established his kindgdom across Bahu fort on the right side of the river Tawi in Jammu region to Sialkot. Those Rajputs who subsquently became the progeny of Sozaldhar came to be known as Charaks. It may also be stated that the clan of the ruler Sozaldhar were known as Jamwals prior to the name of Charak getting prefixed to it.

Since the Charaks of Jammu belong to Rajput lineage, they recall their migration first from Rajputana and then from the valley of Kangra in Himachal Pradesh. But they have settled in the region of Jammu for quite some time. It is, therefore, evident that their migration to the present habitat took place nearly 200 years ago or more.

The Charaks perceive their distribution at a trans-regional level and have a very high self-perception. Other communities also hold them in high esteem. The Charaks are spread in the districts of Doda, Udhampur, Jammu and Kathua. The main regions of their concentrations are Kishtwar, Bhadarwah, Jammu and its adjoining areas. The place of their present habitat records heavy rainfall and non-humid climate. They speak fluent Kishtwari, the native language, besides Dogri, the local language of Jammu region. They also speak English and Urdu among their own folk as well as with others. They communicate in Hindi, Urdu and English with their kinfolk and with others too. However, the majority of them mostly communicate in Hindi and Urdu. Their dress pattern matches the typical Dogri style prevalent in the region. Those who live in urban agglomerations wear modern attire as found in other cities of the country.

The Charak are non-vegetarians. Their staple food is rice and wheat. They consume all types of pulses. Mustard oil is the cooking medium. Their menfolk are reported to consume alcholic drinks besides all types of beverages. Milk and milk products are used in plenty. They smoke cigarettes and *hookah* (hubble-bubble). Fruits are consumed moderately. No changes in food habits were recorded but it is observed that the quality and quantity of consumption pattern is related to the economic conditions of the people.

Social differentiation appears to exist on the basis of economic and social criteria. The Samwals and Katochs are regarded to be at the top of the hierarchy in the Rajput lineage. Most of the marriages are solicited within the broader Rajput clan at the community level. Exogamy exists at the community level. Junior sororate is permissible. Child marriage is no longer in vogue. The age for marriage of the boys and the girls is both over 22 years. Mates are acquired through friends, relatives and *nayees* (marriage-brokers). Monogamy is the prevailing form of marriage. Dowry is paid both in cash and kind. Patrilocal is the rule of residence after marriage. Divorce is permissible with religious and judicial approval. The reasons for divorce are mainly maladjustment, insanity and, to a lesser extent, adultery. Compensation and maintenence is paid to the wife. Children are the responsibility of both the mother and father depending upon the circumstances of the case. Widow, widower and divorcee remarriage is permissible. Junior sororate is allowed, but levirate is not reported among them.

Families are both extended as well as nuclear, the latter being a common feature of urban city life. Avoidence and joking relationships are prevalent among the in-law relations. Elders are paid due respect and regards. Interfamily relations are quite cordial. No conflicts or confrontations occur in interfamilial kin bonds except for property disputes. The parental property is shared equally by the male issues, while female heirs' share is considered to be paid in the form of dowry. Girls are, however, entitled to a share in the parental property though they never demand it. Succession goes to the eldest male issue. Extended families are being slowly replaced by nuclear families.

The Charak women play a significant role in the overall socio-economic-cum-religious spheres of their life. In rural areas, the women actively participate in farm-related activities along with animal husbandary work. In urban centres, they contribute directly to the household income.

Pre-delivery restrictions are imposed on the parturient mother. Her movements are restricted. Post-delivery pollution is observed by them. After twelve days, a ritual known as *surya-darshan* is performed. Naming ceremony is observed, but not in a formal manner. *Mundan* and *janeu* (sacred thread) ceremonies are held for the boys. Marriage rituals are performed at the bride's residence. *Barat*, i.e. groom riding a horse and holding a ceremonial sword, accompanied by a number of guests proceed to the bride's residence for the *lagan* ceremony, after sunset. A feast is given by both the parties. Nuptial rituals are performed at the husband's house. The bride and the groom perform *rakady* (circling around the clan deity) four times.

The dead are cremated after a ceremonial bath. The body is carried to the cremation ground by the relatives and friends. The male heir lights the pyre. The death pollution is observed among them. The *rasam-pagri* ceremony, in which the male family members wear a rouge or pink ceremonial headgear called *dastar*, is held on the fourth day after cremation and it also marks the termination of pollution. Annual *shradh*, i.e. yearly ritual for the dead, is not a common feature though *choubarsi* (fourth year ceremony after death) is also observed among them.

The Charaks are a landowing community in the rural areas. Occupations pursued by them are government service, defence and police service, and self-employment such as business, retail trade, etc. Professor S.D. Charak is a renowned researcher and scholar of repute in the region, who has extensively written on the history and culture of the Jammu region in specific and on the Himalayan belt in general.

The Charak's link with the market exists directly and most of the transactions are in cash. In rural areas, barter system still exists. Neither child labour nor bonded labour exists among them. Priests are drawn from the Brahmanical fold of the region. These priests conduct all their socio-religious ceremonies and rites. Disputes pertaining to property, familial feuds and marriage may initially be reported to the Rajput Sabha, failing which recourse to judicial process may be taken.

The Charaks have a place in the overall Rajput hierarchy. They regularly visit their principal clan deities besides the regional ones like Vaishno Devi, Amarnath, Sarthal Devi, etc. They also visit *pirs* and *faqir*, irrespective of religious affiliations. The community has not witnessed any major change or shift in its socio-religious practices though urbanization has had its impact on the city dewellers. They do not excel in commercial arts and crafts. However, their females have an inborn talent for amateur painting, poetry and cloth embroidery. They possess a rich tradition of folklore and folk tales. Music and dance are enjoyed and performed by either sex, especially on wedding and birth ceremonies. Their clan deity is the goddess Kali. The Charaks accept water and food from all other co-religionists and may accept and exchange *kachcha* food only with the non-Hindus. Interdining among the urban dwellers with other communities is quite common. Marriages are essentially solicited and preferred among their own community members. However, some may be solemnized with other high-caste Hindus as well. A sizeable number of them are administrators, doctors, engineers, scholars, teachers and persons holding white-collar jobs. Political leadership among them does not exist at the regional or national level.

Pursuit of education is encouraged for their boys and girls, without any special preference for either sex. Their male and female usually study up to college level and few of them even beyond that. Economic constraint is the main reason for dropping out of studies. Their attitude towards family planning is positive. They make regular use of modern and traditional medicare. They avail of birth control techniques and sterilization is usually performed on their females. Drinking water is available through tap water supply in urban areas whereas, in rural areas, the same is obtained from natural springs, dug wells and streams. Rural employment is not available to them on a large scale. They are, however, engaged in trade, commerce, business and a few industrial units. They are exposed to all the media of communication, namely radio, newspaper, television and cinema. Roads and post-offices are situated within their easy reach. Railway services are available in Jammu city. They use electricity, wood, kerosene oil, LPG, etc. The attitude towards savings and investment is quite positive and banking-cum-loan facilities are availed by them.

ASHOK AIMA

CHARJI

The Charjis of Jammu & Kashmir call themselves Acharyas while others call them Charjis. The Charji have no other names. In Jammu region, the Charji officiates at the death ceremony. The word 'charji' has been derived from the Sanskrit word *acharya*.

In ancient times, the Charjis were teachers who used to teach students free of charge. People used to give them donations. In this way, the Acharyas were not only able to fulfil their necessities but were also able to bear all the expenses of the pupils such as food, clothing, etc. It was obligatory for the pupils to obey their Acharyas and serve them. Those teaching institutions were at a distance from the place of habitations. According to Dewan Chand Charji of Gura Slithia, the Acharyas led a life of celibacy and treated their pupils as their own sons.

So far as intelligence is concerned, the Charjis were surely endowed with this quality. But with the passage of time, their educational and moral standards deteriorated. They became indolent and lethargic. The degeneration of these Acharyas helped create a new class of intellectuals among the Brahmans who replaced them with the lapse of time . This class came to be known as Upadhyay. They charged fee in cash. In comparison to the Acharyas, the Upadhyays proved themselves to be more intelligent. So people preferred to send their children to them.

Consequently, the monetary condition of the Acharyas weakened. Owing to their weak financial condition they had to adopt the inferior work of officiating at the death ceremony, because auspicious ceremonies such as *jatkarm*, *mundan* and *vivah-sanskar* were already the domain of the Brahmans who were called *pant*, pandit, *purohit*, etc.

The question came up as to who is going to officiate at the death ceremonies? The Charjis remain silent on this question. But up to the time of events in the *Ramayana*, no community like Charji existed. When king Dashratha died, his death ceremony was officiated by his *kul-gurus* Vashishta and Vamdev, and *antdan* was distributed among the Brahmans. There was no special class of Brahmans existing at that time who accepted *dan* of this kind.

The Charjis claim to be the descendants of Dronacharya. According to a myth, once a meeting of the seers was held wherein the question as to who should be given the *antdan* was discussed. Nobody was found competent enough to digest it. Finally, it was decided that a horse should be set free, the person at whose door it would stand, would be entitled to the *antdan*. As it happened, the horse stood before Dronacharya's cottage. In this way, he was found qualified to accept *dan*. However, the veracity of this cannot be verified.

Nowadays, the Charjis' self-perception is low. The community, as it appears from their habitation, feels ashamed of revealing their Charji identity. The members of the community, out of an inferiority complex, call themselves Acharya. There has been a change in their surnames. Now they use Sharma as their surnames. But professional and aged Charjis have no such inferiority complex. They call themselves Maha-Brahman, Maha-Pandit and Maha-Patra. In the justification of the above titles, they say that *antdan* is so vigorous that it cannot be digested easily. Only Sudh and Prabudh Acharyas have, power to accept and digest this type of *dan*. This is the reason why the people of this community are religious-minded and pious. They boast: 'Good ceremonies are performed by many Brahmans but the death ceremony, which is the most important ceremony of life, is officiated only by us. We convert the ghost of the dead into their ancestors.'

The perception of the Charjis by other communities is very low. Other communities do not accept any eatables, cooked or uncooked, from them, because they accept the *antdan*, the *dan* of the death pollution days.

Other communities believe that the Charjis place their cots in an inverted position in front of their own doors because by doing so the Charji expect some one would certainly die and they would earn their livelihood.

There is no doubt that a Charji is a very important person at the time of death, but the people of other communities dislike him. Some thirty years ago, they were considered inauspicious in the society. In normal times, other communities did not allow a Charji to enter their houses because they conduct the death ceremonies. According to other communities, the Charjis are not the original inhabitants of Jammu. They have migrated from Vrindaban, Punjab and Himachal Pradesh years ago. Generally male members of the community speak Dogri but their ladies speak Punjabi. This is so because they marry girls from Punjab and sometimes from Himachal Pradesh. The Charji use Devanagari script in their profession but the educated amongst them use both Devanagari and Roman scripts in writing, and Hindi and

English in speaking. Among themselves their language is neither pure Dogri nor Punjabi. With other communities they converse in Dogri and Hindi.

The terrain of their habitat varies from the plains to the Kalindi (dry) plateau and low hills in the north. Weather varies from warm to temperate with moderate moisture.

The Charjis used to dress like other people of this region. In the past, old women used to wear tight trousers known as *suthan*, *kurta* and *chadar*. In the kitchen they used to wear *dhoti* or *giddi*. They wear earrings, *jhumke*. The men used to wear tight trousers known as *dogra ghatna* and *kurta*. They also used to wear turbans called *safa* or *pag*. Earrings known as *naintian* are worn by the males.

Originally, the Charjis were purely vegetarian, but nowadays they eat various types of meat, except beef. They eat eggs, fish, porks, chicken, goat, etc.; but they avoid cooking the meat in their own kitchens. Previously they were so pious that they did not take even onion, garlic, brinjal, tomato and *masur dal* and *til* (sesame). Onion and garlic sellers did not dare to come in the *mohalla* of the Charjis. Their ladies cook the meal wearing wet *giddi* (one-piece cloth like saree) and they do not come out of the kitchen until all the members of the family, especially the male members, have taken their meal. They wash the firewood with fresh water before using it as fuel in the kitchen.

Wheat, rice and maize form the staple food of the Charjis with occasional *bajra* and barley. They consume almost all varieties of pulses such as gram, *moong*, *kulth*, *rajmah*, *roungi*, peas, etc. At present, they use kerosene oil and gas for cooking. In the villages, they use wood and cow-dung cakes as fuel. The community uses plenty of fruits, vegetables, pulses and cereals because they receive these things from their patrons.

The Charjis have no restriction in using milk and milk products. They have plenty of milk also because they get cow and heifers from their *yajmans*. Nowadays the male members of the Charji habitually take alcoholic drinks, like country wine available in the market. They also smoke. But their women do not take intoxicating drinks.

About thirty years back the Charji women used to take meals once a day for a year after the demise of their kith and kin. Now it has been reduced to one month only; on the other hand, men observe dietary control for eleven days of death pollution, that is till the *kriya* ceremony. The eldest son of the deceased follows dietary restrictions and leads a life of strict purity for eleven days.

The Charjis share the *dan* with the Gujratis in order to provide the latter with some means of livelihood. It was decided that the *dan* given at the time of death, *masik dan* (monthly *dan*), *adh-barkhi* (half-yearly death ritual), *barkhi* (yearly death anniversary) would be taken by the Gujratis and, the *dan* from the first day to the last day of death ritual, would be taken by the Charji. Generally people call the Charji-Gujrati together.

The Charjis have two groups, Charji and Parcharji (Acharya and Upacharya). The Parcharjis are the *purohits* of the Charjis. The Charji have to give all types of *dan* to the Parcharjis and all the rituals of the Charjis are officiated by the Parcharjis. Now in Jammu region there is not a single family of the Parcharjis. There was a Parcharji family at Kangra in Himachal Pradesh who used to conduct the death rituals of the Charjis of Jammu. For the rituals of *pind chhedan sanskar* of the Charjis of Jammu services of the Parcharjis of Punjab and neighbouring areas are sought.

The Charjis are a backward community. But they feel themselves superior to the Vaishyas and Shudras. They dislike taking any *kachcha* or *pukka* food from the Scheduled Castes and Muslims. The Charjis have several *gotras* such as Kashyap, Bhargav, Vasisht, Atri, Koushal, Mudgal and Gautam. Apart from these *gotras*, they have sub-castes,which govern marital relations, like Churamani in Jasrota; Rattanpal in Chanaini; Gour, Tamnot and Jamwal in Udhampur and Katra; Mudgal in Basohli. Bilaloch have two groups: Khooni Bilaloch and Bilaloch. Bilaloch have *chinna* with Khooni Bilaloch. The reason for the *chhinna* is the curse of a Charji girl's ghost to one of her kins who got a rich compensation from a Muslim chief who was the cause of her suicide. She named him *bilalock* or murderer and bade the Charji to observe *chhinna* with his family and their descendants.

There are some surnames which indicate the place names such as Charprar (now in Pakistan), Ghagwalie, Hiranagarie, Marin, Khanoorie, Bhedhue, etc.

The Charjis are an endogamous group. Marital alliances are fixed by their elders. Previously in Jammu region they had very few castes in which they could marry. They had to face great difficulty in acquiring mates. So they had to marry in their own caste. But at the same time they avoid marrying in their own caste, in the same village, tahsil or district.

The Charji observe monogamy. Sororate and levirate are observed in some special cases. Marriages with cross-cousins are not allowed. Marriage is also prohibited with parallel cousins. Legally, sororate is not allowed even in the case of barrenness. There are some examples that show that the husband of a barren woman married a second woman with the consent of his first wife. But the second marriage is not legal, because Hindu Marriage Act does not permit a person to marry another woman while his first wife is alive.

Pre-puberty marriage was the earlier practice among the Charjis, but now the age of marriage is between 20 and 26 for girls and 25 and 30 for boys.

Bindi, *sindoor* and nose-pins are the marriage symbols. *Chura* indicates that the bride has not completed the first year of her marriage. Formerly, dowry among the Charjis was very nominal; but now they give all those things which other communities give. They give clothes in the form of dowry not only to their daughters and sons-in-law but also to maternal and paternal relatives of the bridegroom.

Legal divorce is permitted for adultery, maladjustment, impotency, cruelty and insanity. The law gives right of divorce both to the husband and wife. But the practice of divorce is not considered healthy by the community. The divorced man or woman is at liberty to marry another person. According to the Charjis, there has been no case of either divorce or remarriage till this time. The *dobri* or marriage by exchange and marriage by purchase were common in the past, but now such cases have become rare.

A married couple follows the patrilocal residence after the marriage.

Joint family was an early form among the Charjis. Nowadays, the most common form is the nuclear family. Only those who follow their traditional profession have joint families. Joint families are breaking up, mostly under the impact of modern economic stress.

Both sons and daughters among the Charjis have equal rights to the ancestral property. But generally the daughters do not like to exercise their rights because they dislike any confrontation with their brothers. When a daughter does not have a brother, she has the right to the property.

In the past, the Charji women enjoyed secondary status as compared to men because women were generally illiterate and financially dependent on their husbands, but nowadays they are enjoying equal status with their husbands. They participate in social, ritual and religious activities. In the past, they stitched clothes for others on payment, but now the Charji women are receiving higher education and are employed in government services.

Widow remarriage is permissible but the society dislikes it. Widower remarriage is very common.

They observe a pre-delivery ritual in the eighth month of pregnancy called *reetam*. Forty days of birth pollution is observed after delivery. On the fifth day, *panjale* ritual in case of male and *panjatarora* in case of female neonate is performed with the first bath to the child and the mother. On the eleventh day, the *sutra* ritual is performed with a bath given to both the mother and child. On this occasion, the parents of the woman send sweets, clothes, toys, etc., for the child.

The naming ceremony of the child (son) takes place on the same occasion. The paternal aunt gives the name to the child by speaking the name in his ear.

In the villages, the Charji conduct deliveries in their own homes but in cities the hospital facilities are availed of.

Mundan ceremony is observed in case of male children only in the third or fifth year of his age. Yellow coloured clothes are given to the mother and son by her maternal relatives. After the *mundan* ceremony, on the same day, a vegetarian feast is also given to all the kith and kin.

Among the Charjis, marriage by mutual consent is not very common. The marital alliances are fixed by the elders. After the negotiation between both the parties, parents of the bride fix an auspicious day on the suggestion of the *purohit* for *sagan*. *Sagan* is a formal ceremony in which dry fruit, silver *katoori*, golden *drub*, fruit and sweets are given to the bridgroom's relations. In this function, the elder brother of the bride performs the most important ritual of *tilak* ceremony to the bridegroom in the presence of relatives of both the parties. Family the members and other relatives of the bride give money to the bridegroom and his nearest relatives.

Nowadays a Punjabi tradition is also observed by the Charji which is called *chunni charhana*. In this ritual, *saree*, finger ring, sweets and money, usually Rs. 101, are given to the bride by the bridegroom's relatives. This function is arranged a few months before the marriage.

Nine, seven, five, three or one day before the marriage, *gandi* ceremony is observed in which the *purohit* binds a red thread around the wrist of the bride and the bridegroom separately in their own houses. After this ceremony, neither of them is permitted to move out of their houses till their marriage. But, with the change of time, this restriction is disappearing.

Formerly, marriage among the Charjis was a seven-day affair, but now it is celebrated within a day or two. The first ceremony is *shanti yajna* when *butana* or perfumed cosmetic cream, is applied on the whole body of the boy and girl at their respective houses and a bath is given to them. It is followed by a community feast. Then, on a fixed *mahurat*, the *barat* leaves for the bride's house where the rituals of marriage like *vedi* and *phera* are gone through with the help of the *purohit*. Before *vedi*, *milni* is held and sometimes the bride puts the *jaimala* (garland) around the groom's neck. The female members of the *barat* are also welcomed by the women of the bride's side. Then the *baratis* are treated in a feast and served lunch the following day before they are sent off along with the bride and her dowry articles amidst farewell songs and tears.

The duration of *anḍèrli* and *baharli* bed is of at least five hours. This ceremony starts late at night and ends early in the morning.

Few minutes before death, the person is laid down on the ground which is sanctified by sprinkling *Ganga-jal* (holy water), after which clay from the *tulsi* plant is placed where the dying person is to be lain. After this, Ganga water, *tulsi* leaves and *panjratni* are put in the mouth of the person who is on the verge of death. At the same time *diva batti* (lamp and wick), cereals, pulses and cash are also made to donate by the dying person. All these things and the money are given to a Gujrati. After this, the Parcharji or, on the non-availability of Parcharji, a relative of the Parcharji is called to officiate at the death ceremony.

In hilly areas where the Parcharji or his relative is not available, a Brahman officiates at the death ceremony but he does not take anything for it from them. Moreover he does not perform the *pind-chhedan sanskar*. *Pind-chhedan sanskar* is performed only by the Acharji or Charji whenever he is available. The death pollution continues till *pind-chhedan sanskar*.

The dead body is given a bath by the members of the family. New clothes are wrapped around the dead body. His or her hands and feet are also wrapped with white cloth and then one *shradh* ritual is conducted in the room. When the dead body is brought out of the room, a second *shradh* is conducted. Two more *shradhs* are also conducted on the way to the cremation ground called *ardhmarg shradhs*. They are performed only under the last banyan tree on the way to the cremation ground.

There is one ritual connected with this ceremony which is called *baltah bhanana* wherein an earthen pot is broken on the way under the banyan tree. Two *shradhs* are also conducted at the pyre.

The ritual *tinaka bhanana* signifies final severing of relations by the deceased with his kith and kin.

On the third day the ashes of the deceased are collected by the close relations and kept in a room at the *shamshan ghat* until they are immersed in the holy water of the Ganga. In villages, however, the ashes are preserved in the holes of banyan trees. On the tenth day, the maternal relatives of the widow give white *dupatta* and money called *bura* (bad luck) to the widow.

On the eleventh day, *kriya* ceremony is observed wherein water pot, cereals, cots, bedding, utensils, clothes and umbrella are also given to his relatives (in-laws of daughter) or to the Pracharji. But some poor people give only a few utensils, very cheap bedding, cloth and umbrellas. A very simple feast is given to some of the relatives. With the completion of *kriya*, the death pollution terminates. The members of the breaved family give meals to a Parcharji or his own community member daily which is called *nati*.

Like *kriya*, *adh-barkhi*, *barkhi* is also performed; relatives and neighbours offer fruit and sweets called *naved* in honour of the dead.

Previously the major source of income was officiating at the death ceremony. But nowadays, some of the Charjis are in business and government services. Even those who are performing their traditional job are als employed in government services. Majority of them have left their traditionl occupation for being educated and feel below their dignity to pursue their traditional profession. Only the elderly and uneducated people are pursuing their traditional occupation.

The Charjis are not a rich community.Their work starts with the occurance of death and ends with the ritual performance of *kriya*. From the first to the tenth day, the bereaved family members give them cereals, pulses, sweets, cloth and cash. On the last day of death pollution, that is *kriya*, people of other communities give them essential items such as cot, chappals, utensils, bedding, heifer, clothes used by males and females, umbrellas, fruits, sweets, vegetables, cereals, pulses, etc. Usually, the Charjis sell those surplus items to those who need them for the *kriya* ceremony.

Some members of the Charji are landowners but others are landless. They, however, do not cultivate because they do not know the techniques of agriculture. The land reforms in the state which bestow ownership of land to the tillers have made most of the Charjis landless.

At least 80 per cent of the Charjis are *hakims*, but they are not educated in the field. They have inherited the traditional medical knowledge from their forefathers. Their other source of income is through giving relief to the people from the effect of black magic.

The statutory village panchayats govern the usual community life of the Charjis. It imposes fines for civic crimes. But people generally settle their family conflicts through the elderly persons of the community. The cases of rape and adultery are generally not brought to the notice of the panchayat, but instead try to solve the cases mutually. Nowadays people generally do not care for the panchayat. They go directly to the court of law.

In case of intercaste marriage, the couple is excommunicated.

The Charjis profess Hindu religion. They worship Shiva, Krishna, Rama, Shakti (Vaishno Devi, Sarswati and Mahakali). Besides the regional and village deities, .they also worship their *kul-devis*. As a mark of respect, they do not disclose the names of their *kul-devis*. Sometimes they themselves do not know their names and call them Sajavati and Shilavanti. The Bilaloch Charji used to worship their *kul-devta* named Bawa Kalibeer.

The Charjis visit all those shrines and sacred centres such as Vaishno Devi, Bahu Fort (*Mahakali*) Mansar, Purmandal, Sivkohri, Sudh Mahadev, etc. They observe the fast on the occasions of Purnamashi, Ekadashi and Navratras. In addition they also observe fast on Ahoi, Karva Chauth, Krishna Janmashtami and on Sunday and Monday.

The oral traditions (folk songs, folklore and folk tales) still continues mainly through the elders. They sing folk songs in marriages. The elderly people narrate the folk tales to their children.

Some Charji women of Pirmitta Mohalla of Jammu city are expert in stitching clothes and weaving the waist belt.

In the past, the Charjis used to accept both cooked and uncooked food from other higher castes, but they refrain from eating from the hands of the Scheduled Castes and Muslims. Other higher communities dislike inviting the professional Charji on the auspicious ceremonies, like *sutra*, *mundan*, marriage, etc.

Now the educated people do not hesitate to eat together with others. They share water sources, roads, schools, etc., with other communities even with the lower castes. The Charjis refrain from officiating at the death ceremony of some Scheduled Castes. In case they have to officiate under compulsion, they do not accept anything in return.

The Charjis visit the religious shrines of the Hindus without any objection from higher societies. They also share the crematorium with the other Hindus.

The Charjis have scholars, administrators, doctors, teachers and clerks among them.

The children of the Charjis are getting education without any problem. Their attitude is positive towards modern medicare and they are fully making use of it. They show a favourable attitude towards family planning. Many of them have accepted it and have undergone sterilization after having three children. They have drinking water sources within their vicinity. They are availing the media and communication facilities. They are utilizing electricity for lighting their houses and other purposes.

ARCHNA KESAR

CHEINTZ

Locally known Cheintz are also called Sansi and Gularea. The community is ignorant about its origin. The Cheintz settled down in Kashmir after the Second World War, and live in Gopalpura, Karalpura and Bagimahatab where the climate of the area is cold, humidity is low to medium, rainfall and snowfall are medium during winter. They speak Dogri among themselves, speak in Hindi mixed with Dogri with outsiders and use Devanagari script for writing. The male wear *kameez* and *tambi. Munul*, a woollen trouser, replaces the cotton dress in winter season. The women wear *pyjamas* with narrow ankle openings, frock, *salwar* and sari. Their hairstyle is indistinguishable from the local people. The old pattern of dress is being gradually discarded. They are non-vegetarian and their staple food is rice and wheat; they take all types of pulses and vegetables grown locally. They use mustard oil as cooking medium. Their breakfast comprises salt tea and bread. They enjoy *hookah* and smoke *bidi* and cigarettes. Milk and milk products are also consumed by them. They also consume fruits grown locally.

Kul is the social division which regulates marriage alliances. There has been no change in *kul* names. Economic condition and educational attianment are the major criteria for social differentiation. They recognize the *varna* system and place themselves in the Kshatriya category but others treat them low due to their past occupation. They are an endogamous community but they maintain *kul* exogamy for marriage purposses. Child marriages were common among them but nowadays marriages are performed when the boys and girls become adults. Age at marriage for boys is between 18 and 25 years and for girls it is 16 and 20 years. Marriages are arranged by the parents or elderly relatives. Monogamy is the usual form of marriage. *Bindi* is the symbol of a married woman. *Kanyadan* is performed by the father or brother of the bride. Dowry is paid both in cash and kind. Divorce is permissible but it is rare. In case of adultery and maladjustment either party can divorce. Widow, widower and divorcee remarriages are permissible by the community. In case of divorce, children are the responsibility of the father. In case of remarriage, sororate and levirate are permissible. In case of widow or divorcee remarriage, *phere* ceremony is not performed: only *sindoor* and bangles are offered to the woman in a public place (*gharbasana*). Joint families are on the decline and instances of nuclear families are on the increase. Younger brother's wife avoids the husband's elder brothers. Joking relationship exists between the younger people. Property is equally divided among all the sons. Unmarried daughters also get their share from the paternal property. Brothers have to take the responsibility of their sisters' marriage. Succession pattern is followed in the male line. In an extended family, the eldest male member is responsible for the family management and family functions. Women play an active role in managing the family expenditures; they engage themselves in various economic activities; collect fuel and water and do other household work. They participate in social and religious activities but they do not play any role in political activities. Their status is lower than that of the male members.

Women observe some restrictions during pregnancy and birth of a baby. The first delivery generally takes place at her parents' house. At the time of delivery, services of a midwife or any other knowledgeable elderly woman are utilized. For this, the midwife is paid in cash and kind. After a baby is born, it is given a hot bath. On the sixth day, the baby and the mother take bath and a pandit is asked to prepare the *janam patri* (horoscope). They observe eleven days *haiz* (pollution) after the birth of a child. During this period, the mother is not allowed to worship or offer *puja*. On the eleventh day after taking bath, they perform a ceremony for naming the child. At the age of six month, the baby is given its first cereal in a ceremony. *Zerakasi* (tonsure) ceremony is observed for both the male and the female child.

Regarding marriage, a common friend or a relative makes the proposal when they get suitable information about the bride and bridegroom. In earlier days, they practised child marriage, which is now discarded. Relatives and friends initiate a matrimonial alliance. When agreed it is celebrated through a ceremony called *sagai* or *sagun* in which the bride's father sends a date for marriage along with sweets, clothings, cash and other articles. During *sagai*, some saffron is used for *tilak* on the forehead of the bridegroom. While the ceremony is in progress, the ladies sing in chorus offering their felicitations to the bride, bridegroom and their parents. All the guests attending the function are served meals. After *sagai*, the father of the bride calls on the family priest and decides an auspicious date and time for the marriage functions. The first day of the marriage for the would-be bride is known as *mehndi-raat*. On this day, the bride is anointed with *mehndi* and she is given a bath. The *barat* is received at the main entrance by the elderly relatives and friends of the family. When the ritual of *lagan* starts the bride and bridegroom take their seats close to each other on the *vedi.* The priest then starts to chant *mantras.* The bride and bridegroom go round the sacred fire, which is called *phera*, followed by the ritual of *kanyadan* and the marriage ceremony is over. On arrival of the bride and bridegroom to the latter's house, the bride is received by the mother and other elderly relatives of the groom's house. *Gauna* ceremony is observed nowadays at the same time. Marriage feast is given by both the parties.

The dead are cremated, and the dead infants are buried. When a person dies, the family members observe forty days' *haiz* (pollution). After placing the dead body on the pyre, the Charji prepares the *pindas* and, chanting *mantras*, throws them into the pyre. The eldest son of the deceased goes round the pyre and lights it after touching the fire with the mouth of the dead. No cooking is done in the house when a person dies till the cremation is over. Post-death ritual is held on the thirteenth day. Other rituals observed to commemorate the death include *adh-barkhi*, *barkhi*, *choubarkhi* and *shradhs.* They also worship ancestors during *pitra-paksha* and also at the time of *kriya*, *barsi* and *shradhs.* Nowadays the rituals are curtailed as they have become very expensive.

The Cheintz are landless people and wage labourers, and very few among them are engaged in the government and private services. They have direct links with the regulated daily market where all transactions are made in cash. Owing to various reasons, the number of daily-wage casual labourers has increased. All payments are made in cash.

Traditional caste council exists, but it has become less effective. Heterogeneous statutory panchayat came into existance after Independence and its role is to prepare plans and implement the welfare and development programmes.

The Cheintz are Hindu by religion but some of them have embraced Islam. The Cheintz worship Kali Mata, Durga Mata and Shivji. They visit religious shrines and observe festivals such as Baisakhi, Diwali, Janmashtami and Shivratri. Priests from other communities are engaged for worship and performance of life-cycle rituals. Those who have embraced Islam observe Muharram, Id-ul-Fitr, and Id-ul-Zuha. Local folk songs are sung by both the sexes.

Families assist each other at the time of need. Outside their own community their linkage with other communities varies according to the services rendered. The Cheintz accept water from the Brahmans, Kshatriyas, even Nais and Dhobis but do not accept water from the

Chamar, Dom, etc. No hard and fast norm of exchanging *kachcha* and *pukka* food with others are observed by the community members. They do not have connubial relation with other communities. They share water sources and cremation and burial grounds with other communities.

Formal education is partly favoured for the boys and girls. Owing to the economic and social pressures, the children drop out from their studies. Attitude towards indigenous medicare is positive. They visit the government hospitals and make use of the modern medicines. Family planning methods are accepted by them. They believe in small family norm and adopt various methods of family planning. Piped water facility is available to the community members. They avail themselves of the media and communication facilities available in the areas. For lighting, they use electricity. Cow-dung cakes, dry bushes and kerosene oil are used as fuel. Integrated Child Development Scheme and public distribution system facilities are availed of. They depend on shopkeepers and moneylenders due to non-availability of banking facilities.

D.K. Chakraborty

CHHAN

Chhans are the traditional Muslim carpenters of Kashmir Valley and are also known by the name Nayyar. Though their population figure is not available, they are distributed in almost all the districts of Kashmir. No historical and ethnographic accounts exist with regard to the origin and migration of the community. They claim to be the original inhabitants of the region. They inhabit cold climate with hilly terrain and valleys, experiencing medium rainfall and medium snowfall during the winter months. Kashmiri is spoken among themselves and with other Kashmiris. With the non-Kashmiris, they commonly speak Urdu. Arabic is the script used by them.

Rice is their staple food. Non-vegetarian items are consumed occasionally without, of course, beef and pork. Varieties of roots and tubers are commonly consumed as vegetables. Like most other Kashmiris, consumption of fruits among them is moderate. *Noon-chai* (tea with salt) and *qahwa* are the common non-alcoholic beverages for them. Adults smoke *hookah* and occasionally *bidis* or cigarettes.

Differentiation exist in terms of economic status. They do not subscribe to the idea of status or hierarchy. Their social position is equal to that of any other Muslim community of the region. Though marriage within the community is generally preferred, marriage with any Muslim of the Sunni sect is not a prohibition. Adult marriage is the common practice among them. Most of the marriages are generally settled through negotiation. Consanguinity prevails both at the cross-cousin and parallel cousin levels. Monogamy is the common form of marriage prevailing among them. Residence after marriage is generally patrilocal, wherein the bride comes to live with her husband and in-laws. *Mahr* (dower) amount is generally promised at the time of *nikah* or marriage for future payment, if *talaq* (divorce) is sought. The marital status of a person, male or female, is not symbolized by any marker. *Talaq* is generally a privilege of the husband, though the wife is permitted to seek separation with social approval. Adultery, barrenness and maladjustment are the common reasons for divorce. Divorce compensation is paid to the wife or her parents. The responsibility of maintenance of the children in divorce cases lies with the father. The divorcees, widows and widowers, are permitted to remarry. However, restriction or *iddat* is imposed on the female divorcees for remarriage under the Islamic rules. The period of restriction or *iddat* is imposed on them for at least three months and may be extended till the birth of the child in case the woman was pregnant at the time of divorce. Restriction is imposed to ascertain legitimacy of the expected child. Similarly, under the Islamic rules, *iddat* or restriction is also imposed on the widows wherein they are not permitted to remarry within a period of four months and ten days from the day of their widowhood. Preference is given to remarry the wife's younger sister or the husband's younger brother, as the case may be. Comparative increase in the age at marriage is the only change perceived in the institution of marriage.

Nuclear family, in general, is the predominant type followed by both vertically and horizontally extended families in varied proportions. Love and affection for the young and respect and obedience to the elders are the underlying principles determining interpersonal relationships within the family. Avoidance is maintained between the daughter-in-law and father-in-law and also between the husband's elder brother and the younger brother's wife. The relationship with elder brother's wife, wife's and husband's younger brothers and sisters and with the parents-in-law of sons and daughters is that of joking and friendliness. Paternal property is divided equally among the sons. Unmarried daughters get a share less than that of the sons. Succession is followed through the male line from father to the eldest son.

Besides performing major part of the routine household chores of the family, women participate in agricultural activities, animal husbandry, collection of fuel and bringing potable water. They also participate, directly or indirectly, in different economic activities and thereby contribute to the family income. They play an important role in various socio-religious spheres and equally exercise their authority in decision-making and control of expenditure at the level of family. In terms of the roles and functions mentioned above, and also by virtue of their claim and right in paternal property and *mahr*, women of the community are treated at par with men.

Immediately after a baby is born, a hot water bath and the ritual of *azaan*, or recitation of verses from the Holy Koran in the ears of the child by an adult male member of the family or by a priest, is performed. The ritual of *piaw* is observed on the following day wherein new clothes and some cash are presented to the blessed mother by her in-laws. The ritual of *sunder* is associated with the first bath of the mother on the seventh day of delivery as well as naming of the child, which is celebrated with a feast to the relatives and neighbours. The woman resumes her normal household chores after taking a bath again on the fortieth day. *Zerakasi* is the ritual marked for the shaving of head when the child is about one year old followed by a feast to the female relatives and friends. One of the important rituals for a male child is *khatnahal* or circumcision performed by the family barber just before dawn, generally at the age of three to four years. A feast is hosted by the family on this occasion. Acceptance of a marriage proposal is marked by the ritual of *gandum* through the payment of some token money by the boy's father to the girl's father. After about a month, the girl's father repeats the performance through the ritual of *doon-leij* by presenting an earthen pot full of nuts and some cash, less than that presented by the father of the boy, to the boy's father. The amount of cash is, however, returned to the girl's father. *Dapanbata* is the ritual of formally inviting the friends and relatives for the ensuing marriage. On the third day preceeding the marriage, the ritual of *malas-behoun* is performed at the bride's residence wherein she is not allowed to work, does not take bath and is served dry food only till the day of marriage to make her slim and look prettier. This is followed by the ritual of *massmechravoun* or anointing and hair dressing of the bride by her women relatives and friends. On the day preceding the marriage, the ritual of *menziraat* is marked to beautify the hands and feet of the bride by embellishing them with *henna* or myrtle paste. On the following morning, or on the day of *nikah* or marriage, the ritual of *yenevoul* is marked to send presentation of clothes, ornaments, shoes, etc., for the bride by the groom's party. Only some male relatives and friends accompany the bridegroom for the *nikah* ceremony at the bride's residence. At the time of the *nikah*, the bride and the groom are represented by close relatives as their representatives and witnesses. The marriage contracts and the promised amount of *mahr* (dower) are entered in a written document or *nikah-nama* along with the names and signatures of at least six persons comprising the bride, the bridegroom, two witnesses and two representatives. A priest or *maulvi* conducts the proceedings of the *nikah* which is celebrated through a grand feast. The reception of the bride at her in-laws' place on the following day of *nikah* is marked by a feast, *wathal*, by the father of the bridegroom.

Following the death of a person, the dead body is given a warm water bath by the professional bather called *snangor.* After wrapping the dead body in a white sheet of cloth or *kafan*, it is put in a wooden coffin or *taboot* and then again covered with a piece of white cloth. In the graveyard, the dead body is laid inside the grave, prepared by a professional gravedigger called *malkhos*, with its head facing towards north. Verses from the Holy Koran are recited by a *maulvi* before lowering the dead body into the grave. Two big stones are placed at the two ends of the grave as marks of identification. All through the following four days, called *chaharum,* the mourners of the bereaved family offer prayer at the mosque as well as at the grave in memory of the deceased. On the fortieth day the ritual of *chehallum* is performed through prayer followed by a feast for the neighbours and relatives to mark the end of mourning.

Most of the Chhans possess some amount of land under individual proprietorship. But the size of landholding is not adequate. As traditional carpenters they get employment for about ten days a month at the average wage rate of Rs. 50 per day. Though they are also skilled in making furniture, their expertise in making *khidki* or wooden windows, *dedi* or wooden doors, and *chhat* or wooden roof is hired by most of the Kashmiris when constructing their houses. Carpentry, however, has been the major source of their livelihood which they supplement through agricultural income. Apart from agriculture and carpentry or woodwork, animal husbandry and skilled labour work are traditionally pursued by most of them. They have direct link with fully regulated markets through exchange of cash. Inadequate size of landholding has made them to depend more and more on carpentry for their livelihood.

Traditional panchayat or council does not exist either at the community level or at the level of the village. Problems of adultery, disrespect and insult to traditional norms at the community level are dealt by the informal council of elders of the community, elected by voice vote, through imposition of cash fine. Though they are aware of the existence of modern statutory panchayat for implementing development measures for the public in general, they have not been benefitted much by the panchayat.

They profess Islam and follow the *shariat.* The *dargahs* (sacred shrines) and *masjids* (mosques) are commonly visited by them on various socio-religious occasions. Makhdum Sahib, Shah Hamdan, Naqshband Sahib and Charar-e-Sharif are the important sacred centres for them. Urs-e-Makhdum Sahib, Id-ul-Fitr, Id-ul-Zuha, Urs-e-Pir Dastgir, etc., are some of the fairs and festivals attended by them. Urs-e-Nabi or Id-ul-Milad is celebrated to mark the birthday of Prophet Muhammad. Most of the fairs and festivals are of religious significance to them. Woodwork or carpentry and shawl embroidery are the crafts commonly known to most of them. On various social occasions, women sing folk songs but do not participate in dancing.

Traditional linkages with other neighbouring communities are perpetuated through exchange of food, marriage alliances, sharing of water sources, burial ground, and visiting the common sacred shrines. Exchange and rendering of services in social and economic spheres also promote linkages with the communities of the neighbourhood. The *julus* or processions organized on various religious occasions help to perpetuate linkages with the participating communities of the region. Carrying out woodwork in the construction of houses, and their repair from time to time help them to maintain a type of traditional patron-client relationship with most of the communities of the neighbourhood. Some of them who are teachers and others who are working in the government and private organizations also establish linkages with different communities at their respective levels of interaction in the working places.

Usually the boys fail to pursue their study beyond higher secondary level due to their poor economic condition and need to earn to support their family. Education of girls is only partly favoured. Most of the girls drop out even before reaching the primary level due to poor economic conditions and other social reasons. Though they have not totally discarded their indigenous medicare, modern medicare is commonly used by most of them. They are not receptive to family planning. Drinking water is made available to them through taps within the locality. Majority of them are self-employed in agriculture and carpentry and have not been benefited through any special employment scheme of the government. They are exposed to modern mass media and communication facilities available in the region. Information at the regional and national level is also disseminated to them through the workers of various political parties. They avail the facility of electricity. Their fuel resources comprise firewood, cow-dung cakes, charcoal and kerosene oil. Rain and spring water are the main sources of irrigation for them. Both organic manure and chemical fertilizers are used by them in their agricultural land. They make full use of the fair price shops for obtaining essential articles like sugar and kerosene oil.

B.K. Basu

CHIB

The community goes by the name of Chib or Chibh. It has no other name, nor any sub-groups, except among the Muslim Chibs who are divided into three groups: Mandial, Srahial and Dherial. A fourth group which always ruled the principality *raj* was called Ghanial; but the Hindu Chibs are a heterogenous community. The titles common among them are Mian and Thakur.

The word Chib has been derived from the name of their ancestor Chib Chand. The Chibs claim to be an offshoot, at least in the female line, of the Katoch of Kangra, and their eponym Chib Chand is said to had left Kangra about 1,500 years ago and settled at Maghlora near Bhimbar in the Jammu Hills, receiving from Raja Sripat of Bhimbar his daughter's hand, with part of his country as her dower. Tradition makes Chib Chand's father, Nahar Chand, Raja of Kangra, a contemporary of Timur, but the Jhibhal (Chibhal) was already known by that name to Timur and his historians, which shows that Chibs had settled in that tract long before Timur's invasion in AD 1398-9. The Chib genealogy enters Megh Chand as the Raja of Kangra, who had three sons. One of them was Hari Chand, the founder of Guler state and the Guleria tribe; the other, Karm Chand ruled Kangra; the third was Pratap Chand, father of Narain Chand (Nahir Chand of tradition), and grandfather of Chib Chand.

A variation of the tradition says that the Chibs are of Persian origin. Na'man, a descendant of Darah, son of Bahman, ruled Khorasan, and his son Gauhar Shah came to the Deccan and married Nahir Chand's daughter and their son was named Abdar Chand, a Hindu. His descendant Nahir Chand became the Raja of Kangra.

Raja Sripat was a Thakiyal Rajput who held sway in and around Bhimbar. After marriage, Chib Chand killed the Raja and most of the Thakiyal Rajputs by treachery, subdued the rest of them and usurped the Bhimbar *raj*. His descendants came to be known as Chib. They considerably increased in number and spread over a vast area. In Punjab, the Chibs are found almost entirely in the northern portion of Gujrat under the Jammu Hills. The hills above this territory, within the Jammu province, are their proper home. The tribe has also given its name to Chibhal, or the hill country of Jammu region on the left bank of the Jehlum river, though it appears they no longer occupy those hills and are found scattered mostly in the tahsils of Rajouri, Naushahra, Akhnur, Jammu and Ranbirsinghpura of the Jammu province.

Chib Chand's seventh descendant was Raja Dharam Chand, who was the first of the community to be forced to embrace Islam by Aurangzeb and kept under surveillance in Delhi, from where he escaped with difficulty only to be killed by the pursuing Mughal commander Haibat Khan Qandhari within 5 miles of his capital, Bhimbar, at a place called Adhi Dhak. He died a violent death and is still venerated as a martyr. He was given the Muslim name of Shadab Khan by Aurangzeb and is, therefore, venerated as Bawa Shadi Shaheed by the Muslim Chibs and Sidd Sadi by the Hindus. Both the Hindu and Muslim Chibs venerate his tomb at Adhi Dhak, and offer locks of hair of their male children at the tomb, till the child is not considered a true Chib, nor is the mother allowed to take meat. A Muslim Khokhr is the *mujawar* (caretaker) of the shrine.

After the death of Narain Chand, Bhum Chand ruled Bhimbar. He founded a village called Bhumpur after his name, which later became Bhimbar. When Bhum Chand died, the ruler of Delhi gave the Bhimbar *raj* to Ghani Chand, son of Bhup Chand who agreed to become a Muslim. Thereafter Bhimbar was ruled by the Muslim branch of the Chibs. Most of the Chibs were converted to Islam. Almost all of them migrated to Pakistan during the Partition of the country in 1947. The Hindu Chibs had four strongholds, namely Deva, Batala, Ambriyal and Khadala. There they eked out their existence by plunder of the adjoining British territory of Gujrat and exacted blackmail from all. The most stubborn of them were the Chibs of Deva and Batala, some 5,000 in number, who occasionally raided the villages of Dilawarpur, Gharera and Ajnala. Their chief opponent was Chaudhri Muhammad Yar of Dilawarpur who carried on a guerrilla warfare in which he slew enough Chibs to make a *chabutra* (shrine) for the village Dehra. The spot is said to have been called Sir-i-Katla. But when the Chaudhri was killed in 1847, the Deva, Batala Chibs became more ferocious. Their recalcitrant activities came under serious consideration of the British authorities of Punjab. The matter was taken up with Maharaja Ranbir Singh. Twice their villages were burnt by the officers of the Maharaja and punitive fines were imposed. But the villages were rebuilt and fines were ignored.

On the very night of the battle of Gujrat (in the north-western part of India) in July 1849, the town of Jalalpur was attacked and looted and many other depredations were carried out. The Chibs of Khadala also destroyed the village Assar at the same time. Strong steps were then taken and *chowkis* and thanas were established to apprehend the marauding Chibs. This action checked their depredations. But taking advantage of the mutiny the Chibs of Deva unexpectedly looted the village Dakhua in Gujarat. More stringent measures were taken. At last, the Maharaja sent a force against Deva and Batala in January, 1858, burnt the villages and prohibited their reconstruction on the same site. He recruited the Chibs in the army and channelized their energy in more civic pursuits. Soon the Chibs were tamed to become useful and law-abiding citizens.

The geographical environment of the Chibs can be divided into two types: first, the fertile plain to the south of Jammu which is irrigated by canals since the last quarter of the last century, having temperate climate and moderate rainfall; second, the arid, Kandi plateau, covered with stones and broken by torrents and streamlets, and thirsting for water, with extreme summers and winters, and moderate rainfall in summer just enough for the cultivation of maize and hill beans. Previously, people used to drink rain-water collected in natural tanks but now the Kandi Water Schemes of the state government have reached most of the Kandi villages and hamlets.

They speak Dogri at home and with others. They used to write Dogri language in Tankari or Landa script which was popular in the hills up to the end of the nineteenth century. At present, Devanagari script has been adopted for Dogri. The literate among them communicate with others in Hindi and write in Devanagari script. The highly educated among them communicate in English also. The community does not wear any special dress to distinguish them from the other Rajputs, except the style of the turban. But now that distinction is gradually disappearing, and they mostly look like the Rajputs in dress and demeanour.

The Chibs are a non-vegetarian, but most of their womenfolk usually abstain from taking meat and eggs. The community as a whole abstains from taking non-vegetarian diet on certain occasions and religious days, such as *nauratras* and the *devi* days. They prefer goat's meat but also relish big game and wild fowl. Poultry, eggs and fish are modern additions in their diet. Most of their elderly women are vegetarian but they have no prejudice against preparing and serving meat dishes for their families. Wheat and *makki* (maize) and occasionally rice form their staple food, along with pulses of black beans, gram and *masur*. They use all types of vegetables, roots and tubers grown locally and found wild. Milk and *lassi* are their main non-alcoholic drinks. The Chibs prefer locally made brand alcohol called *rurimarka*, which most of them prepare in their own villages and at home. However, modern drinks are used by those who can afford it, and, on festivals and ceremonial occasions, by most of them.

The Chibs are a homogeneous community without any social or ethnic subdivisions. They are, however, included among the second grade 'jai' or 'jaikariya' Rajputs, being descendants of the ruling clan which was once supreme in their country called Chibhal. Their Muslim counterparts retained the title of Raja and ancestral *jagirs* even to the time of partition of the country. This relegation of the community to their grade was for the purpose of matrimonial alliances and precedence at social gatherings and community feasts. It had no relevance to their economic condition and functional pattern. The Chibs consider themselves Rajputs of the second or Kshatriya *varna* and are recognized as such by other communities of the region, being a part of the ancient Katoch clan of Kangra who claim their descent from Susarma Chandra of the *Mahabharat* fame, and hence one of the original and pure Kshatriya clans of the most ancient standing. However, their claim is contested by the ruling Jamwal and Sambyal clans as some of the Chibs have taken to agriculture.

They follow all the marriage rules enjoined by the *Smritis* and *Dharmasastras* with slight local modifications. The three stages of marriage ceremonies—*kurmai*, or *sagai*, *biah* and *gaona* or *maklawa* are gone through by the usual Brahmanic ceremonies performed by the *purohits*. Formerly early marriages usually took place while the couple were much below the age of 16. The normal mode of marriage was by negotiation through a mediator; usually a *nai* or (barber) of the families acted as the mediator. But marriages by purchase and, in some cases, even by force or kidnapping were also resorted to. Thus, there were three modes of acquiring mates: (i) *dharm-punn*, i.e. through negotiation without any involvement of money; (ii) purchase, in which the wife was acquired by paying to the girl's parents or guardian a stipulated amount of money; and (iii) in some cases girls were forcibly carried away and married. The Chibs exchanged daughters with the Manhas only, or they gave their daughters to the Jamwals whom they considered superiors. In taking brides they followed hypogamy; but while giving daughters they followed the principle of hypergamy or gave their daughters to the Manhas clan whom they considered of equal social status with them, whereas they accepted wives only from the lower grade Rajput communities like the Charak, Langeh, Mahla, Salehria, Rakwal, Sen and others. *Sindoor* and *bindi* are the usual symbols of marriage. Dowry is given and taken mostly in kind, only a fraction being in cash. Sororate occasionally is practised. Marriage with mother's brother's daughter and father's sister's daughter is forbidden. The bride is taken at the time of *maklawa* to live with her husband. The Chibs are monogamous. Remarriage of widows is not encouraged but *karewa* or *chadar-andazi* (marriage by the brother or nearest kinsman of the deceased) occurs in exceptional cases. Divorce is prohibited. The Chibs believe in unbreakable ties of marriage which persists even after death. No marked change has taken place in the institution of marriage except that of the raising of the usual age of marriage.

The Chib family is organized on the extended pattern in which the eldest member of the family holds supreme status, and landed and other property is held in his name. The elders are feared, obeyed and held in veneration, and paternal and filial affection and due regards as per status of the person is the basis of mutual relationship. After the death of father or the elder of the family, the eldest son or his uncle becomes the head of the undivided family. Inheritance is based on the two-fold principle of *pag-vand* and *chunda-vand*. In the former case, when there are offspring of one wife the property is shared equally by all the male children. For instance, in case of two wives, one having one son and the other two or more, half of the property would go to one son and the remaining half to the sons of the second wife which is shared equally between them. Interfamily relations are cordial and they participate in each others' joys and sorrows.

Women are held in high esteem in the Chib community and they are very proud of the honour of their females. The Chibs being descendants of the ruling class and claiming 'Mian' status, their women remained in seclusion and were in no way an economic asset to their families. They don't do any outdoor work and their activities are confined to the household which they entirely manage. Only under the impact of recent developments some Chib women have entered services and become a source of income to the family. But such instances are few and far between.

The Chibs observe all the Shastric rituals prevalent in this region. The birth of a male child is considered auspicious and is marked by great merriment. On the fifth day after childbirth, the mother undergoes the ritual of a purificatory bath called *punjap*. The child is taken out of the room after twenty-one days and the occasion is usually accompanied by some rituals. *Mundan* (tonsure) of the child is celebrated at the age of two. The investiture of the sacred thread, *upanayana*, takes place usually at the age of ten or later and it is conventional to postpone it till the date of marriage, when it is performed a few days before in order to save expenses.

Marriage rites were usually performed at an early age, but now after the attainment of major ages by boys, they are completed in three stages: *kurmai* or *sagai*, *biah* and *maklawa* or *gaona* sometimes called *refaira*. The marriage party accompanying the bridegroom goes to the house of the bride where the marriage rituals are performed; they return with the bride and some rituals are also performed at the groom's parental house.

Death ceremonies include cremation of the dead body attended with *kriya-karam* rituals or funeral rites performed by the family priest and the Gujrati Brahman. On the fourth day, bones of fingers, toes and jaws, called *phul*, are collected and placed in a jar which is thrown in the Ganga before the tenth day. Mourning is observed for thirteen days. On the thirteenth day, the last rituals are performed, the house is purified, and the eldest son or successor wear a turban, *pagri*, in a gathering of the kith and kin who are then feasted and the mourning period comes to a close. One year after death, the *barkhi* (anniversary) of the deceased takes place and his *chabari* or *chaubarkhi* is celebrated after four years. Afterwards, *shradh* is performed for the dead once a year. All these rites are gone through with the help of various categories of Brahmans, such as *purohit*, *pahda*, *charji* and *panda*, and are accompanied by a recital of appropriate portions of the scriptures. But some of these rites have been simplified and shortened, even skipped over or performed without the help of the expert wherever required.

Formerly, marauding and cattle-lifting was the Chibs' main occupation and such activities were the chief economic source of the clan. But in the twentieth century, the Chibs have become progressively law-abiding and have given up their violent ways. They have taken to agriculture and military service in Jammu & Kashmir forces, and now in the Indian army, which has become their chief source of earning. They are mainly a landowning community. Agriculture and service are their major occupations. A few of them have entered business and industry also as owners and factory workers. Only a few of them are farm labourers. Farm labourers receive wages both in cash and kind and the factory workers in cash only.

Formerly the Chib of the village as a whole served as the traditional agent of social control concerning problems of marriage, adultery and inheritance. But now such agencies have lost their value and the members take resort to the law courts and village panchayats which have come into existence since the second quarter of the present century, and have received constitutional recognition and powers after Independence. These gram panchayats are formed on a democratic basis and control civic and social behaviour and intercommunity relations.

A large majority of the Chibs were converted to Islam and they mostly inhabited the areas which have now become a part of Pakistan or have migrated to Pakistan after Partition. Only a few Muslim Chib families reside in the Jammu region. Most of the Chibs profess Hinduism and subscribe to the Sanatanist ideology and faith. They have faith in Vedic and Puranic gods and goddesses, particularly of the Vaishnava group. Their own clan deity is Sidh Sadi, also called Sur Sadi Shaheed at whose shrine they perform *mundan* ceremonies and some rituals concerning marriage. Kali Bir and Gugga are their village deities for which they raise small mounds of earth or set up slabs with horsemen carved on those for worship. They go on pilgrimage to the usual Hindu *tirthas* and shrines, including Vaishno Devi. The Brahmans and family *purohits* perform the religious rites. They participate in the Hindu fairs and festivals held in the region, such as Jhiri and Baisakhi fairs. The special fair or gathering of the community is held once every year at the shrine of Sidh Sadi, which serves as a sort of community get-together called *mail*, when they perform tonsure ceremony of their children and fulfil their vows. They also engage the services of the *chelas* for exorcising evil spirits and adversity attributed to them. Their religious behaviour and precepts have remained unchanged and no socio-religious movement have affected the community. The only change in their religious behaviour in recent years is to be seen in the laxity of most of the puranic rituals and rites, and some type of informal reform has been stressed upon by the elders of the community.

The Chib have been a warlike community ignorant of any type of plastic and graphic arts. Neither have they practised any sort of craft or handicraft. They do not indulge in dance and music as a community. Individuals, however, participate in dance and music on social functions like marriages. The Chib farmers participate in the *bhangra* dance vicearously and publicly at Baisakhi and other fairs. They used to invite the Bhats and Mirasis who sang ballads of their clan heroes and recited family genealogies, but this tradition has vanished with the migration of the Mirasi community to Pakistan.

The Chibs participate in the social and religious rites and rituals of all other communities except those of the fourth *varna* in some cases, some members of that *varna* are specially invited to witness their functions as witnesses and as elders of the village. They also take part in all the festivals and social gatherings of all other Hindu communities, and also invite them for similar participation in their own social and religious rituals. In some of their socio-religious ceremonies, the participation of members of the low castes is necessary. On the occasions of the birth of a son, marriage, *mundan* and similar other rites in their families, the Dums, Mirasis and other fourth *varna* men and women sing songs and ritual hymns and clan ballads to mark the festivity of the performances. They traditionally accept water and food from all the Hindu communities except from the Scheduled Castes. They refrain from eating from the hands of lower castes. They contract alliances only with other clans of the Rajput community. However, putative relations with all other communities, high or low, are permissible among them. If a marriage party while returning with the bride, happens to come by a similar marriage party of any community, the bride and bridegroom of each party, exchange gifts and become *dharm-bhai* and *-sakhi* of each other as the case may be. The Chib share wells, water-reservoirs, roads, public places like schools, panchayat ghars, cremation grounds, etc., with all other communities. But in the matter of temples and religious shrines they prohibit any participation of the fourth *varna* communities and the Muslims. They maintain patron-client relationship with all castes of Brahmans of the region. They themselves are a landowing community, hence they are employed in agriculture and maintain the cultivator-labour relation with other communities of the village.

The Chibs have of late become politically alive, and participate in the politics of the state levels, local, regional and national. They have become members of various political parties and take part in their activities. They have joined the state civil service and police, as well as administrative services at all levels, and have among them administrators of state and IAS cadres. A few of them have become MLAs and, one of them, Rajendra Singh Chib became a cabinet minister in the state cabinet. They are joining all walks of economic life, running small businesses and petty shops, and maintain employer-worker and landlord-tenant relations with other communities.

Most of the Chib families have the benefit of education at the levels of college as well as university; but in far-flung villages and mountainous tracts facilities for higher education are not available. They have scholars, scientists and teachers at all levels among them, but majority of their students drop out at middle and high school level due to economic reasons and absence of educational facilities nearby.

They make use of the modern health and medicare facilities according to their economic resources; but since such medicare is costly, most of them look for indigeneous medicines. Free services are also available at the primary health centres to some extent. Their attitude towards family planning is favourable, and some of them get sterilized after two or three children. Drinking water facilities are adequately available to them, mostly taps and tube wells. They also make use of the natural springs and streams, wherever available. In the hills, tanks are also in use.

Some of them have received benefits of the rural employment schemes and loans for agricultural and industrial purposes, and for setting up fisheries, piggeries, poultry farms and fruit gardens, but such facilities are available to only a limited number. Self-employment schemes have also benefited a few of them. They make use of all type of media, listen to the radio and watch television programmes at their homes or at the community centres set up by the state government. All of them use electricity for lighting their houses and for other purposes, but for cooking purposes most of them still depend on firewood, cow-dung and kerosene oil. Some of them use gas units also. They avail themselves of the irrigation facilities in the plains. Being basically an agricultural community, they make use of chemical fertilizers and insecticides as well as organic manure. In the plains, they make use of mechanical devices for ploughing and harvesting. Majority of those who reside in urban areas, or are landless, get their rations through the public distribution system which is available in all the villages and towns. Banking facilities are available; they make use of these and do not have to depend on the moneylenders. They are used to savings and investment schemes and benefit by them.

The Chibs were earlier known for being lawless subjects. Before the Partition of the country, from their strongholds at Deva and Batala, they made their incursions across the Jammu border into Sialkot and Gujrat territories of the Punjab. It was only during the last quarter of the nineteenth century that their strongholds were burnt and their lawless activities were curbed by the rulers of Jammu Kashmir State on strong protest by the British Government of India. Since Independence, they have reformed their behaviour and become one with other communities in their socio-political behaviour.

Anita K. Billawaria

CHIBALI

The Chibalis derive their name from the territory they occupy, the Chibal region that lies on the southern slopes of the Shivaliks between the Chenab and Jhelum rivers. It was called Chibhal by the Muslim rulers of the medieval period. The Chibalis resemble the Dogras. They are, however stronger than the surrounding ethnic groups. The Chibalis originally were concentrated in Akhnur, Mendhar, Haveli and Rajouri tahsils, and in some parts of Naoshera.

After Raja Dharam Chand was converted to Islam in AD 1465, his descendants and the common public turned to Islam. Some Rajput castes, namely the Jats, Jeehurs, Jhakeers, Mankas, Jarals, Mangdals, Bhawpals, Manhas and Sahus, etc., became Muslims.

The Chibali Rajputs are the descendants of the Rajput lineage of Katoch dynasty of Kangra Valley (Himachal Pradesh). They have migrated from Kangra to the *riyast* of Bimber to Chibhal.

In course of time, these converts started intermarrying with their Hindu counterpart as the Hindu customs were still prevailing among the Muslim Chibalis. Though, initially their women retained their Hindu customs, with the passage of time, the practice of marrying with the Hindus stopped. The Muslim Chibalis sought matrimonial alliances amongst themselves as their size and number grew. The basic occupation of the Chibalis was cultivation and pastoralism. Some of them living in urban areas were engaged in trade and commerce.

In recent times the Chibalis are mostly concentrated in Punch, Rajouri, Naoshera and Jammu tahsils. However, census enumeration categorizes them with the broader Muslim population of the region. They have both written and oral history about their origin. Inter-district migration in pursuit of better job and income opportunities has taken place among them. They live essentially in hot to very warm climate, and the regions of their settlement have both thin to dense forest cover. They mainly speak Dogri among themselves and with others. Arabic is the main script used for correspondence with others and among themselves. Quite a few of them can speak and write English. Their dress pattern conforms to typical Dogri pattern. They do not have any special dress to identify them as a separate ethnic group. They do not enjoy any special privilege as a community. The Chibali are non-vegetarian. They eat mutton, fish, fowl and eggs. However, the average propensity to consume meat is occasional because of hot climatic conditions and the restricted availability of meat products. Their staple food is wheat and maize with occasional consumption of rice. They consume all types of cereals, pulses and vegetables. They use sufficient quanitities of *desi ghee* and mustard oil for cooking. Fruit consumption among them is moderate. They make regular use of milk and milk products, and drink lot of local tea. Alcoholic drink among their males is occasional and they buy it from the market. They also smoke lot of cigarette and loose tobacco by using *hookah*. Tobacco chewing and use of snuff is also found among them. Changes in food habits are noticeable from vegetarians like the Hindus to non-vegetarians like the Muslims.

The Chibali do not have any formal *varna* system prevalent among them now. They have a very strong sense of pride in being Rajputs. However, within Islamic fold, social stratification has disappeared. Differentiation exists on the basis of individual standing of the community members. They now use Khan and Raja as their surnames. Some of them still retain their pre-Islamic surnames like Katoch, etc. They have a high sense of self-perception but the other non-Muslim communities do not have similar view about them.

The Chibali practise endogamy at the community level. They marry with their relations, irrespective of the status; cross-cousin marriages are quite common. However, sororal polygamy has not been observed among them. Pre-puberty marriages are very rare. Nowadays, girls and boys marry after attaining puberty. Marriage age for girls is 14 years and above, and for boys, it is 20 years and above. Marital alliances are mostly solicited through friends and relatives. Fixing of marriages by the professional matchmakers is rare. Monogamy is the most prevalent form of marriage though polygyny is allowed under the Muslim Personal Law. There are no specific marriage symbols for their women except for wearing *nath* (nose ring). Dowry is not as popular among them as it is among the Hindu Rajputs. The system of fixing *mahr* for the bride is prevalent.

The most prevalent form of family is nuclear and the joint family system appears to be on the decline. There is awareness and keeness about leading an independent life. Interpersonal relations are cordial though joking relations are not encouraged. Conflicts and disputes arise in matters of property distribution. The Chibalis follow the Muslim law of inheritance. Male heirs get equal share of the ancestral property whereas females are entitled to a lesser share. Females practically do not get any share of the ancestral property owing to the investment made for their maintenance and marriage expenses. The eldest son succeeds as the head of the family. Interfamily linkages are cordial and friendly. Disputes arising out of land and property may be resolved through mutual negotiations, failing which a recourse may be taken to the state's judiciary.

The Chibali women enjoy secondary status in comparison to their menfolk. They do not get equal share of the ancestral property as the male do. They also have a very restricted role to play in socio-religious spheres of life in their community. Majority of them participate in the farm-related operations, helping to augment the family income. They also act as water-carriers and fuel-collectors for the household. They tend domestic cattle. Their participation in politics is restricted to voting only during elections. They seem to be reconciled to the way of life they are leading and make no special effort to improve their lot and assert their independent identity.

The Chibali women do not observe any pre-delivery ritual though certain protective restrictions are insisted upon. A baby is delivered either at the woman's parents' house or at her in-laws' house, though usually the former is preferred. Wherever hospital or health centre facilities are not available, the services of the midwife are sought. However, people prefer to shift the expectant mothers to hospitals and health centre for safe deliveries. Postnatal restrictions are observed for 40 days. They do not have any formal naming ceremony but their male children undergo circumcision as per the Islamic laws.

Marital alliances are fixed usually by friends and relatives. Invariably, such alliances are formalized within the kith and kin. Marriage ceremonies last over two days. Customarily, marriage ceremonies are held at the bride's place. The groom goes to the bride's home on a horse accompanied by selected number of guests. *Nikah* is performed thereafter. Nuptial rituals are performed at the groom's residence where the bride is brought in a *doli* carried by four persons. Marriages are held after sunset. The bride brings along ornaments of gold and silver, dresses, bedding and furniture as dowry, though it may not be insisted upon by her in laws. Some parents also give cattle and land to their daughters. Marriage feast is given by both the parties.

The dead are given a bath and draped in a white sheet of cloth (shroud) and carried to the *kabristan/mazar* (burial ground) in a coffin. After *fateha-khani*, the dead is buried in a grave as per the Islamic laws. On the ensuing Friday, *jumma-fateha* is performed followed by the *chehallum* (fortieth day ceremony). There has not been any significant changes in their life-cycle rituals. All these occasions have resulted in becoming more expensive. Those who are better-off, observe them with pomp and show.

Their major economic activities are agriculture, animal husbandry and petty trade. The Chibalis are essentially a landowning community, especially in rural areas. Land is under individual proprietorship. Quite a few of them are engaged in government and private services. Most of them are directly linked to the market. Women are also actively involved in farm and animal husbandry operations, thereby indirectly helping to augment the family income. Child labour is extensively used for family-related operations but it is not marketed on commercial basis. Of late, they have sought occupational diversification from the farm sector to non-farm sectors due to growing family size and fragmentation of land.

The village level panchayats exist among the Chibalis. Their elderly persons represent the panchayats which, otherwise, are heterogeneous in nature. Conflicts, quarrels and other social disputes are sorted out with mutual reconciliation and adjustments. Cases of adultery, rape and theft are decided under the state's judicial system. However, such cases are reported to be few and far between. Their panchayats do not have the power to punish or give formal awards but may initiate social boycott. The panchayats also participate in the village welfare and developmental activities though only in an advisory capacity. Among themselves, they do not have any traditional caste counciles, but they do participate in the regional Rajput Sabha which includes the Hindu Rajputs also.

The Chibalis are Muslims and belong to the Sunni sect. They visit the shrines of Pir Baba in Jammu and Hazratbal, Makhdum Sahib, Rishi Peer, Pir Dastgir Sahib, Shah Hamdan Sahib, etc., in Kashmir Valley. They also go to perform *haj* pilgrimage at Mecca. They observe fasting during Ramadan and observe all the Muslim socio-religious festivals like Shab-e-Meraj, Shab-e-Qadr, Jumat-ul-Vida, Id-ul-Fitr and Id-ul-Zuha.

The Chibalis are not specialized in plastic or graphic arts. There are no professional craftsmen among them nor any experts in handicrafts. They have written as well as oral traditions, i.e. folk songs, folklore and folk tales based on historical and religious events.

The Chibali accept both *pukka* and *kachcha* food from the other Muslim communities equal or higher to them in the social hierarchy. There is no restriction in accepting and exchanging *kachcha* food with the non-Muslims. They normally do not refrain from eating with non-Hindus. They share burial grounds, water sources, roads, schools and panchayats with other communities. They visit religious shrines and *dargahs* of *pirs* and *faqirs* and also maintain cordial relationship with other communities. Majority of them live in rural areas and are mostly agriculturists by profession. Cultivator-labour relationship is prevalent among them.

The Chibalis are gradually becoming more participative in market-oriented economy relating to day-to-day business and associated economic activities. Political awareness among them is quite discernible. They have amongst them very few doctors, engineers and senior administrators, however, a sizeable number of them are employed in white-collar jobs and are engaged in petty and retail trade. Some of their females are also employed in teaching and government jobs.

Formal education is spreading amongst the present generation of the Chibalis. Girls usually study up to school level due to socio-economic compulsions. Boys, however, are encouraged to study beyond higher secondary level to become eligible for better paid jobs.

Though the Chibalis' attitude is favourable towards the modern medicare, its utilization is linked to its availability at the right place in right time. Family planning practices among them are not popular and very few of them have accepted it in order to restrict the family size. The average family size varies from six to nine members usually. They prefer to have four or more children. Drinking water facilities are available within their locality through piped water. Other sources of water are ponds, rivers, wells and tube wells.

The Chibalis have not benefited from the state's welfare and developmental projects. However, the present Agrarian Acts (1953 and 1977) have given them the right of land ownership as most of them were tenants in the past. Their houses are mostly electrified. They use firewood, cow-dung and kerosene oil for cooking though some of them are also using cooking gas and electric heaters. Most of them avail of irrigational facilities. A small number of them have so far availed of the nutritional programmes through Integrated Child Development Scheme, Anganwadi and SNP centres. Majority of them make use of the public distribution facilities. They do not borrow money from the village moneylender as a matter of tradition. However, they maintain monthly credit accounts with village grocery shops. They do not have a strong inclination towards savings and investment.

The Chibalis are, in short, a Rajput Muslim community but, in the changing social environment, they have not been able to retain their exclusive identity. They have, by and large, been assimilated into the broad regional Dogra culture. However, they have adapted to the contemporary geopolitical set-up in a successful manner and have been able to economically improve their lot.

INDU BALA DHAR

CHHIMBA/CHIMBE

The Chhimba or Chimbe are a numerically small community of Jammu & Kashmir. Because of various reasons, the community hide their identity and have adopted new surnames.

The Chhimba are distributed in Punjab, Haryana and Uttar Pradesh, and in big urban centres, such as Delhi, Chandigarh, Calcutta, Bangalore, etc. Most of them call themselves Chauhan, Arora and Khatri. Recently, the Chhimba have become the followers of Sri Namdeo. A synonym of Chhimba is Tak Kshatriya. It is likely that in coming years they would like to identify themselves more with the Tak Kshatriya than with any other community.

The Chhimba were in the past engaged in cloth dyeing and printing and got the name Chippa or Chippi, by which other communities referred to them and even addressed them.

It is important to note that Samba had been famous for cloth printing and dyeing. The town was known and described in different records as *chhiton ka shahar* (town of prints). The prints from that place and the cloth dyed by their forefathers attracted the attention of the then kings of Jammu and other places and the long sheets of cloth, curtains and other prints were bought in bulk by the royal courts and used in the palaces. How fast did this craft declined could not be recalled by them at present.

Besides Jammu, the Chhimba also live in Punjab and elsewhere in India. The Chhimba who live in Jammu division fall into two groups: those who had been living here for generations and those who came from Pakistan after Partition. The latter are from Mirpur. The two groups, however, are intermarrying and no discrimination is made in this regard.

They believe that the they are largely an urban community and there are very few agriculturists among them. They are mainly petty traders and many of them are sweet shop owners. The natural environment at Jammu, Kathua, Samba and Udhampur is of warm and termperate climate, hilly terrain, moderate rainfall, high humidity and no snowfall; most of the year, it is warm and, on occasions, heat intensity is oppressive. They speak Dogri and wear the common dress of the land. They are vegetarian, avoid alcoholic drinks and do not smoke. However, there are many exceptions to this general rule.

They consume the local vegetables and fruits. Their staple diet consists of wheat and rice, gram, *urad*, *moong*, *masur* and *rajmah* cooked in mustard oil or in *ghee*.

They are an endogamous community divided into exogamous divisions for the purpose of marriage. They could mention a few exogamous group names, which they call *gotras*. These are: Tagad, Kumbho, Teji, Purwa and Pradhan. The *gotras* commonly found in Punjab are Uttiwal, Jossal, Harad, Kanth and Rehan. According to published literature on the Tak Kshatriya, there were some 172 *gotras* and the number has increased to 209 on recent counting.

The Chhimba who migrated to India after Partition belong to the *gotras* to which the Chhimba already living in India belonged, and hence, intermarriages have not posed any problem. It is also important to note that there are Hindu Chhimba and Sikh Chhimba and these two groups also intermarry without any discrimination, and hesitation. Such intergroup marriages are rather regular. As such, one may say that the Chhimba are one endogamous community and there are exogamous groupings and divisions among them placed equally in hierarchical scale. Differentiation on the basis of migration and religious affiliations are only nominal. Though some Chhimba do adopt new surnames individually, the existing *gotra* names remain unchanged and that is the basis of marriage and identification within the community.

They are largely in business and have been classed as Vaishyas in the Hindu *varna* hierarchy. With recent development of Namdeo following and they being included in Tak Kshatriya Sabha, they identify themselves as Kshatriya but other communities have always considered them an inferior community in the regional hierarchy because of their traditional occupation of cloth dyeing and printing which others considered an inferior occupation. Probably it was for this reason that many of them adopted new surnames such as Chauhan, Verma, etc., and almost all of them tried to hide their real identity. It may be that in coming years the Chhimba as a community may take a new name or totally get merged with the pan-Indian Tak Kshatriya community, based on the following of Namdeo whom they believe to be their ancestor.

Community endogamy and *gotra* exogamy are the marriage rules. In exceptional cases, marriages are contracted also with the Kshatriya community. However, there are no exceptions to exogamy and marriages within *gotra* are considered incestuous. There are no consanguineous marriages among them and all cousins are considered and treated as siblings. The practice of junior sororate and junior levirate do occur occasionally among them. As said before, there is no hierarchy among the different exogamous groupings, hence, there is no hypogamy or hypergamy among them. The Hindu and Sikh Chhimba and those who lived in India and those who migrated after Partition freely marry each other observing *gotra* exogamy. Adult marriage and monogamy are observed as a rule. Boys are married between 25 and 30 years of age and girls between 20 and 25. However, there is a lot of variation in this regard. Most, if not all, marriages are negotiated, hence, there is always delay in a marriage decision and sometimes parents of a girl take long time to find a match of their choice for their daughter. The married women use vermilion, bangles, *bindi*, toerings as marriage symbols and do observe a little avoidance or *purdah*.

They do not hesitate to mention that they give dowry in cash and kind according to their individual economic capacity; marriages are negotiated more or less between families having equal economic status and there are no bargains of dowry. Marriage alliances are negotiated through a middleman belonging to the same community and related to either family and he remains responsible for any complications afterwards, which rarely arise as both parties involved gather all information they require before a match is actually agreed upon.

They are patrilocal and a woman joins her husband's household after marriage. Divorce is not permissible among them and even cases of separation are rare. The elders resolve any misunderstanding between the husband and wife. Since most households consist of extended families, the complications are easily resolved.

Remarriages of widow and widower are permissible and, as said earlier, practices of junior sororate and junior levirate do occur in such cases. However, with a few intercommunity marriages between the Chimbe and the Khatri communities having already taken place, some change may be anticipated to occur in the coming years.

They continue to live in extended families. The grown-up sons continue to live with their father even when they are married and have their own children. In such a situation, there is an elaborate code of conduct which the individual members have to follow. This kind of code of conduct is based on the principle of respect for elders, and youngsters are taught lessons in obedience from an early age. Women observe an avoidance relationship with male elders and observe *purdah*. They avoid direct conversation lest there should be any possibility of disobedience. The menfolk also respect this kind of avoidance relationship. There are, on the other hand, relationships of familiarity and those can be termed as joking relationship. While one avoids his parents-in-law, one jokes with his younger siblings-in-law since junior sororate and junior levirate are permitted practices. These joking relationships are very well explained in this society.

All sons equally inherit their father's property. As said earlier, the Chhimba continue to live in extended families. Family partitions do not occur after the death of the faher, and there are no occasions of confrontation and ill feelings. The daughter is given a dowry at the time of her marriage, in cash and kind, and that is considered as her share in her father's property. The eldest son succeeds and takes the responsibility of the household after the death of the father. The *pagri* (turban) ceremony on the occasion of post-funeral feast after the father's death symbolizes the succession as well as the inheritance. The married son(s) receive the *pagri* from their in-laws while for the unmarried sons, it is brought by the uncle.

The women might have participated in the family occupation and economic activity of cloth dyeing and printing as much as they could before Independence when they engaged themselves in this activity but now the women may, if educated, earn by joining service or remain tied to their household activity only. They have important role in rituals, social and religious functions. In the context of extended families, their importance increases as the household responsibilities are shared among women.

Women neither play any important role in political spheres nor in the mechanism of social control. They are held inferior to men in status. They do have decision-making power but their decisions are subject to men's scrutiny, if these are of vital importance. As said before, women may, and in some cases do, contribute to family income and control family expenditure.

They observe pre-delivery rituals during the eighth month of pregnancy. The ceremony is known as *aathwan*. On this occasion, pregnant woman's parents or brothers bring clothes and other gifts. *Gotra* members gather at the pregnant woman's house, the eldest male member worships the gods and a feast with sweet preparations and *pukka* food is given by her parents-in-law to all who gather on the occasion. With this, restrictions are imposed on the pregnant woman and a kind of confinement commences, which continues even after childbirth. The childbirth is helped by a *megh* or *mahasha* woman who is an experienced midwife. She comes to attend the mother and the child for some twelve days and is given gifts in the form of clothes and cash. She is also given food on all those days. They discriminate between a male and female childbirth and the *dai* (midwife) is given more gifts in case of a male child.

There are certain restrictions on the mother after the childbirth and a pollution period is observed for about one and a quarter month after which she is allowed to participate in her usual household work. There is no name giving ceremony and usually the *bua* (the father's sister) gives a name to the new born. There is no first feeding of cereal ceremony among them and when the child really starts eating solid food it goes unnoticed. However, on Baisakhi (last day of the month of *Baisakh*) which follows a childbirth, there is a celebration and the midwife who helped the childbirth comes and receives gifts from the family.

The *mundan* ceremony takes place in cases of both, male and female children. The ceremony may take place at home or at *kul devta's* place. Among the Tagad *gotra* Chhimbas, *mundan* takes place on Anantchaudas day while among the Kamboh and Agrohi *gotra* Chhimbas this ceremony takes place on Janmastami day. The occasion is celebrated by a gathering of *gotra* members and a feast is given by the parents of the child. They consider *mundan* an important *sanskar* in one's life. The Sikh Chhimba call this ritual *sutra*. In Jammu & Kashmir, there are only Hindu Chhimba and they more or less follow the Dogra culture.

Marriage is an elaborate affair and has as many as five ceremonies of importance. The negotiations are complete with *taka* ritual which declares that the marriage is fixed. The second is the ritual of *mundri* (finger ring) in which gifts are given to the would-be bride by her would-be in-laws. These gifts necessarily include a ring for her, hence, the ceremony is called *mundri*. This is followed by two minor ceremonies known as *sagai* and *sagun* which are more ritualistic in nature rather than feasts or festivities. A day before the actual marriage, a *shanti yajna*, also known as *sandh* ceremony, takes place at the would-be bride and would-be groom's places. The maternal uncle in both the cases officiates and a feast is given to the *gotra* members and other invitees who gather on this occasion. Finally, on the appointed day, the actual marriage takes place at the bride's place and her parents give a feast on this occasion. Consummation of marriage takes place at the husband's place soon after and a ceremony known as *duphera* marks the end of a marriage ceremony among the Chhimba.

They cremate their dead, sharing cremation ground with all other Hindu communities, including the Scheduled Castes. Pollution period is observed for 13 days. Bones are collected and are kept in an earthen pot and preserved at an important place in the house. Ancestor worship is done. After the pollution period the *pagri* ceremony takes place which has already been described earlier. A feast is given on this occasion. Services of a Brahman priest are required on all these occasions. There has been no major change in the observance of different rituals.

The Chhimba are at present largely a landless community who depend on their individual labour for livelihood. There has been a major change in the economic life of these people. They were engaged in cloth dyeing and printing. A very few of them owned some land and were agriculturists. Now they have taken to various trades. Many of them are sweetmeat sellers. There are a few sweet shops at Samba run by them and a few at Jammu are owned by them. The educated among them enter government or private services, or are self-employed as doctors and lawyers.

They have direct relations and link with the market which is daily and fully regulated. All payments are made in cash on the spot. More and more persons, men and women alike, being educated seek service as a source of livelihood.

Minor issues of clash, confrontations and disputes, are resolved by the family elders within the household itself. There are periodical gatherings of *gotra* members to celebrate one or the other occasion, observance of some ritual and when the disputes are sorted out. Statutory panchayats came into existence after Independence to plan and implement the welfare and development activities in the area. They participate in the developmental activities like other communities of the area.

The Chhimba in Jammu & Kashmir state are Hindu. However, there are Sikh Chhimba in Punjab with whom the Hindu Chhimba of Jammu & Kashmir state have marriage relations.

They have household deity and every *gotra* has a *kul-devta* and a specific place where they go for pilgrimage and worship their deity once a year. The Chhimba gather at one place to worship Namdeo which is a religious congregation. Every Chhimba household has a picture of Namdeo for daily worship. They worship the Hindu gods and goddesses with others on festivals.

With change of occupation their social status has marginally changed and improved and the society at large has accepted their claims to be a 'clean' caste. At present they exchange water, *kachcha* and *pukka* food with the Brahman, Rajput, Nai, Lohar and Tarkhan communities. They do not have such relations with the Megh, Mahasha Batwal and other Scheduled Caste communities. They share water sources, shrines, temples, cremation grounds with other communities.

As regards the modern intercommunity linkages, the Chhimba have come up as businessmen and enterpreneurs, scholars, members holding white-collar jobs, teachers, instructors, engineers, doctors and persons serving in the defence services. The Chhimba are a progressive community with a wide range of economic activities.

They favour formal education for both, boys and girls. The boys and girls study upto post-graduate and higher levels.

They make use of the traditional as well as modern medicare. It depends on an individual's choice and also the ailment whether they will go for traditional or modern medicare.They favour family planning and smaller families are more appreciated among them now. There is no special preference based on one's sex as regards sterilization and either mate may go for this according to circumstances.

Drinking water is available to them in the locality. They use communication, transport, postal, electricity, and ration facilities. About 400 households with a population of about 2,000 Chhimba in this state live in towns. Their attitude to savings is good and they do not depend on moneylenders.

In brief, the Chhimba in Jammu & Kashmir are a small localized community and are also found to be living in other adjoining states. They were engaged in cloth dyeing and printing in the past but now they are in service, business and trade. They are town dwellers and educated people.

BAGESHWAR SINGH

CHOPAN

The Chopan are traditional shepherds, who tend the sheep and cattle of the zamindar by taking them to green pastures on various *margs* (meadows) situated at high altitudes. The term *chopan* is composed of two words *cho* and *pan*. The word *cho* means 'four' (legs) and *pan* means the 'keeper'. The main occupation of this community is to keep cattle in their care on contract basis. There are three groups of the Chopan, namely Gamgoor, Ganigoor and Pahal Chopan. The Ganigoor keep the cattle of the villagers on contract basis. The Pahal Chopan keep the sheep of the villagers on contract basis. The members of all the three groups intermarry freely.

The Chopan are distributed in the Kashmir Valley. Harwan and Darbagh of Srinagar are the areas of concentraion of the Chopan. They are sedantary and live in their own houses, constructed by themselves. The area has cold climate, low humidity, medium rainfall, and medium snowfall. They are included in the list of the Other Backword Class (OBC) category of communities.

The usual dress of the male Chopan is loose type *pyjama* and *pheran*. Men wear turban as a sign of respectability and affluence. There is very little difference between the *pheran* worn by men and women. The women wear *kasaba*, a skull cap surrounded by a fillet of generally red colour. A shawl or a white *chadar* thrown over the head and shoulders, completes their headgear.

The Chopan are non-vegetarian and consume mutton but not beef and pork. Their staple food is rice and maize. They take plenty of vegetables but the favourite ones are the *hak* or *karam sag*. Among pulses *moong* (*phaseolus mungo*), *mah* (*phaseolus radiatus*) and *moth* (*phaseolus aconitifolius*) are commonly consumed. The oils used for cooking are rape-seed and linseed. They consume plenty of fruits grown in the area. They consume mulberry, walnuts, almond and *singhara* (water-chestnut) and are fond of tea. *Waha* (coffee) is taken occasionally.

Endogamy at the level of community is followed. Marriages are arranged at the age of eleven to twelve years in case of girls and fourteen to fifteen years in case of boys. The mode of acquiring mate is through negotiation. Cross as well as parallel cousin marriages are allowed. Monogamy is the general form of marriage but polygyny is also allowed. Rule of residence after marriage is patrilocal.

Divorce is allowed. If the couple is unable to adjust due to some reason or when some specific charges are there against any of them, they can ask for divorce. Only the husband can divorce. Divorce matters are settled by the family members and other relatives or villagers. In case of divorce, it is the responsibility of husband to maintain his wife during the period of *iddat*.

It is the duty of the father to maintain the children after divorce, irrespective of whether the children live with the mother or father. The mother is entitled to be the custodian of the children until they are weaned. After the child has been weaned, the custody of a male child passes on to the father, and of a female, to the mother. The mother's custody of a female child continues up to seventh year. Thereafter, the father is entitled for her custody in preference to the mother. Divorcee, widow and widower remarriages are permitted. Remarriages are performed in the same way as regular marriages are performed.

Extended families are considerably less in proportion to the nuclear families. Avoidance relation is observed between father-in-law and daughter-in-law. The daughter-in-law avoids the father-in-law till she is issueless.

Daughters also have the right of inheritance and get the share of the paternal property. But they get less than the sons. Widows have the right of inheritance of parents as well deceased husband's property.

Women are responsible for household work. Besides, they go out for collection of firewood. They are also responsible for bringing potable water. They help their menfolk in the work of poultry-keeping. Women attend the village panchayats and are free to give their statements and stand as witnesses. They cast their votes in elections.

In case of the first delivery, a woman generally goes to her parent's house one or two months before the time of delivery. Immediately after the birth of the child, the *mulla* comes and whispers *azaan* in the right ear of the child. The mother, for one or two days, takes only decoction of certain herbs. On the seventh day after a child is born, the *sonder*(purification) ceremony takes place. On that day, the mother of the newborn baby takes bath and comes out of the delivery room. On the day of *sonder* ceremony, a special dish of mutton and *vapulhak* is prepared and given to the mother.

The name of a child is given by the family *pir*. A baby born in the month in which a great saint died is generally given the name of that saint.

The *zerakasi* ceremony is also observed on the seventh day after the birth. The *navid* (barber) of the village is called to clean shave the child's head. The skin, head and legs of the goat sacrificed on the occasion are buried and the meat is distrubuted to the villagers and the *mulla*. The family members of the newborn child do not eat the mutton of the goat sacrificed at the time of *zerakasi*. The relatives and neighbours are entertained to a feast. The poor Chopan distribute *qahwa* to the guests and villagers.

Circumcision is an occasion of great rejoicing and festivity. Generally at the age of four or five years, the circumcision of the male child takes place. The child's feet are dyed with *mehndi* (myrtle) on the previous night and the relatives and friends are invited. The circumcision is performed by a *navid*. On the day of circumcision, all the friends and relatives kiss the child's hand and offer him cash after which the guests go to a shrine with the boy and return to the house for a feast.

The child is given semi-solid food, *oapsoap*, which is a preparation of milk, sugar and bread or biscuits, after six months.

Marriage negotiations commence when the boy's father goes with a small party of relatives to the girl's house. They are entertained by the girl's father. The priest, in the presence of the party, announces the betrothal. Afterwards on the occasion of Id-ul-Fitr, Id-ul-Zuha, and Milad-e-Nabi, the boy's father sends presents to the girl. A day before the marriage, *mehndi* is sent to the girl from the boy's side for decorating the girl's hands and feet. On the marriage day, the bridegroom's relatives give him presents, the party sets off to visit some neighbouring shrine and then proceed to the bride's house. As the *barat* draws near the bride's house, the women of the bride's side come out singing welcome songs in praise of the bridegroom. When the whole party is assembled, the feast commences. After the feast, the *qazi* proceeds with his business and if the marriage contract was not written earlier, he writes it then and there. Before this, the father of the groom as well as the bride fix the amount of *mahr*, which varies from Rs. 500 to Rs. 900 according to the custom of the family. The main ceremony is the *nikah*. It is a simple ceremony in which the assent of the girl and the boy to marry each other is necessary to obtain.

The last ceremony is *rukhsati* (departure). Before the *rukhsati*, the wedding presents are displayed. At the time of *rukhsati*, *dodmoj* (the woman who accompanies the bride) goes with the bride and stays with her in her in-laws' house at least for seven days till the bride returns to her parents' house. The bride is received with great enthusiasm in her in-laws' house and parties of singing women come to greet her; and she is taken into a room arranged for her reception where she takes her seat. The bride remains for seven days in her in-law's house, after which she returns to her father's house. A feast called *wathal* is arranged by the groom's parents.

On the groom's first visit to his in-laws' house after the marriage, a feast is arranged and he gets presents and cash. The bride also goes along with him and then there is no bar to their visit.

At the time of death, *kalma* and some verses from the Holy Koran are recited into the ear of the dying person. Those around call on the name of Allah and break into tears when he or she dies. A ceremonial bath is given to the dead body, which is then wrapped in a *kafan*. The dead body is carried to the graveyard in wooden *taboot* (coffin), which can readily be procured from a nearby mosque. The *taboot* is covered with a black cloth. The burial is accompanied with recitations of the verses from the Holy Koran. After *namaz-e-janaza*, the body is laid to rest. The mourners then pray for the peace of the departed soul and return to their homes. For some days till the coming Friday, the chief mourner visits the grave daily with the *mulla* and offers *fateha*.

A number of after-death rituals are observed which include *fateha* on the fourth day, *satijihum* on the fortieth day of death and *vaharver* after one year of death.

Fateha is observed on the fourth day after death, but in case Friday falls in between fourth and seventh days, then Friday is preferred for the *fateha* ritual. In no case is the *fateha* observed before four days. On this day, the *peur* (stone piece) is also fixed on the grave. On the day of *fateha*, all friends and relatives of the departed soul assemble at the grave and offer *fateha*.

The traditional as well as hereditary occupation of the Chopan is keeping and grazing the cattle and sheep of the zamindar and other villagers. Besides the above mentioned occupation, they also work as agricultural labourers. Now they have also started poultry business. *Jajmani* system exists among them. They have got particular zamindars and villagers whose sheep and cattle they keep and graze.

Only statutory village panchayats exist in their villages. The community panchayat does not exist these days.

The Chopan are Muslim by religion. They observe the festivals such as Id-ul-Fitr, Id-ul-Zuha, Shab-e-Barat and Shab-e-Qadr. They also celebrate the *urs* at the tombs of some well-known saints of the area and at Hazratbal shrine. Hazratbal *mazar* (mausoleum) of Hazrat Sultan, *mazar* of Pir Dastgir, and *mazar* of Sheikh Wali situated in Srinagar are some of their sacred centres.

Folk songs are sung on the occasion of birth and marriage. Traditional folklores and folk tales are also prevalent.

The Chopan accept food grains as well as cash as remuneration for keeping the sheep and cattle of the landowners (zamindars). They eat in the houses of all communities except the Wattals.

The development programmes, e.g. education, family welfare programmes and health facilities, have not left any significant impact on the life of the Chopan. Children receive religious education and that too in their own house. They do not go for schooling. In recent years, they have started sending their children to the Islamic madrasas for religious education. Modern medical facilities are availed of to some extent besides the indigenous medicines. They are least bothered about the family welfare programmes. Drinking water is available within the locality through taps or streams.

S.N.H. RIZVI

CHUHRA/CHUHRE

The Chuhras are also known as Chamris, Bhangis and Jamadars. The community percieve its distribution all over the state of Jammu & Kashmir where the climate ranges between extreme warm and extreme cold, the terrain is hilly or sub-Himalayan; low humidity, thin forest, medium rainfall, and medium snowfall are other climatic characteristics of their habitat. They speak Dogri among themselves and Punjabi with others and correspond in Devanagari. Cross is the identity marker. In the past men and women used to put on Dogri dress which has now been replaced by other forms of dressing. They are Scheduled Castes with a population of 2,538 (1981 census).

Men and women are non-vegetarian but desist from eating pork and beef. Wheat and rice are the main cereals but the latter is perferred. Gram, *urad*, and *kulthi* pulses are in daily use; mustard oil and dalda are used in cooking. Tuberous vegetables such as *kachalu*, potatoes, onions and garlic are used extensively. The alcohol they take is purchased from the market. Fruit consumption is occasional. A steep rise in the price of mutton and other non-vegetarian food articles is the cause of their shift to vegetarianism and increase in consumption of pulses and vegetables. Fruit consumption has also decreased and they prefer rice to *roti*.

Social division exist on subcaste level and the subcastes found among them are Gill, Mattoo, Khoje, Sotre, Kalyan, Khokhar and Boorat. Differentiation exists at economic and occupational levels and it influences marriage alliances. The community's self-perception is low and other communities too treat them as such. They are aware of the *varna* system but do not recognize it. Endogamy exists at the community level and exogamy at sub-caste level. Cross-cousin marriages are permissible but parallel cousin marriages are not allowed. Junior sororate and levirate, both senior and junior are permissible. Adult marriage is the rule. Mates are acquired through mutual consent, elopement, negotiation, exchange and courtship. Monogamy is the only form of marriage to which they are bound. Vermilion, *lal-chura*, finger ring and *mehndi* (myrtle dye) are the symbols of marriage. Dowry is given in kind. They are patrilocal. Divorce is permissible on grounds of maladjustment, impotency, cruelty, insanity and excessive drinking by the husband leading to maltreatment of the wife. Divorce compensation is paid to the wife. Either party can divorce and children are the responsibility of the mother. Widow, widower, male or female divorcee, junior sororal and leviral remarriages are also allowed. No changes were observed in the marriage rules. There is an increase in the age at marriage and marriage symbols are observed strictly. No changes are observed in dowry and rules of residence but divorce rate is on the decline.

Family types are mixed and extended. Filial, conjugal and sibling relations are smooth. Avoidance is observed between son-in-law and mother-in-law and husband's elder brother, and joking is noticed between elder brother's wife, husband's younger brother, wife's younger sister and wife's younger brother. All male children are entitled to equal share in property. Daughters get less than the sons in case the deceased has made a will to this effect. Women usually do not get a share from the ancestral property. The eldest son succeeds as head of the family. Formation of nuclear families is on increase and extended families are declining.

Women collect fuel, fetch potable water and are mostly engaged in self-employment. They also play an active role in rituals and religious spheres. They have a low status but enjoy decision-making powers, participate in economic activities, contribute to the family income and control family expenditure.

No sooner signs of pregnancy appear, than the pregnant woman is withdrawn from heavy manual work. Post-delivery pollution lasts for seven days. After birth, a priest is called to bless the child and the mother; *mundan* and circumcision are not performed. Nevertheless, when the child attains one year of age, he is taken to a church for baptism or the church priest is invited by the concerned family to perform the above ritual. Confirmation or communion is held when a child attains 12 years of age and henceforth both boys and girls become entitled to attend church services.

Marriage rituals are simple and are mostly performed at a church by exchange of finger rings and readings of verses from the Bible by the priest and extracting a promise of a healthy and smooth married life from the couple. The marriage feast is given by the bride's side.

The dead are buried according to the Christian rites and *daswan* is performed on the tenth day. A prayer meeting and service in the church marks the occasion. Rising prices have affected the life-cycle rituals which stand curtailed.

In cities, the Chuhras neither depend on natural resources nor do they control them. In rural areas, they own small parcels of land under individual proprietorship, but the community is largely landless. Their occupations are scavenging, self-employment, craft (woodwork), and labour. Links with daily and regulated markets exist directly. Bonded and child labour do not exist. Payment for their labour is made in cash. The Christian Biradari Service and the All Jammu & Kashmir Christian Welfare Association, members of which are elected by general consensus, look into the day-to-day affairs of the community, exercise measures of social control and dispute management. Statutory panchayats exist in villages to plan and implement the welfare and development activities. The penalties imposed by the *biradari* panchayat are excommunication and fine. Divorce and beating up of relatives are serious crimes attracting penalties. Good social workers and reformers of the community are honoured and are awarded with citations and prizes.

The Chuhras are Christian, majority of them being Protestants. There are Catholics too, but they are numerically insignificant. Some of their families are affiliated to the Muslim *pirs*. Sacred specialists are from the same community whose functions are to impart religious teachings, perform life-cycle rituals, conduct services in the church and pray for curing of ailments. Christmas and Easter are the festivals of religious significance. Commercial art and carpentry is the common practice with the self-employed. Other than Biblical stories, there are no oral traditions. Carols have replaced folk songs in which both sexes participate. Folk tales, however, exist. Harmonium, flute, tabla and guitar are used in light and Western music. Both sexes participate in dances.

Food and water, if offered to other deities, is not acceptable to them; otherwise they accept the items from all the communities but other communities do not accept either water or food from them in any form. Intercommunity marriages are rare. Patron-client relationship exists. The community claims to have creative artists, teachers, white-collar professionals, administrators, technocrats and defence personnel. Political leadership has emerged at the regional level.

Education is favoured for both sexes. Boys study up to higher secondary level but generally drop out due to economic reasons.

B.R. RIZVI

DANDER

Dander is a Kashmiri word meaning farmer. The Danders affix Bangroo, Bhat, Mir, Nagar, Sofi, Shigan, and Dar with their names. There are two groups in this community, namely Aram and Malyar. Those who grow vegetables with *shali* (paddy) are known as Aram and those who collect night soil, and spread it in the fields as manure and farm are known as Malyar. The members of both the groups intermarry.

The Dander perceive their widespread distribution in the Valley. Chattabal, Noor Bagh, Batmalu, Alochi Bagh and Shalapura are some of the localities of Srinagar where their concentration is more than in other parts of the Valley.

The Danders are settled cultivators and live permanently at one place. The area of this study is Kashmir Valley which has cold climate, low humidity and experiences medium rainfall and medium snowfall. They speak Kashmiri within the kin groups and Kashmiri as well as Urdu with others and use the Arabic script. The subgroup Malyar is included in the category of Other Backward Classes (OBC).

Like other Kashmiris, the Danders wear a long loose gown with buttons at the neck falling to the ankles. Both men and women wear *pheran*. There is very little difference between the *pheran* worn by men and women.

Like other Muslims, the Danders are also non-vegetarian. They consume mutton but do not eat beef. Their staple food is rice. Mutton is consumed in good quantity by the people living in cities but, in the villages, it is still a luxury reserved only for festive occasions. They consume plenty of vegetables. Among pulses *moong*, *mah* and *mothi* are commonly consumed. They use linseed oil for cooking purposes. Fruits such as apple, pear, walnut, mulberry, hazel, cherry, peach, apricot, raspberry, gooseberry, currant and strawberry are consumed. They consume milk and milk products and smoke *bidis*, cigarettes, loose tobacco and chew betel.

Although inhabitants of cold area, the Danders abhor the use of intoxicating drinks. They have, however, found a cheap and harmless alternative in salt tea which they take often.

Endogamy at the community level exist. Marriages are performed at the age of 15-16 years in case of girls and 18-19 years in case of boys. The mode of acquiring mates is through negotiation. Consanguineous marriages are performed. Monogamy is the general form of marriage. Dowry is taken in the form of cash and kind, and the rule of residence after marriage is patrilocal.

Only the husband can ask for divorce. Divorce matters are settled between the family members and other relatives. Among the Danders, divorce takes place in writing. First of all, the relatives try to solve the problem so the husband and wife make a compromise, failing which divorce may be finalized. Divorce does not take place by mere pronouncing the word *talaq* (divorce) thrice but is documented in writing. The amount of *mahr* (dower) is paid at the time of divorce. In case a woman seeks *khula* (separation), she has to forgo the *mahr* and return all the jewellery presented to her by her husband. It is the responsibility of the husband to maintain his wife during the period of *iddat*. Children are the responsibility of the father.

Widow, widower, male as well as female divorcee remarriages are permitted. There is no restriction for a widow or female divorcee to remarry a bachelor. Remarriages are performed in the same manner as marriages performed for the first time.

Extended families are predominant among the Danders. They pay due respect to the elders of the family and the elders love their children. Joking relations are established with *devar* (husband's younger brother) and *bhabhi* (elder brother's wife), *sali* (wife's younger sister) and *bahnoi* (elder sister's husband), etc. Property is the main reason leading to conflicts and confrontations which are generally resolved through compromise.

Both sons and daughters have a right to inheritance and get the share of the paternal property. Widows have the right of inheritance, from parents as well as from their deceased husbands. If a widow is issueless, she is entitled to one-fourth of her husband's property. If there are children, she gets only one-eighth. If the widow is the sole surviving heir of the deceased, she inherits the whole of property. Succession is in the male line and the eldest son succeeds his father.

Women are responsible for household work. Besides, they also do the embroidery work through which they add to the family income. Women can also attend the village panchayats and are free to give their statements and stand as witnesses.

On the seventh day after a child is born, the ritual of *sonder* (purification ceremony) takes place in which the mother of the newborn baby takes bath and comes out of her confinement room. The second bath is given on the fortieth day of the child's birth.

Immediately after birth the *mulla* whispers *azaan* in the right ear of the infant. The baby is given bath on the same day. The name is also given on the same day, usually by the parents of the child.

The *zerakasi* (head shaving) ceremony takes place on the seventh day. A *navid* (barber) shaves the child's head. A goat is sacrificed on the occasion. The skin, head and legs of the sacrificed goat are buried, and the flesh is distributed among the villagers and the *mulla*. The relatives and villagers are invited to a feast. The members of the family do not eat the meat of the sacrificed goat at the time of *zerakasi*. The male child is circumcised after one year and generally at the age of four or five years. After completion of six months of age the child is given a preparation of milk, sugar, bread or biscuits. The ceremony is known as *oapsoap*.

The date for a marriage is fixed by negotiation between the two sides. On the day before the marriage, the boy's father sends *mehndi* (myrtle) leaves for the bride who applies its paste on her hands and feet. On the marriage day, the *barat* (marriage party) first visits a shrine and then proceeds to the bride's house. The *barat* is received at the bride's house with welcome songs sung by women. After the feast is over the father of the groom and the bride fix the amount of *mahr* (dower) according to the family custom. The ritual of *nikah* is performed through the *qazi*. Nuptial ritual takes place at the bridegroom's house. The bride is accompanied by the *dadmoj*, a woman companion, at the time of *rukhsati* and she stays with her in her in-laws' house at least for seven days, after which the bride returns to her parents' house. The son-in-law is invited to a feast by his father-in-law at a convenient time and is given cash, presents, etc.

At the time of death, *kalma* and some verses from the Holy Koran are pronounced in the ear of the dying person. Those who are around call the name of Allah. Among the Danders, dead bodies are buried. A ceremonial bath is given to the dead body and then it is wrapped in a shroud or *kafan*. The dead body is carried to the graveyard in a wooden coffin called *taboot*. The coffin is covered by a black cloth. The burial is accompanied with recitations of the holy verses from the Koran. The mourners then offer *fateha* and return to their homes. From the day of death till the ensuing Friday, the nearest relatives of the departed soul daily visit the grave with the *mulla* and offer prayers. A number of rituals are observed after the death, which include *satijihum fateha*, a ritual performed on the fourth day of death, a ritual observed after forty days, and a ritual performed after one year of the death. A ritual known as *fateha* is observed on the fourth day, but in case Friday falls in between four to seven days, then Friday is preferred for the *fatiha* ritual. In no case it is observed before four days. On the day of the *fateha*, all the relatives and friends of the departed soul gather at the house of the chief mourner and are served food. The *pyur* (engraved stone slab) is also fixed on the grave on the day of *fateha*.

The Danders are settled agriculturists; besides farming they are also engaged in petty business and service. The women do embroidery work at their homes.

Community panchayats do not exist but statutory village panchayats exist.

The Danders are Muslims by religion. They observe the festivals of Id-ul-Fitr, Id-ul-Zuha, Shab-e-Barat, and Shab-e-Qadr. They also annually celebrate the *urs* at the tombs of some well known saints of the area and at Hazratbal. An annual *urs* is celebrated in the month of April at the tomb of Shah Yaqub Batmalu. Hazratbal in Srinagar, the *mazar* of Shah Yaqub Batmalu in Srinagar are some of the sacred centres of the Danders.

Folk songs are sung on the occasions of birth and marriage. Traditional folklores and folk tales are also prevalent.

The Danders do not eat with the Watals. They participate in the functions of other communities and also invite the members of other communities in their functions, e.g. marriage, birth, death, etc. The people of other communities also eat in their houses.

Children of the community avail of the educational facilities. They also send their children to madrasas for religious education. They are not much bothered about the family welfare programmes. Drinking water is available within the locality through taps. Coal and wood are the fuel used for cooking. Wood is collected from the forest if it is nearby.

S.N.H. Rizvi

DAR

The Dar of Kashmir Valley are fishermen and are also known as Ga'd Haenz. The *Rajatarangini* often mentions about the Nishads, boatman, the present-day Haenz. The Haenz who catch fish are known as Ga'd (fish) Haenz. It is said that they were Kshatriyas before their conversion to Islam. Some of the Haenz claim Noah as their ancestor; others claim their gypsy origin. They are distributed mainly in Dal lake, Nagin lake, Wular lake, Manasbal and Ganjabal lake areas. They are found in large numbers in Sopore and Watlab in the Baramula district. Among themselves, they speak Kashmiri. Literate among them write in Urdu using Arabic script. The climate of the area is pleasant during summer but severe in winter. Reliable population figures of the community are not available. *Pheran*, a long coat, shirt and *salwar* is the common dress. On the basis of dress, the community is not distinguishable from the rest of the people in the valley.

They are included in the list of the Other Backward Classes category of Jammu & Kashmir state.

The Dar are non-vegetarians and eat fish, eggs, and meat of all kinds except pork. Rice is their staple food. They take enough pulses such as *masur*, *urad* and *arhar*, and *karam hak* is a favourite leafy vegetable. They use mustard oil as the cooking medium. They take plenty of vegetables. *Nadru* is another favourite vegetable like *karam hak*. Tea is a very common beverage. They also take *qahwa* or green tea. They smoke tobacco. Some of their women also take *hookah* (hubble-bubble) but they do not smoke *bidi* and cigarette. Men smoke *bidi* and cigarette also. Snuff and liquor are avoided.

They are endogamous. The Dar are considered by other communities rather low in the social hierarchy and above only the Watal, Gorkun and the scavanger communites; but they themselve place their position on the medium rung of the hierarchy. Polygyny is permitted, but monogamy is the most preferred and common practice. They settle marriages by negotiation preferably among the relations. Kin marriages such as cross-cousin marriage are practised among them. The bridegroom's father gives first preferance to his brother's daughter in marriage for his son, the preferential practices of parallel cousin marriages. Child marriages are no longer practised. Normal marriagable age for males is 20 and for females it is 16. *Mahr* is promised for future payment. Rule of residence after marriage is patrilocal. Divorce is permissible generally on the grounds of adultery and barrenness of the wife. Only the husband can divorce. If the wife wants separation, she has to forgo the amount of *mahr*. If she has already taken the *mahr* amount, she would have to pay it back. Though there is a positive sanction for divorce, yet it is looked down upon by the community. In case of divorce, children are the responsibility of the father; but if the children are minor, they are the responsibility of the mother. Both widow and widower remarriages are permissible.

Until recent times extended family was most prevalent; but now the common form of family is nuclear. They maintain avoidance between mother-in-law and son-in-law; daughter-in-law and father-in-law. Joking is permitted between elder brother's wife and husband's younger brother; elder sister's husband and wife's younger sister. Sometimes conflict and confrontation arise after the death of the father or after the marriage of a son. Main reasons for such conflict and confrontation may be the issues of sharing property. Male equigeniture is the rule of inheritance. Interfamily relationship is very cordial. Women fetch drinking water and collect firewood. They carry fish to the market for sale. They have a role in parforming rituals and in the management of the family, but they do not have any role in the mechanism of social control and politics. They enjoy a status lower than the male members.

During pregnancy, a woman is not allowed to perform heavy manual work. She is not allowed to pass through the graveyard and such other places which are considered to be the haunting grounds of the evil spirits specially during night. She is also not allowed to participate in a mourning ceremony. Delivery takes place in the husband's house with the assistance of some elderly experienced ladies of the household or neighbourhood. Just after birth, the newly born baby is given a bath in lukewarm water. *Azaan* is whispered by a *mulla* in the ear of the newborn. On the seventh day, the child is given a name. A sheep is slaughtered on this occasion, half of which is reserved for the mother of the child. From the other half, a leg is given as reward to the person who proposes an appropriate name for the child. On this day, the friends, neighbours and relatives are invited to a feast.

Circumcision is done when a male child attains the age of two to three years. The operation used to be performed by a local *navid* (barber) but nowadays they take the help of a surgeon. This occasion is celebrated by inviting relatives, neighbours and friends for a feast. The invitees give a token amount as gift to the father of the child which is known as *katmosh*. Women also participate in the function and sing. After seven days, *hadayu* is performed with pomp and a sheep is slaughtered, cooked and distributed among the gathering.

A marriage may be arranged through negotations conducted by a relative or the *manzymyor*(go-between). The acceptance of a marriage proposal is expressed by the groom's father by placing eleven rupees in the cup in which he takes tea at the bride's house. The visit is reciprocated a few days later. *Nilam* (betrothal) is a ceremony in which the boy's father contracts the agreement in writing. A week before the marriage, the hair of the would-be bride is untied, and *ghee* and scent applied to it after giving her a ritual bath. The bride keeps the hair untied (*malasbehoun*) till the day of marriage. This function is known as *massmechravoun*. The approaching ceremony is observed by singing and playing at *tumbaknar* (a kind of musical drum). One day before the marriage, the bride's hand and feet are stained with *mehndi* (myrtle). Next morning the hair of the bride are finally dressed by a *sazehgaren* (an experienced lady beautician). *Mehndi* is also applied to the hands and feet of the bridegroom.

The marriage party leaves for the bride's place in boats and, in the process, visits the shrines en route. The party is received at the bride's place by the singing women. When the marriage party reaches the door of the bride's house, the *navid* pours out a jar of water. A representative of the bridegroom's party puts a rupee in the empty jar. This ceremony is known as *abdul*. *Nikah* is performed by the *qazi* in which consent of the bride and the bridegroom is obtained and amount of *mahr* is settled. After the marriage, the bride stays with her husband for a period of seven day, after which she visit her parents.

The burial of the dead is done according the accepted practice of the Muslims. Prevaling burial rituals are performed and the fortieth day of death is the final farewell day for those coming to condole the bereaved family.

Being Muslims, they celebrate all the Ids, sacrificing a goat on Id-e-Qurban. During Muharram they abstain from luxuries. They visit well-known shrines such as Hazratbal, Shah Hamdan, Dastgir Sahib, Makhdum Sahib, etc. Visit to Ajmer and Nizamuddin are also undertaken if possible. The religious specialist (*qazi*) performs marriage and death ceremonials and imparts the teachings of Islam. They do not take part in the socio-religious movements. There is no change in the pattern of religious behaviour and organization among them. They believe in evil spirits and take special care not to visit the haunting grounds of the spirits, specially during night. Amulets are tied at shrines for good health of the child. This is called *dash ganden*. Sometimes amulets are obtained from the *faqirs* and tied round the neck of the child to evade evil spirits. They do not have any traditional art or craft. They have folk songs which they share with the rest of the people of the valley.

The major economic resource of the Dar is water, on which they have no individual control. In lieu of a token amount of levy, the Government of Jammu & Kashmir allows them to catch fish. Very rarely do they have land to cultivate and subsist mainly on their traditional occupation of fishing. Some of them have shifted to handicraft work. In their business, there is no middleman. There is no instance of bonded labour among them. Child labour is also absent. With the increase of population and encroachment on Dal Lake, they are facing problems. The Social Welfare Department is helping them by providing nets and other prerequisites for fishing. A few of them are successful businessmen. Some of them are educated and are employed in the university as faculty members.

The Dars have traditional caste panchayats to settle intracommunity disputes. In this court, they settle the disputes through their elders who act as judges. The traditional village level panchayat has a greater force than the statutory panchayat. Wise and respected members of the community constitute the caste panchayat. The disputes referred to are mainly related to marriage, dowry, divorce, etc.

The Dars accept water from any follower of Islam except from the Watal, Gorkan and scavengers. They accept both raw and cooked food from all other communities. There is no putative kinship among them. Intercommunity marital exchange is very rare. None of the communities except those lower to them would agree for marital relation with a Dar boy or girl. Further, the Dars do not like to establish marital relations with the boys or girls from the Watal, Gorkan and scavenger castes. They share public places such as roads, schools, water sources with other communities, and mosques and burial grounds with rest of the Muslim communities except those mentioned earlier. There is no patron-client relationship (*jajmani* system) among them. Modern intercommunity linkages are there, but they have not changed their religious life and marriage customs. The Dars are on the lower rung of the hierarchy, both on economic and social parameters, and have no role in political activity.

They make use of the various facilities offered by the state, though not all are benefited. They are categorized under the category of Other Backward Classes. In case of girls, even those who can afford education are reluctant in sending them to schools out of the fear that education of the girl would make it difficult to get a suitable match for her. Modern medical facilities are available in the area. They hardly use the indigenous medicine. They are quite aware of the family welfare schemes but have a negative attitude towards family planning. Drinking water is available within the locality. They have received negligible benefit of the developmental schemes of the government. There is no initiative to teach them scientific methods of fishing and fish breeding. They enjoy the benefits of mass media like radio, television, etc. The roads are good. The nearest railway station is in Jammu. All of them use electricity for domestic purposes. They avail themselves of the public distribution system. They have a positive attitude towards savings.

B. JOARDAR

DESIL

The Desils are also known as Gilkars. They are distributed in almost all the districts of the Kashmir Valley. They speak Kashmiri among themselves, but write in Urdu with Arabic script. They dress themselves like the other Kashmiri Muslims. They are categorized under the category of Other Backward Classes in the state. The Desils are non-vegetarian and eat beef but not pork. Their staple food consists of rice supplemented by wheat and maize. Pulses such as gram, *urad, moong* and *masur* are taken. Mustard oil is the cooking medium. Potatoes, onion, radish and carrots are some of the tubers consumed by them. Salted and green tea are popular beverages and are taken a number of times in the day. Milk and milk products are also consumed. Aged persons smoke *hookah* (*jajeer*) and rub their teeth with snuff. Seasonal fruits of Kashmir are consumed moderately.

Differentiations within them, if any, are at educational, occupational and economic levels. They can marry any Muslim provided he or she has an equal status and clean occupation. There has been no change in their surnames. They are considered to be in the middle rung of the society. Other communities too consider them in that rank.

Endogamy is practised at the community level, but it is not strictly followed. Consanguinity, both cross and parallel cousin, is practised. Marriage of maternal uncle with his niece is not permitted. Sororate (junior) and levirate (junior) re-marriages are allowed. Adult marriages are preferred. Mates are acquired through negotiation. The other mode is by the exchange of sisters. Monogamy is the usual form of marriage. Keeping more than one wife is allowed but it is not a general practice. There are no symbols of a married woman. Dowry is paid to the father of the bridegroom at the time of marriage. At the time of *nikah* (marriage contract), a commitment is made by the bridegroom regarding the amount of *mahr* (dower) which the bride can claim during her lifetime. A part of the *mahr* is instantly paid and the balance is promised but not paid. After marriage, the bride goes to stay with her husband and in-laws. Divorce takes place due to adultery, barrenness, maladjustment, impotency and cruelty. In case the husband divorces his wife, then he has to pay the amount of *mahr* to the bride; but when separation takes place at the initiative of the wife, then she has to return the clothes and ornaments which she has recieved from the father of the bridegroom. It is always the prerogative of husband to seek a divorce. In divorce cases, children are the responsibility of the father. Widow, widower and divorcee remarriage is permissible. In such cases, marriage with wife's younger sister and husband's younger brother is permitted provided they are of matching age.

Families are generally mixed extended and also nuclear type. Often the nuclear families occupy separate rooms and kitchen in the same dwelling unit. The old parents may cook food in a separate kitchen or share with their married sons. Interpersonal relations within the family are based on respect for the elders and love and affection for youngsters. Avoidance exists between daughter-in-law and father-in-law and between sister-in-law and the husband's elder brothers. Joking relations exist between sister-in-law and brother-in-law; with wife's younger and elder sisters and wife's elder and younger brothers. Points of conflict and confrontation arise mostly on property matters. The father's property is divided among the sons and daughters. The females get less than the males. The father is the head of the family. The eldest son succeeds him. A decline in the extended family has been observed. Women shoulder major burden of the domestic work. Collection of fuel, bringing potable water, cooking food, caring of children, etc., are the jobs to which women attend. Women do not enjoy equal status with men. They do not contribute to the family income.

A pregnant woman is forbidden to carry heavy loads, to meet visitors at night and to come out in the open in the moonlit nights. In case of first pregnancy, the woman does not stay at her husband's place beyond five months of pregnancy. She spends the remaining period at her parental home. The delivery of the child generally takes place at the hands of *dai* (midwife), though nowadays the parturient lady is taken to the hospital for delivery. Immediately after birth, the baby is given a bath in lukewarm water and *azaan* is whispered in its ears. On the birth of the first child, bread with sugar balls, *shirini*, are distributed among relatives, friends and neighbours. On the seventh day after delivery, the mother is given the first bath with lukewarm water and the child is given a name in consultation with the elderly persons in the family or the priest. A second bath is given on the fortieth day of delivery. This marks the end of the pollution period. The childhood rituals are *zerakasi* (shaving of the head) and circumcision of the male child, *khatnahal* which are performed at the age of six months and two years, respectively. Nowadays, the circumcision is done in the hospital soon after birth.

Marriage is an important event. Boys and girls do not enjoy the freedom of selecting their own spouses according to their choice. The selection is the exclusive privilege of the parents or the guardians. Sometimes the services of a *manzymyor* (professional matchmaker) are taken to negotiate a marriage deal. Otherwise, a common friend or relative starts negotiation at the behest of one of the parties. After preliminary negotiations, a convenient date is fixed for the formal announcement. On this day, the boy's father, accompanied by some relatives, visits the house of the girl and offers some money in the cup which is collected by the host signifying the acceptance of the relationship. This ceremony is called engagement or *gandum*. This is followed by the ritual of *doon-leij* formality. On this day the date of marriage is fixed and announced. As the date of marriage draws near several ceremonies are performed in quick succession. The rituals performed at the house of the bride are *malasbehoun* (loosening of hair plaits of the bride) *massmechravoun* (dyeing of hands and feet of the bride with myrtle paste) *malamenz* and ends with (the night of actual wedding) *menziraat*. In the night following *menziraat*, the bridegroom and the *barat* go to the bride's house. The *barat* is received ceremonially and served a feast. *Nikah* is performed and, in early hours, the bride and the bridegroom return to latter's house where the bride stays for seven days. A feast is given by the father of the bridegroom. It is called *wathal*.

A person on death bed is asked to pronounce the name of Allah. The dead body is given a bath by a professional called *snangor* who is paid in cash and kind. The body is wrapped in *kafan* (white cloth) and kept in a *taboot* (coffin). It is taken to the nearby mosque for prayers, before taking it to the final resting place in a graveyard. The grave is dug by a professional gravedigger called *malkhosh*. The body is then placed in the grave and covered with earth and stones. Mourning is held until the following Friday. On the fourth day, the priest, relatives, neighbours and friends are invited to recite the Holy Koran. This is repeated also on the fortieth day. The rituals observed on these two occasions are called *chaharum* and *chehallum*, respectively. The change observed in the life-cycle rituals is their partial curtailment under the changing circumstances.

Land is their main economic resource. They cultivate paddy and mustard in their wet fields and maize in the dry fields. They are owner cultivators. Some are sharecroppers and others work as wage labourers. Their primary occupation is masonry. In the villages they are also engaged as carpenters and make wooden frames for doors and windows. Some of them also make unbaked bricks which are used for house construction. Bonded labour does not exist among the Desils. In the villages, the members of this community own some land. Children above five years are engaged in making bricks. Wages are received in cash. They have also started making wooden boxes for packing fruits.

They do not have a caste council of their own. Disputes of the community are decided by the elders. The statutory panchayat came into being after Independence. It consists of eleven members, of whom eight are elected and three are nominated by the State Development Commissioner from a panel of names sponsored by the outgoing panchayat. It is presided over by a *sarpanch* who holds office for a period of five years. Under the Act, the panchayat is vested with wide powers, such as disposal of suits connected with contracts, recovery of movable property and compensation for wrongful possession of property and damages caused by cattle trespass, etc. In actual practice, however, the panchayats confine their activities to the settlement of petty disputes and execution of minor development projects. Now the crimes and offences are referred to the police and settled in lawcourts.

The Desils profess Islam of the Sunni sect. The shrines and sacred places visited by them are Hazaratbal, Ziarat Dastgir, Shah Hamdan, Jama Masjid, Sheikh Zain-ud-Din, etc. *Imam*, *pir*, and *maulvi* are their sacred specialists. They perform birth, marriage and death rites. All the Muslim festivals such as Muharram, Id-ul-Milad, Rabi-ul-Awwal, Id-ul-Fitr, Id-ul-Zuha, and Shab-e-Barat are celebrated by the people. Making of bricks is the only noticeable craft. Folk songs such as *wanawun*, *wayun* and *rouf* are sung on the occasion of marriage, betrothal, and festival.

They live in the neighbourhood of other Muslim and Hindu communities. They render their services to all of them. They are invited by other communities on the occasion of childbirth and marriage. They accept food and water from all other communities except the *watals* (scavengers). They share the sources of drinking water, shrines, burial ground, etc., with other Muslim communities. They participate in all the Muslim festivals along with their other Muslim brethren. There is no patron-client relations with others. They are paid in cash if employed by others in house construction. There are no engineers and doctors or members holding white-collar jobs from this community.

They have positive attitude towards the development programmes. Facilities of schools up to primary level are available in the villages.

Higher education is not generally affordable and the boys are put to professional trade when still in teens. Facilities of primary health centre are available to the villagers near the block headquarters but, in the interior, the villagers have to go long distances for medicare. Couples prefer to have two to three children and generally the women get sterilized. Piped water is available in the villages for drinking but, in remoter places, springs are the main source of drinking water. Some villages are also covered under Integrated Rural Development programme. They are engaged both as wage earning employees and in self-employment. Only a few have a radio or a television set. Villages are electrified. Firewood, cow-dung cakes and kerosene oil are used as fuel. Irrigation by canal water is available in the villages. The community uses chemical fertilizers and also organic manures. Under the Integrated Child Development Scheme programme, the pre-school going children are given nutrition packets. These facilities are available in villages which are located nearer the block headquarters. Facilities of fair price shops are available and the community members are issued ration cards. The Dehati Elaquai Bank caters to the needs of rural areas but loans are available only to those who have some landed property.

PARMANAND LAL

DHAMALI FAQIR/FAQIR

The Dhamali Faqirs, the folk dancers of Kashmir, are mostly called Dhamalis. The folk dance which they perform is known as *dhambael* and persons who perform this dance are usually called Dhamali Faqirs. The term *faqir* is attributed to them because it is generally believed that they achieve some sort of a trance while dancing. Some people believe that since the Damalis receive alms and move from place to place for begging, they are known as *faqirs.* No historical account of the community exists but they claim to have been patronized by the royal families who ruled Kashmir. The community lives in Zolo Gopal Pora (Chadura), Kaneil Gund, Hum Home, Arigome, Khan Sahib and Aishmugam areas. The natural environment of all these villages is almost the same as in other parts of the Valley. The community speaks Kashmiri languages and uses Arabic script. The Constitution has declared them as a Scheduled Caste.

The Dhamali Faqirs are non-vegetarian and eat beef. They eat eggs, fish and mutton. Rice is their staple food. In the morning and evening, they take salt tea along with chapatis made of wheat or corn flour. Pulses are used during winter season. All kinds of vegetables and fruits are consumed by them. Alcoholic drinks are not taken but some members of the community sometimes smoke *charas.*

Broadly speaking, no social divisions within the Dhamali Fakirs exist. However, the Dhamalis living in Zolo Gopal Pora are believed to be superior to the Dhamalis living in other villages. Shah is a surname used by them and they claim to be superior to other Dhamalis not only socially but also in the quality of the devotional dance. The members of the Dhamali community living in the villages other than Zolo Gopal Pora resort to begging in winter. However, the community as a whole is regarded socially downtrodden by other communities of the Valley.

The Dhamali Faqirs used to be endogamous but now inter-community marriages are also observed. Girls are generally married at the age from 16 to 18 years while the boys are married at the age of 18 to 22 years. The mates are generally acquired within the village but some members of the community have also married outside their villages and even outside their community. In case they do not get the mates within the community, the other communities in which they prefer to marry are the Bhands, carpenters, and professional singers. Neither the women nor men use any symbol of marriage. Dowry is neither paid nor demanded. Clothes and silver ornaments for the bride are offered by the bridegroom. The marriage is performed according to the Muslim customs. Divorce is generally discouraged but divorce can be granted under the Islamic laws. The divorce is generally initiated by the males. Pre-puberty marriages were common in the community but this practice is now being discouraged. Monogamy is the present norm in the community but polygyny is also permitted. Both the males and females can remarry provided they get suitable mates.

The Dhamali Faqirs prefer to live in joint families to form a group for their traditional dancing. However, nuclear family has also started. Interpersonal relations are cordial and the elders are respected. Joking in similar age group is permitted. Conflicts and confrontations do exist. The ancestral property or distribution of money and other items earned through traditional dancing are the main causes of disputes. The rules of inheritance as permitted under the Islamic law and customary laws of Kashmir are followed. The succession as head of the dancing group is made on the basis of merit. The eldest male issue succeeds his father.

Women enjoy secondary status among the Dhamali Faqirs but they do enjoy the rights of inheritance. A married women, besides getting the *mahr* from her husband, inherits a definite portion of her husband's property. She also inherits her share from the property belonging to her father. Women have little role to play in family economy but contribute to family earning by way of spinning woollen yarn, collecting cow-dung and firewood, etc.

The woman generally goes to her father's residence a month before she delivers the baby and is given less workload before and after delivery. She is given complete rest for ten days in case of normal delivery and for forty days otherwise. A few Dhamalis who are in a financially better position observe the naming ceremony. *Aqeeqa* ceremony is also performed by a few members of the community. Circumcision of male issues at the age of three to four years is performed. This ritual is celebrated with pomp and show by such Dhamali Faqirs as are comparatively sound economically. A feast is arranged to which the relations and other members of the community are invited and even a programme of singing and dancing is arranged.

Marriage rituals are performed at the bride's residence. *Nikah khani* is performed by the local *maulvi* and both the bride and bridegroom remain present at that time. The expenditure on marriage is borne by the bridegroom. Dinner is arranged on the occasion by the bride's parents but its expenditure to some extent is borne by the bridegroom. The bride is then taken to the bridegroom's house where she stays for seven to ten days. *Walima* is arranged by the bridegroom. On both these occasions, a feast is given to other members of the community.

No special ritual at the time of death or with regard to the disposal of the dead is observed. Like the other Muslims of the Valley, the dead body is given a bath and wrapped in a *kafan* (shroud) and is taken to an open field for *namaz-e-janaza* after which it is buried in the nearby graveyard. The *jumma-fateha* which is prevalent among the Muslims of the city is not observed. However, the *chaharum* is observed on the fourth day after the death. The practice of fixing a tombstone on the grave was not common in the past but now some Dhamali Faqirs erect tombstones on the graves.

Dancing is the major means of livelihood. They dance at some specific shrines (*ziarat*) where they collect money, cereals, paddy, etc., as alms which is then distributed among the members of the group. During winter they weave *kangris* and *chadars*. Since most of the Dhamali Faqirs do not have their own land, they, work as farm labourers and in return get some cash and a very small percentage of the yield. However, a few members of the community possess some agricultural land. Some Dhamali Faqirs work in brick kilns at Gopal Pora and in nearby areas. During winter when they cannot dance due to the climatic conditions, they move out of the Valley and work in Punjab and adjacent areas where they earn something to eat. The youth of the community do not like to opt for their traditional profession and prefer to serve in the government offices. The members of the community entirely depend on the market for their requirements except for rice and other cereals which they collect at the time of dancing. Child labour is common in the community and the payment of wages is made in cash to those who work in brick kilns, etc.

Traditional council and regional associations do not exist among the Dhamali Faqirs. However, minor disputes are settled among themselves. The leader or head of the dancing group, known as *magun*, generally decides about the minor disputes and his decisions are mostly accepted. Indiscipline during the performance is not tolerated and any member, who indulges in misconduct or indiscipline is suspended from the dancing party or group and is reinstated only after he tenders an apology. In villages where the Dhamali Faqirs are in majority, they come within the purview of the local panchayat, but only a few cases are referred to it as they mostly solve their disputes among themselves.

The Dhamali Faqirs profess Islam and most of them belong to the

Sunni sect. They perform all religious rituals as other Muslims of the Valley do. The Dhamalis mostly visit and dance as an offering on the occasion of annual *urs* at the shrines of saints of Rishi Order of Kashmir. These include the shrines of Baba Gazi at Bijbehara, Lal Bab Sahib at Zakora, Srinagar, and Ziarat Khan Sahib in Budgam district. The Dhamalis feel themselves associated with these shrines. Religious specialists like the *pirs* play an important role at the time of birth and death in the community. They also purify their dead and exorcize evil spirits.

The Dhamali Faqirs are not specialized in plastic and graphic arts. Traditional crafts like *kangri* weaving and handicrafts like shawl embroidery and *chadar* weaving are the means of livelihood of some members of the community during winter. The community has rich oral traditions of folk songs and folk tales.

The dance of the Dhamali Faqirs, known as Dhamali dance, is an age old traditional folk dance of Kashmir. It is a warrior type folk dance and resembles the Dhamali of Haryana and adjoining areas of southern parts of the state. It is reminiscent of martial dance once prevalent in Kashmir but now completely forgotten. It is danced as an offering on the occasions of the annual *urs* at the shrines already mentioned. On such occasions, all the dancers from different parts of the Valley assemble and dance at separate arenas at these shrines. Each party consists of one drummer, one cymbal player and a few dancers, ordinarily fourteen in number. The Dhamalis dance both in groups and individually. Leaps, *rasa* and mock fighting are important features of this dance. A Dhamali dancer has to retain his breath, recite the name of Allah and take leap after leap till he is fully exhausted. He is supposed to dance till the moment of trance. At that moment he breathes heavily and some other dancers take him in their lap. The dancer stretches his body on the beat of the drum with full strength. *Rasa* and mock fighting are important features of this dance and it is exhibited with sticks and not with swords. In olden days, the Dhamalis used to play *dhol* when an army used to march off to war. This is evident from the march-like steps taken by the dancers when they enter into the arena. The Dhamali dancers wear a *kurta*, *salwar*, waistcoat and a turban as their headgear. It is considered auspicious to arrange the dance in one's compound for the prosperity of the family.

They participate and attend all religious, ceremonial and other occasions within and outside their community. Both water and food from other communities are accepted by them. They share the well and water sources, roads, schools, panchayat premises, burial places, etc., with other communities. Mosques and shrines are also shared with the other Muslim communities. They maintain patron-client relationship with the leader of their dancing group who, on behalf of other dancers, receives alms and offerings both in cash and kind and distributes it among all other members of the group.

The members of this community are mostly agricultural labourers. They do not have scholars, enterpreneurs, administrators, engineers, doctors, politicians and businessmen. Some of them are employed in the education and police departments.

Although the Dhamali Faqirs have a tendency towards education and send their children to schools, yet most of the children discontinue at the primary level. Few Dhamalis attend adult literacy programme. Their attitude towards allopathic and ayurvedic medicine is favourable. Some of them have also been benefited by the *Rehabar-e-Shat* scheme launched by the state government. The attitude towards family planning is not encouraging. The Dhamalis of Zolo Gopal Pora have proper drinking water facilities and others mostly depend on natural springs and rivulet water. They have not been benefited by any of the rural employment programmes except from the Food for Work programme launched by the state government. They are making use of the media and communication facilities. Most of them use electricity for lighting their houses but very few use it for cooking. Firewood and cow-dung cakes are used as fuel. Most of them are landless agricultural labourers and do not utilize the irrigation facilities or use chemical fertilizers. Most of them have not availed of the nutrition programmes through midday meals under the ICDS programme. However, in some of their localities Anganwadi centres have been opened. Some of them get ration through the public distribution system. Banking facilities are available to the members of the community living at Zolo Gopal Pora.

The Dhamali Faqirs are socio-economically a backward community. Although they have preserved the rich tradition of folk dances of Kashmir, but nothing is being done for their encouragement. The Jammu and Kashmir Academy of Art and Culture and the Department of Culture, Government of India are encouraging a few Dhamalis living at Zolo Gopal Pora but the dancers of other localities do not get any kind of patronage. They are economically backward and mostly depend on the alms which they receive from the public. They are educationally and socially backward but all of them have at least their own house to live.

REYAZ RUFAI

DHOBI

The Dhobi are also known as Dhob. The term *dhob* means removing spots from the clothes. Earlier there were two divisions of the Dhobis: Pashmin Dhobi or those who were specialized in washing the *pashmina* shawls and carpets, and others who were washing clothes only were simply known as Dhobi. But nowadays, there is no specialized group and any Dhobi can wash *pashmina* shawls, carpets as well as other clothes.

Dhobis are aware of their widespread distribution: Srinagar, Badgam, Pulwama and Anantnag are some of the districts of Jammu & Kashmir, where the concentration of the Dhobis is larger.

Like the common Kashmiris, the Dhobis wear an overdress called *pheran*. In winter they use *pheran* made of wool and, in summer, of cotton. The *pheran* worn by the womenfolk is slightly shorter than the one worn by men. In winter, a *kangri* (portable earthen firepot covered with a basket of wickerwork) is taken under the *pheran* to keep the body warm. They are included in the list of Other Backward Classes communities of Jammu & Kashmir.

The Dhobis are non-vegetarian and consume mutton. Their staple food is rice. They consume plenty of vegetables. Among pulses, *mah*, *mothi* and *moong* are commonly consumed. The cooking oil used by them is linseed. Fruits such as apple, pear, walnut, mulberry, hazelnut, cherry, peach, apricot, raspberry, gooseberry, currant and strawberry are consumed. They do not take alcoholic drinks and other intoxicants. Milk and milk products are consumed regularly.

Earlier the Dhobis were strictly endogamous, but nowadays they have started marrying among the Rather, Dar, Ganai, Bhat and other Muslim communities. They do not marry among the Namdgur, Munjygur and Watal. Marriages are performed at the age of fifteen years in the case of girls and eighteen years in the case of boys. The initiation of a marriage proposal is very important because it opens the way to negotiation and settlement. Consanguineous marriages are also performed. Dowry is taken in kind only. Residence after marriage is patrilocal.

The contract of marriage may be dissolved by the husband at his will, without the intervention of the court, called *talaq*, or by mutual consent of the husband and wife without the intervention of the court, called *khula* (redemption).

It is the responsibility of husband to maintain his wife during her period of *iddat*, the restriction imposed on a woman on the termination of the marriage in order to establish the paternity of a possible child conceived earlier, during which a woman is expected to live a life of seclusion and abstain from all luxuries. The observance of *iddat* is necessary where cohabitation had taken place before the divorce. If consummation of marriage had taken place and the marriage is dissolved by divorce, then the duration of *iddat* is three months and ten days, or, if the woman is pregnant, it is until delivery.

It is the duty of the husband to look after the children even after divorce, whether the children live with the mother or with him. The mother is entitled to the custody of the children without distinction of sex until they are weaned. During this period, which is limited to two years, the children cannot, under any circumstances, be removed from their mother's care without her consent. After the child has been weaned away, the child's custody, if a male, devolves on the father, and if a female, on the mother. The mother's custody of a female child continues till the child is seven years. Thereafter, the father is entitled to keep her in his custody in preference to the mother.

Widow, widower, male as well as female divorcee remarriages are permitted. If a man divorces his wife, he cannot remarry her without submitting to the ordeal of her being married to another person and divorced by him. Then only can he remarry his divorced wife. Remarriages are performed in the same way as the marriages are performed for the first time.

Extended families are common among the Dhobis but nowadays, they are turning towards nuclear families. They pay due regard to the elders of their family and love the children, irrespective of their sex. Joking relations prevails with wife's younger brother (*sala*) and elder sister's husband (*bahnoi*), wife's younger sister (*sali*), husband's younger brother and elder brother's wife (*bhabhi*), etc. Property is the main reason behind conflicts and confrontations. These are generally resolved through familial compromise.

Daughters also have the right of inheritance and get the share of the paternal property. Widows have the right of inheritance of their parents as well as of their husband's property. If a widow has no issues, she is entitled to one-fourth of her husband's property. If the widow is the sole surviving heir of the deceased, she inherits the whole of the property. If she does not remarry, she enjoys the right of support from her paternal or conjugal family. The eldest son succeeds as the head of family.

Women enjoy equal status with the menfolk. Besides doing

household chores, women help menfolk in outdoor activities, e.g. they deliver the washed clothes to the customers at their houses. They do not play any role in politics.

The birth purification ritual is known as *sonder*. It is generally held on the seventh day of the birth. For the first three days after delivery, *sharbat* is served to the mother. For seven days, i.e. till the purification rite, vegetables and *qahwa* are served to the mother. She can also eat bread with tea, *qahwa*, and *sharbat*.

Naming does not involve any ceremony. The name is given by the family *pir* after seven days of the birth. The tonsure ceremony is called *zerakasi* (head shaving). It signifies the removal of the hair that the child is born with. The village *navid* (barbar) is called to perform the shaving. A goat is sacrificed on the occasion. The skin, head and legs of the sacrificed goat are buried and the meat is distrubuted to the villagers and the *mulla*. The relatives and friends are invited in the feast. The family members do not eat the meat of the sacrificed goat. Circumcision (*khatna*) of the boy is performed after one year. A feast is arranged on this occasion for all the friends and relatives.

The elderly ladies of the family consider it their foremost duty to suggest marriage proposals for girls and boys. Other members of the family also look for a suitable match. The initiative is always taken from the boy's side and the help of intermediaries may be sought. The culminating point of negotiations is the fixing of a date. One day before the marriage, the boys's father sends *henna* or *mehndi* which is applied to the hands and feet of the bride before the actual marriage ceremony takes place. There are several ceremonies which are observed during the marriage. The main ones are the *nikah* and *rukhsati*. In the *nikah* ceremony, the invited guests and relatives assemble at the bridegroom's place. The bridegroom and his party members visit some neighbouring shrine and then the *barat* (marriage party) proceeds for the house of the bride. The parents of both the sides fix the amount of *mahr* (dower) before the *nikah* is performed. The *nikah* is performed by a *kazi*. *Daj* (dowry) generally includes clothes, ornaments, furniture, utensils, etc., given to the bride by her parents, as also the presents from her friends and relatives, which are displayed before *rukhsati* or send off. The bride remains for seven days in her in-laws' house, after which she returns to her father's house for a brief stay.

The dead are buried. At the time of death, *kalma* and some verses from the Holy Koran are recited into the ear of the dying person. Bath is given to the dead body and then it is wrapped in white cloth known as *kafan* (shroud). The dead body is kept in a wooden *taboot* (coffin) and the funeral procession proceeds towards a graveyard. Women do not accompany the procession. After the dead body is buried, the mourners at the spot throw *mitti* (earth) on the grave and then recite *fateha* (a *sura* of the Holy Koran). After this, the mourners go back to their respective houses. A number of rituals are observed after the death of a person, which include *fateha* (performed on the fourth day of death), *satijihum* (observed after forty days or on the fortieth day), and *vaharvoor* (performed after one year of death).

The Dhobis are traditional washermen. Besides washing clothes, they are also engaged in business and services.

The community council exists and is known as Dhobi Anjuman. The head of the Anjuman is an elected member. The Dhobi Anjuman still exercises some control in the matter of social behaviour such as marriage, divorce, and mutual disputes. Statutory village panchayats also exist.

The Dhobis are Sunni Muslims. They observe the festivals of Id-ul-Fitr, Id-ul-Zuha, Ramzan, Barawafat and Shab-e-Barat. There are a number of tombs of the Muslim saints where *urs* congregations are held. The following are some of the sacred pilgrimage centres of the Dhobis: tomb of Dastgir Sahib, tomb of Sheikh Nooruddin Wali and Hazratbal.

On all the important social functions of the Dhobis, their Muslim as well as Hindu friends and neighbours take part. They have linkages with the people of other communities of the village. They wash all sorts of clothes of the people of different communities except those of the Watal. They are invited by the people of other communities on different occasions, e.g. marriage, birth and other functions. Similarly, they also invite the people of other communities on different occasions. They eat in the houses of all communities except the Watals.

The Dhobis send their children for schooling. Usually, the girls study up to eighth standard and boys up to tenth class. Education of the children is discontinued for various reasons like poverty, social problems and, some times, non-availability of schools in the nearby areas. They also send their children to *madrasas* for religious education.

The Dhobis are utilizing the modern medical facilities available in the area. They are aware of the welfare programmes but do not accept direct sterilization. Drinking water is available within the locality through taps. Coal and wood are the fuel used for cooking.

S.N.H. Rizvi

DHOLWALA

The Dholwalas earn their living by beating the musical drum (*dhol*) on different socio-religious occasions in the region. The name *dhol* (drum) plus *wala* (the person) together has given them the name of Dholwala as a community. It is reported that the Dholwalas have two sections, Jogis and Gardwachi. While the Jogis play *dhol* on professional basis, i.e. they get paid for playing the instrument, the Gardwachi play the drum only on religious ceremonies, especially those pertaining to Shiva. They believe that prayers offered to Shiva are incomplete without a Gardwachi playing the drum. Hence, they live on the offerings or the doles given by the people on such occassions. Their main subgroups are Malhotra, Jangotra, Balgotra, Jasotra, etc. They are mostly the original inhabitants of Jummu region. They perceive their distribution at the regional level. In the region of Jammu, they are mainly concentrated in Udhampur, Rajouri, Naoshera, Badherwali Katra and the main city of Jammu.

Social differentiation among them appears to exist on the basis of economic status and employment pattern, which influences the marriage alliances. They do not go for marriage alliance with the Hindus who are lower to them in the overall hierarchy. Endogamy exists at the community level. Junior sororate is permissible but its occurrence is very rare. Children are married after attaining puberty; boys usually marry after the age of 20 years while for girls it is usually around 18 years and above. Mates are acquired through friends and relatives. Monogamy is the prevailing rule of marriage. Dowry is mostly paid in kind though it is not as ostentatious as among the high caste Hindu. Patrilocal is the rule of residence. Divorce is permissible with religious and judicial approval. The reasons for divorce are adultery, maladjustment and insanity. Compensation and maintenance is paid to the wife. Children are the responsibility of both mother and father, as the case may be. Widow, widower and divorcee remarriage is permissible. Junior sororate is permissible though levirate in the form of *chadar dalna* is a very rare phenomenon.

Families are extended as well as nuclear, the latter being a common feature among the urban dwellers. Avoidance and joking relationships are prevalent. Elders are paid due regards and intrafamily relations are cordial. No conflict and confrontations prevails in intrafamily bonds except for property disputes. The paternal property is divided equally among the male issues as the female's claim over the same is considered to be paid in the dowry. Girls are, however, entitled to a share in the paternal property though they never demand it. Succession goes to the eldest male issue. Extended families are being slowly replaced by nuclear families.

Women have limited roles to perform. In the rural area they have a role in agricultural operations and other economic activities but, in the overall context, they are put in relative seclusion. However, they participate actively in socio-religious spheres. The women's role in politics is restricted to voting only. Their status is low as compared to their menfolk. They usually do not contribute to the family income but do have a part to play in its expenditure. Some of them contribute to the family earnings by undertaking petty jobs while a few of them are also teachers and holding white-collar jobs.

Pre-delivery restrictions are followed by the parturient mothers. Their movements are restricted. The post-delivery pollution period is observed by them. Naming ceremony is not of a formal type while *mundan* ceremony is only practised in case of the male children. First feeding of cereals is not ceremonial though *janeu* (sacred thread) ceremony is celebrated. Marriage rituals are performed at the bride's residence. The *barat*, i.e. the groom riding a horse and holding a ceremonial sword is accompanied by the relatives and friends who proceed to the bride's residence for the *lagan* ceremony in the evening. A feast is given by the bride's side to all the guests. The groom's side throws a post-*lagan* feast.

The dead are cremated. The body is carried to the cremation ground by the relatives and friends. Male heirs lit the pyre. Death pollution is observed among them. *Uthala*, i.e. the ritual marking formal end of the death pollution, and *rasam-pagri*, i.e. wearing of saffron or pink colour headgear by the male members of the family, is performed among them. *Choubarsi* (fourth year's death ritual) is practised by them.

The Dholwalas are mostly landless in the urban areas but a number of them have small pieces of land in the rural areas. Occupations pursued by them at present are self-employment, business and retail trading. Their links with the market exist directly and most of the transactions are made in cash. Priests are drawn from the upper caste Brahmans who conduct their socio-religious rites. Disputes pertaining to property, familial fueds and marriage are referred to the law courts.

The Dholwalas are divided into two main sections of Jogi and Gardwachi. The differentiation among these two group is occupation-related. While Jogis among them are professionals charging for playing drums on socio-religious occassions, the Gardwachi depend on the alms given by the people. They observe all the Hindu religious festivals and the local regional festivals. They also visit the regional deities and shrines of *pirs*. They do not excel in any art or craft though their females are engaged in occassional cloth embroidery.

The Dholwalas accept water from the other Savarna Hindu communities but do nto exchange water. They exchange *kachcha* and *pukka* food with the above mentioned communities. Marriages take place among their community members and is exceptional cases even with high caste Hindus. The community does not have significant number of administrators, businessmen, scholars and creative artists, but a few of them hold white-collar jobs as teachers and clerks. Political leadership has by and large been confined to the regional level.

Education is favoured for both boys and girls who normally study up to school level. Girls often drop out due to econmic-cum-social reasons. Boys usually aim to be graduates. The community makes use of both traditional and modern medicare. Their attitude towards family planning is favourable and modern methods of birth control are also used. Drinking water is available through tap in the urban areas and rivulets and streams in rural areas. Rural employment programmes are not available to them but they are self-employed in running petty retail trade and business. They are exposed to all media of communication—radio, newspaper, television and cinema. Railheads, roads and post-offices are situated nearby. They use electricity, wood, kerosene oil, LPG, etc., as fuel. Attitude towards saving is positive and banking facilities are availed of by them.

ASHOK AIMA

DHYAR

The Dhyars of Jammu who claim a Rajput origin, used to extract iron ore from the mines of Sanghad-Kalakot area of Jammu region in the past. They left iron pits open and uncovered, wherein animals and cows grazing around would fall and die. Consequently, they were called *hatyare*, i.e. murderers and cow slaughterers. The word *hatyare* over the period got corrupted into Dhyar. After Independence they were included in the Scheduled Caste category and were treated as outcasts by the Rajputs. However, recently the Dhyars have applied to the state government for their derecognition as a Scheduled Caste and to be included in the general unreserved open category of Rajputs. According to 1981 census, their population was 4,797.

Over a period of time, they have spread out from Sanghad-Kalakot area in Riasi region to the neighbouring area of Moher, Budhal, Rajouri, Rausu, Teot, etc. Consequently, most of them have migrated to their present places of habitat and their distribution is essentially perceived at the local level. They live in the warm and temperate climate of Jammu province. Most of the Dhyar settlements are located on hilly terrain with high humidity and thin forest cover. The region experiences medium rainfall. They speak Dogri among themselves and communicate with others in Dogri and Hindi while they write in Devanagari and Arabic scripts. They do not have any specific dress for either sex as ethnic identification markers. They wear clothes which are more close to the Dogra pattern.

The Dhyars are occasional non-vegetarians, with no prejudice for fish, eggs and meat except beef. Wheat, rice and maize form their staple food. They take all kinds of pulses and vegetables available to them. The consumption of milk and milk products is normal while that of fruit is very low. Men take alcoholic drink occasionally and procure it from the market. Their womenfolk are teetotallers. Cigarette smoking and use of loose tobacco is common among these people. A small number of their menfolk chew tobacco and use snuff. There has not been significant change in the overall food habits but there has been an improvement in the quality of food of the affluent amongst them.

The Dhyars, are conscious of being low in status. However, stratification among the Dhyars seems to be more on occupational and educational levels. Subcastes among the Dhyars are Nag, Nagoti, Jhakhar, Sangadh, Katiyar, etc. There have been no changes in either surnames or clan names. Self-perception of the Dhyars is low and the same is true of the perception of other communities about them.

The Dhyars do not have consanguinity. Consanguinity among cross-cousins on mother's side (MBD) was prevalent earlier. However, sororal polygyny is not reported among these people.

Pre-puberty marriage was the earlier practice among the Dhyars. Nowadays, their girls are married after puberty. The marriage age of girls varies between 16 and 18 years and for boys from 20 years and above. Marital alliances are negotiated by the marriage brokers or by friends or relatives. Monogamy is the present and common norm of marriage. Symbols of marriage of the Dhyar women are vermilion, bangles (lac), *mangalsutra*, *bindi* and nose ring. Practice of dowry is prevalent but involves very little cash transaction as usually kitchen utensils, bedding and furniture coupled with a few dresses for the bride and the groom are given. Gold or silver component of the dowry is quite modest. Divorce is permissible with legal and religious sanction. Divorce may be mainly due to adultery or barrenness. Divorce compensation is given to the wife and it is usually the husband who divorces. In fact, divorce is governed by the Hindu Marriage Act. However, either party can initiate divorce proceedings. Children are the responsibility of either mother or father, as the case may be. Rules regarding remarriage are quite flexible as there are no specific restrictions on remarriage. Sororate alliances is permitted but levirate is prohibited.

Family types are mixed extended though now nuclear families are becoming gradually popular. An urge to lead an independent life is catching on. Interpersonal relations are cordial among the household members and joking relationship prevails among consanguineous and affinal relatives. Avoidance relationship is observed between mother-in law and son-in-law and also between daughter-in law and father-in law. Conflicts arise mainly due to property disputes but such cases are very few. The Dhyars usually follow the Hindu tradition of inheritance and succession. Females have a share in the parental property but they seldom claim it. Interfamily linkages are cordial. If any dispute arises within the community, it is sorted out through mutual negotiation, reconciliation and discussion sponsored by village community elders. Except for the tendency for a rise in the formation of nuclear families, no major changes are reported in the family set-up.

The Dhyar women have a secondary status compared to men in almost all walks of life. Though they have an equal right over the ancestral property, yet in practice they do not get their share as they do not insist on it. Women participate in most of the social activities but do not enjoy same status in religious matters. Living in predominently rural agrarian setting, women participate in most of the farm work and related pursuits with their menfolk. They perform all household as well as outdoor work, upkeep of the house and domestic cattle. Besides enjoying voting rights, women do not play any role in the local or regional politics. They seem to be quite docile, and contented in letting the menfolk play the dominant role.

No pre-delivery rituals are observed except for a few restrictions. Women may go to their parental house for delivery if circumstances require. Deliveries usually take place at home with the help of an experienced midwife (*dai*), but delivery at a health centre or hospital, if these facilities are available, is also common. A post-delivery pollution period, is observed for 21 days, but no postnatal restrictions for the mothers are observed. No *annaprashan* ceremony is observed. However, they perform *mundan* ceremony of boys. *Janeu* (thread-wearing) ceremony for the male children is duly performed but no puberty rites for their girls.

Marital alliances are arranged and fixed by marriage brokers, relatives and friends. The entire marriage ceremony is brief, i.e. one or two days' affair. *Mehndi-raat* is celebrated before the wedding day. Customarily, the marriage ceremony is held at the bride's residence. The bridegroom's party called *janj* goes to the bride's house where the marriage ritual takes place at night according to the Hindu tradition and both the parties entertain guests with feast in their turn. The residence after marriage is patrilocal.

The dead is given a bath and wrapped in white cloth, and is then carried on bier to the cremation ground for cremation. A thirteen days' death pollution period is observed among them. *Rasam-pagri* or *uthala* is usually performed on the thirteenth day by installing the eldest son as the head of the family. Annual *shradh* for the dead is optional. No significant changes in the life-cycle rituals have taken place except that some of them have grown expensive and elaborate. They follow the Hindu way of life.

The Dhyars are a landed community and agriculture is their main occupation. Previously mining, quarrying and irons mithy was their traditional occupation. But now, agriculture and allied activities is the mainstay of the community. Working as daily wagers or farm or factory labourers is their subsidiary occupation, as also government and private service for the educated among them. Some of them have taken to trade at the retail level. Animal husbandry is more popular among them. Their women participate in agricultural and cattle-rearing activities and perform all types of domestic work. There has been a rise in the number of casual and agricultural labourers among the Dhyars. Child labour is neither hired nor marketed though some children are used in domestic, farm and non-farm operations. The people receive their wages both in cash and kind. Link with the market exists both directly and through middlemen, and is based on daily to monthly transactions. The Dhyar are gradually taking to trade and commerce.

Panchayats exist at the village level. Elderly persons of the village belonging to other communities usually form a village panchayat which is heterogeneous in nature. These panchayats are of statutory formal nature and are usually involved in settling disputes relating to social problems as well as those concerning land. These panchayats are also responsible for implementing the village developmental plans and welfare activites. It may also initiate social boycott or excommunication proceedings against the defaulters. Adultery and disputes over land and water are the main offences.

The Dhyars are Hindu by religion. They worship village and regional deities. Individual affiliation to a *pir* is a common phenomenon. Religious specialists are from the Brahman community who perform the birth, marriage, and death rites. Regional deities like Vaishno Devi, Raghunath Mandir, Bahu Fort, etc., are worshipped by them. Festivals are of socio-religious nature and they celebrate all the major Hindu festival such as Shivratri, Janmashtami, Navratras, Diwali, Holi, Lohri and Rakshabandhan.

Folklores and folk songs exist in which both men and women participate. Local instruments of music like *dhol* (drum) and harmonium are used by them, and music is based on local and classical patterns. Both men and women participate in dance. Folk songs and folklore are usually of religious and romantic nature.

The Dhyars traditionally accept both cooked and uncooked food from the high caste Hindus and co-community members except from the other Scheduled Castes such as the Chamiyars or Malgis. No restrictions have been put on acceptance of uncooked food from co-religionists. They normally refrain from eating with non-Hindus. They maintain marital relations with all the high caste Hindus. They share the well and water sources, roads, schools, and panchayat ghar with other communities and non-Hindus. They share the cremation grounds with other Hindu communities. They visit the religious shrines of *pirs* and *faqirs*. They maintain cordial and informal relationship with other community members. Being an agriculturist community, they have cultivator-labour relations. They receive the services of the barber, carpenter, mason, etc.

Political awareness is also fast catching up with these people. They do not have entrepreneurs or creative artists, but administrators, teachers and other white-collar servicemen are found among them. Political leadership is confined to village panchayat level only.

Formal education is gradually becoming popular among the Dhyars, both for boys and girls. However, it is the boys who study mostly upto matriculation or college level but they dropout from schools or college due to socio-economic constraints and to supplement their family income. Though the Dhyars' attitude is favourable towards modern medicare, they are not making optimum use of it. They have started to show positive attitude towards family planning. In practice, however, it is yet to become popular at the mass level. Average family size varies from five to eight members. They have drinking water facilities available to them through tap. Their water sources are springs and streams besides tap water being made available by the government.

The Dhyars have not, by and large, been benefited under the government sponsored welfare-cum-employment schemes. Cooperative societies help in the distribution of essential commodities and other farm-related input requirements. Almost all the households utilize electricity. They use firewood and cow-dung as fuel for cooking. Most of them own land and avail of the irrigation facilities. They have now started to use modern cheimical fertilizers and insecticides in their agricultural field. Local manure is still used in bulk for agriculture. Very few of them have availed of the nutrition programmes through ICDS, Anganwadi and SNP centres. Most of them are getting rations and other essential commodities from the public distribution centres or the fair price shops. Occasionally they borrow from the local moneylenders to meet social or unforeseen contingencies but they try to abstain from taking loans from the banks for business and other commercial ventures.

The Dhyars are trying hard to regain their social status as proud Rajputs and to shake off the social stigmas on account of their forefathers. They have, therefore, practically given up iron ore mining and shifted to agriculture, trade and commerce for pursuing more socially accepted jobs. This has partly rehabilitated them socially among the Rajputs. They have requested the government to de-recognize them as a Scheduled Caste and treat them at par with the Rajputs under the open category. The community is undergoing a phase of socio-economic transition.

INDU AIMA

DOGRA

The Dogra, has only one synonym, 'Rajput'. However, the members of the community may be addressed by any of the three titles, Mian, Thakur and Kanwar. The ruling clans among them were sometimes addressed as Rajaji and their agriculturist brethren have the title of Chaudhary.

The word 'dogra' has been derived from the Sanskrit term *durgara* which was first used in two Chamba copper-plate title-deeds of Raja Ashtavarman (1030-40) mentioning events of the days of his ancestor, Raja Shailavarman (AD 930-40). Amir Khusrau writing at the close of the fourteenth century, mentions in his work *Nausipihir* the separate language spoken in 'the Duggan country'. The import of the word Durgara (Duggar = Dogra) is only a matter of conjecture. In Sanskrit, the term stands for difficult terrain. As the highly broken and rugged formation of the Jammu territory very well answers the definition of the term, so it came to be popularly called 'Durgara' which later changed to Duggar, and the inhabitants acquired the name Dogra. Historically, this original name was applied to the country and its people, at least from the beginning of the tenth, or even the earlier century.

The Dogras have several groups, some of which are *als* or sub-branches of the main ruling family of Jammu, while others belong to separate groups who have retained their traditions after migration from distant parts of India during the early middle ages. These are listed as: (1) Main Dogra, or stem: Jamwal. Its *als* or branches: Manhas, Charak, Shau, Bhatial, Baghal, Mandla, Harchandar, Tangral, Jasrotia, Lakhanpuria, Sambyal, Sangramia, Mankotia and Salathia; (2) Stem: Balauria with the branches: Bhadwal, Bhadarwahia, Sumbria; (3) Ambaraiyan and Shonkla; (4) Chib; (5) Bhalwal, Rajial and Rasial; (6) Langeh; (7) Rakwal; (8) Andotra and Bohdala; (9) Jamal and Salehria; (10) Bandrahl; (11) Kishtwaria; (12) Galian; (13) Hiuntal; (14) Thakkar; (15) Gaddi.

All these Dogra groups have different traditions of their origin and migration to Jammu hills. The Jamwal group claim to have migrated from Ayodhya sometime prior to the *Kaliyuga*, but most probably they came to Jammu Hills during the fourth or fifth century AD. The Bhog-Pal, the ancestor of the Balauria group, migrated to Vallapura

(Balaur-Basohli) region from Kulu in the first quarter of the eighth century. The Ambaraiyan are a branch of Panwar or Parmars of Dharanagari (Ujjain) and seem to have migrated to Akhnur region during twelfth century AD. The Chibs are a branch of the Katoch of Kangra and their ancestor, Pratap Chand, migrated to Bhimber-Rajouri region. As Pratap Chand is said to be the youngest of the four sons of Raja Megh Chand of Kangra (1390-1405), the community seems to have migrated to Jammu region about AD 1400. The Bhalwal, Bajial and Rasial trace their origin from the house of Udaipur, Mewar, and their common ancestor, Mani Man, is said to have migrated to Jammu Hills probably during the sixth or seventh century AD. Lang Pal, the ancestor of Langeh tribe, is said to belong to the line of Karna of *Mahabharata* fame and he migrated from Kashmir to Jammu in about AD 1350. The Rakwals seem to have migrated from the Punjab and they first find mention in Jammu annals about AD 1450. The Andotras and Bohdalas had descended from Gahl, the elder brother of Rana Bhet, ancestor of the Pathania Rajputs who founded Pathankot (ancient name Pratishthan) State in about AD1095. The ancestor of Andotras, Anandji, migrated to Kathua region during the thirteenth century.

Several other clans of the Dogras, namely Bhamotra, Malkhotra, Mahotra, Jaghi, Lallotra, Gohotar, Katal, Saroch, which are minor subdivisions of the Dogras, have lost the traditions of their origin and migration to their present abode.

The natural environment in which the Dogras live is of three types. First is the strip of plain to the south of hills, some 180 km long and 5 to 20 km wide, a fertile soil, fed by rivers and streams crossing it southwestwards and irrigated by canals. The bulk of the Dogras live in this tract. Second is the arid broken uplands, called Kandi, which is stony land thirsting for water, covered by bushes and sparse forests subsisting on periodical rainfall, moderately inhabited by the sturdy hill Dogras, comparatively short in size but possessed of greater martial spirit. And the third type of environment is that of the mountains of the Middle Himalayas ranging in height from 1,000 metres to 5,000 metres, covered by dense forests of lofty pine and deodar trees, rich in forest yield and subsoil water, but sparsely populated.

The language spoken and written was previously Dogri, with its own script called Takari. But now Hindi and Urdu have taken place of written Dogri. In their homes and amongst the community itself, they speak Dogri. In communicating with others also the Dogra speak Dogri, but the literate and urban population communicate with others through Urdu and Hindi.

Almost all the sections of the Dogras, with the exception of the Gaddis, were identifiable by their dress. They wore *pyjamas* (tight trousers) and turban worn in a particular style characteristic of them.

The food habits of the Dogras are similar to those of other Hindu communities except that there is greater emphasis on consumption of mutton by the males. The community is known as non-vegetarian, although it is only partially true. Most of the Dogra women are vegetarian. Even some men are also vegetarian, and some become so in later life. Almost the whole community takes to vegetarian diet on certain religious days, such as Navratras and other fasting days. The concept of vegetarianism is based on ahimsa and religious or spiritual merit.

However, the Dogras are known for their vociferous non-vegetarian habits, a fact which is primarily based on the concept that such a course strengthens *shakti* and martial prowess. This concept draws some religious sanction from the ritual of animal sacrifice to the deities like Durga, whom the Dogras hold in the highest reverence. Taking of fish and eggs is considered as part of non-vegetarian diet. Formerly, domestic fowl and eggs were considered unclean and seldom taken. Beef is a sacrilege to them as to all other Hindu communities.

Cereals, including rice, wheat and maize form the staple food of the Dogras, and in uplands coarse millets called *maodil* and *sawak* form a regular portion of their food. Maize is a favourite grain and from September to May is in constant consumption. In the evening supper, rice is seldom eaten. In rice-growing valleys and canal-irrigated tracts of Ranbirsinghpura and Andhar, people subsist for greater part of the year on rice. When wheat harvest is matured in May, it becomes the common diet for about half of the year.

The usual beverages of the Dogras are milk and *sharbat*. Milk products like buttermilk (*lassi*) and *sattoo* (parched grain flour mixed with sweet water) are popular among all the classes of Dogra. Alcoholic drinks and liquors have never been popular among the Dogras, particularly the Mian and high class (*swaran*) Dogras. Indulgence in alcohol and drugs, except opium, were discredited, though their lower classes were fond of these in spite of discredit attached to their use. Most of the agricultural groups of the Dogras consume liquor, particularly on happy occasions such as the birth of a son, marriage of males and fairs like Basoa (Baisakhi). Very few among them extract their own liquors, but they mostly use country-made liquors.

On most of the religious occasions such as Navratras, Nirjala Ekadashi, Ramnavami, Janmashtami, Karva Chauth, Channan-shastha,

Gugga and marriages of girls, abstention from all types of food, and some days even from water, and complete fasts are observed, or *falahar* (fast on fruits) is resorted to. All types of non-vegetarian diet is abstained from during Navratra days by all classes of the Dogras. On *shradh* days also, and for thirteen days following the death of a relative, non-vegetarian diet is usually not taken. But in recent days, some deviations from such observance have been noticed though no major change in food habits is observable except that the intake of liquor is much on the increase and most of the previous food taboos have disappeared.

The Dogra community was highly stratified in hierarchical order at the top of which stood the Mian group, consisting of about 22 ruling tribes of Jammu and their *als* (sub-branches). Below them were a number of clans, graded as second in social hierarchy as inferior to the Mians. All the Dogra clans were arranged in these two main stratas which were further subdivided into a number of grades. The dividing factor was the 'plough'. The Mians did not put their hands on the plough. A Mian to preserve his name and honour unsullied must scrupulously observe the following four maxims: (1) He must never handle a plough, (2) He must never give his daughter in marriage to an inferior, (3) He must never accept money in exchange for the betrothal of his daughter. (4) The females of his house must be strictly secluded and observe *purdah*. The prejudice against plough is perhaps the most inveterate of all. The probable reason for this prejudice was that 'the legitimate weapon of the Rajput is sword and the plough is an insignia of a lower walk of life', and adoption of a lower profession tantamounted to loss of caste status.

The non-Mian Dogra were considered inferior and relegated to the second grade, and being ploughmen, were called *halbaha*. The Mian who put his hand on plough was at once reduced to the second grade. No Mian will marry his daughter to a second grade Rajput and he must go a step lower in social scale to obtain a wife for himself. In a meeting of the community and at marriages the non-ploughing Dogra refused to sit in the same *pangat* (seat) with the *halbaha*.

Another feature of this gradation was the mode of salutation. When addressed by an inferior, a Mian should be greeted with the salutation of 'Jai Diya' from the Sanskrit *Jayatu Devah*, meaning, 'May our gods be victorious'. On this account, the Mians in the hills were called Jaikaria. Even among the Mians, for there were endless gradations even among the Mians, the inferior must be the first to offer the salutation which is then returned.

The families with whom the Mians usually intermarried consisted chiefly of the descendants of those families or other ruling families or branches of royal clans. From those the Mians took wives and for reason of honour of alliance, they were given the privilege of the salutation of *Jai*. The second grade Dogras were sometimes further subdivided: (1) the superior class enjoying the privilege of 'Jai' (2) the inferior class, the clans of which were only entitled to a 'Salaam' or 'Ram-Ram', and were called Ram-Rami or Salaami, and were relegated sometimes to third grade. The Salaami clans were further subdivided into two classes, the Kahri and the Dohri. The Kahri only intermarried with certain families and were considered as being of slightly higher social status than the Dohri, who intermarried on terms of equality and practised widow remarriage or *karewa*.

Of late, however, all the Dogra clans, high or low, have disregarded their old caste rules. They now have adopted the common salutation of 'Jai Diya', do operate the plough and intermarry among all the grades indiscriminately.

The Dogra are exogamous, i.e. they marry into the clan's *gotras* other than their own. The lowest castes were as strict in this as the highest. Marriage within the clan was impossible and was regarded as incest. *Got* in their case differed from the Puranic *gotra*. Most of the Dogra clans belong to Bharadwaja *gotra*, and some to Attri. But they intermarry, irrespective of the *risi-gotra*. For example, the Manha, Bhau, Charak, Jasrotia not only belong to the same Bharadwaja *gotra*, but are also the branches of the Jamwal clan. These clans intermarry without any consideration of the *risi-gotra*. However, they consider their clan as a separate *got* and do not marry within their own clan or *got*. Besides, although a Dogra boy might accept a bride from a class of inferior status similar privilege was denied to a Dogra Rajput girl whose husband must be her equal or, if possible, her superior. In this connection, the general rule regarding marriages among the Dogras, whether of the hills or the plains, was that each class married the daughters of the class next below its own. Marriages between persons of the same status were called *dohra*; those in which the husband was of higher rank than the bride were called *akahra*.

The Dogras, in common with the respectable Hindus, bar marriage within the following degrees of kinship; the *got* (clan) of mother's father and maternal grandfather and the *got* of father's maternal grandfather, and any *bans* (tribe) which had common ancestor with their own. It was also unusual for a man to marry into a family, of whatever clan it may be, that is settled in his own village on any adjoining village.

Among the Dogras, child marriages were customary, the only exception being the very high caste Rajput girls for whom it was difficult to find a suitable match. The usual age of marriage varied from six to ten years in the case of males. The marriage contract was of three kinds: *dharm* or *punn*, in which no payment or exchange of any kind was made, *batta-satta ka nata*—or exchange involving two or three families, e.g. A will give his daughter to B on the condition that B gives his to C, and C to A. The exchanges were very common and sale-purchase, which is marriage for money that was common among the lower classes of the Dogras who had taken to cultivation or who lived in remote hills. A cash payment was made for the bride varying in amount according to the circumstances of the family.

Dahej (dowry) was invariably demanded and given, sometimes settled at the time of betrothal. It was usually in the form of kind, partially in cash in some cases. The symbol of marriage among the Dogra women was *balu* and *natha* (nose-string). Among higher classes *sindoor* and *mangalsutra* served the same purpose.

Though marriage took place usually at an early age but the *maklawa* or *phera* (home-taking of the bride) took place when the bride was about twelve and the boy was of 15 to 18 years of age. After *maklawa*, the bride lived at the husband's home and was allowed to visit her parents for a short time on important occasions. Among the Mians, the bride was seldom allowed to visit her parents' house after *maklawa*.

Divorce was almost unknown among the Dogras as marriage was considered an unbreakable spiritual bond after its consummation. Widow remarriage was also not permitted except among the third and fourth grade agriculturist Dogras, who practised *karewa* by the custom of *chadar dalna*, a privilege allowed only to the brothers of the deceased husband. The concept of marriage has of late undergone much change among the Dogras. The barriers of hierarchy in marriage have almost disappeared and now inter-*got* marriages take place without discrimination. There are several instances of divorce mutually arranged, and legal widow remarriages have also taken place without any stigma. But such instances are still uncommon.

A Dogra family is invariably a jont patriarchal institution headed by the eldest member, the father or grandfather (if alive). All members of the family respect and love each other. There is usually lack of wilful confrontation with elders or equals in the family where congenial conditions prevail. The Dogras were usually monogamous, but high class and landlord families were sometimes polygynous, having two or three wives.

The Dogras were very particular about the honour of their females, and girls were particularly held in reverence and considered as *kanjaks* or something divine. Married women had the right to a share of the property of the deceased husband for their sustenance. Mostly women were not allowed to go out to work in any form for the family. However, in the hills, women did all types of outdoor work. Usually, the Dogra women managed the household but had little share in raising family's income; but the harvest and grain coming to the house was their entire responsibility and they took good care of these all through the year. Among the high class families and Mians, who did not operate the plough, women had little to do and remained mostly in seclusion, confined to the four walls of the house.

The life of a Dogra is crowded with various Hindu *sanskaras* (rites). On the birth of a male child the *purohit*, or family priest, is summoned, who prepares the *janam-patri* (horoscope) of the child. If the birth is propitious, a Brahman or a barber is sent round to summon relatives and friends, who thereupon tender their congratulations to the family. Feasting and rejoicing is held for a couple of days. A Dogra household remains ceremonially impure for ten days after the birth of a child. On the fourteenth day a *pandit* is sent for, who purifies the household by sprinkling *Ganga-jal* (water of the Ganga) and reciting of *mantras* from the *shastras*. Immediately after, on an auspicious day, the child is given a name according to his *janam-patri*; but the original name is kept a secret till the boy is eight or ten years old. Meanwhile, he is addressed by a pet name. About six weeks after birth, the child is carried outside the house. When the child is about two years, an auspicious day is selected for the *mundan* (ceremony or tonsure), on which occasion his hair is shaved for the first time, leaving on the crown of the head a small tuft called *bodi* or *choti*. On the birth of a daughter, all feasting and rejoicing is dispensed with; only the bare rites are observed. The investiture of a Dogra with the *janeu* represents his formal admission into the ranks of his caste. Among the wealthy classes, the thread is usually assumed at the age of ten but, among the poor, *upanayana* (investiture) is often deferred until marriage so that the two ceremonies may be combined to save expenses.

Among the Dogras, infant marriages were customary. The negotiations which preceded a *kurmai* (betrothal) were generally conducted by the Brahmans. In the plains, it was the concern of the girl's father to send an envoy to seek a husband for his daughter. When the matches were found, a date of the *kurmai* was fixed by the *padhas* or *purohits* of the two families, who exchanged visits to ascertain whether the position and pedigree, etc., of the contracting parties were satisfactory. On the fixed day, a *tikka* or *tilak* was marked on the would-be bridegroom's forehead and some *sagan* (offerings) were made, usually a large scarf and one silver rupee and some sweets. The members of the brotherhood were usually invited to witness the ceremony, among whom sweets were distributed and the *kurmai* ceremony was complete. Sometime after, the date of the marriage (*beah*) was fixed. The *barat* (marriage party) led the bridegroom to the bride's house where the marriage ceremony was completed in front of sacred fire, accompanied by the recitation of concerned sections of the *shastras*. The bridegroom, followed by the bride went round the *havan* (fire) for seven times. The marriage party was entertained there for three to four days, after which they returned along with the bride. The date of marriage was called *lagan*, and usually feasting and rejoicing was carried on by both the families fifteen to twenty days before the *lagan* day. In due course of time, on the day set for *maklawa* or *phera*, the bride was carried by the boy to his house, and the marriage was consummated. The marriage rituals, beginning with *kurmai* and completed with the second *phera*, was a comprehensive affair and a number of rituals had to be performed from time to time.

The death rituals among the Dogras are as elaborate as those of marriage. Near death, the dying man is laid down on the ground specially prepared after some rites. The attending *purohit* performs certain rituals, sprinkles *Ganga-jal* on the dying man who is made to give something in charity, *dan-punn*, such as cow, grain, etc., before he breaths his last. He calls upon the dying man to repeat the god Vishnu's names like Rama, Narayan or Hari. After the man is dead, his *kriya karam* (funeral rites) are performed by a special class of Brahmans called Acharajs or Gujratis. Under certain rituals common to all the Hindus, the dead body is taken to the cremation ground (*shamshanghat*), usually on the banks of a river, where the corpse is burnt on the funeral pyre, accompanied by certain rituals. Four days after, the *phul*, or the burnt bones and ashes, are collected in an urn and kept to be immersed in the Ganga any time before the expiry of four years. But usually this takes place within thirteen days of death. For thirteen days after death, the Dogras observe mourning for the dead. On the thirteenth day, the Acharaj Brahman performs the rituals of first *shradh* and the *purohit* purifies the household, and the next of the kin (usually the son) is made to wear *pagri* (turban) in the presence of nearer ones gathered for the purpose. *Barkhi* and *chaubarkhi* are the death rituals performed annually and fourth-yearly, respectively. *Pitra-paksha* is the death ritual performed yearly in the month of September.

The Dogras, are primarily a landowning community which is now the mainstay of their economy. The land is owned by the family and, in hills, there are small forest plots attached to their holdings. The main occupation of the community is military service; but they have now joined other civil services also, even some have taken to business and trade. In the hills, their holdings are very small, and a very small minority among them have become landless and taken to labour also; but there are bonded labourers among them. However, boys from the hills and *kandi* go to towns to serve as domestic servants. Since Independence, the Dogras have lost most of their lands under legislative ceilings and have been forced to adopt other occupations for supplementing their income. Most of them are running after services, government or private. Majority of them are poor, particularly in the hills and *kandi* tracts, and have to work as labourers in order to add to their incomes, both as farm labourers and as mill workers, wherever alternatives are available.

Previously there were informal *biradari* panchayats which considered social problems only and had nothing to do with law and order situation or crimes. In some villages, and especially in hilly areas, such community bodies still exist, and even decide cases of social and moral crimes. But in most of the Dogra villages, statutory bodies have taken the place of *biradari* panchayats. As the Dogras have been an important and controlling section of the population of Jammu, they have, from at least the days of Maharaja Ranbir Singh (AD 1857-85), been ruled by the statutory law framed by the Maharaja and called Ranbir-Dand-Vidhi (Ranbir Penal Code), which is even operative today. Formal panchayat bodies have been formed in all the villages, which have been given legal powers and play an important role in economic and social development, and health and sanitation work in the village. But these have not proved very effective organs, being very heterogeneous in formation and overridden by local and regional politics. In only hilly and remote villages, *biradari* panchayats still play useful role.

The religion of the Dogras is the popular form of Hinduism and they hold all the three members of the Hindu trinity and *Shakti* in the form of Durga in highest veneration. The two avatars, Rama and Krishna, are the idols of worship, in addition to Kali or Kalka Devi and the goddess Bhagvati called Vaishno. Temples and shrines have been raised for their consecration which the Dogras visit daily or on the days set apart for worship.

Almost every house possesses its *penates* in the form of *siddha* or *nag*, who are supposed to repel witches and to propitiate fortune. Besides, they worship Kala Bir and Mahar Singh, whose images are generally stamped upon silver plates worn as charms round their necks or upper arms. For the ceremonial worship of these, a black and white goat is kept in each house. These tutelary divinities are believed to be constantly plaguing mortals with every kind of ill. They are ministered to by a certain class of priests called *chelas* who are supposed to be acquainted with their intentions, and thus able to avert their wrath. Nearly every village has two or three godlings of its own, called *devtas* or *devis*. These are generally deceased local celebrities, deified for the occcasion, or worshipped in the form of a mound of earth called *dehra* or *dehri*. Some villages have *sati* shrines, a few of which have gained local celebrity by the efforts of attending *jogis* who go about singing praises of them from village to village.

All the Dogra clans have their clan deities known as *kul-devta* who are propitiated on religious and social occasions. For example, the Jamwal clan has Rani Parmeshari as their *kul-devi*, the Chibs have their ancestor-martyr Shadi Shaheed, Charaks have their martyr priest Bawa Ranpat, and, strange enough, the Sambyals have an ass as their *kul-devta*.

All these deities or divinities are attended to by the specialists who may be classified into two groups. Firstly, the priests in temples and shrines who, besides performing worship, officiate at socio-religious *samskaras*, *havanas* and *yajnas*. Then there are *chelas* and *jogis* who feign inspiration by the deity and perform the acts of exorcizing evil spirits and soothsaying. They represent the persisting vestiges of occultism and are very much in demand in uplands where the fear of ghosts and witches strongly prevails.

The Dogras have several regional deities. The most important and ancient amongst them are: Hari-Hara at Balor, Sudh Mahadev, Siva shrine at Purmandal, Kameshwara temple at Akhnur, Buddha Amarnath near Rajouri, Siddha Gauriya at Swankha, Vasuk Nag at Bhadarwah, Bawa Jitto at Chiri, Malla Devi at Sarthal, Vaishno Devi at Katra and Sheetla Devi. The shrines of these deities are the chief places of Dogra pilgrimage, in addition to Pir Khoh and Raghunath temple complex at Jammu and Sakrala Devi. Of these, Vaishno Devi and Bawa Jitto's shrines have of late acquired national fame.

The Dogra participate in most of the Hindu fairs and festivals which are widely celebrated in the country, like Sivratri, Basant Panchami, Holi, Ramnavami, Dussehra, Diwali, etc.

A socio-religious movement among the Dogras was started by the Arya Samaj which, however, could not be popular and had only a few votaries. Change in the pattern of religious behaviour has been quite negligible, though a few Dogra reformers preached liberal reformative ideas through their verses and socio-religious gatherings. There was some awakening against social evils.

The Dogras are primarily a martial race and a serving group, some of whom are agriculturists and a few, like Gaddis who are only a fraction of them, are pastoral and migratory, tending sheep. None of them are craftsmen and artisans. Hence, they do not cultivate any form of plastic and graphic arts except as a hobby on a limited, individual level. However, they have rich oral traditions and enjoy listening to martial ballads, called *baran*, and singing emotional songs known as *pahkhan* and *karkan*, which they enjoy singing in chorus in the evenings. Their long utterances notes echo the lone hill tops and valleys. The heroic ballads of Mian Deedu, Ram Singh, Bawa Jitto, General Hoshiara and several others are popular among them. The ballads of Gugga-Mandlik, Raja Salvahn and Puran Bhagat are sung and heard all over the Dogra land; but these are not sung by the people but by particular families of bards, called Dres and Garari, who also compose and preserve them.

The Dogras indulge in dance and music only on festive occasions, such as the birth of a son or a marriage. In such semi-religious rites, it is mostly the womenfolk who sing and dance. Mixed group dances among the Dogras are unknown except among special sections like the Gaddis and inhabitants of remote hills.

Traditionally, all Dogras had intercommunity linkages with all other *varnas* except the fourth *varna*, and participated in their social and domestic functions and ceremonies, mixed with them and communicated at all levels. However, they would not accept water and any form of food from the hands of the artisans, craftsmen and menials except domestic servants. Nor would they share a *pangat* (common seat) with them at community or ceremonial dinners. Separate seats had to be provided for them. Some such classes were the Tarkhans (carpenters), Lohars (blacksmiths), Kumhars (potters) and Chimbas (textile workers). Previously the Dogra community shared their wells, tanks and other water sources and community buildings, like *dharmashalas*, panchayat ghars and temples with all other communities except the fourth *varna*.

On connubial level, intercommunity relations were simply exceptions and rare, and were not liked and approved. Putative relations with other communities, even with the fourth varna, were common and were resorted to on ceremonial occasions, such as marriage and *mundan-sanskars*. If a marriage party happened to come by another marriage party on the way, irrespective of *varna*, both the bridegroom and bride contracted putative relationship of *dharma-bhai* and *-sakhi*. Similar relationship was established at home with those who untie the *gana* (the red ceremonial thread) off the wrists of the bride and the bridegroom. Patron-client relationship or *jajmani* system still prevails but has lost most of its need and popularity. Even today, the same system of intercommunity linkages prevails, except that now the public places and property are shared even with the fourth *varna*, with some reservations in connection with the religious shrines. In villages, crop is shared with the tillers who usually belong to the fourth *varna*. The Dogras are generally landholders. Landlord-tenant relationship exists in the community based on age-old traditions which have been modified by legislation during the last half a century. Cultivator-labour relationship with other communities also exists based on tradition and legislation. Employer-worker relationship too exists where the Dogra community stands both as employer and employed, as the case may be.

The Dogras participate in political activities and public functions at all levels: local, district, region, state, and national; but no political or ethnic movements are recorded within the community.

The Dogras are generally receptive and responsive to all types of development plans and programmes. They are quite alive to health and medical care problems and measures. Scarcity of drinking water in tracts inhabited by the Dogras is a usual phenomenon.

Electricity has become an indispensable part of the everyday life of the Dogra but they have not yet become alive to the importance of environmental conservation and consume energy resources available to them indiscriminately. Irrigation facilities in the form of canals and *kuhls* (water ducts) are available to them in plains and natural sources of water in the mountains; but in *kandi* area they have to depend on periodical rains. They make the best out of the irrigation facilities available to them. They frequently use chemical fertilizers, country made compost manure and also insecticides where it is necessary.

Rural employment programmes in the Dogra areas have not yet been introduced. However, some youngmen have been benefited by the self-employment programmes started by the Jammu & Kashmir government. The Dogra community is receptive to the banking facilities and savings, which are now available to them adequately. There has been a public distribution system in this state for over a century and it has become a part of the everyday life in spite of inconvenience involved in the system.

The Dogras react favourably to media and communication from which they draw great benefit. Nutrition programmes are still unknown to them, as these have not been included in the educational and social upliftment programmes of the government.

Of late, some cultural revivalism is noticeable among the Dogras in the field of religion, re-emergence of reverence for their heroes and emphasis on the adoption of the basic Hindu ideals and *sanskars*. There is some move towards consolidation of the Dogra society and infusion of patriotism and sense of equality and fraternity with other tribes and communities.

S.D.S. Charak

DOGRA BRAHMAN

The Dogra Brahmans are simply called Brahmans by themselves and by other communities. It is the highest caste among the Dogras. The surnames idenitifying them as Brahmans are Pandit or Pant, Purohita and Sharma. Sharma is a wider term for addressing the people of this community. The members of this community are addressed by the terms like *purohitji* or *panditji*.

The region between the rivers Ravi and Chandrabhaga is known as Duggar where its inhabitants are called 'Dogras' and their speech 'Dogri'. The word Duggar is derived variously from the Sanskrit words *durgara*, *dwigarta* (two-lakes), *durgrhas* and *doongar*. As per the phonetic laws of sound-change, the word *durgara* alone can claim to be the scientifically correct. It means 'a region of difficult terrains', 'un-conquerable', 'difficult to be subdued'. Historically also this derivation seems confirmed by the Chamba state copper-plate titledeeds of Raja Ashtvarman (1030-40) when a con-frontation with the Durgaras is mentioned. Duggar has three terrains—*kandi* which is a dry, sandy, stony, hardsoil, full of thorns and cacti; plain-cum-riverine, and *pahari* (mountainous) . The soil or *kandi* has played the most important role in building the Dogra character. Since it is the land of craggy hillocks and rugged rocks, the Dogras had to work hard to earn their living and are, therefore, sturdy and hardworking. The Dogra Brahmans are disciplined persons and are known for their honest and truthful character.

Among the Dogras, the Brahmans are considered as the highest of all other Hindu castes because of their spiritual character and knowledge of the holy books. Hence, community pride is in the very blood of the Brahmans. They would prefer to 'break than to bend'. The Dogra Brahmans are adamant and firm-minded by nature. The famous *als* among the Dogra Brahmans are: Kohdie, Nale-*ale*, Galbaden-*ale*, Karlupie, Kalithie, Kalhe-*ale*, Udhampurie, Khanurie, Amli-*ale*, etc.

The Dogra Brahmans have several subgroups of the main branch; whereas others belong to separate tribes who have retained the traditions of their own stems after migration from other parts of the state as well as the country hundreds of years ago.

The Dogra Brahmans have a number of *gots*, which are exogamous.

The known *gots* of the Brahmans are: Badeal, Badgotra, Badkulia, Bakhshi, Bali, Balotra, Bamhal, Banathia, Barkulia, Baru, Bannotra, Basotra, Bhakhari, Bhareyal, Bilanloch, Datta, Dharmatt, Dobliya, Dubey, Gabgotra, Gandalgal, Gaur, Gautam, Goswami, Hadotra, Jamwal Pandit, Kak, Kalsotra, Kerni, Kesar, Khajuria, Lalotra, Magotra, Mamolie, Misra, Modi, Naad, Padhe (Upadhyaya), Padhe (Spolie), Pandotra, Parasher, Pateha, Plashar, Rasgotra, etc.

Of these, the *gots* such as Kashmiri Pant, Razdan, Raina, Kak are the migrants from Kashmir region; Sathe *got* claims to have migrated from Maharashtra to Jammu hills, Gaurs have migrated from West Bengal. The Jamwal Pant who have adopted this name migrated from UP. Several other groups of the Dogra Brahmans have lost the traditions of their origin after migration to the valley.

The language of Dogra Brahmans is Dogri which has a significant status in the linguistic map of north India. It has its own script known as Dogre *Akkhar* (Takri), but now it is written in two scripts—Devanagari and Arabic. Dogre *Akkhar* is sometimes used by the trading community. The Dogra Brahmans speak pure Dogri amongst themselves in homes and while communicating with others, but illiterate and urban population comm-unicate with others through the language of the later.

The Dogra Brahmans are identifiable by their dress. Traditionally they wore *dhoti* and loose *kurta* and placed a *parna* (*angocha*) on their left shoulder in summer. In winter, they wear *achkan* (coat) and a pair of shoes. While attending auspicious occasions such as marriages, elderly males wore coloured turbans dyed pink or lemon. The Brahmans rarely moved out bareheaded. They applied white or yellow sandalwood paste in summer and red sandalwood *tilak*, vertical or horizontal, on their foreheads, earlobes, and chest. Females wore colourful *churidar*, tight Dogra *pyjama* (*suthan*), dyed peacock-blue, green and maroon shirts falling down to the knees. The village women at homes, mostly in the kitchen, wrap themselves in long white cloth around their bodies which is called *giddi*. This dress is still prevalent among old ladies in the village. Men wore *naintian* (gold earring) and a silver bangle known as *naint*. It was compulsory to wear *naint* above the elbow of the left arm. At present no such custom is practised. Tatooing is rarely found to be popular in the community. The Dogra Brahmans do not enjoy any special constitutional status in the state or at national level. However, *purohits* have been recognized as a Backward Class according to the information available.

The food habits of the Dogra Brahmans differ from those of other Hindu communities. The community is known to be pure vegetarian, although it is now partially true: Many of the male members of the Dogra Brahmans are occasional non-vegetarians and some are regularly non-vegetarians. Even some females are also non-vegetarians. They take either mutton or chicken. Some women cook meat for the male members of the family while others totally abstain from even touching it. Those women who otherwise are non-vegetarians give up eating meat later in their life. Nursing mothers are permitted to take meat only after the *mundan* ceremony of their sons. The concept of vegetarianism is based on *ahimsa* and religious and spiritual merits. Taking eggs is considered as semi non-vegetarianism. Orthodox Dogra Brahmans not only abstain from consuming eggs, meat and fish but even abhor garlic and onion. Those who take non-vegetarian food occasionally avoid it every Tuesday besides certain religious days such as on every Puranmashi and Amavas, Ekadasi, Chaturdas, Navratras, during mourning and *shradh* days, Janmashtami and Ganesh Chaturthi, etc.

The staple food of the Dogra Brahmans consists of wheat, maize, *bajra*, rice and pulses and, in uplands, coarse millets form a regular item of their food. Maize is also consumed by them. The Dogra Brahmans seldom cook rice for the evening meals while, in the midday meals, it is a must. Pulses like black gram are necessarily cooked on Saturdays, *rajmah* (kidney beans) on Sundays, gram pulse on Thursdays. *Masur* is not at all taken by this community.

The main drinks of the Dogra Brahmans are milk, *sherbat*, *lassi* (buttermilk) and *sattoo*; which is a mixture of parched barley flour and sweetened water. They are very fond of a sweet dish, *khir*, prepared with rice and milk. It is taken only during the day time. Sweetened rice called *mitha bhatt*, cooked with milk and *desi ghee*, *sripalao*, *auria ambal* and *madra* are some other sweet dishes. *Madra* is a fine liquid preparation of dryfruits, milk and other compounds and is a heavy diet in character. Dogra *dham* (community lunch) consists of two pulses, *chane ki dal* and *mah ki dal*, one *madra* of *rajmah* with *ambal*. The community meals are served on *pattals* (leaf plates) made of the lotus or *palash* leaves.

The community meals of other Hindu groups were prepared mostly by the Brahmans who were called *siyans*. Before engaging themselves for the duties of *siyans*, they have a bath and then put on clean *dhoti* and *kurta*.

The Dogra Brahmans have been non-drinkers but, after 1947, many nave developed a taste for alcoholic drinks and younger generation freely drink liquor in an urban society. Some take liquor on special occasions like the birth of a son, marriage of males and fairs like Baisakhi (Basoa) and Lohri, etc.

The Dogra Brahmans, otherwise, are considered to be fond of eating but there are special religious days on which either nothing at all is taken or in place of cereals, fruits, roots and milk and milk products only are taken, while on some days even water is avoided both by some males as well as females. During Navratras, on Ekadashi and Janmashtami, they take fruits, roots, milk and milk product called *phalahar* in place of cereals. On the full moon day of the month and on Tuesday, some Brahmans take one meal without salt while on days like Karva Chauth, Shivratri, Ganesh Chaturthi and on the marriage day of the daughter, even water is not taken by the parents of the bride, till she gets ceremonially wedded, i.e. circled four times around the sacred fire. The maternal uncles and aunts of the bride observe fast till she wears the auspicious red bangles. They smoke *bidi*, cigarette and also use indigeneous pipe, i.e. *jhari*. *Jhari* is shared with people of the same social stratum. Almost all the groups have *chhinna* (boycott) with one or the other group community.

The Brahman community is highly stratified in hierachical order at the top of which stands that clan of the Brahmans who claim to be the descendants of King Porus. Datta, Bali, Vaid *gots* are considered as the superior Brahmans. They mostly join either military and police service or prefer to run business. They do not enter into marriage alliance with the Brahmans of other groups. As per oral tradition some ancestors of the Brahmans had married Rajput girls and their issues were called *purohits* who enjoyed all the favours of the ruling class. Some ceremonies are exclusively performed by the *purohits*. Next come the Pandit clan graded as second in hierarchy. They perform the functions of a priest and earn their livelihood. All the Brahmans were arranged in these two prominent strata which were further subdivided into a number of grades. In north India, one of the dividing factors was the handling of plough. Those Brahmans who work with their ploughs are called *halbaha*. The Brahmans of upper class do not marry their daughters to a *halbaha* Brahman. Earlier the high class Brahmans did not share their *pangat* even with the *halbahas*.

Another feature of the gradation was the mode of greeting. When two Brahmans of the same social strata meet together they salute each other by saying '*pairipouna*' but when a high class Brahman is addressed by an inferior Brahman, the former replies 'Ram-Ram'.

The Jogis and Bawes also claim to be Brahmans. A Jogi is a *pujari* of a Ram temple while a Bawa is a priest in the Shiv temple and accepts *dan-punn* of the dying minors. They write the word Sharma for their caste identification whereas the fact is that the Jogi used to bury their dead and raise a *samadhi*. The social stratification of Brahmans also took place on the basis of *karma*. Those who performed death rituals and accepted *dan-punn*, left by the dying person, came to be known as the Charjis and Gujratis. They are considered as the lowest class of the Brahmans. Similarly, the Dubes are also inferior Brahmans who had migrated from Maharashtra. The *purohits* and pandits do not enter into matrimonial relations with them. Neither do they dine with them nor permit them to share seats with the high-class Brahmans.

The Dogra Brahmans are monogamous and endogamous and, as such, marrying into their own *gots* or class is necessary for them. Here the *got* is different from the *gotra* of the Puranas. Most of the Dogra Brahmans have Bharadwaj *gotra*, so the marriages do take place in the same *gotra*. But the class or subcaste is considered as a separate *got* and hence people of the same *got* do not intermarry. Even the *got* of one's mother's parents is not permitted for marriage. Secondly, the bridegroom should be older than the bride. Earlier, in the Brahman families, it was unusual to marry into a family settled in the same village; but now the traditions are breaking down and intercaste marriages are gradually increasing. Among the Dogra Brahmans, child marriage was customary.

The marriage system was of three types: (1) *dharm* or *punn*, in which nothing was accepted from the bridegroom's side, (2) *dohari* or *batta-satta*, i.e. exchange involving two or three families, which were very common amongst the Brahmans of lower strata and the (3) sale-purchase marriage in which a payment was made for the bride. The last form of marriage was prevalent only among the low caste Brahmans. Now intercaste and widow remarriage is becoming more common among the Brahmans. A widower is permitted to re-marry. Sororate system is prevalent among the Dogra Brahmans.

Daj (dowry) system is prevalent. It is demanded and given. Dowry is given both in cash and kind. It is displayed for the view of the *biradari* and *baratis*. Some gifts are given to the groom at every stage of the betrothal process such as *akha* (request), *thaka*, *tika*, *sagan*, and also after marriage on the occasion of *daphera*, *raphera* or *maklawa*. This *maklawa* or *daphera* now takes place two or three days after marriage, but when child marriage was prevalent, it took place when the girl was 12 and the boy 15 to 18 years of age. Even afterwards, gifts in the form of clothes, victuals, etc., were sent to the daughter and her in-laws on all important religious and social occasions, particularly on Basoa, Karva Chauth, Lohri, Diwali and Sakolare. Divorce was almost unknown among the Brahmans since marriage was thought to be an unbreakable holy bond. But in the urban areas of Duggar these barriers are disappearing. Divorce cases are being reported now for reasons like barrenness of the woman, maladjustment, impotency, insanity on either part as well as cruelty of the husband. Divorce can be given by either party but divorce compensation is given by the husband to the wife.

A Brahman family is of patriarchical nature in which the grandfather or father holds all the authority. Property of the family is held in his name. He is respected and feared. He looks after the family, and showers love and care on all members of his family. But things are changing very fast. Joint families are disappearing giving birth to nuclear family system which is on the increase though it is not very common in the village society. Avoidance exists between mother-in-law and son-in-law, daughter-in-law and father-in-law. Joking relationships exist between sister-in-law and brother-in-law and grandchildren.

Balu or *besar* is the symbol of marriage of a Brahman woman. They are held in high esteem but they enjoy no freedom of speech and movement, except *panditains* among them who visit the houses of their *jajmans* on auspicious occasions. They get some fees on every occasion which augments their family income. All other Brahman women are only domestic aids. Girls are revered as *kanjaks* (worshipable) but birth of a female child is not welcome. A widow has the right to the property of her deceased husband for her maintenance. Women have a vital role to play in the performance of some rituals, in the household activities and in controlling family expenditure. Women of agricultural families amongst the Brahmans play a great role in the agricultural operations.

The Dogra Brahmans are generally Sanatanis and are known for their *karam-kandi* character. All the sixteen Hindu *sanskars* are performed by them.

On the eighth or fifteenth day of the *shukla-paksha* (bright forthight) of eighth month of conception, the woman carrying a child is made to sit on a *peera* or wooden stool and wear a coloured, mostly pink, suit gifted by her parents. A female barber combs her hair and some rites are performed. *Bihaiyan* songs are sung by the ladies. It is a function of the womenfolk. On the birth of a child, a *jyotishi* (fortune teller) is consulted for knowing the *graha* of the child and *mahurat* (auspicious time) to feed the child. *Sootak* (pollution) is observed for ten days after delivery. On the fifteenth day, the *punjap* ritual is performed. *Karah* (sweetened milk cooked in dry nuts) is offered to those who come to congratulate on the occasion. On the fifth and eleventh days, the infant and mother are purified by tasting *guntra* (cow's urine) and *Ganga-jal*. The child is given a name by his *bua* (paternal aunt). This original name, given according to the *janam-patri* (horoscope) is kept a secret for fear of getting the child affected by the black magicians who may intend to do harm to the child. Someone with a good temperament or sometimes the midwife writes 'Om' with a gold string on the tongue of the child during these eleven days, preferably before offering him his first diet. *Suraj darshan* (sun-sighting) by the child on the fortieth day of his birth, *annaprashan* (feeding him cereals in the sixth month) are the other important ceremonies. In the third year, on any auspicious day of Uttarayan period, the *mundan-sanskar* of the male child is performed. All the hair is removed. In the Dogra Brahman families, keeping of a small tuft of hair called *bodi* is compulsory. Hence immediately after *mundan* day *choti* or *bodi* keeping known as *argha* is marked by the barber with a razor. On both the ceremonies *sutra* and *mundan* the maternal parents give valuable dresses, eatables and other items to the child, his mother and his paternal relatives.

Among the Dogra Brahmans, it is the girl's father who approaches the boy's father through a middleman, mostly *purohit* or barber, for the settlement of the marriage of his daughter. At the satisfaction of both the parties, the ritual of *kurmai* is fixed and *tika* or *tilak* (*sagan*) is sent to the boy's residence. The brother of the girl, along with some cousins and friends, takes the *sagan*, which consists of dry nuts, sweets, fruits, at least one silver rupee and a large pink or red scarf. A band is engaged by the boy's parents to play music, sweets are distributed amongst the invited relatives and friends and *tilak* is applied by the girl's brother to the bridegroom's forehead with the chanting of the *mantras* by the pandit. The date of marriage is fixed and communicated to the boy's parents. In both the houses marriage ceremonies start with the installation of temple-shaped wooden frame in which the framed photos of Radha and Krishna are placed.

This ceremony is also called *gandhian*. The *baratis* (marriage party) follows the bridegroom riding the horse to the house of the bride with the beating of the drums and playing of the band. As per the *mahurat*, the *lagan* ceremony takes place with the recitation of *shastric mantras* in front of the sacred fire. The bride goes around the fire four times—thrice she is followed by the bridegroom and once she follows the bridegroom. She is then given a send-off along with her dowry. In the house of the in-laws, she is seated in front of *dehri* and made to distribute handfuls of *gurhara* (fried and sweetened rice flour) to the receptionists. The lunch is hosted in connection with the reception of the bride. It is called *chaab*. The marriage rituals commencing with *kurmai* conclude with *daphera* or *raphera* and in between various rites are performed.

The third important *sanskar* of the Dogra Brahmans is of death. The dying person is laid down on the ground purified by sprinkling of *Ganga-jal* (holy Ganga water) and dust from *teeraths* (pilgrimage centres) and of *tulsi*. Offerings, in the form of cow, grains, clothes, cash, etc., are made to donate by the dying person. This offering is called *dan-punn*.

Panjratni (five *ratnas*) and Ganga water is put in his or her mouth. A burning *diya* (lamp) made of wet flour is placed on the palm of the dying persons and he or she is asked to repeat any name of Lord Vishnu, i.e. Ram, Hari Om, Hare Krishna, Narayan, and so on. *Dan-punn* is given to the Charji or Gujrati. *Dah-sanskar* (cremation) of the deceased is performed by the eldest son at the *shamshan-ghat* (cremation ground). As among the Hindu communities, the dead is laid on a pyre which is lit by the eldest son. On the fourth day, the remains are collected to be immersed in the Ganga or any other river. Thirteen days are observed as *mutak* (pollution due to death). Till recently, mourning by women was performed all through the thirteen days. Much expenditure had to be incurred. The kith and kin (males) had to get their heads shaved. But these customs are disappearing with the passage of time. On the eleventh day, *kriya-karm* is performed by the Charji Brahman. In the name of the departed person a cot with bedsheets, mattress, grains, fruits, vegetables, clothes, shoes, utensils, umbrellas, sweets, etc., are put together and offered to the Charji who acts as a *purohit*. This gift is known as *chaj*. Afterwards, *ardh-barkhi* and *barkhi* and *chaubarkhi* are performed in the name of the dead after six months, a year and four years, respectively. On all these occasions, gifts similar to that of *kriya-karm* are offered to the *purohit*. However, the death of a very old person is celebrated with beating of drum, band and music, though his or her family members observe mourning in the usual way for eleven days. The married daughters and sisters of the deceased were given clothes and sweets. *Garud Puran* is read out during the mourning days by a *pandit* at the time convenient to all. But with the arrival of modernity the observance of death ceremonies have also changed a lot. Formal ceremonies are no longer prevalent. People do not find time to sit all together for ten consecutive days.

The Brahmans are basically a priestly class and earned their livelihood by ministering at socio-religious functions, worship and imparting education. But in Duggar, some of the Brahmans are engaged in the agricultural profession also. Preparation of horoscopes, soothsaying and astrology too have been the sources of income for them. But now most of them are in services, government and private. Some are running business and carrying on trade.

The Dogra Brahmans had traditional *jati* (caste) councils and regional *sabhas* (councils) which settled the disputes amongst the members of the community. Such *sabhas* were formed through elections. These *sabhas* decided social problems and extended help both financial and moral. Awards were conferred upon the persons of the community for their distinct services to the community. Punishments too were inflicted on those who defied the decisions of the *sabha*. The violators of community taboos were not permitted to share *pangat* or *hookah* and were not allowed to establish matrimonial relations with the Brahmans. It was called *chhinna*, a very common practice among the Dogra Brahmans. Since Independence, the mechanism of social control has changed much, yet *chhinnas* are strictly adhered to. The Kesar subcaste have *chhinna* with Mamoaliye and Badgotras. The Jalotre Brahmans have *chhinna* with Takhiya, Karlupiye with Hadotras, and Badiyal with Dubeys, Sapolie; Padhe with the Rakwal Rajputs.

The Dogra Brahmans worship the gods and goddesses of Hindu pantheon. Local deities also find favour with them. There are several prominent places of pilgrimages in the land of Dogras. Some of these are the holy shrines of Vaishno Devi at Katra, Sukrala temple near Billawar, Shiv temple at Billawar, Shiv temple at Sudh Mahadev near Chanaini, Narsinha temple at Ghagwal, Raghunath temple, Shiv temple, Panjvaktra and Pirkho temple in Jammu city. Here the regional deities are worshipped by them. Of these, Vaishno Devi and Bawa Jitto have acquired state and national fame.

They are staunch Sanatanists and have full faith in the Sanatan form of Hinduism and the religious *karm-kand* (ritualism).

Every Dogra Brahman family has its own deity called *dehra* or *dehari*. Clan deities known as *kul-devtas*, besides the two *avatars* Sri Ram and Sri Krishna, are also worshipped. The modern generation visits the shrines of *pirs* also. Almost all the Brahmans have a place of daily worship in their houses where many symbols or idols of deities are kept. Every new eatable is first offered to the deity before the family consumes the item. The Brahmans who attend these deities can be classified into two groups. First, the priests who worship and perform *havans* and *yajnas* in temples, and second, those who are called *chelas* and get inspiration from the deities for doing away with the evil spirits and for soothsaying.

The Dogra Brahmans participate in all the Hindu festivals celebrated all over the region, such as Dussehra, Diwali, Holi, Sankrant, etc. Some festivals like Karva Chauth, Bhugga, Bachh-doab, and others are exclusively meant for the females when women decorate their houses. On such festivals people take bath in rivers and canals and in the Dewaka at Purmandal.

The Dogra Brahmans are mainly associated with the duties of priesthood and some of them are agriculturists. Though they have no particular training in any kind of art and craft yet they have traditionally inherited the art of preparing *janeu* (sacred thread), *paintra* (grass ring) for worship and *tulsi*-beads. They are adept in preparing, *bhumi-chittra* for *nava-grah puja* and *vedi-mandap* (altar).

The Dogra Brahmans did not have any linkage with all other *varnas* and did not participate in their social and domestic functions and ceremonies. However, some of them did perform the duties of a pandit on the ceremonies like naming, *mundan-sanskars* and marriage ceremonies and that too in the upper three *varnas.* They did not accept water or *pukka* food from the hands of the artisans, craftsmen and the people of the fourth *varna.* They did not share *pangat* (seat) with the people of other three castes. They did not share their wells, tanks, *dharamshalas*, temples, etc., with people of the fourth *varna.*

Folk ballads certify that the Dogra Brahmans had fraternal relations even with the people of fourth *varna.* Eso (a Scheduled Caste) was a close friend of the famous Brahman Bava Jitto. The Brahmans did accept *kachcha* food or dry fruits from the people belonging to the fourth *varna*, while they accepted *gyasan* (cooked food) also from the other two *varnas*, i.e. Kshatriya and Vaishya. In spite of keeping their isolation, the Dogra Brahmans received full respect and love from the other *varnas* and guided them in the hour of difficulty. These taboos are disappearing now among the youth of this generation.

Being an educated and learned community, the Dogra Brahmans have favourably responded to all types of development plans and programmes. The community shares common hospitals, holy shrines, transport and water pipes from common tube wells with other communities. They are entering into marriage alliances with the other two *varnas*, i.e. Kshatriya and Vaishyas also. Similarly, they are willingly adopting the family planning measures and programmes. They have no prejudice against allopathic medicines. They are participating in the fairs and festivals of other communities also. Electricity has become an indispensable part of their daily life. The agriculturist group of the Brahmans is making full use of chemical fertilizers, canal irrigational facilities and *gobar* gas, etc.

The youth have been benefited by the self-employment programmes started by the Jammu & Kashmir government. Banking facilities are being utilized by them.

The Dogra Brahmans are favourably reacting to the mass media benefits. They are now taking a scientific attitude towards the Hindu mythology. Cultural revivalism is gaining ground amongst the Dogra Brahmans.

CHAMPA SHARMA

DOGRA JHEER

The Dogra Jheers call themselves Kashyap Rajputs whereas other communities call them Jheer. In this region, both the words Jheer as well as Kashyap Rajput are understood as synonyms and signify the same commuity.

They have no title to affix to their names, but some educated members of the community working in government services and other employments are suffixing Dogra to their names. The word *jheer* is derived from the Sanskrit word *dheevara.* In the process of language development, different connotations of the word *dheevara* have come forth. In Sanskrit, it is meant for a 'partly mixed caste'. In *Gautam Dharamshastra* and *Mahabharata* it has been used for 'fishermen' while in *Kathasaritsagara, teevara* (*dheevara*) connotes a caste of hunters which has been explained by R.L. Turner in *Comparative Dictionary of Indo-Aryan Languages* as an offspring of the Kshatriya with Rajput woman. In Prakrit, also *dheevara* is referred to a caste of fishermen. In Awankari dialect of Lahndi, *dheevara* stands for a 'cook'. In the age of modern Indo-Aryan language, the uses of the word *dheevara* appears in various forms like dheevara, dheemara, jheevara, jhiur, jheer, etc. In Punjabi, Dheevara is uttered as Jhiur while, in Dogri, it is pronounced as Jheer. As such, the development of Dogri word *jheer* can be traced out from the Sanskrit *dheevara*, Prakrit *dheevara*, Hindi *dheevra*, *dheemara*, *jheevara* and Punjabi *Jhiur*, or Dogra Jheer.

The Dogra Jheers adopted different modes of labour to earn their livelihood. Fishing, running of water-mills, carrying of load on their shoulders (including *baihnqi* and palanquin), roasting of grams, groundnuts, etc., are some of the occupations taken up by them.

Regarding the origin of the word 'Kashyap Rajput', two legends are prevalent. According to one legend, some tortoises on the seashore were transformed into men who carried Sita in a palanquin to Ayodhya. Thus, because of this transformation from *kashyapa* (tortoises) to men, those palanquin bearers were called Kashyap Rajput. In Duggar, the use of palanquin at the time of marriage and *dafera* (*gauna)* was very popular in olden days and the palanquin bearers who were known as Kahara, always belonged to the Jheer community. Still the custom of palanquin exists in remote areas and the Jheers are performing the service of palanquin bearers.

According to a second legend, Kashyapa Rishi took upon himself the duty of serving water to thirty-three gods invited to a *yajna* by the rishis. Hence those who performed similar duty in society came to be called Kashyapa. However, the Jheers have other *gotras* like Bhardwaj, Atri, Kaushal, etc., so the Kashyapa Rishi's theory does not hold water. The *Kathasaritasagara* view of Jheevara as a mixed caste may be true.

The Jheers are mostly concentrated in the Dogra region of Jammu. The terrain inhabited by the community varies from fertile plain to arid *kandi* and sandy hills of Udhampur, thinly covered by low bushy forest. The climate ranges from dry to moderately moist with seasonal rainfall; weather varies from warm to temperate. Fertile plain and arid *kandi* characterize the land.

Their medium of communication among themselves and with the people of other communities is Dogri, the native language. For reading, writing and learning purposes, old generation was using Urdu, the state language, and Arabic or Dogre *Akkhar* (which was very much in use up to earlier twentieth century) scripts. The modern generation also speaks Dogri as their first language, but their medium of communication of reading and writing is Hindi, English and, to some extent, Urdu. Therefore, Devanagari, Roman and Persian scripts are being used by them.

The Dogra Jheers used to dress in a simple way. Being a working class, they used to wear second hand clothes given by their *jajmans*. Men used to wear *kurta* (shirt) and *tahmad* (loincloth) along with a *parna* (an extra scarf). They are often found barefooted and put on shoes on special occasions. They wore *naintian* in their ears. Now they wear clothes same as other communities of the Duggar. Their women used to wear *kurta, churidar suthan* and a wide *dupatta* with all types of silver ornaments. Now they put on modern dress including *kameez, salwar and dupatta.*

The Dogra Jheers are non-vegetarian and very fond of eating meat, fish, eggs, etc. The biggest source of livelihood of this community is catching and selling of fish, besides cooked fish, *siri, kharore* meat and fried eggs. They do not take beef. Their women also take meat.

The Dogra Jheers' staple food is wheat and rice. Seasonally, they also take maize and *bajra.* They eat all varieties of pulses and beans available in their region. They use mustard oil, dalda (hydrogenated oil) and refined oils for cooking. A few of them who are economically sound, also use *desi ghee* for *chapatis.* Among vegetables all types of roots, tubers and leafy varieties locally available are consumed by them. Fruits are used occasionally.

Milk and milk preparations like *lassi* and tea are also consumed by them. Menfolk use alcoholic drinks frequently, which they get locally or from wine shops. They smoke *jhari*, i.e. *hookah*. Old Jheer women smoke *jhari*, but young and old refrain from alcoholic drinks.

The Dogra Jheers of Jammu region have been divided into several subcastes, such as Khisku, Phounti, Bera, Tak, Bamhotre, Doe, Athgotre, Sukhajange, Manhotre, Baspurie, Balgotre, Allar, Sountre, Manni, Sarmutte, Sangotre, Chikkardubbe, Samhotre, Lunjh, Jalandhari, Lakhotre, Dain, Bahri, Seotre, Malgotre, Maski, Koonj, Gadari, Jassam, Poonchhi (Jheer), etc. They are having *gotras* like Bhardwaj, Kaushal, Bashal, Kashyap, Atri, etc. Mostly the *gotra* is common for two or more subcastes, e.g. Bera, Doe and Bamhotre groups have common *gotra* of Bhardwaj. Similarly, the *gotra* of Phounty and Tak groups belong to Kaushak, while Khisku comes under Bashal *gotra*, Athgotre in Kashyap *gotra*, Laghotre in Atri *gotra*, etc. Both the subcaste as well as the *gotra* govern the marital relations. Even the *gotra* of mother is to be avoided. Therefore, cross-cousin marriages and the marriages between parallel cousins are not permitted. After marriage, the caste as well as *gotra* of a girl is changed from parental to her in-laws' *gotra* and subcaste.

The Dogra Jheers recognize four-fold *varna* system and place their own status higher than that of the Shudras from whom they never accept food and water. In Jammu & Kashmir, they are considered as an economically backward class.

The Dogra Jheers are endogamous at community level and cases of exogamy are rare. Blood relations on the side of mother as well as father are avoided.

Sororate and levirate marriages are allowed in case of wife's death and husband's death, respectively, usually with the consent of the bride and the bridegroom. In olden days, levirate marriages were very common and were known as *chadar dalna*.

Prior to Independence, girls and boys were married at a young age. Generally the marriage age for girls was 10-14 years and, for boys, it was 15-18 years. At present, the girls usually get married after attaining puberty. The matrimonial age is between 15 and 20 years for girls, and 20 and 25 years for boys. In remote areas, there still are cases of pre-puberty marriages but the custom of early marriage is fading away. Being a Hindu community, monogamy is socially and the legally accepted norm of marriage in the society. Few cases of polygyny may be noticed in case of barrenness, but only with the consent of the first wife. *Bindi*, *sindoor* and nose pin are the marriage symbols. Though unmarried girls may also have nose pins on their noses, it is a must for the married. In case of widowhood, all the three signs, namely *bindi*, *sindoor* and nose pin are removed at once. Besides these the Jheer women usually wear bangles, necklace, finger rings, earrings, *shrangarpatti*, *tika*, nose ring, *bicchue*, etc.

The system of bride price is not prevalent among the Dogra Jheers. In olden days, a noteworthy aspect of marriages in Jammu region was exchange marriage called *dohari*. This was prevalent either among the people of backward and remote areas or among the people of lower status. Dowry system like other upper clan communities is becoming a more common practice. In spite of the social and legal restrictions, the demand for dowry is on the increase and the amount ranges between 10 and 25 thousand rupees. Marriage is performed at the bride's residence.

According to tradition, the Dogra Jheers follow patrilocal residence after marriage. Nowadays divorce is permissible with the decision of a court under the Hindu Marriage Act. Divorced women are entitled to get divorce compensation or maintenance. The children are the responsiblity of their father in such cases. In olden days, it was less prevalent in the community. In case of maladjustment, barrenness, impotency and chronic sickness, the brides were sent back to their parents for ever without any notice and maintenance.

Joint family system is gradually declining among the Dogra Jheers owing to their credence and faith in *jadu-jarhian* (black magic). Under the influence of *jadu-jarhian*, the illwill among the members of a joint family generates prejudice, family tensions and quarrels, which result in partition of the family. Therefore, at present the family is generally seen in its nuclear form. In rural areas, still a few joint families can be noted. Interpersonal relations among the family members are of several types on the basis of mutual behaviour and dealings with each other; but all the family members respect and honour the authority of the eldest or head of the family often combined with awe and fear. In return, the eldest family member also reciprocates with the feeling of responsibility and sincerity on his part. Joking relations are permitted between *der-bharjai, sali-jija and salehar-nanoia.* Such jests or teasings are a source of entertainment at marriages or on other happy occasions, when there is generally a free interaction and direct communication amongst the members. *Sithnian*, the popular joking songs, are also sung on these occasions. *Nanad* also has joking terms with her *bharjai* if they are of the same age group.

Conflicts and confrontations generally exist due to misunderstandings among the relatives often on account of one being under the impression that he or she is being subjected to *jadu-jarhian* by some other relative. Under these conditions, even affinal as well as consanguineous relations are severed. The interfamily relations between the supposedly victimized family and the family accused of vicitimizing are terminated. The Dogra Jheers, follow the Hindu law of inheritance, but only their male children inherit the ancestral property. Daughters never put a claim over it. In case of there being no male issue to their parents, they inherit their parental property. After the father's death, eldest son takes the responsibility as head of the family but the examples of putting up together of the brothers' families after the father's death are noticed rarely. Generally, all brothers prefer their separate families.

The status of women among the Dogra Jheers is lower in comparison to men. Though the womenfolk are legally entitled to inherit their paternal property, as a matter of practice, they are not given their shares; rather while distributing the property amongst the sons, a power of attorney in favour of their brothers is usually taken from the daughters. Birth of a daughter is not considered to be a happy affair. Often a girl is taken as a liability in this community. In orthodox families, the girls are treated indifferently and they are denied normal educational facilities that are available to the male members of the family. A good majority of Jheer girls are made to work and labour from their childhood to support and strengthen the family economy. As a matter of common practice, they go to clean the utensils of upper castes or wealthy people in their houses. They also perform other types of labour like washing the clothes and cleaning the houses of those who are economically well placed. The daily urgent family needs are met with the earning of the daughters. In urban areas, they get their wages in cash as well as in kind on monthly basis, accompanied by other gifts on special occasions and ceremonies. In the same way, they also shoulder the family income of their in-laws after marriage. Womenfolk of this community share all sorts of religious and social activities with men but the decision-making power rests with men only.

An antenatal ritual called *reetan* is celebrated in the eighth month of pregnancy when the pregnant woman's parents send her gifts comprising of fried and cooked eatables. The woman also undergoes a ritual bath and hair dressing for safe delivery of a male child. Delivery is normally helped by an experienced *dai* (midwife) at home. Child-birth pollution is observed for 13 days, but in some groups it is for 21 days. At the end of pollution period, *sutra* rite is celebrated, when the neonate is named and the mother and child get a bath of purification along with some other rituals. A feast is also served to the kith and kin on this occasion. But usually this feast is deferred till the *mundan sanskar*.

Mundan rites, in case the child is male, are observed with great ceremony and mostly at the shrine of some deity or the other which is a special object of worship for the family. This ceremony is always marked by a sumptuous feast to the *biradari*.

Marriages are settled by negotiation between the parents of the bride and the bridegroom. The negotiation is initiated by a middleman, then it is fixed with the consent of both the parties. After betrothal, the *sagun* ritual is performed.

Elaborate marriage rituals were previously held by the Jheer community and the whole process lasted for several days. From *sagun* to *vedi*, a number of minor rituals are even today performed at the homes both of the boy and the girl. The usual ritual of *biah* takes place in a *mandap* and *vedi* witnessed by the sacred fire and accompanied by *ved-mantras* recited by the attending *purohit*.

Antyeshti sanskar (death rites) are performed with several minor rituals. The dying person is made to lie on the floor and gift away some articles like grain, cow, some coins, etc. The dead body is carried on a bier to the cremation ground. The eldest son lights the pyre. It is accompanied by a series of rituals performed by a *charji*. On the second or third day *phool* (ashes) is collected and immersed in a river, the Tawi or Ganga. On the tenth day, *daswan* rites are performed. Death pollution is observed for thirteen days. The last day is marked by the performance of *kriya-karam*, and *rasam-pagri*. Then follow the periodic death rites, *masats* (four month), *ardh-barkhi* (six months), *barkhi* (one year) and *chaubarkhi* (four years) ritual which are accompanied by the performance of *shradh* and giving of gifts to the attending *charji*.

The economic activities of the Jheers are multifarious. They serve mostly by carrying loads and cleaning utensils and drawing water for their *jajmans* in the villages, for which they are paid in kind and cash. Some of them have joined the defence services. In towns, they sell eatables such as *rehris*, *chaats*, etc., and catch and sell fish. The Jheer women are also an economic asset to the family. They do menial domestic work in other households in various ways for daily and periodic wages.

Before 1975, the members of the panchayat, *sarpanch*, *panches*, secretary, etc., were elected. But after 1975, they are nominated by the state government. Though they are delegated the powers to decide about conflicts, quarrels, thefts, misconduct, etc., the limit of their power is to a lower extent. For example, they can adjudicate the cases of theft where the value of property stolen does not exceed Rs. 1,000. In case of damages caused by a cattle trespass, they are empowered to adjucate where the amount of loss does not exceed Rs.150. Similar is the case for crimes like fouling the water of public spring or reservoir, wrongfully taking away or injuring movable property, obscene acts, etc. The mode of punishment is usually a cash penality. Under the Ranbir Penal Code 1889, the fine does not exceeded Rs. 25 or double the amount of loss caused up to a limit of Rs. 40, Rs. 20. for gambling, Rs. 5 for cattle trespass, etc. Cases falling beyond the panchayat jurisdiction are referred to a court of law and, ultimately, people have to go to courts for claiming full compensation.

The cases of rape and adultery are generally not brought to the notice of the panchayat. People try themselve to solve these cases.

The Dogra Jheers are followers of Hindu religion. They have their *kul-devtas* like Baba Bhair, Baba Sidh Gauria, Kalibeer, etc., and *sajaivaties* such as Bua Tripta, Bua Jiuni, Bua Ghani Rani, etc., at their *gotra* and subcaste levels. Stories of these *sajaivaties* have been connected with certain sacrificial incidents which live in oral traditions. To atone and immortalize the sacrifice of these *sajaivaties* (holy places), where the symbolic statues of these clan deities have been installed, *dehries* have been constructed at different places either connected with the incident or of religious popularity. A number of *dehries* related with the Jheer *kul-devtas* have been found at places of Bawe de jar at Jhiri, near Akhnur tahsil of Jammu. To commemorate the sacrifice of these *kul* deities and *sajaivaties*, fairs known as *melas* are held on traditional and customary days at these shrines once or twice in a year by various groups of Jheers. It is noteworthy here that fairs at every shrine have great relevance with harvesting. At the outset of every harvest, people of different groups offer the harvest to their respective *kul-devtas* first before consuming it themselves.

Polytheism has an important place in the Dogra Jheers' worship and devotion. They believe that there are thirty-three crore deities, but their personal choice of deities generally falls between Shiv and Devi (*Shakti*). The deities of local importance also represent Shiv and Shakti (Kali, Mahalakshmi, Durga and Vaishno) along with Vishnu, Hanuman, Ganesh, etc. Most of the womenfolk observe fasts on Mondays (for Shiv), Poornima and Ekadashi (for Vishnu) and during Navratras (for Shakti). On these days, they go to temples of the respective deities for worship. One fact worth mentioning is that their devotion rests around Devi. During Navratras, majority of the people visit the shrine of Vaishno Devi at Katra and Mahakali at Jammu (Bahu Fort). The most popular form of their devotion is to hold a *jagraata* (full night devotional sitting) in her honour. In this holy act, they erect a pandal and decorate it with a variety of flowers, wreaths, photos, balloons, etc., and burn incense. All relatives and close friends are invited to attend and participate. Devotees skilled in narrating *katha* (story) of the devis and reciting *bhettan* (devotional songs) composition of *katha* and *bhettan*. This devotional observance of *jagraata* lasts upto four in the morning and concludes with singing of concluding recitation (*aarati*) and distribution of *prasad* comprising of *halwa* (*karah*) and fried *chana*. People also visit the *dargahs* (shrines) of *pirs*. In Jammu region, a number of *pir dargahs* have become the centre of devotion and worship. Among these, the *dargah* of Baba Vudhan Shah Wali at Pir Baba Satwari, Roushan Shah Wali at Gumat, Jammu, Baba Pir-Mitha and Panjpir near Nagrota, are of greater significance. People visit these *dargahs* every Thursday. It is common belief among the people that the desires expressed at these places are fulfilled.

The Dogra Jheers observe Diwali, Lohri, Holi, Baisakhi, Rakhi and Dussehra with great zeal like other Hindu communities. They join and participate in all the fairs held in the region such as Baisakhi, Shivratri, Chaitra Chaudash, Sudh Mahadev, Siddh Suankha, Thara Kalval Jhiri Purmandal, Bachhduah and Drubari (both female fairs), Mela Bahu Fort, etc.

In addition to Haridwar, they visit all the regional holy places like Vaishno Devi, Bahuwali Sukrala Devi, Sudh Mahadev, Purmandal, Uttervahini Devika, Pir Khoh, Siva-Khori, Buddha Amarnath in Jammu region and Sri Amarnathji in Kashmir province.

Basically being labourers, the Dogra Jheer are not specialized in the field of plastic and graphic arts, yet their interest in singing, dancing and painting is gradually increasing. Their old generations were skilled in making fish nets. Their women are experts in traditional painting. On the occasion of *ahoi* fast, people of all the three upper castes get their baskets and planks, etc., painted by the Jheer. They put cooked food, sugar cane, brinjal, with other fruits, clothes and cash in these painted baskets and give to the Jheers as alms.

The Dogra Jheers are famous for their sweet voice and musical accent. On marriages and other ceremonies, the Jheer singers, known as *gataran*, are invited to add colour to such functions. Men of this community are also popular for singing *chhinjan*, the Dogri folk songs.

Even today, the talent in singing and dancing can be observed among the boys and girls of this community.

The Dogra Jheers accept both cooked and uncooked food from the Brahmans, Kshatriyas and Vaishyas (Mahajans). They are invited for per-forming the tasks on religious and ceremonial festivals, and on other auspicious and inauspicious occasions. They receive money and gifts. They are also not hesitant to accept water and food from their parallel communities like the Nai (barber), Tarkhan (carpenter), Lohar (blacksmith), Kumhar (potter) and Chimbe (washerman), etc., besides participating in their ceremonial and religious activities. Cooked food and food products form part of their wages at the time of ceremonial occasions. It is, however, noteworthy that the community refrains from taking food and water from the Megh, Dum Mahasha, Chamar and other low castes. They do not also participate in their ceremonies.

The Dogra Jheers also keep away from maintaining marital relations with other communities. They share water resources, wells, hand pumps, tube wells, ponds, religious places, temples, schools, roads and panchayat ghars with higher and parallel communities and not with other lower castes. They are Hindus by faith; so they share the cremation ground with the Hindus.

In urban areas, the Dogra Jheers have established their hotels and *dhabas* where people of higher communities eat and drink freely. Some retired cooks from defence services of this community work as cooks for the higher communities on ceremonial and religious occasions. Some of them deal in tent houses and render the services of decoration, erecting of *pandals* on marriage ceremonies and on other important occasions.

With the awareness of modernity, some of them are taking interest in educating their children with the result that some Jheers are working as doctors, engineers, teachers, judicial officers, etc., while some others have proved their skill in the art of dancing and singing. The participation of this community in political activities cannot be overlooked at different levels in the state politics.

On account of general awareness and facilities provided to the economically backward classes by the government, the Dogra Jheer are marching forward with the help of the developmental programmes. They are taking interest in the education of their children but only a few children are the beneficiaries of these developmental programmes because of their preoccupation with farming in their own localities. Hence, while still of school-going age they give up their studies. A few who can carry on, achieve their aims in obtaining professional education and occupy higher places in the state and central services.

Though the Dogra Jheers' attitude towards developmental programmes, like modern medicare, family planning is favourable, yet only a few among them are making use of these. In case of illness, majority of the people (living in rural areas) prefer to consult the *jogis*, *gararies* and *doalas* to detect the spirits responsible for illness. The family planning programme has its impact in urban areas. The city dwellers commonly undergo sterlization after having three to five children. They avail of drinking water facilities within their houses, streets and *mohallas*. Tube wells, handpumps, and wells are the main sources of water supply in plain areas. In *kandi* areas, the facility of handpumps is not possible. In hilly areas, besides tube wells, rivulets and springs mainly fulfil the need for water.

Under the self-employment scheme of the government, some of the Dogra Jheers have secured loans and advances and have managed to start different kinds of business enterprises, such as poultry farming and plying autorikshaws, etc. Some of the families belonging to urban areas have also been allotted pieces of land and houses under the housing scheme for the homeless. Majority of the Jheers are availing of media and communication facilities and use electricity for lighting their houses. Rural dwellers use cow-dung and firewood for cooking, whereas in cities mostly kerosene is consumed. A few of them manage to use cooking gas for this purpose. Being mainly a landless community, they are not making use of the irrigational facilities, chemical fertilizers, insecticides and organic manure, etc. Their school-going children receive midday meals under the Nutrition Programmes. The main source of their food supply is through fair price shops at nominal rates.

Most of the Dogra Jheers are living hand to mouth with meagre savings, which reduces their chances of availing of any banking facility. Only a few of them who are economically sound utilize the banking facilities.

The Dogra Jheer belong to a caste considered lower than the Brahman, Kshatriya, and Vaishya (Mahajan) in the social hierarchy of the Dogras. Most of them render their services to the upper castes. Still they are earning their livelihood through their traditional occupations. Their women also work and support their family income. They are economically and educationally backward. But nowadays, some of them have established hotels, tent houses, tailoring shops, small scale business activities, etc., and a few are employed in government services.

VEENA GUPTA

DOGRA MUSLIM

The Muslims inhabiting a small hilly tract of land popularly known as *Duggar Des*, now the Jammu region, are called the Dogra Muslims. Frederic Drew's contention that those of them who have retained their Hindu faith bear the name Dogra cannot be accepted. It is, however, necessary to understand that the Muslims inhabiting the entire Jammu region are not Dogras. This name can rightly be applied to the Muslims of the three districts of the Duggar Des only, namely Udhampur, Jammu and Kathua. The Muslims inhabiting other areas of the land are either Kashmiris or Chibalis, who have migrated to this hilly terrain from time to time.

Being mostly converts from the Dogra Hindus—conversion having taken place mostly during the Mughal period—they carry with them the remnants of their earlier faiths or communities. The communities that can be found common among both the Hindu and Muslim Dogras are the Chibb, Manhas, Chaudhury, Rathore, Thakkar, Mian, Jaral, Pal, etc.

The Duggar Des, excepting the lower areas of the region falling in proximity to Punjab, is a hilly terrain. Its climate is, therefore, varied. In areas adjoining Punjab, it is almost tropical, between the middle hills almost moderately warm, and around the upper reaches, almost cold. Agriculture is their main occupation. All these factors have contributed to make the Dogra Muslims, like their Dogra Hindu brethren, physically attractive, well-built, stout and wheatish in complexion.

The Dogra Muslim, other than the Gujjars and the Bakarwals, speak three to four languages, i.e. Dogri, Punjabi, Kashmiri and Urdu. Well-educated Dogra Muslims, in addition to these, speak English. Arabic is the script used by them for writing purposes, both at home and with the kin groups. Well-educated Dogra Muslims correspond in the Roman script. The Gujjars and Bakrwals speak Gujri and Bakarwali, respectively. For writing purposes, they also use Arabic both at home and with others.

The Dogra Muslims wear the same dress which other communities of the Duggar Des wear. The typical dress which was previously regarded as the symbol of Dogra culture is now rarely seen. In hilly areas, however, the people of old generation are still seen wearing *kurta*, *churidar pyjama*, turban, *waskat* (waistcoat), etc. The educated lot is now considerably Westernized and is seen wearing pant, coat, suit, bush shirt, and T-shirt. The traditional *pyjama* and *kurta* are now relegated to the four walls of home only. Recently, *salwar* and *kameez* have also gained currency among the Dogra Muslim males.

Women normally wear *salwar*, *kameez* and *dupatta*, but *sari* is also occasionally seen. Young ladies of the well-to-do families are seen wearing jeans and other modern Western dresses. The Gujjars and Bakarwals wear their traditional dresses and ornaments. The Gujjar menfolk usually wear *kameez*, multicoloured *dhoti* or *tehmad*, bedecked waistcoat, turban and a particular type of *pahari* shoe called *jora*. Educated young Gujjars are, however, equally Westernized and wear the same dresses which others wear. The Bakarwals are normally seen wearing typical *kameez*, *salwar*, waistcoat, turban and *jora*. Women of both the communities have almost identical dresses, i.e. typical *salwar*, *kameez*, *chadar* and *jora*. There is, however, a vital difference in the manner in which their hair are braided. The hair of a Bakarwal woman is braided in numerous thin strands which differentiate her from the Gujjar woman. The Dogra Muslim are a non-vegetarians and, if available, eat beef. This should, however, be kept in mind that cow slaughter is legally banned in Jammu & Kashmir. Hence, normally only mutton is available to them. Other constituents of their diet are wheat, rice, maize, pulses, vegetables and fruits. Milk and curd are also frequently taken. All sorts of drinks, alcoholic or non-alcoholic, are liked by them. They, however, use only those brands which are available in the market. They have no food inhibitions except that they eat only *halal* meat (the meat of the animal which is slaughtered in accordance with the Islamic tenets).

The Dogra Muslims have no categorical social divisions or strict hierarchical order except the one that is specified by the state government for its administrative convenience. Some disparities, based on economic and caste considerations are observed, but they are not of any vital consequence.

Institution of marriage is governed strictly by the Muslim Personal Law. Marriage is considered a contract. *Mahr* is fixed in accordance with the demands of time and with the mutual consent of the parties. They also practise cross-cousin marriage, sororate, levirate, polygamy and polygyny (sororal). The Gujjars and Bakarwals are, however, endogamous.

Child marriage has also been common among the Dogra Muslims; but with the passage of time, and particularly after Independence, the spread of education has brought a lot of change in them and now the age limit specified by the law is strictly adhered to. Among the Gujjars and Bakarwals, however, early marriages still persist.

The main mode of acquiring mates previously was through middlemen or matchmakers, who were usually eunuchs or barbers. They frequented houses for this purpose and kept a complete record of the entire community always ready with them. Hence the parents took their help in this regard. Arranged marriages were always preferred. In hilly areas, however, a custom prevailed in which disgruntled married young women used to take recourse to elopement with some young men of their choice, and later obtained divorce from the first husband by paying some compensation money to him. In some hilly areas, this custom still thrives and is known as *muamla*. *Dohri* is another custom prevalent among them in which two girls are exchanged in marriage. Both girls are actually kept as hostages for each other's security. The husband of one girl does not dare to maltreat her under the fear that his sister wedded to the brother of his wife would also receive the same treatment in return. With the spread of education, however, this custom is also slowly disappearing. But it can still be seen in the hilly areas.

Dowry is accepted but not demanded. After marriage, the new couple lives with the groom's parents. Joint family system still continues among the Dogra Muslims. Recently, however, it has started breaking. Husband and wife are both free to obtain divorce and can remarry in accordance with the Muslim Personal Law. Post-divorce maintenance is also granted under rules.

Interpersonal relations among the family members are cordial. Respect and love is still the main source of strength for the family. Conflicts and confrontations are mostly avoided. Issues of inheritance and succession are governed by the Muslim Personal Law. Both male and female members have the right to the ancestral property. Before Independence, however, the law of inheritance was not uniformly practised. It was presumed that after marriage a girl forfeited her right of inheritance. But, with the spread of education and political and social consciousness, this illegal practice is also being slowly discarded and now ancestral property is divided among both the male and female children in accordance with the tenets of Islam. The eldest son succeeds as the head of the family. But, in the absence of any male child, the same right is conferred upon the eldest daughter. The will of the parents, however, can confer the right of succession or inheritance upon any child, male or female. Interfamily linkages are also cordial.

Conflicts are usually amicably resolved with the help of the religious leaders, mostly the *mulla*. But in the event of their failure to resolve the issue, recourse to law is the normal alternative.

A Dogra Muslim woman is a hard-working person. She renders great help to her husband in maintaining the family. Whether in the fields, at home or in the office, she is considered to be the right hand of her husband. She participates in all the social, religious or ritual activities along with her husband or other menfolk. They have also started taking part in the state politics. But, inspite of all this, they are still treated as second-rate citizens. With the spread of education, a lot of change has occurred, yet much remains to be done to ameliorate their condition.

A majority of the Dogra Muslim women like to deliver their children at their houses with the help of a midwife or a nurse. With the spread of nursing homes and maternity homes, the upper-and lower-middle class families prefer to make use of them.

After the birth of a child, the mother remains in bed for five days. She is not allowed to take cereals during these days. Only liquid diet, particularly the one which is more nourishing, is served to her. On the fifth day, she takes bath and is free to come out and move around. This ritual is known as *panjap*. If the newborn baby is a boy, then on the fifth day after bath a special sweet known as *korha* made of ground almonds, coconut, ginger, raisins and sugar cooked in *ghee* and milk is distributed among the relatives and neighbours. If the newborn baby is a girl, then this ceremony is not held. No ceremony is held for naming the child. Children are usually named after their parents or ancestors. Tonsure ceremony is also held but no day is fixed for this purpose. Another important ritual is that of the circumcision of the male child, which is held as and when the parents decide. It is, however, followed by a feast in which relatives and friends eagerly participate. The child is fed only after obtaining six months of age.

During menses, however, a girl is not allowed to enter into the kitchen or touch anything sacred. She resumes her routine after taking bath and changing clothes at the termination of her periods.

Marriage ceremony is held at the bride's residence but it is preceded by a few other rituals like *tel*, *mehndi* and *sehrabandi*. *Tel* and *mehndi* are held at both the places, whereas *sehrabandi* is performed at the groom's place only. During *tel*, mustard oil is applied to the hair of both the bride and the bridegroom one or two days before the marriage. Similarly, *mehndi* is also applied to the hands and feet of both but it is held first at the bridegroom's place and then his sisters and other women of the family come to the bride's place with *henna* and apply the same to her also. *Sehrabandi* of the bridegroom takes place on the day of marriage, an hour before the *barat* leaves for the bride's place. If the distance between the two places is great, then this ritual is performed a day or two earlier. At the bride's place, the *barat* is received with songs. In olden days, it was greeted with songs full of abuses called *sithnian*. Now this ritual has almost vanished. Before the *barat* is allowed to enter the house, *milni* ritual is performed during which the elders of the two families exchange greetings by garlanding and embracing each other. After *nikah*, the *barat* and other invitees are treated to a sumptuous feast. Then the *rukhsati* takes place and the bride departs amidst much wailing and crying. Consummation of marriage is followed by a sumptuous feast at the bridegroom's place known as *walima*.

The dead are buried during the day time. The dead body is bathed and wrapped in *kafan* (white sheet) and carried to the graveyard on a *charpai* (cot), where it is lowered into the grave dug according to the Islamic law. All this process is accompanied by recitation of *kalma*. The dead is placed in the grave with his head to north after the *namaz-e-janaza*. After burial, the relatives return by a different route. On reaching the house, prayer is once again recited and the people then leave.

The major economic resource for the Dogra Muslims is agriculture. But with the spread of education, government service has also becomes a prominent means of income. A negligibly small number of them is engaged in business. The Gujjars and the Bakarwals earn their livelihood by tending flocks of sheep and goats and herds of cattle.

The Dogra Muslim are mainly a landowning community. Even the Gujjars and the Bakarwals, who lead a sort of nomadic life, also possess pieces of land which are their permanent habitats. Property rights are exclusively conferred upon individuals.

The Dogra Muslims are a part of the socio-political system of the state. Hence, they are also governed by the same institutions which govern other communities of the state. At the village level, for instance, panchayats exercise control over them strictly in accordance with the provisions of the Jammu & Kashmir Village Panchayat Act No. XXIII, 1958. With regard to matters falling out of their jurisdiction, they also have recourse to law as their other Dogra brethren do.

Islam is the religion they profess and an overwhelming majority of them are Sunni. They also pay frequent visits to the shrines of the Muslim Sufi saints which are spread over the entire area. These visits are usually undertaken on Thursdays, when every shrine is swarmed by its devotees belonging to all religions. They also believe in the spiritual powers and the talisman. Hence the *pirs*, *faqirs*, astrologers, astronomers and soothsayers flourish. Their major festivals are Id-ul-Fitr, Id-ul-Zuha, Shab-e-Barat, Shab-e-Milad, Shab-e-Miraj and Shab-e-Qadr. Besides, they also have some festivals associated with the local shrines of the Muslim Sufis known as *urs*. Spread of education has, however, made them conscious of the evils which have crept into their life. Hence incessant efforts are being made to introduce suitable reforms into their social and cultural life.

The Dogra Muslims have among them fine craftsmen. Pottery making, knitting, wood carving, embroidery and weaving are their popular crafts. They manifest keen interest in fine arts and have produced some fine singers and playwrights. Malika Pukhraj (now in Pakistan) and the late Sahibzada Mohammad Umar and Noor Ilahi are a few examples. They are fond of music and dance. The Gujjars and the Bakarwals have shown much ingenuity in composing folk songs and folk tales in their own languages, which mostly deal with chivalry or the erotic element.

The Dogra Muslims have cordial intercommunity and interethnic relations. Intercommunity marriages do take place but they are usually avoided. With the spread of education, however, these barriers are slowly breaking. The Dogra Muslims have produced reputed persons in all professions like medicine, engineering, teaching, judiciary, army and business. They are politically conscious and have produced national leaders.

Literacy rate among the Dogra Muslims was very low before Independence. The free education policy of the state government implemented after Independence has rendered a great service in this regard and, though the literacy rate, even now, is not satisfactory, the situation is much better and continously improving. Health and medical care facilities have also increased tremendously after Independence and improved their standard of life. Drinking water facilities are available to all. They are drawing maximum benefit from the family welfare and self-employment schemes, besides benefiting from the bank loan schemes for establishing business, industries and transport companies. Self-employment programmes and other welfare schemes of the state and central governments are also popular among them. They are also availing themselves of the media and communication facilities. Electricity is now available to most of them. Previously, they used firewood, coal and cow-dung cakes for cooking but now, in addition to these, kerosene and cooking gas are also gaining popularity. Irrigation facilities are available to most of them. Use of chemical fertilizers, insecticides and organic manure is common. Ration facilities are available to them. They are also taking interest in saving and investment schemes initiated by the government and commercial banks. All these measures have proved highly conducive to improving their standard of living.

ZAHIR-UD-DIN

DOKHPA/DROKPA

The literal meaning of Drokh or Dokh is a meadow, and Drokhpa or Dokhpa refers to the people of the meadow. The term is associated with them as they have been living on higher reaches of mountains with water and fodder available in abundance.

The Dokhpas, it is believed, are the direct descendants of the Dards, said to have migrated from Gilgit. Most of the Dards who had migrated from Gilgit have retained their cultural and ethnic identity in spite of the sway of Tibetan culture. The history of their migration from Gilgit is preserved in their folk literature.

Historians refer to the Dokhpas as a brave people. Their Tibetan or Dogra masters have not been able to subjugate them. The Ladakhi saying is that two things are impossible, loading a dog and forced labour by a Drokhpa, speaks of their stubborn nature.

The Dokhpa population is spread over four villages, namely Hanu and Da in Ladakh, and Darsik and Gorkone in Kargil. The natural setting is the gorges of high and barren mountain peaks on or around the banks of the river Indus. They are a Scheduled Tribe. No census records are available to suggest their population.

Agriculture and horticulture are the main occupations of the Dokhpas as water is available in abundance. The main crops grown are naked barley, buckwheat and millets. Tomatoes, apricots and grapes are their cash crops which form the main source of their income.

The Dokhpas speak Droskhat amongst themselves but with others they converse in Ladakhi or Urdu. The script used by them is Bodhi. The distinguishing features of the Dokhpa dress are their headgear, peculiarly half-shaven head and the gown. Women are specially interested in needlework. They decorate their gowns and trousers by embroidering beautiful floral designs on them. In the traditional way, both men and women cover their backs with goatskin, keeping the fur inside.

Roasted barley flour is the staple diet of the Dokhpas. They consume meat, rice and vegetables as well. Cow's milk and its products, eggs and poultry are strictly prohibited. They neither rear cows nor fowls as it is considered offensive to their gods. They do not keep dogs either. *Gurgur chai* (salted tea) is included in their diet. Fruits, especially apricots and grapes grown in abundance, are consumed in large quantities. *Chang*, a alcoholic drink brewed locally from barley, is consumed by every member of the community. They also prepare wine from grapes and consume it in large quantities. No social or religious function is complete without a drink, especially *chang*.

The Drokhpas comprise of a few clans called *phasphuns* among whom intermarriage is permissible. Members of one's own clan are supposed to belong to the same blood and marriage between them is taboo. Clan members have a few social obligations such as accompanying a *barat* or lighting the funeral pyre. Marriages are endogamous. The major forms of marriages practised among them are monogamy and fraternal polyandry. They generally follow patrilocal residence after marriage. Both men and women have a right to break the marriage and the initiating party pays the compensation. Widows, widowers and divorcees are permitted to remarry.

Joint family is the rule and nuclear family an exception. Relations among the members of a family are generally cordial.

Women in good health help men in the fields besides doing the daily household chore. Wool spinning is a common hobby. They have a right over the ancestral property in case there are no male issues. They participate equally in all social and religious activities but have no say in making important economic decisions like sale and purchase of the assets such as land, cattle or cash crops.

Marriages are generally arranged. Acceptance of *chang* and a rupee by the girl's father from the boy's father symbolizes their commitment to the future relationship. Betrothal takes place when the boy and the girl concerned reach adolescence.

This is an occasion of great festivity marked by singing, dancing and drinking. Betrothal is followed by a chain of feasts from relatives and friends in honour of the prospective bride and groom. The first feast is given by the maternal uncle of the girl.

Marriage ceremony is marked by singing and dancing in which the newly weds also take part. Feasting is an integral part of the exercise.

After delivery, a woman is not supposed to move out of the house at least for a month. Even the father of the neonate is not expected to go out during this period and visitors are not welcome.

The newborn babies are exclusively breast-fed. Breast feeding is supplemented by *sattoo*, roasted flour and tea from the age of six months.

After death, a lama recites *mantras* at the side of a dead person. The dead body is cremated in sleeping posture. Remains are collected after four or five days which are buried in the burial ground of the clan.

Agriculture is the main occupation of the Dokhpas. Their villages are situated on or around the banks of the Indus river in the gorges covered by high and barren mountain peaks. The cultivable land-holdings available to them are very small. However, these lands produce two crops. Cattle and sheep rearing is another area of the Dokhpas' economic activity. Competition, healthy or otherwise, is completely absent in their system of values. Moreover, people are reluctant to go out of their habitat in search of employment. Craftsmen and artisans like barbers, tailors; etc., are conspicuously absent among the Dokhpas. Even some semi-skilled men like carpenters and blacksmiths do not have an exclusive profession but a subsidiary one as they spend most of their time in agricultural activities. Children contribute their own mite in the economic activities. It is from a very early age that they accompany their parents to fields and orchards.

The headman, called *makdom*, is the only authority known to the Dokhpas. He is democratically elected. It is he who takes important decisions concerning the community as a whole and looks after the community's interests. He approaches the authorities for welfare works. He decides the festival dates. He, in consultation with elder members of the village, plays the role of a judge. Courts and litigations are unknown to these people. Fines imposed on culprits are spent either in the community's interest or in compensating the victim. Cases are generally decided after thorough investigation by the *makdom*.

The Dokhpas claim to be Buddhists. But on a closer examination of their beliefs and practices, one finds it rather difficult to associate them with any particular faith. It appears to be an admixture of various systems of beliefs. Offering of animal sacrifices, worshipping of animals, deities and the sun, and also following Sakiyamuni are the basic religious precepts.

They believe in gods, spirits and demons. Three important gods worshipped even more than the Buddha are La, Dogla and Sapdak, who have an overwhelming impact on their lives as their wrath and displeasure cause death, disease and misery while their pleasure and goodwill lead to health, long life, prosperity and other joys of life. The three godheads are represented by three uncarved stones in every household. The Dokhpa kitchen is not only a sacred place but a prohibited area as well.

The Dokhpas follow a ten-day week. It is at the end of the week that one of the residents invites a few of his neighbours for a prayer meeting. Every other member follows him at his own turn. Thus there would be ten prayer meetings in ten different houses during a course of ten weeks. The host provides them with *chang* and the evening is spent in enjoying *chang* and reciting hymns.

Given to music and dance, the Brokhpas recount the story of their migration in the bygone days through folk songs.

There is no restriction on accepting food (cooked and uncooked) or water from members of other communities. A girl outside the community is not admitted to their fold though a Dokhpa girl may choose a boy from other community.

Educational facility at the lower levels is provided. The percentage of boys and girls attending schools is very low. Even those who attend these schools do not seem to be benefited much.

The government has established a carpet weaving centre in one of the villages to train young boys and girls in this craft; but only few persons attend the centre. Family planning is unknown to them. The Indus river provides water for drinking. There are no arrangements for the supply of potable water. Wood and kerosene oil are the major fuels. Use of cow-dung as fuel or manure is considered sinful. There are no hospitals but a small dispensary does exist. Drinking water is available from the river. Chemical and natural fertilizers are put to use. Electricity is not available. Inter-village link roads are not developed. People are not making use of the banking facilities. The community members benefit from the public distribution system.

M.I. NAZKI

DOMAL

The Domals are Rajputs converted to Islam inhabiting the Jammu division. It is said that once a Mala Rajput went to Kargil in Ladakh and married a Buddhist Dum woman. The man later on adopted Islam. The community Domal has thus originated from the marriage of a Muslim man and a Buddhist woman. The community is mainly distributed in Rajouri and Punch districts of Jammu & Kashmir state. It is reported that Domals were once the rulers of Chilas and Gilgit. The community occupies the south-western slopes of Pir Panjal ranges. Their villages are found along the slopes of hills overlooking a number of tributaries falling in the Chenab and the Punch rivers. The hills are of moderate elevation. The climate is moderate with low rainfall. The forests are thin and confined to the upper slopes of the hills. They speak Dogri among themselves and Urdu with others. Their script is Arabic. The community is identified by the suffix Khan. They dress themselves like other Muslims of the region. The men wear *salwar*, *kameez* and turban. The women wear *salwar*, *kurta* and *dupatta*. They are listed as an economically and educationally backward class in the state.

The Domals are non-vegetarian but do not eat beef. Their staple diet consists of wheat, maize and millets. Milk and milk products are important items of daily food. Pulses consumed are gram, *urad*, *moong*, peas and *masur*. Mustard oil is the main cooking medium. They smoke *bidis*, cigarettes and loose tobacco. The roots and tubers consumed by them are potato, turnip and radishes. The fruits commonly eaten are pears, apples, oranges and plums. They do not consume alcoholic drinks. Tea is a popular beverage.Rice consumption is increasing in their diet.

The Domals have no social division. Differentiations are due to education, occupation and territory, which play important roles in the settlement of marriage alliances. The community belongs to a *khandan* (lineage) within which there are families, *kunbas*, belonging to a particular territory such as Punch or Rajouri, etc. The Domals belonging to Punch are called Punchia. Similarly there are Rajouria. The community perceive themselves as Muslim Rajputs. Others consider them of middle rank in the social hierarchy and equal in status with the Jaral, Basith and Gujjar.

The Domals are endogamous but endogamy is not strictly followed.

The other community whom which they have marriage alliances is the Jaral. Consanguineous marriages both with parallel and cross-cousins are avoided. Sororate (junior) and levirate (senior) remarriage is possible in case they are of matching age. Marriages generally take place after attaining adulthood. Boys and girls do not enjoy the freedom of selecting their mates. Marriages are settled through negotiations. Marriage by exchange of sisters is also prevalent. Monogamy is the usual form of marriage. A second wife is taken only in case of barrenness, insanity or serious disease, but without divorcing the first wife. There are a few cases where a man keeps three wives at three separate places without divorcing any one of them. The system of dowry is creeping into the community due to their contact with others. It is paid by the father of the bride both in cash and kind. The *mahr* (dower) is fixed at the time of *nikah* (marriage) and the bride can demand it any time. In practice, however, the amount of *mahr* is promised but not paid. The difference in the marriage rules of the Domals and other Muslims of Kashmir Valley is that the *nikah* or marriage contract and the *mahr* is verbal in the former and written in the latter case. The bride goes to her husband's house after marriage. Only the husband is free to divorce but it is not practised at all in the community. Widow and widower remarriage is permissible.

If the bride becomes a widow soon after her marriage, then she can marry the younger brother of her deceased husband provided they are of matching age. Otherwise, she may go to her parents and get married to some other person. A widow with children prefers to stay in the house of her deceased husband. A widower with children prefers to marry the younger sister of his deceased wife because she can lookafter the children as her own. Changes observed in the marriage are an increase in the incidence of dowry, decrease in the incidence of polygyny and liberalization in the rules of remarriage.

Families are generally mixed-extended type. The married sons may live in separate dwellings but the ownership of property rests with the father. The sons also perform their obligations towards the parents. Interpersonal relations are based on respect for the elders and love and care for the young. There is no *purdah* by women but the daughter-in-law avoids her father-in-law and the elder brother of her husband. Joking relationship is observed with sister-in-law and with the elder brother's wife. Conflict and confrontation arise over property matters and challange to the authority of the father who is the head of the family. It results into the division of the landed property and the son with his family shifts to a new dwelling. All the children get equal share in the father's property but, generally, the daughters do not claim it after marriage. The succession is from father to son. Owing to urbanization, the families are gradually becoming nuclear. In the family, women play a great role. They play a part in agriculture, tend the cattle, milk the buffaloes, collect fuel, bring potable water and do other domestic duties. In spite of shouldering major responsibilities in the family, the women have lower status than men.

Life-cycle rituals connected with child birth, marriage and death are common with other Muslims of Jammu region. Post-delivery pollution or *sootak* is observed for forty days after which the parturient mother resumes her normal domestic duties. The rituals observed are *zerakasi* (first hair cutting) at the age of six months and the *khatnahal* (circumcision) at the age of two years. Bachelors and unmarried women do not enjoy the freedom of selecting their spouses according to their own choice. The rituals performed in marriage are engagement (*gandum* and *doon-leij*) observed after one month of engagement, *malasbehoun*, *massmechravoun*, *malamenz*, *menziraat,* etc. *Nikah* or marriage contract is performed by a *maulvi* in the presence of at least ten witnesses from either parties involved in the marriage. The amount of dower is fixed according to the status of the family.

The dead bodies are buried. The *maulvi* (priest), relatives and neighbours are invited on the fourth day for offering prayer for the deceased person. This ritual is repeated on the fortieth day also. These rituals are called *chaharum* and *chehallum*, respectively.

Agriculture is the primary occupation of the Domals. Due to hilly terrain, steep slopes and non-availability of irrigation facilities, agriculture is supplemented by secondary occupations such as animal husbandry, horticulture and forestry. Other occupations in which the community is engaged are wage labour, selling goods such as milk, firewood and vegetables, construction and services. Land is the chief economic resource of the community. The land is hilly with steep slopes, hence cultivation is possible after making terraces. The community uses two types of land, viz., hilly land and valley land. The former type of land is used for the cultivation of maize, millets, barley and wheat. In the valley land where water is available, paddy is grown. The village forest provides valuable timber and other minor forest products to the community. They domesticate buffaloes, cows, sheep, goats and donkeys, which are of great economic value. The milk is sold in the market. Sheep and goats are also sold for money. The donkey and ponies are used for carrying loads from the village to the town. The community has direct link with the market. The agricultural and forest products are sold either to the village *bania* (grocer) or in the towns of Rajouri and Punch. It was observed that men and women carry a lamb or a goat, or a fowl to the market and barter it for clothes, edible oil, sugar, matchbox, *bidi*, cigarettes, kerosene oil, etc. Since Independence, various road building agencies such as GREF, Vertak and the defence forces have provided employment opportunities to people in construction work.

Formerly the traditional caste council headed by a *chaudhury* used to decide the disputes of the Domals, but nowadays it has become defunct. Statutory panchayat is the only organization responsible for looking after the interests and welfare of the inhabitants. The panchayat which was set up in accordance with the provisions of Jammu & Kashmir Village Panchayat Act of 1958 consists of one *sarpanch* or village headman, one chairman and eight members who are all elected. The panchayat is empowered under the Panchayat Act to decide suits for money due to contracts, recovery of moveable property, compensaton for a wrongful behaviour or causing harm to property and damages caused by trespass. The panchayat *adalat* is authorized to take cognizance of some of the cases such as spreading infection of any disease, fouling waters of public reservoir, theft, etc. The panchayat is not empowered to sentence any person to imprisonment but can impose fine up to Rs. 25.

The Domals profess Islam. They place themselves under the Sheikh category and generally belong to the Sunni sect. The religious specialists (*maulvis*) are Sayyad who perform their life-cycle rituals. In case of non-availability of a *maulvi*, any literate person of the community can perform these duties. The community observes all the Muslim festivals and visit the *idgah* and mosques with other Muslims of the region.

The Domals do not have any plastic or graphic art of their own. The crafts practised by the community are basket and rope making. The women knit woollen pullovers. Folk songs are sung on the occasions of childbirth and marriage.

The Domals maintain cordial relations with other Hindu and Muslim communities of the region. In the village, the Domals live in the neighbourhood of other communities such as the Jaral, Basith, Mirasi, Gujjar, Nai, Rajput, Brahman, Bania, Megh, Mahasha, etc. These communities live in mutual interdependence and participate in the ceremonies of childbirth, marriage and death. The Domals work in the fields of the Rajputs, Brahmans, and Banias as wage labourers and sharecroppers. The Gujjar tend the cattle. The Mirasi render their services on the occasion of childbirth, marriage and death. They are musicians and play on flute and drums. They exchange food with all other communities except the scavengers. Connubial relations are maintained only with the Jaral. They share the sources of drinking water, roads, schools, mosques, panchayat ghars and burial ground with other communities. Owing to backwardness, illiteracy and poverty, there are no businessmen, doctors, engineers or administrators from this community.

As a result of various development programmes, there is a marked improvement in the socio-economic conditions of the Domals since Independence. The boys and girls are literate and are generally matriculate. The girls drop out from studies after matriculation because of marriage or the parents not being able to afford higher education of their children. There are a few boys in the community who have studied up to the intermediate level. Facilities of doctors and nurses are available at the primary health centres but often their services cannot be availed of due to poor transport network and communication facilities. Patients from distant villages are carried on a cot by four persons to a town for treatment. The community is aware of the family welfare programmes but they do not practice sterilization. It was reported that they use indigenous methods of family planning. Natural springs are the only source of drinking water. Sometimes, the women have to walk as far as 2 km to fetch potable water. The roadside villages have facilities of tap water which are connected with the springs. Radio is available in the villages. The villages are electrified but only a few houses of the community have electric connections. Firewood is the only fuel available to the community. Cow-dung is used as manure. Irrigational facilities are not available to the community. The community uses chemical fertilizers and insecticides as these are available from the Development Block, Manjhakot. Fair price shops are available to villagers near the roadside but the community prefers to purchase food items from the village *bania* as it is available on credit. The community has not received any benefit from the rural banks because bank loans are available only to the business entrepreneurs. They depend on the village *bania* for borrowing money.

PARMANAND LAL

DOSALI

The Dosalis, a small community of the Rajputs in Jammu, are the traditional maker and seller of *donas* (leaf cups) and *patals* (leaf plates). The term Dosali is the changed version of *doswale* (persons who have committed some sacrilege) and therefore excommunicated by the Rajputs. The community has no titles and subgroups. They were identified by their occupation of making *done* and *patal* which they have now discarded and have taken up other occupations such as business, trade, service, transport, etc. According to Ibbetson, the Dosalis are a small caste found in Hoshiarpur but not east of Satluj. Its members make dishes of leaves often of *tawar* leaves for the Hindus. At weddings, their services are in great demand to make leaf platters and that appears to be their principal occupation. They sew the leaves together with minute pieces of dried grass straw as is done in Shimla Hills by the Dumnas. The Dosalis are considered to be an impure caste and the Rajputs do not drink water from their hands. It is deemed higher than the Sarera or the Banjara but below the Bahti or Girth and nearer to the Chimba. The Dosali rarely or never married outside their own caste (Ibbetson and Rose, 1919: 247).

The origin and history of migration of the community is not known but it is reported that their ancestors belonged to Rajasthan. Their stay in Jammu is very old and their ancestors used to serve the Maharajas. The community has been included among the Rajputs by a resolution passed in 1984 by the regional Rajput Sabha presided by Dr. Karan Singh at Jammu. The community is mainly distributed in Jammu and Samba tehsils of Jammu district of Jammu & Kashmir. A few families are also found in Himachal Pradesh, Punjab, Delhi and UP. Their natural environment consists of foothills having warm and humid climate. They speaks Dogri within the family and kin groups, and Hindi with the outsiders. Their script is Arabic. The men dress themselves in Dogri *pyjama* (trousers), *kameez* (shirt), *kurta* and turban. Their women wear *salwar*, *kurta* and *dupatta*. They come under the Other Backward Classes category.

The Dosalis are non-vegetarian. Their staple diet is wheat but rice is also taken in a lesser quantity. Pulses taken are *rajmah*, *mash*, *moong*, *urad*, *masur*, gram and peas. Milk and milk products such as *lassi* and *chhena* are taken by the community. They smoke tobacco in the form of cigarettes, *bidis* and *hookah* (hubble-bubble). Alcoholic drinks are also taken. They take all the seasonal vegetables and fruits. Mustard oil is their cooking medium. The change observed in the food habits is that they are becoming vegetarian and take rice more frequently.

There are no social divisions within the Dosalis and the differentiations are on the basis of economy, occupation, education and territory. Making leaf cups and plates is being considered a low job by the members of the community. A well-to-do Dosali will not give his daughter in marriage to a Dosali boy engaged in the manufacturing of leaf cups and plates. The members of the community conceal their identity and do not affix Dosali titles after their names. The community's self perception at the regional level is that they are equal to the Rajputs. But the Rajput consider them as inferior. They neither give their daughters to, nor take brides from, the Dosali. This has forced the Dosalis to marry their daughters in other communities such as Khatri, Brahman, Vaish, etc.

The Dosalis are endogamous but practise exogamy at the *gotra* level. Their *gotras* which they call *jati* are the same as found among the Rajputs such as Chauhans, Rathors, Jamwals, and Samyals. The Jamwals belong to Jammu while the Samyals are from Samba tahsil of Jammu district. Marriages are generally settled between families of equal status and occupation. Sororate (junior) and levirate (senior) are allowed if the spouses are of matching age. This type of marriage is performed after the death of the partner. There are no elaborate rituals in such a marriage. It is called *chadar*. In most of the cases, marriage takes place when the boys and girls attain adulthood though child marriage was in vogue in the past. At present the age at marriage is between 18 and 21 years in case of girls, and from 21 to 25 years in case of boys. The mode of acquiring mates is through negotiations in which the respective parents play a dominant role. Marriage by exchange of sisters was prevalent in the past but it is no more practised now. Such marriages lessen the risk of harassment by the respective in-laws. Nowadays, the Dosali girls are getting educated and some of them have taken jobs. In such cases, they select their own spouse. Normally such marriages are approved by the parents. Generally a *bicholia* (middleman), who may be a common relative or friend, settles the marriage through negotiations.

Roka or *thaka* is the selection of the boy who is offered some gifts on this occasion. The *purohit* fixes the date for *sagan* and *lagan* (marriage). *Sagan* is sent to the boy in form of presents and some cash. *Shanti havan* is performed before the departure of the *barat* and then *butna* and *sehra* rituals are gone through. The *barat* is received by the girl's father and others at the *milni.* The marriage ritual is performed at a *vedi* accompanied by chanting of *mantras* by the *purohit.* Next day, the *barat* and the bride is given a send-off.

The community practice monogamy but, in case of barrenness or serious disease, a second wife can be taken. In such a case, the consent of the first wife is taken. In case of death of the first wife with minor children, marriage with the wife's younger sister is preferred as she will look after the children properly. Marriage with the widow of the elder brother permitted in case she is young and issueless. The symbol of a married woman is vermilion mark on the forehead, bangles, *bindi*, toe ring, nose pin, etc. Dowry, both in cash and kind, is prevalent but it is not demanded. The custom of *kanyadan* exists and is preformed by the senior male relatives of the girl. After marriage, the bride goes to live with her husband and in-laws. Divorce is permissible but it is not commonly practised. In case of maladjustment, the elderly members of the community persuade the partners to live amicably. No case of divorce was reported in the community during the last fifty years. Widow and widower remarriage is permissible. Changes observed in the marriage system with emergence of dowry system and liberalization in the rules of remarriage are increase in inter caste marriage, love marriages, age of marriage, cases of neolocal residence after marriage, and decrease in exchange-marriage and incidence of divorce. The Dosali households are nuclear. Relations between the young and the old are cordial. Elders are respected and feared. Father is supreme in the family. Avoidance usally is practised. Joking relationship exist between elder brother's wife and husband's younger brother, with wife's elder sister; with brother-in-law and wife's younger brother. Points of conflict and confrontation arise in the family on property and check on the freedom of the youngsters. Father's property is equally divided among the sons. According to the new Act, the daughters also get a share in the father's property but they generally do not claim it. If there are no sons, then the property goes to the son of the daughter. Succession pattern is followed from father to son. The change observed is an increase in the number of nuclear families. The extended families are found mostly in rural areas. Daughters now claim their share in the father's property after marriage and all the sons assert their equal right to inherit after father's death.

Status of women among the Dosalis is inferior to men. They have a share in the father's property and have started demanding the same after marriage. The wife has full right on the *stridhana* (property and valuabes owned by the wife independently of her husband) which cannot be disposed of even by the husband without her consent. Women have an important role to play in all spheres of life. They participate in agricultural operations and do all the jobs except ploughing. They milk cows, collect fuel, bring potable water and do all the household jobs. It is the women who prepare leaf-cups and plates. They have a pivotal role in social and religious functions. Women do not contribute but control the family expenditure.

They follow the usual life-cycle rituals celebrated by Hindu communities. In case of delay in the first pregnancy, the couple visit local shrines to get divine blessings for a child. The educated couples consult the doctor in such cases. The news of pregnancy is first given to the parents of the girl. The rite of *reetan* is performed in the eighth month of pregnancy when her parents offer her gift of sweets and fruit. A local *dai* helps in delivery. On the fifth day of childbirth, *panjap* is celebrated when the mother and child are given a bath. It is followed by more rituals on the twelfth day. On the twenty-first day, the period of pollution terminates and the woman is free to do her household work.

Childhood rituals are *annaprashan* at the age of six months. *Mundan* is observed at the age of five years. It is done only for the male child. Some of the couples go to the temple of Balak Nath in Himachal Pradesh or to Vaishno Devi for this purpose.

They cremate their dead in the usual Hindu way of *antyeshti sanskar*. The nearer ones still get their heads shaven. The eldest sons lights the pyre. One the third day, ashes are collected, to be immersed in the Ganga or Tawi. After six and twelve months, *ardh-barkhi* and *barkhi* rituals are performed when the *charji* and *purohit* are given *chhajji* or offerings. In some cases, fourth yearly anniversary is celebrated likewise. Some rituals, however, are being curtailed.

The traditional occupation of the Dosalis was preparation and sale of *donas* and *patals* hence the forests having *blungari* trees were the main natural resource of the community. Gradually they left this traditional occupation and took up other occupations such as agriculture, business and services. In urban areas, the members of the community are engaged in the government and private services. Some of them own shops of leaf cups and leaf plates, particularly in Moti Bazar of Jammu. A few are contractors for the supply of leaves of *blungari* trees. Before 1947, they had direct contract with the Muslim Gujjars who used to collect leaves from the forest, tie them into bundles and sell to the Dosali contractors. The cost varied from Rs. 100 to Rs. 150 for 25 to 50 bundles of leaves. Now the forests have been declared reserved and leaves are auctioned by the government to the contractors, which requires an investment of Rs. 25,000 to Rs. 50,000. This is beyond the capacity of the Dosali. Now most of the contractors of leaves are the Brahmans. The Dosalis purchase leaves from them and distribute it among the weaker sections who may be the Brahman, Rajput, Dosali or Jheevar for the preparation of leaf cups and plates on wages. In Samba tahsil, they have some land for agriculture. At present some of the Dosalis run shops of general items and stationery, tea stalls, shops of electrical goods, and have taken to teaching, government and private services, skilled and unskilled labour and cultivation. The community has direct links with the market. There are no bonded labourers in the community. A few of them have sold out their property in the villages and migrated to Jammu city for business. Extent of child labour is negligible as the parents want their children to be educated. Payment of wages is made in cash. A change observed in the economy of the community is that they are taking over to business and services from the land-based economies.

In earlier days, the Dosalis used to have their own traditional caste panchayats, but those are completely defunct nowadays. Now disputes over land and matrimonial matters are solved by the elders in the community or the village. Sometimes cases are taken to the court of law. The community has its representation in the regional Rajput Sabha, at Jammu. They have their representation in the statutory gram panchayats. These panchayats look after the plans and developmental activities of the village and the communities.

The Dosalis are Sanatani Hindus. A few of them are Arya Samajis. They worship Radha and Krishna; Ram, Lakshman and Sita; Hanuman; Shivji and Durga. The deity of the community is Baba Balak Nath in Himachal Pradesh, which is visited on different occasions. They worships Baba Surgul. On the occasion of Nag Panchami, the women keep fast the whole day and offer vermicilli (*sewain*), *puri* and *halwa* on the serpents mound. They also visit the temple of Vaishno Devi. The Pandits, *purohits*, and *acharjees* who belong to other communities perform their birth, marriage and death rituals. Festivals observed by the community are Janmashtami (birthday of Krishna), Karva Chauth, Nag Panchami, Dussehra, Holi, Diwali, etc., which have socio-religious significance.

The Dosalis have a tradition of folk arts. Drawings on the wall and floor are made on the occasions of childbirth and marriage. Women have been observed doing embroidery on cloth. They do not have any oral tradition. The women sing folk songs on the occasion of childbirth and marriage. There is no particular folklore, folk tales, and musical instrument of their own. Light music is popular in the community.

Intercommunity relations are based on mutual dependence and understanding. Being involved in business, they maintain good relations with all the occupational castes of the Hindus and Muslims. In villages, they accept food and water from all the communities except the Dum, Mahashe, Chamyar and Chuhre. The services of the pandit, *purohit, acharjee,* Jheevar, Nai, Dhobi, Tarkhan, Megh, and Mahashe are available to them on the occasion of birth, marriage and death. The Dosalis, too, render their services to other higher and lower castes of the Hindus. The services of the Saryara, Batwal, Mahashe and Megh are available to them in the construction of their houses. The Saryara have the expertise in whitewashing and colour painting of the houses. The Dosalis have economic relations with the Muslim Gujjars as they are the main suppliers of the leaves for making leaf cups and plates. Intercommunity marriages take place with the Brahmans and Khatri. Before 1947, there were separate wells for the members of Untouchable castes but now all the communities share the same well and other sources of water. They visit the same religious shrines with other communities. They visit Panch Pir and Satwari Pir with the Muslims. They participate in the traditional festivals and festivities with other communities. They participate in the fair of Baba Bua at Jhiri which draws people from all parts of India. Partron-client relationship exists among the Dosalis. At present the members of the community are in different government and private services. Some are big businessmen.

The Dosalis have been benefited by the different development plans and programmes adopted by the government for the upliftment of the communities and betterment of the area. The boys and girls are availing themselves of the school facilities in the villages. For higher education, they have to go to the cities. As a result, the boys and girls in rural areas are educationally backward compared to those living in cities. Owing to transport facilities boys and girls from Samba tahsil daily commute to Jammu for higher education. Drop-outs both among the boys and girls have increased due to the rising cost of higher education. Further, the boys have to earn and contribute to the family income. The girls drop out from studies generally due to marriage. Facilities of primary health centres are available in the villages. The community is aware of the family welfare programmes. Now couples prefer to have only two or three children. Generally, men get sterilized. Drinking water is available through taps and handpumps in the locality. The source of water is from natural springs and streams. Provisions for employment are available under the IRDP but none of the members of this community has availed of these. A few of them community are self-employed and own shops and tea stalls. They listen to the radio. A few own television sets and visit the cinema. The facilities of roads, railways and post offices are available to them. Firewood, cow-dung cakes, coal, sawdust and kerosene oil are the main fuel resources. Sources of irrigation are rainwater, wells, tube wells and ponds. They use chemical fertilizers and insecticides. Under welfare programmes, ICDS centres for distribution of nutrition kits to the children are available. The members hold ration cards and get wheat, sugar and kerosene oil through the fair price shops. Banking facilities are available in the rural areas and investment is positive. In the villages, they are dependent on the moneylenders and shopkeepers to some extent.

The Dosalis are struggling to regain their rightful place among the Rajputs, but they are not getting equal treatment from them. The Rajputs still hesitate to take brides from the Dosalis. It has forced them to marry their daughters outside the Rajput community. During the regime of Bakshi Ghulam Mohammad, a section of the Dosali community made a representation to be listed under the Other Backward Classes (OBC) of Jammu & Kashmir state. But only about 12 per cent of its members took advantage of this facility. Later on, they preferred to go back to the Rajput fold.

PARMANAND LAL

DUM

The community identify themselves as Mahasha or Dum-Mahasha. The name Dum and Mahasha are interchangeable and stand for the same community. The original name of the community is Dum and other communities mostly address them by this name. In course of time, due to some reason now forgotten, they came to adopt the synonym Mahasha which has become popular now. The term Mahasha no doubt is the same as the Sanskrit word *mahashay*, meaning a gentleman, *mahatma* or noble person. The meaning of Dum, also pronounced as 'dome' is not clear. However, according to some Western scholars, the original form of the name Dum or Dome is 'Domb' or 'Domba' which in Sanskrit means 'a low caste man'. The community has preserved no etymology of the word Dum. However, one scholar, J. Przyluski, attempts to explain the term and its origin and opines that it has been derived from the name of an ancient non-Aryan tribe Odumbara, also written as Audumbara in ancient literature. The Odumbaras appear in the list of Mlecchas in Jain books, and probably belonged to the Austro-Asiatic race; at least they were non-Aryan according to the ancient Indian tradition. The Audumbaras were a part of the larger confederacy of the Salavas including the Madras, and have been mentioned in the works of seventh century BC. The Salava Madras were the descendents of Vyusitasava, which is the Sanskritized form of the Iranian name Vistaspa. Thus the Salavas and their confederates including the Madras and Audumbaras seem to belong to the Saka race and were of non-Indian origin.

The Dums preserve a very vague tradition of their origin. According to the tradition, the Domes were created by Lord Shiva himself. It is said that in order to get Shivji as her husband, Parvati brought into use several herbs with *jarhian* (occult power) and *jadoo* (spells). Consequently, the god used to feel highly indisposed and lethargic. He thought of curing himself by playing *jarhian*. For that purpose he needed a drum for the creation of which he first created a carpenter, who manufactured the drum, and then he created a drummer, who became the ancestor of the Dum. With the help of the Dum or Mahasha, the god played that mysterious dance called *jarhian* and got rid of the malady engendered by the occult herbs. The Dum claim that they were formerly known as *jogis* who ministered the mysterious dance called *jarhian* and *karkan*. In rural areas, they are usually known as the Dum. Hence, the community has acquired three names, Dum, Mahasha and Jogi.

The Dums have no known tradition of their migration. If their derivation from the Audumbara stock is accepted, they can be attributed a republican, tribal rule during the centuries before Christ. Their claim of creation by the god Shiva and their exclusive partiality for Shiva worship may lead us to believe that they descended from Audumbaras. According to the *Rigveda* Shambar, the leader of a people inhabiting the sub-montane upper reaches of the Purushini (Ravi) had offered tough resistance to the early Aryan adventurers for forty long years. He belonged to the race of dark-skinned people, who worshipped *sisna* (phallic symbols). The Rishi Vashishta calls them Sishnadevah, i.e. worshippers of the symbolic phallus. They were snub-nosed people with short stature and dark complexion. The Dums possess these characteristics to this day. They are commonly dark in colour. They are usually small in limb and short in stature; they are less bearded than the other castes; and their countenances are of a much lower type than those of the Hindus generally.

There are a large number of Dums in Jammu district, and they are scattered all over the region, both of the outer hills and the next higher plains. There are a few Dum families in almost all the villages of Jammu province. They form about 20 per cent of the total population of the Scheduled Castes in the state. The total population of the Dum in Jammu & Kashmir was 78,986 according to *Census of India*, 1971 which rose to 1,00,296 in 1981. They have the constitutional status of Scheduled Caste in this state. As they have been non-agriculturist serving class, they are found in all types of natural environment available in this region. In arid *kandi*, in the fertile plain south of Jammu, and in the lofty northern ranges they are found following the ancestral profession and serve the village community. They speak the local dialects of the tract they live in: Dogri in Jammu, Punjabi in areas adjoining Punjab, and Pahari languages in mountain areas. The literate among them use Hindi in their correspondence. They do not wear any distinctive dress nor they carry any distinctive marker, except their dark complexion which marks them out as a distinct community from all other Hindus. They dress and behave like all other Hindu communities.

The Dum are both vegetarian and non-vegetarian. Those who take meat strictly abstain from taking *halal*, i.e. meat of animals slaughtered according to the Muslim convention, and take only *jhatka* meat. Beef is prohibited. They abstain from taking non-vegetarian diet on certain religious days like other Hindu communities. *Makki* (maize) and wheat form their staple food with occasional dish of rice, along with *dals*. Pulses used include black and green beans, gram, *masur* and *moth*. All of them cannot afford to take fruits but vegetables available locally are consumed by most of them. The Dums do not have any particular liking for drinks. Only a few of them use alcoholic drinks. Wine is not drunk on any rituals, and they take it only on some festive occasions. The *desi* or locally prepared liquor is mostly used by them. Milk, *sattoo*, and sugar cane juice are the popular non-alcoholic drinks among them. The Dums do not have partiality for any special item of food.

They belong to the fourth *varna* of the Hindu society. They are a homogeneous community without any hierarchy, but they have certain subcastes like Sivotre, Balgotre, Kalotre and Vila-loch. These subcastes are exogamous and belong to different *gots*. Sivotre belong to the Deval *got*, Balgotre to Bhardwaj *got*. They do not marry within their subcaste and *got*. As a community, they are endogamous. The community has been related to the Shudra castes since its known antiquity and they still retain that status. They believe in the Hindu *varna* system and recognize the superiority of other castes, though modern changes in the Hindu social system have bred new aspirations among the community and they are claiming equality with other *varnas* though they function in the prevalent social set up and continue scavanging as their traditional occupation. Some of them who are literate, however, are entering other professions and services reserved for the community under the constitutional provisions.

As a rule, the Dums are monogamous. They are endogamous, and marriages outside the community are still very rare. However, they have exogamous subcastes and *gots*, and they follow the rule religiously. Previously child marriage among them was the usual custom, but now marriages are celebrated only after the girls and boys attain adulthood. Marriages are normally arranged by the parents. Even though the community is poor, the system of bride-price, etc., was never popular among them. A humble dowry in kind is given to the daughter at the time of marriage like all other Hindu communities. *Sindoor*, *thali* and *bindi* are the symbols of marriage, as also a set of *lal chura* (red bangles). Like other Hindu communities, cross-cousin marriage is prohibited among them. Levirate is permissible. They follow the patrilocal rule of residence after marriage. Previously child marriage, *sati* and other customs pertaining to marriage were current among them. All stages of a Hindu marriage are followed, i.e. the rituals of *kurmai*, *biah* and *maklawa* are performed. Marriage is accompanied by *havan* and recitation of *Ved-mantras* by the Brahmans. Some literate among the Dums sometimes perform this duty. Formerly, the Brahmans attending on the marriage used to take bath and wash clothes for purification after the service. But now this is not done. The Dums follow all the rules of divorce and remarriage of the Hindu *shastras*. Remarriage of widows within the family of the deceased husband is encouraged. Cases of divorce are rare. The right of initiation of divorce is with both the parties. The latest changes in the society and betterment of the status of the fourth *varna* and statutory provisions regarding marriage, women's right to property, etc., have made no remarkable change in their marriage and divorce rules except that incidence of child marriage has become an exception now.

A Dum family is mixed nuclear unit, converging into a joint family, in which the eldest member is considered to be the head of the family. After the death of father, the eldest son becomes the head. All the members are shown respect and veneration according to age, status and the relations of family members are based on mutual love and affection. The elders are feared and, normally, joking with elders is not liked. However, joking in family is reserved towards the youngers and between brothers-in-law and sisters-in-law. The family usually remains undivided after the death of the father and the property is inherited by the mother, while the eldest son becomes the head and looks after the family property. On division, equal share goes to all the male children of the family according to the Hindu custom of inheritance. As the community has been economically very backward and poor, the incidence of inheritance was of little importance. Most of the families did not have any landed property at all, and the houses in which they lived belonged to some zamindars of the village. Their interfamily relations are cordial and they participate in each other's joys and bereavements. At social and ritual performances, the presence of the *biradari* is sometimes considered very necessary, and the concerned family is expected to reconcile with any other family which, due to any reason, is reluctant to participate in their social function. The community attaches great importance to the participation of relative and close friends in social functions.

The Dum women belong to the working class group. Hence *purdah* and seclusion are unknown to them. They go out to work in houses of the zamindars and other well-to-do people of the village and town. They share equally with their men the task of earning livelihood for their families. In their parental houses also, they help their parents in looking after cattle and in gathering fodder and firewood, etc. The women participate freely in all types of social, religious and political activities. They are an economic asset to the family and add to the family income by their labour. Their right to inheritance is governed by the Hindu law of inheritance. They do not possess special rights and obligations other than those enjoyed by the women of other working class Hindu communities.

The Dums observe all the Hindu rituals from birth to death. The birth of a male child is celebrated with great festivity. The first five days of childbirth are observed as pollution days, which terminate with the ritual of *panjap* on the fifth day when the mother and the child are given a bath of purification. After twenty-one days, the ritual of *sutra* takes place when a sacred thread is tied round the waist of the baby and the days of confinement for the mother are over, and the child is taken out of the house for the first time. The *mundan* (tonsure) ceremony is performed after the age of two years in accordance with the Hindu custom. The performance of marriage takes place with special merrymaking and rituals. The celebrations open with the sending of *neondra*, that is, invitation to the relatives, after *sagai* has been contracted and *muhurat* or date for the marriage has been fixed. When the boy is apparelled in bridegroom's dress and *sehra* (head-dress of strings) the participating relatives offer *tamol*, i.e. gifts of cloth and money, to the boy. The marriage party then leaves for the bride's house where the marriage rituals are performed. The bride is then carried to the bridegroom's parental house but is sent back in a day or two. Some time after, *maklawa*, also called *refaira*, takes place when the bride is permanently taken away from her parents to live with her husband. The death of a person is also attended with all the Hindu rites of *antyeshti*. The dead are cremated. Condolence pollution is observed for thirteen days. The *ardh-barkhi* (half-yearly) and *barkhi* (first anniversary) are celebrated in the usual Hindu manner, followed by *chaubarkhi* after the fourth year of death. They also observe *shradh* of the dead annually. No change in the performance of these rituals has been marked in the recent years except that most of these are now celebrated with greater show as a result of the economic uplift of most of the Dum families.

The Dums are a landless community. Only recently, some of them have purchased a couple of acres of agricultural land. They have been a serving, menial class throughout and scavenging has been their only occupation, to which most of them still adhere. They have no resources of their own except physical labour, that too unskilled in most cases.

They serve as cleaners of others' houses and village and town streets. They remove cow-dung with filth. In exchange for such services, they get seasonal or annual wages in kind mostly, and in cash occasionally. They work as farm labourers also at the time of harvesting season. Now they also work as factory workers where such opportunities are available. A small fraction of them now own their small pieces of agricultural land and such families have taken to agriculture. As they are reckoned unclean in villages, they are not engaged in occupations other than the unclean ones. In villages, they are even now considered untouchable to a large extent. Hence, most of them are still economically quite backward and handicapped. Their traditional occupation is singing, dancing and beating *nagara* (drums) at the time of festive occasions such as marriage and birth of a son and also at the funeral procession. In villages, most of them perform similar service even today. Some of them have organized bands in the towns for the purpose. The subsidiary occupation for some of them are preparation of bamboo baskets, hand fans, mats and *sirkis* (bamboo trays for *chapatis*) and other containers. Most of their articles are sold in villages, but some finer things get their way into the towns as well. Both barter and cash systems of payment are in practice. Some of them worked in the houses of village zamindārs as bonded labourers but the system has now gone out of practice. A large number of them work as labourers and are landless. Opportunities for working as factory labourers are very limited as the state has only a few big industries and mills. After Independence, some of them have become landowners and some who are literate among them have joined various government services. Even before Independence, the Maharaja employed them in the army as sappers and miners, in which capacity, they performed their duties nicely; and even on battle front, they proved as brave and fearless as the martial classes of the state.

Formerly, the Dums had caste councils or panchayats at the regional level, but now their place has been taken by the community *sabhas* organized at the tahsil level which are called Mahasha Sabhas. These have presidents, secretaries, cashiers and ordinary members, and are democratically elected. They have their central council with its headquarters at mohalla Rehari in the Jammu city, situated in a temple of the community called Guru Nama Mandir. This *sabha* pursuades its people away from social and economic evils. It imposes fines on those who transgress the accepted customs and indulge in unsocial behaviour. In serious cases, the culprits can even be ex-communicated. In addition, they are also subject to the gram panchayats which have been set up in the state by the Maharajas much before Independence. Now these village bodies have been given more powers for the uplift and development of the village community in general.

The Dum profess Hinduism. They believe in the whole pantheon of Hinduism and worship Sri Rama and Krishna as *avatars*. They worship Vaishno Devi also. They have their own *kul-devtas* whom they propitiate in their socio-religious occasions. After marriage they go to pay homage to their *kul* or community goddess Mall Mata, Kayi Devta, and Shivji (Shiva). They approach these deities for the resolution of difficulties and problems and to seek their aid in successful performance of their socio-religious activities. They go on pilgrimage to the regional and national pilgrim centres of the Hindus. The Brahmans serve as religious specialists for them and help them perform the social and religious rites and customs. However, there are some *jogis* and *chelas* among them. The *jogis* usually put on white or saffron *tehmad* or *dhoti*, shirt and turban, and hoist a triangular yellow flag in front of their houses. They are supposed to be able to pacify supernatural and evil spirits and are believed be capable of removing maladies and bad luck. They have no special fairs and festivals of their own and participate in those of other Hindu communities. Change of religion among them has not been recorded. The community is striving for social reforms and the special rights given to them are going a long way in uplifting the community, but there has not been any socio-religious reform movement worth mentioning among them. In early stages, the Arya Samaj movement had influenced them and probably it is the result of that organization that the Dums got the more respectable name of Mahashas.

The humbler among them practise handicrafts connected with bamboo works and straw and *kharh* (long grass) out of which they prepare mats, bamboo vessels, fans, *sirkis*, winnowing fans, baskets, and fine articles of domestic use. They excel in bamboo handicrafts. As mentioned earlier, singing and dancing and beating drums is their traditional profession and most of them inherit the musical sense. They perform both on happy and sad occasions. They are not a colourful people and do not sing or dance by themselves. It is only for others that they do so, and have provided the village community this lighter strain since known antiquity.

The Dums have linkages with other communities on occupational basis. They accept water, *kachcha* and *pukka* food from other Hindu communities, but not *vice versa*. However, putative kinship may be contracted with any other community. Previously, the Dums were not allowed access to water sources as they were considered unclean, but now tap water and water reservoirs have been opened to them. Similarly, they have access to roads, schools, cremation grounds, panchayat ghars and other public places and temples.

Under the impact of modern democratic set-up and legislation, the Dums are becoming politically conscious and enlightened. They take part in political activities both at the regional and state levels, and they have their due share in political set-up of the state. Of course, they have not participated in any political or ethnic movements of the region. They share the crop with the landlords for whom they work as farm labourers but, being landless, they do not enjoy that privilege themselves. Thus their relationship is mostly that of cultivator-labour. Employer-worker relationship also exists, as some of them are factory workers, and the literate among them have got white-collar jobs in factories and various similar organizations.

The various development plans are having some good effect on the Dums. The number of educated among them has increased, and there are many graduates and post-graduates among them who have joined high government jobs. They are benefited by the health and medicare facilities provided to them in rural areas. Their attitude towards family planning is also somewhat favourable. They have got drinking water facilities and use electricity. Some self-employment schemes like that of poultry and piggery farming, fisheries and other crafts have been introduced for them, but these have not much benefited them. Rural employment schemes are not available in the state. For communication, they are using the various media to their benefit. There are community radios and televisions in the villages. For energy they have resources like firewood and cow-dung. Those among them who own a few acres of agricultural land make use of canal irrigation facilities wherever available. Nutrition programmes for their children have not been introduced in the state so far. Public distribution system and fair price shops are available to them as to the other communities. The facilities of chemical fertilizers and insecticides are available but only a few of them can benefit by them. Banking, savings and investment facilities are available and are being made use of by them.

ANITA K. BILLAWARIA

GADDI

The Gaddis are shepherds who inhabit mostly the mountainous region of Jammu. Most of them are spread around the regions of Badherwah, Basoli, Ram Nagar, Udhampur, Bilawar, Ramban and Batot. Their origin and history is shrouded in mystery as no authentic evidence is available. According to a popular belief, they originally lived in the plains of the united Punjab and Sindh province. However, they had to flee from their places during the reign of Aurangzeb to save themselves from persecution and proselytization. Moving from one place to another, the Gaddis reached the landlocked region of Bharmour (Himachal Pradesh) and settled there. Lord Shiva blessed them with *gaddi*, i.e. the reign, and ordained that nobody else except them would rule and live in the region. That is how these people were later known and called as the Gaddi. Over the period of time, they moved out of the region to various parts of Jammu province when conditions became more congenial and normal for their return. They do not have any subtitles or synonyms and outsiders also call them as Gaddi. They have various subcastes such as Chuhan, Baloria, Katoch, Lalhal, Parihau, Shundal, Charak, Veerpuri, etc. They have now been grouped with the local Hindu population in the census records. They possess oral account of their origin and genealogy. They have migrated to their present habitat and their distribution is essentially perceived at the regional level, though their migration is not very recent. They live in both extreme cold and temperate regions of Jammu in hilly terrains at a relatively high altitude. Their place of settlements records both high and low humidity with dense and thin forest cover. They speak Gadiyali among themselves but correspond and communicate with others in Arabic and Devanagari scripts. They can speak Dogri, Badherwahi and Kashmiri as and when the need arises. The community, over the period of time, has got assimilated into various subregional cultures, mainly into Dogri, and does not have a special dress for either sexes as identification markers. In the recent past, a *chola* (a type of loose gown) tied with *dora* (rope) and *khadi* (cap) were their special identification markers. Now one comes across any Gaddi wearing this traditional dress very rarely. They wear dresses which are more close to the Dogri pattern. They are covered under the Backward Classes.

The Gaddis are non-vegetarians but they abstain from eating beef. Their staple food is maize and wheat, and rice to a lesser extent. They consume cereals and all types of pulses, and they use mustard oil for cooking. They also consume *grim* (baked barley). They take all types of locally available vegetables, roots and tubers, and make moderate use of fruits. They use lesser quantities of milk and milk products but tea is a popular drink with them. Consumption of alcoholic drinks is occasional. They smoke a lot of cigarettes and cheroot. They chew tobacco and use snuff also. There has not been any significant change in their food habits but the rich amongst them have improved the quality of their food.

The Gaddis are divided into a number of subcastes such as Aralu, Beloria, Katoch, Chaak, Hrokar, Jarwa, Lalhal, Shundal, Parihar and Veerpuri. Stratification of these subcastes appears to be based on the Brahman and Rajput lineages. They do not have a high self-perception but are aware of the *varna* system. People of other communities too do not have a high perception about the Gaddis at the regional level. They still consider themselves low in status in comparison to other Dogra communities of Jammu.

The Gaddis practice endogamy at the community level and exogamy at the *gotra* level. Consanguinity is not reported among them. Sororate polygyny is also not practised by them. Pre-puberty marriage was the earlier practice among these people. Now girls are married usually after puberty. The marrying age of girls varies between 14 and 18 years and, for boys, the marriage age varies from 18 years onward. Marital alliances are negotiated by the middlemen. Polygyny has also been reported among a few. The marriage symbol used by their women is *long* (nose-stud). The custom of *kanyadan* exists among them and dowry is usually paid in kind such as kitchen utensils and bedding, etc., and very little cash is given. Residence after marriage is patrilocal. Divorce is permissible among them according to the Hindu traditions under the causes and conditions prevalent amongst other Hindu communities. Rules regarding remarriage are quite flexible. Male and female divorcees or widow, widower remarriage is permissible, and marrying age for either sex has gradually increased.

Nuclear family is the most common form as the joint family system is gradually breaking up due to an urge for leading an independent life. Interpersonal relationships are cordial among the household members, joking relations exist among affinal relatives. Reasons for conflict and confrontations are attributed mainly to the property disputes. Eldest son succeeds his father. Though inheritance is based on equigeniture, females seldom press for their share. Interfamily relationships are cordial. Disputes are usually resolved through mutual reconciliation unless they are of criminal nature to be dealt with by the state judical laws.

Women have a secondary status as compared to men in all walks of life, though they participate in all socio-economic activities, yet they do not compete with their menfolk on equal terms. Majority of women participate in agricultural and animal husbandary and other farm-related activities. They act as water carriers-cum-fuel collectors for their households. Most of the women have also taken to weaving of woollen blankets and clothes. Active participation of women in politics is practically absent though they enjoy their voting right. They are docile and submissive but at the same time are hard working. They appear to be reconciled to play secondary role to their male counterpart. They make contribution to the family income but enjoy no command over the household expenditure.

No pre-delivery rituals for the pregnant women are observed. Babies are delivered either at own home or at in-laws' house; there is actually no precondition for it is more a matter of convenience. The delivery of babies is usually conducted at home. Very few go to the nursing homes or hospitals. Help of an experienced midwife is sought for delivery of the child. A twelve-day post-delivery pollution period is observed among these people while the same is of seven days for postnatal restrictions on the mother. Naming ceremony is observed among Gaddis, while there is no *annaprashan* (first feeding of cereals) ceremony being observed by them. *Janeu* (thread wearing) ceremony is aslo reported for male children among the Gaddi.

Marital alliances are fixed by negotiation through family head or marriage-broker. Marriage ceremonies are brief, i.e. one-or two-day affairs. The ceremony usually starts with *mehndi-raat* followed next day by *lagan*. Customarily, the marriage ceremony is held at the bride's place. The bridegroom's entourage called *barat* leaves for the bride's residence in the evening and marriage rituals are performed early in the morning the following day. Feast is given by both the sides in the marriage. The bride's parents give it to the guests accompanying the bridegroom while the bridegroom's side gives a feast for the relatives and friends.

The dead are given a traditional bath and then wrapped in a white cloth. Thereafter, the body is carried on a bier to the cremation ground to be cremated as per the Hindu religious rites. Death pollution is observed for 13 days. The dead bodies of a small children, however, are buried. *Shradhs* (death anniversaries) are also performed by the Gaddis in reverence to their dead.

There has not been any significant changes in the life-cycle rituals of the Gaddis though these rituals have become more expensive and elaborate to demonstrate their social standing.

The major economic resources for the Gaddis are land and forest. Shepherds by occupation, the Gaddis invariably have to move from one pasture to another and from one region to another with their livestock which comprises of sheep and goats. Settled agriculture and trade in selling of livestock are other economic activities pursued by them. It is not really a landowning community though individual proprietorship-cum-tenancy is reported among them. In recent times, a small number of the Gaddis are found in government services and petty business. They can make good money if their livestock survives epidemics and other calamities but, if the livestock dies, they are financially ruined. A small number of the Gaddis are also engaged in wool and wool-processing trade. They are not directly linked with the market as most of their market transactions are made by middlemen, periodicity of market varies from weekly to monthly wherein both barter and cash transactions are made. The Gaddis, besides pursuing their ancestral occupation, are also settled agriculturist and their dependence is considerably less on the formal market. The female participate in almost all farm and non-farm activities besides collection of firewood and fetching of drinking water. Their women are also engaged in making woollen garments and blankets. Child labour is not hired or marketed though it is used in farming and non-farming operations. The mode of payment for labour is both in cash and kind.

Village panchayats exists at the village level among the Gaddis. Village panchayats are of heterogeneous nature and their main job is to exercise social control though they have now no statutory power. Panchayats help in implementing the developmental work in villages.

The Gaddis profess Hinduism. They worship family and clan deities besides regional deities common to all the Hindus. At the village level, individual affiliation to *pirs* is reported. They observe all the major Hindu religious festivals such as Diwali, Lohri, Janmashtami, Shivratri and Rakshabandhan. They also celebrate seasonal festivals like Pitrolu and Shari.

There are no professional craftmen but weaving is the major activity in which both sexes excel. Wool and woollen blankets made by them are quite popular and famous in the region. Cloth embroidery is another popular past-time of their womenfolk. The oral traditions pertain to religion, kings, queens and romantic characters. There are no experts in fine arts among the Gaddis though music and dance is popular among them. A few poets writing religious and romantic verses are reported among them. They play on a traditional musical instrument called *ponoth*. Both men and women participate in dances.

The Gaddis accept both cooked and uncooked food from other Hindu communities. No restriction has been reported on acceptance of uncooked food from other religious groups also. They participate in all socio-economic and religious festivals of co-religionists as well as festive occasions of regional nature. They maintain economic relations with almost all cross-sections of the society. They share wells and other water resources, schools and panchayat *ghars* with other communities and non-Hindu members. They share the cremation grounds with other caste Hindus. They visit the religious shrines of Muslim *pirs* and *faqirs*. They maintain cordial and business-like relationship with other members of the community. The Gaddis are semi-sedentary, especially those who have taken up government jobs, opened their own business establishments and do not now pursue their traditional occupation, but others still move from one pasture to another in order to feed their livestock. However, the Gaddi women do not usually accompany their males and they remain at their permanent habitat. Over the period of time, they have taken to farming. They maintain cultivator-labour relationship and receive services of the barber, carpenter, masons, etc.

The Gaddis are becoming more conscious of market-oriented trade related to buying and selling of livestock. In fact, emergence of voluntary cooperative agencies among them has led to better marketing and remunerative prices for their herd. Political awareness is also fast catching up. They do not have entrepreneurs, creative artists, administrators, engineers or doctors, though quite a few male and female teachers are there among them. Some of them are employed in the police and defence services.

Formal education is becoming popular among them, though boys are given preference over girls in its pursuit. Boys study up to high school level mostly and quite a few of them go to colleges. Girls usually study up to primary level but, a few also reach high school level. The girls drop out from school due to social and economic factors. Boys have to give up their formal studies mainly due to economic reasons and for augmenting the family income. Though their attitude is favourable towards the modern medicare, due to its non-availability, the Gaddis predominantly depend on traditional medicare. Family planning has yet to catch up with them in full measure. Family size varies between five and eight persons per household. Generally, it is their women who get sterilized. Drinking water facilities vary from region to region; at one place they have it within their vicinity while at other places they have to fetch it from a great distance. Their water sources are streams and springs though tap water is now being made available by the government.

The Gaddis have not been benefited under the various developmental welfare schemes launched by the government for alleviation of poverty. Cooperative agencies facilitate procurement of essential commodities like sugar, cloth, etc. Mobile dispensaries have helped them to overcome and reduce livestock mortality. Electricity is also available to them. They use firewood and cow-dung cakes as fuel. Those who own land use river and stream for irrigation, depending on rainfall. They use chemical fertilizers and insecticides in their fields although local manure is in common use. Very few of them have so far availed themselves of the nutrition programmes through ICDS and Anganwadi schemes. They enjoy public distribution facilities for getting rations and other essential commodities. They still seek loans from the village moneylenders and shopkeepers. Only a few of them make use of the banking facilities. They do not seem to have propensity to save and invest in an organized manner.

The Gaddis, as an exclusive shepherd community, are gradually fading. The onslought of modern life and ambitions of attaining higher socio-economic living standards have made a dent on the profile of this community. Not only vertical but horizontal shifts in occupation patterns have started occurring. The younger generation does not seem to be willing or inclined to hold on to the age-old occupation of shepherding. They are seeking new avenues and opportunities for improving their social and economic life. However, the Gaddis who are still in livestock trade of sheep and goats (they do not deal with any other type of animals) are trying to organize themselves for better marketing. Sale outlets and remunerative prices have resulted in emergence of cooperative societies. The community seems to be on the move for socio-economic transformation.

INDU AIMA

GALWAN

The Galwan is a combination of the two Persian terms, *galah* and *ban*, literally meaning the 'keeper of the herd of quadrupeds'. People who tend horses are called Galahban in Persian and Galwan in Kashmiri. Since horse was the most important animal for the olden society—as a means of transport and as war material—there appeared a community which took upon itself the task of tending horses, exchanging them, purchasing and selling them, even taking care of some ailments of horses like back wounds called *mudaw* in Kashmiri.

The Galwans can trace their history to distant times. In Kalhana's *Rajatarangini*, we often come across the term 'lord of horses', which shows that the Royal Stable was an important institution in ancient Kashmir. Until recent times, there were many prominent places in rural Kashmir where the Galwans conducted their activities. From ancient records, we may infer that many Galwans conducted their activities along the Pir Panjal mountain ranges, from Uri in the west to Shupian in the south. The Galwans do not have separate localities for themselves but live with other communities in villages and hinterlands. They are not dwellers of towns or cities but are strictly restricted to villages, particularly highlands of Kashmir. As such, they live in natural surroundings without being distinguished from other people in the locality or the village. They speak Kashmiri, which is their mother tongue, and many communicate in Urdu with those who do not know Kashmiri. If at all, they use Arabic script though at present the population of literates among them is not more than 3 to 4 per cent. There is no specific mark of identification of the Galwans. They dress just as any other Kashmiri as is the case with their families. *Kameez*, *salwar*, waistcoat and *chappal* is the common dress they wear. The younger among the Galwans have a peculiar sturdy highland appearance giving them a slightly arrogant counternance. They don a cap and not a turban. Their womenfolk are not at all distinguishable from the ordinary Kashmiri women. They wear *kurta* and *salwar*, and a *pheran* as an overdress. The ancient headgear called *kasaba* has become obsolete now. The women may wear an ordinary necklace of stones or an earring of silver or a bangle of silver. Gold ornaments are not worn at all. The State Constitution has recognized the community as socially backward.

The Galwans are non-vegetarians but they have no specific philosophy about their being non-vegetarians. It is just the custom. They eat mutton and beef, eggs and chicken but they do not eat pork as it is forbidden in their religion. Their staple food is cereals, pulses and oil seeds. Mustard oil is preferred as a cooking medium and fruits may be taken occasionally. Vegetables are taken in abundance. Rice is the most common food grain though occasionally bread made of cornflour is also consumed. They are averse to alcoholic drinks but they take salt tea in plenty. Sometimes it may be without milk, which is called *teuth* in Kashmiri. They are not used to drinking mineral water or milk but *lassi* is drunk during the hot days of summer. No home-made beverage is used. Common vegetables such as *hak* (green leafy vegetables), turnips, cucumber, carrots, peas, *nadru* (lotus roots), spinach, potatoes, tomatoes, brinjals and mint form a part of their diet. Among the fruits eaten are apples, pears, peaches, grapes, watermelons, melons, apricots, cherry, etc. There are no specific likes or dislikes of food for them; all depends on availability and afffordability. No significant change in their food habits has been observed. One thing which is to be mentioned is that they prefer local products like local rice, flour and mutton rather than anything imported from outside the Valley, but it has not been possible for them to keep up this habit owing to non-availability of local eatables.

There exist no social divisions among the Galwans nor are there any subgroups. There is no hierarchical order. They have close links with other community members on the basis of their occupation. What may make a particular person of the community more prominent than the rest is the capability of tending horses. One head Galwan in a particular village has many Galwans under his command. It is the head Galwan of a given locality who takes the responsibility of tending horses entrusted to him. He in turn gives these horses into the custody of his subordinate community members who may be scattered over a vast area and villages. There is no hierarchical system in the community. It is only the convenience of profession. The main function of the Galwans is to tend horses in pastures and take care of their safe custody.

A Galwan is essentially known by his name to which the term Galwan is appended, e.g. Muhammad Galwan, Aziz Galwan, etc. Even the Galwans themselves like to be called by that name. They consider themselves inferior to other communities though not inferior to some lower communities like barbers, butchers, etc. Other communities consider them low. A Galwan is a responsible person who takes care of a large herd of cattle. He is regularly paid in kind and, sometimes, in cash for the services he renders. He is also familiar with some apparent diseases and treatments of horses. He is conversant with branding, called *dag*, and he is also the person who is engaged in breaking the colts. He has a fine eye for distinguishing a good breed from the ordinary, and advises on the maintenance of horses. He also undertakes the duty of getting a mare mated to a horse of good breed if approached by the owner of the horse. A Galwan is a tremendous rider who can control even the wildest horse.

Marriages of boys and girls are contracted at an early age, at about 18 for a boy and 15 for a girl. These are always arranged marriages; arranged by the parents after mutual agreement. The boy and the girl generally have no say in the matter. A Galwan, when fully grown in physical strength and economic stability, loves to behave like a cavalier and carry away by force the woman he loves even if she is married to another person. They have no symbols of marriage except *mehndi* applied to the foot and palms of the girl and fingertips of the groom. On marriage, the bride wears new clothes and bangles which indicates that the marriage has taken place. *Mahr* is settled by mutual agreement. It is generally a very modest sum, ranging between Rs. 500 and 2,000. Marriage takes place at the bride's house on the fixed night. The bride's father serves a feast to the guests accompanying the groom. Meat cooked in rice is the common dish served at this occasion. The *mulla* (priest) performs *aqd* or *nikah*, in which the consent of both the sides is sought. The *nikah* having been performed, the party along with the bride and the groom returns to the house of the groom but the guests go to their respective homes. The bride stays in the house of her husband for seven days and then returns to the house of her parents for about a month, during which period her husband would pay her occasional visits. There is no custom among them to ascertain the celibacy of the bride on the nuptial night. The marriage party is generally accompanied by musicians called *bhands* in Kashmiri. The women sing together when the groom leaves along with guests to proceed to the house of the bride and when the bride leaves the house of her parents along with the groom. This singing is called *vanvun*. Minor changes are recently noticeable stereo tapes are used instead of *bhands*, metallic utensils have replaced earthen utensils in which food used to be served in olden days or the dresses now are more fashionable. The number of the guests accompanying the *barat* is also restricted and usually does not exceed forty.

Generally, the Galwans have a mixed-extended family. Joint family system is very common among them. Usually the son after getting married does not leave the house of his parents but lives with them as long as it is possible. Relations between the newly wed and their in-laws are normal and cordial. There is no familiarity beyond resonable limits between them. The daughter-in-law shows respect to her father-in-law. Joking relations exist between the bride and her husband's younger brother. Also, good relations and even joking relations exist between the bride and the sister of her husband. Towards grand-parents, they do not show undue familiarity that might be mis-understood as disrespect for them. Relations with them are formal and reserved.

Conflict and confrontation between the married couple and their parents or brothers, can occur for property. The Galwans are small holders of land and this can be the source of conflict when the question of distribution of property arises after the death of the father or one in whose name the property existed. The elder Galwan would not like anybody to challenge his authority. By profession, he develops a sort of strong personality and does not like anybody to dictate to him. The eldest son is the person who occupies the position of his deceased father in the social circle. Two-thirds of property of the father is divided equally among male issues and one-third among the female issues. But if the dead person is survived by only female issue, the issue has the right of inheritance. In case a person dies issueless, he is succeeded by his brother's son or younger brother or anyone from the line of his brother or sister or daughter, as the case may be. Families are linked through matrimonial alliances.

A woman in a Galwan family has an inferior status in comparison to the menfolk. Except for very few matters, a woman has no decision-making power. When there are no elders and the husband and wife have to bear the brunt of life direct, the woman is a partner in the decisions along with her husband, but such cases are rare. Women do the household jobs besides helping in the field and outdoor activities related to the supplementing of family income.

No definite rituals have been prescribed for pre-delivery period. Certain customs are observed which are a hangover from the past. For example, a pregnant woman is not allowed to carry heavy burden; she does not go out in the dark, meet a stranger, or climb a tree. These restrictions are perhaps imposed only to safeguard her from mis-carriage. On becoming pregnant, the news is secretly circulated among the closest of relations some of whom then secretly convey their felicitations to the pregnant woman. The first ritual to a newborn baby is to recite the Islamic prayer into its ears. The parturient mother observes the forty-day pollution period. She takes bath with warm water on the eleventh day and then on the fortieth day when the period of pollution is over. Thereafter, she slowly returns to normal life. A black thread may be tied round the neck of the newborn baby to ward off the evil eye. Naming ceremony is quite simple. Ordinarily, the elder of the house proposes a name which is a very common one, but, in rare cases, a *mulla* may be approached for the name of the baby. If a baby is struck with illness, the parents approach a *pir* or a *mulla* for an amulet which is tied round the neck or the arm of the infant. The first shaving of the head of a male baby is accompanied with a ceremony. Cooked rice with turmeric is distributed among the neighbours. The parents of the mother bring some clothes for the grandchild whose head is being shaved for the first time. It is called *zerakasi.* Then in the case of the male children comes the time for circumcision which is normally done when the child is of the age of five or six. In Kashmiri it is called *khatnahal* or *behnawun.* The *mulla* is invited on the occasion and the operation is done by the *navid* (local barber). He also applies some ointment after the operation to the wound. However, some of the Galwans now prefer to take their child to a professional surgeon for circumcision. When the baby is slightly grown and can digest some semi-solid food a small ceremony is performed called *oapsoap.* It is only mentioned but not observed and no ceremony accompanies it. The Galwan are mostly illiterate and they do not send their children to local schools, but now the trend has changed.

There is no specific ritual during the adolescent period. No puberty rites exist in the community. Marriage is perhaps the most important ritual in the life of the Galwans. It is performed in the house of the bride and during the night only. Marriage means a big feast for the guests and for the local people as well. Expenditure of the feast is entirely borne by the parents of the bride. The groom's parents also throw a feast but that takes place after the marriage is solemnized. It is called *wathal.* The Galwans observe the marriage feast in a modest way since they are economically a backward community.

The dead body is bathed in warm water, wrapped in the shroud and placed in a coffin which is carried by close relative on their shoulders to the graveyard. The *gorkan* digs the grave in the village graveyard. Mourners and those who come to mourn the death, walk behind the pall bearers slowly till the site of the grave is reached. Then the coffin is placed on the ground, the dead body lifted out of it and placed gently by the side of the grave and, when the *mulla* has finished reciting of verses, *namaz-e-janaza* is performed and the body is slowly lowered into the grave. It is covered with soil and a tombstone or an ordinary slab is placed atop. The *mulla* receives some money for performing the funerary rites. There is no ancestor worship among the Galwans nor do they pay regular visits to the grave of their dead. On the fourth day of the death, tea is served to the people who come to condole the bereaved family. After that, there is no condolence and the normal work of life continues. When death has occurred in a family, no food is cooked on that day or night and the neighbours bring food for the bereaved family. The tradition continues as before. The dead may be remembered on the day of Id by giving out a dirgeful wailing.

Land and forests are the main sources of economic sustenance. The Galwans require pastures and grazing fields where the horses can graze. Land is the property of the state and they make use of it. The Galwans are partially a landowning community and may sometimes act as cultivators of land belonging to other people. Only a small number of the Galwans are landless. Some of them who have become prosperous for one reason or the other are now holding big patches of land and have developed orchards in them. It may be said that the Galwans are a mixed community of landless and landholding community. The main occupation of the community is to tend horses, but with the advent of mechanized form of transport, keeping horse has fallen out of use, and the Galwans have steadily been taking to other occupations to earn a livelihood in case they have no land. Tilling the land, carrying on small transactions, petty fruit business and selling of timber, are some of the subsidiary occupations for these people. For these occupations they entirely depend on the market. Barter system of trade does not exist. All transactions are made in cash. There are no bonded labourers in the community. Child labour is by and large uncommon but teenagers work for the household. They look after the cattle, carry food to the working men, assist in tending cattles, cows, horses, etc. Wages are paid in cash.Very rarely an exchange of goods agreement may be struck. Many changes have appeared in the traditional economic activities of the Galwans, as horses are steadily becoming rare in the state because of the mechanized transport system, roads and the high cost of maintaining a horse. Forty years ago, horses could be seen frequently in the markets of the towns, not to speak of villages, but now they have totally vanished. Consequently, it has its impact on the Galwans. Tending of horses as an occupation is no more there. Though the Galwans are called by that title but they have taken to other professions. Modernization is having its impact on them.

They subject themselves to the directives of the panchayats of local villages wherever these exist and do not have their own panchayats separately. Rewards or punishments are what the law may give them.

The Galwans are the Muslims of Sunni faith and of Hanafi sect. They observe the *shariat* laws prescribed for the Muslims. There are no family, clan or regional deities though they observe certain customs like burning a candle in the hollow of a tree. Major shrines of religious importance are the tombs of local saints, like Makhdum Sahib, Charar-e-Sharif and Hazratbal in Kashmir; Baba Rishi Sahib in Tangmarg is an important shrine to which they pay a visit whenever they get an opportunity. *Pirs* are the religious specialists for them. The *pir* is invited now and then to perform certain rites or to recite from the Holy Koran. Once a year, they may present a fowl to the *pir* as a mark of respect. He gives them his blessings and amulets to the children to ward off any evil. Two Ids in a year are the major festivals observed by the members of the Galwan community. Then there are the festivals connected with the death anniversaries of the local saints and holy men. Ramzan, the month of fasting, is observed by them with all sincerity. There has not been any significant change in observing these festivals or the manner in which these are being observed. On festival days, the children and also the grown ups are provided with new clothing and other amusements.

The Galwan are illiterate. Art and aesthetics are unknown to them and they are prone to starting a quarrel. When a Galwan comes of age, he likes telling exaggerated stories of his adventures.

In all rituals, social functions and interactions, the Galwans are connected with the other Sunni Muslim communities of Kashmir. There are absolutely no restrictions on sharing civic facilities with other communities. Food and water are freely offered to others and accepted, and in social functions all are invited to participate. A prosperous Galwan would like to establish links with more affluent families of the Kashmiri Muslim society and this could be by entering into matrimonial alliances. No ethnic movement has been noticed among the Galwans. They have never formed any political group of theirs nor have they any strong position in political matters. They cast their vote as any other voter and, beyond that, are not interested in politics. A Galwan follows the decision of his fellow villagers in choosing the candidate and voting for him. Seldom has he an independent opinion about the candidate. The Galwans have small landholdings which they usually till themselves. As such, the tenant-landlord relation is out of question. They may till the land of another villager but it is a mutual understanding and relationship, and is not marked by tenant-landlord relationship.

The Galwans are very backward and the literacy rate among the children is very low. After Independence, they have been sending their children to local schools but their schooling generally terminates after having passed primary class. They mostly depend on tending horses, tilling fragments of land, doing farming exercises or growing small orchards. Some have had the luck of finding some jobs of Class IV category and leading a settled life. For health and medical care, they depend on the facilities provided by the governemnt like dispensaries and hospitals. Being poor, a wholesome diet is not available to them and they suffer many physical infirmities. They do not observe family planning. For drinking water, they depend on running streams and brooks. But now the government has provided tap water to many villages, and those who can derive benefit from it, do so. While in pastures, they take drinking water from the running brooks.

There has recently appeared a trend among the Galwans to send their children to school regularly. The rate of literacy is increasing among them and they want to take the benefit of many government schemes. They make use of local transport such as buses, trucks, motor cars, etc., as riding a horse to go on a long journey is only hazardous. They have not so far been able to get responsible government jobs. They now keep transistors but television sets are a luxury which they cannot afford. Electrification has been carried out in almost all the villages and the Galwans are benefiting from it. Where there is no electricity, they burn wood to give light, warmth and ward off the wild animals at night. For fuel energy they depend on wood, cow-dung and kerosene oil. Gas or *gobar* gas is unknown to them. Water from streams and canals is used for irrigation purposes. There are no wells or tube wells for them to utilize. Chemical fertilizers are used sparingly and insecticides are used for orchards. There is no scheme of midday meal for the school going children. They take the advantage of existing public distribution system in the state. They obtain rice, flour, sugar, kerosene oil and cloth on subsidized rates from the cooperative stores. Some remote villages in which they live are out of the jurisdiction of the public distribution system. Though banks have been opened in remote areas also, yet they do not usually make use of the banking facilities as they are economically poor.

The Galwans as professional horse tenders are fast vanishing. They are quickly taking to other professions. It may be a skilled or unskilled labour but they must for the sake of existence do something else.

K.N. Pandita

GANAI

The Ganais, traditionally a community of meat sellers in Kashmir Valley, comprise four categories; each laying claim to its illustrious ancestory. Professional butchers in the Valley are called Ganai. The community perceives its distribution at regional level with concentrations at Srinagar, Anantnag, Badgam, Baramula and Kupwara. Climate of their habitat in Kashmir is cold, humidity low, forests thin and heavy snowfall occurs in winter. In the 1891 census, their population was shown to be 37,987, and they were returned as Brahman cultivators. The census figures of 1911 and 1931 mentioned their population as 46,424 and 59,241, respectively. They speak Kashmiri with the kin whereas with others they speak Urdu and use the Arabic script. They dress themselves like the other Kashmiri Muslims, e.g. *pheran* (long gown), *pyjama* or trousers and skull cap. Their women wear *pheran* of printed cloth, *salwar*, *kameez* (shirt) and a scarf of printed cloth to cover the head.

The Ganai are non-vegetarian. They eat mutton and beef. Fish is eaten occasionally. Chicken, ducks and eggs are also consumed. Their staple food is rice and wheat. Besides pulses, a number of vegetables such as potatoes, tomatoes, cabbage, carrot, turnip, pumpkin and leafy vegetables locally called *karam* or *hak* are taken. A few people smoke tobacco and many rub their teeth with snuff.

There is no social division within the Ganai. Differentiations, if any, are due to education, occupation and economic status which regulate their marriage alliances. They are considered to be of middle rank in the hierarchy by other communities. Those engaged in the selling of meat are considered rich by other members of the community.

The Ganai are endogamous but it is not strictly followed. Cousin marriages are preferred. In case of non-availability of a suitable mate, they take bride or groom from distant relations. Sororate and levirate remarriages are arranged if they are of matching ages. Mates are acquired through negotiations. Marriage by exchange of sisters is also practised. Monogamy is the usual form of marriage. In case of barrenness, a second wife is taken but only with the consent of the first wife. There are no marriage symbols for married women in their community. Matrimonial alliances are initiated and conducted by a common relative. The ceremonies between agreement and wedding are *gandum*, *doon-leij*, *dapanbata*, *menziraat*, *nikah* and *rukhsati*. *Nikah* (formal deed) can be *wakalatan* (through attorney) or *asalatan* (in person). *Phirsal* is the first formal invitation to the son-in-law by his father-in-law. Dowry is given. *Mahr* is fixed at the time of *nikah* according to the status of the families involved in the marriage. The bride goes to stay with her husband after marriage. A husband can divorce his wife for reasons of adultery, barrenness or chronic sickness. A period of *iddat* is observed in case a divorced woman is to remarry. Children are the responsibility of the father in case of divorce. Changes observed in the marriage rules are increase in the age of marriage and decrease in the incidence of divorce.

Families are generally mixed-extended type. Often a joint family comprises members ranging from fifteen to thirty individuals. Interpersonal relations within the family are based on respect for the elders and love and affection for the youngers. Joking relations are confined to women relatives only. Father's property is divided into three shares for the widow, sons and unmarried daughters. Succession is from the father to son. Changes observed in family are that they are becoming nuclear due to urbanization and increasing opportunities of employment. Though women bear a major burden of domestic chores and do other work, their status is inferior to men. They do not have decision-making powers. The family expenses are controlled by men only. Nowadays, due to education and employment, the women have become self relient to some extent.

Life-cycle rituals connected with childbirth, marriage and death are similar to other Muslim communities of the state. Issueless women seek benediction at the holy shrines. Pregnant women are not allowed to carry heavy loads, receive visitors and family members arriving late in the evening. Women who are pregnant for the first time do not live for more than first five months of their pregnancy with their husband, and spend the remaining period at their parental house. The delivery generally takes place at the hands of a *warin* (midwife). In serious cases, the pregnant woman is taken to the hospital. The baby is given a bath in lukewarm water and *azaan* is recited into its ears. Parturient mother receives the first cleansing bath on the seventh day and the final on the fortieth day of delivery, whereafter she resumes normal work of life. *Zerakasi* or headshaving is done after the child has completed six months and *khatnahal* (circumcision) sometime between the age of two and three years.

The dead is given a bath by the *snanagor* and the grave is dug by the *gorkan*. Fourth and the fortieth day are observed as remembrance days for the dead. The *mulla* recite from the Holy Koran and those who condole are served food.

Land is still the major economic resource of the Ganai in the villages. Those living in towns like Srinagar, Anantnag, etc., are engaged in business and services. Members of this community are mostly engaged in selling mutton.

There are three categories of people in the meat selling trade. The first category is of traders who purchase sheep and goats from the Bakarwals. The second category of traders is of those who own meat shops in villages and towns. The third category is of those who purchase skins of the slaughtered sheep and goats and sell it to skin traders. The meat trade in Kashmir is generally controlled by the Ganai community. They are considered quite rich by other Muslim communities. Their social status is, however, low because of their occupation. Owing to their education, services and other businesses, they are becoming prominent in the area.

Traditional caste councils have become defunct. They have been replaced by the statutory panchayats that are responsible for settlement of disputes and execution of minor developmental works. The Ganai are the Muslims of Sunni sect. The shrines and sacred places visited by them are Hazratbal, Shah-i-Hamdani Mosque, Jama Masjid, Ziarat Dastgir, etc. Sacred specialists like the *pirs* and *imams* are from other Muslim communities. They observe all the Muslim festivals. Some of the important festivals observed by the community are Moharram, Urs-e-Nabi, Id-ul-Milad, Rabi-ul-Awwal, Meraj-e-Alam, Id-ul-Fitr, Id-ul-Zuha or Id-ul-Qurban and Shab-e-Barat, etc.

Embroidery and carpet weaving are the crafts found among the Ganai. Folk songs and special singing are performed on marriages and circumcision.

The Ganais' relations with other Muslim and non-Muslim communities are based on mutual interdependence. In the village, the services of artisans are availed of. Most of the Hindu communities in the village participate on the occasions of marriage, childbirth, etc. The Muslim communities help each other on the occasion of transplantation of paddy and harvesting of crops. The community accepts food and water from all other communities except the Watals. Connubial relations are maintained with all other Muslim communities provided the spouse is of equal status or occupation. The Ganai are called by other families in the villages for slaughtering sheep or goats on certain occasions.

As a result of various development programmes, there is a marked improvement in the general conditions of the Ganai. Literacy among the boys and girls has improved since schools are available to them. They prefer to go to the hospital for treatment of diseases. Pregnant women prefer to deliver in hospitals. Even the circumcision of male child is done in the hospital. The couples, nowadays, prefer two or three children, which is a marked change. The women now adopt various family planning methods. Tap water has been made available to the villages. Under the Integrated Child Development Schemes, children from early childhood to six years of age are given nutrition packets free of cost. A few members of the community have availed of employment under the Integrated Rural Development Programme. Radio and television are available in the villages and a few members of the community own television sets. Most of the houses are electrified. The fuel used are kerosene oil, cow-dung, wood and coal. Irrigation facilities are available in the villages through a network of canals. Chemical fertilizers are available to the farmers through cooperative societies. Ration shops provide the cardholders sugar, kerosene oil, rice, etc. Facilities of Dehati Elaqai Banks (rural banks) are available in the villages.

PARMANAND LAL

GANZ

The Ganz are involved in the occupation of taxidermy. In Persian, *ganz* means 'skin' and persons dealing with skin and stuffing animal skins are also called the Ganz. There are four groups, namely Balle, Dianposh, Baba and Rather involved in this occupation. They are settled in Ganz Khod area of Srinagar and also in Tangmarg.

The Ganz live in urban areas. They speak Kashmiri language within family and also with others. However, they communicate in Urdu using Arabic script.

Staple foods consumed by the Ganz include wheat and *batta* (rice); pulses eaten are *moong, masur* and *razmah*. They are non-vegetarian and consume mutton and beef but not pork. Women are also non-vegetarian. *Kavdaari saag*, a leafy vegetable, is consumed in large quantity. They supplement their diet with milk and milk products. Alcoholic drinks are strictly prohibited by religion.

There are no social divisions among the Ganz. They have individual group affiliation and are placed in the middle order of the Muslim social hierarchy. Marriages are usually performed within the group. Consanguinity of both types, i.e. parallel cousin and cross-cousin, are prevalent. Sororate and levirate (junior) are also practised. There is no bar in marrying outside their own community. They marry in all the Muslim groups excepting the Goor, Ganai and Watal communities. The usual age of marriage for males is 25 to 30 years and for female 20 to 22 years. Marriages are usually settled through negotiations. The usual form of marriage is monogamy. There are no marriage symbols, though earlier *kasaba* (headgear) did served as a symbol.

Marriages are settled through a mediator (*manzymyor*) who may be a relative or any other person belonging to a different community. *Manzymyor* gets some cash from both the parties. In the marriage rituals, *pakarlee* (first betrothal) is done in which the girl is seen by the parents and relatives of the boy. On this occasion, jewellery is given to the bride. This is followed by *nishani* at the bride's place and she is given jewellery, fruits, sweets and cash by the bridegroom's parents and relatives. *Nishani* is followed by *hazri* in which ten to twelve of the bride's relatives come to the bridegroom's place and present jewellery and other articles to the persons who visited them in the *nishani* ceremony. Between *hazri* and *shadi*, the bride is given clothes, etc., on festivals. Marriage rituals are performed at the bride's place. *Nikah* is performed by a *maulvi* and the *nikah-nama* is issued by him. *Mahr* money is fixed at the time of *nikah*. The feast is given by the bride's parents. At the time of marriage, *vanvun* singing and dance are performed by the women. *Bidai* (*rukhsati*) is done after marriage. The bride accompanies the bridegroom and comes to stay at the in-laws' house. Nuptial ceremony is performed at the bridegroom's residence. *Wathal* ceremony is performed on the next day of marriage at the groom's place. A feast is given on this occasion and the bride's relatives also are invited. After seven days of marriage, both the bride and bridegroom, and some relatives visit the bride's parents. The bridegroom offers *salaam* to the elders and gets some cash or presents. All party mem-bers are given a feast. This ceremony is known as *firsal*.

Both *mahr* (dower) and dowry are prevalent among the Ganz. In dowry, usually jewellery, garments, household articles and copper utensils are given. *Mahr* money is fixed at a minimum of Rs. 40,000. The *mahr* is payable on demand, but it is usually condoned by the wife. It is demanded at the time of divorce. The rule of residence is patrilocal.

Divorce is permissible and it can take place on grounds of adultery and maladjustment. Divorce case is decided between the elders of the two families and has social approval. The *talaq-nama* is issued by the *maulvi*. A divorced woman observes a period of *iddat*. Divorce can be sought by either party. Children become the responsibility of the father in divorce cases. Remarriages of the divorcee, widow and widower are permissible in this society. Sororate (junior) and levirate (junior) forms are also permissible. Nowadays, the Ganz take a liberal view of such remarriages.

Generally there were extended families in the community, but, nowadays, there are more separate nuclear households. The conflict and confrontation in the family is mainly on property matters. The inheritance in the family is permissible both to males and females. The males get more share and two-thirds of the property is distributed equally among them. The succession goes to the eldest son.

Women among the Ganz enjoy equal status with men. They do not have decision-making powers but are consulted on family matters, e.g. marriages and purchase of property, etc. Women contribute to the family income and participate in wage earnings. They do embroidery work and spinning. They have a role in social functions, rituals and religious matters. Females in the community do not perform the job of taxidermy.

At the stage of birth, post-delivery pollution is observed and the mother and the infant are given a bath on the seventh day (*satwan*). Naming ceremony is observed on the same day. The *maulvi* gives the name to the infant and gets some cash. No feast is usually given on this occasion.

Head shaving ritual is performed within one year the birth of the infant. *Zerakasi* (tonsure) is done by a *navid* at some sacred place, for example at Rishi Sahib. A feast is given on this occasion and four *maulvis* are invited. *Khatnahal* (circumcision) is performed on male children. It is usually done by a qualified surgeon who gets his fees. This ceremony is performed before the child's three years of age.

When a person dies, the dead body is given a bath and wrapped in a *kafan* (shroud). *Namaz-e-janaza* is performed in a mosque and the dead body is kept outside the mosque. A gravedigger digs the grave and gets Rs.50 to 60. The corpse is placed in the *lahad* (grave) which is closed thereafter. *Fateha* is read four times on Friday (*jumma*) after death at the *kabristan* and a *pyur* (stone) indicating the name and the birth and death dates is placed on this day. *Satijihum* is performed on the fortieth day of death. In this, the *maulvi* reads *kalma* and is offered food and other articles. The rituals have become more expensive.

The Ganz have the traditional occupation of taxidermy. These days, they are also engaged in business and have found jobs in the government and private organizations. Besides, they work as skilled labourers too. They have a link with the market which is fully regulated. They purchase articles of their daily use from the market by paying in cash.

There is no bonded labour among the Ganz. Child labour exists and is employed in shawl making and other embroidery work. Payment is made to them in cash.

The Ganz do not have any traditional caste council or panchayats. Earlier, there was one fur-cum-leather union which used to supply them fur and also solved business disputes. Statutory or formal panchayat came into being after Independence and takes care of planning and implementation of welfare and developmental activities in the villages.

The Ganz belong to the Sunni sect of Islam and have *silsila* affiliation to Pir Dastgir, Makhdum Sahib and Shah-i-Hamdan.

The Ganz observe Id and other festivals at Charar-e-Sharif (Rishi Sahib), Ramdan, Makhdum Sahib and Dastgir Sahib. The festivals are of socio-religious significance to the community.

The Ganz do weaving and embroidery work on cloth. This is done mainly by the womenfolk and children.

In the traditional intercommunity linkages, the Ganz accept and exchange water, *kachcha* and *pukka* food with other communities excepting the Watals. They get the services of other communities during rituals. The modern intercommunity linkages show growing social relationship with other communities.

Formal education is favoured for both, boys and girls. The boys normally study up to secondary level and drop out from studies because of economic reasons as they have to look after the business and earn for the family. Their attitude towards modern medicare is favourable and they make full use of it. They prefer four children or more. Family welfare programme has had no significant effect on them.

The facility of drinking water is available in the locality and the Ganz get tap water in their houses. There is no special provision for employment of the Ganz. The community members avail of media and communication facilities available in the locality.

The Ganz have electricity in their houses. Fuel resources are mainly firewood, coal and LPG. Their children avail themselves of the midday meal scheme and ICDS programme of the government. Their attitude towards savings is positive and they do not depend on the money-lenders.

A.C. SRIVASTAVA

GARA

The origin of the Gara, a community of blacksmiths in Ladakh and known as Garba in Kargil district, may be traced to Mongoloid stock. Their concentration is in Leh, and they are also sparsely distributed in Kargil district. Their habitations in Leh are perched at a high altitude on the Ladakh range overlooking the Indus river and its tributaries. The climate of the arid zone is extremely cold and the region remains snow bound from six to eight months in a year. They speak Ladakhi; a few can speak Urdu. Their written script is Bodhi. They dress themselves like other Buddhist Ladakhis. Men wear *goncha* (long coat), *shakten* (shirt), *sherak*, a belt around the waist, and boots made of leather and wood. The women dress themselves in *goncha*, *perak*, *firoza* which is a scarf on the head and *chertor*, a woollen or leather boots. They are listed in the category of Scheduled Tribes in the state.

The Garas have prominent cheekbones, broad and flat faces with some obliquity in the eyes. The mouth is large with prominent lips. The nostrils are quite wide and the nose is broad and also flat. They have scanty hair growth on the face. The hair of the head are straight and slightly wavy. The men have medium height while women are short statured.

The Garas are non-vegetarian and eat beef. Their staple food consists of *grim* (naked barley) and wheat. Pulses taken are gram, *urad*, *moong* and peas. Mustard oil is the cooking medium. *Sattoo* made from the flour of roasted wheat and barley is the main food item. Men and women are fond of *gurgur* (salty tea) , taken a number of times in a day. *Chang* prepared from barley is a popular alcoholic drink. Seasonal fruits like apricots and pears are eaten. Rice has become popular as a food item although it is not produced locally. Smoking is not popular among them.

Social divisions do not exist. There are, however, *gyuts* (blood relations) and *rikanum* (occupational group) which are exogamous. The *gyuts* have no specific name but the villagers know of their respective *gyuts*. No part of an individual name is inherited from any member of a senior generation. *Phasphuns*, which are small brotherhood of the community mutually renders some social service when needed.

Endogamy is practised at the community level. Under normal

conditions, the Garas neither give nor take brides in marriage from the Mon, Beda and Bhotos (Ladakhi Buddhists). Consanguinity, both cross and parallel, is not practised. Junior sororal marriage is permitted in case of death of the first wife. Marriage with the husband's younger brother is not permitted. Marriages are arranged and exchange of *khatak* (white scarf) symbolizes confirmation of the proposal. Marriage by choice is also practised by elopement. This, of course, is formalized later on. Another practice of acquiring a mate is through exchange of sisters.

Monogamy is the usual form of marriage. Polyandry has been discarded now. *Goncha* and *firoza* are the marriage symbols. Bride-price and dowry are prevalent in the community. The bride price paid in cash or kind to the father of the bride varies according to the health and appearance of the girl. Dowry consists of a number of household articles. After marriage, the bride lives with her husband and in-laws. In case the girl's father has no male siblings, his son-in-law may take care of the family. The practice of *pharsak* (servicing husband) is fast dwindling.

Divorce, desertion, and separation are common in the community. No stigma is attached to a divorced woman and she is free to marry anybody else. Separation and desertion are revocable. Divorce, however, is irrevocable in all cases. Matters of divorce are referred to the *goba* (village headman). He tries to resolve the matter or deliver a decision. Adultery, barrenness, maladjustment, impotency, insanity and inability to meet the expenses of the wife are some of the major reasons of divorce. Husband and wife are free to divorce each other, compensating the aggrieved party by giving a horse or a cow as the case may be. The children are the responsibility of the father in divorce cases. Widow, widower and divorcee remarriage is permissible. A childless widow prefers to go back to her parents' house. Marriage with wife's younger sister is permissible, but marriage with husband's younger brother is not practised. Changes observed in marriage rules are increase in the age of marriage, decrease in the incidence of divorce due to heavy compensation, and discarding of polyandrous marriages.

Families are generally of mixed-extended type. Interpersonal relations are based on respect of elders and affection for youngsters. Avoidance relationship between mother-in-law and son-in-law; daughter-in-law and father-in-law, etc., does not exist. Joking relations exist with the sister-in-law and brother-in-law; with the wife's younger and elder sisters and between grand parents and grand children. Conflict arises on matters like property, check on the freedom of youngsters and challenge to the authority of elders. Youth of the community have developed revulsion for their ancestral profession. Rule of inheritance is male equigeniture. Formerly, the eldest son used to inherit the property from father but now all the sons get equal share. Succession is from father to son. In the absence of a male issue, the daughter inherits the property including land, house and mother's ornaments. The head of such a family would like to keep a *maqpa* (the husband who goes to live at his wife's house) for his daughter.

Women shoulder a major burden of the household duties. Tending of children, cooking food, fetching drinking water and collection of fuel are the major domestic works. They also work in the field at the time of sowing and harvesting. The status of women is equal to that of men. They are not secluded. They do not observe *purdah* (veil) and freely consume the local drink called *chang* in the company of men. They are free to keep a *phorsak* (an additional husband) if they like. They are free to marry outside their own community.

Rapshit (a barren woman) is not a welcome person. There are no pre-delivery rituals. The pregnant woman is forbidden to carry heavy load, cross a river or stream, go out in the field or garden after sunset and in the moonlit night. *Dhunuche* is a formal occasion marking the seventh month of pregnancy. The lama recites the holy verses. A woman in labour pain is attended to by the *amchi* (female medical practitioner). Delivery confines the mother and father of the baby to the four walls of their room for seven days. On the seventh day, the lama performs *laf-tsang* (purification of the house) ceremony. On this occasion, members of the *phasphun*, relations, neighbours and friends are invited. The next ritual observed after one month of the delivery is called *da-tsang*. The relatives, *phasphun* members and friends bring dresses, *chang* (barley beer) and food materials. On this occasion, the *onpo* (soothsayer) is invited to forecast the future of the child and prepare a horoscope. He also suggests a name for the child. *Ralchang* (shaving of head) is performed on the male child before the age of two years. There is no ritual connected with the adolescence.

Marriage rituals are performed at the bridegroom's residence. The bridegroom does not accompany the marriage party but sends his *nyopa* (representative) who is dressed like the bridegroom.The marriage party is received by the parents of the bride. The *nyopa* performs all the marriage rituals and brings the bride to the residence of the bridegroom. The bride is seated close to the family kitchen and is later joined by the bridegroom. They are blessed by the lama and elderly relatives. The *nyopa* formally hands over the charge of the bride to the bridegroom who dine together. The bride stays in her husband's house for three days. The parents of the bride invite the bridegroom and his parents and relatives to their residence. A feast is given and thereafter the bride comes back to her in-laws' house.

The Garas cremate their dead. A child below five years is buried in case of death. When a person dies, blood relations and members of the *phasphun* are first informed to make the necessary arrangement for the disposal of the dead and death rites. The Bhotos or Ladakhi Buddhists do not participate in the death rites of the Garas but the Gara must participate in mourning the death of a Bhoto. During three days for which the dead body is retained, the lama chants hymns. Cremation of the dead body is performed in a sitting posture. Thirtieth and forty-ninth day of death are observed for recitation of hymns. *Sizak* is observed after one year of the death in which a feast is given to the relatives, friends and the lama.

The Garas are a landless community. They serve the village community by repairing agricultural implements, utensils, iron hearths, etc., and, in return, they get a fixed quantity of food grains from the families they serve. They prepare plough shares, sickles, spades, hammers, knives, iron stoves, windows and doors. Besides meeting the needs of the village folk, they also sell their finished articles in the Leh market. They also visit other villages for the job and get remuneration in cash and kind. Bonded labour does not exist. Child labour is prevalent.

The traditional caste council does not exist. Because of the Garas' low social status, they do not hold any position of authority in the village council. They cannot hold the position of a *goba* or village headman. They settle the disputes through the elders of their own community and hardly take their disputes to the village council. In case of disputes with the Bhotos or Ladakhi Buddhists, a Gara is always at disadvantage. Statutory or formal panchayat exists but the Garas are not represented in it. Village panchayats are heterogeneous and are represented by all the upper castes except the Garas. Post-Independence statutory panchayats plan and implement the welfare and development activities. They settle disputes of minor nature. Offenses are now referred to police and settled through the courts of law.

The Garas are Buddhist by religion. Each family has a *chotkang* (place of worship) in the house, generally in the kitchen where an oil lamp is kept burning. At the village level, there is either a small *gompa* (monastery) or a big *gompa* and the regional *gompa* with which these are associated. The members of the community have access to the *gompa* but they are not allowed to become a lama. Lama is their religious specialist who performs for their birth, marriage and death rites. *Gompas* are woven into the socio-economic fabric of Ladakhi society.

There is no particular art of the Garas. They make cooking ovens from iron sheets which are used in every Ladakhi house. In the snowclad mountainous region, extreme hardship of life is reflected in many different folk songs.

Intercommunity relations are based on mutual interdependence. In the village, the Garas are considered as a service community by the dominant population of Bhotos (Ladakhi Buddhists). They live with the other communities in a specific type of relationship. Customary norms of behaviour and interrelationship exist, and the same are reflected in different ways of life.

The Garas are not treated as a respectable community and do not receive equal treatment from the Bhotos. The community does not have entrepreneurs, scholars, members holding white-collar jobs, doctors and engineers. The Bhoto do not want a Gara as school teacher because the Bhoto children will have to wish and salute, *zu-zu* to him.

The Garas are aware of the various development programmes. Formal education is favoured for the boys and girls, but the community is unable to send its children to schools due to prejudice from the members of the majority community. Drop-outs are found more in this community. Their attitude towards health and medicare is favourable. They now prefer to send their patients to the hospitals and primary health centres. Couples prefer four children. Villages are provided with tap water for drinking. Employment under the various rural employment programmes is available but its main beneficieries are the majority community. A few members of the community are self-employed as ironsmiths. Facilities of transport and communication are available to them but none has a radio or television set. Electricity is available to the villages but not a single Gara house is electrified. Firewood and dung are the chief sources of fuel. Facilities of fair price shops are available and they get rice, sugar and kerosene oil through such shops. Banking facilities are not availed of.

PARMANAND LAL

GARDI

The Gardis are professional musicians who sing and recite *bhajans* and folk tales on the occasions of birth and death among the rural Hindu communities of Jammu. They bear a close similarity with the Jogis of the same region who are also professional singers but the latter sing religious and devotional songs in the temples or places of worship. The Gardis are a Scheduled Caste. They are better known for the type of profession they have been pursuing for long past. In fact, this has given the community an exclusive identity and they receive alms for rendering such type of services . They are found all over the Jammu province. The community perceives its distribution at the regional level. No ethnographic background is available nor are their references found in *Jati Puran*. They claim to possess a historical background which has reportedly been forgotten. The community has not migrated to its present habitat. They live in extreme warm to moderately warm and temperate climate in and around plains and semi-arid terrains. The region records high humidity, medium rainfall and thin forest cover. There were 771 Gardi individuals according to *Census of India*, 1961 which increased to 2,181 in 1981 census. They are a Scheduled Caste. They speak Dogri amongst themselves and correspond by using Gurmukhi, Devanagari and Arabic scripts. With others, they usually speak in Dogri and use Devanagari script. The community does not have any specific identification markers but their menfolk, being professional musicians, are identified by their musical instruments.

The Gardis are occasional non-vegetarian but they abstain from eating beef. Fish, eggs and fowls, are also included in their diet. Meat consumption is essentially linked to the level of economic affluence. Their main staple food is wheat, rice and maize. All types of pulses and beans are consumed by them. They eat moderate quantities of vegetables. Fruits are consumed occasionally. Milk and milk products are also used in plenty during festivals and on religious occasions. They take tea mixed with milk and sugar. They use mustard oil and *ghee* for cooking. Their menfolk consume alcoholic drinks occasionally and purchase the same from the market. Cigarette smoking is common among menfolk who also make use of cheroot. Betel and tobacco chewing depend on their availability. They now prefer rice to *roti*. On the whole, there has not been any significant change in the food habits though its quality has improved for those who have become financially resourceful.

The Gardis do not have any formal stratification on the basis of social hierarchy. Differentiation among them has now crept in on the basis of better occupational and educational status. They are conscious of the *varna* system but, among themselves, they do not have any clear-cut and formal demarcation in this regard. The community's self-perception is very low and so is the image and status they enjoy in the eyes of others. The main subcastes among them are Saugril, Gardi and Angurana.

The Gardis are exogamous at the surname level and do not marry with other communities. They practice consanguinity with the exception of seeking matrimonial alliances with first cousins. There is no restriction on seeking sororate alliance (junior) but levirate marriages of either type are prohibited. Pre-puberty marriages were common in the pre-Independence era and the system of *gaona* was prevalent but now adult marriages are common. The mode of acquiring mates is by mutual consent and negotiations. Usually friends, relatives and family heads arrange the matche. Age at marriage for the girls is 18 years and above and for the boys 22 years and above. Monogamy is the most prevalent form of marriage. Marriage symbols are vermilion, bangles made of lac and glass, *mangalsutra*, *bindi* and finger rings. But there is no strict rigidity in this regard. Practice of dowry exists marginally. It comprises kitchen utensils, bedding and a few dresses for the bride and the bridegroom. *Kanyadan* is also practised by them. The marriage ceremony is performed at the residence of the bride after sunset. The bridegroom alongwith the guests, *baratis*, comes to the residence of the bride on a horseback holding a ceremonial sword. After the *jaimala* ceremony, *lagan* is performed. Feast is given by both the parties at different occasions. Nuptial ceremony is performed at the residence of the bridegroom. In most of the cases, the rule of residence is patrilocal and, in exceptional cases, uxorilocal. Divorce is usually sought with judicial approval, the reasons of divorce being adultery, maladjustment and barrenness. Compensation is given to the wife as it is usually the husband who seeks the divorce. Children can be the responsibility of either party depending upon the circumstances under which divorce is sought. Rules regarding remarriage are quite flexible. Widows, widowers, divorcees can remarry with ease. Junior sororate is permissible. There has not been any significant change in the rules and customs of marriages or remarriages. Marriages, however, have become costlier and the marriage age for both the boys and girls has increased significantly since Independence.

Family composition of the Gardis at present is both nuclear and vertically extended. Joint family system is still the common family type. Interpersonal relationships are cordial among the household members. Joking relationship is reported among affinal relatives. Avoidance prevails between daughter-in-law and father-in-law. Conflicts and disputes arise on account of property and challenge to the authority of elders. The Gardis follow male equigeniture though, according to the existing Hindu Personal Law, female heirs are also entitled to equal share of ancestral property. The women generally forgo the share of property in favour of male heirs. Eldest son succeeds the deceased father as the head of the family. Interfamily linkages are formal and cordial though they do not exhibit any emotional bond or tie-up. Disputes are usually settled through mutual negotiations and mutual agreements through the efforts of friends, relatives and elder members of the community. Offences and crimes are dealt with under the existing judicial laws. Except for growing preference for having nuclear families, no other significant changes in the institution of family are reported. Women play a very significant role in the overall socio-economic milieu yet they are given a secondary status in comparison to their menfolk. Though women are entitled to equal share in the property yet they are deprived of it and are not even allowed to stake their claim. The women participate in the social functions and religious ceremonies. They are an active partner with the menfolk in income-generation. They take part in farm and non-farm activities and tend the domestic livestock. In rural areas, women collect fuel, carry water and attend to all other domestic chores. Though they enjoy voting rights, yet their participation in active politics either at the village or regional level is virtually absent.

The Gardis do not observe any pre-delivery rituals though some informal restrictions are observed. Lifting of heavy objects or travelling during night hours or opening doors to strangers is avoided. Children are usually delivered at home with the help of an experienced midwife. Wherever hospital facilities are available, they prefer to make use of them. They observe twenty-one days' post-delivery pollution but there are no postnatal restrictions on the mother. The naming ceremony is not observed. *Mundan* is performed for the male children while the same is not done for the female children. *Annaprashan* (first feeding of cereals) is not observed by them. Thread wearing ceremony is not carried out by them nor do they have any puberty rites for the females.

The dead are given a bath and then wrapped in a white shroud and taken on a bier to the cremation ground for the last rites. They observe ten days' death pollution. Those dying under five years of age are buried. *Rasam-pagri* or *uthala* ritual is usually performed after the death pollution is over. There have not been any significant changes in the life-cycle rituals of the Gardis but rituals have become more expensive and, for the well-to-do, these ceremonies have acquired a fair amount of exhibitionism.

Land, the main resource for livelihood, is controlled by individual owners. Though professionally they are musicians who sing at religious and social functions of the various Hindu communities, the majority of them over the period have now shifted from their traditional occupation. Owing to economic compulsions, they have sought job diversification to sustain and supplement their household income. Now agriculture has become the mainstay of their economic life. However, most of them still claim to be landless. Their present occupations are cultivation, animal husbandry and working as unskilled labourers while government and private service are their new vocations besides their traditional profession as musicians. Link with the market exists directly and also through middlemen. Market transactions are regulated by barter and cash, depending upon the time and place. Practice of bonded labour is not prevalent as also it is prohibited under the state law. However, a rise in the daily casual workers has been observed among them coupled with a steep increase in the number of agricultural labourers. Child labour is neither hired nor marketed though some may be used extensively for domestic works. Mode of payment of wages is in both cash and kind.

Traditional caste councils or panchayats do not exist among the Gardis but they have village panchayat system which is heterogeneous in character. Elections to such bodies are based on voicevote. Statutory formal panchayats exist after Independence but frequency of their tenure is intermittent and their impact quite restricted. Role of such panchayats is to monitor implementation of the government plans within the regions, keep track of other social and welfare developmental activities, render services of an arbitrator in solving disputes arising out of social and economic frictions and punish the guilty by social boycott. Adultery and land disputes are major offences. Panchayats do not institute any awards.

The Gardis profess Hinduism as their religion. They worship village and regional deities. Individual and family affiliation to *pirs* is a common phenomenon. Religious specialists are drawn from the Brahman community who perform their birth, marriage and death rites. Regional deities are worshipped at Vaishno Devi, Rughunath Mandir, Bahu Fort, Sudh Mahadev and Amarnath. Festivals are mostly of socio-religious significance. Besides all Hindu festivals, they also observe Shivratri, Lohri, Janmashtami, Rakshabandhan, Navratras, Holi and Dussehra. Neither any change in religion has been reported among them nor are they involved in any socio-religious movement.

Their womenfolk do cloth embroidery as a pastime. They make crude musical instruments of one or two strings attached to bowl shaped ends. Folk songs are sung by their menfolk for making a livelihood and usually these songs and folklore are in praise of old heros and brave warriors of the region. They also sing romantic and religious songs. They render public narration of folk tales pertaining to kings and queens or about some martial race of the region. Being essentially a musician community, they use light classical music for singing in public. No traditional dance is performed either by the Gardi men or women.

The Gardis accept cooked and uncooked food from the high caste Hindus as well as from other such communities which stand hierarchically at par with them. They accept cooked and uncooked food from the Bhagats, Meghs, Jogis and Ramdasiyas. They also accept uncooked food from non-Hindu communities. They normally do not interdine with the Mahashas, Saryaras, Chimyars and Barwalas though there is no formal prohibition in this regard. They maintain marital relations at the intercommunity level within the Hindu fold. They share cremation ground with other co-religionists. They also share schools, panchayat *ghars*, water sources, roads and wells with other people living in and around their habitats. They visit shrines of *pirs* also. They have a specific role, especially playing of musical instruments and singing of devotional songs on death rituals among Hindu communities. They maintain cordial and businesslike relationship with other communities. With the introduction of land reforms, they have become a typical agrarian community and as such maintain cultivator-labour relations wherever such reforms have led to individual proprietorship of land. They receive the services of barbers, carpenters, masons, etc.

The Gardis are trying to come out of their traditional ethnic identity of village singers for collecting of alms. They are trying to improve their socio-economic conditions by seeking new professional avenues which are socially more honourable and lucrative. They do not have enterprenuers or businessmen, creative artists, administrators, scholars or teachers among them, while there are some white-collar job holders, engineers, doctors and a few in the police and defence services. Political leadership has essentially remained confined to village block level. As a community, they have not been able to make any perceptible impact on the political scenario of the region.

Formal education has yet to assume an important role among the Gardis. They do not show any interest in the education of their children. Under the existing conditions, boys are given preference in schooling and pursuing higher education. Usually boys study up to secondary level and very few of them reach college level. Boys have to drop out from studies due to economic constraints and also because of their need to supplement the household income. Girls study up to secondary level but they have to drop out from studies because of social and economic reasons.

Their attitude towards modern medicare is favourable but its use depends upon its availability in predominantly rural areas of the region. Consequently, they have to fall back upon the traditional medicare which is easily available in their localities. Their attitude towards family planning is also favourable but they have yet to grasp fully the implications and benefits of a planned family life. They still prefer three to four children. Use of modern methods of family planning has recently been reported among them. It is generally their women who get sterilized.

Drinking water is available within their localities and its main sources are ponds, wells and tap water. They have not benefited from the various government sponsored schemes for the creation of employment opportunities. Mostly they are self-employed in agricultural and allied sectors besides working as professional singers. Their awareness about most of the government sponsored schemes seems to be quite marginal. They listen to the radio and also watch television occasionally. They also go to cinema as and when they visit the city of Jammu. Roads and post offices exist in and around their settlements. They make use of electricity for lighting purposes. Their fuel resources comprise firewood, cow-dung cakes, kerosene oil and cooking gas. Irrigation sources are canals and rainwater. Those who own farmlands make use of organic manure, chemical fertilizers and insecticides. None of them avail of the facilities of nutritional programmes launched by the official agencies. Facility of food supply are made through ration depots and cooperative stores. Their attitude towards savings is favourable but only a few can save due to their poor economic conditions. They are partly dependent on the moneylenders and shopkeepers.

The Gardis, being a Scheduled Caste are trying to come out of the social and economic backwardness which has engulfed them for a very long time and are trying to seek socio-economic emancipation by diversifying their economic and educational pursuits. Most of them are conscious of their status in the socio-religious hierarchy. Consequently, all efforts of the younger generation are directed towards achieving better living and social acceptability.

ASHOK AIMA

1. Dogra Brahman of Jammu

2. Domal of Rajouri, Jammu

3. A Family of Jat Sikh, Jammu

4. A Rattal couple of Jammu

5. Barwala of Jammu

6. The landscape in the Valley

11. A Banduk Khar or gun-maker at work in Kashmir

12. Manjygur or the eatable sellers of Kashmir

5. Barwala of Jammu

6. The landscape in the Valley

7.
Watal the shoemakers of Kashmir

8. Shaksaz, the basket weavers of Kashmir

9.
Sangtarash (stone-cutters) of Kashmir

10. Chopan or cattle herders' family

11. A Banduk Khar or gun-maker at work in Kashmir

12. Manjygur or the eatable sellers of Kashmir

13. Hanji women selling apple in Kashmir

14.
A carpet weaver of the Valley at work

15. A Panyạch or priest at work in Srinagar

16. Bakarwals of Jammu & Kashmir with their flock of goats

17. A Bakarwal family in a transit camp

18. Mon and Beda musicians of Ladakh

19. Buddhist ladies in traditional attire at the Thiksey monastery in Ladakh

20. A view of Beda kitchen, Ladakh

GORKAN/GORKUN

The Gorkans are a community of *gor* (grave) diggers in the Kashmir Valley, traditionally an occupational category of the Muslim distinct from other Muslim communities. The history and origin of the community is not known. It is believed that on the advent of Islam in the Valley, the ancestors of the community converted to Islam and adopted the occupation of grave-digging. They are scattered in Srinagar, Pulwama, Badgam, Anantnag, Baramula, Kupwara and other districts of Jammu & Kashmir but their main concentration is in Srinagar district. The average altitude of Kashmir Valley is between five and six thousand feet and is surrounded by the Pir Panjal and greater Himalayan ranges. The climate is cold. Natural vegetation is moderate and rainfall is medium. The area is thinly forested and confined to hill ranges below the snowline.

The language of the Gorkans is Kashmiri. They use the Arabic script for communication. They are in the category of Other Backward Classes of Jammu & Kashmir. They wear, like other Kashmiris, *pheran*, *goompochh*, trousers and cap. Women wear *salwar*, *kurta*, *pheran* and *putz*, which is worn on the head and is made of long plain cloth. They are non-vegetarian and eat mutton and eggs. Beef is not consumed by the community. Their staple food is rice. Wheat and maize are also consumed but not as a substitute for rice. Bread is taken with tea in the morning and afternoon. Pulses like gram, *moong*, *urad* and *masur* are consumed, and mustard oil is used as a cooking medium. They consume roots and tubers also. Vegetables like cabbage, potatoes, carrot and brinjals are consumed frequently, particulary in the rural area. *Hak* or *karam sag* is their favourite leafy vegetable. Fruit is consumed in plenty. Tea is more popular than any other drink. They are very fond of taking tea with salt. Tea with sugar is called *qahwa* is occasionally taken. Milk consumption is low due to its scarcity. *Ghee* (clarified butter) is also not consumed as it is considered harmful because of the climate. They do not take alcoholic drinks, but smoke *bidi*, *hookah* and cigarettes.

No social division has been reported among the Gorkan except on the basis of occupation, economic and educational status. In the local social hierarchy, they are put in the lower rank but in their perception they are of a middle rank. They belong to both the Shia and Sunni sects. Though they are endogamous, this rule is not strictly followed. They prefer to marry off their sons and daughters within their own community, but if the match is not available, they may marry outside. While selecting a girl, preference is always given to the cousins. Consanguinity prevails both at the cross cousin and parallel cousin levels. Nowadays only adult marriages take place but in the past child marriage was a regular phenomenon. The age for marriage at present is between 18 and 25 years for both boys and girls respectively. Marriages are settled by negotitation and sometimes arranged by a common friend or by a mediator (*manzymyor*). Though monogamy is commonly practised, polygamy is permissible according to the *shariat* or Islamic rules. There is no symbol of marriage for the Gorkan women. Bride-price is not in practice, but the system of fixing dower for the bride exists. *Mahr* is fixed at the time of *nikah* (marriage) for the bride and promised for future payment. They are patrilocal, i.e. after marriage the bride goes to live with her husband at his house. Divorce is permissible in the community. Only the husband can divorce on grounds of barrenness, adultery, maladjustment and insanity. The husband is more privileged than the wife in the matter of divorce. Divorce may be given either orally or by written document called *talak-nama*. In the Muslim law, when a marriage is dissolved by divorce the woman is prohibited from marrying for a specified time called *iddat*. If consummation of marriage has taken place and there is divorce then the duration of *iddat* is for three months, if the woman is pregnant, it is until the delivery. But the cases of divorce are still rare in the community. It is the duty of the father to look after the minor children after divorce. Remarriage for widow, widower and divorcee is permissible, but a widow is allowed to remarry when the *iddat* period is over. Remarriages are performed in a simple manner. Two major changes which have occurred in recent years are decrease in the rate of divorce, and the emergence of dowry system. Most of the families are nuclear, though in rural areas, mixed extended families are also found. In most cases, a newly married couple establishes a new household after marriage. Interpersonal relationship is amicable among the family members. Love and respect are paid to elders of the family. Avoidance relationship is maintained between the daughter-in-law and in-laws, and between younger brother's wife and *jeth* (husband's elder brother); likewise with outsiders and other elderly relations. Joking relationship exists between the husband's younger brother and sister-in-law and between the husband and his wife's younger sisters.

Property is divided among the sons, daughters and widows. The daughters get a smaller share than their brothers and the widowed mother. The succession pattern is followed in the male line from the father to the eldest son. No changes have been reported in these rules. The only change observed is the breaking up of the joint family system and emergence of nuclear families. In the Gorkan community, women have an equal status with men. They have full right on *mahr* which is fixed by the husband at the time of *nikah*. It can be claimed any time when the husband seeks divorce. Women play important role in all spheres of life. They participate in agricultural activities, collection of fuel, carrying of potable water and other household chores. Their role is pivotal in social and religous functions. Though they do not directly contribute to the family income, they certainly help supplementing it. They participate in the decision-making and exercise control over the expenditure of the family.

Among the Gorkan life-cyle rituals start from the first pregnancy of the woman, when certain restrictions are imposed. Women are not allowed to carry a heavy load or do strenuous work. They live with their husbands for more than first five months of their pregnancy. In rural areas, delivery takes place at home with the help of the *warin* (midwife), who assists the parturient mother and is paid in cash and kind such as sweets, rice and maize according to the economic status of the family. The *warin* could be from any community. Generally, they are old and experienced women of the village or the neighbouring area. In urban areas nowadays, women prefer hospitals for delivery. Immediately after birth and warm water bath, a senior male member recites *azaan* in the ears of the child. In the first delivery, bread and sweets are distributed among the relatives, friends and neighbours. If the delivery takes place at the girl's parental house, sweets are sent to her in-laws also. Her mother-in-law sends sweets, cash and clothing for the baby in return. This ritual is called *piaw*. On the seventh day of the delivery, the mother of the child takes her first bath after the delivery. On this day, the child is also given a name either by the family priest or any elder person of the family. The ritual is called *sunder*. This is usually followed by a feast. After forty days, the mother is given another bath and then she is allowed to do all normal household jobs. The next ceremony, *zerakasi*, is performed when the child is seven months old. In this ceremony, the hair of the child is shaved by the family barber. A feast is also arranged on this occasion. *Khatnahal* or circumcision is the next ceremony. This is done by the family barber, but in urban areas it is done in hospital or at home by an expert surgeon. A grand feast is arranged on this occasion.

Among the Gorkans, marriages are settled by negotiation and the first preference is given to the cousins. The boys and girls may also be selected from outside the community in case suitable spouses are not available within the community. Sometimes the help of a *manzymyor*, a matchmaker, is also sought for negotiating a marriage proposal. After the preliminary negotiations between the concerned familes, the father of the boy along with some relatives visits the residence of the bride and offers some gifts in cash and kind to the bride and her father. After this, the ceremony *doon-leij* is performed. In this ceremony, an earthen pot full of nuts and cash money is presented to the father of the bridegroom by the bride's father. Thereafter, the members of the family go to their relatives to invite them to the marriage and there they are served tea or lunch. The ritual is called *dapanbata*. In the house of bride, *malasbehoun* ritual is observed in which the bride is not allowed to take bath and do household jobs for atleast three days before marriage. *Massmechravoun* is the ritual, in which the hair of the bride is combed by the female relatives. On the first day of marriage, *menziraat*, hands and feet of the bride are dyed with *mehndi* paste (myrtle). In *yenevoul*, the second day of the marriage, the father of the bridegroom sends a few copper plates containing sugar candy, sugarball, almonds, dresses and ornaments for the bride. When the marriage procession (*barat*) starts, it is followed by two or three rows of women singing in chorus holding each other for distance. At the residence of the bride, the groom's party is received by the women. *Nikah* (marriage) ceremony is performed at the house of the bride and is presided over by a *maulvi* (priest). There are two types of *nikahs* among the Gorkan as in the other Muslim groups. One is *nikah asaltan*, in which the bride and bridegroom are present and a marraige contract is written with the consent of both in the presence of witnesses. *Mahr* money is also fixed which varies from Rs. 9,000 to 21,000. The other is *nikah vilaitan*, which is performed when the boy and girl are minors. This type of marriage was prevalent in the past. In such cases the parents used to give their consent on behalf of the bride and bridegroom. When the *nikah* ceremony is over, a feast is served. At the time of departure the bride's female relatives follow her for some distance, singing in chorus. The bride stays with her husband for seven days. A big feast called *wathal* is arranged on the marriage night. After the marriage, the bride starts living with her husband and in-laws.

The dead are buried. A bath is given to the dead body by the *snanagor*, a professional man, in the presence of relatives and friends of the deceased. He is paid money and given the clothing of the deceased. After wrapping the dead body in *kafan*, a white cloth, it is placed in a *taboot* or coffin and laid on the ground facing Mecca. The *mulla* recites prayers. Thereafter, the *taboot* is carried to the graveyard where a *lahad* (grave) is dug by the *malkhos* (gravedigger). He is paid money for his services. The dead body is placed in the *lahad* and covered with stones and clay. On the fourth day after the death, the *mulla*, relatives and neighbours are asked to recite the Holy Koran for peace of the departed soul. The same ceremony is repeated on the fortieth day. These rituals are called *chaharum* and *chehllum*, respectively.

The primary occupation of the Gorkan is to dig graves in the graveyards for their dead clients and give other services required on this occasion. Almost all the familes of the community are engaged in their traditional occupation of digging graves. In village areas, they are involved in agriculture also, but in cities they mostly depend on their traditional occupation. Besides their involvement in traditional occupation, members of the community are also engaged in different government and non-government jobs. Those who practise agriculture, own their lands and the resources are controlled by the individual or the family. They are directly linked with the local market, which is fully regulated. Child or bonded labour is not prevalent. There is no *biradari* or caste panchayat and disputes, if any, are resolved either by the head of the family or old persons or relations in the village. In village areas, this is done by the village headman or *chaudhury*. Sometimes, disputes within the community are taken to the court of law. They are aware of the role and function of the statutory panchayat.

The Gorkans are followers of Islam and follow its dictum, *shariat*, like other Mulsim communities of Jammu & Kashmir. There are serveral sacred shrines and mosques which are visited by the community members on specific occasions. Shah Hamdan, Charar-e-Sharif, Makhdum Sahib, Dastgir Sahib, Naqshband Sahib are their sacred places. The community has its own *pir*, the *mulla* or *maulvi*, who is called to perform birth, marriage and death rites. They observe different Muslim festivals in different months. Urs-e-Nabi, Prophet Muhammad's birthday, also known as Id-ul-Milad is celebrated on twelfth of Rabi-ul-Awwal. On this day, the Prophet's hair relic is displayed at Hazratbal shrine. Meraj-e-Alam is celebrated on twenty-sixth of Rajab and the hair relic is displayed on this day also. Id-ul-Fitr, Id-ul-Zuha and Shab-e-Qadr are other festivals which are celebrated with great zeal by the communtiy. Besides, there are certain *urs*, like Urs-e- Shah Hamdan, Urs-e-Batmaloo, Urs-e-Naqshband and Urs-e-Rishi Sahib, in which the members of the community participate. Festivals are of socio-religious importance. The Gorkans do not have their own art and craft, but a few members of the community are involved in shawl embrodery, wood carving, papier-mâché other traditional crafts of Kashmir. Women sing folk songs and dance on various social occasions.

Members of the Gorkan community maintain their relations with all other communities, particularly with the Muslim communities. They offer their services even to the lowest castes of the Valley, like the Watals. They accept *kachcha* and *pukka* food from all the Hindu and Muslim communities and never hesitate in mixing with the lower castes. The services of *pir*, Barber, Waza, Tarkhan and other communities are utilized on the occasions of childbirth, marriage and death rituals. They share water sources, burial grounds, religious shrines with the other Muslim communities. Patron-client relationship exists in the community.

Various developmental programmes adopted by the government have left a good impact on the Gorkan community. In urban areas, the members of the community pay more attention towards education than in the village areas. Children have to cover a distance of at least 2 to 3 km for reaching their schools. For higher education, they go to cities. Generally, they study up to primary level and only few of them reach college level. Education of girls is less favoured than that of the boys. The Gorkans prefer modern rather than their traditional medicare in the urban areas, where such facilities are available. In villages, however, the indigenous traditional medicare system still prevails. The attitude of the community towards family planning programmes is not favourable. Electricity and drinking water facilities are available in their locality. Tap water, streams and springs are the main source of water. Most of the members of the community are self-employed. The media of communication is radio in rural areas. In cities, people watch television and visit cinema. Cow-dung cakes, wood and kerosene oil are used as fuel. Irrigation facilities are poor and they have to depend on rain or stream water for cultivation. Nutritional programme of the government have not been implemented properly. Facilities of food distribution system through fair price shops are available to the community. They have a positive attitude towards savings and are not dependent on the moneylenders or shopkeepers.

ANAND SARAN

GUJJAR

The Gujjar are a well known semi-nomadic, pastoral community. Before embracing Islam, they were all Hindus but during the reign of Aurangzeb, they changed their religion. However, a small section of them still continue to be Hindus. They derive their name from Gujarat from where they migrated to Jammu & Kashmir. They claim to be the descendants of ancient Yuchi or Kushan but it is still controversial. They are spread over Srinagar, Anantnag, Pulwama, Doda, Kishtwar, Jammu and other districts of the state. The climate of the region where they live and move in search of pasturage is cold with low humidity, and has low rainfall, thin forests and medium to heavy snowfall during winters. The terrain is hilly and surrounded by the Pir Panjal and Himalayan ranges. The population figures of the Gujjar are not available. The language of the Gujjar is known as Gujri. Now, they can speak either Kashmiri or Hindi and Punjabi while communicating with others. They use the Arabic script. In the state, they are categorized as a Scheduled Tribe. *Dastar*(long turban), beard, *salwar* and *kameez* (shirt) are the dress and identification markers of the community. Women put on a special type of cap (*topi*) on their head. Most of the adult members have their beard dyed with *mehndi* or *henna*.

The Gujjars are non-vegetarians and consume meat of goat, sheep, chicken and fish. Their staple food consists of maize, rice and wheat and pulses such as *moong* (green gram), *urad* (black gram) and *moth* (brown gram). Besides seasonally available vegetables, roots and tubers are also consumed by them. They do not take alcoholic drinks because of religious prohibition but consumption of milk and milk products is high among them because they always have suffiicient number of buffaloes, the rearing of which is their main occupation and also the main stay of their economy. They are fond of taking salty tea with bread. Consumption of tea with sugar is rare among them. Smoking of *hookah* (hubble-bubble) is common among the old, but the new generation smokes *bidis* and cigarettes.

Social divisions among the Gujjars exist on the basis of religion and occupation. There are both Hindu and Muslim Gujjars but in Kashmir all are converted Muslim Gujjars. The Hindu Gujjars are found in Himachal Pradesh and Uttar Pradesh. Among the Gujjars of Kashmir, there are two sections, Jamindar and Dodhi. The Jamindar Gujjars are mostly engaged in cultivation while the Dodhi Gujjars subsist on the sale of milk and milk products and rearing of buffaloes on contract basis. Marriages between the two religious groups are prohibited. Further, the Muslim Gujjars are divided into various exogamous sections or *gotras* such as Kasana, Chechi, Padhana, Lodha, Khatana, Paswar and Bangri, which regulate the marriage alliances. They perceive themselves in the middle order of the regional social hierarchy and others also recognize them in the same way. Endogamy at the religious and the community level is always maintained and considered the rule of marriage. Both parallel and cross-cousin marriages are practised and preference is given to the cousins while selecting a bride for marriage. To avoid heavy expenditure on marriage, *badla* (marriage by exchange) is common among them where the marriage expenses are mostly met reciprocally. Most of the marriages are performed when the boys and girls attain adulthood. The ideal age of marriage for boys is between 18 and 21 years and for girls between 16 and 19 years. Child marriage, though common in the past, is a rare phenomenon nowadays. Marriages are settled through negotiations but love marriages also take place. Monogamy is the norm though polygyny is also permissible according to the *shariat* (Islamic rules). There is no symbolic indicator of marriage. Bride-price and dowry systems are not prevalent among them. Rules of residence are patrilocal after marriage, i.e. the bride goes to live with her husband and her in-laws. Cases of divorce are rare though it is permissible for either of the spouses. However, the husband has more rights and privileges than the wife. Divorce is possible on the grounds of barrenness, adultery, maladjustment and insanity. Likewise, the wife can also seek divorce if the husband is absconding, not taking proper care of the wife and children or has not had sexual contact for more than three years. Divorce may be granted either orally or by written document called *talaq-nama*. According to the Islamic rules, after divorce the woman is not permitted to remarry for a specified time period called *iddat*. It is for three months and ten days after the grant of divorce and it is till delivery if the women is pregnant. The father is responsible for maintaining the minor children after divorce. Remarriages for widows, widowers, and divorcees are permissible and are practised.

The Gujjars prefer to live in extended families. Newly married couples normally establish a new household after marriage. Interpersonal relationship among the family members is established with due love towards youngsters and respect towards the elders. The eldest member of the family is treated as the head and he takes the responsibility of looking after the family affairs. Avoidance relationship is maintained between the daughter-in-law and parents-in-law, and between the younger brother's wife and husband's elder brother. Joking relationships exist between the sister's husband and wife's brothers and sisters, between elder brother's wife and husband's younger brothers or sisters. Property is divided among the sons, daughters, and widows, but daughters get a smaller share than their brothers. Succession is followed in the male line, from the father to the eldest son. Among the Gujjars, the women have equal status and play important roles in the economic, social and religious spheres of life. They remain engaged in household works. Milking of cattle, collection of fuel and fodder, and bringing potable water are their duties besides assisting their menfolk in agricultural activities. Besides controlling the family expenditure, they contribute to the family income by engaging themselves in productive work.

Among the Gujjars, the rituals connected with childbirth, marriage, death and other social functions are observed with great zeal and enthusiasm. There are certain restrictions imposed on the expectant mother. She is not allowed to carry heavy loads and do tedious work after five months of pregnancy. In most of the cases, delivery takes places in their camp with the help of a *warim* (local midwife) who is either an old experienced woman of the same community or any other knowledgeable woman available in the area where they camp. She is rewarded both in cash and kind. Just after birth, the baby is given a bath and a senior male member recites *azaan* in the ears of a baby and sweets are distributed among relatives and neighbours. A feast is served on the third day. *Sunder* ritual is celebrated on the day the parturient mother is given her first bath and, on this day, the child is also named by the family priest or any old member of the family. On the fourteenth day, the parturient mother takes her final purificatory bath and starts doing the normal house-hold work. When the baby is six months old *zerakasi* ritual is observed, in which the head of the male child is shaved by the family barber who is paid money and given new clothes. Sometimes a feast is also arranged on the occasion. *Khatnahal* (circumcision) is another important ceremony observed according to the Muslim religious doctrines. It is performed by the family barber, and a grand feast is arranged to mark the occasion.

Marriage ceremonies start with *gandum* (engagement) and, on this occasion, the bridegroom's father presents money and other gifts to the bride and her father, and the former through the ritual of *doon-leiz* receives money and an earthern pot full of nuts, in return. Marriage invitations are sent to the relatives and friends after the engagement. At least three days before the actual marriage ritual of *malasbehoun* is performed at the bride's place, in which the bride is refrained from doing household jobs and taking bath. This is followed by another ritual called *massmechravoun*, when the women relatives comb the bride's hair. On the first day of marriage called *menziraat*, the hands and feet of the bride are dyed with *mehndi* at night. On the second day of marriage called *yenevoul*, the bridegroom's father sends dry fruits, sweets, clothes, and ornaments for the bride. When the marriage procession starts, it is followed by the women relatives singing in chorus. The bridegroom is received at the bride's place by the female relatives of the bride, where all the participants are served tea and snacks. *Nikah* is the most important ceremony of the marriage and is presided over by the *maulvi* (priest). There are two types of *nikah* in the community. One is *nikah asaltan* in which the bride and bridegroom are present and give their consent for the marriage in presence of the witnesses. The second type is *nikah vakaltan* which is performed when both the bride and the groom are minor and the consent is given by their parents. The custom was prevalent in the past when child marriages were in practice, but now it is losing its importance. *Mahr* is fixed at the time of *nikah*. It varies from Rs. 9,000 to 21,000 and is promised for future payment. Generally, it is demanded by the bride's party at the time of divorce. After the *nikah* ceremony, a grand feast is arranged by the bride's father. When the *barat* departs, the bride's female relatives follow her for some distance, singing in chorus. The bride stays with her husband for at least ten days. On the fourth day, a grand feast called *wathal* is served, in which relatives and friends are called to have a dinner and all the participants give presents to the new couple. After the marriage the bride starts living with her husband and in-laws.

They bury their dead. The dead body is given ritual bath by the *snangor*, a professional bath giver. The body is then placed in a coffin, *taboot*, and wrapped in white cloth, *kafan*. Then it is laid on the ground facing Mecca and a prayer is recited by the family *maulvi* (priest). Thereafter, the coffin is carried to the grave (*lahad*), placed in it and covered with clay and stones. *Lahad* is dug by a *malkhos* or *gorkun* (professional grave-digger) who is paid money and given tea with bread. On the fourth day, relatives friends and the *maulvi* recite the verses of Koran for the peace of the departed soul. This is repeated on the fourteenth day. These rituals are known as *chaharum* and *chehallum*. Polluntion is observed for forty days.

As mentioned earlier, there are two types of Gujjars in Jammu & Kashmir, Jamindar and Dodhi. The primary occupation of the Jamindar Gujjars is agriculture, besides animal husbandry, but the Dodhi Gujjars are exclusively pastoral people. They still move from low to high and high to low altitude hills in search of pastures for their buffaloes on which their whole economy is based. They live mainly on the sale of milk and its products. Sometimes, they rear buffaloes on contract basis. Agriculture is also taken up by them as a secondary occupation and is done only in winter when they stay in their original habitat. During other seasons, they give the land to the sharecroppers. Most of the milk and milk products are sold in the cities, but during their summer pasturage the products are sometimes exchanged with other essential commodities. The Jamindar Gujjars possess larger size of land than the Dodhi Gujjars. There is no bonded labour system among them but child labour of the family is sometimes engaged for paddy and maize cultivation. They also work as graziers. Pastoralism is still considered their traditional occupation, but they are now taking up other occupations such as business, government and private jobs, and even defence services. A few of them are engineers, doctors, school teachers and in administrative services. They are directly linked with the market and do their business mostly in cash, but sometimes exchange of goods is also followed. Payment of wages to labourers employed by them is made both in cash and kind . Changes in their age-old occupation of cattle herding have occured after Independence and they have adopted new types of occupations for their livelihood.

The Gujjars have their own *biradari* panchayat to resolve the disputes within the community. *Nambardar*, who is the head of the panchayat, is selected by a voice vote. Generally old, knowledgeable and sometimes educated persons are selected as *nambardars* of the group. There are caste associations at the regional level also, besides the *biradari* panchayat, to look after the grievances of its members. The headman, in consultation with other elderly persons of the community, gives his verdict when disputes arise among the members. Social boycott or imposition of cash fine are the general modes of punishment for the accused. Statutory village panchayats are also there of which they are members. These panchayats plan and implement the welfare programme and work for the development of the village as a whole. Because of the nomadic life, no changes have been reported in their political organization of the Gujjars.

The Gujjars follow Islam. On different occasions, they visit the mosques and other sacred shrines. All the Muslim festivals are observed by them. Besides, Id-ul-Zuha, Id-ul-Fitr, Shab-e-Qadr, Urs-e-Nabi, the Prophet's birthday, Id-ul-Milad, and Miraz-e-Alam (Sharif) are also celebrated. On the birthday, the Prophet's hair relic is displayed at the Hazratbal shrine. They participate in the *urs* such as Urs-e-Shah Hamdan. Urs-e-Batmaloo, Urs-e-Naqshband Sahib and Urs-e-Rafimal are celebrated with others. Besides these, another *urs* which is very important for the Gujjars is celebrated every year in the month of July at Wangat valley of Srinagar district. It is held on the fifth day of Rajab on the death anniversary of father of the Gujjar leader Mian Bashir. All the festivals are of socio-religious and socio-economic significance. There is no exclusive art or craft of the Gujjars, but a few members have the skill of making certain woollen articles from sheep wool. On different social occasions, folk songs are sung by women, but there are no traditional musical instrument of the community.

Since they move from one place to another from high mountain range to low, along with their cattle in search of green pasture, they establish cordial relations with all the Muslim and non-Muslim communities of the region where they camp. Their relations with the Bakarwal are very close as they are considered a section of the Gujjar and who originated from the same stock. Business relations are amicably established with all the Hindu and Muslim communities as they supply milk and milk products to them and also rear their cattle on contract basis. Services of the Tarkhan, Nazzar, Shaksaz and Sangtarash are made use of for different purposes. There is no restriction on accepting *kachcha* (uncooked) or *pukka* (cooked) food from other communities except the Watals whom they avoid to some extent. Intercommunity linkages are established with other neighbouring communities through exchange of food, sharing of water sources, burial grounds and sacred religious shrines. Landlord-tenant and patron-client relationships also exist among them.

The attitude of the Gujjar towards formal education is not positive, particularly towards the girl's education, because they lead a nomadic life. Boys study upto the primary level and a few of them have reached higher level. Girls do not study due to social reasons and nomadic way of life. Though a few mobile primary schools have been introduced by the Jammu & Kashmir government to provide education to their children, the scheme could not be successful due to their short stay in one camp and their frequent movement to new places having extreme climate and difficult access. They do not pay much attention towards modern medicare system and still prefer the traditional indigenous medicines. The modern medicare facilities of the primary health centres are also not available to them in certain areas where they live. Family planning programmes are also not favoured by them due to their nomadic life and their traditional occupation as it requires more and more helping hands to work and cope with the arduous conditions of life. Drinking water and electricity facilities are available in their original homeland, but during the winter season when they return to their homes, the supply of electricity is generally poor. Tap water, streams and springs are the sources of drinking water. They are self-employed and only a few of them are serving in the government or private organizations. Radio is the only meduim of communication and they occasionally visit cinema. Firewood, cow-dung cakes and kerosene oil are the main fuel resources for them. Though the Jamindar Gujjars depend on agriculture and Dodhis too have lands for cultivation, they lack proper irrigation facilities. They use organic manure in their fields. Chemical fertilizers and insecticides are rarely used. Neither any nutritional programme nor employment schemes have benefited the Gujjars. Facilities of food distribution system through fair price shops are available in their areas, and they avail themselves of them only during the winter season. In summer they move from one place to another to graze their cattle and do not get facilities of the fair price shops. The attitude of the community towards saving is positive and they do not depend on the moneylenders or shopkeepers.

ANAND SARAN

GUJARATI BRAHMAN

The Gujarati Brahmans are the immigrants from Gujarat. There are three distinct sections of the Gujarati Brahmans, namely Nagar, Audhich and Barad but the former are more prominent and numerically dominant. The people identify themselves as Nagar whereas the local population refer to them as Gujarati. Another synonym for them is Vedvays. They are divided into six major subdivisions in order of hierarchy: Vadnagara, Visnagara, Sathodra, Chitroda, Krishnora and Prashnora. Their surnames are Dave, Mehta, Jani, Pandya, Joshi and Rawal. The community assumes a national identity. Ethnographic and historical accounts on them exist. Historians claim that they are of purely Aryan stock belonging originally to Southern Europe or Central Asia. They travelled from Hindukush to Tibet and then through Kashmir and settled around Kurukshetra. Risley regards them as Greaco-Scythian or Dravido-Scythian in origin. Some of their families had remigrated from Gujarat to north India either at the time of the second Gujarat famine or during the reign of Akbar. During the Sikh regime in Punjab, one of them, Pandit Shyamji, held the rank of military officer-in-charge of the army of Jammu. Thus, the community perceive its distribution at inter-regional level. They mostly live in Jammu and speak Gujarati and Dogri amongst themselves, but shift to Dogri, Punjabi and Hindi while speaking with others. Devanagiri is the only script which derives its existence from the Nagar Brahmans. Male headgear and *dhoti* are the identity markers besides the symbolic *kalam* (pen), *karchi* (spoon) and *barchi* (spear) qualifying the community as a blend of intellectual acumen, hospitality and martial prowess. The Gujarati Brahmans are vegetarians and do not eat even onions and garlic. Cereals used by them are wheat, rice and maize. Gram, *toor*, *moong* and *kulthi* are the pulses consumed by them. Mustard oil and *ghee* are used in cooking. They drink only non-alcoholic drinks like soda and *sattoo*. Vegetables and fruits are also consumed by them. They prefer rice to unleavend bread. Men smoke cigarette, *bidi* and *hookah* (hubble-bubble) but women do not smoke.

Among the Gujarati Brahmans, social divisions exist at sub caste level which regulates marriage alliances and indicate soical status. No changes have occurred in surnames or titles. The community perceives a high status of itself but other communities assign it a low status.

They are aware and recognize their place in the *varna* system as Brahmans. Endogamy exists at the community level but *gotras* are exogamous. Marriages can take place among the six above mentioned subdivisions only if *gotras* are different. Hypergamy is permissible but hypogamy is strictly prohibited. Consanguinity is absent but junior sororate is permissible. Marriages are performed in adulthood through negotiation and mutual consent. Monogamy is the general rule. Vermilion, bangles, *mangalsutra*, finger and toe ring, ear and nose rings and studs and *pajeba* are the symbols of marriage. *Kanyadan* exists and dowry is given both in cash and kind, but it is never demanded. They are patrilocal. Divorce is not permissible. Sororate is tolerable but levirate is disallowed. There are no changes in marriage rules. There is an increase in age at marriage and marriage symbols are observed strictly. The families are nuclear and mixed-extended. Avoidance and joking relation-ships exist among specified kins. Sons receive equal share in the property but daughters do not. The eldest son succeeds the father. There is a rise in the formation of nuclear families and extended families are declining.

Being purely urbanites, their women have no role in agriculture but they do have a role in animal husbandry and in fetching potable water. They participate in social functions, rituals and religious spheres. They are prominent in political sphere too and have a place in the mechanism of social control. Nevertheless, their status is low although they have decision-making power, contribute to the family income and control the family expenditure.

During the advanced stage of pregnancy (eighth month), a *havan* is performed for the well-being of the mother and the unborn child. *Chhatti* ritual is observed on the sixth day after birth and *chalima* or pollution lasts upto forty days. On the eleventh day, the father's sister swings the neonate on a *patola* sari and announces the name. Green *pipal* leaves are strung on the four conners of the swing. Birth pollution ends with the offering of *panchamrit* to the mother. Male children between the age of three and five years undergo tonsure ceremony called *mundan*. *Yajnopavit* (wearing of the sacred thread) is performed at the age of eleven years with great fanfare. Girls between the age of seven and twelve years perform *Gauri vrata* or *goryo* by eating saltless food and worshiping Gauri Mata. They also perform *surya-puja* to propitiate the sun god. In the age group of twelve to sixteen years, the girls observe *candla vrata* wherein they apply saffron marks to the forehead of five *suhagins* or married ladies. The marriage rituals are *shagun*, *Ganesh bana*, *kurksar*, *karahi pujan*, *phool ki holi* and worship of *isht dev* Hatkeshwar and *kul-devi* Ambika, besides *kanya-dan*, *varmala* and *saptapadi*. Marriage rituals are performed at the bride's residence where a feast is given. Nuptials are performed at the groom's residence.

When the signs of death approach, the dying person is given *snan*, a purificatory bath, and he is made to offer a variety of alms. Agnates have hair cut on the *daswan*, tenth day, and *kriya* is performed either on the eleventh or thirteenth day. The dead bodies of children less than three years of age are buried. These rituals are now being curtailed as they have become more expensive.

The Gujarati Brahman are traditionally an urbanite and landless community. Members of the community earn their livelihood through priestly services, practice of Ayurveda and business. Link with the daily regulated market is direct and all the transactions are made in cash. Bonded and child labour do not exit.

In the Gujarati Brahman community, the Jammu & Kashmir Prantiya Nagar Mandal aims at simplification of rituals, integration of various subgroups and exercising measures of social control. The luminaries of the community are given *samman* (honoured). The Gujarati Brahmans are Sanatanist orthodox Hindus and worship *kul-devi* Ambika. Chait Purnima is devoted to the worship of their presiding deity Lord Hatkeshwar. *Panchayatana puja* involves worship of the deities of wider pantheon order: Ganesh, Vishnu, Surya, Shiva and Shakti. They regard Vishnu and Shiva as the manifestation of one Brahman. The sacred specialists are from the same community, who guide them in worship, perform life-cycle rituals, inculcate religious teachings, protect against evil spirits and confirm theft and guilt. Diwali, Lohri, Shivratri, Maghi Sankranti, Hatkeshwar Jayanti, Navratras, Sravani and Bhaiya Dooj are festivals of socio-religious significance. Change of religion has not taken place. The community has been actively involved in socio-religious movements under the leadership of Hakim Pandit Parsuram Nagar of Jammu. They have a deeply embedded tradition in arts and crafts especially floor and wall paintings. Women's pastime is embroidery. The community's attachment to music is traditional; Baiju Bawra, the reputed singer, was a Nagar Brahman. Once they attracted the displeasure of Akbar by refusing to hand over two musician sisters, Tana and Riri, whom the Emperor wanted to serve as singers in his court; the girls refused and set themselves aflame as the royal forces attacked Vadnagar. Women participate in traditional dances and singing of *stuti* in honour of Ambaji. Musical instruments used are *dholak*, *tabla*, harmonium, sitar, guitar and flute.

They traditionally accept and exchange water from the other high order Brahmans, Kshatriyas and Vaishas, but do not accept *kachcha* (uncooked) food from any other community. *Pukka* food cooked in milk is accepted and also exchanged with other communities. *Siddha* is accepted but not exchanged. Inter community connubial norm is absent. They share the cremation ground with the *savarna*. They visit the same religious shrines and participate in traditional socio religious festivals without playing any specific roles in them. Patron-client relationships exist. The community has businessman, scholars, creative artists, white-collar personnel, teachers, administrators and defence personnel. Political leadership has also emerged at the national level.

The Gujarati Brahmans perceive formal education favourably for both sexes and they study up to postgraduate level. Dropping out of school or college is due to economic and social reasons. Both traditional and modern medicare are considered useful and are fully availed of. They favour family planning, prefer three children norm and use modern methods of birth control. Sex-wise preference for sterilization is absent. Water supply is through tap. They are engaged both in employment and self-employment. Listening to the radio; watching television and visiting cinema are the common means of entertainment. Roads, railways and post offices are situated nearby. Electricity, firewood, cow-dung cakes, coal and LPG are the main sources of energy. They avail public distribution facilities through the fair price ration shops, have positive attitude towards saving and are not dependent on the moneylenders and shopkeepers.

BAQAR R. RIZVI

GUJRI

The Gujri or Goor is an occupational title of persons who tend cattle and sell milk and milk products. It has not been possible to trace the origin of this word, nor to determine whether it is a distortion of the name Gujjar. The fact, however, remains that, like Gujjars, the Gujris are also sturdy people and are used to hard labour. Other segments of the Kashmiri population do not intermarry with them due to their low social status. The community is distributed in all the districts of the Kashmir Valley. Their major concentration is in towns and sparsely distributed in the villages. The environment is characterized by cold climate and mountainous terrain. The average altitude is 1,600 metres from sea level and the region experiences snowfall for four to six months in a year. Kashmiri is spoken within the family and with the kin groups. With the non-Kashmiris, they speak Urdu. They write in Arabic script. Majority of them are illiterate. They dress themselves like the other Muslims of the Valley. The men wear cotton shirt, and trousers, and the women wear *pheran*, brocaded near the collars, *salwar*, *kameez* and put potch or scarf on the head. In the towns, the members of the community are identified with selling of milk and curd in the shops. The community is listed as a Backward Class in the state.

The Gujri are non-vegetarian. Their staple diet consists of rice, wheat and maize. The pulses used are grams, *urad*, *moong*, peas and *masur*. Mustard oil is the cooking medium. Roots and tubers consumed are potato, onion, carrot, radish and turnip. Salty tea is taken a number of times a day. Milk and milk products are taken regularly. They smoke *bidis*, cigarettes and hubble-bubble. They also rub their teeth with snuff. They take seasonal fruits like apples, pears, apricots, cherry, *khubani*, walnuts, etc.

There are no social divisions among the Gujri. Differences, if any, are due to education, occupation and economic status which also regulate their marriage alliances. They occupy low social position; hence the other Muslims do not intermarry with them. They consider themselves superior to the Gujjars, who have migratory habits.

They practice community endogamy. Marriages with cousins, both cross and parallel, are preferred. In case of non-availability of a suitable bridegroom within close relatives, they go to distant relatives. Marriages are arranged after attaining adulthood although, in the past, child marriages were prevalent. The spouses are acquired through negotiations and exchange. Monogamy is the usual form of marriage. Junior sororate is possible only in case of death of the first wife. Senior levirate is possible provided both are of matching age. There is no symbol for a married woman. No marriage is possible under the Islamic Law unless the *mahr* and the *than* (clothes) are settled in advance. The former means a cash ranging from Rs. 900 to 9,000 according to the status of the family. *Mahr* is both prompt and deferred, but, in normal circumstances, it is not paid unless marriage is dissolved at the instance of the bridegroom. The bride, after marriage, goes to stay with her husband and the in-laws. A few instances of *khanadamad* wherein the husband goes to live with his bride and her parents, have also been reported. Only the husband can divorce, but it is permitted under special circumstances. The husband seeking divorce expresses his desire in front of a *maulvi* or an *alim* (learned person). The reasons for divorce are adultery, barrenness and maladjustment. The wife, on the other hand, can seek separation from her husband in case of impotency, cruelty, inability to meet the wife's expenses and chronic sickness. She has to observe *iddat* for a period of one hundred days before remarriage. When the husband seeks divorce, he has to pay the *mahr*, to the wife. But when the wife separates from her husband, she has to return the ornaments and *than*, the clothes she received from her husband. The children are the responsibility of the husband in case of divorce. Widow, widower and divorcee remarriage is permissible. Sororate and levirate is possible provided both are of matching age. The change observed in the marriage rules is that the incidence of divorce has decreased considerably due to the increase in the amount of *mahr* and other social reasons.

The families are generally mixed-extended in villages, but in the towns, they tend to become nuclear. The aged parents are respected. The wife does all the domestic work and gives a helping hand in the business of her husband. The daughter-in-law does not observe *purdah* from her father-in-law and the elder brothers of her husband. Joking relationship are observed with sister-in-law, brother-in-law and with the maternal uncle. Father's property is divided among all the sons and daughters. Succession is from father to the eldest son. Although women share major responsibility of the family, yet their status is inferior to men.

The life-cycle rituals connected with childbirth, marriage and death are similar to the other Muslims of the Valley. The birth of a child usually takes place at home. The new born baby is indoctrinated by the recitation of holy verses (*azaan*) in its ears. Pollution is observed for forty days after the birth of the child. At the age of six months, first tonsure (*zerakasi*) ceremony is observed. At the age of two years, the male child is circumcised called *khatnahal*. Formerly, the village barber used to perform this ritual, but nowadays it is done in hospital soon after the child's birth. *Aqeeqa* ritual is performed by those who can afford it. Marriage takes place after attaining adulthood. Marriage is arranged through the middleman (*manzymyor*) or through a common friend or relative. The initiative is taken by the father of the girl or the boy. When a suitable match is found, the ceremony of *nishani* (betrothal) is performed. Sometimes on this occasion, *nikah* (marriage contract) is documented and commitment is made. Afterwards other rituals that follow are *doon-leiz*, *malasbehoun*, *massmechravoun*, *melamenz* and *menziraat*. In case of death, pollution is observed for four days. The *snangor* gives a bath to the dead body. It is carried in a *taboot* to the grave. The *malkhos* prepares the grave. The rituals observed are *chaharum* and *chehallum* on the fourth and fortieth day after the death of a person.

The economic activities of the Gujri are tending of cattle, selling of milk and milk products. They also domesticate cows and sell the milk in villages and towns. In the cities, they own shops and sell milk and milk products. Owing to illiteracy and general backwardness, the members of this community are not found employed in services. Their women work as wage labourers in the villages. Traditional caste councils have become defunct. There are, however, statutory panchayats to look after the interests of the village communities. The community is Muslim by religion and belongs to the Sunni sect. The services of a *pir* and *imam* from other Muslim communities are available to them. They perform and participate in all the important festivals like Id-ul-Milad and Id-ul-Fitr and visit the shrines of Hazratbal, Shah-i-Hamdani, Jama Masjid. There is no particular art or craft of the community. Folk songs like *vanvun*, *wayun*, and *rouf* are sung on the occasions of engagements, marriages and festivals.

Intercommunity relations of the Gujri with the Hindu and Muslim communities are based on mutual interdependence. In village, the Gujris live in the neighbourhood of the other communities. There is no separate locality for the Gujris. Services of the carpenter, mason, barber, ironsmith, potter, gravedigger and scavenger are available to them. They are invited on the occasion of marriage by other communities. They accept food and water from all the other communities except the Watal. Intercommunity marriage does not take place due to their low social position. They share the burial ground and shrines, and participate in the traditional festivals with the other Muslims. There is socio-economic interdependence with the Sofi, Ganai and Gujjar communities. The Gujris always keep their milk shop adjacent to the shops of the Sofi bakers and the Ganai butchers. The community have no big enterpreneurs, scholars, members having white-collar jobs, engineers or doctors. There are no political leaders from this community.

The development programmes have a postive impact on the social and economic conditions of the Gujri community. Their boys and girls are getting formal education. In the villages, there is hardly any girl who has not read up to class eight. The boys also study at least up to class eight, only a few do their matriculation. The reason for dropping out is the need for additional helping hands for economic activities. Medicare is available at the primary health centres. They prefer to go to a hospital in case of disease and childbirth, but the villages which are far away from the main roads are deprived of such facilities. Couples now prefer to have limited children. Generally, the women get sterilized. Most of the villages are provided with tap water. Some have expanded their business to towns. Radio sets are common. Television is available in the village panchayat *ghar*. The villages are electrified and the community avails itself of the facility. Firewood, cow-dung cakes, coal and kerosene oil are the main sources of energy available to the community. Public distribution system is available to the villagers. There are rural banks, but the loan is available to those who have some landed property. The community still depend on the moneylenders and shopkeepers.

PARMANAND LAL

GUMAR

The term Gumar seems to be derived from the Hindi term *kumhar*, i.e. potter. The Gumars live both in rural and urban areas of the region. Their traditional occupation has been making earthen pots of different types, such as, utensils for cooking and containers of water and other materials. They are spread all over Jammu province comprising the districts of Kathua, Udhampur, Doda, Rajouri, Punch and Jammu. They have been living in their present habitat for a long time and those who have migrated to the cities, look out for job opportunities. Their main section is Prajapati, while various subcastes among them are Manawa, Badiyal, Dafara and Dab. They speak Dogri and write in the Arabic and Devanagari scripts. A few of them can also read and write in the Roman script. The Gumar do not have any separate ethnic dress and conforms to the local Dogri attire. They live in hot and humid climate, with predominently thick forest cover and medium rainfall.

The Gumars are vegetarians, though they eat meat occasionally. Those who eat meat also consume eggs, fish, fowls, mutton, and pork but refrain from beef. Their staple food is wheat and occasionally rice. They consume cereals and pulses of all types and use mustard oil and *ghee* (clarified butter) for cooking. They consume potatoes and all types of vegetables. Partial absence of roots and tubers in the region has restricted their consumption among these people. They make regular and adequate use of milk and milk products. They drink local variety of tea mixed with milk. Alcoholic drinks are consumed by their male members which are purchased from the local market. They smoke cigarettes and tobacco by using *hookah*. Few of them chew loose tobacco and use snuff. There has not been any significant change in their food habits except a gradual shift to non-vegetarianism.

The Gumars do not have any formal social divisions, but they are aware of the *varna* system. They are placed low in the overall hierarchy. They have not changed their surnames. They consider themselves low in status in comparison to the other communities of the region. Differentiation is on the basis of their economic status. The Gumars practise endogamy at the community level as well as within the Hindu-fold. They do not marry among their blood relations. Sororate and levirate forms of marriages are not prevalent. Observence of marriage symbols is not essential among their women, though toering, earring, nose stud and nose ring, *mangalsutra*, *bindi* and vermilion are used more for cosmetic purposes. However, most of their married women use vermilion and *bindi*. Among the Gumars, pre-puberty marriage is not practised for either sex. Marriage age for the girls and the boys is 17 years and above. Marital alliances are fixed by common friends, relatives and middlemen. Monogamy is the present norm among these people. Dowry is prevalent among them, which mainly comprises dresses, kitchen utensils and few articles of furniture. Cash transactions and gold ornaments are not, in most cases, included or demanded in dowry. Rule of residence is patrilocal and divorce is permissible with legal as well as religious approval. Divorces are mainly on account of maladjustment. Childrens' maintenance is fixed by the court if judicial separation is sought and, in such a case, their council acts as the arbitrator and both the parties have to abide by verdict. Maintenance is given to the wife and, in case the husband decides to desert her, then the children are the responsibility of father. Rules regarding remarriages are quite flexible for the divorcess and the widows.

Among the Gumar the most common form of the family is the nuclear type. Joint families have declined rapidly. Since most of them are engaged in business of various kinds, they want to pursue independent ventures, thus facilitating breaking up of joint families. Agrarian reforms have conferred individual land proprietorship to the farmers, which has also contributed to the emergence of nuclear families. Interpersonal relations are cordial among the family members and joking relations are permitted between affinal relations. Conflicts and disputes are rare among them and the ones which occur are mainly due to division of property. They follow the Hindu law of inheritance. All their male heirs get equal share of the ancestral property, to which females are also entitled. However, as a matter of tradition, the women forgo their share in favour of males. However, a few of them give equal share to the heirs irrespective of their sex. Eldest son succeeds as the head of the family. Interfamily linkages are informal and cordial. Disputes within the community are usually sorted out by the community association, failing which recourse to law may be taken.

The Gumar women live and function within the traditional social norms prevalent since centuries. They accept the supremacy and dominance of their menfolk in all spheres of life. Though they enjoy equal rights over the ancestral property, yet in most of the cases they either forgo it or are deprived of it. However, they participate in all socio-religious functions. They take part actively in farm and non-farm activities, and contribute to the household income. They act as water carriers and fuel collectors for the household, besides looking after their cattle. They utilize their leisure time in embroidery, knitting and stitching. Their participation in active politics is restricted only to casting of their votes, that too on the direction of menfolk.

The Gumars do not observe any pre-delivery rituals. Women can deliver either at their natal house or in-laws' place, though the former is preferred to the latter. Deliveries, when conducted at home, are carried out with the help of an experienced midwife (*dai*). However, where modern medical facilities or health centres are available, delivery of the babies takes place there. Few of their women go to the private or government maternity homes. Postnatal pollution of twenty-one days is observed by them, but no specific restrictions are imposed during this period. They do not have any formal naming ceremony. There are also no adolescent rites observed for either sex. Marital alliances are solicited through close relatives, friends and other community members besides the marriage brokers. Marriage ceremonies last for two days. On the wedding day after sunset, the bridegroom riding a horse with a ceremonial sword in hand comes to the bride's house along with the guests. The wedding ceremony is conducted at the bride's residence according to the Hindu tradition. The groom returns to his home along with the bride either in the early hours of the next morning or during the following midday. Feasts are given by both the parties during the marriage celebrations.

The dead is given a bath and then body is wrapped in a white coffin to be carried on a wooden bier to the cremation ground. They usually observe 13 days' death pollution. *Uthala* or *rasam-pagri* rituals mark the end of the mourning period and succession of the family head respectively. This is usually done by sporting new turban by their male members. They observe the first year death rites but thereafter no *shradhs* (annual rites) are performed by them. There have not been any significant changes in their life-cycle rituals though they have become more expensive. People of means observe these rituals with great pomp and show.

The traditional occupation of the Gumars has been that of making earthenwares especially in the vast hinterlands. Even in urban centres, a few of them are carrying on with their traditional occupation. Agrarian reforms in the state have conferred on a few of their individuals land proprietorship, thus making them a land-owning community as well, particularly in villages. They are also engaged in grain trading, retail sales in utensils including those made of aluminium and steel, supply of construction materials, petty contractorship, government and private service, etc. In villages, they are not linked to the market directly. The female also participate in the family, farm and non-farm activities, wherever required, to augment the family earnings. They also collect firewood, fetch water and look after the domestic cattle. Child labour is extensively used for family-run business or farm-related operations, but is not commercially marketed. They receive their wages in cash and kind as barter system of exchange still prevails in the rural areas. However, of late, they have diversified occupationally in all spheres of economic activities and, as such, are no longer exclusively dependent on pottery making.

Panchayats function at the village level to take care of issues concerning all those living in it. These panchayats are mainly involved in the welfare-cum-developmental works initiated by the various government agencies. Intercommunity conflicts are also resolved by the panchayats in most of the cases. However, at community level, they have the Gumar Association of Jammu & Kashmir state to which elections are held every year. They have president, vice-president, secretary and treasurer in the executive body, besides members affliated to it. They also have district level chairman who participates in the state level association. This association has taken up issues advocating anti-dowry and simplicity in marriage ceremonies that restricts the number of guests to the minimal. Welfare activities like gifting sewing machines and financial assistance to widows and the poor is also undertaken by the association. Both at the panchayat and association levels, social boycott or excommunication is affected but there is no formal system of giving awards or punishments.

The Gumars profess Hinduism. They mostly belong to the Vaish category of the *varna* system though few of them also claim to belong to the Brahman fold. They do not have clan deities, but at regional level they visit Vaishno Devi, Amarnath, Kheer Bhawani and Pirbaba. Affiliation to *pirs* and *faqirs* is common among individuals as well as families. They observe and celebrate all socio-religious festivals of the region like Shivratri, Navratras, Diwali, Rakshabandhan, Holi, Lohri and Janmashtami.

The Gumar are not specialized in plastic or graphic arts. They are however professional craftsmen in making earthenware. The oral traditions are drawn from folk songs, folklore and folk tales, based on the religious and historical events. There are no experts in fine arts, music and dance among them. However, their ladies do stitching, wool knitting and embroidery on non-commercial basis.

The Gumars accept both cooked and uncooked food from the other Hindu communities, but refrain from doing so from the Shudras. They accept uncooked food from the non-Hindus as well. They participate in all socio-religious festivals of their co-religionists. They also maintain marital relations with the Hindu communities except for those who stand lower to them in the hierarchy. They share the wells and water sources, schools, panchayat *ghars* with all the communities. They also share the cremation ground with others. They visit the shrines of *pirs* and *faqirs*, irrespective of their faith. They maintain cordial and business like relations with others and among themselves. Majority of them are agriculturists, earthenware makers and petty traders. Cultivator-labour relationship is also exists among them. They receive services of the barber, carpenters, masons. The Gumar is gradually evolving themselves to match with the socio-economic conditions prevailing in the region. They participate in the market-oriented trade and commerce in the region. Political awareness and participation is modest and limited. They do not have creative artists. However, a few doctors, engineers and administratiors have come up from among them. Few of them are teachers as well.

Formal education among the Gumar is not popular. The girls and boys usually study upto primary or secondary levels only. Very few of them pursue higher studies. Economic constraints are the main reason for high illiteracy rate among them. Boys at a young age have to start earning to sustain the family. Their attitude towards modern medicare is moderately positive and same is also the case for adopting family planning norms. Mostly, they depend on traditional medicare methods. It is their women who usually have to undergo sterilization. Usually, each couple prefers to have a minimum of three children. They have drinking water facilities within their localities. In urban areas, tap water is the main source of drinking, whereas in villages, tap water, tube wells, wells and canals are the main water sources. This community has not been benefited significantly from the welfare cum development projects sponsored by the various governmental agencies. Cooperatives and ration shops help them in procuring essential commodities and other farm-related inputs. Most of them make use of electricity for lighting and other purposes. They also use firewood and cow-dung for cooking. A negligible number of them have been benefited from the various nutritional programmes like ICDS, Anganwadi and SNP centres. They do not take loans from the moneylenders to the extent they used to do before Independence and also before seeking employment diversifications. Increasingly, banking loans are sought for the promotion of their business. They exhibit a significant tendency to save and invest. The Gumars are losing their identity as potters. Modern technology has given the consumers better choice of products of the utensils earlier purchased from them. Consequently, they suffered a setback. This has led them to seek diversification from traditional occupation. Even in making earthenware, they are facing difficulty in procuring good quality soil due to rapid urbanization which has resulted in loss of supply of the raw materials. They appear to have adapted well in the face of socio-economic changes in the economy as a whole. However, as an ethnic group, they appear to just assimilating in the broad Hindu ethos of the region.

ASOKA AIMA

HANJI

The Hanjis or Hanzas are essentially riverine dwellers, living in boats of various shapes, sizes and types in and around different water bodies of Kashmir Valley. Their origin remains a controversial point. Kalhana identifies them with the term Nishadas which got converted into *henz* in Kashmiri language. It is also reported that King Pravarsena Kashmiri (AD 112-72) brought some boatmen from Sangaldeep (Sri Lanka) to regulate riverine transport in Kashmir and the present Hanjis sprang from them.

The boat a Hanzi owns for earning his livelihood is indicative of the class to which he belongs in the hierarchy of the Hanjis. Their major concentration is in the navigable course of the Jhelum river in Srinagar city, Bijbehra Khanabal, Avantipora, Sopore, Sumbal, Baramula, Pampore, Shadipur and Shalateing. They also live in Wular, Anchar, Dal Lake and in the localities such as Navpora, Chinar Bagh and Kralyar in the vicinity of Dal Lake. Even in the city of Srinagar, the Hanjis live along the river banks in Amira-kadal, Habba-kadal, Zamina-kadal, Kayria-kadal, Zero bridge, and Safa-kadal. They move from one place to another along the water-bodies in the Valley. The natural environment of the Valley is cold.

The Hanji have various subgroups and the stratification is essentially on the basis of occupational pattern. The subgroups include Dun Hanz, Gas Hanz, Mak Hanz, Bachi Hanz, Gad Hanz, Shali Hanz, Houseboat Hanz, Phear Hanz and Mat Hanz. They are also known as the *kishti-bash* or (boat dwellers) and perceive their identification at the local level. Living around water bodies, they are settled in the plains that experience heavy snowfalls. Language spoken within the family and with the kin groups is Kashmiri and the script used is Arabic. Of late, the Hanjis, connected with tourism can speak in English and correspond in the Roman script. There are no identification markers exclusive to these people as they, by and large, conform to the dresses worn by the local Muslim population. Womenfolk of the Gad-Hanz (fishing community) can be identified by *kanvej*, which are very big earrings. They do not enjoy any special constitutional status.

The Hanjis are non-vegetarian consuming meat, eggs and fowl. Pork is not eaten. Pulses of different kinds are consumed; and *hak*, a type of leafy fresh vegetable and *nadru* (lotus root) are commonly consumed. Fruits available in the market are consumed, but they do not favour milk and milk products. Only males occasionaly take alcoholic drinks and smoke cigarette or *hookah*. The habit of chewing betel is absent though snuff is used.

Varna system is not known to the Hanji and stratification is based on occupational pattern. Houseboat owners are at the top of the social hierarchy whereas the God-Hanz are at the lowest level. They do not have a high perception of their community nor do others have so about them.

The Hanjis are essentially endogamous even at the subgroup level, but do not prohibit exogamy. Preference is usually given for seeking matrimonial alliance within one's own subgroup though this rigidity is fading away. They marry with their cousins, irrespective of the status of blood relations. Cross-cousin marriages between father's sister's daughter and mother's brother's daughter are common. Sororate and levirate forms of remarriage, though not prohibited, are not common. Monogamy is the common form of marriage with few cases of polygyny.

Pre-puberty marriages are common. Age at marriage for the girls is usually between 14 and 15 years, while for the boys, it is between 17 and 30 years. Marital alliances are negotiated by the *manzymyor* (middlemen) or by the family elders. There is no practice of bride-price but dowry both in cash and kind prevails. System of *mahr* (dower) is also prevalent, but there is no rigidity about the amount or mode of payment. It is payable on demand and can also be paid instantly. Patrilocal rules of residence after marriage predominate and divorce is permissible. Divorce is mainly due to maladjustment or cruelty. Divorce compensation is given to the wife and it is the husband who can divorce. Children are the responsiblity of the father in the event of divorce. Rules regarding remarriage are according to the Islamic laws. Divorcee and widow can remarry without any socio-religious ceremony. The *mahr* amount varies usually between Rs. 300 and 9,000.

Among the Hanjis, nuclear family is common and joint families are gradually breaking up. Avoidance exists between mother-in-law and son-in-law, and daughter-in-law and father-in-law. Frequent confrontations take place on account of property disputes and, to a lesser extent, due to challenge to the authority of elders. Interpersonal relations are cordial among the family members though joking is not permitted between consanguineous relatives. All male children have equal right in their ancestral property and the female receive lesser share than the male. The eldest son succeeds as the head of the family after the father's death. Interfamily linkage are cordial though there are conflicts between the lower graded Hanji. Offences of criminal nature are dealt with under the state law whereas social disputes are usually resolved through mutual reconciliation.

The Hanji women enjoy a secondary status compared to the men in all walks of life. They do not have unequal right over the ancestral property and do not enjoy the same standing on religious matters. Majority of the women participate in catching fish and its marketing. Womenfolk of the other Hanji sections also supplement the household income by pursuing various types of economic activities like fishing, vegetable cultivation, transportation of sand, timber and household embriodery. For most of the migratory Hanjis, women also take an active role in rowing. They have also taken to weaving of wool. However, their participation in politics is negligible. Entire household chores are attended to by the womenfolk. The Hanji women do not seem to be as submissive and docile as the womenfolk of other Muslim communities, but they neither control the family income nor its expenditure.

The woman delivers the baby either at her natal house or at in-laws' house. The delivery at home takes place with the help of an experienced *dai* (midwife). However, in urban areas, deliveries of babies take place in hospitals or maternity homes. Seven to eight days' post-delivery pollution is observed. They do not observe any child-naming ceremony but male children have to undergo the ritual of circumcision. *Aqeeqa* ceremony is performed by them. They do not observe any adoloscence rites.

Marriges among them are arranged by negotiations through family heads or the *manzymyor* (marriage broker). *Mehndi-raat* is celebrated before the wedding day. The marriage ceremony is held at the bride's place. Bridegroom's party leaves for the bride's home at night. Marriage ceremony is confirmed by *nikah*. After spending the nuptial night at the grooms's residence, the bride returns to her parent's house for a minimum of seven days. Thereafter, a messenger goes to the bride's parental house carrying with him some gifts and escorting the bride back to her in-laws house. The bride's parents give a feast to the guests accompanying the marriage party, while the bridegroom's side invite their friends and relatives. As among all the Kashmiri Muslims, the Hanjis also eat in a batch of four from a common plate. *Wathal* is a return social call by the bridegroom to his in-laws wherein he is accompanied by few selected guests. It is a post-marriage ceremony observed by the people.

The dead is given bath and draped in a white cloth. Thereafter, *fateha-khani* (religious prayers) is recited and then the dead is carried in a wooden coffin to the family's private *mazar* (burial ground), and buried in a grave according to the Islamic laws. *Jumma-fateha* is performed on the Friday following the death. Forty day mourning known as *chehallum* is observed by them. Customarily, till the day of *jumma-fateha*, relatives of the deceased family arrange food for the bereaved family. On that day, tea and bread are served to all the community members assembled at the grave of the departed soul and the same is repeated on the ritual of *chehallum* on the fortieth day. There has not been any significant change in the life-cycle rituals, though now these have become more expensive and the tendency to show off appears, especially among the neo-rich section of the Hanjis.

The major economic resources for the Hanji originate from water bodies spread all over the Valley of Kashmir. A few of them own agricultural plots for growing vegetables. Such landowners are known as the Hak-Hanz. Fishing in rivers and lakes is another activity restricted to the Gad-Hanz only. The families engaged in extracting weeds and grass from the lakes to sell as fodder are known as the Has-Hanz. Those involved in renting out their boats to serve as ration depots are known as the Shali-Hanz. Those who supply sand collected from the riverbed and supply of timber for construction are known as Bachi-Hanz. The Hanjis who carry and supply earthen pots are known as the Mat-Hanz, while those who trade on their *shikara* (small boats) are called the Phere-Hanz. The Hanz who own house-boats are involved with the local and foreign tourism trade and are the most prosperous ones. Doonga-Hanz are those who live in small to medium sized boats permanently around different water bodies and are engaged in trade, service and other activities. In fact, economic activities pursued by the Hanjis have created various hierarchies among them. Hunting and gathering fish, labour, trades related to sand and timber supply for construction, weeds and grass collection, growing vegetables on floating garden on the lakes have been the traditional occupations of the Hanjis. However, tourist house-boats, business, government service, private service, tourist trade and house-hold weaving and embriodery, transport, carpet weaving, shawl weaving, boat making, carpentry, rope-making, blacksmithy, tailoring and handicrafts are some of the recent occupations. They have direct and indirect links with the market and have a fully regulated market system with daily/weekly/fortnightly and monthly forms. Cash transactions predominate all other forms of business transactions. Being an essentially landless community with the exception of Hak-Hanz, the mode of payment of wages is essentially on cash basis. Child labour exists among the Hanjis, and is employed for rowing of boats.

The Hanjis do not form a homogeneous group having centralized mechanism for social control. In fact, different classes of the Hanjis have their own separate social organization. Conflicts, quarrels and divorce cases are resolved within the community. Cases related to adultery, rape and theft are decided by the state law. Social boycott, punishment or awards are not prevalent among these people.

The Hanjis are predominantly Sunni Muslims with a small group of them belonging to the Shia section. They visit Hazratbal shrine, Makhdum Sahib, Rishi Peer, Pir Dastgir and Shah Hamdan. At the local level, affiliation to individual *pir* or family *pir* exists. Fasting during Ramzan and pilgrimage to Mecca to perform *haj* are religious obligations performed by them. They observe all the Muslim festivals like Id-ul-Fitr, Id-ul-Zuha and Ramzan. They also participate in the local fairs like Nauroz, Shab-e-Meraj, Friday following Shab-e-Meraj, Shab-e-Qadr, Jumat-ul-Vida, Urs Shah Hamdan, Urs Sheikh Nooruddin Sahib, etc.

The Hanjis have not specialized in plastic or graphic arts. There are no professional craftsmen, but carpet weaving and other handicrafts are being developed within the community. Hand embriodery is popular among the women. The community has oral traditions, which are derived from the religious text and some are based on local events and history. They learn religious verses from the *maulvis* (learned persons). The community does not have experts in fine arts, music and dance. Mat weaving is common among the poorer Hanjis.

The Hanjis accept both cooked and uncooked food from the other Muslim communities. There is no restriction on acceptance of uncooked food from the non-Muslims. They participate in all the socio-religious festivals of the co-religionists. They normally refrain from eating from the hands of non-Muslims. They do not maintain marital relations with most of the other Muslim communities with few exceptions. They share common burial grounds with other Muslims communities though, normally, burial grounds are reserved and privately owned. They maintain cordial and business-like relationship with other communities. The Hak-Hanz are essentially an agricultural community, while the houseboat owners have joined tourism, carpet and handicraft trade. A small number of the Hanjis are now employed in the government services as well as in the police and defence services. They also perform services of barber, carpenter, masons, etc. The community is gradually envolving into a more organized participative and market-oriented community. Since the Hanjis are predominently a service rendering community, they try to develop more professional approach towards their respective trade. Political awareness is also gradually developing among them. Though they do not have entrepreneurs, doctors, engineers or even administrators, with few exceptions, they are modernizing and seeking new avenues of business especially related to tourism.

Formal education is becoming popular among them. Literacy rate among females is low, while among the males, it is around 20 per cent. Imparting formal education is viewed favourably. The girls usually study up to primary or secondary level and the boys even reach upto higher levels. The reason for not pursuing higher education in case of boys is the economic constraints and the need to support their family. Girls are discouraged from seeking formal education due to social reasons. Though their attitude is favourable towards modern medicare, they are not fully making use of them. They still do not react favourably towards family planning. The average family size is between nine to twelve persons. They avail both modern and traditional medicare. Generally, it is the women who get sterilized. They do not have adequate drinking water facilities within their vicinity. Only those who are permanently stationed at a particular place now get tap water for drinking. Even now their main water sources are rivers and lakes. They are not covered under any of the rural development programmes and are essentially self-employed in fishing, weaving, vegetable cultivation, household crafts, transport and trading in general merchandise. The Hanjis who are permanently stationed along the river banks and lakes use electricity for lighting. They use firewood and cow-dung cakes as fuel for cooking. Most of them are landless. A few of them have availed of the nutrition programmes through ICDS, Anganwadi and SNP centres. The majority of them are getting rations through public distribution system. For developing their respective trades, the Hanjis are now gradually seeking financial assistance from the government. Now the Hanjis are trying to acquire landed property and have, in fact, started construction of lodges around the Dal, Nagin and Anchar lakes. They still borrow from the traditional moneylenders and shopkeepers. Their attitude towards savings is favourable.

INDU AIMA

JAIN

About four or five decades back, the Jains were called Bhavra, and the name Jain was not much in use for the community. The term Jain was used only to refer to their religion. But now, the community exclusively calls themselves Jain and others also address them by the same name. The term Bhavra has almost gone out of use in Jammu region. Even a market which was called Bazaar Bhavra for the last few centuries where they had established shops and trade since their arrival in this town, has now been changed to Jain Bazaar. The etymology of the word 'Bhavra' is not very certain, yet it is believed that it is the corrupted form of *bhao-bhala*, from *bhao* (motive) and *bhala* (good), i.e. 'those of good intent'. Their chief aim is not to injure any living creatures and to attain *nirvana* or peace. Jain is a generic term for all those who belong to the Jain sect, which arose out of Brahmanism by a religious movement probably in the sixth century BC by a Jina (spiritual conqueror) named Parsvanath. The religion so formed was reformulated by Mahavira, a contemporary of Gautam Buddha. The Jains being the followers of Jina, the word Jina is derived from the Sanskrit root *ji* 'to conquer', hence, Jain means 'conquer'. The community is divided into two groups: Swetambara and Digambara, the latter being the older and original group. The Oswal Banias are the principal section, which follows the Swetambara doctrine. The priests or religious men among them are of two classes *sadhus* and *yatis* or *jatis*. The remaining Jains are called the Saraogis.

Presently, as in the past, the Jains being a rich trading community live in big towns like Jammu, Srinagar, Doda and Udhampur, and only some families are scattered in a few more small towns. In the beginning of this century, their number in this state was limited.

The Jains of this state do not have any language of their own nor any script. They usually speak the dialect of the region they inhabit, for instance, they speak Dogri at home and with others in Jammu, Kashmiri in Srinagar and Punjabi in areas predominated by the Punjabi speaking population. They also speak and write Hindi and English when necessary. They use Devanagari script and Hindi language for correspondence and trade. The Jains do not wear any distinctive dress or marker except for their *sadhus* or *jatis*. Like the other Hindu communities, they usually go bareheaded, and put on the local Dogra or Western dress.

Their *sadhus* go bareheaded, and put on spiked shoes, wear white *dhoti* and *kurta* by the Swetambara and coloured garment by the Digambaras, who sometimes go half-naked, tie a cloth to cover their nose and carry *chauri* over their shoulders. They always keep their heads shaven.

The Jain are purely vegetarian out of religious conviction. They do not take meat or any diet involving destruction of any living creatures, such as honey. The use of liquor is forbidden. Their chief tenet is not to injure any living creature, so they follow the principle of *ahimsa* in every sphere of life. Among the Jains, therefore, it is a strict rule that no flesh or intoxicant should ever be touched. Wheat and rice form their staple food. They consume pulses, beans and vegetables, and use oils, *ghee* and butter as the cooking medium. Except for alcoholic drinks, they have no reservation for any drink, home-made or commercially prepared. *Sharbats*, aerated peprations, *lassi* and milk are freely used by them. They use milk and all other preparations of milk and dairy products, though these may be avoided by the *sadhus* among them. Like the other Hindu communities, the Jains observe *vrats* (fasts) and, on such occasions, they abstain from taking their normal food in normal form and may take only fruit or simply go without food, or take any item speical for the occasion. The ascetics (*jatis*) among them never eat or drink in the dark in order to avoid destruction of insect life.

There are two main socio-religious divisions of the Jain community, namely Swetambara and Digambara. This division was chiefly based on differences of faith regarding the dress. The Digambaras worship naked idols and their *sadhus* also remain naked; the Swetambara ascetics wear white garments and their idols are also clad in white clothes. The Swetambara were further subdivided into Bis-tolas and Tera-panthis. The Bis-tolas revered the 32 *sutras* of Mahavir, but the Tera-panthis have scriptures of their own consiting of 52 verses (*slokas*). The Digambars were also bifurcated into two divisions: Bis-panthis and Tera-panthis. The Bis-panthis revered the 24 *arhats*, the guru and *shastras*, while the Tera-panthis deny that there is any guru and save the *shastras* themselves. The Bis-panthis are orthodox Digambaras who worship standing before naked idols and refuse to burn lamps before them. At present, the Jains of Jammu & Kashmir are subdivided into three separate groups namely, the Sithaneek-basi, Murti-puji (idol-worshippers) and Tera-panthi. Most of the Jain *sadhus* and *saraogis* are recruited from the various groups of the Banias, such as Aggarwal, Oswal, Shrimal and Khandelwal, the last three of whom were also called Bhavras. Thus, the Jains also observe caste system to some extent. These castes or subgroups serve as a sort of endogamous units. The Jains are considered among the high class and wealthy people of the society of Jammu region and the Hindus equate them with the third *varna*, i.e. the Vaishya. No doubt they themselves also claim Kshatriya origin. They, being a wealthy and leaders in local trade, are held in high esteem by all the other communities and they themselves are conscious of such status. In the society, their role against violence in any form and their liberal charities for common welfare are much appreciated. In Jammu & Kashmir, no change of religion is known to have taken place among the Jains, nor was there any socio-religious movement among them. No marked change is noticeable among them except that they now behave more like the other Hindu communities and have become modernized in their living and profession, though they strictly stick to their dietary rules.

The marriage rules of the Jain are similar to those of the Hindus with minor variations. Marriage once solemnized is considered indissoluble. With the legalization of divorce, slight change in ideals have occurred, but the incidence of divorce is rare among them. The usual age at marriage is above 20 years. They have never been in favour of child marriage. In the case of boys, marriages may take place even at the age about 30 years. The accepted mode of marriage is through negotiation between the contracting parties, i.e. the parents or guardians of the boy and the girl. When negotiations mature, the consent of the boy and girl is secured in some form by arranging a meeting between them. Then the boy is reserved through the *thaka* ceremony, which culminates into *kurmai* (betrothal). The only from of marriage current among them is that of negotiated marriage. Sometimes, marriage through choice or love may also take place. Some preliminary ceremonies take place at the bridegroom's house a few days before the marriage. On the fixed day, the bridegroom arrives at the bride's house accompanied by the marriage party. Marriage ceremonies take place at the bride's house on the *vedi* in front of sacred fire. Usually, the services of a Brahman are taken for the performance of the rites. Then *pheras* (circumambulation) takes place. The marriage party is feasted and returns the same night leaving behind the bridegroom for further rites. Dowry may consist of both kind as well as cash to the convenience of the bride's parents. Marriages are performed at the bride's house. The symbols of marriage are *sindoor* (vermilion), *bindi*, red bangles, *nath* (nose ring), and finger ring. Earlier, divorce and remarriage were not permitted; now divorce takes place but rarely, remarriage of widow is permitted if she is very young or has no support. The only change visible in the institution is that some rites have been cut down or simplified, and new provisions of the Hindu Code have been introducted.

The Jain family is patriarchal and usually extended, nuclear, and sometimes mixed. Cordial relations exist between the young and elder members of the family. The elders are venerated, obeyed and usually feared. Joking relationship exists between brother-in-law and sister-in-law. Conflict within the family seldom occurs and confrontation of the youngers and elders is also never heard of. The relations with other families are always cordial. Inheritance of family property is in the male line and followed by the Hindu law of inheritance. Now female members too have a right of share in parental property under the new startutory provisions. But according to the Jammu & Kashmir state constitution, a girl married outside the state loses state citizenship and forfeits the right to immovable parental property. After the death of the father, usually mother, if alive, succeeds and, in her absence, the elder son becomes the head of the family. In case of division, all brothers get equal share in the ancestral property, both movable and immovable. A widow too gets her share, but if she remarries, she loses that right. No new changes in the family set-up and rules of inheritance and succession have occured.

Women are held in high esteem in the Jain community. They have the right of inheritance. They get education. Some of them have received high education and occupy high government posts. They are administrators, doctors and advocates. In middle class families, women have little role to play in the economic shpere except those who have entered any job or profession. However, in family management, they are unsurpassed. Few women earn money through domestic craft, like weaving or knitting. They participate in all types of social and religious function equally with the men.

Among the Jains, childbirth is usually an occasion of rejoicing, particularly when the child happens to be a boy. First five days after the childbirth are observed as pollution days. On the fifth day, both the baby and the mother are administered a bath of purification. On the thirteenth and twenty-first day after the birth, some rituals are performed and, on the twenty-first day, the child is taken out of the house for the first time. The mother starts doing all types of domestic work after that day. Naming ceremony is not performed. Some people do not perform even the *mundan* ceremony as a social function. They simply take the child to the barber and get his hair cut without any ceremony. But some of them perform *mundan sanskar* according to the *shastras* and hold celebrations on this occasion, to which they invite their relatives and friends. Wearing of sacred thread is no longer prevalent among them. Marriage takes place usually after the age of 20 years and, in this ceremony, almost all the rituals of a Hindu marriage are gone through, commencing with *thaka*, *kurmai* and *sagan* and culminating in *phere* round the sacred *vedi* fire. Consummation of marriage takes place at the house of the groom's parents. The Jains are strictly monogamous. Dowry is practised, but it is never demanded but is left to the free will of the bride's parents. In performance of the *vedic* rites, usually the services of the Brahman are sought.

The Jain death rituals are the most simplified affair. The *arthi* (bier) of the dead is carried to the cremation ground in the form of a procession. No particular rituals are performed for the *arthi* at the cremation ground. The dead body is burnt on a pyre of wood. They share cremation ground with the other Hindu communities. On the second or third day, the burnt bones are gathered in a *kalas* (vessel). This ritual is called *uthala*. The *kalas* is not taken to Haridwar, but is immersed into a local river. After *uthala*, no other death rituals are performed. There is no fixed tenure of mourning period. It may last so long as relatives come for condolence.

The Jains of Jammu & Kashmir state is basically a trading community, who have so far nothing to do with land and agriculture. They claim that in Rajasthan some of their relatives are agriculturists but, in this state, they are non-agriculturists and a landless community. The chief occupation of the community is trade and shopkeeping. This is their traditional as well as present occupation. In addition to this primary occupation, they have now adopted the subsidiary occupation of service. Most of their youngers get higher technical, vocational and general education and training, and they prefer to join the government services, professional and technical jobs. Some of them are in the state as well as in central government administrative and medical services. There are administrators, political leaders, teachers, lawyers, doctors, finaniciers, jewellers and bankers among them and the remaining of them run cloth or general merchandise shops. A few families are in the industrial field and run factories. Thus, their dependence on the market is but natural. Their form of exchange is cash. They pay wages in cash whenever they employ labour. After Independence, the only change visible in economic field among them is that they have adopted service also as their occupation to which they were formerly indifferent.

In industry and trade, they are employing the latest technology and have discarded their age-old traditional system.

For the purpose of social control, the Jains have formed an organization called Jain Sabha with its headquarters at Jammu city. It is formed of members from various localities and its officer-bearers are president, vice-president, secretary and treasurer. This *sabha* lays down rules of social behaviour, rites and rituals for the Jain *biradari*, which the whole community faithfully observes. Some form of *prayashchit* (punishment) is imposed on non-conformers, but such cases occur rarely. The religious and moral tenets are prescribed by their *sadhus* and other religious leaders. The *sabha* guides and controls their social pattern, which mostly corresponds in many respects to that of the other Hindu communities, excepting a few rituals and customs. The community remains unaffected by modern statutory councils. However, it is fully responsive to the latest legislation on marriage and inheritance like other constituents of the Hindu community. In Jammu & Kashmir, there are only a couple of Jain temples where there are images of one or more of their *Tirthankaras*; before them the worshippers place candles, incense and flowers; hymns of praise are chanted in their honour. They go on pilgrimage to the places sacred to their memory, such as the temples of Abu. They also go on pilgrimages to the Hindu sacred places like Vaishno Devi shrine, Varanasi, and participate in the Hindu fairs and festivals. The existence of Hindu gods is accepted, and some of these, which are connected with the legends of their saints, are admitted for worship in the Jain temples. They revere the gods of origin of the *Vedas*. As a matter of faith, they revere certain saints or holy mortals whom they hold superior in stature to the gods. Though Jainism is silent about god, Jammu Jains worship Bhagwan and participate in the Hindu ways of worship and visit the Hindu temples with reverence. They do not employ the Brahmans for any of their *sanskaras*, religious rites and functions. For that purpose, they employ their own religious persons. They lay great stress on the preservation of animal life.

As a community, the Jains of Jammu & Kashmir do not practise any art and craft. Professionally they are traders and shopkeepers. However, some of the families have adopted the jeweller's trade and hence some of them are adept in the art of ornament making. They do not have folk songs or oral traditions. They do not indulge in singing on religious festivals. However, on social functions like marriages and birth, they sing and dance like the other Hindu communities. Being an exclusively urban community, they prefer the latest music and songs of the Hindi cinema.

As financiers, traders and *sahukars* (shopkeepers), the Jains came in contact with all sections of the society since their arrival in Jammu. They have, therefore, a long tradition of close intercommunity linkages. Their commensal norms were similar to those of the Hindu community. They did not accept water or food from the fourth *varna* and Muslim communities in accordance with their conception of the principle of *ahimsa.* Connubial relations were rare and that too were with the trading Hindu communities. They shared wells and other water resources with all other communities which commensurated with their ideal of *ahimsa. Jajmani* (patron-client relationship) do not exist among them. In modern times, some change in their linkages with other communities have taken place. The attitude of untouchability towards the Shudra group and Muslims, which was previously observed, is no longer practised. In matters of exchange of food and water also, some liberal attitude has developed. They participate in all types of political activities and local and public functions. They have made their contribution to various political movements in this state and continued to play its role even today. They own large houses and mansions which they let out to others on rent. They have set up factories and trading houses. Hence landlord-tenant and employer-worker relationships exist in the community. They come in contact with other communities as suppliers of goods and as customers at all levels and, as financiers, they have closer links with other commercial groups and communities. This type of relationship is perhaps more vital in their case.

The Jains are alive to its educational needs and draws full benefit of such facilities provided by the state and union governments. They are getting all types of higher education at college and university levels and also go in for technical and vocational training. They get benefit of the health and medical care facilities available through the government and private agencies. The community has shown keen interest in the family welfare programmes and adopted various family planning methods available. Being an urban community, they do not benefit by the rural employment schemes, but they have made use of self-employment schemes offered by the government agencies. Majority of the community members are engaged in self-employing businesses. They make an extensive use of all kinds of media and communications like radio, television, newspapers, roads, and posts and telegraph system. They use electricity in their homes, shops and business premises for the purpose of lighting, heat and energy. They also use cooking gas and electric cooking ranges in their kitchens. Of course, before the introduction of cooking gas firewood was extensively used as fuel for cooking, heating and energy purposes. Coal was also used and is still used to some extent. Sawdust is also in use in some families. Banking facilities in various forms are available to them which they use for their business and domestic purposes, and for savings and investment. Facilities of the public distribution are also available to them in common with the other inhabitants of the towns. On the whole their attitude towards the development plans and family planning and health programmes is favourable.

ANITA K. BILLAWARIA

JANGAM

The Jangam trace their origin to a place called Chirani in the Udhampur region of Jammu. They seek alms from people by singing and reciting *Shiva Vivah Katha*, a narration of the marriage of Lord Shiva, every day by roaming from place to place. The word Jangam according to the mythological version is derived from two words *Jang*, thigh of Lord Shiva, and *amh*, part of the thigh. In other words, they believe that they have been created by Lord Shiva from the flesh of his thigh on the eve of his hundred and eighth marriage. According to them reference to history of their origin can be found in *Shiv Puran* and the book called *Shiv Vivah*. The Jangams, therefore, are the people who normally move in a group of three to five singing *Shiv Vivah kathas*, i.e. the song about the wedding ceremony of Lord Shiva and Parvati. They perceive their distribution at medium range, i.e. they are found in the states of Gujarat (Rann of Kachch) and Haryana, besides Jammu region. They have ethnographic accounts about their origin and history to which references are cited in the *Jati Puran*, but there is no such literature available at the moment. The *gotras* they have are Tanwar, Mamar, Chouhan, Gutam and Koushal. Surnames used by them are Daru, Shivmool, Langouch, Shiv-leeg, Gupt, Shil, Mool. They speak Urdu and Haryanvi among themselves and with others they speak in Urdu and Hindi. They correspond in Hindi and English. The Jangam wear a formal saffron dress while seeking alms. Besides they use *mukat* (crown), a symbol of Lord Shiva, *Nag* (replica of a Cobra), *kanandhul* (earrings) symbolizing Goddess Parvati and *ghanti* (hand bell). They can be easily identified by their dress. Thus, each part of the robe is symbolic of *isht devs* (deities) i.e. *mukat* of Lord Shiva, *kalangi* of Lord Vishnu, nag of Lord Shiva, *kanandhul* of Goddess Parvati and *ghanti* of Nandikeshwar.

The Jangams are pure vegetarians and abstain from eating meat of any kind. Wheat and rice are their staple food. The medium of cooking is mustard oil and *ghee*. Green vegetables are consumed by them regularly. Sweet tea is drunk a number of times in a day. Though they deny drinking alcohol, they are reportedly taking it. They also consume opium and *bhang* (hemp), as it is believed that Lord Shiva consumes it. Rice is now preferred to the traditional *roti* (unleavened bread). They use *cheroot* or *hookah* for smoking.

The Jangams do not have any formal differentiation on the basis of hierarchy. They are aware of the *varna* system and perceive themselves low in the social order. In the overall hierachical system, the Jangams are considered lower in order than the other communities. Monogamy is generally followed. Marriage alliance is not sought among the blood relations. There is no restriction in seeking alliance within the broad Hindu community-fold. Since most of them are not natives of the region, marriage alliances are not made with the local co-religionists. However, marriages are settled through friends and relatives and also with the help of marriage brokers. Demand for dowry is a common norm though quantity or quality of the same is not insisted upon. There are no strict rules about marriage symbols for the women. Residence is patrilocal after marriage. Incidence of divorce are few. Bigamy is prohibited and remarriage is permissible. Age at the marriage is mostly above 20 years. Families are slowly breaking up into nuclear families. Elders are given due regard. Joking relationship exists among them except for observance of a formal relationship between the daughter-in-law and father-in-law. Close interfamily linkages in terms of rendering of reciprocal physical labour and mutual economic exchanges portray them as a closely knit community. Primogeniture is not strictly adhered to; the eldest male issue succeeds his deceased father. Their main source of income is from alms given by the people. However, those who are in the government and private service sector go in groups to seek alms after the office hours. Of late, they have started to seek occupational diversification mostly by joining the government services and petty trade and commerce. Women have a right in the parental property but they do not necessarily get it or demand it. Their women have no direct role in the management of family affairs or decision-making. They do not contribute to the family earnings and enjoy a secondary status to their menfolk. Childbirth takes place at the parental house or in a maternity hospital. *Mundan* ritual is performed for their male children. They observe pre-delivery restictrions and post-delivery pollution of seven to twenty-seven days depending on the birth stars of the child. *Annaprashan* (first feeding of cereals) is observed by them. Marriage rituals are performed at the bride's residence. Feast is given by both the families in marriage. Nuptial ceremony is performed at the groom's residence. The dead are given a ceremonial bath and then cremated.

The Jangams are a marginal landholding community and that too in their native place of Haryana and Rajasthan. Individuals hold land ownership titles. A few of them are employed in the government service, trade and self employment, which are secondary occupations. Market is fully regulated and the community is fully dependent on it. Payment to labourers is made both in cash and kind. They have a traditional caste *sabha* which is more of an advisory body dealing with day to day problems faced by the community. Statutory panchayats have no significant part to play in the affairs of the community.

The Jangams profess Hindu religion. There are no family dieties, though at the clan level they have a deity. Individual and family affiliation to *pirs* and *faqirs* prevails among them. They visit the shrines situated within the state and outside. Sawan Shivratri is celebrated as Goddess Parvati's birthday whereas Shivratri in the month *Phagun* marks the wedding of Lord Shiv and Goddess Parvati. They also celebrate the other Hindu religious festivals. Handicraft is practised by some young girls and ladies occasionally. They have rich oral traditions in the form of folkore, folk tales and folk songs. They use bell and *damru* while seeking alms from people by reciting narration of *Shiv-Parvati Vivah*.

The Jangams accept and exchange food and water from all other communities as they depend on alms. Marriages are performed only with the co-believers, irrespective of their ethnic identity. They share cremation ground with others. They participate in traditional festivals. Patron-client relationship exists among them. The community has a small number of people who are employed in white-collar jobs.

The Jangam's attitude towards the developmental programmes is positive. They are in favour of small family. Schemes of employment and self-employment through bank loan is partially availed of. They use all modern media of communication and avail modern media facilities. They avail the irragational facilities through canals, wells and tube wells besides making use of chemical fertilizers. Facilities of public distribution system are availed of by them. Their attitude towards savings is favourable. They have formal caste *sabha*, which collects all offerings and alms at a central place and then distribute them equally among individual group members. In the region of Jammu, they live in temples or *deras* in groups while their families stay at their native places. In this region, they live without their families and visit them periodically. They have now constructed two or three buildings for their stay in Jammu. They still pursue their traditional occupation as the singers of hymns of Lord Shiva and Goddess Parvati and the narration of the divine wedding.

INDU BALA DHAR

JARAL

The Jarals are Muslim Rajputs living mainly in Rajouri district. Their traditional occupation is cultivation and tending buffaloes, sheep and goats. The Jaral Rajputs were the rulers of Rajouri state for centuries. They adopted Islam during the invasion of Mohammad Ghori. It is also mentioned that a major section of the Jaral Rajputs adopted Islam during the Mughal rule in India. According to another tradition based on Fouq and supported by Narsinh Dass, the Jarals got their name from Raja Jaisar Rao, who was the eighth descendant of Raja Parikshit, the grandson of Arjuna. The fifth descendant, Raja Neel Singh, along with his followers, adopted Islam during the invasion of Mohammad Ghori. According to another story, Emperor Akbar, while returning from Multan with a large retinue of army, halted near a settlement of *jaal*, weavers. Impressed by their art, the king offered to marry one of the Jaal girls. It is said that the present Jaral community originated from that union.

Their villages are found on the hill ranges of moderate elevation overlooking the Barot, Kalali Jamole and Ramgarh tributaries of the river Chenab. The climate is cold with occasional snowfall from December to March. The region has thin forests. The communities living in the neighbourhood of the Jaral are the Domal, Basith, Thakur, Gujjar, Brahman, Nai, Bhagat and Mahashe. The Jarals live in houses made of stone, mud and wooden planks. The roof is flat and made from wooden poles covered with leaves and plastered with mud. Every house has a cattle shed and a verandah in front of the house. Dogri is the *lingua franca* of the community. With others they speak in Urdu. The script used by them is Arabic. They dress themselves like the other Muslim communities. The men wear *salwar*, *kameez* (shirt) and a turban. The woman dress themselves in *salwar*, *kurta* and *dupatta*. The Jaral men keep beard and moustache. They are listed as an economically and educationally backward class in the state.

The Jarals are non-vegetarion, but do not eat beef. Their staple diet is maize. They also eat wheat, rice and millets like *jowar* and *bajra*; pulses, such as, *moong*, *masur*, *rajmah*, beans, *rongi* and *urad* are consumed. Mustard oil is the cooking medium. Roots and tubers consumed are potato, onion, turnip, radish, *banda*, *arwi* and ginger. They take only non-alcoholic drinks due to religious considerations.

They take tea, milk and milk products as common drinks. They smoke *bidis*, cigarettes and loose tobacco. Fruits generally taken are apples, pears, apricots, oranges and bananas. Changes have been observed in their food habits. The village dwellers prefer to sell their sheep, goats and chicken in the market for money rather than slaughtering them for consumption.

There are no social divisions within the Jaral community. The Jaral belongs to a *khandan* (lineage) within which there are *kumbas* (families). Each family keeps a *shajra* (geneology) of its own. Differentiations, if any, are due to occupations, education, territory and economic status. It regulates the marriage alliances. There are no surnames. The titles common among the community are Mirza and Yusuf, which are affixed after the names. The community's self-perception at the regional level is of middle rank and they belong to the Sheikh Muslim category. Others consider them equal to the Domals.

The community is endogamous. Marriages outside the community are rare, as such instances of hypergamy and hypogamy are not found. Cousin marriages are preferred. Consanguineous marriages among the brother's and sister's childern are allowed. Consanguinity with cross-cousins, particularly Father's Sister's Daughter, Mother's Brother's Daughter and maternal uncle-niece, is avoided. Marriage with the wife's younger sister is allowed only after the death of the wife. Levirate remarriage is allowed. Marriage takes place after adulthood. Child marriage was prevalent in the past, but it is no more found now. Spouses are acquired by negotiation. Marriage by exchange of sisters also prevails in the community. Monogamy is the usual form of marriage. According to the Islamic law, a man is allowed to marry four times. There are few instances of polygyny in the community. A second and third wife is taken only due to barrenness. A second wife is brought with the consent of the first wife. Divorce is generally avoided. There is no marriage symbol for married women. At the time of marriage, the amount of dower, *mahr*, is fixed according to the status of the families involved in a marriage. The agreement of *nikah* and *mahr* is verbal. The *maulvi* (priest), in the presence of ten persons from either side, presides over the ritual of *nikah* and declares the amount of *mahr* which can be demanded any time by the bride. After the marriage the bride goes to live with her husband and in-laws. Generally, the son makes a new residence for himself after marriage. This is necessary for looking after the cultivated fields which are scattered on the hill slopes. The houses are made in the midst of the cultivated fields. In case, where there are only daughters, the father may keep the husband of the eldest daughter as *khanadamad* to look after the property. Divorce is permissible, but rarely pracitised in the community. In case of barrenness, the husband may bring a second and even third wife without divorcing any of them. He may keep all the wives at separate places. Divorce is done in exceptional cases. The husband may divorce his wife due to barrenness, maladjustment, chronic disease and insanity. The wife can also seek separation due to impotency, cruelty and inability to bear the family expenses. In case the husband seeks a divorce, then he has to pay the *mahr* to the wife. But when the wife seeks separation, she has to forego *mahr*. Children are the responsibility of the father in cases of divorce. Cases of divorce are rare. Widow, widower and divorcee remarriages are permissible. If the bride, soon after the marriage, becomes widowed, then she can marry the younger brother of her deceased husband if they are of matching age, otherwise the wife may go to her parents and get married. A widow with children prefers to stay in the house of her husband. Similarly, the widower with children prefers to marry the younger sister of his deceased wife because she can look after the children of her deceased sister. Changes observed in marriage rules are an increases in the age of marriage and decrease in the incidence of polygyny. Among the Jarals, the families are generally extended both vertically and horizontally. The married sons live in separate houses and away from the parents but the ownership of the property rests with the father. The sons also perform their obligations towards the parents. The women do not observe *purdah*, and perform all the outdoor work with menfolk. Avoidance relationships are observed between the mother-in-law and son-in-law, daughter-in-law and father-in-law and between the younger-brother's wife and the husband's elder brother. In fact, a new bride in the village avoids all the elderly members of the village. She turns her face to the other side when encountered by any elderly person of the village. Joking relationship exists between the elder brother's wife and husband's younger brother, with the wife's elder and younger sisters and with wife's elder and younger brothers. Conflict and confrontation arise on matters of landed property. Conflict also arises between the mother-in-law and the daughter-in-law. The son may demand to separate his share of the landed property and cattle. The rule of inheritance is from father to son. According to the new rules, the daughters have a share in the father's property. It is usually given at the time of marriage. Rule of succession is in the male line. In case of only daughters, the daughter's son inherits the property. Change observed in the family since

Independence is an increase in the formation of nuclear families. The Jaral women play important role in the family and outside. In agricultural operations except ploughing and mud-crushing, the women have a role in sowing, manuring, irrigating and harvesting the crops. They tend the cattle and milk the buffaloes, collect cow-dung and fuel from the forest. They bring potable water from the springs. The women make things for domestic use such as baskets, ropes, woollen caps and sweaters. They attend the rituals connected with birth, marriage and death. Even then, their status is inferior to the men. The men are allowed to keep more than one wife. The women do not get a share in the father's property, although by law, they have equal right in the property. The women, generally, do not work on wages. The family expenses are controlled by the men only.

A pregnant woman is restricted from doing arduous jobs such as bringing potable water from the streams, tending the cattle and bringing head loads of firewood or harvested crops. The birth of the child takes place in the house and only in complicated cases, she is taken to the hospital. After the childbirth, a pollution period is observed for forty days. On the fortieth day, the mother is given a bath. After this the mother resumes her normal domestic duties. The newly born baby is given its name according to the advice tendered by the *maulvi*, village priest. Sometimes, an elderly person of the family or of the village suggests a name for the child. *Zerakasi*, hair cutting, of the child is celebrated after the child attains the age of at least six months. Hair cutting is done by the village barber or by the local hairdresser. On this occasion, the female relatives and neighbours are invited for a feast. While the hair cutting operation is in progress, the women sing in chorus praising the qualities of the child, the skill of the barber and even his razor and other implements. After the haircut, the child is given a bath and clothed in new dress. *Khatnahal*, the circumcision ceremony, is usually performed when the child is more than two years old. It is done by the village barber. A large fowl is kept in a basketand the child is made to sit on its inverted belly. His arms and legs are held firmly by one or two persons so that the child does not make any movement when the barber applies the razor. After the circumcision, the fowl is given to the barber together with some money and *shirini*, sugar candy and cereals. The circumcision ceremoney takes place before the dawn. During the course of operation, female relatives sing in chorus. Bachelors and unmarried girls do not enjoy freedom of selecting their spouses according to their own choice. A common friend starts the marriage negotiations at the initiative of one of the parties.

The ceremonies connected with marriage start with the *gandum*, or engagement. This is followed by *doon-leij* about a month after the engagement. On this occasion, the bride's father accompanied by two or three relatives calls on the house of the bridegroom, where they are feasted. The period between this function and the actual marriage varies according to the circumstances of each case depending upon the convenience of the parties to the marriage. If during this interval, any of the four principal religious festivals takes place, the bridegroom's father sends some gifts, such as a silver bangle for the bride together with some *shirini* or sugar candy in plates. In return, the bride's father also sends some sweets with cash money. The date of marriage is announced by the intermediary in consultation with the parties concerned. The marriage ceremonies begin with *malasbehoun* in which the bride is not permitted to take any bath or to attend to any work and is kept on solid food. This continues for three days. The second ritual is *massmechravoun*, loosening of hair plaits. On the penultimate day before marriage, the female relatives are invited and served *malamenz*, dinner. The hands and feet of the bride are dyed in *henna*. The first day of marriage is called *menziraat*. Both male and female relatives are invited and served with dinner. The second day of marriage is called *yenevoul*. It starts with the presentation of a number of copper plates containing sugar candy, sugar balls, almonds and dresses and ornaments by the groom's father for the bride. On this day, a feast is served in the evening to the bridegroom and the guests accompanying him. Women keep on singing for the whole day in the house of the bridegroom and perform the rituals of ceremonial haircut and bathing of the bridegroom. The bridegroom wears new dress, a turban and a pair of new shoes. Then he, accompanied by a *barat* (marraige procession), goes to the house of the bride where the *barat* is received by bride's parents. The guests are entertained with *qahwa* and specially baked cakes. This is followed by the *nikah* ceremony, which is presided over by the *maulvi* (priest). It is not necessary that the *nikah* should take place on the day of wedding. The fixation of the date of *nikah* is determined according to the convenience of the parties. Some people celebrate this as a separate function, several months before the date of wedding. Others hold the ceremony only a day before and many others in the afternoon of the day on which the wedding is to take place. On such occasion, the bridegroom is represented by his attorney (*vakil*) and at least ten witnesses before the *maulvi*. Similarly, the bride is also represented by her attorney and ten witnesses. The priest makes enquiries from the two attorneys and their witnesses to confirm that the authority has been given and that the marriage bond would be governed by the conditions which he has announced before the audience. The conditions consist of the offering of jewellery, clothing and payment in cash of a specified amount of *mahr*, 33 per cent of which is to be paid immediately and the balance to be paid on a future date which is left to the choice of the bride. The priest then recites certain verses from the Holy Koran. This kind of *nikah* is called *vakalatan* i.e. through attorney. The only difference of *nikah* of the Jaral and other Muslims of Kashmir Valley is that the document of *nikah* and the conditions of *mahr* is not written in the former case while it is written and signed in the latter. When the departure is announced, the bridegroom rides on a pony followed by a palanquin, in which the bride is seated. The palanquin is arranged by the bridegroom's parents and is carried by four persons. The bride stays with her husband and in-laws for seven days. During this period, she is visited by her relatives, who present gifts of cakes, sweets and walnuts. This is called *khabar*. On the seventh day, the bridegroom's father invites five to seven persons from the bride's house for dinner who, along with two or three servants, bring cooked meat and breads to the bridegroom's house. After dinner, the bride returns to her parental house. After sometime, which may vary from a week to a year, the bridegroom is invited by his in-laws, where he stays for three days and nights. This is called *phirsal*.

A dying person is asked to say or call out the name of Allah. Then a hot water bath is given to the dead person. The bath is given by a professional man called *snangor*. The body is washed three times. It is then wrapped in a piece of *kafan* (white cloth) measuring about 19 to 20 yards. The body is placed in a *taboot* (wooden coffin) and is carried to the graveyard for burial. The grave is dug by a professional *malkhosh* (gravedigger). Mourning period is observed until the following Friday, during which period people keep visiting the bereaved family to offer their condolences. On the fourth day after the death, the priest, relatives and neighbours recite verses from the Holy Koran to bless the soul of the deceased person. This ceremony is repeated on the fortieth day. The two functions are called *chaharum* and *chehllum* respectively. The only change in the life-cycle rituals is that they are being curtailed.

Agriculture is the primary occupation of the Jarals. Owing to hilly terrain, steep slopes and non-availability of irrigational facilities, agriculture is supplemented by rearing of cattle, and pursuing horticulture and forestry. Migration of the local Muslims to Pakistan and immigration of the displaced persons caused economic hardships to them. Only a few families of the Jarals are engaged in the government service. The economic condition of the community is poor. The subsidiary occupations followed by them are agricultural labour, cattle rearing, vegetable selling, priesthood, confectionery, mat-making, oil extraction, carpentry, ironsmithy and as casual labourers in road building. Land is the main economic source available to them. Owing to hilly terrain and steep slopes, cultivation is done after making terraces. The *nalas* (water of rivulets) is available for irrigation. The community has direct links with the market. The agricultural products, such as maize, wheat, barley, rice and pulses, are sold either to the *bania* (village grocer) or in Rajauri town. Men and women carry sheep, fowls and ducks to the market and exchange them for clothes, edible oil, sugar, salt and other items of domestic use. Changes observed in their economic activities are their employment in GREF, a road building agency in the town of Rajouri and Punch.

Formerly, the head of the *biradari* panchayat, *chaudhaury*, used to decide disputes in the community, but nowadays it has become defunct and is replaced by the statutory panchayats which are presided over by the village *pradhans* and assisted by five to ten members representing different communities of the village. The *nambardar* and *chowkidar* are its other office-bearers. The role of the statutory panchayat is to plan and implement the welfare and development activities. Disputes of criminal and civil nature are referred to the court of law. Disputes, generally, arise over land infringements and cutting of grass from the field of others. Such disputes are settled by the *pradhan*.

Saiyids are the religious specialists who perform the life-cycle rituals for the Jarals. Though *maulvies* are generally Saiyids, in case of non-availability of a Saiyid *maulvi*, any literate person from the community can perform the duties of a *maulvi*. The community observes all the major Muslim festivals like Id-ul-Zuha, Id-ul-Fitr and fasts during the month of Ramzan.

The crafts of the Jaral are basket and rope-making. The women knit woollen garments in their leisure time. Folk songs are sung by them at the time of child birth and marriage.

The Jarals live in mutual interdependence with other communities and participate on the occasions of childbirth, marriage and death. They work in the fields of the Rajputs and Brahmans as wage labourers and sharecroppers. The Jaral also render their services to other communities living in the neighbourhood. They exchange and accept food and water from all other communities except the scavengers. Intercommunity marriages of the Jarals are limited to the Domals only. They share the sources of drinking water, roads, schools, mosques and panchayat ghar with the other communities. They are paid in cash or kind for working on the fields of the Rajput and Brahman landlords (*zamindars*). Owing to illiteracy and poverty, there are no businessmen, administrators, doctors and engineers from this community. Political leadership has not emerged in this community. As a result of various development programmes, there is a marked improvement in the general social and economic conditions of the community since Independence. Primary and junior primary schools are found in practically all the villages. As a result, the boys and girls of the community are getting educated at least upto junior primary level. Facilities of higher education are available in the towns such as Rajouri and Punch. The Jaral girls study up to matriculation and some boys study up to intermediate level, but due to lack of employment opportunities, they discontinue their studies. The poor parents are unable to afford the high cost of education of their children. The villages situated close to roads are in a better position to avail of the facilities of school, dispensary and post office. The members of the community living in distant villages have to depend on the indigenous medicines. The community is aware of the family welfare programmes, but they employ their own methods of birth control.

PARMANAND LAL

JAT

The Jats are the representative cultivating caste of undivided Punjab. They are also called Jati, Get, Jaut, Jit and Jut. Some include them among the great Rajput tribes; while others hold that the Rajputs belong to the original Aryan stock, and the Jats to a later group of immigrants from the north-west, probably Scythian race. They are distributed in the whole of Punjab, Haryana, border areas (with Pakistan) of Jammu & Kashmir and in Uttar Pradesh. The climate of the area in which they live is moderate with low humidity and medium rainfall. Among themselves, the Jats speak in their own regional dialect. In Jammu & Kashmir, they speak in Punjabi and sometimes in a mixture of Dogri and Punjabi. In Jammu and Kashmir, they use Gurmukhi as their script. With outsiders, they speak in Hindi or in the local language. Majority of the Jats are Sikhs and a few of them are Hindus. They have migrated from Pakistan to India after Independence. They do not have any particular dress to differentiate them from other communities. Men of older generation use *dhoti*, *lacha*, *lungi* and *kurta*, and wear a turban. The women wear *salwar*, *chunni* and *kameez*. Nowadays, men generally wear *lungi* or *pyjama*. Young boys wear trousers and shirts, while young girls wear the traditional *salwar* and *kameez*. Those children, who go to school wear either trousers and shirts or *kurtas* and *pyjamas*. The Jats are non-vegetarian, but they do not eat beef. They eat eggs, onion and garlic. Wheat is their staple food. Maize comes next. They consume pulses such as *masur*, *urad*, *moong*, *arhar*, *chana* and *rajmah*. They relish leafy vegetables like *bathua* and *sarson*. They, generally, use vanaspati as the cooking medium. Sometimes, they cook in mustard oil. During winter, they relish baked bread made of *bajra* and *jowar* accompanied with *sarson sag*. They consume plenty of milk and milk products. During summer, *lassi* (buttermilk) is a must in their diet. There is no stigma attached with liquor. The females rarely consume liquor. They purchase the liquor from the market. In the olden days, some of them used to brew liquor. All of them except the Sikh Jat smoke *hookah*, *bidi* and cigarette.

The Jats are endogamous and maintain clan exogamy. Monogamy is the general rule of marriage and polygyny is rare. Intermarriages between the Sikh Jat and the Hindu Jat is a common practice. In reality, the Jats, irrespective of their religion, follow similar social customs and beliefs. They settle marriages by negotiation through a *nai* (barber) or a family friend, and well wishers. Junior sororate and junior levirate marriages are legitimate in their society. Wearing of green bangles and the use of lipstick are the marriage symbols of a woman. Customarily, the Jats spend large sums of money on weddings. A man can neither marry from his *patri*-clan nor that of his mother or grandmother, nor from those of his father's sister's. During marriage *havan* (sacred fire) is performed with butter, barley, sugar and sesame wood around which the bride and bridegroom take *chaonri* (circumambulation) seven times with their right hand inwards. The Jat Sikhs place the *Guru Granth Sahib*, the holy text on the *chauki*. They also perform marriage in a gurudwara. Bride-price is not given; rather the bride in given dowry by her parents. The amount of dowry varies depending on the economic condition of the bride's family. Marriage by purchase is rare. Divorce is permissable, but is rare in practice. It is granted on grounds of a adultery, insanity, barrenness of the wife by the court of law or the *biradari* panchayat. The divorced wife is compensated. The children are the responsibility of the father. Widow or widower remarriage known as *kareva* is permissible. Formerly child marriage was in practice, but now marriage takes place between the age of 18 and 20 years, respectively, in the case of girls and boys.

A few decades ago, extended form of family was prevalent in the community but, nowadays, nuclear form of family is common. They maintain avoidance relationship between mother-in-law and son-in-law; daughter-in-law and father-in-law; and husband's elder brother and younger brother's wife. Joking relationship exists between elder sister's husband and wife's younger sister; elder sister's husband and wife's younger brother; elder brother's wife and husband's younger brother. Conflict and confrontation is not appreciated, but these usually arise after the death of the father or after the marriage of a son. Among them, male equigeniture is the rule of inheritance, but, in the case of death of the father, the spinster gets a share of her father's property. Succession is by the eldest son. Both intra- and interfamily relationships are cordial. Nowadays, there is a marked decline in extended family, while there is a sharp rise in the formation of nuclear families. The Jat woman enjoy the right of inheriting the property of her husband or her father. They perform all domestic chores, tend cattle, bring fodder, and help their husbands in farm activities except ploughing. Thus they contribute to the income of the family. They also participate in socio-religious functions, but have neither any role in the social control mechanism nor enjoy higher status in the society. They have no control over the family expenditure nor do they take any part in socio-political activities.

A few pre-delivery restrictions are observed among the Jats. They take special care of the pregnant women, who are not allowed to go to the places supposed to be haunted. They do not observe any pre-delivery ritual, but, during pregnancy the women are fed with nutritious food and are not allowed to perform any heavy work. The pregnant mother is given *panjiri*, a mixture of *sonth* (dried ginger); *ajwain* (omum seeds), sugar, *desi ghee* and almonds, with the belief that this would provide extra nourishment to the expectant mother. Generally, the birth of a child takes place at the girl's parental house. After the birth of a child, the parents of the girl send a chunk of *gur* (jaggery) to her husband's house. *Laggi*, a man of low caste, carries the *gur* to convey the good news. On receiving the news, the mother-in-law goes to see the child and the mother along with the *laggi*. Gifts are exchanged between both sides. On the tenth day of the *sootak* (pollution period), the child and mother are given a bath and the friends and relatives are feasted. The mother is allowed a forty-day rest and, on the fortieth day, she is administered a bath of purification and given new dress to wear. After bath, the mother takes the child to the courtyard. She cooks food for the whole family. This ritual is known as *chauke charna*. Then she is permitted to do all the household activities. The *dai* (midwife) gets the discarded clothes of the mother and a cash gift. The Jat Sikhs give name to the child by reading a *vak* (hymn) of *Guru Granth Sahib* opening at random. This name giving ceremony takes place one and a quarter month after the birth of a child. In case of the male child, either they go to the gurdwara or arrange *akhanda path* at home and distribute *prasad*. The Hindu Jats, in case of male child, observe the *mundan* ceremony. Marriage rituals such as *vatna malna* or annointing body of the bride and the bridegroom with the paste of turmeric, oil and wheat flour, *gharoli* (filling of pitcher), *jadkatna* (to cut a twig) are observed at the house of the bridegroom, while *vatna malna* and *phera*, circumambulation, are observed in the house of the bride. The marriage is complete with a feast in which womenfolk of both the sides eat together in the house of the bridegroom after the marriage.

The dead are cremated and they observe mourning period for sixteen days. But the dead bodies of children are buried. The bier is made by the members of the *biradari*. Sons and relatives carry the bier on their shoulders to the cremation ground. The body of the deceased is wrapped in a white cloth by the son. The female relatives throw some money on the deceased during the last glance. This money is taken by a man of low caste. The bier is carried to the cremation ground, performing all the usual Hindu rituals on the way. The pyre is lit by the eldest son. Three days after the cremation, the persons who carried the bier, go to collect the ashes (*phul*) to be later immersed in the holy water at Amritsar or Hardwar. During the mourning period, they observe ancestor worship. After sixteen days, the Sikh Jats arrange *akhand path*, a continuous recitation of the Holy *Guru Granth Sahib* for seven days and arrange a great feast. The Hindu Jats also, sometimes, arrange the *akhand path* of the Holy *Guru Granth Sahib*.

Most of the Jats have land and only a few are landless. They are well-to-do farmers. Control of land is by the individual members, who owns the land. Their primary occupation is cultivation. But, nowadays, a few of them are in service, specially in defence, or as truck drivers and the like. They directly sell their agricultural produce in the market and there is no intermediary.

The Jats have traditional *biradari* panchayat to settle the intra-community disputes. In this court, they settle disputes through the *panchs* (members) and the *sarpanch* (head). The guilty are fined. The amount of fines thus collected is spent for the development of the community. The panchayat looks after the interest and rights of every member of the community. This *biradari* panchayat plays an important role and has a greater force than the statutory panchayat within the community. Generally, five wise and honest persons of the community constitute the panchayat. The disputes referred to this body are mainly related to marriage, dowry, sex crimes and divorce. The person who wants to lodge a complaint against someone approaches the *panches*, or one of the *panches*, for justice. He names his opponents and states his complaints. Then the panchayat fix up a date for hearing and passes the verdict. Punishment is given in the form of fines in cash. Sometimes, light physical punishment is also given. The role of statutory council lies in the implementation of the developmental activities of the government. It is worthy to note that the role of statutory council is not satisfactory as far as this community is concerned.

The Jats are followers of both Hinduism and Sikhism. They belive in all the Hindu gods and goddesses. The Hindu Jats also visit the gurdwara and chant the hymns of *Guru Granth Sahib*. In every household, the images of Guru Nanak, Tegh Bahadur, Sri Krishna and Lord Rama adorn the living room. They take special interest in *akhand path* of *Guru Granth Sahib*. Baisakhi is celebrated with great festivity during which the ancestors are worshipped, sweets distributed and children are dressed in new colourful clothes. Those who can afford, go to some sacred place for a holy dip. Some of them visit Amritsar on this day. They also observe Holi, Diwali and Lohri with equal zeal. After this worship, the children are given sweets. They believe in evil spirits and take special care not to visit the haunting grounds of the spirits. They also believe in evil eye. To neutralize the effect of evil eye and the spirits, they recite the *mantras* (magical words). Change of religion from Hinduism to Sikhism among the Jat is not uncommon. The Jats do not have any traditional art and craft. They do not have any folk songs of their own. They sing the folk songs prevalent in their native place before the Partition. *Bhangra* dance is favourite among them.

The Jats traditionally accept water from all the castes except from the Balmikis, Chamars, Chuhras and Muslims. Intercommunity marriage is not permitted. They share wells and other sources of water with the rest of the high caste communities. They share the cremation ground with the higher castes. The Jats are numerically and economically a most powerful community. In Jammu & Kashmir, they are not actively involved in politics and ethnic movement. Since, they are a good landowning cultivator community, they employ the agricultural labourers in their field. But the Jat would not give his land to a share cropper.

There is lack of facility for the education of Jat children. Though they are economically well-off, college education is yet to take its roots among them. Only a few boys and girls go for higher education. The boys drop out to help the family in cultivation and the girls drop out to help the family in domestic work. They are reluctant to send their daughters for higher education. They are afraid that higher education of the daughters would make it difficult to find a suitable match for them. Modern medical facilities are not available in the village, but, within reasonable distances, they have medical facilities of high order. They avail the modern medicare facilities. They do not use the indigenous traditional medicines. They are aware of the family welfare schemes and go in for family planning and adopt the latest methods available. Drinking water is available within the locality. In fact, in all the Jat households, tube wells are common. They have received a negligible benefit from the Integrated Rural Development Plan or such other schemes. The government agriculture officers help them in testing soil and prescribe the remedy in case the soil needs any treatment. They receive good variety of seeds from the government departments on payment with or without subsidy. They enjoy the benefits of modern communication systems like radio, television and cinema. The village roads are *kachcha*, unmettaled. The nearest railway station is at Jammu, which is about 20 km from the village Rohi. There is a river nearby. Post Office is not far-off. Nearly all of them can afford and use electricity. They use cow-dung cake called *kandi*, wood and such other fuel. They do not avail of the public distribution system. They are hard-working and sincere in their occupation, and hence earn a handsome amount. They save a portion of their income and majority of them have bank accounts. They rarely depend on the moneylender.

B. JOARDAR

JOGI

The Jogis live on the alms given to them by the people in temples and other places and on socio-religious occasions. They play on a single stringed musical instrument called *kank* or *iktara* in local language. Jogi is a Hindi word meaning 'one who has renounced the worldly possessions and moves from place to place reciting and singing *bhajans* (religious songs)'. In the rural areas of Jammu, they are entitled to receive the head and legs of the animals sacrificed to the village deities and also get a share in the annual harvest. They are a branch of the Dholwalas of Jammu region. While the Dholwalas play drum (*dhols*) to make a living, the Jogi play *kank* or *iktara* to seek alms. They use the surname Nath, but claim to have subgroups of Chib and Minhas, which are also the subgroup of the Rajputs in the region. The reason attributed is that they must have initially acquired these surnames or that some of the Rajputs might have become Jogis. A few of them are also known to be the village magicians, warding off the evil spirits, ghosts and curing various types of ailments. They perceive their distribution at trans-regional level. The Jogis are scattered all over the Jammu province, but their concentration is more pronounced where the regional deities and famous temples are located. Their self-perception is very low and other communities also treat them so.

The Jogis are non-vegetarians and eat pork, but abstain from eating beef. They consume all types of pulses. Mustard oil is the medium of cooking, though *ghee* may also be used occasionally, especially on socio-religious ceremonies. Menfolk consume alcoholic drinks besides non-alcoholic ones. Milk and milk products are used regularly. They smoke cigarettes, *bidis* and *hookah*. Fruit consumption is occasional.

Among the Jogis, there is no stratification based on social, economic or political factors. However, in relation to other communities like the Dholwalas, they enjoy a better status. They marry mostly in their own community because, in comparison to the other high caste Hindu communities, they virtually are treated as an outcaste. They are closer to the Dums, who are recognized as socially and economically backward. Junior sororate is permissible in specific cases rather than as a general phenomenon. Child marriage is gradually being replaced by adult marriages. The marriage for both the girls and boys is solemnized after 18 years of age. However, in few cases girls get married even earlier. Boys usually marry around 23 years of age. Spouses are acquired through friends, relatives and other community members besides the *nai* (marriage broker), who does it on a professional basis. Momogamy is the prevailing form of marriage. Dowry is more of symbolic nature comprising few dresses for the bride and the bridegroom plus furniture and kitchen articles. Patrilocal is the rule of the residence. Divorce is permissible. The reasons for divorce are adultery, maladjustment and insanity. Compensation is paid to the wife. Children are the responsibility of either parent depending upon the specific circumstances of the case. Widow, widower and divorcee can remarry without any socio-religious restrication. Junior sororate is permissible, while levirate is not.

Among the Jogis, the families are extended as well as nuclear. The latter being a common feature of people living in the cities of Jammu region. Avoidance and joking relationships are observed among them. Elders are paid due regard and respect. Intra-familial relations among them are cordial and warm. Parental property is divided equally among the male issues as females claim is considered to be paid in the form of marriage expenses incurred on the wedding of a girl. Even then, girls can claim a share in the parental property but, as a matter of tradition, they forgo it in favour of the male issues. Extended families are being slowly replaced by nuclear ones as economic independence has swayed the joint family system.

The Jogi women have limited roles to perform. In rural areas, where they own agricultural lands, the women are engaged in farm activities besides tending the cattleheads. Their participation in socio-religious spheres is ritualistic. Political participation among the women is restricted to voting in elections. The status of women in comparison to menfolk is low. The Jogi women have a marginal role in contributing to the family income and have no direct control over the family expenditure. A few of them are in service as teachers in primary schools or are doing clerical jobs in the government departments.

Among the Jogis, pre-delivery restrictions are imposed on the parturient mother. Her movements are restricted and she is not supposed to talk to strangers, especially during night hours. Neither naming ceremony nor *annaprashan* (first-feeding of the cereals) is a formal affair. Birth pollution period is observed among them. *Janeu* ceremony is celebrated in a formal manner. The marriage is solemnized at the bride's residence. The groom, accompanied by the *baratis* (marriage party), rides a horse holding a ceremonial sword in hand

and arrives for the *lagan* (wedding) at the bride's house. Feast is given by both the parties on the marriage occasion. Nuptial ceremony is performed at the groom's house.

The dead are cremated after a ceremonial bath. The dead are carried to the cremation ground by friends and relatives. Male heir light the pyre. Death pollution is observed among them. Annual worshipping the dead (*shradhs*) is not practised by them but after four years the ritual of *chaubarsi* is observed. *Rasam-pagri*, i.e. wearing of new headgear of pink or saffron colour after the ritual of *uthala* (formal mourning), is practised by them.

In the rural areas, the Jogis have marginal and small landholdings besides their traditional occupation. They are self-employed and are in petty business. Their links with the market are direct and most of their transactions are made in cash. However, in rural areas, barter system among them is still prevalent. Priests are drawn from the Brahman, who perform all their socio-religious functions and rites. Disputes pertaining to property, family feuds and marital discords are referred to the judicial authority.

The Jogi visit the villages and local dieties besides the regional and state ones. Visit to the *pirs*, *faqirs*, and *dargahs*, irrespective of religious affiliations prevails among them. The community is not involved in any socio-religious or political movement on a significant scale. The Jogis do not excel in arts, painting or crafts on professional basis. However, their womenfolk are engaged in occasional cloth embroidery. They possess a rich tradition of folklore and folk tales, especially based on the mythology of Lord Shiva. Both men and women are engaged in music and dance. Their menfolk perform musical recitals on a professional basis.

The Jogi traditionally accept water and food from all the other Hindu communities and even from the non-Hindus. Since they are essentially dependent on the alms given to them, they have no inhibitions in accepting water and food from others. Marriages take place among their own community members, but there is no ban on soliciting it from the broader Hindu fold. The community does not have a sizeable number of administrators or white-collar job holders. Political leadership is confined to village level only.

Education, though considered good, is not popular among them. The present generation is acquainted with it, but higher education among them is not present. Girls study up to primary or secondary level and drop out thereafter, mainly due to economic compulsions. Boys, generally, study up to high school level though a few of them reach up to the college level. They make use of the traditional and modern medical facilities subject to their availability. Their response to family planning is favourable, but it is their women who generally get sterlized. Drinking water is available through tap in urban areas and in rural areas, its sources are ponds, tube wells and canals. Rural employment programmes have not benefited them though IRDP has rendered financial assistance to a few of them. They are self-employed in petty trade and small businesses. They are exposed to all media of communication such as radio, newspaper, television and cinema. Railway exist and roads and post offices are situated nearby. They use electricity, wood and kerosene oil. Their attitude towards savings is favourable though their capacity to save is nominal. They are fast losing their ethnic identity as the imperatives of present day life compel them to migrate to cities and seek employment. Thus, gradually, they are relinquishing their traditional occupation in favour of other economic pursuits.

ASHOK AIMA

KASHMIRI PANDIT

The Kashmiri Brahmans also known as Pandits and Bhattas, which is the corrupt form of the Sanskrit word *bhattarika* are the indigenous people of the Valley. The present Hindu population of Kashmir comprises besides the Pandits, consists of some members of trading communities and Setch, Chintz, Panyach, etc., besides we were told about two minor groups namely the Buhur and Purbi which were not studied. Although the Kashmiris claim to be the descendants of the Aryan race (in a linguistic sense), yet the last authoritative word about their origin has not been said so far. However, many Western and Indian scholars have argued that the Kashmiri Pandits, without any doubt, belong to the Aryan race who migrated from Central Asia, as indicated by their features and fair complexion. The Kashmiri Pandits, with a few exceptions, belong to the category of Sarasvat Brahmans. The Kashmiri Pandits are spread all over the Kashmir Valley, though their number is small. At the time of Partition of India, the Kashmiri Pandits consitituted nearly 2 per cent of the total population but, with gradual migration to other parts of India, especially to Jammu province, today they constitute under 1 per cent of the total population of the Valley. The natural environment is formed by Valley, surrounded by mountains most of which remain covered with snow. The climate is cold. In the past, service sector used to be the mainstay of the Kashmiri Pandits in the urban areas and agriculture through absentee-landownership and sharecropping in rural areas. However, with the land reform laws abolishing absentee landownership and with the land-to-the-tiller practice, a sizeable part of their rural population has started looking for jobs in the service sector both within and outside the state. Being a highly literate community, they essentially prefer white-collar jobs. However, in recent time, the younger generation is trying other avenues like business and self-employment ventures. Those engaged in agricultural operations are cultivators and have assured means of canal irrigation. The areas where they live are well connected with transport network. They speak Kashmiri among themselves in the Kashmir Valley, but in Jammu region, they communicate in Urdu. The Kashmiri Pandits use the Urdu, Devanagari and Roman scripts. A few of them are also conversant with Persian and Sanskrit. The womenfolk, in the past, could read and write Hindi and Urdu, but the present generation is quite proficient in English as well. They correspond and communicate with the other communities in English, Urdu and Hindi, and quite a few of them who are settled in Jammu can converse in Dogri and Punjabi as well.

The Pandit women apply a forehead mark (*tika*) and wear a pendant (*dehjore*) as distinguishing markers of a married woman from a spinster. A *sari* or *pheran* with a long headdress called *puts* distinguish them from women of other communities. Unmarried girls usually wear *salwar* and *kameez*. Married women traditionally wear *dehjore* as a marriage symbol and generally do not use *sindoor* on their head as the other Hindu married women. The Kashmiri Pandits wear *janeu* (holy thread) and have changed their way of dressing according to modern fashion. In the past, and even now, a few of the Kashmiri Pandits wear turban as against a cap made of *karakul* (sheep skin) worn by the Kashmiri Muslim. There is no special status or privilege enjoyed by this community under the state or union Constitution. In fact, over a period of time, this community has become highly competitive and mobile in the pursuit of better jobs and income opportunities. Bio-anthropological information is available for the community.

Most of the Kashmiri Pandits are non-vegetarians. They eat mutton, fish, eggs, fowls, ducks and chickens. Meat is consumed during birth and death rites, too. *Roganjosh*, *yakhni*, *kaliya*, *mutch*, and *kabergah* are some of the exclusive meat dishes cooked in the Pandit families. Their staple food is rice. Usually, all varieties of pulses including beans are consumed. They consume vegetables and fruits too. *Hak*, a green leafy vegetable, is popular and common vegetable cooked in the Kashmiri households. *Nadru* (stem of lotus) is another popular vegetable consumed by them. Milk and milk products are also used, especially during the religious functions. The Kashmiri Pandit drink *qahwa* and *sheechai* (black tea). Tea made of salt and milk is another popular beverage. Alcoholic drinks are consumed by men occasionally. Women are teetotallers. Menfolk smoke mainly cigarette though *hookah* was used earlier. Betel and tobacco-chewing or use of snuff is rare.

The Kashmiri Pandits are heterogeneous with *gotras* and segments. The founders of these *gotras* are said to be *rishis*. The Kashmiri Pandits are said to have originally belonged to only five *gotras*, Dattatreya, Bhardwaj, Paladeva, Mudgalya and Dhaumyayana. By intermarriage with the other Brahmans the number of *gotras* multipled to 199. The Brahmans of Kashmir are divided into two subcastes—the Karkun and the Bhasha-Bhatta (Gor/Gaur). The former included those who studied Persian and entered the government service and the latter those who studied Bhasha, i.e. Sanskrit and took charge of religious affairs of the community. Among the Brahmans of Kashmir, the Karkuns who are said to have rededicated themselves to the study of Sanskrit and religion without taking up the priestly duties, especially during the Sikh rule, came to be known as the Pandits. Those who were well versed in astrology and drew up calendars and almanacs were known as the Jyotshis. Presiding priests of Shiva worship were called Gurrins. A section of the Karkun were called Panyach, who were considered untouchables both for a Karkun and a Gor as they performed death rites and who live in the city of Srinagar alone. During the Muslim rule, those Pandits who went into exile and later returned when normalcy was restored came to be known as Malamasi and those who stayed back were known as Bavamasi.

The Kashmiri Pandits are an endogamous group. Marriage between the members of the same *gotra* is not normally solicited though these days the principle of 'same *gotra*' is not strictly followed. However, the principle of *sapindi* is respected by all. They strictly prohibit the marriage with the parallel cousins or even among the distant relations.

Marriage age for the girls varies between 20 and 25 years and for the boys between 24 and 28 years or even later. Matrimonial alliances are normally negotiated by the *manzymyor* (middlemen). Monogamy is rigidly observed. *Dehjore* is the main marriage symbol. Giving *daaj* (dowry) is prevalent and, in fact, the more the dowry, the more the social prestige enjoyed by the father of the bride. Gold forms the main component of dowry among the Kashmiri Pandits. During the first year of the marriage, the parents of the bride have to pay in cash and kind on all religious festivals and birthday of the bridegroom and his near relations. Both husband and wife have a right to divorce and can initiate the divorce proceedings under the Hindu Marriage Act, but in practice, it is rare and is socially looked down upon. Divorced woman can marry any person within her own community. Remarriage of widows is also allowed. Divorcee and widower remarriages are a recent phenomenon and were practically non-existent in pre-Independence times. A woman, if she has conceived, will not normally be divorced in that state. Care of infant is usually the responsibility of the mother, but about grown-up children it is mutually arranged or decided by the court of law. The divorced woman is usually entitled to maintenence allowance until she remarries.

Nuclear family is common among them in urban areas but joint family system still continues in rural areas. Their families are strongly attached and interpersonal relations are firm and cordial. Joking relationship exists between affines. Conflicts and confrontations exist to a lesser extent. The Kashmiri Pandits follow the Hindu law of inheritance. Boys and girls have equal right to the property. However, this is not the commonly practiced norm. Sisters, generally, surrender their right to property in favour of brothers. Interfamily linkages are cordial. Any dispute over property or otherwise is usually settled through mutual agreements, failing which recourse is taken to a court of law.

The Kashmiri Pandit women enjoy practically equal status with the menfolk in all walks of life. They enjoy equal right over parental property. They participate in all social, ritual and religious activities along with their menfolk. Women are almost 100 per cent literate and support and supplement the family earnings by seeking empolyment in the government or private organizations. A few women actively participate in politics. Young generation of the Kashmiri Pandit women are competing alongside with menfolk in professional and highly specialized services such as engineering, medicine, computers, applied sciences and management. In fact, the amount of encouragement for all round development, which a Kashmiri Pandit woman enjoys is phenomenal when compared with women of other ethnic groups.

There are pre-delivery restrictions like not going out in late hours, not seeing the bridegroom, not receiving a guest directly and not moving out during an eclipse. Upto ten days after the delivery, the parturient mother does not change for reason of *hoonts* (pollution), nor does she take a bath. On the eleventh day, both the mother and child receive a bath in boiled water in which specific herbs have been added. After the bath, fresh clothes and bedspread are provided to the mother and infant. The mother suckles the child immediately after its birth and in the evening, the ritual called *shran sunder* is performed. The food served comprises fish and *hun*, spinach. A part of postnatal ritual is burning of a few leaves of papyrus. In the past, name-giving ceremony was also observed but it has almost been done away with. The *sabhas* control the socio-religious activities of the Kashmiri Pandits all over India without being affiliated to each other. Elections to the *sabha* are based on secret ballot and single adult franchise. These *sabhas* have a role to play in the politics of the state by advising the community members on the issues and problems confronting them. Its role is essentially advisory, as they cannot enforce any statutory edicts on the community members. The community is highly individualized, consequently these *sabhas* have little controlling power.

These *sabhas* cannot award punishment or order excom-munication. Incidence of crime and related offences is practically absent in this community.

The Kashmiri Pandits as mentioned above are Saraswat Brahmans and profess Hindu religion of the Valley. Though there is no difference between the Sarasvats of the plains of India and that of Kashmir, a wide difference exists in religious beliefs, practices and social customs. The Brahmans of Kashmir practise some 'local' beliefs like naga (snake) worship. After the decline of Buddhism in Kashmir, Shaivism with all its vigour dominated the minds of the Kashmiri Pandits. Pandits are also worshippers of the Sakti, the consort of Shiva. Each family professes devotion and allegiance to one of the three manifestations of the goddess Durga, i.e. Sharika, Ragiya and Jwala. Some of the religious rites performed by the Kashmiri Pandits are said to be in accordance with Charanaia Kathka School. The *sutras* of *Laguksha* follow this school and guide all the rites from birth to death. Certain aboriginal beliefs and practices like *yaksha puja* and *daiptya puja* are also observed strictly. The Kashmiri Pandits are referred to as *saktites* or *tantriks* and even some of the Western scholars have also referred to a host of *tantrik* practices being followed by them. *Tantras*, a later religious development, are generally devoted to one of the manifold forms of Devi, the Shakti of Shiva. The *tantrik* worship by the Kashmiri Pandits seems to have been more influenced by the *Vamachar* than by the *Dakshanachar*. Thus the Kashmiri Brahmanism has essentially evolved around Shiv and Shakti worship.

Certain places of the Kashmir Valley have village deities, generally, raised in reverence to holy persons or saints of the past. Shivratri (the day of Shiva's marriage with Goddess Parvati), Navreh (beginning of new year) and Janmashtami (the birthday of Lord Krishna) are the major religious festivals observed by Kashmiri Pandits. Shravan Purnima (Rakshabandhan) is celebrated by worshipping Lord Shiva. *Soonth*, beginning of spring, *Kamber-pach*, a fortnight in early autumn is observed for *shradhs* for the dead ancestors, Khichi-amavas, the first day of the ensuing winter and Pun, is the culmination of rainy season and welcome to fruit season. Over a period of time, there has not been any significant change in the religion or religious practices. However, in ritualistic aspects, there has been a gradual change, resulting in discarding of some of the rigid practices. Religious ceremonies and rituals have been made easier and the days of fasting are not strictly adhered to. Religion is not allowed to interfere with daily life.

The Kashmiri Pandits are not specialized in any particular art or craft for the simple reason that they always preferred government service. Cloth embroidery as a pastime is done by the Pandit women. *Bhajans* are popular in every Pandit household. Songs and recitations on marriage ceremonies are common and indispensable. Sitar and harmonium are the principal musical instruments played in their homes. There are, however, no dances performed by either sex of this community. *Bhajans* of famous Kashmiri poetess Lal Ded called *Lalvakh* are popular among them. *Tumbaknari* an elongated drum type of musical instrument is played in marriages.

Strict isolation from other communites, especially the non-Hindus, was adhered to by the Kashmiri Pandits in respect of food sharing. Though *kachcha* food could be accepted from the non-Hindus, sharing of cooked food was strictly probihited. However, water could be shared from the same source. Garlic and onion are sparingly consumed. They visit some of the religious shrines of the Muslims of the Valley like Makhdum Sahib, Baba Rishi and Shah Hamdan Wali. Cremation ground is shared with the other Hindu groups. Cultivator-tenant relationship and cultivator-labour relationships exist among the Pandits.

The community has a number of scholars and a large number of male and female members are holding white-collar jobs. Teaching was the exclusive domain of the Pandits in the past and, even now, some are employed as teachers in schools, colleges and universities. The number of the Kashmiri Pandits in administrative jobs in the state government is now on the decline. Constituting under 1 per cent of the total population, the Kashmiri Pandits have an insignificant role in the state politics. Doctors and engineers are found in very large number in this community. Professionals of the community can be found anywhere in India and in foreign countries.

The student population of Kashmiri Pandits in high schools, colleges, and universities is high. Boys and girls are given equal opportunity to pursue education. Economic constraints are the only factor stopping students from seeking higher education. Minimum qualifications on an average for both boys and girls is graduation. The Pandits have taken to modern medicine and practise family planning methods. Drinking water is available through springs and streams in the rural areas and, in the urban areas, tap water is a common feature. Since the Kashmiri Pandit is not covered by any beneficiary category, they, by and large, seek government or semi-government employment through open competition both at the state and national levels. However, some of them are self-employed in small-scale industry, general merchandise, contractroship, etc. Listening to the radio, watching television, reading newspapers and going to the cinema are popular modes of entertainment. Most of the settlements where they live are connected by roads and have post offices nearby. Electricity is used by them for lighting and heating purposes. Traditional fuel-use pattern comprising firewood and cow-dung cakes is being replaced by kerosene oil and LPG (cooking gas). Wherever they still own agricultural land, canals form the main source of irrigation. They use organic manure, chemical fertilizers and insecticides for food and fruit crops. Mother infant immunization is a common practice but midday meal scheme is not availed of. The Kashmiri Pandits make use of the public distribution system for ration and have a healthy attitude towards saving. In case of financial crisis, they may borrow from friends and relatives though in a few cases for business enterprises, they take loans from the banks.

INDU AIMA
ASHOK AIMA

KATOCH

One version of the meaning of Katoch, a Rajput community, is a combination of *kot* and *ouch*, i.e. forts and defenders of a higher order; in other words, they are the descendants of those upper class warriors who defended the forts located in present day Pakistan. Another meaning of the Katoch is derived from the words *kat* (army), and *ouch* (upper class), i.e. people in king's army belonging to a higher order. References to the Katochs are found in the *Mahabharata*, where Susaram Chand's defeat by the Pandavas at Multan is mentioned. The Katoch claim to be Surajvanshi, i.e. people belonging to sun race and are stated to be sun worshippers. Arab geographers, too, thus called them of solar race (*Surajvanshi*). The people record their migration from Trigarth region mainly from Kangra Valley, Himachal Pradesh to their present habitat Badherwah in the district of Doda in Jammu & Kashmir. Their migration took place on account of the Mughal Emperor Aurangzeb's invasion of Kangra. They took away the idol of their clan deity Goddess Durga. While passing through Hambal village in tahsil Doda, the *palki* (palanquin) carrying the statue of Goddess Durga become heavier and, despite increasing the number of carriers, it could not be moved further. Thus it was inferred that their deity wanted them to settle in that very region. Hence, the Katoch's first place of settlement in the Jammu region is stated to be the village Hambal. Some of them had to flee from this region when the ruler of Badhrwah from the adjoining region attacked them. Thus, some of them settled in Banihal and Doda where most of them got converted to Islam. These people percieve their distribution at trans-regional level and have a high self-perception. Other communities also hold them as being in a high position in the hierarchy. They live in the districts of Doda, Udhampur, Jammu and Kathua. Other regions of their concentrations are Kishtwar, Badherwah, Jammu, Kathua, and Rambañ (especially the region of Pogal, Pakistan). The place of their present habitation records heavy monsoon and hot humid climate. Their habitats in the plains have a thin forest cover. Their exact population number is not available. They speak their own Kisthwari language, Dogri and English within their own family group, while with others they also communicate in Urdu and Punjabi. Their mediums of correspondence are Urdu, Hindi and English. In modern era, they have a dress pattern close to the urban culture prevalent in the rest of India, while in rural areas, their dress conforms to the traditional Dogri styles. They do not enjoy any special constitutional status.

The Katochs are non-vegetarian. Their staple food is rice and wheat. They consume all types of pulses. Mustard oil is used as a cooking medium. Their menfolk consume alcoholic drinks besides all types of beverages. Milk and milk products are used in plenty. They smoke cigarettes and hubble-bubble (*hookah*). Fruits are consumed moderataly.

Among the Katoch, social differentiation appears to be existing on the basis of economic and social criteria. The Katochs and Jamwals are considered to be on top in the Rajput social hierarchy. Most of their marriages are solicited within the broader Rajput clan. Endogamy exists at the community level. Junior sororate is permissible. Children are married after attaining puberty. The boys usually get married after the age of 22 years and the girls around 20 years. Spouses are acquired through the help of friends, relatives and the *nai* (barber) as marriage broker. Monogamy is the prevailing form of marriage. Dowry is paid both in cash and kind. Patrilocal is the rule of residence. Divorce is permissible with religious and judicial approval. The reasons for divorce are mainly maladjustment, insanity and adultery. Compensation and maintenance are paid to the wife. Children are the responsiblity of both mother and father, as the case may be. Widow, widower and divorcee remarriage is permissible. Junior sororate is permissible but levirate is not.

In the Katoch community, families are both extended as well as nuclear, the latter being a common feature of urban city life. Avoidance and joking relationships are prevalent. Elders are paid due reverence and regard. Interfamily relationships are cordial. No conflict or confrontations generally occur in intra-familial kin bonds except for property disputes. The paternal property is shared equally by the male issues, while the female heir's share is considered to be paid in the form of dowry. Girls are, however, entitled to a share in the parental property though they never demand it. Succession goes to the eldest male issue. Extended families are being slowly replaced by nuclear families.

The Katoch women have a significant role to play among the city dwellers, but it is limited to agricultural activities in rural areas. In cities, they contribute to the family earnings. They also participate actively in socio-religious spheres. Their role in politics is essentially restricted to exercising their voting right only. Their overall status is low as compared to their menfolk. Only a few Katoch are employed in white-collar jobs as teachers, administrators, doctors and engineers.

The Katochs have a social stratification in the overall Rajput caste hierarchy. Differentiations on account of economic standing and educational background does not enjoy any significant congnisance. Among the Katochs, pre-delivery restrictions prevail. They regularly visit their principal clan deity, the Goddess Durga, in village Hambal, besides the other Hindu deities of the region like Vaishno Devi and Amarnath. They also go to the *pirs* or *faqirs*, irrespective of their own religious affiliations. The community is not involved in any socio-religious movement on a significant scale, though modern urban life and culture have made an impact. The Katochs do not excel in any art or craft, though their females are engaged in occasional cloth embroidery and painting. They possess a rich tradition of folklore and folk tales. Music and dance is enjoyed by either sex, especially on wedding and birth ceremonies.

The Katochs accept water and food from all other co-religionists, but only *kachcha* food is accepted from the non-Hindus. Interdining among these people in urban areas is a common feature. Marriages are mostly solemnized among their own comunity members and with the other Hindus of equal social rank, if required. They have a significant number of administrators, businessmen, scholars, engineers, doctors, teachers and persons holding white-collar jobs. Political leadership has emerged at the state level.

Education among them is considered favourable for both boys and girls, who normally study up to college level. Dropping out from school is more on account of economic reasons than anything else. Their attitude towards family planning is favourable. They make frequent use of both the traditional and modern medicare. They make use of the modern methods of birth control. Drinking water is available through taps in urban areas, and springs, wells and streams in rural areas. Rural employment programmes are not available to them in any significant manner, but they are self-employed in running trade, commerce, business and medium scale industrial units. They are exposed to all the media of communication such as, radio, television, newspaper and cinema. They use electricity, wood, kerosene oil, LPG, etc. Their attitude towards saving and investments is positive and banking facilities are available.

Ashok Aima

KAVOJ

The Kavojs, a little known community of the Kashmir Valley, are the traditional cremators of dead bodies of the Hindus and Sikhs. The word *kavoj* appears to be of Sanskrit derivation. The Kavoj are sporadically distributed in Nathipora, Dal, Noor Bagh and Kamarbari areas in Srinagar. They claim to be the original settlers of the region. They inhabit the region characterized by cold climate with hilly terrain and valleys experiencing medium rainfall and medium to heavy snowfall during the winter months. Kashmiri language is spoken amongst themselves and with other Kashmiri people. Arabic is the script commonly used by them. The staple food of the Kavojs is rice. Non-vegetarian items are consumed by them occasionally, excepting beef and pork. Roots and tubers of different varieties are taken as vegetables. Fruit consumption among them is moderate. Like most of the Kashmiris, they are fond of drinking tea without sugar prepared in the *samawar* kettle. Alcoholic drinks are avoided. They are habituated to smoking tobacco in their *fajit* (hubble-bubbles), some of them also smoke *bidis* and cigarettes.

There are no social divisions in the Kavoj community. No differentiation or hierarchy prevails among them at any level. They do not have any concept of status. Their social standing is equal to and at par with any other Muslim community of the Valley. Butt is the surname commonly used by them. Though endogomy at the community level is preferred, marriage with any other Muslim community of the Sunni sect is not prohibited. Adult marriage is the common practice prevailing among them. Most marriages are settled through negotiations. Consangiunity is permitted at both the cross-cousin and parallel-cousin levels. Monogamy is the general form of marriage existing among them, though they are permitted to marry up to four wives under the Islamic rule. After marriage, the bride comes to live with her husband and in-laws. The amount of *mahr* or dower, is generally promised at the time of *nikah* for future payment, as and when *talaq* (divorce) is sought. No symbol is used to indicate the marital status of a person. Commonly, it is the privilege of the husband to divorce; the wife is entitled to seek separation with social approval. Adultery, barrenness and maladjustment are the common reasons leading to divorce. Divorce compensation is generally paid to the wife.

The children, especially the minors, in divorce cases become the responsibility of the father. Widows, widowers and divorcees are permitted to remarry. However, certain restrictions under the Islamic rules are imposed on the widows and female divorcees in this matter. Normally, a female divorcee is permitted to remarry only after completion of *iddat* which is the restricted period of three months. The *iddat* period is extended till the birth of the child, in case the woman was pregnant at the time of divorce. This is done to legitimize the paternity of the expected child. A widow's restricted period, is limited to four months and ten days within which she cannot remarry. Both junior levirate and junior sororate prevail as preferential choice in remarriage. Comparative increase in the age of marriage is the only change perceived in the institution of marriage among them. Extended family, both laterally and vertically is the predominant type of family followed by nuclear types. Relationship of avoidance exists between the daughter-in-law and father-in-law, husband's elder brother and his younger brother's wife and also between wife's elder sister and her younger sister's husband. The relationship between elder brother's wife and her husband's younger brothers and sisters, and the in-laws of sons and daughters is that of joking and friendliness. Though paternal property is inherited both by the sons and the daughters, the latter's share is always lesser than that of the sons. Succession follows in the male line and the eldest son succeeds as the head of the family. No change is being perceived in the institution of family and extended system of family still continues to predominate.

Besides doing major part of the routine household chores, the Kavoj women participate in animal husbandry, collection of fuel, bringing potable water and, at the same time, play important roles in various socio-religious functions. Most of them directly or indirectly contribute in the decision-making process with the men at the family level and also excercise control over the family expenditure. From the point of view of the above considerations, the women enjoy equal status with men in the community.

No ritual is associated with the pre-delivery condition of the Kavoj woman. Following the birth of a child, warm water bath is given to the baby and verses of the Holy Koran are recited in the ears of the baby. This ritual is called *azaan*. On the following day, presentation of some clothes and cash is made to the blessed mother by her inlaws in connection with the ritual of *piaw*. On the seventh day of delivery, the woman takes her first bath in warm water which is followed by the ritual of *sunder*. A *maulvi* is invited to recite verses from the Holy Koran and give a name to the child on this occasion. The ritual of *sunder* is celebrated through a feast to the neighbours and relatives. On the fortieth day, the women takes a similar bath and resumes her normal household chores. The ritual performed for tonsuring of the child, *zerakasi*, takes place after about one year of its birth, which is marked by dinner for the female neighbours and relatives. The important ritual of *khatnahal* (circumcision), is observed for the male child at the age of about two years. This is generally conducted by the family barber just before dawn and the occasion is celebrated through a feast for the neighbours, friends and relatives.

The ritual performed for finalization and acceptance of the marriage proposal by the bride's party is called *gandum*. Ritually, the father of the bridegroom visits the house of the bride and presents a token amount in cash to the father of the bride, who in return entertains the party to a dinner. After about one month, the ritual of *doon-leij* is observed wherein the bride's father, along with some other relatives, visits the house of the bridegroom and presents an earthen pot full of nuts and some cash to the father of the bridegroom. The father of the bridegroom entertains the party in the house with a dinner. He retains only the pot full of nuts with him and returns the cash amount to the father of the bride. Once the date of marriage is fixed through mutual consent of the two parties, the ritual of *dapanbata* is observed in connection with formal invitation to the relatives and friends for the marriage. On the third day preceding the marriage, the ritual of *malasbehoun* is observed at the bride's house, after which the girl is not allowed to do any household work. She does not take bath till the date of marriage and is fed with only dry food to make her slim and look pretty. This is followed by the ritual of *massmechravoun*, in which the women neighbours and relatives loosen the hair plaits of the girl and comb the hair to make her look beautiful. On the day preceding the marriage, the ritual of *menziraat* is observed to adorn the hands and feet of the girl with *henna* paste by the women neighbours and relatives, who are entertained to a dinner in return. On the following morning, or on the day of *nikah* (marriage), the ritual of *yenevoul* is performed, wherein the bridegroom's party sends presentation of clothes, ornaments and shoes for the bride. By the evening, the bridegroom along with his friends and male relatives, proceeds to the bride's house for the *nikah* ceremony. Women do not accompany the party. During the *nikah*, the bride and the bridegroom are represented by one of their respective relatives, who communicate the response on behalf of the bride and the bridegroom. The amount of dower promised is entered in a *nikah-nama* document in which the names of the bride and bridegroom, their respective representatives and two witnesses are also enlisted. The whole proceedings of *nikah* are conducted by a *maulvi*. The occasion of *nikah* is celebrated with a feast. *Wathal* ritual is observed on the fourth day after *nikah* wherein the father of the bridegroom hosts a feast for the relatives and friends to mark the arrival of the bride at her in-laws' house.

The dead are buried. After the death, the dead body is given a bath in warm water by a *snanagor* (profesional bather). Then a *kafan* (a piece of white cloth) is wrapped up from the head to the toe of the corpse. The body is then put in a wooden *taboot* (coffin) and covered with another piece of white cloth. At the graveyard, *malkhosh*, the professional sexton, digs the *lahad* (grave). A *maulvi* recites the verses from the Holy Koran before laying the dead body in the grave with the head facing north. Stones and clay are poured into the grave to cover it. Two stones at the two ends of the grave are kept as markers. For the following four days of the ritual of *chaharum*, the mourners and relatives of the bereaved family offer prayers at the mosque and at the grave in memory of the deceased person. The ritual of *chehallum* is observed on the fortieth day to mark completion of the mourning period by hosting a feast for the neighbours, friends and relatives.

Among the Kavoj, some of the families of the Sunni sect have been traditionally working as cremators for the Hindus and Sikhs. Their part of the work of cremation does not involve any religious performance. The religious part associated with cremation is the privilege of the Gor Brahman who acts as the priest. The Kavoj's work of cremating the dead bodies comprises of three main aspects, namely, *lakdi-dena*, arranging firewood for the funeral, *kapda-uthana*, removing clothes from the dead body, and *jalana*, burning the dead body. Their remuneration for cremating a dead body generally varies from Rs. 100 to 300 or more, depending on the economic status of the deceased person's family. If the relatives of the deceased person put a shawl on the bier, it is taken by the Kavoj. It is he who prepares the pyre. On the following day of cremation, some member of the bereaved family come to receive the *sur* or *phool*, i.e. the ashes from the cremator at the cremation ground on payment of some amount in cash. The cremation ground is established and maintained privately by the Hindus and Sikhs of the region. The firewood needed for cremation is obtained from the government at controlled rate in addition to cutting or splitting charges paid to the Kavoj. Most of them own some land with individual proprietorship. Besides these, many of them also engage themsleves as wage labourers or in shawl embroidery work to supplement their income. They have direct link with the fully regulated daily market through exchange of cash. Inadequate size of landholding has compelled many of them to depend on secondary sources. The number of persons attending to the profession of cremating the dead is dwindling fast since they are earning through other lucrative engagements. The Kavojs have a low perception of themselves; others too have a low perception of the community.

No traditional caste council or panchayat exists either at the community level or at the level of village or locality. Disputes of adultery, disrespect for traditional norms and insult to the informal council are dealt with by the informal council of elders of the community through imposition of cash fine. The members of the council of elders are elected by voice vote. They are of the opinion that the statutory formal panchayat exists to implement the welfare and development activities in the region as a whole.

The Kavoj profess Islam and belong to the Sunni sect. Allah is the supreme power for them. They strictly follow the dictums of the *shariat*. On various socio-religious occasions, different *dargahs* (sacred shrines) and *masjids* (mosques) are visited by them. Affiliation to the *pirs* exists both at the individual level as well as at the level of family depending on their choice. Charar-e-Sharif, Shah Hamdan, Makhdum Sahib and Naqshband Sahib are some of the sacred places commonly visited by them on various socio-religious occasions. Id-ul-Milad, Id-ul-Fitr, Id-ul-Zuha, Urs-e-Batmaloo, Urs-e-Charar-e-Sharif, Urs-e-Makhdum Sahib and Shab-e-Qadr are some of the fairs and festivals commonly attended by them along with most of the Muslims of the region. Embroidery on shawl is the only craft known to the Kavojs and shared with most of the Muslim communities of the region. They sing folk songs on various social and religious occasions, but neither the women nor the men participate in any traditional dance.

Among the Kavojs, exchange of food, marriage alliances, sharing of water sources, graveyards and visiting the common sacred shrines are the areas of interaction through which they establish and perpetuate traditional linkages with the different Muslim communities of the region. As pro-fessional cremators, the cremation ground happens to be the unique place of interaction facilitating establish linkages with most of the Hindu and Sikh communities of the region. Apart from these, the *julus* (processions) taken out on various socio-religious occasions also happens to be the place for interaction to establish linkage with various other Muslim communities of the neighbourhood.

Receiving and rendering of services in various socio-economic spheres are the important factors in establishing linkages with most of the communities of the neighbourhood. A kind of patront-client relationship with the various Hindu and Sikh communities prevails and is perpetuated through their occupation of cremators of dead bodies. Patron and cliental relationship also prevails with the dealers of shawls for whom they do the embroidery work on payment in cash. The teachers and persons holding white-collar jobs also help to a great extent in establishing linkages with various other communities at their respective levels.

Education of girls is generally not favoured by them. However, a few of their girls do study up to primary standard and then drop out due to socio-economic reasons. Though they favour education for their boys, normally, they pursue their study up to the secondary level and, only in few instances, the boys manage to study up to the college level. Poor economic condition and the need to support the family through earning are the main reasons for the boys to drop out from their schools and colleges. Though they have not completely discarded their indigenous medicare, in practice, most of them generally depend on and make use of modern medicare facilities. The idea of adoption of any indigenous or modern family planning method is not at all favoured by them. Drinking water is available within the locality, supplied by the state government through tap. Most of them earn their livehood through self-employment as cremators, agriculturists, shawl embroideres and as wage labourers excepting a few who are employed as teachers and in some other service. They make use of the mass media and communication facilities such as radio, cinema, newspaper, roads, and post offices, which are available in and around the region. The nearest railway station is, however, located at Jammu which is far-off. Information is disseminated to them through the workers of different political parties of the region. They make use of the facility of electricity. Their fuel resources normally comprise firewood, charcoal and kerosene oil. Rainwater and the water from springs and streams are the sources used by them for irrigation. Organic manure, chemical fertilizers and insecticides are used by them in the fields to increase crop productivity. Most of them are benefited by the public distribution system in procuring articles such as wheat, sugar and kerosene oil. They do not favour banking system, and at the same time, they generally do not depend on the moneylenders and shopkeepers for credit and borrowing.

B.K. BASU

KHATRI

The Khatris are a business community and are so addressed by the people. But, as they have numerous subdivisions and sections, members and families of every subsection are known, and generally, addressed by their sectional names. The titles used with their names are Lala and Shah. The community, in general claim their origin from the Kshatriya, which was second in the order of the *varna* system of the ancient Indian society. This also explains the etymology and the origin of the name. Khatri appears to be an adaption into Prakrit of the Sanskrit *Kshatriya*. Indian literature assigns various origins to the Khatri. According to the *Vishnu Purana*, Bharata had nine sons, whose mothers put them to death, fearing that he would disown them as they had no resemblance to him. Thus, left without a son, Bharata offered sacrifice to the Maruts and they gave him a son known as Bharadwaja, son of Brahaspati by Mamta. Bharadwaja had four grandsons, of whom two became Brahmans while the other two remained Kshatriyas, though all continued to be of the Bharadwaja *gotra*. There is another legend current among the Khatris about the origin and etymology of their name. This popular legend tells how Parsuram, the Brahman and the sixth incarnation of Visnu, exterminated the Kshatriyas twenty-one times and, not content with slaughtering them, he started destroying even the foetus in the wombs of Kshatriya women. So the Kshatriya women fled to the Sarasvat Brahmans of Kurukshetra on the banks of the river Saraswati and when Parsuram demanded their surrender the Brahmans declared them as their own daughters. Parsuram in his wrath bade the Brahmans to take *kachcha bhojan* (unlawful food) from their hands as a test of their relationship and, only when they did so, did he spare the women. So their children were called Khatri instead of Chhatri. Thus, there was a time when the Brahmans intermarried with the Khatris on equal terms, but this has long since been discontinued. The Agniras-*gotri* Khatris are said to have descended from Agni or Havishmat and Havirbhuja, as he is also called. The Kausika-*gotri* Khatris are of lunar descent, through Kusha, the king, who was eleventh in descent from Soma and ninth from King Pururavas. The Kausilya of Kausalya-*gotri* Khatris are of solar race, King Kausalya or Hiranyanabha Kausilya their eponym, being the twenty-second in descent from Raghu. To this *gotra* belong the Mihira Khatris, the Kapura *gotra* being by *gotra* Kaustika. These historical legends indicate clearlyenough that the Khatri is made up of at least three racial elements, solar, lunar and the *agni kula* (fire race). Of these races, some families became Brahmans and others remained *Kshatriya* and later got corrupted into Khatri.

The Khatris preserves no tradition of their migration to Jammu & Kashmir. It is probable that, being an important trading and administrating part of the Hindu community in general, their presence is inseparably associated with the Hindus. However, their movement within this state, and ingress and egress, largely depended on economic conditions and prospects of trade and services. A large number of the Khatri families came to Jammu province during the middle of the eighteenth century when Maharaja Ranjit Dev had established peace and security in Jammu territories and business and trade flourished. In later times also, the Khatri families, particularly those of the *diwans* of Eminabad and their retinue, migrated to Jammu & Kashmir where the eminent among them became commanders, *diwans*, generals and revenue officers of all cadres as well as administrators. They are sparsely scattered all over the Jammu province with large concentrations in towns and cities. No village could get on without the Khatris who kept the accounts, did the banking business and bought and sold the grain. Somehow, the Khatris were altogether excluded from Kashmir.

The Khatris seem to have come to this region from the adjoining Punjab plains, hence they mostly speak Punjabi in their homes and also with others of the local population. However, the Gaddi Khatris speak their own Gaddi dialect. Those inhabiting higher mountains speak Rambani, Kishtwari and Bhadarwahi dialects with the local people. They maintain their accounts in the Lunda or Takari script. They correspond in Hindi, and those who are literate among them, speak Hindi and English when necessary. They do not wear any distinctive dress or mark. Of course white turban had been their usual head wear which is still worn by the elderly people and the rural Khatris. But most of their urban and literate population has now discarded it and use it only on festive occasions like marriage.

The Khatris are non-vegetarian with mixed eating habits. As a community, they have no prejudice against taking meat, fish and eggs, but individually, they may of their own or under some sectarian influence, like that of Arya Samaj or Radhaswami ideology, abstain from taking meat in any form. Their women, like those of the other

Hindu communities, are vegetarian, though they prepare meat dishes for their families. On several religious days like Ramnavami, Janmashtami, and *nauratras* and *shradhs* fortnight or *pitra-paksha*, the Khatris abstain from taking non-vegetarian diet as a religious duty. Similalry, alcoholic drinks and beverages are avoided on such days. Otherwise, Khatris have no prejudice against taking of alcoholic drinks of any type. Most of them occasionally take drinks on festive occasions like betrothal, marriage, birthday celebrations and social festivities. Most of their families are well-to-do so they use high quality alcoholic drinks available in market. Rice and wheat form their staple food along with all types of *dals* and vegetables available in the market. The Khatris of rural areas have a special taste for *makki* bread and *sarson* or mustard leaves. They rear cows and buffaloes and make liberal use of milk, *ghee*, *lassi* and other milk products. In towns also, the Khatris prefer to keep a cow or buffalo for liberal supply of milk and milk products. *Halwa* is also their favourite dish, along with *poories*. No particular change is noticeable in their eating and drinking habits.

The Khatris are divided into three main groups: Bari, Bunjahi and Sarin. The Bari comprises eleven exogamous sections and the name is derived from twelve (*barah*). These sections are: 1. Kapoor, 2. Khanna, 3. Malhotra, 4. Kakkar or Seth, 5. Chopra, 6. Talwar, 7. Sehgal, 8. Dhawan or Dhaun, 9. Tannan (Tandon), 10. Bohra and 11. Maindhru. The first four sections are *bara* (senior) and the remaining are considered *chhota* (junior). The Bari group contains four *dhamas* (subgroups) based on the status of families in each. These are: Dhaighar, Charghar, Chheghar and Bara-jato.

The families of the Dhaighar subgroup are of the highest status and their status depend on the fact that they can only give their daughters in marriage in *dhai* (two and a half) families. The Charghars are below the Dhaighar in status, because they give their daughters in marriage to four sections, and so on. The Bunjahi theoretically comprise, fifty-two sections as the name derived from *bawanwaja* implies. The names and numbers of the sections are, however, variously stated. They too have their subgroups, Khokhran, Bunjahi Khas or Kalan, which are subdivided into Asli, Pakka or Bara (superior) Bunjahi, and Chhota (younger) Bunjahi. The Chhota Bunjahis used to give their daughters to the Bunjahi Khas subgroup.

The Sarin comprise a large number of sections. At present there are two subgroups: Bara Sarin and Chhota Sarin. The Khatri had territorial subgroups also, which makes it exceedingly difficult to give a clear account of their organization. However, Jammu region had two endogamous territorial groups: the Jhikli of the plains and Dugri of the lower hills, and in both these the Bari and other social groups do not appear to have existed. The general principle underlying the Khatri organization was that the higher the circle within which a daughter might be given in marriage, the more exalted the social position of the family in its own group. These are social divisions with a sense of high and low in status for managing marital relations mainly. They are separate from each other because of certain social rites special to each group. The recent change observable among the Khatri social system is the loosening of the *gotra* distinctions. The Khatris hold themselves high in local social hierarchy.

The Khatris usually avoid four sections of the *gotra*, namely those of the father, mother, father's mother and mother's mother, but because of narrowing down of the circle of allliances due to hypergamy, this rule has given way. Thus the Dhaighar families of Kapur, Khanna, Malhotra and Seth sections are no longer bound by this rule, and avoid only the father's *gotra* and the near relations of the mother. Further, the rule forbidding intermarriage between the descendants of a common ancestor is not rigidly observed. The Khokharan avoid only the *gotra* of the father and mother because they have few sections to marry into. The Bais appear to avoid both the parents' *gotras* and the relations of their mothers within seven degrees, but no general rule can be laid down. A common Brahmanical *gotra* is also, as a rule, a bar to intermarriage, but though the Kapur and Khanna sections are both of Kaushal *gotra*, they intermarry.

Like the other Hindu communities, the Khatri boys and girls were betrothed and married at an early age, though they did not normally practise infant or child marriage. The age of betrothal depended upon the status of the group. It was stated to be from four to eight years in the case of girls among the Khokharan and Baris, and eight to ten years among the Bunjahis. The married life usually commenced at the age of thirteen to sixteen years in all the groups. The predominant form of marriage was *dharam*-marriage, i.e. through negotiations, and consummated according to the Hindu *shastras* prevalent all over India. The negotiations were started by a Brahman *purohit* (priest) or *nai* (barber) attached to the families. Marriage by purchase was also common, particularly in case of an old person or a widower. The Khatris were usually monogamous, but the rich among them had more than one wife. *Sindoor*, *bindi*, a set of red bangles, *balakru*, *nath*, and toe rings were symbols of a married woman. A sort of gold head-ornament worn in hair on the crown and known as *chauk*, a round conical piece, was a special symbol first worn at the time of marriage and continued throughout the lifetime of the *suhag* (husband). Dowry was given both in cash and kind, and the higher in status was the *gotra* of the boy, the costlier had to be the dowry. Both divorce and remarriage of widows were forbidden. Now the Khatris are wholly monogamous. In recent years, cases of divorce and remarriage of widows are on the increase, and the Khatris have given up polygamy. Some symbols of marriage like *chauk* has gone out of fashion. But, on the whole, the Khatri marriages have become more costly affairs than before. Formerly, the Khatri families were vertically extended units consisting usually of grandparents and their offspring; but now the tendency is towards nuclear families. Cordial relations exist between all the old and young members of the family. The elders are venerated, feared and obeyed. The usual Shastric rules of inheritance prevailed among the Khatris. All the male offspring shared the paternal property equally in *pag-vand* tradition, but in case of male offspring from two or more mothers, division followed the *chunda-vand* system, in which the whole of the movable or immovable property was divided in equal shares corresponding to the number of wives whose male offspring were alive, then each share was divided equally among the male children of that wife. After the death of the father, the eldest son succeeded him and became the head of the family. The Khatri family had cordial relations with other families and social groups of the locality and participated in their joys and sorrows, and social and religious celebrations. Under the impact of modern conditions and recent legislation, rules of inheritance and pattern of families are undergoing a change. Female offspring and widows are getting their share in the paternal property. There is a growing tedency towards nuclear type of family.

The Khatri women were held in high esteem in their community and society, in general. They participated in all the social and domestic rites, rituals and celebrations equally with men. However, they did not have right of inheritance in paternal property and had only the right of sustenance in husband's property in case of the latter's death. They shared responsibility with men in the family management. Although they were not a major source of income for the family, most of those belonging to the families with low economic status earned some money by producing some commercial goods on a small scale at their homes. In villages, they used to earn interest by lending small amounts of money to the villagers. Those who had fallen on evil days did not hesitate even to work as maidservants in the houses of the rich. Under recent legislation, they have got the right of divorce and inheritance; remarriage of widows has also become more common now. They take part in all types of political activities, get education up to the highest level and have joined the local and national services. They have among them medical practitioners, advocates, public representatives and administrators.

Most of the Khatri families celebrate the wife's first pregnancy by the custom called *reet*. Her parents send her sweets, clothes and cash. Sati is specially worshipped on this occasion with other deities. After the birth of a child, thirteen or twenty-one days pollution period is observed, accompanied by the ritual of *punjap*, which is the first bath of purification of the mother and child on the fifth day. Meanwhile, the child is named and, on the twenty-first day, it is taken out of the house for the first time. On the birth of a child, the mother is made to sleep on the ground. Seven thorns of a *kikar* or *jandi* tree are buried in the earth under the pillow. Bread or corn in any form is avoided for the first three days and only milk is served to her. On the fourth day, a mixture of flour, sugar and *ghee* (*churma*) is given to her. On the thirteenth day, she puts on a barber's shoes, leaves her room and resumes her household duties. The tonsure ceremony is a significant rite among them. It is known by various names, such as *mundan*, *munnan*, *bhadan* and *jandian*. The age for the performance of this rite differs with numerous Khatri sections and ranges from the age of 2 to 11 years. The Chopras, Kakkars, Bhandaris, Malhotras and several others perform this rite at five years; Dhands at 3, 4 or 5 years, Duggal at 5, 7 or 9 years and Wadehras at eleven years. Sometimes, a halfway tonsure ceremony is observed by cutting the hair and leaving three top-knots on the head of the boy, to be removed at the full *mundan* ceremony. It is known as *jandian* or *jhandan*. Among the Bhandaris and a few other sections, a *jandi* tree is cut on the occasion from which the rites got their name. Most of the Khatri sections venerate *aak* (kite), and eagle on the occasion. Several other rituals are observed by them before the ceremony of *janeu*. For instance, the Wadehras make offerings of *luchis* at the shrine of Baba Tomba when a boy at the age of one and a quarter years wears a shirt for the first time and a *dan* offering is made to kites. When the boy puts on shoes for the first time at the age of 6 years, the ear of a he-goat is cut and water is sprinkled on the animal; shivering of the animal is considered a good omen. It is known as *bijna*. The thread-wearing ceremony is performed usually between the age of 8 and 11 years, and is marked by some curious symbolic celebrations like slaughtering of a goat and marking a *tilak* on the boy's forehead with its blood, feasting of kites, mock fight between boy's father and mother and the latter's leaving the house and going to a neighbour's house, the husband appeasing her and bringing her back after making suitable presents. Child marriage was not practised among the Khatris. However, early marriage was the rule of the day. It was celebrated from 8 to 10 years for girls and 10 to 12 years in case of boys. The marriage rituals passed through all the stages of negotiations current in all other Hindu communities, such as *thaka*, *kurmai*, *sagun* and family *barat* and *vedi*, with a variety of minor variations here and there. The performance is accompanied by the Vedic rites and recitation of sacred *mantras* before the *havan* fire which is fed by *ahutis*.

The *antyeshti sanskar* or death rites, also follow the general Hindu pattern. The dead person is cremated and, on the fourth day, *phools* (burnt bones) are collected in a *kalash* (urn) and a ritual called *chautha* or *uthala* is performed. Then the *asthis* (ashes) are carried to Haridwar to immerse in the Ganga river. *Kriya-karam* is observed on the tenth day and, on the thirteenth day, the ceremony of tying of turban on the head of the eldest surviving male member of the family is performed. Most of these subsidiary rituals have now been simplified but the necessary skeletal observances of the *antyeshti sanskars* are still observed by all sections of the Khatris.

The Khatris are a trading community. Their major economic resources are factories, shops and mercantile goods. Some of them are forest contractors and deal in timber. The community has owners of large mills and big factories, cinema houses and business establishments as also petty shopkeepers and petty village traders. In villages, some of them own lands, and hence the Khatris are a combination of both of landless and landowing people. However, the main occupation of the community is trade, which is their traditional occupation. Service and agriculture are subsidiary occupations for them. They entirely depend on the market for operation of their trade. Their dealings are wholly in cash, and barter, which was long ago a usual practice of exchange, has gone out of fashion. In fact, a labourer class hardly exists among them. However, most of their boys start working with their parents as apprentices at an early age and, after school hours, help their elders in their family trade or occupation. Under the modern economic stress and strain, some of them have taken to work as factory labourers or workers. They receive and pay wages in cash.

The Khatris have no powerful and organized body for social control. Only tradition and the *shastras*, as well as the conventions of the various sections of the community excercise such control. However, there are the Khatri *sabhas* organized in various towns and cities on local level which provide some sort of social control. Such bodies do not have much power to reward or punish, but only to disapprove actions of individuals and families transgressing the social conventions. In villages, they, as a part of the larger village community, are under the jurisdiction of the gram panchayats so far as their civic behaviour is concerned. In solving the major problems concerning divorce, inheritance and individual's rights, they are governed by the recent legislations and they can have recourse to legal courts.

The Khatri community professes Hinduism and its various subsects. Some of them profess Sikhism, as Guru Nanak, the founder of the Sikh faith, belonged to the Bedi Khatri family. His immediate successor was also the Khatri of the Trehan section. Most of the other Gurus also belonged to the various sections of the Khatris. Hence, some of the Khatri families became converts to Sikhism but have retained their sectional names to this day. Arya Samaji ideology has also influnced the community as Swami Dayanand Saraswati, the founder of Arya Samaj, belonged to the Khatri community. Majority of them, however, are still Sanatanists and stick to their traditional totems like kite, eagle, and *kikur* and *jandi* trees which they still propitiate on social and religious rites. Baba Tomba, Bawa Lalji, Baba Farid and Satis are venerated by them. The symbolic sacrifice of a goat is still prevalent among a number of their sections. A Brahman *purohit* or an Arya Samaji *purohit* performs their social and religious rites. They visit all the local and national places of the Hindu pilgrimage, and they immerse *asthis* (ashes) in the Ganga as well as in local rivers like the Tawi and Chenab.

The Khatris being a trading and moneylending community, had very close linkages with all other communities of the locality, irrespective of religion, creed or caste. They used to cater to the economic needs of all communities of village and town, hence they had developed a secular outlook in commercial affairs. However, in the social sphere, they observed the usual caste conventions and restrictions ordained on the Hindu communities, like that of untouchability and prohibition of social linkages with the Muslim community. All types of exchange of water and food with the Muslim and fourth *varna* communities was prohibited and strictly observed. However, with the Brahman, Kshtriya or Rajput and other Vaishya communities, they had closer commensal linkages and free exchange of water and *kachcha* and *pukka* food, and *purohits* accepted *sidha* (religious uncooked offerings) from them. Intercommunity marital exchanges were not approved of, but such exchanges took place occasionally with the Mahajan, Rajput and Brahman families and were unwillingly accepted. Putative kinship was allowed with all the Hindu communities including those of the fourth *varna*. At certain social rites, such kinship was contracted according to tradition, such as on the occasion of *mundan* and *maklawa*. The Khatris have access to all public places, temples, water reservoirs and markets, and they share their public places with all other communities like the Muslims and Shudras. Patron-client relationships also exist and all their sections have their *kul-purohits* for whom they serve as *jajmans*.

The Khatris are one of the most awakened communities of this state. They participate in all the political activities and movements, both on regional and national levels. The community has among them members of the state legislature and the parliament as well as political leaders and ministers. The community is partially landowning and mostly commercial, so production and landlord-tenant relationships exist, as also cultivator-labour and employer-worker relations are a necessary part of their socio-economic organization.

The Khatri community is highly responsive to the developmental programmes introduced in this state. In the field of education, they have an outstanding position. The community is totally literate. Most of their boys and girls go for higher education and for technical and professional training courses. They have medical practitioners among them and the community, as a whole, is alive to the problems of health and the benefit from proper medicare. In the towns and villages they inhabit, they have facilities of drinking water. They are responsive to the family planning programmes. They, however, do not get any benefit of the rural employment programmes and, as such, the programmes have not been introduced in this state. They get the benefit of self-employment schemes, and government loans and aids given for this purpose. They make use of the media of information like newspapers, radio, television and telephones and telegraph systems and roads and railways. Most of them use electricity and gas as the source of energy for domestic and commercial use. However, in rural areas, they make use of firewood, kerosene oil and cow-dung as fuel. Nutrition programmes are still unknown in this state and boys do not get the benefit of such amenities, but the community has the facilities of public distribution in towns as well as in villages. The landowners among them in villages make use of chemcial fertilizers, irrigation facilities and insecticides. They also use organic manure. Banking facilities are now available to them even in rural areas.

S.D.S. Charak

KRAAL

Kraals are an artisan community of the Kashmir Valley. The term *kraal* is the Kashmiri corruption of the Persian word *kalal*, meaning potter. They believe that Allah, the Supreme Power, is the greatest Kraal, being the creator of earth and, call themselves Kraal because they make earthern pots. History of origin of the community is not known but they believe that they were Hindus before the advent of Islam in Kashmir Valley. They are concentrated in Charar-e-Sharif in Badgam district, but are also distributed in other districts of Jammu & Kashmir. The climate of the region is cold and the terrain is hilly with medium rainfall, low humidity and medium to heavy snowfall during winters. The region is surrounded by the Pir Panjal and Himalayan ranges with an average altitude of five to ten thousand feet, and is moderately forested. The total population of the community is not known. They speak Kashmiri language among themselves and use the Arabic script while writing in Urdu. While communicating with others, they speak Kashmiri and Urdu languages. There is no identification marker of the community and they wear the dresses like the other Kashmiris. *Pheren*, *pochh* and trousers are the common dress for men while women wear *salwar*, *kurta*, *pheran* and *puts* (headgear). The Kraals are non-vegetarians and consume mutton, fish, eggs and chicken, beef being restricted in the Valley. Rice is their staple food but wheat, maize and millets, seasonally available, are also consumed. Pulses, like *moth* (brown gram), *urad* (green gram), black gram and *masur* and *moong* are consumed in their daily diet. Seasonal vegetables are consumed in plenty but *hak* or *karam sag* is their favourite leafy vegetable. Fruit consumption in the community is high. Salty tea is very popular among them and is taken with bread. Tea with sugar is occasionally consumed. They do not take any alcoholic drink which is prohibited in their religion. Milk and milk products are consumed in lesser quantity due to its searcity in the region. They smoke *bidis*, cigarettes and *hookah* (hubble-bubble), and occasionally chew betel.

Social divisions do not exist among the Kraals, but differentiation on the basis of educational attainment, economic status and occupational status of high and low rank is maintained. There is no change in their surnames and, being clean occupational community, they put themselves in the middle rank in the regional social hierarchy. Others also recognize them as such.

Among the Kraals, endogamy at community level is the rule of marriage, but marriages outside the community are not prohibited and they may accept girls or boys from the community of equal status like the Sofi, Wani, Malik, Dar, etc. First preference is always given to cousins either cross or parallel in the selection of the bride or bridegroom. In case of non-availability, they select the bride or groom from outside their kin. Ideal marriageable age for boys and girls is considered to be between 18 and 25 years and 16 and 20 years, respectively. Though sporadic cases of love marriages do occur, most of the marriages are settled through negotiation either by a common friend or *manzymyor* (a mediator). Monogamy is the general practice, though polygamy is permissible. There is no symbol of marriage in the community. *Mahr* is fixed at the time of marriage and promised for future payment to the bride. After marriage, the bride goes to live with her husband and in-laws. The husband enjoys more rights in divorcing his wife on the grounds of barrenness, adultery, maladjustment and insanity. The wife can seek separation if the husband absconds and does not take proper care of the wife and children, or does not have any sexual contact for more than three years. According to the Muslim rules, divorce may be given either orally or through *talaq-nama* (written document). According to the Muslim law, when a marriage is dissolved by divorce, the woman is prohibited from remarrying for a specified period called *iddat.* If consummation of marriage had taken place before a divorce, then the duration of *iddat* (restriction period) is for three months and ten days; if the woman is pregnant, it is until the delivery of the child takes place. The cases of divorce are rare in the community. It is the duty of the father to maintain the minor children after divorce. Widow, widower and divorcee remarriages are permissible in the community but are performed in a simple manner. Widows are allowed to remarry after the *iddat* period which is for four months and ten days. Decrease in divorce cases, emergence of dowry system and monogamy are the major changes which have occured in recent times.

Most of the families are nuclear though, in villages, extended families are also found among them. Newly married couples establish a new household after the marriage. Interpersonal relationship among the family members is amicably established and due love and respect is paid to the elders. Avoidance relationship is maintained between the daughter-in-law and parents-in-law and between younger brother's wife and husband's elder brother, likewise with outsiders and elders of other category of relations. Joking relationship is prevalent between the husband's younger brother and sister-in-law and between husband

and his wife's younger sisters. Property of the father is divided among the sons, daughters and widows, but daughters get lesser share than their brothers. Succession pattern is followed in the male line from father to the eldest son. Breaking of joint family system and emergence of nuclear families is the change noticed in recent years.

The Kraal women enjoy equal status with men and have full right on *mahr*, the amount which is fixed at the time of *nikah* by the husband and can be claimed by the wife at any time after marriage. Generally, it is demanded at the time of divorce. In all the spheres of life, women play an important role. They assist in agriculture, collection of fuel, bringing potable water, making of earthen pots, and do other household jobs. They are fully involved in all the social and religious functions and contribute to the family income besides controlling the expenditute.

Life-cycle rituals of the Kraal start from the first pregnancy. A pregnant women is not allowed to carry heavy loads or do strenuous work during pregnancy. Delivery takes place generally at home and a *warin* (midwife) is called to assist the parturient mother and is paid in cash and kind. She may be from any community. Generally, they are old women who are experts and have knowledge about delivering babies. Immediately after birth, the child is given bath and a senior male member recites *azaan* in the baby's ears. If the delivery takes place at the residence of the bride's parents, sweets are distributed among the relatives and friends and the largest share goes to the boy's father's house. Her mother-in-law also sends clothings, cash and other gifts in return. This ceremony is called *piaw*. *Sunder* is celebrated on the seventh day of the birth and the mother is given her first bath. The child is named on this day either by the family priest or any elder person of the family. After forty days, a final purificatory bath is given to the mother and then she is allowed to resume her normal household works. *Zerakasi* ceremony is observed when the baby is over six month of age in which hair of the male child is cut by the family barber and a feast is arranged. Another important ritual of the child is *khatnahal* (circumcision). It is performed by the family barber when the child is about two years old. In urban areas, it is done either in hospital or at home by an expert surgeon. A big feast is arranged to mark the occasion. Marriage ceremonies start with the ritual of *gandum* (engagement). The bridegroom's father visits the place of the bride with some relatives and offers some money to the bride and her father. This is followed by *doon-leij*, in which an earthen pot full of nuts and cash money is presented to the father of the bridegroom by the bride's father. After the engagement, marriage invitations are sent to the relatives and friends. *Malasbehoun* is another ritual in which the bride is not allowed to take bath and do household jobs for at least three days prior to marriage. Then, the second function, *massmechravoun* or loosening of hair plaits, starts. On this occasion, the bride's hair is combed by the female relatives. The first day of the marriage is known as *menziraat*, in which, the hands and feet of the bride are dyed with *mehndi* (myrtle) paste at night. The second day of marriage is called *yenevoul*, when the father of the bridegroom sends few copper plates containing sugar candy, sugar balls, almonds, clothes and ornaments for the bride. When the *barat* (marriage procession) starts, it is followed by two or three rows of women singing in chorus holding each other following the party for some distance. At the bride's house, the procession party is received by the women in the same manner. After this, *nikah* ceremony is performed and presided over by the *maulvi* (priest). There are two types of *nikah*; one is *nikah asaltan* in which the bride and the bridegroom are present and a marriage contract is written with their consent in the presence of witnesses. The other one is called *nikah vilaitan* and is performed when the bride and bridegroom are minor and consent on their behalf is given by their parents. This type of *nikah* was prevalent in the past when child marriage was in practice. When the *nikah* ceremony is over, a grand feast is served to all the participants. At the time of departure, the bride goes with her husband and her female relatives follow her for some distance singing in chorus. The bride stays with her husband for seven days and a big feast called *wathal* is arranged. After marriage, the bride starts living with her husband and in-laws.

The dead are buried and the period of mourning lasts for 40 days. When the relatives and friends assemble, a bath is given to the dead by the *snangor* (a professional bather), and the body is placed in a *taboot* (coffin), wrapped in a *kafan* (white cloth). It is laid on the ground facing west and the priest recites prayer. Thereafter, the *taboot* is carried to the graveyard where a *lahad* (grave) is dug by the *malkhosh* or *gorkan*.

The primary and traditional occupation of the Kraal community is preparing earthenware which is the primary source of their livelihood. They make earthenware of different shapes and sizes and other articles of daily need according to the choice of the customers. They make earthenware both for retail and wholesale. *Kundal, nut, dagul, antu, takar, jajir, chilam, tav, mad, thalbau*, king flower pots and *kangri* are some of the articles made by them. Few families are engaged in the traditional occupation as well as in agricultural activities, particularly in rural areas. Besides their traditional occupation, a few members of the Kraal community are empolyed in the government and private jobs, or are running their own businesses. Local market is fully regulated and the entire business transaction is in cash only. There is no bonded labour in the community but child labour does exist. People are now trying for new occupations as their traditional occupation has lost its economic viability due to the advent of metalware and scarcity of raw materials.

The Kraals do not have any caste panchayat to settle the disputes within the community. At the regional level, there are associations which take care of minor disputes. Disputes, if any (other than business) are resolved either by the village headman or *chaudhury* or an elderly person of the family. Sometimes, they go to court of law also.

Being Muslims, the Kraals follow the *shariat* dictum like the other Muslim communities of the Valley. They visit several sacred shrines and mosques on different occasions. Shah Hamdan, Charar-e-Sharif, Makhdum Sahib, Dastagir, Naqshband Sahib are the sacred shrines which they visit. They have their own *pir*, who supervise performance of the birth, marriage and death rites. Besides, they observe different Muslim festivals in different months, Urs-e-Nabi, the Prophet's birthday, also knwon as Id-ul-Milad, is celebrated on 12th of Rabi-ul-Awwal. On this day, the Prophet's hair relic is displayed at Hazratbal shrine. Meraj-e-Alam is celebrated on the twenty-sixth of Rajab. Id-ul-Fitr, Id-ul-Zuha, Shab-e-Qadr are other festivals which are observed with great zeal and enthusiasm. They participate in the *urs* celebrations like Urs-e-Shah Hamdan, Urs-e-Makhdum Sahib, Urs-e-Pir Dastgir, Urs-e-Naqshband Sahib, and celebrate these festivals with the other Muslims of the areas. All the festivals are of socio-religious and socio-economic significance. Pottery is the main craft of the Kraal community. A few members of the community are also involved in other crafts like carpet weaving, shawl embroidery and wood carving, besides their traditional craft. Folk songs. are sung by the men and women on different occasions. Women participate in the traditional dance of Kashmir called *rouf*, but they do not play on their traditional musical instrument.

Being involved in a traditional and important occupation of pottery, the members of the Kraal community establish and maintain good relations with other communities of the region and extend their services even to the lowest castes like the Chamar and Watal. They are placed in the category of clean occupational castes. The relation of the Kraal with the Shakhsaz community is of important significance because of their allied occupations. The wicker case of the *kangri* is made by the Shakhsaz whereas the *kundal*(pot) is provided by the Kraal. The Kraals accept *kachcha* and *pukka* food from all the communities but to some extent avoid the Watals. Other communities too exchange water, *kachcha* and *pukka* food with them. Services of the Pir, Hajjam, Gorkan, Najjar, Wani, Sofi and Ganai are taken on different occasions. Other linkages with the neighbouring Muslim and non-Muslim communities are established through intercommunity marriages, interchange of food, sharing of water sources and burial ground. Now, the members of the community have entered the government and private organizations and are holding white-collar jobs. Though the Kraals have a positive attitude towards education yet, living in remote and difficult areas under poor economic conditions usually prevent them to study beyond primary level. They do not pay much attention towards the education of girls for social and economic reasons. For higher education, they have to go to the cities which is not possible for all the families. Development programmes adopted by the central and state governments have not had much impact on the Kraal community. They favour modern system of medicare but have not discarded their indigenous traditional medicare system as the facilities of modern medicare are not properly available in their areas. Family planning programmes have not attracted them much, particularly in the rural areas. Electricity and drinking water facilities are available in their localities. Tap water, springs and streams are their sources of drinking water. Most of the members of the community are self-employed, being involved in their traditional occupation of pottery. In rural areas, radio is the medium of information while, in urban areas, some families have their own television sets. They occasionally go to the cinema. Firewood, cow-dung cakes and kerosene oil are the main fuel resources. They depend on the rain and stream water to irrigate their land as the irrigation facilities are not available in their locality. They use chemical fertilizers and organic manure to boost the crop production. Neither any empolyment scheme nor nutritional programme has been properly implemented in their area. Facilities of food grain distribution system through the fair price shops are available, and they avail themselves of it.

ANAND SARAN

KUL FAQIR/FAQIR

The Kul Faqirs are a band of mendicants who derive their identity from a Kashmiri term *kul* meaning a tree. Those who used to meditate under trees came to be known as the Kul Faqirs. The process of parochialization (McKim Marriot, 1955) turned the term *kul faqir* into *kuli* (porter), *faqirs* (beggars) who move with their bag and baggage from one place to another. The Kul Faqirs, however, subscribe to the former theory of their origin. They are mostly settled in Janbazpora, Nadihal and Binner in Baramula district of Kashmir. They are also known by the term Bodel. Some suffix the title Shah to their names. The community perceives its distribution at local level. Ethnographic and historical accounts exist and were found to be true. The community has migrated to its present habitat from North-West Frontier and the migration is recalled in their oral traditions. They live in a cold hilly terrain with low humidity, medium rainfall and medium to heavy snowfall. Population figures are not available. Amidst their own kin, they speak Pushtoo and Kashmiri whereas with others, they speak in Urdu and Kashmiri. They use the Arabic script. The adult male wear a long and loose *chola* and long white sheet of cloth hanging on their left shoulder typifying their Sufi style of living. Under the *chola*, they wear long shirt and *salwar* or *lungi*. They grow long beard and flowing locks of hair on their head. They always carry an artistically carved long staff in their right hand and a begging bowl, *kashkol,* in their left hand and keep on moving the beads of a rosary. They belong to an economically and educationally backward class. The Kul Faqirs are non-vegetarian and the cereals they eat are wheat and rice besides pulses like *moong, masur* and *moth*. Medium of cooking is mustard and rapeseed oil. They consume only non-alcoholic beverages like tea. Fruit consumption among them is moderate. Now they prefer rice to *roti* (unleavened bread).

Social divisions do not exist among the Kul Faqirs, but the basis of differentiation are social, economic, occupational and educational. The community's social perception is low; they are not aware of the *varna* system and other communities too consider them low in the regional social hierarchy. Endogamy is observed at the community level. Intermarriages with the local Muslims are usually discouraged in case of daughters, but hypergamy and consanguineous marriages are allowed. Marriages are solemnized through mutual consent and negotiation. Monogamy is the predominant form of marriage. Marriage symbols are lacking. The amount of *mahr* ranges between Rs. 10,000 to 20,000 and is payable on demand. Dowry is not practised. Residence is partilocal. Divorce is permissible with judicial approval because of barrenness, absence of male issue and maladjustment. Divorce compensation is paid to the wife. Only the husband can divorce and children are the responsibility of the father in such cases. Widow, widower, male or female divorcee, sororate and levirate remarriages are allowed. There is an increase in the age at marriage.

Among the Kul Faqir, the family type is nuclear and mixed-extended. Avoidance and joking kin behaviour are absent. Intrafamilial relations are governed by an authoritarian father, but there are no conflicts or confrontations in the realm of family. Property is divided among the sons and daughters according to the Islamic rules of inheritance and the eldest son succeeds his father. Nuclear families are replacing extended ones. The Kul Faqir women collect fuel, fetch potable water and do other household chores and are given a low status. No pre-delivery rituals are observed by them. Post-delivery restrictions last for 40 days. First tonsuring ceremony, *mundan* or *aqeeqa*, is performed on the male children and a goat or ram is sacrificed for the well-being of the child. Circumcision is performed on male children before the child attains three years of age. Marriage is performed in accordance with the Muslim personal law at the bride's residence whose parents host a feast after the ritual of *nikah*. The dead are buried in accordance with the Islamic rituals.

Receiving alms, soothsaying and giving amulets and *tabarruk, piri* and *muridi* were some of the activities around which the economy of Kul Faqir revolved. It is mainly a landless community now involved in business, government service, besides begging. Links with the regulated daily markets are direct and transactions are made in cash. They have neither traditional *jati* panchayat nor are they under the influence of the statutory village panchayat. Minor disputes are resolved by the *biradari* elders.

The Kul Faqirs profess Sunni Islam of the Hanafi school and observe all the Islamic tenets such as *namaz*, *roza*, *haj* and *zakat*. They visit the Muslim *pirs* and are affiliated both individually and family-wise with them. The sacred places of pilgrimage for them are Hazratbal, Baba Nooruddin Rishi, Saiyed Malik Janbazpora Sahib, Saiyed Salim Chishti's tomb at Agra and Khawaja Nizamuddin Aulia's at Delhi. Sacred specialists are from the same community, who inculcate *waaz*-

o-nasihat (religious teachings), perform life-cycle rituals and cure ailments and diseases through amulets. They celebrate all the Muslim festivals of religious significance such as Id, Shab-e-Barat, Shab-e-Qadr and *urs* of the Muslim saints. Neither has any change taken place in their religion nor is the community involved in any socio-religious movement. The community has oral traditions. Folk songs are sung by the women. Folklore and folk tales are a part of their lives. The degree of internal conformity to religion has increased. The only craft prevalent in the community is blanket weaving on handlooms. Their dances may be divided into meditative and ritual dancing. *Hal* or *dhamal* (meditative dancing) is performed by elderly persons, whereas ritual dancing is performed by young boys and girls who dance separately.

The Kul Faqirs accept water and exchange food from all other Muslim communities. Intercommunity connubial ties do not exist in case of daughters. Putative kinship exists and the people share water resources and burial grounds, and visit religious shrines with other communities. They participate in all the traditional festivals and festivities. They receive from and render services to other communities on reciprocal basis and maintain a patron-client relationship. A few members of the community are now employed as school teachers.

Among the Kul Faqirs, education is considered favourable for boys, who study up to post-graduate levels and drop out due to economic reasons, and for girls who seek education up to higher secondary level but drop out due to social reasons. Tubectomy, however, is gaining ground among the people slowly. Sterilization is considered un-Islamic for both the sexes. Drinking water is available to them through streams, springs, rivulets and water taps. Provisions for empolyment and self-employment for them are not available. They listen to radio and watch television, but do not go to cinema. Roads and post offices are located nearby but not a railway station. Electricity is used for lighting, and wood, cow-dung cakes, sawdust and kerosene oil are their main fuels. Nutrition programmes for their mother and children are not available. They are the beneficieries of public distribution system. Their attitude towards saving is positive and the people are not dependent on the moneylenders and shopkeepers.

BAQAR R. RIZVI

LOHAR

The Lohars, an occupational community of Jammu & Kashmir, manufacture iron implements used in agricultural activities and also other iron works. They are also known as Khar and Ahangar. The Ahangar is generally used as surname by them. Hazarat Mir was the first Ahangar of Zainakadal, Srinagar. He got converted to Islam about six hundred years ago. The community is identified at regional level and it is dispersed in Shalimar, Nishat, Chesebal (Srinagar), Safapora, Sopore, Baramula and Bandipora. Their maximum concentration is in Chesebal area. No census figure is available for the Lohars. They speak Kashmiri language within the family and also with others, and use the Arabic script. The Lohars have no identification marker and are included in the Other Backward Classes and Backward Classes category of the state.

Staple foods consumed by the Lohars are wheat (*gandum*), rice and grams; and *moong, masur* and *rajmah* are the pulses consumed by them. They are occasionally non-vegetarians and consume fish and meat. Women are also non-vegetarians. A leafy vegetable *kavdaari sag* is consumed in large quantity. They supplement their diet with milk and milk products.

Among the Lohars, social divisions exist which are based on occupational considerations . There are four divisions, Banduk Khar, Jongl Khar, Jamidar Khar and Cycle Khar. Thus, the type of occupation of the Ahangar indicates their social status. They are placed in the middle of the social hierarchial order.

The Lohars usually marry within the community. There is no bar in marrying with other communities such as the Dar, Bhat, Mir, Rather and Lone. Consanguinity is practised. Sororate and levirate forms of remarriage are also prevalent. Adult marriages is the practice in the community. The usual marriage age is 25 years for the boys and 18 years for the girls. Marriages are settled through negotiations. Monogamy form of marriage is the common. There are no marriage symbols, but, at the time of marriage, *door* (earrings) are worn by the bride. Both *mahr* and dowry are prevalent in the community. In dowry, usually a gold ring, suits and household articles including copper utensils are given. *Mahr* money is fixed at a minimum of Rs. 5,000 and maximum of Rs. 10,000. *Mahr* money may be condoned by the wife.

However, in some cases it is demanded at the time of divorce. The rule of residence is patrilocal. Divorce is permissible in the community and it is on the grounds of adultery and maladjustment. Either party can divorce. Divorce cases are decided among the family elders and a *talaq-nama* is issued. During the *iddat*, a woman stays with her parents and gets maintenance of Rs. 200 to 300 per month. Sometimes, food and other means of sustenance are also provided to her during this period. Children are the responsibility of the father in divorce cases. Divorcee remarriage is permissible and a liberal view is taken for such remarriages in the society. Levirate and sororate forms are also permissible. Change in the marriage institution is that *talaq* shows an increased tendency.

Among the Lohars, the family type is mainly nuclear, although extended form also prevails. Conflicts in the family occur on property matters and sometimes on the challenge to the authority of the elders. Property distribution is equal to all sons but daughters receive their property share in a lesser proporation than the sons. The succession in the family is usually to the eldest son. In the changed circumstances, there is a rise in the formation of nuclear families.

The women in the Lohar community enjoy equal status with men. They have decision-making powers and are usually consulted on matters of marriage and purchase of property. Women contribute to the family income by doing embroidery and spinning. Besides, they have a role in agricultural operations, collection of fuel, social functions, rituals, religious affairs and economic activity. Women also take up jobs in the government or private organizations.

Among the Lohars, after the child birth, both the infant and mother are given bath on the seventh day called *satwan*, and fortieth day known as *chaliswan*. Naming ceremony is observed after one month and the infant is taken to a *maulvi* who gives a name to the child. In return, the *maulvi* receives some cash.

The first hair cut ceremony (*zerakasi*) is performed for which no time is fixed. Circumcision is performed in the case of a male child. It is usually performed by a doctor. First-feeding of cereals is performed after the sixth month of child birth. Marriage is settled through a *manzymyor* who may be a relative or a person belonging to another community. The *manzymyor* gets Rs. 100 to 200 from both the parties for his social service. Among the marriage rituals, the first is *nishani*, in which the groom's relatives go to the bride's place and present jewellery, fruits, sweets and cash to the bride. *Nishani* is followed by *hazri*, in which the bride's relatives come to the groom's place and give jewellery and other articles to the persons who had attended the *nishani* ceremony. Between the rituals of *hazri* and *shadi*, the bride is given clothes on all festivals. Marriage rituals are performed at the bride's place. In *shaadi*, *nikah* is performed in presence of a *maulvi*. The *Nikah-nama* is issued by the *maulvi*. A feast is given by the bride's parents to the invitees. *Bidai* (*rukhsati*) is done after marriage. The bride comes and stays with her in-laws. The nuptial ceremony is performed at the groom's residence. After seven days, both the bride and the bridegroom, and some relatives of the groom, visit the bride's parents and they are served a feast. The groom offers *salaam* to the elders and is paid cash by his in-laws. This ceremony is known as *firsaal*. On the second day of marriage, the *wathal* ceremony is performed at the groom's residence and a feast is given to the invited guests on this occasion.

On the death of a person, the dead body is given a bath and wrapped in a *kafan* (cotton cloth). *Namaz-e-janaza* is performed in a mosque. The *malkhos* digs the grave and gets Rs. 50 to 60. The dead body is placed in the grave (*lahad*). *Fatiha* is read four times on Friday (*Jumma*) after death at the *Kabristan* (burial ground) and a *pyur* (tombstone) indicating the name, birth and death dates of the deceased is placed on the grave on this day. *Chehallum* is performed on the fortieth day of death. On this occasion, the *maulvi* reads *kalma* and is offered food and other articles. There has been no change in the ritual observances. The life-cycle rituals have become more expensive.

Land is the main natural resource for the Lohar community. Landownership is controlled by the individual proprietors. Besides, they do metal work as their traditional occupation. Nowadays members of the community are also engaged in business, trade, weaving, government jobs and have set up industry as well as self-employed business. They depend on the market, specially the local market, for their daily needs and the markets are fully regulated. The Zamindar Khar have barter system with the big zamindars in the village. They do not have traditional caste council or panchayat. Statutory panchayats came into existence after Independence and it takes care of the planning and implementation of welfare and developmental activities.

The Lohar (Ahangar) belong to the Sunni sect of Islam and are *silsila* affiliated to Makhdum Sahib and Miraq Shah. The religious specialists are from outside the community and they perform the birth, marriage and death rites.

They observe Id, Bakr-Id, Id-ul-Milad and other festivals which are of socio-religious significance. Baisakhi is also observed by them.

Singing called *vanvun* is performed by the Lohar women at the time of marriage. They also sing traditional Kashmiri songs.

In the traditional intercommunity relations, the Lohars accept and exchange water, *kachcha* and *pukka* food with other communities, excepting the Watal (Sheikh). The patron-client relationship exists in the community. They cultivate fields on sharecropping basis also. The community has businessmen, scholars, teachers, engineers, doctors and persons in white-collar jobs.

Among the Lohars, the attitude towards formal education is favourable for both the boys and girls. They generally, study up to graduation level. Their attitude towards modern medicare and family welfare programme is also favourable. Tap water facility is available to them. They make use of electricity, irrigation facilities, ICDS and public distribution facilities available in the area. Thier attitude towards saving is also positive.

A.C. SRIVASTAVA

LONE

The Lone, a corrupt form of the Sanskrit word *lavanya*, is a Kashmiri community whose traditional occupation was to trade in rock salt. The members of the community own shops dealing in grocery, rock salt, etc. The origin and history of migration of the Lone is shrouded in mystery. The 1891 Census mentions Pare and Lone and few other communities as Rajputs and Warriors. The Census of 1911 has mentioned Lone as Kashmiri Rajputs. According to others, the term Lone is a distorted version of Raina which was pronounced as Run and which later become Lun. According to Lawrence, the Lone are converts from the Vaishyas, a Hindu community of Kashmir.

The Lone live in all the districts of Kashnmir Valley. However, their major concentration is in the district of Baramula. The natural environment is characterized by an altitude from 5,000 to 19,000 feet above sea level, drained by the river Jhelum inbetween the Pir Panjal and the greater Himalayan ranges. Climate is cold and remains snowbound for four to six months in a year. They live both in the villages and towns. They speak Kashmiri language within the family and with the kin groups. Their script is Arabic. While talking with others, they speak in Urdu. Their dress is identical with the other Muslim communities of the Valley. The men wear *pheran* (long gown), *pyjama* (cotton trousers) and skull cap. The women wear *pheran*, *salwar*, *kameez* (coloured cloth shirt) and a printed scarf on the head. The Lone come under the Other Backward Classes category.

The Lone are non-vegetarian. Their staple food is rice. But, they also eat wheat and maize. Pulses such as gram, *urad*, *moong*, peas, and *masur* are also taken occasionally. They consume all the seasonal fruits and vegetables. They are fond of milk and milk products. Mustard oil is used as the cooking medium. They consume roots and tubers. Alcoholic drinks are forbidden in their religion. Beverage like *gurgur chai* (salty tea) and *qahwa* (sweet tea) are taken a number of times in a day. Older persons smoke *hookah*, while the young smoke cigarettes and *bidis*. There is no change in their food habits. But now, they also take *roti* (unleavened bread) more often. There is a decrease in the frequency of meat consumption due to rising cost of mutton.

They belong both to the Shia and Sunni sects, the latter being numerically dominant. The differentiation is due to economic, occupational and educational reasons. In the region, the Lone are considered in the middle rank of the social hierarchy. The differentiation at occupational level regulates marriage alliances. They can marry among any of the Sheikh title (Krams) provided both are of equal status and occupation. Some of the Krams with whom the Lone have marriage alliance are Bhat, Dar, Malik and Rather. Marriage with the *kamzat* (inferior Krams) are avoided. The inferior Krams are Tarkhan, Watal, Ganai, Desil, and Doom.

The Lone are endogamous, but the role of endogamy is not strictly followed. They prefer to marry off their sons and daughters within their close relatives. If the same are not available, then they select a suitable match from the other Krams title of equal status. They give first preferance to the cousins. In most of the cases, marriage takes place when the boys and girls are adults though, in earlier times, they used to perform child marriages. At present, the age at marriage is between eighteen and twenty years in the case of girls and twenty and thirty years in the case of boys. Generally a common friend or relative starts negotiations but sometimes, it is done through a mediator *manzymyor*. In Srinagar the the *launts* (eunuchs) are engaged to search for a suitable girl. Though polygamy is permissible according to Islamic rules, the same is rarely practised. Monogamy is thus the usual form of marriage. There is no symbol of marriage for women. Likewise, being Muslim both bride-price and dowry are not in practice, but nowadays, dowry is creeping into the community. *Mahr* is fixed at the time of marriage. It is of two types, namely *mahr-e-muajjal* (prompt dower) and *mahr-e-muajjil* (deferred dower). Being a patriocal society, the bride goes to live with her husband and in-laws after marriage. *Gharpet*, the system when the husband goes to live at the house of the bride and in-laws is also practised. In case there are only daughters, the father may ask the husband of the eldest daughter to become *gharpet*. In this case, the husband shares the expenses of the family. According to Islam, only the husband has the right to divorce, but there are certain conditions on the basis of which separation or divorce can be sought. If the husband fails to bear the expenses of wife and children, suffer from serious disease, or does not have sexual contact for more than three years, the wife may seek separation from her husband. Likewise, a husband may also divorce his wife in case of adultary, maladjustment, barrenness and insanity. According to the Islamic rules, divorce may be given either orally or by written document, called *talaq-nama*. A divorced woman has to observe the period of *iddat* before remarriage. If consummation of marriage has taken place but followed by a divorce, then the duration of *iddat* is for three months or, if the woman is pregnant, the *iddat* period extends till the delivery of the child. Widow, widower and divorcee remarriage is permissible. Marriages are performed in the manner as of the first marriage. The changes observed in the marriage rules are a decline in divorce cases, increase in monogamy, decrease in practice of *gharpet* and emergence of dowry system in the community.

Their families are of two types: nuclear and extended, both vertically and horizontally. Interpersonal relations within the family members are based on love, respect and mutual understanding. Old parents are respected and receive due attention from the young. The father treats his adult sons and daughters as equals. They are free to express their views before their father. The guests visiting the house receive full attention from the inmates. There is no avoidance relationship between mother-in-law and son-in-law. The daughter-in-law does not observe *purdah* (seclusion) from the father-in-law and the husband's elder brothers. Joking relations exist between sister-in-law and brother-in-law, with wife's elder sister and wife's younger sister and younger brother. Conflict may be on account of allocation of domestic work among all the wives of married sons, or property distribution among the brothers. The father's property is divided equally among the sons. The daughters get lesser share in the property. The father's property is first divided into three parts. The first share is given to the widow, the next share goes to the unmarried daughters, which is earmarked towards their marriage expenses. The rest is divided equally among all the sons. Succession pattern is followed from father to son. The major change which has been observed is the fission of joint family system.

The Lone women play an active role in the domestic sphere. They do all the domestic work. In the villages, women collect cow-dung, leaves and twigs for firewood. They bring potable water from the public watertaps and look after their younger siblings. They also tend the cattle. In agricultural field, they do all kinds of work except ploughing and clod crushing, which is the responsibility of men. In all agrarian activities, women contribute physically. They enjoy equal status with men and educated ones find employment in the offices, schools and private institutions. There are a few lady lawyers and even judges from this community.

Life-cycle rituals are similar to those of the other Muslim communities of the Valley. An issueless woman is not welcome in the community.

During pregnancy, a woman is not allowed to carry heavy loads. She is not allowed to go out on a moonlit night. During the first pregnancy, a women does not remain with her husband for more than the first five months. The first delivery of the child takes place at her parents' house. Help of a *warin* (midwife) is sought at the time of the delivery. Immediately after the birth, the child is given a bath with warm water. A priest or an elderly person of the family whispers *azaan* in the ears of the child. A message is sent to her in-laws announcing the birth of the child. The first birth is marked with distribution of bread with *shirini* (sugar balls) among friends, relatives, and neighbours. In return, the mother-in-law makes a personal call and offers three pairs of new clothes to the baby, *traem* a large-sized plate full of bread, *shirini*, and some cash. This ceremony is called *piaw*. On the seventh day, the parturient mother takes her first bath with warm water. Tea is served to the neighbours and relatives. The priest is invited to recite prayers and served with dinner. On this day, the child is given a name. This is called *sunder*. A period of pollution is observed for forty days after the birth of the child. During this period, the woman does not offer *namaz* or keep fast. On completion of forty days, the woman is given a second bath. From this date onwards, the mother resumes her normal work. *Zerakasi* (first hair-cutting) of the child, is done at the age of six months or even earlier. A Ganai is called to slaughter a goat. The skin, head and legs of the goat are buried and the mutton is given to the priest and other poor people. Close relatives and members of the household abstain from eating the mutton of the sacrificial goat. The barber performing *zerakasi* gets gift of rice, wheat, and some money. It is believed that the child on whom *aqeeqa* has been performed will not die by an accident. The child is then presented to the womenfolk, who shower small sugar balls, almonds and dates on him. The copper bowl of the barber goes round the guests, who put some coins or cash in it. Circumcision or *khatnahal* is performed before the child attains the age of two years. Formerly, this was performed by the village barber, but now it is done by a qualified surgeon immediately after birth. Marriages are usually settled through negotiation. Boys and girls do not enjoy the freedom of selecting their spouses. The selecion is the exclusive privilage of the parents. Generally, a common friend starts the negotiation at the initiative of one of the parties. The ritualistic stages of marriage are *gandum* (engagement), *doon-leij* (confirmation), *dapanbata* (formal feast), *menziraat* (*mehndi-raat*) and *yenevoul* (wedding). As the date of marriage draws near, several rituals are performed in quick succession, such as seclusion of the would-be bride a practice known as *malasbehoun*, and loosening of her hair *massmechravoun*. On the day preceding the marriage, *malamenz* is observed wherein the female neighbours are invited, served with a dinner and they dye the hands and feet of the bride with *henna*. The relatives and friends of the bridegroom present him *gulmeth* (money) and the bridegroom leaves for the bride's house, formerly on a horse, but now in a taxi in a procession. Before the bridegroom leaves for the bride's house, he sends ahead of him some presents and a hired car for the bride to come along with him after marriage. As the *barat* (marriage procession) draws near the bride's house, the women of the house come out singing *vanvun* (songs of welcome). Then a feast is given. At times, when the *nikah* ceremony is not written by the family elders, a *maulvi* or *imam* of a nearby mosque is called to write it and receive some money. Before this is done, the two contracting parties fix the amount of *mahr* according to the customs of the family. The amount varied from Rs. 800 to 900 in the past, but nowadays, it has gone up varying between Rs. 50,000 to 1,00,000. If the amount of *mahr* fixed is Rs. 50,000 then Rs. 10,000 is paid; the balance of Rs. 40,000 can be demanded by the bride any time, even without divorce. The bride departs with her husband accompanied by one of her female relatives or *dadmoj*.

At the groom's house, the mother-in-law receives the bride and *wathal* or a big feast, is given on this occasion. The bride stays for seven days at the husband's house, after which she goes to her father's house. After a few months, the father of the girl invites his son-in-law to a feast called *firsal* at his house.

When a person dies, a *snangor* (professional bath giver), is called to give bath to the dead body. It is then wrapped in a *kafan* (white cloth), kept in a *taboot* (coffin) and carried to the nearby mosque for *namaz-e-janaza*. If the dead person belonged to the Shia sect, then *marsia* (dirges) are recited. The coffin is taken to the graveyard. The *malkhosh* (gravedigger) digs the grave and the body is laid to rest. Mourning is observed for three days. Close relatives offer cooked food to the members of the bereaved family. During this period, the close kins go to the graveyard and recite *fateha* for the deceased person. On the fourth day, *chaharum* is observed. Relatives, friends and neighbours are invited and offered bread and tea. The *pir* or any religious person is invited for reciting the Holy Koran (Quran *Khwani*) everybody, and which continues for forty days. On the expiry of the fortieth day, *chehallum* is observed and the *pir* and other religious persons are offered a dinner. There is no change in the life-cycle rituals except their curtailment.

The traditional occupation of the Lone community was to trade in rock salt, which was brought from Peshawar before Independence; but it came to a halt after 1947, which caused a great economic set back to this community. The members of the community took up other occupations, such as carpet weaving, embroidery on woollen shawls, fruit growing, business and service for wages. In the villages, the members of this community are engaged in cultivation and growing orchards. Members of this community serve in the police and in military services. With the growing family size, the agricultural land is being fragmented into small holdings, which become uneconomical to operate. Weaving of carpets has provided new avenues to this community. They also keep cows, sheep, goats and fowls to supplement their income by selling milk, wool and eggs. The community has direct links with the market. Child labour is found in the community. Wages are paid in cash. Contractors and middlemen dealing in carpet and woollen shawls visit the villages and engage them for this work on daily wages. A majority of the contractors and wholesalers of carpet belong to the Shia sect, while the majority of skilled labourers are from the Sunni sect. Child labour constitutes 50 per cent of the labour force engaged in the weaving of carpet and shawl embroidery. Disputes over land and matrimony are solved by the elders. Sometimes, cases are referred to the court of law. The Lones have their representatives in the *gram* panchayat. This also looks after the plan and developmental activities of the village.

The Lones profess Islam. Majority of them belong to the Sunni sect, and the fundamentals of their religion are strictly followed. In order to protect themselves against troubles, such as disease, accidents, barreness, and for the welfare of the family, they visit the *asthan* (shrines) and take advice from a *pir.* The sacred shrines visited by the members of the community are Hazrat bal, Dastgir Sahib, Khanqah-e-Mulla, Charar-e-Sharif, Shah Zain-ud-Din and the shrine of Makhdum Sahib. They observe Id-ul-Fitr, Id-ul-Zuha, Shab-e-Barat and Shab-e-Qadr festivals.

A few members of the community are trained in carpet weaving. Some of them are engaged in *rafoogiri* (darning) on woollen shawls for which they get daily wages. Only men are engaged in this type of work. Folk songs are sung on the occasion of child birth, marriage and on festivals. Only women participate in the folk songs and dances. Men have separate folk songs. The musical instrument is *tumbaknari*, which is generally played by women.

The shawl hawkers and representatives from various art emporia of Srinagar visit their villages and engage employ them for *rafoogiri* and carpet making. They give plain woollen shawls and materials for embroidery to the villagers and pay them at the rate of Rs. 20 to 25 per day. This has certainly improved the economic condition of the village people.

The Lones are in favour of education. Facilities of school education are available in almost every village. Boys and girls are studying at least upto the primary and middle levels in the villages. Those who are keen to continue their education go up to college standard. Girls generally drop out from their studies because of economic constraints. Facilities of primary health centres are available to the villagers. Besides, under the ICDS programmes, health visitors (*gram sevikas*) visit the villages and provide medical attention to the nursing mothers and nutrition kit for children who are under six years. They also advise the families on sanitation and health care. Open latrines and lack of proper drainage in the villages are the main problems. Family planning is now popular with the villagers. Generally, men get themselves sterilized. Drinking water is now available in the villages through taps. The UNICEF has helped in providing clean drinking water to many villages. Provision for employment through IRDP is available to them. Stipends are given for vocational training in tailoring and carpentry to boys and girls whose parents' income is low. Loan is given to the poor for the construction of house under the house building programmes. Electricity is now available in most of the villages. It has benefited the rural industries. Dehati Elaqai Banks have contributed to the general improvement of the rural people. They provide loans to small and marginal farmers for the purchase of tractors, milch cattle, seeds and fertilizers and for small scale industries. Fuel resources available in the villages are cow-dung, firewood, leaves and twigs of willow, *safeda*, and *kikar*, which are preserved for the winter season when everything is covered with snow. Kerosene oil is an important source of fuel in the villages. Irrigation facilities are available through canals. There are cooperative societies through which the farmers get fertilizers. Facilities of food articles distribution through the fair price shops are available in the villages. Dependence on the moneylenders and shopkeepers has been reduced to a large extent due to banks. The panchayat ghars are equipped with television sets, which is a powerful medium for mass communication. The improved variety of milch cows has improved the economic condition of the community.

PARMANAND LAL

MAHAJAN

The community calls itself Mahajan, and is addressed by others also by this name. The literary meaning of the term is 'great folk' and has been in use in ancient literature, though with a different shade of meaning, denoting a great or respectable person, and has nothing to do with any caste name. How the term came to be applied to a caste or sub-caste belonging to the third *varna* in the Hindu social hierarchy has not been known. This name or title has been bestowed throughout the state on the Banias or the trading community. As such, it is synonymous with *shah* meaning king; the popular term for a moneylender in the hills of Jammu. Sometimes, in these hills, they are known as *pahari mahajan*, who are considered a true caste and the term is no longer an honorific or title. Not long ago, they were generally styled as *Karar* or *Kirar*. Now the community has given up this name and adopted the title of Gupta. The Mahajans seem to be a mixed community sprung from the intermarriages of immigrants from the plains, belonging to the Bania or Kayasth castes. Thus a Brahman shopkeeper was also called as Mahajan, though most of the Mahajans appear to be the Banias or Kayasths who had married girls of the lower Rajput grades, such as the Rathis and Rawats. Now, Gupta and Mahajan are the terms commonly used for them.

The Mahajans are spread all over the state, but their greater concentrations are in Jammu and Udhampur districts. As they are found scattered all over the state, they inhabit all types of climatic conditions and terrain found in the state. To the north, they inhabit the high mountains and valleys of the Himalayas, which receive good share of snowfall in winter, in Bhadarwah, Kishtwar, Kashmir Valley and Punch-Rajouri belt. They are found in the *kandi* belt of the lower Shivalik.

In the matter of food, the Mahajans are of mixed habits. Some of them are vegetarian on philosophical grounds rooted in the tenets of non-injury or *ahimsa*. Some are vegetarians on the basis of faith or sect of which they are votaries, but most of them have no prejudice against taking meat and other forms of non-vegetarian diet permitted for the Hindu castes. Eggs, fish, mutton, and occasionally pork and *shikar* are relished. Wheat and rice form their staple food along with all types of *dals* like green gram and *masur*. All types of vegetables are consumed by them. Wild roots, greens and fruit are occasionally consumed by the village Mahajans in *kandi* tract when available in special seasons. Fruits are moderately used by them. The rich among them have a large share of dry as well as fresh fruit. Generally, they are not favourably disposed towards alcoholic drinks, but the rich and agriculturists among them of rural areas consume both country-made and costly drinks. The use of alcoholic drinks amongst them is on an increase. On some religious days, like Janmashtami, Ramnavami or Shivratri, they abstain from taking staple food and observe complete fast and take some wild grain like *seul* and *dreyu* flour which is used sometimes instead of usual grain. During Navratras (nine days Devi worship), non-vegetarian food is altogether avoided. The most outstanding change in their food habits is marked in their tendency to disregard some dietary injunctions of the *shastras*.

The Mahajan community of Jammu & Kashmir is divided into two distinct groups, one is called Mirpuri and the other Dogra Mahajans. They differ not only in name, but also in some social features and ritualistic observations. The Dogra or eastern Mahajans have the following main *gotras*: Jandial, Beotre, Lamme, Manath, Mohotre and Phagotre. The Mirpuri subcastes (*gotras*) are Bagotra, Kabotra, Khangal, Khariyal, Sadavartiye, Bhagial, Gadya, Garnal, Khanna, Pandi, Kalshotre, Pakshotre, Phanial, Paharu, Rotre, Rasotre, Ragarly and Thathar. All these *gotras* of both the groups are exogamous but while the Dogra Mahajans can marry in any other Mahajan family outside their own *gotra*, the Mirpuris may marry their sons and daughters only in Mirpuri families. However, these *gotras* are not hierarchical, involving any sense of high and low. Their classification seems only to reflect the fact of their different origins and ancestry. The Mirpuri Mahajans have titles of Chaudhari, Lala, Shah and Raja. The community considers itself superior to the other communities in the economic field and in the affairs of trade and commerce, particularly in the matters of counting and accountancy. They recognize the *varna* system, and in that hierarchy, they include themselves in the third *varna*, i.e. Vaishyas. Their special role as petty shopkeepers, traders and moneylenders has been recognized by the society since ages.

The Mahajans are generally monogamous, but the rich among them were polygamous. The Mirpuri Mahajans were mostly polygamous. Formerly, early marriage between the age of 8 and 12 years in the case of girls and 10 and 16 years for boys took place, and *gaona* or *rafera* usually took place when the bride was about 16 years in age. Negotiated marriage was the only popular mode of acquiring spouses. Old and polygynous persons sometimes sought brides by purchase.

Even in such cases, all the formalities of the negotiated marriage were observed. Negotiation was initiated by the party of the girl, except in the case of the Mirpuri Mahajans, among whom the parents of the boy pursued the negotiations for a considerably long time in order to seek the hand of the girl. Negotiations were conducted through the *kul-purohit* or the village barber, or a mediator, known to both the families, called *rawara*. After the negotiations were successful, *kurmai* (betrothal) took place and *sagun* was sent to the boy's parents by the parents of the girl. According to the *gandian* ceremony, in return, the parents of the boy also sent a sort of *sagun* for their would-be bride a fortnight or a week before the day of marriage which was conveyed finally with the *gandian* ceremony. After *gandian*, the boy and girl were not allowed to go out of their houses. The marriage ceremony was performed at the house of the girl according to the Vedic rites in the *vedi* according to the rules of the Hindu society. Then, the bride was taken to live at her husband's house. The Mahajans are patrilocal. *Sindoor*, vermilion, *bindi*, *lal chura* (red bangles), finger and toe rings were symbols of marriage along with *chauk*, a form of conical head ornament. Some of these have now fallen out of use, particularly the latter one. Dowry was given both in cash and kind, mostly in latter form. Divorce was not recognized before the introduction of Hindu Marriage Act. Remarriage of widows was not allowed and some cases of *sati* are also known to have occurred. There are some *sati samadhis*, which are venerated even today. However, a widow was allowed to marry her *devar*, the younger brother of her deceased husband. The rite was known as *chadar dalna*. Among recent changes in marriage rules, legal divorce has come to stay, but yet in rare cases. Not much change in the marriage customs has taken place except in simplification of some rites.

The Mahajan family is a horizontally extended unit in which the elders are respected, feared and obeyed, and relationships are properly maintained. Joking relationship exists only between sister-in-law and brother-in-law. Conflicts in family sometime arise out of overbearing behaviour of the elders in suppression of social and economic rights of the youngers. Inheritance rules are governed by *pag-vand* and *chunda-vand* systems. In case of only one wife, all the sons of the deceased share his property equally among them at the time of division. In case of more wives, the *chunda-vand* system is followed, where the property is divided into equal *dheries* (shares) corresponding to the number of wives. Then each son of a wife receives equal share in the *dheri* of his mother. In inheritance, the rule of primogeniture is observed. Some changes have been observed in these aspects in recent years as a result of constitutional and social legislation as well as under the impact of modern influences. Families are breaking up into nuclear units. The youngers have become less respectful towards their elders.

The Mahajan women are given a respectable place in the family and community at large. They participate in all social, cultural and religious activities. However, they do not play a significant role in the economic activities of the family. Among the poorer families, the women prepare some simple saleable articles of domestic use for others or for their own shops and add a little to the family earning. Barring few instances, they do not contribute much to the family income. But in family management, they shoulder greater responsibilities than men. They have now got social and political rights and receive good education. Some of them are doctors, lawyers, and representatives elected to the local bodies. They have also joined the government service and factory jobs. This applies to the younger generation. Majority of them are still housewives and look after the domestic affairs.

The Mahajans observe all the usual Hindu *sanskars* with only minor variations. The birth of a female child passes without much rejoicing, but the birth of the boy is celebrated with great feasting and rejoicing. Songs are sung on *dholak*, and *gurh* (molasses) is distributed among the whole village community. Twenty-one days of pollution is observed. On the fifth day, the first bath is given to the baby and the mother. The ceremony is known as *punjap*. On the twenty-first day after birth, the child and the mother are given final bath of purification and the mother is allowed to join her domestic and social activities. The child is subject to a rite called *sutre*; on that day, a thread is tied round the child's girdle, and then the child is taken out of the house for the first time. An astrologer is called to prepare the horoscope of the child and find out the *rashi* (zodiacal name) which is incorporated in the horoscope, but it is kept a secret and a nickname is given to the child. *Yajnopavit* rite was performed usually between the age of 7 and 11 years, but now it is mostly deferred to the date of marriage when both the rites are celebrated at the same time, probably with a view to saving time as well as expenses. Marriages were formerly performed at an early age, usually between the age of 12 and 16 years but now adult marriage has become the normal fashion. For the purpose of marriage, consanguinity and *gotra* are prohibited. Marriage out side the community is also not approved, although there are several intercaste marriages among the Mahajans and the number of such marriages is on the increase. Marriage rites are performed at the house of the bride. Nuptials are performed at the husband's house. The bride after marriage lives at her husband's house.

The *antyeshti* (death rites), closely follow the Hindu vedic system. The dead body is cremated. On the fourth day after death, the *phool* (burnt bones) are collected by the family members in an earthen jar, and are usually carried to Haridwar to be immersed in the Ganga before the tenth day. *Oke* (mourning) is observed for thirteen days and closes with the *kriya-karam* rites on this day when the *biradari* is also feasted. *Barkhi* and *chaubarkhi* rites are performed after one and four years, respectively, after death. Afterwards, annual *shradh* is observed during the *pitra-paksha* fortnight.

The Mahajan is primarily a trading community; so the major economic resource of the Mahajans is shopkeeping and inter-village trade. In every village and town, a few of the Mahajan families are found who run petty provision shops there. Moneylending was their subsidiary profession and they used to lend money against mortgage of land and ornaments. Consequently, they came to acquire land and agriculture became their subsidiary occupation. Such land is controlled by the elder of the family, as the sole proprietor of the family property. The Mahajans own big or small pieces of land. Hence, the community may be considered partially landowning although most of the petty shopkeepers in villages and towns do not possess any agricultural land. The community is thus a combination of landowning and landless categories. Some of them were big farmers, but recent agricultural reforms in the state have subjected ownership of agricultural land to a meagre ceiling, thereby abolishing big landlordism. Their subsidiary profession of moneylending has also suffered due to extension of the banking and government lending facilities to villages and small towns. The Mahajans have, therefore, concentrated all their energies towards developing their traditional trading profession and business of all types. They have entered industry, interstate trading, technical professions and the government jobs. Marketing facilities are available to them everywhere. They transact all types of business in cash. Barter or exchange system is unknown to them. Mostly, they buy consumer goods from Jammu city or some other big town and sell these at their village shops on profit. Their expertise in the profession of trade and shopkeeping as well at computing figures has become proverbial in this region. Most of their school-going children help their parents after school hours, mostly, as apprentices. Those who employ salesmen or keep apprentices pay wages in cash. As a result of the incidence of higher education and technical and professional training, youngmen are joining the government services and professions like those of doctors, lawyers and contractors, and are setting up production units and industries, with the result that there is a visible shift from the primary to the secondary sectors of occupations and professions.

The Mahajans have organized their associations called *sabhas*, which serve as an instrument of social control in a loose manner. They have a central Mahajan Sabha at Jammu housed in the large Mahajan Hall. Mahajan Halls have been constructed in other towns also, where marriage parties are housed and other social functions and gatherings of the *biradari* are held. The Central Sabha lays down rules of social behaviour and carries reforms which are generally observed by the Mahajan *biradari*. Those who fail to abide by these rules are punished to undergo some *prayashchit* in the form of fines or punishment called *donn doda*. In serious cases, it results in *samajik* (social) boycott, of the person or family, in which no *sabha* member maintains any social and ritual connection with them and they cannot become member of any of the Mahajan *sabhas*. In villages, gram panchayats settle disputes of the villagers including the Mahajans. Mahajan *sabhas* offer help to the deserving Mahajan students for higher education in India and even abroad. The recipients are expected to refund the money when they are settled in their career. The *sabhas* also help their *biradari* members in setting up big and small businesses. Consequently, there is no unemployment among them. The young are helped to set up their business as and when they come of age. During recent years, the Mahajans have grown richer and their *sabhas* have come to play more important role in the economy of the community, and thus are wielding greater power of social control.

The Mahajans are ardent votaries of Sanatan religion. However, some of them are reformists and have joined the fold of Arya Samaj and Radhaswami Satsang. Most of the Mahajan *gotras* have their own *kul-devtas*, whom they propitiate on the occasion of socio-religious rites. For instance, the Jandials are votaries of Guru Sehaj Nath, a disciple of Guru Gorakhnath, one of whose temples is at Talab Tillo, Jammu, and another at Jandi village. The Manath section has a sati shrine near Samba town. Most of the Mahajan sections have their *sati samadhis*. Among the regional shrines, they visit the Chirhi of Bawa Jitto and the *samadhi* of Bawa Pohto in Jammu district. They also go on pilgrimage to the shrines of Vaishno Devi and Amarnath and the other Hindu *tirathas* (holy places) all over India. Religious specialists for the community are usually the Brahmans who perform all their socio-religious rites and functions and have no other role to play.

Some of the village Mahajans, particularly those inhabiting the hills, have faith in *jadoo jarhian* (charms and spells) and take services of the *chelas* in cases of mental and physical ailments and adverse situations, which they attribute to evil influences and charms. The *chelas* and *jogis*, who are adept in the art, conduct sittings of occult dance *jatra*, and *jarhian khedana*, supposed to lead to health and well-being. Annual fairs are held at the shrines of Bawa Pohto, Bawa Sehaj Nath and Chirhi which the Mahajan attend in large numbers as votaries, while in all other local fairs and festivals, they cater to the needs of people gathered on such occasions by setting up temporary shops during the fairs. No change of religion has been ever reported among the Mahajans of this state. The local Mahajan leader, Mahatma Hans Raj, a pleader and popular reformist, led social reform movement among the Mahajans and other Dogra *biradaris* and founded a Dogra Sadar Sabha. The reforms he introduced among the Mahajans are contained in a booklet published by the Central Mahajan Sabha, Jammu. They have also been influenced by the social reforms advocated by Arya Samaj and Radhaswami Satsang. These movements have made the Mahajans liberal in their social outlook and much progressive in their ideas.

Their traditional profession is of different nature. They do not practise any crafts. However, the talented among them are good artists, painters, sculptors and radio artists. They have preserved oral traditions and legends about their own heroes and also folklore and folk tales current in the region, but most of these have now been forgotten, as the custom of story telling has gone out of fashion. Every section of the Mahajans has a legend about some of their heroes or ancestors.

The Mahajans were governed by the traditional Hindu principle of untouchability which they observed towards the Shudra class and the Muslims. Within such framework of their social behaviour, they have had cordial relations with all the communities and, as shopkeepers and traders, they served all the communities in fulfilling their needs. In that capacity, they were respected by all the communities, but, they did not have commensal relations with the Shudra *varna* and with the Muslim community. Though they served food and water to these communities, they did not accept these from their hands. However, they have commensal relations with all the other Hindu communities. Connubial norms were also governed by tradition or *reeti* which prohibited such linkages with even the other Hindu communities. Intercommunity and inter caste marriages were disallowed, nevertheless such marriages took place though rarely. Putative linkages are formed with members of any other Hindu or Muslim communities depending on chance or choice of the person concerned at the time of ritualistic occasions, such as *gaona*, *mundan*, a *dharm-bhai* or *-sakhi* may be from any community, irrespective of caste and creed. They share the public buildings such as schools, panchayat ghars, cremation grounds and inns with other communities such as the Muslim and Harijans, but they do not share water resources with the Muslims and Harijan communities. However, the Mahajans had relations of economic interdependence with these and all other communites. They were shopkeepers and traders and all others were their clients and customers. They had patron-client relations also with the Brahman community. Under the impact of recent legislation and liberal ideas, the traditional linkages are undergoing a change. Except connubial linkages, they now have all types of inter community linkages with all the Hindu and non-Hindu communities. They participate in all types of political activities and public functions at the local, regional and national levels. They not only elect but also get elected to the local and national democratic institutions. They participate in the political movements and agitations in the state. As landlords, they have sharecropper linkages with their tillers and agricultural labourers as well as landlord-tenant relations with those to whom they let out their farm lands. Some of them engage farm labourers on daily wages or seasonal basis for various agricultural operations, and hence have cultivator-labour relations with other communities, particularly with the Scheduled Castes who mostly supply the farm labourers and workers. Most of them are shopkeepers, traders, businessmen and owners of big and small production units where they employ workers, apprentices and clerks whom they pay monthly salaries and observe all the formalities of empolyer-worker relationship. The community plays an important part in the multifarious activities of socio economic life of the region, therefore, they have comprehensive inter-community linkages most of which are now guided by the modern ideals.

The Mahajans have a high percentage of literacy. Their boys and girls receive education up to the highest standard and also undergo all available training and professional courses. Majority of them study upto graduation. Health and medical care facilities are fully available to them in the towns as well as rural areas. Government dispensaries and civil hospitals are at their disposal. They avail of both the indigenous and the modern systems of medicine. They contribute to the family planning programme and make use of the usually available methods. They believe in having a small family of two or three children. Tap water for drinking purposes is available to them, even in *kandi* and hill areas. Few employment schemes have been introduced in this state. Hence the Mahajans do not enjoy the benefits of rural employment programmes such as IRDP and Employment Guarantee Schemes. Only minor self-employment programmes are available under which the Mahajans get small government loans on easy terms to set up petty production units, such as poultry, fishery, piggery, bakery, fruit and vegetable gardens, and small cottage industries. Most of them are engaged in their traditional trade. They make use of the communication media for their everyday conveniences and for their business. Radio, television, telephone and newspaper services are available to them. They get electricity for their domestic as well as business uses. Electricity, kerosene oil, soft coke and wood are the usual sources of energy. In towns, most of them are making use of LPG for domestic use and in villages, kerosene oil is taking place of wood for cooking purposes. Coal is also becoming popular for such uses, but cow-dung is still being used by the rural Mahajans for domestic purposes. Of late, some movement against denudation of forests and atmospheric pollution has been set up which is receiving favourable response.

S.D.S. CHARAK

MALIK

The Maliks inhabit the higher part of the Darhal Valley and other parts of Kashmir. It is an Islamic title given by Emperor Akbar. The Maliks were appointed by the Emperor as in-charge of the passes that led to Kashmir. Villages were granted to them on tenure for this service. They were to defend these passes and appear in the field, when required, with an army of their own people ranging from one hundred to five hundred men. The charge became hereditary, and the Maliks of Darhal as well as those on the other frontiers of Kashmir represented the original officers of Akbar. Those of Darhal, though in some respect resembling the rest of the Chibbalis, still have something distinctive in their appearance; for instance, their beards are long and wavy. They give their daughters in marriage to the Jarals of their neighbourhood. They are distributed throughout the Kashmir Valley. They speak Kashmiri and use the Arabic script for writing in Urdu. The climate of the Valley is cold, with low humidity, thin forest, medium rainfall and medium snowfall in winter. There is no special dress to distinguish them from the other Kashmiris. The Muslim women wear a skull cap surrounded by a fillet of red colour. The Malik are non-vegetarian, but they do not eat pork. They take all types of seasonal vegetables. *Hak* or *karam sag* is their favourite dish. Their staple food is rice and wheat. They take pulses like grams, *urad* and *moong*. They use mustard oil as cooking medium. They do not take alcholic drinks. They often take salty tea. Their consumption of fruit is moderate. They take milk and milk products and enjoy *bidi*, cigarette and hubble-bubble. They chew betal leaves.

The Maliks are termed as Sheikhs in *Tarikh-e-Hasan* and *Tarikh-e-Aqwam-e-Kashmir*. They place themselves in the middle order of the Muslim hierarchy. Marriages are usually performed within the community, but there is no bar in marrying with the Dar, Mir and Bhat. Marraige is settled by parents through negotiation when the children become adult. Consanguineous marriage is in practice. Junior levirate and junior sororate are permitted. Though the usual form of marriage is monogamy, polygyny also exists. There is no marriage symbol among the Maliks. The *mahr* is fixed according to the status of the bridegroom. The rule of residence is patrilocal. Divorce is permissible. Women cannot divorce, but they may seek separation on certain grounds. According to the Muslim law, when a woman wants to remarry after divorce or also after the death of her husband, she cannot marry before completing the *iddat* period, that is four months and ten days, which is, in fact, to establish the paternity of a possible child conceived. Compensation is given to the wife in case of divorce. Remarriage is permissible for widows, widowers and the divorcees. The usual family type is extended, but these days separate households within the family are formed. In the family, the younger brother's wife avoids the husband's elder brother and also all other elderly male members. Joking relationships exist between the husband's younger brothers and sisters and younger brothers and sisters of the wife and elder sister's husband. Both sons and daughters inherit paternal property though daughters get lesser share. Succession is from father to the eldest son.

Status of women in the community is lower as they have no decision-making power. They participate in all economic activities and contribute to the family income. Women play an active role in the family management, they collect potable water and fuel and perform rituals, participate in the social and religious festivties. They do not have any pre-delivery rituals. Pregnant women are treated carefully and affectionately. They generally go to their parents' house for the delivery. Assistance of some experienced woman in the household or neighbourhood is sought during the delivery. After the birth of the child, the *mulla* recites *azaan* into the ear of the new-born baby. On the seventh day, the mother takes a bath. The baby is also cleaned and a name is given by the *pir* of the family. This ceremony is known as *sunder*. *Zerakasi*, is one of the chief ceremonies, usually perfromed within one year at some sacred place wherein the barber is called to shave the head of the child. *Khatna* (circumcision) is performed on male children within three years of age. It is an occasion of great rejoicings and festivities. The child's feet are dyed with myrtle paste (*henna*) and a feast is given to relative and friends. On the next day, the child is seated on a basket under which a cock is cooped. The basket is covered by a piece of new cloth. The surgical operation is performed by the barber.

Marriage is settled through a *manzymyor* (middleman). Marriage ceremonies initially start with the pre-betrothal ritual called *roopay pilnavin* or *sagan paytravithyun* ceremony. It is on this day that the two parties start direct negotiations with one another. Prior to marriage, singing of songs continues for the whole night and the ladies apply *henna* on the hands of the bride on this occasion, and a cash present is collected and given to the barber. The bridegroom wears, shirt, coat and *pyjama* with a *sehra* on head. Tying of *sehra* on the head of the bridegroom is an important ritual of marriage. The dress of the bride consists of *salwar* and *kameez*. The marriage party, *barat* leaves for the bride's residence, where a feast is served to them. After this, the *pir* or *qazi* writes the *nikah-nama* (marriage contract) and the amount of *mahr* is fixed with the consent of both the parties. *Rukhsati* wherein the bride bids farewell to her parents, friends and kin is the last marriage ritual. Next day at dawn, the bridegroom comes back to his residence with the bride. Nuptial ceremony and feast are held at the bridegroom's place on this occasion.

The dead body is given a bath and wrapped in a *kafan* (white cloth). It is carried to the graveyard in a wooden *taboot* (coffin) which can readily be procured from a nearby mosque. The *taboot* is covered with a black cloth and taken to the nearby mosque where the customary prayer, *namaz-e-janaza* is performed. The grave is dug by the relatives and neighbours of the deceased. After placing the corpse in the grave, all those who are present there throw a handful of soil into the grave. After reciting *fateha* on the grave, the mourners return home. On the fourth day, *fateha* is again read at the grave of the deceased. After performing the rituals at the grave, the mourners are served light refreshments. *Koran-khani* is observed on the tenth and fortieth day. Many rituals and ceremonies connected with birth, marriage and death have, however, undergone reforms as a consequence of modern socio-economic necessities.

Among the Maliks, land is the main natural resource which is controlled by individual proprietors. Their primary occupation nowadays varies. They are engaged in horticulture, business, trade and government and private service. They are self-employed in textile weaving and printing, and in handicrafts. Many of them participate in agricultural and horticultural activities in the rural areas. Young boys, after completing their education in the cities, either join the government service or start business. The local market is fully regulated and the entire business runs on cash transactions. Owing to the increase in the number of family members and the pressure on agricultural land, many in the family shift from villages to towns in search of livelihood.

There is no traditional caste council among the Maliks. Social disputes are solved either by the family elders or by the well-wishers. If the need arise, they may go to the court of law. Statutory panchayats are heterogeneous and take care of implementation of the welfare and development programmes in the village.

The Maliks profess Islam and follow the Islamic rules and regulations. They attend mosque for *namaz* prayers specially on *Jumma* (Friday). Sacred shrines associated with the name of saints are the source of attraction and inspiration to them. Prayers are offered at these places. They visit Charar-e-Sharif, Hazratbal and Ajmer Sharif on different occasions. Their religious specialists are from other communities. They perform birth, marriage and death rites. They celebrate different Islamic festivals like Id-ul-Fitr, Id-ul-Zuha, Shab-e-Barat, Muharram and Nauroz. Also some local festivals like Urs-e-Shah Hamdan, Urs-e-Makhdum Sahib, Urs-e-Charar-e-Sharif and Ziarat-e-Hazratbal are observed by them. All these festivals have socio-religious and socio-economic significance. Traditionally, the Maliks are not craftsmen, but a few of them who have received training are engaged in carving, engraving, and weaving work. They sing folk songs on different social festivals. Traditionally, there are no musical instrument associated with them.

In Kashmir, both the Muslim and Hindus Maliks equally share one another's joys and sorrows. Social consciousness on common tradition and cultural unity are preserved inspite of penury and economic subjugation through the ages. Their common language and dress strengthens the ties of integration. In the traditional intercommunity linkage, they accept and exchange water, *kachcha* and *pukka* food with the other Muslim communities excepting the Goor, Ganai and Watal. They visit and participate in the Hindu festivals. Being land-owners and businessmen, they maintain good relations with the workers and the clients. The modern linkages are based on political inclinations and affiliations which brought them closer to the members of other communities. They have scholars, businessmen, teachers, doctors, engineers, members in defence service, etc., among them. Political leadership from among them has emerged at the state level.

In the past, the Malik children were sent to a *madrasa*, generally at the age of five for Islamic education. Later, the traditional sciences were taught to them. Those included the study of theology such as *Ilm-e-kalam*, *Ilm-e-tawhid* and education of the Koranic verses called *tafsir*, *hadis* (traditions) and *fiqah* (jurisprudence). But nowadays, formal education is fairly widespread and considered favourable for both boys and girls. They study up to postgraduate and higher levels. Some of them drop out from studies due to social reasons. Their attitude towards modern medicare is positive. They use both traditional and modern medicines. They are not receptive to family planning. Tap water facilities are available to the community. They enjoy media and communication facilities in the area. They have electricity in their house. For fuel, they use firewood, cow-dung cakes and kerosene oil. They use organic manures, chemical fertilizers and insecticides in their fields. They avail of irrigation facilities from the canals. ICDS and public distribution facilities are availed by them. Their attitude towards saving is positive.

D.K. CHAKRABORTY

MANHAS

The Manhas once formed a part of a large Rajput community inhabiting the country below the Jammu border, i.e. the districts of Rawalpindi, Jhelum, Sialkot and Shakargarh, now in Pakistan, and Jammu, Rajouri, and Kathua districts of Jammu province. After Independence, the Manhas of the districts in Pakistan migrated to India and have settled in Gurdaspur, Hoshiarpur and Una districts. They were also distributed in the districts of Shahpur and Montgomery. The derivation of the name of the community also explains its origin. The Manhas claim to be of solar origin (*surya-vanshi*) or by direct descent from Sri Ramchandra, whose descendant Ukalghar took up his abode in the Doab (Sialkot). His son Jambu Lochan, became powerful and famous and defeated Raja Chandra Hans (Haus) of Madra-desh and built the present city of Jammu. The last ruling house of Jammu and Kashmir was their lineal descendant and they owe their family or clan name, Jamwal, to him. One of his successors was named Jogi Rai, also called Jog Raj and Jaggu Rai in their tradition. He ruled Sialkot during the fourth-fifth century AD, and is said to be the contemporary of Anang Pal, the Tanwar, who founded Delhi in about AD 372. He had two sons, Malhan Hans and Suraj Dhar. Malhan Hans, also called Man Haras, ruled Madra-desh from its capital Sialkot. He had a large number of sons amongst whome he divided a number of villages as *jagirs* for their sustenance. In due course of time, their numerous offspring took to agriculture. Hence the whole of their clan came to be called Manhas or Malnhas and Manharsas after Raja Malhan Hans. The villages of Pargowal, Chaprar, Thub, Ghorsuha and others traditionally belonged to them. As they grew in number, they were compelled to migrate to other places. Bara Manga and Darya Pind were their main habitations. On account of their adoption of the occupation of agriculture, they were looked down upon by their colateral brethren Jamwals, who continued to stick to their traditional vocation of a soldier.

The Manhas are one of the larger Rajput communities and majority of them are spread over the tahsils of Ranbirsinghpura, Jammu, Akhnur, Samba, Hiranagar and Kathua, but are also sparsely distributed all over Jammu province. The members of the community do not put on any distinctive mark of dress other than that of the Rajputs of this area. Normally, they wear tight trousers, *ghatanna* or *pyjama*, with a long coat, called *achkan*, falling down up to the knees. The poor sections of the community wear *dhoti* and *kurta* of coarse cloth, usually of homespun fabric. White is usually worn by the elderly and ploughmen. Turbans dyed in light colours, such as almond, rose and *ferozi* (azure) are worn by the well-to-do persons among them. *Kesari* colour is worn on special occasions and considered a distinctive mark of all classes of the Rajputs of this area. Long upturned moustache was their distinctive mark. Now most of them have changed their dress habits. For footwear, they put on country-made shoes of coarse leather as well as sophisticated shoes.

The Manhas are non-vegetarian abhoring beef or buffalo meat, but are fond of pork. However, their usual meat item is goat's meat and poultry. As among the other Hindu communities of the region, most of their females are vegetarian, but prepare meat dishes for their family. Men also abstain from non-vegetarian diet, including egg and fish, on certain occasions like fasting days, *vrats*, *navratras* and *shradhs*. Rice and wheat with all types of *dals* and beans produced locally form their staple food. The only roots and tubers used are the sweet potato and *tarrar*, a long natural root found in low hill tracts. All types of fruits and vegetables grown in the area and available in the market are consumed by them. Carrots, spinach, turnips, radish, tomatoes, potatoes, *methi*, *karam* and cauliflower are the greens and tubers of everyday use, with green gram, green peas and *sarson ka sag* for seasonal use. Milk and milk products are abundantly in use as the commmunity is primarly agriculturist. Among non-alcoholic drinks, *lassi* and sweet water treated with lemon juice and *sattoo* mixed in water are occasional drinks. The community has no prejudice against use of alcoholic drinks and most of them indulge in drinking freely on festive occasions, but only a few of them are regular consumers. Country liquor is freely available and, on festive occasions, costly and superior alcoholic drinks are also served.

The Manhas are a homogeneous community without any social divisions. However, they themselves are part of a stratified social system to which the Rajputs of the hills are subjected. In Jammu region, the Manhas belong to an inferior grade. They claim to be the origional Jamwal clan which ruled at Sialkot and Jammu but, as their ancestors took to the plough, they fell in social status and, because of some special social customs, they are relegated to the second grade of the *jaikaria* Rajputs of the Dugar group who are divided into three or four grades. Being akin to the ruling clan of Jammu, they are entitled to the salutation of *jai*. Though they are part of the Jamwal ruling clan, the latter look down upon them for their taking to inferior occupation of agriculture and for adopting degraded social customs like *karewa* and *dohari*. The gradation is social and meant mostly for marital purposes and in social gatherings of the Rajputs; but since Independence, a tendency is observable among the Rajputs to disregard such distinctions to a large extent and now these hardly exist. The Manhas belong to the second *varna* system of the Hindu society and they are recognized as such by all other communities.

The Manhas community is exogamous and, usually, monogamous. They gave their daughters to superior Rajput clans of the first grade, and took their wives from inferior graded clans. However, they intermarried with the Salaria and other second graded Rajputs of the neighbourhood. They are, therefore, classed among the *dohari* group for matrimonial purposes. Among the Rajputs of Jammu and neighbourhood, there are minute distinctions as to who can give and who can take girls in marriage and these distinctions were adhered to with great pride. It is this practice which has led to the distinction which exists between the *ekahri* and *dohari* groups. The *ekahri* sections contract only one-sided match, they take wives from certain clans, but do not give their daughters to those clans. The *dohra* clans exchange their sons and daughters between them without any restrictions. In fact, marriages among them are settled on a system of exchange, usually involving two or three families. The Manhas belong to the category called *dohari* and also practise widow remarriage through *karewa*. They follow the usual rites connected with marriage custom, such as *tika* (reserving the boy), *kurmai*, *biah* and *maklawa*. A special event connected with the Manhas marriage is the custom of *neejana* or *bijana*, wherein the bridegroom's family sprinkles water on a he-goat. If the animal shakes, it is considered to have been accepted by the deity. It is then, killed, cooked and served to the *biradari* in the marriage feast. Widow remarriage in the deceased husband's family or his kin is recognized and is known as the ritual of *doahl*. Divorce is not permitted. The *dohari* system entailed even child marriage, when an adult boy or girl was not available in the families for exchange. With the improvement in socio-economic conditions of the community and introduction of the constitutional laws concerning divorce and female inheritance, the Manhas has also given up most of the older customs, but the change is comparatively slow.

The Manhas family is patrilineal and the father or an elder male member of the family holds the proprietary rights over all types of moveable or immoveable property. The elders are usually feared as well as respected and obeyed. Two systems of inhertiance are practised among them. Where there is offspring of only one wife, *pag-vand* system is followed, in which the sons equally share the property of their father. Where there are children from more wives, the property is divided into equal shares according to the number of wives, and among the children of each wife their respective share is equally divided among them. This is known as *chunda-vand*. Previously, wives and daughters were excluded from inheritance and they had only the right of maintenance, but in the light of the modern statutory provisions, claims are invoked by the parties to indicate their right of inhertance in the father's property.

The Manhas women hold an honourable status in their community as well as in the village society. Previously, the females had the right of maintenance and widows, if they decided to avoid *karewa*, were provided a share in the agricultural produce for their sustenance. Such exigency was usually evaded through *karewa* and *doahl* customs. Among the poorer families, the women help their men in outdoor activities, but to a limited extent. However, they manage the household and look after the milch cattle. They have right over their *dahez* (dowry). Now their females are getting educated and are also entering the government and other services. The community is undergoing a change under the impact of modern influences which are reaching them rather slowly in this state.

The Manhas observe all the Hindu rituals from birth to death current in this region. The time of the birth of the child is noted and a *patri* (horoscope) is got prepared. On the fifth day after the childbirth, the mother is given a purificatory bath. On the fourteenth day, a priest (pandit) is called and the household is purified through sprinkling of *Ganga-jal* (holy Ganga water) and recitation of hymns accompanied by appropriate rituals. After a few days, the child is named and, six weeks after the birth, the child is taken out of the house for the first time. The *mundan* (tonsure) ceremony is usually performed at the age of two years, and *janeu* is worn under the connected ritual at the age of ten, or later if desired. This *upanayana* ceremony is usually postponed till a few days before marriage. The marriage, usually, takes place between the age of twenty and twenty-six years, although formerly child marriage was common. The event is attached with the rituals of *tika*, *kurmai*, *bedi* or *biah* and *maklawa*, also called *rafera* and *gaona*. Death ceremonies are equally elaborate. Mourning period extends over thirteen days, *phool* (burnt bones), are gathered on the fourth day and immersed in the river Ganga during the days of mourning. The first *shradh* of the deceased is called *barkhi*. On the fourth death anniversary called *chaubarkhi*, elaborate ceremony is performed with *dan-punn* (donations) to the Brahmans and sumptuous feast to the *biradari*. Afterwards the annual *shradh* is usually performed.

The Manhas are mainly a landowning community, hence land is their major economic resource. Formerly, they held large chunks of land, but now due to agrarian reforms in the state, their holdings have been reduced to the limits fixed by the provisions of land ceiling, which is only sufficient for the maintenance of a moderate-sized family. Most of the individuals, particularly, the younger generation, has therefore taken to other professions like service, self-employment and small trades and cottage industries. The land is held in the name of the father or eldest male member of the family. The Manhas do not work as farm labourers in agricultural operations for others, hence bonded labour is unknown to them. In some cases, children of ten to twelve years of age and beyond render only part time help to their parents after school hours.

The village community as a whole served as an organ of social control in case of the Manhas community also; but in their particular social problems, their own *biradari* in general was there to adjudicate. The traditional village panchayats also existed in their villages, which punished social transgressions, normally, by fines and penalties, and sometimes, by a limited excommunication called *hukka pani chhakana*. For a grave crime by one family or group against the other, *chhinna* was imposed, breaking away all contacts with the offending family which lasted for generations. This system, however, has died out. During the twentieth century, gram panchayats came into being with statutory powers which now control the social and inter-community behaviour of the village communities including the Manhas.

The Manhas belong to the Sanatanist section of the Hindus. Only a fraction of them have embraced Islam. The Hindu Manhas are devoted to the Hindu pantheon, particularly to Shiva and the Goddess Kali in the form of Durga, and Vishnu's incarnations Narsimha, Rama and Krishna. They have their family and village deities also, among which Kali Bir is much popular. *Kul-purohit* helps them perform religious and social rites and customs. The illiterate and less cultured among them believe in evil spirits and seek the services of the *chelas* for the solution of their health, mental and even economic problems. The Manhas participat and celebrates all the fairs and festivals held in this region by the Hindus. Now some of them have come under the influence of Arya Samaj and Radhaswami movement, but these influences have failed to bring about a major change in their religious behaviour.

They, being agriculturists, feel hesitant about adopting crafts and handicrafts. They do not indulge in any special dance or music except those on the socio-religous occasions like *sagai*, *biah*, *rarho*, *swan-khan* and *navratras*, when their womenfolk indulge in group singing and *giddha* dance. Men also enjoy participating in the popular *bhangra* dance on Baisakhi day and speical festivals. Songs known as *sohag*, *bishan-patey*, *ghori* and *sithnian* are fervently sung during the marriage ceremonies. *Dirges* are also sung when there is a death. Now, most of the traditional songs are dying out and giving way to popular cinema songs and tunes.

The Mánhas accept water and cooked food from the other Hindu communities, except from the low castes. They do not, however, exchange daughters with all other communities, but only with the *dohari* group from whom they take wives. They employ the Brahmans for religious and ritualistic performances. Putative kinship is also practised among them. They share wells, tanks and temples with the other communities except with low castes. Panchayat houses and other community centres are, however, shared with all, irrespective of caste or creed. *Jajmani* system is present and there are regular *kul-purohits*, though the system is now losing ground.

They participate in all types of political activities and public functions on local as well as regional levels. They also take part in the political and social movements. Production and landlord-tenant relationship with other agriculturist communities also exists. They employ labour for various agricultural operations and share the crop with them or pay the wages in cash and kind.

Their attitude towards the developmental plans is favourable. Their children have got educational facilities above matric level. Some of them join colleges and university for higher education. Most of their girls, however, drop out after middle standard. The community shares the benefits of health and medicare and has no prejudice against the family planning and welfare programmes, which have reached them through the health centres. Some of them have been benefited from the village employment and self-employment schemes, and have received loans and other facilities for starting small trades and cottage industries. They use the media and communication. They have been benefited by the supply of electricity, kerosene oil and gas, but most of them still depend on cow-dung cakes and wood for heat and energy. Canal irrigation has been made available to them in plains. They use chemical fertilizers, improved seeds and some of them own tractors and threshing appliances. They have got banking facilities for savings and loans, and benefit from the public distribution agencies. They have become free from the traditional village agencies, but most of the government agencies and plans meant for rural development have not yet been made available to them.

ANITA K. BILLAWARIA

MANJYGUR

The Manjygurs prepare and sell different eatables such as fish *pakora*, *nadru*, *gooji* (chestnut) and *chak*. They affix Bhat, Saudagar and Chikla to their names. They are distributed all over the Kashmir Valley. Nauhatta, Lalchowk, Hazratbal and Wantpuri are some of the localities of Srinagar district where there is greater concentration of the Manjygur. Like the other Kashmiris, they wear a *pheran* which is a long loose gown with buttoning at the neck and falling down to the ankles. Both men and women wear *pheran*. In winter, *kangri*, an earthen pot of about 6 inches diameter covered with a basket of wicker work, is kept under the *pheran* to remain warm.

The Manjygurs are non-vegetarian and consume mutton as well as beef. They do not eat pork. Rice is their staple food. They consume a good quantity of vegetables. Among pulses, *mah*, *moth* and *moong* are commonly consumed. Mustard oil is their cooking medium. Fruits such as apple, pear, walnut, peach, apricot and strawberry are also moderately consumed. They do not take alcoholic drinks or other intoxicants. Milk and milk products are consumed regularly.

The Manjygurs are exogamous. They marry among the Mir, Bhat, Beg, Baba, Dhob and the Navid. They do not prefer consanguineous marriages. They do not marry among the Ganai, Goor and the Watal. Marriages are performed at the age of 14 years in case of girls and 17 years in case of boys. The invitation of a marriage proposal as such is important, because it opens the way for negotiation and settlement. Dowry is given and accepted in kind only. Residence after marriage is partilocal. The contract of marriage may be dissolved by *talaq* (i.e. by the husband at will); without the intervention of the court, or by *khula*, i.e. mutual consent of the husband and wife. In case of divorce, it is the responsibility of the husband to maintain his wife during her period of *iddat*. It is the responsibility of the husband to maintain the children even after divorce, whether the children live with the mother or with him. The mother can keep the children in her custody until they are two years old. During this period, the children cannot, under any circumstances, be removed from the mother's care without her consent. After the child has been weaned away, its custody, if a male, devolves on the father, and if a female, on the mother. The mother's custody of a female child continues up to seventh year. Thereafter, the father is entitled for her custody in preference to the mother. Remarriages are allowed in all the cases, i.e. widow, widower, male and female divorcee. Remarriages are performed in the same way as regular marriages are performed.

The Manjygur nowadays favour nuclear families, but the extended families still exist among them. Due respect is paid to the elders of the family. Joking relations exist with *devar*, the husband's younger brother and *bhabhi*, elder brother's wife; *sala*, wife's younger as well as elder brother; and sister's husband; *sali*, wife's younger sister, and *bahnoi*, elder sister's husband. Property is the main reason behind conflicts and contradictions. These are, generally, resolved through familial compromise. Both sons and daughters have the right of inheritance, but the daughters do not get equal share. Widows also have right of inheritance of the parents, as well as their husband's property. If a widow has no children, she is entitled to one-fourth of her husband's property. If there are children, she gets only one-eighth share. If the widow is the sole surving heir of the deceased, she inherits the whole property. If she does not remarry, she enjoys the right of support from her paternal or conjugal family. The eldest son succeeds his father as the head of the family.

Besides household work, the Manjygur women also help their menfolk in preparing different items for sale. They do not play any role in politics.

Among the Manjygur, the first purificatory bath is given to the parturient mother on the seventh day of the birth. This is known as *sunder*. After delivery, *sharbat*, mixture of water and sugar, is served to her for the first three days. For seven days, that is till the *sunder*, first purificatory bath, vegetables and *qahwa* are served to the mother. She can also take bread with *qahwa*, tea and *sharbat*. Naming does not involve any ceremony. The name is given by the family *pir* after seven days of the birth. *Zerakasi* (tonsure ceremony), is done by the village barber. A goat is sacrificed to mark the occasion. The meat is distributed to the villagers, friends and the *mulla*. The family members do not eat the mutton of the sacrificed goat. Circumcision is usually performed after one year. A feast is arranged on this occasion. Marriage proposals are suggested by the elderly ladies of the family when a suitable match is found following which the ritual of *nishani* (betrothal), is held. The boy's father goes to the girl's house with a small party of relatives and friends. After betrothal, the final date of marriage is fixed. On this occasion, the boy's father sends presentation to the girl's father. For a week before the marriage, festivities and rejoicings are held. On the marriage day, the bridegroom with the *barat* (marriage party) proceeds for the bride's house. The *nikah* ceremony is performed at the bride's house. A feast is arranged for the marriage party as well as for the invited relatives and friends of the bride. After everything is over at the bride's house, the marriage party departs along with the bride. In her in-law's house, she is received with great enthusiasm. The bride stays for seven days in her in-law's house and then she returns to her father's house. After this, the father of the girl invites his son-in-law to a feast at his house, where the latter is presented cash and gifts. After this ceremonial visit, both the bride and the bridegroom are free to visit the house of the girl's father.

Among the Manjygurs, the dead are buried. At the time of death, *kalma* and some verses from the Holy Koran are recited into the ear of the dying person. The *ghusl-e-maiyat* (ceremonial bath) is given to the dead body and then it is wrapped in a *kafan* (shroud). The dead body is placed in a wooden *taboot* (coffin) and then the mourning procession proceeds towards the graveyard. Women do not accompany this procession. After the burial, the persons present there throw *mitti* (soil) and then recite *fateha*, a *sura* of the Holy Koran. Afterwards the people go back to their respective houses. A number of rituals are observed after the death of a person which include *fateha*, performed on the fourth day of death, *satijihum*, observed after forty days of death, and *vaharvoor*, performed after one year of death.

The traditional as well as present occupation of the Manjygur is to prepare and sell different fried food items. Besides their traditional occupation, they are turning towards other businesses and agriculture.

These days, the Manjygur community council is not in existence. Statutory village panchayat exists.

The Manjygurs are Sunni Muslims. They observe Id-ul-Fitr, Id-ul-Zuha, Shab-e-Barat, Bara Wafat and Ramzan. There are a number of tombs of the Muslim saints where *urs* congregations are held. The sacred centres of the Manjygurs are tomb of Baba Rishi, Baba Makhdum and Hazratbal.

On all important occasions, such as marriage, birth and different festivals, the Manjygurs participate along with the villagers. They also invite the villagers on these occasions. Not only the Muslims, but the Hindus also purchase and eat the items prepared by them. Except the Watals, they eat in the house of all other communities of their area.

The Manjygur send their children to school. Usually the girls study up to high school level and boys up to graduation level. Girls do not study further due to social problems. Modern medicare facilities are available in the area and the same are availed of by the people of this community. They are aware of the family welfare programmes but do not practise the family planning devices. Drinking water is available to them through taps within their own locality. Wood collected from the forest is utilized as fuel.

S.N.H. RIZVI

MEGH

The Megh are one of the most numerous communities of the state. The accepted name of the community is Megh, which sometimes is pronounced with a nasal sound, converting the term into something like Mihngh. The Meghs claim an ancient origin and they seem to be the original inhabitants of the Jammu region and the owners of land in this tract. The local chronicles of Jammu support this view and they are stated to be the original occupants of Jammu territory before the migrating Jamwal ruling clans ousted them from power and subjugated them. This, according to the Jamwal *vanshavali*, happened much before the Christian era. In some details, the Megh traditions support their close connection with the Jammu region since a hoary past.

The Meghs are the inhabitants of the plains and hills between the Ravi and the Chenab rivers, except Akhnur which lies to the west of the latter river. Over 60 per cent of them live in the fertile plain irriagated by canals and *kuhls* (water ducts), whereas over 20 per cent of them inhabit the high forest covered tract to the north and north-east of Jammu. They are found distributed over the dry *kandi* tract also. Inspite of difference of natural invironment, there is practically no difference in their life pattern. The community speaks Dogri language in oral communication amongst themselves and with other communities except the few well-read amongst them, who communicate with others in Hindi. Communication in writing is invariably done in the Devanagari script. Previously, they used to communicate in Dogri, written in the Tankari script. They are a Scheduled Caste with a population of 1,99,242 (1981 census).

The members of the community do not wear any distinctive dress or marker, but like the general working Hindu classes of low castes, they wrap a short rough cloth, usually homespun, round their loins for *dhoti* and a short half-sleeved *kurta* of the same fabric, mostly of khadi or of similar home-made stuff. For footwear, they use country-made rough leather shoes. Mostly, they go bareheaded, but when required, they wind small white piece of rough cloth round thier heads for turban. Humility is writ large on their countenances. In dress and complexion, they are not much different from the rural caste Hindus. The state government has now accorded them constitutional status of a Scheduled Castes and they have been enjoying special benefits and privileges under the provisions. Owing to this and other favourable circumstances, their standard has improved, particularly of those living in plain and fertile areas, and their dress habits have now become almost similar to those of the other Hindu communities.

The Megh are vegetarians. The Meghs, with the exception of their subcaste Basith, used to eat the flesh of dead animals, but by a contract or decision concluded and signed in 1879 through the influence of their Guru of Keran in Jammu tahsil, who had been the religious head of the Megh community, they pledged total abstention from it. A breach of this agreement made a man liable to pay Rs. 25 to the government, Rs. 5 to the head of the village and a sum fixed according to the means of the offender, as a penalty to the *biradari.* In default of payment, he was liable to be excluded from the community. With this change, the Meghs are also becoming vegetarian like the other Hindu communities. Their womenfolk usually, and men on certain occasions, avoid taking non-vegetarian diet. Rice and wheat and *makki* (maize) form their staple food; pulses, particularly *mah* and *masur*, and all types of vegetables are now available to them in the villages. They have no particular liking for alcoholic drinks, but occasionally indulge in it publicly on festive occasions, such as birth of a son, marriage, fairs and festivals. They used country-made alcoholic drinks and did not have any prejudice against preparing some at home. Now, with the spread of modern ideas in the community and as a result of constitutional benefits, the community has come out of much of its backwardness and has adopted food habits as in all the other Hindu communities of the state.

The Meghs gave their daughters in marriage to men of another *gotra* other then their own. Similarly, they took wives from other *gotras.* But now this custom has lost much of its hold, though normally they follow the obligations of *gotra* incumbent upon them. The origin of these *gotras* is not known now as traditions about them have been forgotten. A number of their *gotras* are in common with the Brahman community of this region, and this supports their Brahmanic origin as claimed by their traditions.

The basic tenets governing the marriage customs of the Meghs are those of Hinduism. The ceremonies, however, differ to some extent. At the boy's marriage, the Meghs observe no ceremony at their own house, but collect a few leading members of their *biradari* (community), and go to the house of the girl's father, accompanied by the bridegroom. There, they perform some of the necessary rituals and the next day bring the girl to their own house. On the following morning, the members of the *biradari* carry the bride and bridegroom to a *malah* (mulberry tree), where they make the couple seat. A long thread, *mauli*, is wrapped round the trunk of the tree and all present, together with the couple, walk seven times round it. Afterwards, a quantity of bread and sugar pounded together called *churan* is distributed to the gathering. After that, they return home and the bridegroom's father serves a sumptuous feast to the invited *biradari*. All the Hindu rites are gone through with the assistance of a *panda*. Although, they have the Brahman priests and give them *birt* (offerings), they do not engage them. Widow remarriage is permitted. But the choice is limited to the deceased husband's elder or younger brother, failing which, she can, with the consent of her guardians, marry any man belonging to the *gotra* of her deceased or *biradari*. If she wants to marry a man of a *gotra* different from that of her deceased husband, the man must bear all the expenses of the marriage, or he must give his sister or daughter or any other near relative to some male member of the widow's household in exchange. When a widow declines to remarry, provision for the necessities of her life is arranged out of contributions made by the *biradari* of the village and she is held in high esteem.

The Megh family is patrilocal in which proper reverence and respect and affiliations are observed according to the status of all the members. Elders are usually feared and obeyed. The respect and obedience is extended to uncles and their families also who in several cases are considered a part of the larger joint family. All the male issues have equal share in the property of the family. A widow has the right for maintenance.

The Megh women are usually held in high esteem and they participate even in outdoor activities with men. They collect fodder for their cattle and fuel for their hearths. They not only take care of all the indoor household activities but also go out to work in other homes and outdoor jobs in order to earn bread for their families. They help their husbands in all the farming operations and rearing of cattle. Hence, the Megh woman is an economic asset to the family. She takes part in social, ritual and religious activities like women of all the other Hindu communities.

The Meghs perform all the Hindu rituals from birth to death, except the *yajnopavit* ceremony for which they had no *shastric* right. But now the *purohits*, which have risen from their community, wear and make the Meghs wear *janeu* at the time of marriage. The rituals of *namkaran*, taking the child out for the first time, when 21 days old, and *annaprashan* are performed during the first year of birth, *kurmai* or *sagai* and *vivah-sanskars* are performed when boys and girls come of age. Previously, child marriage was almost a universal convention among the Meghs and other such comunities of this region. The *anta-sanskar* (death ceremony) followed by the *shradh*, is performed according to the rituals current among the other Hindu communities. They employ the Brahmans for the ritual purposes, but these Brahmans are looked down upon by the other Brahmans. Failing to get the services of such Brahmans, the Meghs employ the *pandas* who are also called *gorais*. Now some of the literate Meghs have taken to the profession of a priest.

The Meghs are primarily an agricultural community. Formerly, they were owners of land in this tract but, because of the highhandedness and oppression of the ruling tribes, most of them have been deprived of large tracts of agricultural land. Till recently, the Megh families were petty landholders; but majority of them had been rendered landless, though they still stuck to the agricultural occupations and mostly work as tillers and agricultural workers. However, under the recent agrarian reforms in the state and also as the result of constitutional benefits, there has been much amelioration in their economic condition. Most of their families have received small agricultural lands and have purchased additional tracts. The land in the Megh family is owned, as in case of the other Hindu communities of the area, by the eldest male of the family, and is equally shared by all the sons after the death of their father or elder. In addition to working on their own fields, they work as farm labourers and tillers of land. They receive wages both in cash and kind according to the nature of the job or agricultural operation. They mostly work in their own or nearby villages, and there is limited mobility among them. Children and women help their menfolk in agricultural operations and in rearing cattle. Children of 14 or 15 years and above are sent out to earn wages. Previously the Megh men and women worked in the houses of the village zamindars and moneylenders against repayment of their own or ancestral debts. A limited type of bondage labour was prevalent in this region too. But since Independence, conditions have undergone much changes and this custom has disappeared from this region. By profession, the Meghs are largely weavers and they profess to have learnt this craft from Kabir, the *bhagat*. The members of the community are, therefore, sometimes addressed as Bhagat and some among them write Bhagat as caste with their names. They practised this craft as a part-time work, in addition to agriculture and the older among them, when weakened by age, mostly confined their activities to weaving; but, of late, they have given up this craft as the khadi is little in demand in the villages. Now the craft is being revived and power-driven handlooms have replaced the older, out-of-date manual *khaddies.* Being primarily a rural community, their economic activities are conditioned by the conditions prevailing in their respective villages.

The Meghs had their community organization to serve as an organ of social control which was formed by the elders of their own community whenever an occasion arose. Sometimes, they had recourse to adjudication or arbitration of the zamindras of their village, even in social problems. But in religious and in community affairs of consequence, the community was guided by their *guru* of the village Keran in Jammu. The accused person had to pay some fine or serve a feast to the village *biradari* and, in case of socio-religious offenses or non-fulfilment of penalties, excommunication was imposed. Now *gram* panchayats usually, regulate their social and intercommunity relations. In socio-religious cases concerning their own community, they still refer to their community elders. They seldom take their case to the court of law

The Meghs are Hindu by faith but Arya Samaj's influence has also penetrated into the community. In most cases, they are guided by the Brahmans called *pandas* and *gorais.* By sect, the Meghs are Kabirpanthis. They also worships the *guru.* His decision is final with regard to every matter whether social, ceremonial or religious. The Meghs accept food from other communities except by one of its subcastes, the Basith. They participate in all the Hindu fairs and festivals held at various religious places, such as Jitto-ki-Jhiri, Ghagwal Purmandal, etc.

The Meghs are fine craftsmen weaving fine cotton fabrics, exclusively homespun khadi, and khadi bedcovers known as *khes* of charming designs and beautiful borders. They have no special traditional folklore or folk songs particular to the community, but share these with the other Hindu communities of the area. Though their womenfolk indulge in dance and music on social ceremonies like marriage, their menfolk generally do not partake in this finer side of social life. At the most, their youth take part occasionally in the traditional *bhangra* dance on Baisakhi and other occasions.

The community has occupational linkages with other village communities from the ancient ages. On social level, they interact with other communities though to a limited extent. They accept food and water from all the communities. Other communities, however, have limited commensal intercourse with them; but now, they are invited to participate in community dinners even if they are provided separate sitting mats. Ties of friendship could be established with the Meghs on certain occasions, such as when a marriage party returning with the bride the newly-wed Megh couple comes by a newly married couple of other Hindu community in similar circumstances. The Meghs were deprived access to watersides and wells as they were known to take flesh of dead animals. Later, when they gave up this habit, they were allowed to draw water from wells and tanks. They were denied entry in temples, but in 1930, Maharaja Hari Singh of Jammu & Kashmir opened temples to all sections of the Scheduled Castes, including the Meghs. In villages and towns, landlord-tenant and employer-worker relations exist. In the panchayats and elected political bodies and in the government and public services, they have reservations as part of the Scheduled Castes. In local politics, they are active. They have formed their social associations in order to look after their common interests and work out social reforms in their community.

The response of the Megh community towards the development programmes is positive and they have benefited by these. The level of literacy and education among the Meghs has gone up. They have no prejudice against family planning and take full benefit of the health and medical facilities available in their villages. They have also got their share of rural self-employment programmes. They have got proper representation in all types of the state services reserved for them. They have risen high in service cadres, got representation in the state ministries and other public institutions. Electricity and media of communication are available to them. They are benefited by the public distribution system. Chemical fertilizers are available to them everywhere, in villages and towns. Canal irrigation facilities and drinking water sources have been made available to them.

S.D.S. Charak

MOCHI/CHAMAR

The Mochis are considered an offshoot of the Chamars, who are specialized in the craft of shoemaking and repairing. The word *chamar* is derived from *charmkar*, a worker in leather, hide or skin. The word *mochi* is applied to those who make shoes, leather articles and are considered more skilled workers then the *chamars*. In Jammu & Kashmir, they call themselves Ram Dasi, Raidasi or Ravidasi and claim their descent from Ravidas and Guru Ramanand. They are distributed in Jammu, Kathua, Udhampur, Doda and Srinagar Valley of Jammu & Kashmir, their highest concentration being in Jammu. They perceive their distribution at the national level. They inhabit in warm and temperate climate in the Jammu region. The terrain is hilly with low humidity. Rainfall is medium and there is no snowfall in the Jammu region. The area is thinly forested. They are one of the major Scheduled Caste, of the state. Total population of the Mochis is not known, while the population of the Chamars of which the Mochis are an offshoot, was 1,22,292 according to the *Census of India* 1981. They speak Dogri among themselves and in Hindi or Punjabi while talking with others. The script used by them is Devanagari.

Earlier, they used to wear *dhoti*, *kurta*, *pagri*, *sadri* and *chadar*, but now they wear *kurta*, *dhoti*, *pyjama*, pant and shirt. They are included in the list of Scheduled Castes of Jammu & Kashmir. The Mochis are non-vegetarians and eat eggs, mutton and fish with the exception of beef. The families who are worshippers (*bhagats*) of Rama have turned vegetarians. Their staple diet is wheat, rice, *urad* (black gram), *moong* (green gram) and *masur*. Roots, tubers and seasonal vegetables are also consumed according to their availability. Fruits are occasionally used. There is no restriction on taking alcoholic drinks and old women also consume liquor occasionally. The use of milk and milk products is moderate. They smoke *bidis*, cigarettes, *hookah* (hubble-bubble), and chew betel and tobacco. Alcoholic drinks are purchased from the market, but in villages, they often brew the drink themselves. The most significant change which has come recently in their food habits is a shift from non-vegetarianism to vegetarianism.

There is differentiation based on occupation, education and economic status. In Jammu region, the Chamars have given up the job of skinning dead animals, and those who are still in this menial job are known as Chandal by the Chamars as well as by others; and they are placed below the Chamars. Intermarriage is also prohibited between the two groups. There has been no change in surnames or clan names, but they are divided into various exogamous groups called *jati* or *gotra*, such as Midie, Thap, Batson, Kalsi and Bahoch. There is no hierarchy among these *gotras* and all are considered equal. The Mochis are perceived as low by other communities of the region, and the Mochis too perceive themselves as low in the hierarchy. They are placed in the Shudra rank of the *varna* order.

The Mochis are an endogamous group. *Jati* or *gotra* exogamy is in practice and is strictly followed. In earlier days, most of the marriages used to be performed between the age of 10 and 15 years; but nowadays, the age of marriage for a boy is between 18 and 25 years and, for the girl, between 18 and 21 years. Child marriage is still in vogue in rural areas. Marriages are arranged by the partents or relatives, though sporadic cases of love marriages are also there. Marriage by exchange was a common practice till a few years back, as it helped to curtail the marriage expenses, but nowadays it is not observed. Monogamy is the usual form of marriage and only in the case of barrenness, a man can remarry with the consent of the first wife. The symbols or *suhagchinha* for married women are *sindoor* (vermilion), bangles, toe ring, and nose pin. *Kanyadan* has been the practice and is still prevalent. In the past, there was a custom of paying bride-price, but it is not prevalent now and is being replaced by dowry in cash and kind, i.e. utensils, ornaments and clothing. Being patrilocal, the bride after marriage goes to live with her husband and in-laws. Divorce is permissible and can be sought by either of the partners. It is effected with the consent of the panchayat, on grounds of impotency, adultery, maladjustment or insanity. Sometimes, the cases of divorce are taken to their traditional *sabhas* or courts of law. Widow, widower and male and female divorcee remarriages are permissible in the community. Divorce compensation is given to the wife. In case of divorce, children are the responsibility of the father. Junior levirate and junior sororate is permissible. In case of widow or divorcee remarriage, no elaborate marriage ceremonies are performed; only *sindoor* and bangles are offered to the woman in public. It is called *ghar baithana*. The recent changes which have been noticed in marriage system are the emergence of dowry system and decrease of divorce cases.

The urban Mochi families are nuclear, whereas those in villages are mostly extended. After marriage, in most of the cases, the newly married couple establishes a separate household. Personal relations within the family members are cordial. Love and respect are paid to the elders. Avoidance is maintained between the daughter-in-law and father-in-law, and between the younger brother's wife and *jeth*, husband's elder brother. Likewise, joking relationship exists between the *bhabhi*, elder brother's wife and the *devar*, the husband's younger brother, and between brother-in-law and wife's younger sister. Property is equally divided among all the sons. If the father divides his property during his life-time, the unmarried daughters also get a share. After the father's death, it is the responsibility of the brothers to get their sisters married. The eldest son succeeds his deceased father. Changes have not been noticed in the rules of succession and inheritance. Extended family system is, however, declining due to the impact of urbanization and industrialization.

The Mochi women play an important role in all spheres of life and enjoy equal status now, but in earlier days, they were always considered inferior to men. Widows have the right to inherit their share from the deceased husband's property. They are engaged in various economic and household activities like agricultural operations, animal husbandry, collection of fuel, bringing of potable water, etc. In social and religious functions, they play a pivotal role. Except but casting of votes, they do not have any other role in political field. In the mechanism of social control, they participate only when they are called.

The life-cycle rituals of the Mochis do not differ much from the Dogra customs. Pre-delivery rituals and restrictions are observed in the community. The first pre-delivery ceremony, *reetan*, is performed in the eighth month of pregnancy, in which the father of the pregnant lady sends sweets, dry fruits, fruits and clothing for his daughter and son-in-law. A *dai* (midwife) who comes from the Batwal community or, sometimes, a female relative who is specialized for this job, assists in the delivery. For this, the *dai* is paid in cash and kind. The first bath to the child is given on the third day, and the next on the fifth day.

The dead are cremated. Burial is done in cases of the dead bodies of children below the age of eight years. The dead body is carried to the *shamshan ghat* (creamation ground) where the funeral pyre is lit by the eldest son or the youngest son, or by the close relatives in the absence of sons. The ashes of the dead are collected on the third day to be immersed either in the Tawi or in the Ganga at Hardwar. On the tenth day, *tam* or *daswan* is observed. All the close relatives get their heads shaved. On the thirteenth, fourteenth, fifteenth or seventeenth day, the relatives of the deceased have *jags* (community feast). *Adh-*

barkhi and *barkhi* are performed in the sixth and twelfth month, respectively. Curtailment of the rituals has been observed in the community.

The primary occupation of the Mochi was skinning the dead animals and shoemaking. Now, the job of skinning the dead animals has been completely given up and they only do the job of shoe-making and shoe-repairing in urban areas. In villages, they are involved in agriculture as their primary occupation, supplemented by leather work. The community is mainly landowning, but they are not large landholders. Land resources are controlled by individuals. In earlier times, the Mochis rendered the traditional services to the landlords, for which they were paid in kind, but it has now been replaced by cash. The new generation have taken up different jobs, for example, working as labourers, industrial labourers, businessmen, government services, etc. The Mochis have their own *biradari* panchayat to solve the disputes within the community. Generally disputes over land and matrimonial affairs are solved in these panchayats. There are *sarpanch* and *panch* in the panchayat, and they are elected by voice vote. In the cities, they also have Ravidasi Sabha. Social boycott or ex-communication or cash fine is imposed on the offenders. Persons ex-communicated are readmitted only after giving a feast to the *baradari*. The Mochis have their representations in the statutory gram panchayat, which looks after the planning and implemetation of welfare and development activities of the village. They are Hindu by religion. The community has its own deities and specific places for annual worship. Baba Surgal, Kali Bir, Buababa, Baba Mansar and Nag Devta are worshipped on different occasions by the Mochis. Each clan has its own deity. They sacrifice goats and offer sweets on occasions such as marriages or curing of diseases to propitiate the deities. The Mochis have reverence for Sant Ravidas whose picture decorates their houses. Jhiri ka Mela is an important fair of the Mochis. It is held in the month of November at the Jhiri village in Jammu, where their *kul* (clan) deities are worshipped. Besides, there are other temples and sacred places like Raghunath Mandir, Vaishno Devi which are visited on certain occasions. The Mochis employ the Brahmans to perform the birth, marriage and death rituals. Their festivals and fairs are of socio-religious and socio-economic significance and are celebrated with great zeal and enthusiasm. The Mochis also believe in *bhoot/pret/jinnat* (ghosts and spirits). The changes which have taken place recently are that they are becoming *bhagats*, thereby adopting vegetarianism. The community has oral traditions, but possesses no folklore or songs of its own.

Because of their involvement in the business of leather, shoemaking and repairing, the Mochi maintain good relations with all the communities of the region. In earlier days, they used to serve their clients by supplying leather articles and shoes and by removing dead animals, for which they were paid in cash and kind. In villages, the Mochis still serve their *jajmans* and get a share at the time of harvesting. They had a direct link with the Brahmans, Rajputs, Dhobis, Kahars, Malis, Lohars, Barhais, etc. In urban areas, where they are economically better off, social distance is not maintained to that extent. They sit, eat and chat together because of their business. They accept cooked and uncooked food from all the lower and higher communities except the Bhangis. The Brahmans or Rajputs still avoid them and do not accept water and food from them. Intercommunity marriages normally do not take place, but stray cases occur. They share well, temple, cremation ground and other important places with other communities, but it is a recent phenomenon which has emerged after Independence. In villages, patron-client relationship and landlord-tenant relationship exist as the members of this community are employed as labourers to work in the agricultural fields. *Batau*, sharecropping, also prevails. The sharecropper keeps half of the gross produce. Putative kinship also exists among them. At present, the community has established more contacts with all other communities of the region as they are now engaged in various economic pursuits such as hotel business or dealing in cloth.

Developmental programmes of the government for the betterment of the Scheduled Castes have a good impact on the Mochis. They too are responding well. Education has improved the status of the community in the region, though in villages, the situation is different mainly due to the non-availablity of schools. The children are not sent out for higher education as their economic conditions do not permit. Attitude of the community towards modern medicare is favourable and they avail of the facilities more than their indigenous method. Family planning programmes have a good impact on them, and now they prefer only two or three children. Facilities of water and electricity are available in the localities, though not adequatly. Cow-dung cakes, wood and kerosene oil are the main fuel used by the community. Bulk of their population are self-employed. The medium of information for them is radio, but only few members have it. Roads, post offices and facilities of railways are available. Irrigation facilities are not available in all the regions and, for this, they have to depend on rain-water. They use chemical fertilizers, insecticides and organic manure to boost their crop producton. Though the facilities of food distribution system through the fair price shops are available in the locality, their services are unsatisfactory. Thier attitude towards saving is positive and the community do not depend on the money-lenders and shopkeepers.

ANAND SARAN

MOHYAL BRAHMAN

The Mohyal Brahmans maintain a separate identity *vis-a-vis* other Brahman communities of Jammu region. Prior to independence of the country, they were concentrated in Peshawar, Rawalpindi, Pera, Kriyala, Meerpur, Jhelum, Gujrat, Norwal tahsil, Sialkot, Gujranwala, Lahore and Amritsar. However, after Partition, they migrated en-bloc to India and settled mostly in Delhi. In Jammu region, the Mohyals are found in Jammu (proper), Rajouri, Naoshera, Punch, Udhampur, Badherwah, Kishtwar and Akhnur. The Mohyals are also settled in Srinagar. A special mention may be made of the Hussaini Brahmans. They are the people whose ancestor Rahib Dutt settled in Arab region, offered his seven sons to fight along side Hassan and Hussain in the battle of Karbala. Consequently, it was decided by the loyalist of Hassan and Hussain to confer on them the title of Syeeds because of the sacrifice made by them in the battle of Karbala. Some of them also use the word Bhai with their names on account of the slaying of Mati Dass Chibber by the Mughal Emperor Aurangzeb for refusing conversion to Islam. Thereafter, Guru Tegh Bahadur conferred the title of Bhai and made Bhai Kitab-Chibber his *wazir*. In Jammu region, the Hussani Brahmans are settled in Samba region in district Kathua.

The Mohyal Brahmans have *gotras* after the names of seven *rishis*, which include Bhardwaj, Kashyap, Parasram and others. While the Duttas belong to Bhardwaj *gotra*, the Mohans have Kashyap as their *gotra*. In the recent past, the Mohyal Brahmans were recognized by their *dastar* (headgear), *raftar* (speed) and *guftar* (way of talking). However, these days their traditional dress pattern and dialect has become almost obsolescent though their native language has been Punjabi. They speak Punjabi and Dogri amongst themselves, but switch over to Urdu and English while talking with others. The scripts they use are Devanagari, Arabic and Roman to correspond among themselves and with others.

The Mohyal Brahmans are essentially non-vegetarians. Wheat and rice are their staple food. They consume all varieties of pulses. The medium of cooking is mustard oil and *ghee*. Green vegetables are consumed regularly. Occasionally, alcoholic drinks are also taken by them and they are bought from market. Rice is now preferred to *roti* (unleavened bread).

Monogamy is, generally, observed. Marriage alliance is mostly arranged within seven *gotras* prevalent among them. Cross-cousin marriage or marrying within blood relations is not permissible. Marriages are usually arranged, and few cases of courtships also exists among them. Dowry is quite common among them. Residence is patrilocal after marriage. Divorce is rare among these people. Bigamy is prohibited and remarriage is permissible. Marriages are mostly solemnized in the Sanatani or Arya Samaji rules. Age at marriage is about 20 years for both sexes. Among the Mohyal Brahmans, extended families are slowly breaking up into nuclear ones. Elders are given respect. Joking relations prevails among all types of relations, though the same is avoided between daughter-in-law and father-in-law. Close interfamily linkages based on cordiality and reciprocity are also observed among them. Primogeniture is not strictly adhered to; the eldest male child succeeds his deceased father. Authority of the family elders is still observed and recognized. The Mohyal Brahman women have a right in the parental property and play a role in the family management. They contribute substantially to the family earnings and enjoy better status in comparison to the women of other communities in the region. Among the Mohyal Brahmans, birth pollution is observed. *Mundan* and *janeu* rituals are practised by these people for their male children. First feeding of cereals, *annaprashan*, is observed by them though puberty rites for their family are not practised. Marriage ceremony is usually held during the evening, i.e. the *barat* alongwith the bridegroom depart for the bride's house. *Lagan* is performed by the family priest, while *jaimala*, exchange of garlands by the groom and bride, is performed first. Consumation of marriage is performed at the groom's residence.

The dead bodies are cremated on a funeral pyre. Death pollution period is also observed by them. The funeral pyre is usually lit by the eldest son of the deceased first and then followed by others.

Traditional occupations of the Mohyal Brahmans prior to the Partition of the country was mainly restricted to farm pursuits along with a few of them serving in the police and defence forces. However, in the present setting, they have occupationally diversified into business, trade and commerce, agriculture, government and private services, etc. Individuals hold the landownership titles. The market is fully regulated and the community's depedence on it is absolute. Payment to labourers is made both in cash and kind. The Mohyal Brahmans have a *sabha* known as Mohyal Mitra (Mohyal Friends) and also known as All Jammu & Kashmir Mohyal Sabha. The *sabha* usually tries to extend financial help to the widows, orphans and, in case of death rites, and needy ones. Statutory panchayats have no significant part to play in the affairs of the community.

Among the Mohyal Brahmans, land is the main source which is individually owned. They are mainly a landowning community in rural areas, though, in urban areas, they pursue occupations in business, industry, trade and commerce, and in government services. They visit the regional deities such as Vaishno Devi and Amarnath. They participate in all regional festivals coupled with various religious festivals such as Diwali, Shivratri, Rakshabandhan, Holi and Janmashtami.

The Mohyal Brahmans have close links with the other Hindu communities and other occupational groups. Marriages are performed according to the Hindu rituals and customs, irrespective of their ethnic identity. Patron-client and landlord-tenant relationships exist among these people. They have enterpreneurs, scholars, teachers, administrators, defence personnel, engineers and doctors among them.

The Mohyal Brahmans' attitude towards the development programmes is favourable. They favour small family norms. Oppotunities of employment and self-employment through bank financing are freely availed of. They use all the modern media of communication. Rainwater and canals are the main sources of water for irrigation and fertilizers, both organic and chemical are freely used by them. Public distribution system is effective enough to take care of their needs. Banking facilities are fully availed of and there is a healthy trend among them to save and invest their savings in better and more remunerative business pursuits.

INDU BALA DHAR

MON

The Mons are a community of musicians and flute players of Ladakh. They have no sub-groups, titles or synonyms. The Ladakhi Buddhists call them Dolba. The *Census Report* of 1911 categorized the Mons as Rungnum (lower class). The major concentration of the community is in Leh district while in Zanskar and Kargil districts their population is sparse. The Mons inhabiting Leh are found on high terraces overlooking the Indus Valley and its tributaries. Climate is extremely cold. They speak Ladkhai, which is of Tibeto-Burman origin. The script used by them is Bodhi. A few of them speak in Urdu with others. The script used with others is Arabic. They dress themselves like the other Ladakhi Buddhists. Men wear *goncha* (long coat), *shakten* (shirt), *sherak* (trousers), belt of white coloured cloth around the waist, shoes made of leather or wool and Ladakhi cap. The women wear *goncha*, *perak*, *cherton* (woollen boot) and scarf on the head. They have prominent Mongolian features. They are categorized as a Scheduled Tribe in the state.

The Mon are non-vegetarian and eat beef. Their staple food consists of *grim* (barley) and wheat. Pulses taken are gram, *urad*, *moong* and peas. Mustard oil is the cooking medium. The main food item is *sattoo*, made from the flour or roasted wheat and barley; potatoes, turnips and cabbage are also eaten. Drinks common among the people are *gurgur* (salty tea) and *chang* (barley beer), which are taken a number of times in a day. They also take curd and milk. Seasonal fruits such as cherry, apricots and pears are consumed. Rice is becoming popular as a food item although it is not locally grown.

Among the Mons social divisions do not exist. There are, however, *gyuts* (blood relations), which are exogamous. The *gyuts* have no specific names, but the villagers know of their respective *gyuts*. The members of the community do not have specific surnames. They have their own *phasphuns* (brotherhood pools), whose services are available at the time of marriage and death. The *phasphun* cannot be equated with a clan as its members are not connected through a common ancestor. Differentiations exist on grounds of educational, economic and occupational levels, which regulate their marriage alliances.

Endogamy is practised at the community level, though not strictly followed. There are a few cases of marriage outside the community. Under normal conditions, the Bhotos or Ladakhi Buddhists do not give or take brides from the Mons, as they are considered of low social position. Consanguinity is not practised. Junior sororal marriage is permitted in case of death of the first wife. Junior levirate is permitted. Adult marriage is preferred. When the boys and girls attain adulthood, the boy's father with a few close relatives approaches the girls's father with a proposal for marriage. They offer *chang*, *khatak* (white scarf) to the girls's father with the proposal. Spouses are acquired generally through negotiation. Other modes of acquiring mate are through elopement, intrusion, exchange of sisters, mutual consent and courtship. Monogamy is the usual form of marriage. Polyandry has now disappeared. Married women wear *goncha* (long gown) and *firoza* (scarf). Both bride-price and dowry are prevalent in the community. The bride-price is paid to the father of the bride at the time of negotiation of marriage. The amount of bride-price varies according to the health and appearance of the girl. The bride's father brings dowry on the day of marriage. It consists of *goncha*, *firoza*, utensils, ornaments and other household articles. The bride after marriage goes to stay with her husband and in-laws. In case of *maqpa*, the husband goes to stay at his wife's residence. Sometimes, the newly married couple make a new residence for themselves and live separately from their parents. Both the husband and wife are free to divorce. It is a simple affair. Elders sit together with the couple and decide the case on terms favourable to the parties. It is only recently that the divorce cases are taken to the court of law. Divorce takes place due to adultery, barrenness, maladjustment, impotency, cruelty and insanity. After divorce, the dowry and presents given by the bride's parents are returned to them. In divorce cases, children are the responsibility of the father. Widow, widower and divorcee remarriages are permitted. Changes observed in marriage rules are increase in the age of marriage, decrease in the incidence of divorce due to heavy amount of compensation and absence of polyandry.

Families among the Mons are mixed-extended. Apart from the family, the individuals also belong to the *nang-chang* (household). Sometimes, members of different *gyuts* stay together and constitute the group. At times, the extentions are wide. Interpersonal relations are based on respect for the elders and love and affection for the youngers. Joking relationship exists between the sister-in-law and brother-in-law; with wife's younger and elder sisters; between grandparents and grandchildren. Conflict arises on property matters, restrictions on the freedom of youngsters, and challenge to the authority of elders. The rule of inheritance is male equigeniture. As against the previous practice, now all males are equal shareholders in the property. The father is the head of the family. The eldest son succeeds him. The sons after marriage prefer to have a separate house for themselves. Due to urbanization and wide employment opportunities, there is a rise in nuclear families. The Mon women are not secluded, but play their roles equally with men. They have a role in agricultural operations and animal husbandry, collection of fuel, bringing potable water, caring of children, cooking food, cleaning the house etc. Compared to the boys, the girls are nurtured with care as they bring bride-price. Women enjoy equal status with men.

Among the Mons, a childless woman is looked down upon in the society. She is nicknamed *rapshit* (barren). *Amchis* (medicine women) are frequently consulted in case of delay in pregnancy. It is believed that religious specialists like the lamas, *chemas* and *kushaks* can help in causing pregnancy. As suggested by the religious specialists, the couple make human figures out of *sattoo* which is flour of wheat and barley. It is belived that it causes pregnancy to a barren woman. Pre-delivery rituals are not observed. A pregnant woman is advised against carrying or heaving load, crossing a stream and going out after dusk. In the seventh month of pregnancy, a ceremony involving reading of the sacred scriptures and worship is performed by the lama. *Amchi*, help a woman in labour pain. After the delivery of the child, both the husband and the wife are confined in a room for seven days. On the seventh day, a lama performs the ritual *laf-tsang*, which is the purification of the house. On this occasion, the members of the *phasphun*, neighbours and friends are invited. After one month of childbirth, *da-tsang* is observed. The relatives bring presents of dresses and food materials. The *onpo* prepares a horoscope of the child and gives a name to the child. Within two years of a childbirth, shaving of the head, *ralchang*, is done. Marriage rituals are performed at the bridegroom's residence. The distinguishing feature of marriage is that the bridegroom does not accompany the marriage party. *Nyopa*, who is a representative of the bridegroom dresses himself as the groom and brings the bride to the house of the bridegroom for marriage. The bride is seated close to the family kitchen and is joined by the bridegroom later. The *nyopa* formally hands over the charge of the bride to the bridegroom. The lama reads the sacred books and showers blessings on the couple. The *nyopa* places a silken scarf around the head of the bridegroom marking the culmination of marriage ritual.

Pakhtun, a feast, is given at the house of the bridegroom after marriage. The bride stays at the house of the bridegroom for three days. They are then invited by the bride's parents for a feast. Nuptial ceremony is performed at the bridegroom's residence.

The dead body of a child below eight years is buried, but elder children and adults are cremated. When a person dies, the body is kept in the house for a week for performance of rites and prayers. It is belived that the spirit of the dead takes time in travelling from earth to heaven. Lamas remain in the house during this period. They eat and sleep where the dead body is kept in lying position. Later on, it is tied up in a sitting position. The body is brought out, usually by the eldest son on his back and then put in the coffin and carried to the cremation ground. The dead body is put on an oven built above the ground. Weeds and twigs are burnt from below so that lesser quantity of fuel is consumed in cremation. Usually, the *phasphun* members provide help in performing the death rites. The ritual observed after one month of cremation is called *langanj*. On the forty-ninth day after the death, the ritual of *zarju* is observed. *Turen* or *sizak* corresponds to the death anniversary involving ceremonial worship for the deceased person. The life-cycle rituals have been considerably curtailed.

Among the Mons, land is the main economic resource. In the past, it was the raja or the monastery that provided some land to the Mons in return of the services rendered by them. Their primary occupation is playing on flute on the occasion of festivals and rituals. The members of the community are also engaged as wage labourers, or doing business or are employed in services. A few of them are in the armed forces. The Mon families receive an annual gift of grains from all the peasant families after the harvesting of crops. They get their land cultivated by the Bhoto (Ladakhi Buddhist) who have the necessary implements for the purpose.

Owing to their low social status, they do not hold any office of authority in the village council. They settle their own disputes through the elders of the community. In case of some dispute with the Bhotos, the Mon is always at disadvantage because the village council is dominated by the Bhotos. Statutory panchayats do exist, but the Mons are not represented in them. The main function of these panchayats is to plan and implement the welfare and developmental activities. Crimes such as adultery, rape, elopement and theft are non-existent. Disputes over land and water occur quite often. Disrespect for traditional norms invites *malem-chulem* or stoppage of water from the Bhotos.

They Mons are Buddhist by religion. They have access to the *gompas* where they can worship and pay offerings to the idols of Lord Buddha. The services of the lama are available to them. The lamas visit their houses to perform the rituals on the occasion of childbirth, marriage and death. But the Mon can never become a lama or a *chomo* for their low social status. In almost every Buddhist house, there is an altar on which a lamp is kept burning. Besides the family worshipping place, there is a village *gompa*, which is attached to the regional *gompa*. The religious specialists are the *kushak* and lama, who perform the birth, marriage and death rites. The Mon participate in all the Buddhist festivals like Losar, Strupla (harvesting festival), and the *gompa* festivals are celebrated round the year. They also provide musical performances on such occasions.

Intercommunity relations are based on mutual interdependence. The Mons live in the neighbourhood of the Buddhist and non-Buddhist communities. Set customary norms of behaviour and inter relationship exist between the Mons and the other Buddhist communities. The Mons render their services to all the communities in the village and, in return, get a fixed quantity of grain at the time of harvest. On the occasion of Losar festival, the Mon offers an arrow to the male and a spinner to the female of all the families he serves. It is reciprocated by the offerings of food and *sattoo*, flour of baked wheat and barley, to the Mon. During the course of *gynd*, a dance performed on the occasion of marriage, the Mon musicians get some money after every round of dance. At the start of sowing of crops, the Mon sing *goru* songs and are offered grain. They accept food and water from all the communities but the Bhotos do not like to take food in the house of the Mon. In a social gathering of the Ladakhi Buddhists, the Mon has to take his seat in accordance with his low status. The Ladakhi smokers do not offer their cigarettes to the Mon. The same restriction is observed in the distribution of drinks such as *chang* and *gurgur*. Members of all the communities make use of the common drinking water source. No regular marriage can be contracted between the members of two different communities. The male members of the other Ladakhi group do not aspire for a Mon bride. The other Ladakhi female after marrying the Mon becomes Mon for all practical purposes. The Mon can never join the Ladakhi *phasphun* group as a member. Usually, the *phasphuns* share a common cremation ground. At the time of death, families from all the groups utilize the services of lamas in the matter of carrying the dead body. The Ladakhis do not help in carrying the dead body of a person belonging to any group lower than them. The Mon, like the other Buddhist, have access to the *gompa*. They can make offerings and are free to consult the lamas and the *kushaks* as and when required. The community has not produced professionals such as doctors, engineers, administrators and teachers. The Ladakhi boys and girls do not want to be taught by teachers belonging to the Mon community if there are any. Since they have no voice in village affairs, political leadership has not emerged in this community.

The Mons avail of the facilities of schools, primary health centres, family welfare, transport and communication. Boys and girls study, at least up to the primary level. Dropping out of school among the boys and girls is mainly due to poverty. The Mons residing in remote villages still depend on the *amchi* in case of illness. Most of the villages are now provided with tap water. The sources of water are aqueducts and springs. The villages are covered under the Integrated Rural Development Programmes (IRDP). Under this programme, the families below poverty line are indentified and recommended for subsidy from the banks. Avenues of self-employment are thus made available in their villges. The DRD Agency provides loans for the procurement of cows. Media of communication such as radio and television are available. Motorable roads connect most of the villages. In the interior, however, pony tracks are the only links of communication. They have not availed themselves of electrification facilities. Firewood, cow-dung cakes and kerosene oil are their source of fuel. Facilities of fair price shops are available and they get rice, sugar and kerosene oil through them.

PARMANAND LAL

MORAVIAN

The emergence of the Moravian Christians as a community in Ladakh is a recent phenomenon. The Moravians are also known as Mashikapa among their neighbouring Ladakhi groups. The Moravian Mission has been functioning at Leh since 1885. The community traces its origin to Moravia, which was a province of the present Czech Republic.

They speak Ladakhi amongst themselves, but switch over to Urdu and English while talking with others. The scripts they use are Bodhi and Roman, the latter is being used while corresponding with outsiders. No constitutional status is being conferred on them.

The Moravians are non-vegetarians and eat yak meat. Wheat and barley are their staple food. The medium of cooking is mustard oil. Green vegetables are consumed occasionally, especially during summer. *Gurgur cha* (salty tea) and lipton *cha* (sweet tea) are consumed a number of times in a day. Their alcoholic drinks are *chang* and *arrack.* Their *chang* is either brewed from barley at home or purchased from a kiosk in the market. *Arrack* is invariably purchased from the market. Special cakes and biscuits are baked on Christmas and Easter. Rice and lipton *cha*, considered a luxury in the past due to their non-availability, are now commonly consumed. In fact, rice is more preferred to traditional *tsampa* and *skiu* (steamed *sattoo*).

The Moravians are hierarchically arranged into *skootak* (aristocracy), *mangrik* or *yengbadpa* (farmers) and *riknun* (occupational groups) but in the overall regional status hierarchy most of the Moravians belong to the middle order of the *mangriks*. They possess only a diluted concept of social differentiation avoiding connubial and commensal interaction with lower occupational groups. Titles used earlier have been replaced by the Christianized titles. The community perceives for itself a middle position in the social hierarchy. Other communities too consider them accordingly. They are neither aware of the *varna* system nor claim a position in it. Monogamy is generally observed. Marriage alliance with father's brother's daughter, mother's sister's daughter, wife's sister, and husband's brother are not permissible. Cross-cousin marriages are allowed. Marriage by *maqpa*, and by courtship (*skus khoyangches*) are the usual modes. Married women put on skirts (*sulma*). Demand for dowry is a recent phenomenon. Residence after marriage is partrilocal. No case of divorce has ever been reported. Bigamy is prohibited; remarriage is permissible. Age at marriage is above 20 years. Among the Moravians, extended families are slowly breaking up into nuclear ones. Elders are given due regard; smoking, drinking and loose talks are avoided in their presence. The youngsters invariably concede to the wishes of the elders. Joking and avaoidance kinship behaviours are absent. Close interfamily linkages in terms of rendering of reciprocal labour and mutual ecomomic exchanges portray them as a close knit community. Primogeniture is not strictly adhered to; the eldest male issue succeeds his deceased father. Fresh employment avenues and greater mobility has made youngsters assertive in family matters, causing a decline in the absolute authority of the family elders. The Moravian women have a right in the parental property and play an effective role in family management, affairs of the church and the community. They contribute substantially to the family earning and enjoy a high status in the society. Childbirth in the Moravian community takes place either in the paternal house or in a maternity hospital. Baptism commences after seven months; naming ceremony is done by the parents. At the age of 13 years, the children are imparted religious education and are confirmed as full-fledged members of the church and are entitled to participate in the Holy Communion held once in a month in commemoration of the Last Supper. Marriages are performed during the day time at the church where the Pastor confirms marital union of the intending spouses. Wedding rings are exchanged and feasting follows. Consummation of marriage is performed at the bridegroom's residence. When a person dies, the dead body is kept for 24 hours to ascertain actual death. Thereafter, it is given a ceremonial bath and buried in the cemetry.

The Moravian Christians are a landowning community of Leh and are primarily agriculturists. Individuals hold the landownership titles. Government service, trade and self-employment activities are their secondary occupations. Market is fully regulated and the community's dependence on it is absolute. Payment to labourers is made both in cash and kind. There has been a a new vigour in their economic activities as new job avenues opened after Independence. The church plays a significant role in exercising political control over the community through the *garnme*, a church elder's council, where all disputes of personal or collective nature and the necessary measures for the community welfare are discussed. The five church elders are elected by a voice vote. The *garnme* is not authorized to impose any social sanctions. Statutory panchayats have no significant part to play in the affairs of the community.

The Moravian Christians are Protestants and believe in the edicts of the New Testament. The Moravian Church is one of the oldest but still one of the smallest of the Protestant denominations. There are no family, clan and village deities. Church is the place of worship and Jesus Christ is the object of veneration. The shrines are situated within the state of Jammu & Kashmir and outside, but they do not have the tradition of making pilgrimages. The Pastor is the religious specialist who plays an important role in the life of the believers right from baptism to burial. He also presides over the conclaves held to discuss the overall welfare of the community. Christmas and Easter are their major festivals. The people still bear on overall cultural melieu of the Ladakhi Buddhists, they neither share the Buddhist faith nor any vestiges of the old faith remain amongst them. They have brought about evolutionary changes not only in their own community, but in the whole of Ladakh. They were the first to introduce smokeless steel ovens, start a Mission hospital and run a Mission Public School at Leh. They are, however, well versed in the Christian oral traditions such as choral hymns which are sung in the church during periodic services and festivals.

The Moravians are closely linked with the Buddhists, Muslim Argons and other occupational groups with the ties of economic cooperation and a fuller participation in other socio-economic activities. They do not observe any commensal taboos either with the Buddhists or with the Argons, but avoid interacting with the Gara, Beda and Mons. Marriages are performed only with the believers irrespective of their ethnic identity. They enjoy free access to the places of public interest and water resources. *Jajmani* system exists no more but *shus* (sharecropping), is still a source of interethnic interaction.

The Moravians' attitude towards the development programmes is enthusiastic. They are however against small family norms. Schemes of employment and self-employment through bank financing are fully availed of and they use all modern media of communication besides making efforts in conservation of environment and harnessing solar energy for self-consumption. *Kuhls* supply water for irrigation, and fertilizers, both organic and chemical, are fully made use of. Programmes on nutrition have been effectively introduced and well received. Public distribution system is effective enough to take care of their needs. Banking facilities are fully availed of and there is a healthy trend among the people to save and reinvest their savings in profitable economic pursuits.

BAQAR R. RIZVI

MUGHAL

Origin of the Mughal of Jammu is reportedly traced to the ruling Mughals, who came to India with Babar. There had also been a tendency among the people of low caste to call themselves Mughals. The Muslims of Jammu who claim to be Mughals can possibly belong to this class. Of the Mughal tribes, only the Chughatta and the Bartas are probably true Mughals, and the Mughals of Jammu do not claim their descent from any of these. Their claim to Mughal descent is, therefore, doubtful. A few so-called Mughal families seem to have come to Jammu during Maharaja Gulab Singh's time, especially after the revolt of 1857. Information reveal that Mirza Jan Beg was that the first Mughal to settle in Jammu. Belonging to the ruling family, the Mughal Muslims of Jammu controlled one of the zones of 22 divisions in Delhi which was known as Mohalla Bangish at that time. Quite a few of them migrated to Pakistan on the eve of the Partition. Even after the 1965 Indo-Pakistan war, some of them migrated to Pakistan. Most of them are reportedly living in zila Mirpur in Pakistan. Some of them preferred to shift back to India even after their migration to Pakistan and are now settled in the main city of Jammu. The Mughal Muslim settlements in Jammu region are in Jammu (proper), Naoshera, Rajouri and Punch. They use the surname Mirza or Baig. They speak Punjabi and Urdu amongst themselves but switch over to Urdu and English while talking with others. The scripts they use are Arabic and Roman for corresponding with each other as well as with outsiders. Their dress pattern comprises *salwar* and *kameez* for their menfolk. No constitutional status has been conferred on them.

They are non-vegetarians and consume beef. Wheat and rice are their staple food. They consume all varieties of pulses. The medium of cooking is mustard oil and *ghee*. Green vegetables are consumed regularly. Sweet tea, is consumed several times a day. Alcoholic drinks are occasionally consumed by their menfolk, who purchase the same from the market. Menfolk are regular smokers of cigarette and use of cheroot is also found among them. They prefer rice to *roti*. The men chew tobacco and betel, besides occasional use of snuff. Regular and sufficient milk and milk products is used by them. There has not been any change in their food habits.

The Mughals do not have any hierarchical division, neither are they aware of the *varna* system. Differentiation among them is essentially in relation to ecomomic and occupational status rather than any socio-religious factor. The community percieves itself to be in middle position in the social hierarchy. Other communities too consider them accordingly. Monogamy is generally observed. They practice both exogamy and endogamy at the community level. Consanguinity among parallel cousins and other blood relations is permissible. The practice of junior sororate and junior levirate also exists among them. The marriage age for their males is usually above 22 years while for their females, it is above 18 years. Marriage is arranged through mutual consent and negotiation. There are no formal symbols of marriage observed by their women though they use finger ring, toe ring, earring, nose ring and nose stud pin. *Mahr* is promised in the form of *muajjil*, part cash and part *ghain-muajji*, promised but not actually paid. Marriage rituals are conducted by a *maulvi*. Demand for dowry is a recent phenomenon. Residence is partrilocal after marriage. Divorce cases are few. Bigamy is permitted and remarriage is permissible. No changes were reported in the rules of marriage which are strictly conducted according to the Islamic practices. Among the Mughal Muslims, extended families are still a common family form, though they are now slowly breaking up into nuclear types. Elders are given due respect as smoking, drinking and loose talks are avoided in their presence. Joking relationship among formal relations is usually avoided. Close interfamily linkages are reported to be cordial. In practice, rules of inheritance favour the male equigeniture, though females are also given some share of the ancestral property depending upon the wishes of their male relations. The eldest son succeeds his deceased father. Their women have a right in parental property and play a restricted role in the family management. They also contribute to the household income, specially in urban areas, whereas they help in farm and non-farm activities in rural areas. There are neither pre-delivery restrictions or rituals observed by their women nor is there any post-delivery pollution or naming ceremony performed by them. Circumcision is performed in case of male child only and *aqeeqa* ceremony is prevalent among them. Marriage rituals are performed at the bride's residence. The groom, accompanied by guests, arrives at the bride's residence, where ritual of *nikah* is performed. A feast is given by both the parties and nuptial ceremony is performed at the groom's residence. The dead are given a ceremonial bath and buried in the *kabristan*. For the first three days after the death, the family's relations arrange for the meals of the bereaved family members and all those present at home.

The Mughals are essentially a service class community in the region of Jammu, while a few of them have land-related occupations. Among those who have land, it is held under individual proprietorship. Besides, a few of them are also in petty trade and commerce. Market is fully regulated and the community's dependence on it is total. Payment for labour is made both in cash and kind. Self-employment opportunities in the community are limited. They do not have any separate caste *sabha* or *majlis*, but are members of the village panchayat, which is heterogeneous in its composition. Statutory panchayats have no significant role to play in the affairs of the community.

The Mughals are Sunni Muslims by religion. Individual affiliation to *pir* is there among these people. They usually have *maulvis* drawn from the other Muslim communities to perform their religious functions. They visit the shrines located within the state as well as those in other parts of the country. They make pilgrimage to Mecca to perform *haj*. They observe all the Muslim religious festivals especially, Id-ul-Zuha, Id-ul-Fitr, Id-ul-Milad-ul-Nabi and Shab-e-Qadr. Handi-crafts are absent excepting their ladies doing occasional embroidery. They are, however, well-versed with the Muslim oral traditions and *ayaats* from the Koran recited during the religious meetings. Since, they belonged to royal family of the Mughals in the past, they have folk tales about bravery and victories in the wars by their ancestors.

The Mughals accept food and water from their co-religionists, while quite a few of them also interdine with people of other faiths. They are closely linked with the Sunni Muslims of other ethnic stock. Marriages are performed with all communities of co-believers, especially the Muslim Rajputs of the region. They enjoy free access to the places of public interest and water sources. Patron-client relationship exists among them. There are doctors, teachers and government servants among them. Political leadership is virtually absent at the community level and is, by and large, restricted to voting in elections.

The Mughal's attitude towards the development programmes is favourable. The average family size is seven members and above. Schemes of employment and self-employment through banking facilities are partially availed of. They use modern media of communication. They use firewood, coal, kerosene oil and LPG as fuel resources. Since they are predominantly a landless community, they do not make use of irrigational or fertilizer procurement facilities offered to the farmers by governmental agencies. Nutritional programmes are also not availed of. Facilities of the public distribution system are made use of and their attitude towards savings is favourable. They partially depend on the moneylenders and shopkeepars. They reinvest their savings into remunerative business pursuits.

INDU BALA DHAR

NAGVANSHI

The Nagvanshis of Reasi tahsil, in the district of Udhampur of Jammu & Kashmir, are reported to have migrated from Ayodhya via Hastinapur and Punjab during the reign of Aurangzeb. Nagvanshis of Reasi perceive their distribution in Himachal Pradesh, Madhya Pradesh, West Bengal, Assam and in southern India. There are places in Kashmir, the names of which end with nag, such as Seshnag, Anantnag, etc. So far the history of their origin is concerned, they could only mention that there is reference to the Nagas and their Kingdom in the *Mahabharat.* 'Nag' is commonly used as the surname. Pahari, Dogri and Hindi is spoken at home and with others respectively. Devanagari and Arabic script is generally used by them and some of them are conversant in English as well.

Rice, wheat and maize are their staple food. They are occasional non-vegetarian and eat mutton, fish, egg, chicken and pork. Home-made alcoholic drink is consumed occasionally. *Mehra*, a mixture of rice, *lassi* and *ghee* is a special dish relished by them during festive occasions.

Brahman and Rajput are the two subdivisions recognized among the Nagvanshi. The Nagvanshis of Reasi region claim to be Rajputs and are popularly called the Thakkar Nag. They all belong to the Sandilya *gotra*, akin to that in Himachal Pradesh. The Brahmans are considered superior, while they claim equal status with the Lohar, Teli, Bania, etc. The Thakkar Nag ascribe a lower social status to the communities such as the Megh, Chamar, Nadiala (musicians), Ramdasi.

The Thakkar Nagas are exogamous at the level of *gotra* and lineage. They marry in all the local Rajput groups, excepting those of Sandilya *gotra.* Adult marriage through negotiation is the common practice. Sometimes marriage by exchanging daughters is also preferred. *Sindoor* (vermilion) and nose-stud are the symbols of a married woman. Both patrilocal and neolocal residence after marriage are found to exist among them. Both husband and wife are permitted to seek divorce. Remarriage of divorcees, widowers and widows are allowed in the community. Paternal property is inherited and equally shared by the sons only. Apart from their routine load of household chores and childcare, the women lend economic support to the families by earning as teachers, agricultural labourers, etc.

Birth pollution is observed for twenty-one days. On the last day the child is named by the *kul-purohit* (family priest) through the rituals of *havan* (sacred fire) and worshipping *kul-devta* (family deity), the serpent Nag. The ritual of *annaprashan* (first rice feeding) is performed for the child between the age of six months to one year, followed by *mundan* (tonsuring) on the first or third year. The rituals of *bia* or marriage commence with *sant* or *natrod* at the bridegroom's house wherein relatives from nearby villages visit the house dancing and singing all the way. The ritual of *janibarat* marks the procession of the bridegroom's *palki* (palanquin) for the bride's house accompanied by relatives and friends as *barati* (bridegroom's party). The marriage rituals at the bride's residence are conducted by a Brahman *purohit* through *havan*, around which the bridegroom and the bride are made to circumambulate. Return of the couple to the bridegroom's house on the following day is called *pajoki*. Consummation of marriage is performed at the residence of the bridegroom. The Thakkar Nagvanshis cremate their dead. *Marna* (death pollution) is observed for thirteen days. The ritual of *daspindi* is performed on the tenth day wherein all the affinal relatives wash their clothes for the first time after the death. The rituals of *pind-dan* and *sogtorana* is performed on the thirteenth day to ritually offer food to the mourning family members by the affinal relatives of the deceased and to mark completion of the pollution period. *Adh-barkhi*, *barkhi* and *chaubahri* are the death rituals performed on the sixth month, one year and fourth year respectively.

The Thakkar Nagvanshi is a landowning community and agriculture has been their traditional occupation and primary source of income. Most of them are owner-cultivators, but sharecroppers and agricultural labourers are also not altogether absent among them. They have the facility of regulated daily local market to transact in cash. Child labour continues to exist among them. Welfare and development activities in the region are carried out by the statutory panchayat. During the annual *yatra* (festival) of Nag-devta they perform the traditional *kud* dance with *dhol* (musical drum) and *bansuri* (flute). The Thakkar Nagvanshis are Hindus, having followers of Saiva, Shakta and Radhaswami sects, but Nag-devta (serpent Nag) is the *kul-devta* (family deity) for all of them. The priest who invokes and appeases Nag-devta must always be a Thakkar Nagvanshi Rajput, not a Brahman Nagvanshi. Vaishno Devi is regarded as the regional deity while *pagan* or Nag-devta is the village level deity for all of them. Apart from the perpetual traditional linkages with other neighbouring communities, of late they have established modern linkages through employment as the government servants, lawyers, shopowners, teachers, doctors, etc. The Thakkar Naga take food and water from the Brahmans, Rajputs, Bania, Kumhar, etc. They do not accept food from the Nadiala, Saria, Megh, Ramdasi, etc. The Thakkar Naga of Reasi traditionally accept food and water from the Lohar, Kumhar, etc., but they do not have connubial relations with them and also do not share the *hookah* (hubble-bubble) with them.

Education of sons and daughters is an important concern for the parents. They make use of both traditional and modern medicare system. Springs and rivulets are the main source of drinking water in most of the villages. Firewood, kerosene and LPG are the fuels used by them. They often use chemical fertilizers and insecticides to increase agricultural output. They avail the benefit of the government controlled fair price shops.

B.K. Basu
M. Hazra

NALBAND

The term Nalband is composed of two words, i.e. *nal*, a horseshoe, and *band* which means fastening. The traditional occupation of the community is fastening the horseshoe. Now they have turned towards other occupations such as cloth weaving and wood carving. They are distributed throughout the Kashmir Valley as well as in other parts of the country. They are a settled community and live permanently at one place. Their habitat has cold climate, low humidity, thin forest, and medium snowfall. They speak Kashmiri as well as Urdu and use the Arabic script. They enjoy the status of Other Backward Classes.

Like other Kashmiris, the Nalbands wear a long loose gown called *pheran* which has buttoning at the neck and falling down to the ankles. In winter, it is made of wool and, in summer, of cotton. Both men and women wear the *pheran*. There is little difference between the *pheran* worn by men and women.

Like the other Muslim communities, the Nalbands are also non-vegetarian. They consume mutton but do not consume beef and pork. Their staple food is rice. They consume plenty of vegetables. Among pulses, *moong*, *mah* and *moth* are commonly consumed. Their medium of cooking is linseed oil. They do not take alcoholic drinks and other intoxicants. Milk and milk products are also consumed. They smoke *bidi*, cigarette, loose tobacco and chew betel.

Among the Nalbands, endogamy at community level exists. Marriages are performed at the age of 18 to 24 years in case of girls and 22 to 26 years in case of boys. The marriages are settled through negotiation. Consanguineous marriages are also performed. Monogamy is the general form of marriage. Dowry is taken in the form of cash and kind. Rule of residence after marriage is patrilocal. Divorce is allowed among them. If the couple is unable to adjust owing to one or the other reason, or some specific charges are there against any of them, they can ask for divorce. But, in fact, divorce cases are rare and the matter is settled by the family members and other relatives. In case of divorce, it is the responsibility of husband to maintain his wife during her period of *iddat* or a period of continuance imposed on a women on the termination of her marriage in order to establish the paternity of the possible child conceived earlier, during which a women is expected to live a life of seclusion and abstain from all luxuries. The observation of *iddat* is necessary where cohabitation has taken place and the marriage is dissolved by divorce, the duration of *iddat* is three months and ten days. If the woman is pregnant, the duration of *iddat* is till the delivery. It is the duty of the father to maintain the children after divorce, irrespective of whether the children live with the mother or father. Widow, widower and divorcee remarriages are permitted. The remarriages are performed in the same way as regular marriages are performed.

Among the Nalbands, there is a marked increase in the formation of nuclear families. Extended families are also in existence, but are considerably less in proportion to the former. They pay due regards to the elders of the family and love the children. Joking relations prevail with *devar* (husband's younger brother) and *bhabhi* (elder brother's wife); *sali* (wife's younger sister) and *bahnoi* (elder sister's husband). Avoidance relation is observed between the father-in-law and daughter-in-law. The daughter-in-law avoids the father-in-law till she is issueless. Property is the main reason behind conflicts and confrontations, and these are generally resolved through familial compromise.

The Nalband daughters enjoy the right of inheritance and get a share of the paternal property; but they get less than the sons. Widows have the right of inheritance not only of their parents property but also that of their husbands. If a widow has no children, she is entitled to one-fourth of her husband's property in cash and kind. If there are children, she gets only one-eighth. If the widow is the sole surviving heir of the deceased, she inherits the whole property. Succession is in the male line and the eldest son succeeds his father.

Besides household work, the Nalbad women go out for collection of firewood and for bringing potable water. They also do embroidery work through which they supplement the family income. Women can attend the village panchayats and are free to give their statement and stand as witness. They can cast their vote in the elections.

Among the Nalbands, when a baby is born, the *mulla* (religious priest) comes and whispers *azaan* in the right ear of the child. A bath is given to the baby on the same day. The name is also given on the same day. Usually, the name is given by the father and mother. For one or two days, the mother takes only a decoction of certain herbs. The *sunder* (purification) ritual, takes place on the seventh day after a child is born. On that day, the mother of the newborn baby takes bath and comes out of the delivery room. The second purification bath is given on fortieth day of the child's birth. The head shaving ceremony (*zerakasi*), is observed on the seventh day. The *navid* (barber) performs the shaving. A goat is sacrificed at the time of *zerakasi*. The skin, head and legs of the sacrificed goat are buried and the meat is given to the villagers and *mulla*. The family members of the newborn baby do not eat the meat of the sacrificed goat. The relatives, friends and neighbours are invited and a feast is arranged. Generally, at the age of four or five years the ritual of *khatna* (circumcision) of the male child takes place. It is an occasion of great rejoicing and festivities. The relatives, friends and neighbours are invited on the occasion and a feast is arranged. The *oapsoap* ritual is observed after six months, wherein the child is given a preparation of milk, sugar, bread or biscuits.

The marriage negotiations commence when the boy's father goes with a small party of relatives to the girl's house. They are entertained by the girl's father. The priest, in the presence of the party, announces the betrothal. Afterwards, on the festive occasions, the boy's father sends presents to the girl. On the marriage day, the *barat* (marriage procession) starts from the bridegroom's house. First, they visit some neighbouring shrine and then proceed for the bride's house. As the *barat* draws near the bride's house, the women of the bride's side come out to welcome the *baratis*, or members of the marriage procession. The main ceremony is *nikah*. The *nikah* is performed by a *qazi*. After the marriage rituals are over at the bride's house, the *barat* returns with the bride to the groom's house. This ceremony is known *rukhsati* (departure) of the bride. In *rukhsati*, the *barat* returns with the bride along with a *dadmoj* (woman) who accompanies the bride. The bridegroom and bride are received with great enthusiasm. The parties of singing women come to receive the bride, and she is taken into a room arranged for her reception where she takes her seat with her gaze fixed on the ground. The bride remains for seven days in her-in-law's house after which she returns to her father's house. *Wathal* is ceremonial feast performed at the groom's house. After marriage when the son-in-law is invited for the first time by his father-in-law, a feast is arranged and the son-in-law gets presents and cash. The bride also goes with him and then there is no bar for them to visit the house in future.

At the time of death, the *kalma* and some verses from the Holy Koran are recited into the ears of the dying person. The dead are buried. The relatives and friends recite the Holy Koran till the dead body is kept inside the house. The *ghusl-e-maiyat* (funeral bath), is given to the dead body and then it is wrapped in *kafan* (shroud). The dead body is carried to the graveyard in wooden *taboot* covered with a black cloth. *Namaz-e-janaza* is performed before the dead is buried.

They are slowly giving up their traditional occupation and turning towards occupations like wood carving, cloth weaving, etc. Since the number of tongas is decreasing day by day, it has become difficult for them to depend on their traditional occupation of shoeing the horses.

Statutory village panchayats exist in their areas.

The Nalbands are Sunni Muslims. Besides celebrating the Muslim festivals, such as Id-ul-Fitr, Id-ul-Zuha, Shab-e-Barat and Shab-e-Qadr, they participate in the *urs* (fairs) held to mark the birth anniversary of well-known saints, namely, the tombs of Ghulam Nabi Baig and Mohammad Usman Qadri. Hazratbal is another sacred centre for these people.

Among the Nalbands, folk songs are sung on the occasions of birth and marriage. Traditional folklore and folk tales are prevalent in the community.

They eat in the house of members of other communities except the Watal. Intercommunity marriage, participation in social and religious functions are some of the avenues of developing mutual understanding.

A large number of the Nalbands are educated. Not only boys, even the girls also study up to college level. Their attitude to modern medicare is positive and they make moderate use of medicare. They are aware of the family welfare programmes and generally their women get sterilized. Drinking water is available within the locality through taps. Thier attitude towards saving is also positive. Cow-dung cakes and kerosene oil are the fuel used for cooking.

S.N.H. Rizvi

NAMDAGUR

The Namdagurs are craftsmen engaged in producing *namda* (felt), a kind of warm woollen fabric. The word 'namdagur' comprises two terms, *namda* and *gur*, both Persian in origin. *Namda* is the corrupted form of Persian *namad* meaning felt used in warm clothing, caps and footwear; *gur* is the Kashmiri corruption of the Persian noun *gar* meaning doer or maker. Hence *namdagur* in Kashmiri is the corruption of Persian *namdgar*. *Namda* is coarse wool beaten into felt and perfected by dying, washing and embroidery.

The craft of making felt in Kashmir is shrouded in mystery. The popular legend is that the craft was imported to Kashmir from Central Asia or Iran by persons adapt in it during the reign of the mid-fifteenth century Kashmiri Sultan Zainu'l-Abidin or Badshah (the Great King). In the historical accounts of medieval Kashmir, there are references that certain crafts were brought by the said Sultan from Samarkand and Bukhara in the present-day Republic of Uzbekistan. But as far as information goes, there is no specific reference to the craft of making *namda* having been imported by that ruler. Nevertheless, the very name of the commodity suggests that it is either Iranian or of Central Asian origin, the latter place being a more dependable probability in view of Kashmir's close cultural contacts with it in the medieval period. In Iran and in Central Asia, there existed the use of a felt hat *kulah-i-namad* or 'wearer of felt', *namad posh*. Also the possibility of Kashmiri craftsmen having learnt the craft in the towns of Eastern Turkistan (present Sinkiang or Zinjiang in China) such as Khotan, Yarkand and Kashghar cannot altogether be ruled out because of brisk commercial interaction between Kashmir and that part of Central Asia in medieval times. However, there is no oral history or legend which could indicate any group of *namda* craftsmen having migrated from any part of Central Asia to Kashmir at any point of time in history. Hence, on the basis of absence of any such evidence and also in view of perfect ethnic and anthropological traits of the Namdagur community in Srinagar, it should be quite safe to state that they are Kashmiris for all intents and purposes. Unfortunately no mention of the community exists in any published or unpublished source of the last two hundred years.

There is only one locality in Srinagar called Namdagur Mohalla near

Naohatta, where the community is concentrated. The locality derives its name from the craft in which most of its inhabitants are involved. From some of the knowledgeable persons contacted, it was learnt that this is said to be the only locality in the city of Srinagar where the community is concentrated. However, quite recently some craftsmen have come up in rural areas of the valley not too far away from Srinagar, for instance, in Watehkol in Chandura tahsil, Sandeb in Badgam tahsil and Bujoi in Chadura tahsil. Possibly the workers in the workshops having learnt the trade, left their workshops in Srinagar, and set up their own manufacturing units in their respective villages with only modest success. But their number is almost negligible. The oral tradition has it that more than a hundred years ago, a Kashmiri craftsman named Mohi-ud-Din Khan brought the craft from Yarkand in eastern Turkistan and, after settling down in the present Namdagur Mohalla near Naohatta in Srinagar, popularized it and expanded the industry to the extent of its commercialization. But just a hundred years appears to be too little a time for popularization of the craft in Kashmir when it is several hundred years old in Central Asia.

Namdagur Mohalla where the community is concentrated is a very congested area. There is no park or open space in the locality and the houses are made of wood, bricks and clay, and wear a perfectly medieval look silhoutted against the backdrop of the Hari Parbat hillock on the top of which stands the famous Hari Parbat fort of the sixteenth century. The total population of the community is estimated at about 25,000 (census data being not available, results of a field study are relied upon) with a ratio of 52:48 between the male and female population. Their mother tongue is Kashmiri but they can speak Urdu also to the limits of their professional requirement. Wherever necessary, the members correspond with one another in Urdu. There is no specific identification mark for the community in the matter of dress. *Kameez, salwar*, coat and *pheran* (Kashmiri gown) is the common dress. The community has not been given special status under the Constitution of India or the state of Jammu & Kashmir.

The Namdagurs are non-vegetarians but because of their weak economic position and high cost of meat, they cannot afford to be exclusively non-vegetarian. Rice is their staple food and *chapati* is seldom consumed. It is considered a sign of poverty to eat or serve *chapatis* and *dal*. There is a good intake of vegetables. Previously, pure vegetable oil was consumed but, owing to rising prices, they now use rapeseed oil. Fruit eating is not a regular habit nor is fruit considered an essential part of diet. Alcoholic drinks are forbidden by religion nor is there any practice of taking *sharbat* or soft drinks. However tea, particularly salt tea, is a regular part of their diet. It is taken twice a day at breakfast and during the afternoon. Invariably bread from the baker's shop is eaten along with salt tea. There are varieties of baked bread, for example, *bakerkhani*, *tschochur*, *kulcha*, *nan*, *lawaseh*, *girdeh*, *katlam* and *shirmal*. Usually, about two or three persons partake of food from a platter, a big round tray called *traem* in Kashmiri, derived from copper *tram* in Kashmiri and *tamra*, in Sanskrit. *Tashner* is the water jug and container, a two-in-one utensil, for washing hands before they sit down to have their food. Food is always eaten sitting crosslegged on the floor over a spread-out sheet called *dastarkhwan*. Green pepper is consumed invariably and condiments are frequently used. Since the community is economically weak, it cannot afford the delicacies of Kashmiri cuisine, but marriages do afford such opportunities, rare though they be. Eatables are purchased from the market whereas food grains, sugar, kerosene and flour are purchased from the supply depots of the government food and supplies department.

The Namdagur belong to one group only and they have no sub-groups or divisions. The question of stratification in social terms, therefore, does not arise, though in economic terms there are comparative differences. They are essentially a labour class and have only one category. However, as far as the production stages of the craft of making felt is concerned, there are other groups called the Naqqash (designers), Jalaqdoz (embroidery workers), Rangrez (dyers), Dhobi (washerman) and packers. Between these subprofessional groups, there are intercommunity links. Change in lifestyle is connected with the level of income which is not satisfactory as far as the actual workers are concerned. In the general sweep of economic advancement of the country, only a peripheral change has taken place. For instance, a worker today can afford a second pair of dress or shoes, or occasionally visit the cinema when bored by his monotonous work. Also the use of a baggy *salwar khan dress* and a longish *kurta* (an imitation of the traditional dress of the Pathans) is often worn as a fashionable attire. In the same way, they may give a somewhat stylish name to their children after some well-known Pakistani cricketer, sportsman, film actor or popular figure indicating a clear departure from traditional names, particularly shortened names like Lassa from Ghulam Rasul, Sideh for Muhammad Siddiq, and Museh for Mustafa.

In terms of self-perception, they suffer from a sense of inferiority complex which is not only absent but is replaced by a feeling of superiority in the case of communities engaged in more lucrative and sophisticated handicrafts like shawl weaving, papier mâché and wood carving. The members of this community are conscious that they are considered socially inferior, and a Namdagur does not easily attract a mate and a life partner. The perception of other communities about the Namdagur is also not very high. The reasons for this phenomenon are twofold; this craft involves great manual labour in unhygienic conditions and it is a non-remunerative craft, at least for the basic worker.

Marriage between parallel cousins, cross-cousins is the general marriage norm. Eighteen and above is the normal age of marriage for girls but it can be higher for boys. The mate is acquired by parental intervention and arrangement. Monogamy is prevalent and polygamy is extremely rare. There are no special symbols of marriage except that for first few weeks after the nuptials, the bride is usually ornamentally dressed with a lot of make-up. Dowry is generally given in kind (household goods, pieces of furniture, electric gadgets, television, bedding and furnishing) and only a small fraction is given in cash under some name like *tchochih hareh* (bread money). The bride lives with her husband in the house of her in-laws unless it has been otherwise arranged previously. The rules of divorce are strictly those stipulated in the Muslim *shariat*. Marriage rites are performed at the house of the bride in the presence of close relatives and are solemnized by the priest. Divorce can be given by either of the two, but it is a complex process. Usually the matter of divorce is discussed at length by the relatives and friends or neighbours, and efforts are made for reconciliation. Sometimes, good offices of the elders in the community are sought to persuade the parties to accept a negotiated settlement. In some cases, local political personalities are approached to intervene and bring about rapprochement. But when all efforts fail, the case is referred to a priest who issues a formal decree leading to the dissolving of the marriage bond. Occasionally, a court of law may be moved for the issuance of the decree. The divorced woman has to wait for at least a period of three months and ten days, called the period of *iddat*, before she can marry again. She can remarry the previous husband, or he can remarry the previous wife provided the priest decrees it; but, in such a case, the common practice is that the woman must first becomes the legal wife of a third person, then divorce and finally remarry her first husband. The divorced woman is entitled to receive the dower called *mahr* as stipulated in the marriage deed. If the divorced woman has conceived before the divorce takes place (conception revealed within the period of *iddat*), the expected baby is to be taken care of by its own father, meaning the first husband of the divorced woman. The infant may be brought up by the mother. Grown-up children may remain with their father, or as mutually agreed upon. A very significant change which has been noticed is that divorces are extensively discouraged since it is somewhat difficult for both the man and woman to get married again. One of the Namdagurs said that they were considered an inferior category of craftsmen and, therefore, finding a mate was usually a tedious matter.

The family is generally of vertically extended type, though in many cases it is a mixed-extended one. As regards interpersonal relationships, one finds mixed relationship of respect and fear working in conjunction in the family. Avoidance has not been noticed because the bride is usually from among the blood relations and is invariably exposed to manual work besides having to do daily household chores. Property is inherited equally by the sons, and the daughters are entitled to their share called *koreh-har* or daughter's money. However, daughter's share is not equal to the share of the son. The eldest son is normally the successor to his deceased father's status in the family and not the daughter even if she happens to be older than her brother. A rise in the extended family system has been noticed. The change which has taken place during the last one or two decades is that there is a trend towards a nuclear type of family.

The woman enjoys the right to inherit the property of her deceased father if the latter is not survived by a male issue. In case there are more than one daughters, they enjoy equal right to the property of their deceased father. If a man is survived by four sons and one daughter, the entire property will comprise nine equal shares, two shares going to each son and one share to the daughter. Among the Namdagur community, the women have an active role in the economic life. They also work along with their husbands in the manufacture of felt or the basic material. Besides, women do all the cooking and take part in the management of the household. They have a say in the day to day life of the family and their suggestions and decisions in the household are hardly ignored. A woman considers it her duty to take care of her parents-in-law, particularly if they are old and infirm. The woman's role in the selection of mate for a grown-up child in the house is of vital importance. In fact, in the selection process, viz., enquiring about the prospective mate's family antecedents, the mate and his or her behaviour and character, the woman plays the main role.

The Namdagur community has no antenatal rituals though, of course, there are some pre-delivery taboos like confinement within the house during the time of solar or lunar eclipse, not receiving a visitor or a guest directly, avoiding going out at late hours or carrying heavy burden. At the birth of a baby, *kalma* or the Muslim call for prayer is said into its ears by any elderly person present on the occasion. It can be an elderly woman also. For the christening ceremony, no specific ritual is observed but the baby's name may be given after opening the Holy Koran and finding a name on the open page. The ritual observed during childhood is circumcision. A day is fixed (generally avoiding third, thirteenth, and twenty-third day of the month) when the *maulvi* is called. Then, after reciting prayers from the Holy Book, the child has to wear new clothes and is taken for circumcision. Previously the operation was done by the barbers, but now in urban areas, this is done by doctors in their private clinics. In remote villages, however, barbers still do the operation. There may be a small feast restricted to close relatives only.

Till marriage, there are no other rituals, though occasionally the family may visit the shrine at Hazratbal, Srinagar on some auspicious religious day. Cooking of rice mixed with *haldi*, called *tehar* in Kashmiri, may take place on some day and then handfuls of the cooked food is placed on the threshold of a nearby shrine, or on the wall with a red chillie placed on top of it. Handfuls are distributed among children and even elders who may happen to pass by. Usually the yellow coloured cooked rice is brought out on a big platter to the shrine or burial place or tomb of a saint in the locality and distributed there. Marriage is the important ritual which must be observed according the custom of the local Muslim population. The dead are buried in the ancestral or the community burial ground. The death rites are performed by a *maulvi*, and the dead body is carried in a wooden coffin and kept at one side in the compound of the nearby mosque. The mourning ends on the fourth day, on which tea or *halwa* and bread are served to the visitors coming to condole the bereaved family. The fourtieth day is the day of final farewell and no more condolences are expected. Some male members may visit the grave of the dead sometimes, particularly on some festive day, and offer *fateha*, the prayer for peace to the departed soul.

Land resource is essential in the sense that raw material is obtained from sheep and goats which are raised in pastures. Namdagurs producing felt need space not only to live on but to use it for manufacturing of the product. They conduct most of their activity within the small space of their own compound or some small open space in the locality. Namdagurs are not a landowning community and in most cases they are landless. Manual labour is the main occupation, and they are the producers of handicraft items which have a good export market. And, obviously they work for the exporters. There is no question of subsidiary occupation for the reason that making of *namda* or felt occupies their entire time. Their dependence on the market is complete.

Unless there are buyers, they cannot sell their produce. As a general rule, buyers are generally exporters and they exploit these poor craftsmen. There are no bonded labourers but the workers occasionally ask for credit from the monopolists and, in most cases, loans are offered. Ancestral debts are also there and have to be paid through offering labour. There is a definite rise in the number of workers engaged in the industry. Child labour (below 15 years) is also prevalent. There is minimal literacy and children are put to work. Wages are paid in cash and in a lump sum if loans are asked for. The change in the above phenomenon has been witnessed in the quantitative aspect. Though production has increased, wages are hardly commensurate with the rising prices or return from sale of the product to the monopolist. There has only been marginal increase in their standard of living and, out of sheer economic necessity, children are forced to the work of producing felt. To a very minor degree, there has been a shift in the primary occupation; some have shifted to carpet making.

It is a group localized in a *mohalla* in Srinagar only and has no regional or local council. They are a part of large community of handicraft workers of Kashmir whose economic and social interests are reflected in that organization. Of course, they have their *biradari* and occasionally common issues are discussed but there is nothing like a panchayat. There are no punishments or rewards except that, on occasions, advice or admonishment may be administered to an errant member.

The community professes Islam of the Sunni sect and Hanafi school. As Muslims, they have the family spiritualists, *pirs*, not necessarily in their own locality. The *pir* may be stationed at some distant village or town. However, they owe unswerving allegiance to Mir Waiz of Kashmir (at preset Molvi Muhammad Farooq). The sacred shrines are the graves or tombs of some saints in the locality, the shrine of Naqshband Saheb in Khanyar, Makhdum Sahib in the immediate neighbourhood of the locality and on the southern slopes of Hari Parbat hillock, Dargah Hazratbal in Srinagar where the holy relic of the Prophet remains enshrined, Baba Rishi on the northern slopes of Gulmarg mountain ranges, Batmol Sahib in Srinagar, Kalashpora shrine and elsewhere in the city and the valley. Obviously, the rich people dealing in the craft and exporters who fall in that category can afford to go for pilgrimage to Mecca.

The *pirs* with whose name *bab*, meaning fatherlike is generally appended, are charged with the duties of performing the circumcision rites, marriage rites and death rites of the members of the community. They are approached to give amulets to ward off evil. They recite prayers to ward off the ghosts. For illnesses such as fever, jaundice, delirium and nausea, they give *menther*(corruption of sanskrit *mantra*) to set right some intestinal disorder by touching their heel on the naval of the patient. The community has no special fairs or festivals other than those observed by the general Muslim population of the Sunni sect in the Kashmir Valley. The community has identified itself fully with the life and active religious activities, and reacts enthusiastically to the religious preachings, practices and propaganda.

The Namdagurs are essentially one of the components of a larger Muslim, Sunni community and, as such, their linkages with other groups of Muslim community are quite natural and normal. In fact, as has been pointed out earlier, because of their unsatisfactory economic conditions, they are considered somewhat socially low perhaps because of the nature of their work, that is beating the dusty and dirty wool felt. However, acceptance of or exchange of food is freely done. They marry the members of other communities if mutually accepted. Putative kinship is very uncommon. They share water with others. They have no special linkages or relationships and, in political affairs, they are just like other normal citizens. The employer-worker relations are not very happy because of the fact that the wages of workers are not in reasonable proportion to the income of the employer.

The percentage of literacy is very low. Most of the children drop out after they have cleared their eighth standard, which means at the age of 13 or 14. There are no special arrangements for medical and health care, though it is extremely essential because of the nature of work they do. They are born, grow and die in dust-filled rooms and space. As such, respiratory diseases are very common. The family welfare programme is not effective for reasons of conservatism and religious constraints. There is no government agency or social organization which could extend any assistance to the workers like loans, technical improvement programme, marketing facilities and elimination of monopolists and middlemen. A Namdagur is given the material at fixed rates, out of which he manufactures *namda* and sells it to the supplier and the accounts are settled. The labourers receive no special facilities as a matter of right. Water, electricity and food supplies are common to all without any discrimination. Wood and coal are the sources of fuel energy besides electricity, kerosene oil and cooking gas.

Making *namdas* is a very hard profession and is fraught with tremendous health hazards. According to reports received, this was not a lucrative craft for them. A labourer normally puts in twelve hours work to produce one *namda*. Foreign buyers come directly to the wholesale suppliers and place bulk orders with them.

Wool is generally procured from Kullu and Kangra in Himachal Pradesh, yarn is obtained from Panipat and cloth comes from other parts of the country. The women sometimes lend a helping hand to the men and teenagers are also put to work. Felt has varieties with 32 per cent and 100 per cent wool. In fact, quality control personnel are easily bribed to put higher percentage seal on an inferior stuff. A labourer puts in just 15 days' work in a month and for the rest 15 days, is confined to bed owing to respiratory ailments caused by the dust.

K.N. Pandita

NAQQASH

The Naqqash or Jalaq-Doz derive their identity from the word *naqqash* which is of Persian origin meaning a drawer, painter, engraver and designer. Hence, Naqqash signifies a designer and a drawer. There are three groups of the Naqqashs whose actual work, though identical in principle, differs from one another in some respects. They are: those who design a motif-floral, animal and engrave it on a metallic or wooden plate, those who imprint the design on plain sheets of cloth or on shawls and those who imprint the design on *namdas* and do embrodiery on them. The last mentioned group of craftsmen is called the Jalaqdoz in local terminology, which is also of Persian origin.

The history of the beginning of the craft or the migration of the community is not recorded. However, since the terms are of Persian origin, it is presumed that the community came into being when the craft of designing and drawing developed in Kashmir. History tells us that Sultan Zain-ul-Abidin, the fifteenth century ruler of Kashmir introduced into Kashmir a number of arts and handicrafts from Central Asia. But it cannot be ruled out that the possibility of existence of some sort of designing in Kashmir before the advent of the Sultans in early fifteenth century. The community has not migrated from outside because there are no visible ethnographic traits of a foreign race among the members of this community.

The community is spread over a vast area of the Srinagar Valley but its members are mostly settled in towns and not in villages. Among these towns are Srinagar, Pattan, Baramula, Sopore, Anantnag, Pulwama and Bandipore. However, there is major concentration in some localities of Srinagar such as Noor Bagh, Kamarbari, Jamalatta, Naohatta and Khwaja Bazar. The group engaged in designing and not in printing is concentrated in Maharaj Ganj, Srinagar, and they are only a handful of families. In Srinagar, they are found in a larger number in comparison to other towns. The Naqqashs speak the Kashmiri language but they write letters in Urdu in Arabic scripts. They speak Urdu also.

The community has no specific dress to identify it or to distinguish it from the rest of the population. A shirt and *pyjama* called *vezar* is their common dress for summer, with warm and woollen clothes in winter, and a *pheran* as an overall. Though a weak section of the society, the government has not allotted to them any specific category.

The Naqqashs are occasional non-vegetarians and usually subsist on pulses and vegetables. Beef is taken when available but not pork. They do not have any particular conceptional reason behind their being non-vegetarians. Their staple food comprises cereals, pulses and oil seeds. Rice in preference to *chapati* is consumed. They do not use any kind of alcoholic drink or soft drink except tea with milk and salt, which is a common beverage in Kashmir. On particular occasions, they may have a cup of *qahwa* which is taken without milk. Bread is invariably eaten with salt tea. Vegetables and fruits when available are eaten. Fresh dates are consumed during the fasting month of Ramzan.

No special divisions exist among the Naqqash. It is essentially an artisan class, the only possible difference being in terms of economic standards which again is very marginal. Social subdivisions being non-existent, there is no concept of clan functions or obligations. Professional brotherhood is a factor which binds them together. There has been a modicum of change in names and surnames in recent times. Instead of the short names used previously, now they use the expanded full names. Today the popular names given to the newborn babies are based on the outstanding religious or historical personalities. As such, they have no illusions about their descent. Having imbibed the spirit of equality among men as stipulated in Islam, they do not have any inferiority complex of being a community of lower status in any respect. Other communities think of them as labourers and craftsmen who earn their livelihood through the sweat of their brows.

Marriage is performed under the Muslim customs and *nikah* is one of the important rituals. The amount of *mahr* is settled before the marriage is solemnized. It is generally in cash and not in kind. Divorce by the husband, or separation by the wife, though allowed under the tenets of Islam, is not very common. However, if it becomes unavoidable, the aggrieved party may take the initiative and pay the price as per the commitment made before the marriage contract was signed. In the case of a divorced woman, she can marry a second time only after the completion of the period of *iddat*. Infants go to the divorced mother but the grown-up children may be looked after by their father if the matter is settled through negotiations. The only change in the system which may be noted today is that divorce is becoming more and more rare.

There is a growing tendency towards a small and independent family and the joint family system is gradually declining. The elders receive respect from the youngers. A daughter-in-law does not have joking relations with her in-laws, though with the younger brother and sister of her husband she may have such relations. Conflict between the daughter-in-law and father-in-law or mother-in-law may appear for several reasons such as property, jealousy, disrespect and maltreatment. The husband of a woman has joking relationship with her younger brother and sister. Family bonds are strengthened by marriage among relatives for example uncle's daughter, maternal uncle's daughter.

The sons have equal rights to the property of their deceased father, but daughters have an unequal share called *koreh-har* in local language. If a son receives two parts a daughters will receive only one. The eldest son assumes the status of the head of the family when his father dies, but if there is no male issue, the female issue becomes the legal heir to the property.

A woman participates in the economic activity of the family. This depends on her capacity to work. She does all the daily chores such as cooking, washing, cleaning, caring for the children, and meeting social and religious obligations. She is consulted on all vital matters of the family. She does not, however, join her husband in helping him in his professional work as it is an art in which she has not been trained.

The first ritual observed on the birth of a child is the whispering of *azaan* into its ears. Then the naming ceremony takes place. A *pir* or an elderly person suggests the name. On that occasion, tea and cakes are distributed among the family members and a handful of guests. Then follows the first head-shaving ceremony called *zerakasi.* The barber is invited, and after he has performed the operation, he is given some money and new clothes. A feast is also given to the gathering. *Khatna* (circumcision) is an important ritual for male children which is performed usually before the boy reaches ten years of age. Now trained and recognized surgical practitioners do the operation.

The marriage rituals take place at the house of the bride where the *barat* arrives late at night. The guests sit for a midnight feast. The bride and the bridegroom are married through ritual of *nikah* conducted by the *mulla.* The entire party returns home before dawn. The bride stays in her husband's house for seven days. Thereafter, her parents come to see her and take her with them for a week or two. Each time when the bride returns to her in-laws, she brings with her presents in the shape of cakes, dry fruits and candies. The news of the newly married woman having conceived does not entail any ritual but may be announced in confidence to the close relatives only.

The death rites are performed according to the provisions of the *shariat.* The body is given a bath with warm water, wrapped in shroud and carried in a coffin which is taken to the graveyard by relatives, friends, neighbours and other mourners. Before it is lowered into the grave, prayer for the dead called *namaz-e-janaza*, is offered by those who are present at the burial ground. The fourth day of death is the farewell day to the mourners. Those who come to convey their condolences are served *halwa* and bread. The *mullas* who recite from the Holy Book are given alms and may be asked to undertake the complete recitation of the Koran called *khatm-e-sharif.*

The Naqqash is mainly a landless community. Their occupation is to print sheets or shawl fabric. In the case of the latter, the print is followed by embroidery work done by the embroiders called the Rafgar. In this comm-unity of craftsmen, the craft has been carried on from generation to generation. This is the primary and the only occupation of the community. The community depends entirely on the market. Shawl and cloth merchants bring to them stocks for printing. They give them instructions of the type of printing required and the Naqqash does the job for them. The reason why the community exists in towns only is that their craft has more demand in urban areas. Child labour is on the decrease because now the community has become conscious of the need of being literate. Wages are received daily unless there is a contract for a lump-sum payment between the parties. Payment is always made in cash.

No doubt their wages have gone up, but the wages are not commensurate with the price index of the necessities of life. Only a few families have left their ancestral locality and settled in new localities. This is an economic issue and migration to new localities depends on the economic strength of the family. However, it has been observed that there is a growing tendency among the members of the community to shift to larger towns.

There are no traditional councils of the community for exercising social control. However, previously there did exist a union of the Naqqash, which is defunct now. Besides attending to the economic aspects of the community, that union sometimes would exercise social influence on its members. Their disputes are settled locally by their elders. The Naqqash do not live in exclusive and separate localities but in *mohallas* having a mixed population. For the punishment of defaults of minor nature, the elders in the family take some action but, for a serious default, the law takes its course.

The Naqqash is a community of the Sunni Muslims of the Hanafi

School, though in some pockets of the city of Srinagar, the Shias are also in this profession. As Sunni Muslims, they have no clan or regional deities, but they show veneration to the *pirs* and holy men. A *pir* is the family priest and this is a position which he holds over a number of families. It is hereditary in most cases. Among the shrines which the members of the community visit are those where relics of the holy men of faith are preserved. These are called *ziarats* in local language. The *ziarats* of some sufis, saints and *rishis* are well known among the Muslims of Kashmir, like those of Baba Rishi. Hazratbal shrine is the biggest and the most popular and important among numerous shrines in the Valley. The place is frequently visited by the faithful, particularly on Friday's congregations.

The religious specialist plays his role in more than one way. He is present at the circumcision, *nikah* (marriage) and death rites. He visits the family occasionally but especially to give an amulet to ward off the evil from a member afflicted by some ailment. He recites the *Ism-e-Azam* (holy name) so that the evil spirits are exorcized and frightened away. He suggests the name for a new-born baby. He signs documents as a witness to an agreement in the family which is recorded in writing. He may even arbitrate in a dispute arising in the family.

Ids, local *ziarats* and *urs* are the major festivals. Id is a religoius festival, *urs* is the death anniversary of a saint, and *ziarat* is a festival to perpetuate the memory of a good saint. The only socio-religious movement that had some impact on the community is that of Ahl-e-Hadith, which is a movement laying stress on the pure Islamic traditions that have come down from the Holy Prophet. It is not that the Naqqash is a specific community influenced by this movement; it became popular throughout the Valley in the post-Independence period. There has been a perceptible change in the religious behaviour of the community, resulting in the resurgence of religious fervour in Kashmir. Strict adherence to the Islamic practices like fasting during Ramzan, five *namaz* daily, consultations with a doctor of divinity in matters of personal and social importance, consciousness of a wider base of Islamic brotherhood and interest in the affairs of the Muslim world are some of the new realizations of respect for religion. Printing and drawing is the only art known to the Naqqashs. By printing is meant imprinting motifs on fabrics of different kinds. There does not exist any oral tradition nor is there any tradition of dance and music to be found among them.

Intercommunity linkages go back to olden times. Marriages in other communities do take place but, in such matters, the decisive factor is the economic standard of the families. However, matrimonial alliances within the community are given preference. In such matters, it is the professional skill and adeptness which are important. They exchange water and food with the communities of other craftsmen in the Valley. Putative relations with the other groups of Islamic community are there. They share their graveyard with other sections of the Muslim community. They earn a day to day living. They are becoming politically conscious, consider voting in the elections as their pious right and exercise it. Some of the younger people take active part in politics by attending meetings, listening to speeches and discussing issues.

The Naqqashs are receptive to the development programmes and plans offered at various levels and in various forms. Literacy is becoming popular among them and more boys and girls now attend school; but they leave schools generally before doing matriculation, the reason being their poverty and the necessity to earn a living. The community members are becoming health conscious, and medical facilities provided by the government are being increasingly utilized as also other facilities like the public distribution system. There is a growing response to the family planning programmes. They make use of tap water in town but spring and well water in places where tap water is not available. Some of them who have acquired education up to graduation level seek goverment jobs which, however, are not forthcoming. In view of large scale unemployment in the state, they revert to their traditional occupation despite the fact that through this activity they can at best make both ends meet. The community has not benefited from various schemes offered by the government, perhaps because they are not fully acquainted with them.

For communication purposes, they make use of public and private transport. Telephone is not found in their homes. Kerosene is the main source of energy and they get it through the public distribution system. Some of them use the gas for cooking purposes. Firewood is becoming very rare and its use as fuel is now out of question. There is only marginal banking activity among the members of the community though branches of different banks are not at a great distance from their residential or working sites.

K.N. PANDITA

NAVID/HAJJAM

The Navids are also called Hajjam. Other communities also know them by this name. Most of the Navids are called so because of their occupation as barbers for other communities. The Navid or Hajjam are traditionally engaged in this occupation for generations.

They do not have any titles, but affix Hakim to their names. They identify themselves at the regional level and historical account about their origin, has been forgotten. They are the original settlers of Kashmir, being low caste Brahmans of the Valley. Presently, they are spread all over Kashmir in almost all villages, towns and cities. The community perceives its distribution at local and trans-regional levels. The Valley of Kashmir being cold, they face the harsh winter of the region. They are settled in the hilly terrains in rural areas, while in urban centres they live in plains. The region has low humidity and very thin forest base in urban centres coupled with dense forests in the rural areas. The Valley records medium rainfall as the region does not experience tropical monsoon. The population of the Navids in Kashmir is estimated to be between one and five lakhs. They speak Kashmiri, their native language, among themselves and with other groups. Arabic is used as the script to correspond and communicate with others.

Till recently the Navid had a distinctive dress. They wore a white overall called *potch*, a white turban, white shawl and threw a white sheet on their shoulders, called *kapar chadar*. They slung a barber's kit over their shoulders, called *kheus* in Kashmiri (corruption of *kesch*). This has now been replaced by coat, trousers and shirt.

In the past they rendered crude medical assistance, particularly in curing wounds, blisters, carbuncles and also performing *nester* or *cheer* (minor external surgeries) such as opening of vein and *toriheh*, akin to acupuncture. Circumcisions were exclusively done by them. But now people prefer modern surgical operations under trained medical supervision.

The Navids are essentially non-vegetarians and eat meat except pork, which is strictly prohibited under the Islamic law. They eat eggs, fowl, mutton and fish. Their staple food is rice. Sometimes, they consume wheat and maize. *Moong*, peas, beans, *moth* and *masur* are the main varieties of pulses consumed. Mustard oil is used as the cooking medium. They take potatoes, *hak*, a green leafy vegetable, roots and *nadroo* tubers besides a variety of other vegetables locally produced. Their consumption of milk and milk products is nominal. They drink *noon-chai* which is black tea brewed with salt in which milk is also occasionally added. Tea with milk and sugar is also consumed. They do not observe any dietry restrictions during the death pollution period. The men are regular smokers. They use *hookah* or *jajer*. Some of the men chew tobacco and take snuff. There has not been any significant changes in food habits, though level and quality has improved with the rising of living standard.

The Navids are considered to be one of the lowest communities in the hierarchy of the Kashmiri Muslim communities. There are no social divisions among them. A change has occurred in the surname from Hajjam to Hakeem. The community's self-perception is low at the village and regional level.

The Navid are an endogamous group. Consanguinity with parallel cousins is allowed, either on father's side or on mother's side. Sororate marriage is not practised. Polygyny is permissible under the Muslim Personal Law but monogamy is the most prevalent form of marriage.

The marriage age is from 16 to 20 years for girls and 24 to 30 years for boys. Marital alliances are negotiated by their elders normally through a *manzymyor* (middleman or marriage broker). As per the Islamic law, marriage is solemnized by mutual consent of the bride and the bridegroom through the ritual of *nikah*. Their women do not wear any symbol of marriage. Dowry is not insisted upon by the groom's parents as a pre-condition to marriage among these people. Among the poorer sections, dowry transaction is almost negligible. However, the bride's parents may give dowry in cash and kind according to their economic status. *Mahr* is payable on demand and may be paid instantly. It may be promised for future and not paid eventually. They follow the rule of patrilocal residence after marriage. Both the husband and wife have the right to seek divorce. The main reasons for divorce are maladjustment, adultery and cruelty. A divorced woman can remarry any person within their faith and community. The male divorcee or widower can also remarry.

The most common form is the nuclear family. Joint family system is gradually breaking up. Interpersonal relations are cordial among the household members but joking relations do not exist between the consanguineous and affinal relatives. Conflicts and confrontations exist only to a lesser extent. All the male children have an equal right to the parental property. The daughters too have right of inheritance but their share is not equal to that of the male members. The eldest son succeeds as the head of the family after his father's death. Interfamily feuds are usually settled through mutual consultations by the village elders or through the panchayat. They also go to the courts of law to settle their disputes which relate mainly to land and property. Over the period, there has been a significant rise in the formation of nuclear families.

The Navid women enjoy a secondary status compared to men in all spheres of life. Though they participate in all the social and religious activities yet they do not enjoy equality in religious affairs. A majority of them participate in agricultural activities, collection of wood and drawing of water. They do not play a major role in decision making, neither do they control the family expenditure. Most of the women are housewives and mostly remain busy only in household jobs. Though these women enjoy voting rights yet their participation in active politics is nil. Very few women are employed in the government jobs. The younger generation exhibits tremendous inclination to seek formal education whereas there is total illiteracy among the older generation.

A Navid woman can deliver the child at her natal or at in-law's house, though the former is given preference over the latter. A majority of them have their deliveries at their homes, with the help of an experienced *warin* (midwife). The women in urban areas go to local hospitals. The christening ceremony is not observed in a formal way but the *maulvi* (local clergyman) simply names the child. *Aqeeqa* ceremony is also performed by the Navids.

Circumcision is performed on male children between the age of three and seven years. *Zerakasi* (shaving off the head) is observed for both boys and girls.

The marital alliances are fixed by negotiation conducted by elders of the prospective in-laws or a middleman, *manzymyor*. Marriage is usually a two day affair, i.e one day for the ritual of *menziraat* or *mehndi-raat* and one day for the wedding. On the wedding night, the bridegroom accompanied by a fixed number of guests arrives at the bride's house for the *nikah*. A *wazwan* (feast) is given by the bride's side. The marriage is consummated at the groom's residence but, next day, the bride returns to her parent's home for a minimum period of seven days. A return call (known as *firsal)* by the bridegroom along with a few selected guests is made on the bride's house. They take sets of dresses and gold ornaments as gift for the bride. Thereafter, no gifts are exchanged except on Id days.

The body of a dead person is given a bath and wrapped in a shroud and carried in a *taboot* (coffin). After offering prayers, the dead is taken to the *kabristan* or *mazar* and buried in the privately owned family plots. Before the burial, once again *fateha* is offered for the dead. If the person dies three days prior to Friday, then Friday prayer (*jumma fateha*) is offered on the graveyard of the dead person on the ensuing Friday. If death takes place later than that, then the next Friday is chosen for this. After this, tea and bread, *jumma chai*, is offered either at the graveyard or at the home of the deceased. No death pollution is observed. On the fortieth day ceremony known as *chehallum* community tea is offered to the friends and relatives who assemble to offer *fateha*. All death rites including *fateha-khani* are performed by a *maulvi*.

Though the community has undergone socio-economic transformation, there have not been any perceptible changes in the life-cycle rituals. These rituals have now become more expensive.

The major economic activity of the Navid is *hajamat* or shaving and trimming of hair in the urban areas, whereas in rural areas this occupation is supplemented by agricultural pursuits. In urban areas, most of the Navids own their saloons or work for the other Navids as casual and seasonal barbers. In rural areas, besides working as *hajjams* they also attend to their farm activities. In cities, the Navids also try to do side business like working as property brokers, petty contractors, or even seek government jobs. With the growing literacy ratio, the men try to seek settled jobs and at the same time carry their trade in the mornings and evenings. Some of the saloons have installed modern Westernized equipments, especially in Srinagar city, to attract more clientele and modernize their profession. In rural areas, the Navids conduct their work on traditional basis using the old techniques. They are a landowning community with individual proprietorship. The women in rural areas have taken to embroidery of shawls and scarfs to augment the family income.

The Navids still continue to pursue their traditional occupation and attempt to modernize their saloons in the urban centres or by seeking part-time diversification in rural areas. The young generation of the Navids find their traditional job unattractive, unremunerative and socially ostracized. Owing to this, they seek job opportunities in other respectable professions. This has resulted in their taking to petty trade and seeking government jobs. In urban areas, a direct link exists with the market on a day to day basis. In rural areas, the local market is regulated on a fortnightly or a monthly basis and transactions are made both in barter and cash. On the whole, the Navids want to develop their traditional occupation on modern and scientific line and the same time at number of them also seeking to move away from this profession. Wages are earned in both cash and kind.

Village panchayats exist in rural areas and consist of elderly persons. These members meet at a place to decide mainly about conflicts, quarrels and divorce cases of the entire village. There is no separate social mechanism for these people in rural areas or in urban areas. Adultery, rape, theft and other related offences are settled through the local courts. Since panchayats are not of a homogeneous character, such institutions, themselves are not effective to control the Navids.

The panchayats work for the benefit of the entire village community, but not for this particular community. These panchayats are not empowered to enforce any punishment nor can they give awards. However, panchayats do participate in the government-sponsored welfare-cum-development activities. The community is sparsely spread in the Valley of Kashmir, but not as a socially cohesive group.

The Navid are Muslims. They predominantly belong to the Sunni sect. They do not have any family or clan deities. There are however, regional saints and *pirs* like Hazratbal, Makhdum Sahib, Rishi Peer, Pir Dastgir Sahib and Shah Hamdan. At the village level, affiliation to individual *pir* or family *pir* prevails. Fasting during Ramzan and pilgrimage to Mecca to perform *haj* are the main religious obligations performed by the Navid. They observe all the Muslim festivals such as Id-ul-Fitr, Id-ul-Zuha and Ramzan. They also participate in local fairs like Nauroz, Shab-e-Meraz, the Friday following Shab-e-Meraj, Shab-i-Qadr, Jumat-ul-Vida, Urs Shah-e-Hamdan, Urs Sheikh Nooruddin Sahib. These festivals are of socio-religious significance.

The Navids are not specialized in any plastic or graphic arts. There are no craftsmen among them. Oral traditions like folk songs, folklore and folk tales exclusive to this community do not exist. Songs and folklore are essentially religious. There are no experts in fine arts, music and dance among them. Oral songs are sung mainly by men and *ruf* (a group dance by ladies) is quite popular.

They accept cooked and uncooked food from the other Muslim communities and take only uncooked food from the non-Muslims. They participate and attend all the religious, ceremonial and other festivals of the Muslims of Kashmir. They do not normally maintain marital relations with the high caste Muslims as the latter do not allow it or encourage it. They share wells and water sources, schools, panchayat ghars, etc., with other communities and non-Muslims. They share the burial grounds with other Muslim groups. Mutual alliances are made within the community as far as possible. They maintain patron-client relationship with the high caste Muslims and non-Muslims. They render their services during festivals and ceremonial occasions and receive *bakhshish* (tips) in both cash and kind. From ancient times, the Navids stand low in the social hierarchy of the Muslims and are also treated as such.

The members of the community supplement their income by seeking diversification in other areas like petty trade and commerce, petty construction contractorships, small village shops, agricultural and horticultural pursuits. The traditional occupation of the Navids has not been able to meet the growing socio-economic needs of the community in the wake of transformation occurring in their society. They do not have scholars, creative artists, doctors, engineers or administrators among them. Some of them are employed as peons or clerks in the state government. They have not been able to emerge as a politically cohesive unit as they are scattered all over the Valley.

The student population in high schools is growing in the post-Independence years. Economic compulsions are the main restraining factor in their desire for higher education. Social taboos discourage girls from seeking formal education beyond primary level. The attitude towards modern medicare is quite positive among the urban Navids, whereas in rural areas, they are yet to accept it without any reservations. Some of them are responsive to family planning but most of them consider it un-Islamic. Generally, their women get sterilized. They have drinking water and electricity facilities within their vicinity. Their water sources are rivulets, springs and streams in rural areas, and tap water in urban areas. Some of the Navids have been benefited by obtaining loans under the self-employment business and schemes through the government banks, but other government-sponsored welfare measures have not benefited these people. They avail themselves of the media and communication facilities. They use firewood and cow-dung cakes as fuel for cooking. In rural areas, most of them are landowners and utilize irrigational facilities. They have not, by and large, availed themselves of the nutrition programmes through midday meal scheme for children. Majority of them are getting rations through the public distribution system. They marginally depend on the moneylenders and shopkeepers to meet their requirements. In the urban areas, the Navids make use of the banking facilities and have developed the habit of saving. In rural areas, the propensity to save and invest has yet to develop among these people.

INDU AIMA
ASHOK AIMA

PANYACH

The Panyachs, a group of the Brahmans, could not explain why they are called 'Panyach'. There are no historical or ethnographic accounts available about this community. They use Acharya as a surname. The climate of the Valley where they live is cold with low humidity. The average rainfall is not much and, at the end of December, they experience snowfall.

They are non-vegetarians. They eat eggs, fish and mutton, but do not eat pork or beef. Thier women have no restriction on food items. Rice is their staple food. They prepare bread from wheat flour which is taken with tea in the morning and afternoon. Vegetables such as cabbage, potatoes, carrot, turnip, cauliflower and brinjal are taken regularly. They are very fond of taking salty tea.

They do not consume alcoholic drinks. Milk and milk products are occasionally taken as part of their meal. Their fruit consumption is moderate. Smoking of *bidi*, cigarette and *hookah* is common.

The social division is based on *gotra* which regulates marriage alliances. Nowadays the younger generation have started to write their surnames as Sharma instead of Acharya. They consider themselves higher in the social hierarchy. They also recognize that, among the Brahmans, their position is lower than others. They are an endogamous group. Owing to their traditional occupation and small population, they are facing great difficulty in acquiring mates from their own group. Sometimes they are unable to maintain *gotra* exogamy. Matrimonial relations with the Khatris are not disallowed. Alliance for marriage is proposed by parents. Monogamy is practised and *dejhor*(ear pendants) is the marriage symbol. The age for marriage varies from 25 to 30 years for boys and 20 to 25 years for girls. The age for marriage has considerably increased. Dowry is paid in cash and kind. Residence after marriage is patrilocal. Divorce and levirate are not permissible while a widow can remarry. A widower can remarry his late wife's younger sister. They live in extended families. Joking relations between the members of younger age-group exist and avoidance relations with elders are noticed. The relation between brothers' wives is sisterly, but it sometimes becomes strained as a result of disputes connected with the sharing of property or economic resources in a joint family. Under the Hindu law, property is equally shared by the sons and daughters after the demise of their father. Succession among them is through the male line. However, the women's movement within and outside the family is free and they go out to work in the government or private offices to supplement the family income and share economic burden. They do the household chores. Participation of women in the religious and social function is necessary. Their status is considered equal to men. In family management, their decision receive due consideration. They contribute to the family income and control the family expenditure.

Ritan is the antenatal ritual observed in the seventh or eighth month of pregnancy. Eleven days' pollution period is observed after the birth of the child. The house where the birth has taken place, as well as all those who are blood relatives, are considered polluted during this period. On the eleventh day, the clothes that have been used during this period are given to the washerman and the house is purified. The mother observes postnatal restrictions. On the day of delivery purificatory bath, giving a name to the child and a *havan* is performed. Before this on the sixth day after the birth, both the mother and child are given warm water bath. This is called *sharan sunder* and after this lighted torches of birch bark are passed round the head of the child and all those present. *Mundan* ceremony (*zerakasi*) is performed when a boy is between three and five years of age. A *havan* is performed and the boy's head is shaved for the first time after birth. *Annaprashan sanskar* is observed in the sixth month before the child cuts his first tooth. They do not observe puberty ritual but the girls are not allowed to enter the kitchen and offer prayers during menstruation. The *yajnopavit*, or sacred thread ceremony, is one of the most important ceremonies in their life. It is performed before a boy is twelve years old but now it may be observed even a day before the marriage. In this ritual, the sacred thread is put round the boy's neck by his *guru* after a very elaborate and complex ritual and he is declared to have been initiated into the Brahmanic faith.

Marriages are generally arranged by the parents. At the beginning of negotiations, the parents first study the horoscope and then make an enquiry about the social status and economic position of the family. The girl's father also makes enquiries about the education, health and occupation of the boy. Finally, both the parents agree to the marriage of their children, which is called *vakdan*. A day is fixed for the *sagan* (engagement). The bride's elder brother puts the *tilak* on the bridegroom's forehead. After this, a red thread is tied round the wrist of the bride and bridegroom in their respective houses. The marriage ceremony starts with the ritual of *menziraat* and *divgon*. Then the ritual of *shanti* is performed to ward off the evil effect of the planets. On the wedding day, the bridegroom is dressed in a gorgeous suit and a coloured turban. The oldest woman in the house waves lighted lamps in a circle round his head and then the bridegroom proceeds towards the bride's house in a procession. In the compound of the bride's home, the *vyug* rituals are performed and the wedding party is given a feast by the bride's father. The marriage ceremony is performed by the family priests of both the parties. The father or the elder brother of the bride performs the important ritual of *kanyadan*. The bride and the bridegroom hold each other's hand and walk around the sacred fire seven times. Thereafter, observing the *lokachar* the marriage functions comes to an end. The bridegroom returns to his home with his bride, and they are received by the mother of the bridegroom and elderly ladies of the house. A feast is given by the parents of the bridegroom to introduce the newly arrived bride to the relatives and friends.

The dead are cremated and the bereaved family observes thirteen days pollution period. Before the dead body is put on the pyre, the *nirvana* ritual with invocations to the *bhairvas* and chantings of hymns is performed. The eldest or the youngest son lights the pyre first and all other relatives present also follow suit. The mourners collect the ashes and keep it for immersion in the Ganga at Haridwar or Prayag in Kashmir. Those who had been to the cremation ground take a bath on returning to their houses. On the tenth day, sons of the deceased shave their head and offer *pinds* to the deceased and worship the ancestors. On the eleventh day, the *shradh* ceremony is performed. Every month on the day of the death for the first year, the *masik* ritual is performed. After this yearly *shradh* ceremonies are performed. A feast is also arranged for the relatives and friends during the ceremony. Nowadays the rituals are curtailed owing to the high expenses involved.

Their main occupation is to officiate during the death ceremonies for the other Hindu communities. They accept the offerings made in the name of a deceased person. They are mainly landless. Many of them have shifted to business or government services. The educated ones feel it below their dignity to perform their traditional occupation. Their link with the daily regulated market is direct and the transactions are made in cash. Statutory panchayats came into existence after Independence to plan and implement the welfare and development activities.

They worship Lord Shiva, Lord Krishna, Goddess Bhagavati and Goddess Kali Mata. Now they have forgotten about the *kul-devta*.

Thier religious specialists are from the same community for performing the birth, marriage and death rituals. They visit the shrines and sacred centres such as Vaishno Devi, Amarnath, Haridwar, Mathura, Brindavan and Kashi, and observe fast on Purnamasi, Ekadashi and Navratras. They observe festivals like Holi, Diwali, Shiv-Chaturdashi and Makar Sankrant. Their ladies sing folk songs during marriage, birth, and at the time of *upanayan* ceremonies.

The Panyach accept water and cooked food from the other Brahmans and Khatris but they do not take cooked food and water from the Muslims. They accept uncooked food and water from other higher Hindu communities but not from the Scheduled Castes. Traditionally, they do not maintain marital relations with other communities. They share wells and water sources with other communities and visit the same religious shrines. They participate in the traditional festivals and festivities. They share the cremation ground with other Hindu communities. They maintain relations with their *jajmans*. The community has businessmen, teachers and members holding white-collar jobs. The current major linkages are based on political alignments and affiliations, and these linkages, through the exercise of adult franchise, extend far beyond their immediate neighbourhood and cut across various ethnic groups. These have brought them socially closer to many other ethnic groups.

The formal education is considered favourable for boys and girls. Technical education among them is encouraged. Some of their children drop out from studies due to social or financial reasons. Their attitude towards modern medicare is favourable. The traditional medicare, though less practised, is not despised. Their attitude towards modern methods of family plannings is also receptive. Drinking water is available through taps. They are availing of the media and communication facilities. They use electricity for lighting their houses, and firewood, kerosene oil and gas as fuel. The community has been categorized as a backward community in Jammu & Kashmir state. There is no special programme of development for the community as such. There is no midday scheme in schools for their children. They are engaged both in employment and self-employment. They enjoy all the modern facilities like radio and television. They visit the cinema halls for entertainment. They make use of the public distribution system and buy ration from the government ration depots. Their attitude towards savings is positive. They do not depend on the moneylenders and shopkeepers.

D.K. CHAKRABORTY

PARA

Para is a Persian word meaning a millstone. In Kashmiri, *par* means a heavy stone or a heavy stone hammer. It appears that the people carving either a millstone or cutting a rock to turn it into a millstone or a stone hammer were called Paras. The practice of cutting stone for turning it into millstone is their traditional occupation. Even today, this practice continues in the villages of Kashmir, but some of the artisans engaged in this occupation have migrated to the towns when their skill was no longer needed in the village. They continued to be called Paras. Eventually they took up other occupations for earning their livelihood. The most common occupation adopted by them was darning, which some of their families continue even today. They have now forgotten their traditional occupation of cutting millstones.

They are spread all over the Valley of Kashmir in the districts of Anantnag, Baramula, Badgam, Kupwara and Srinagar. They have only an oral account of their historical background and perceive their distribution at the local level. They live in severe cold and hilly terrains and also in the plains of the Valley. The region records a low humidity with dense forest cover. Population estimates of them are not available. They mainly speak in the Kashmiri language among themselves but write in Arabic script. Quite a few of them can speak and write English. They do not have any distinct dress or identification marker. They do not enjoy any special status listed by the state goverment.

The Paras are essentially non-vegetarians. They consume meat except pork and eat eggs, fish, fowl, mutton, etc. Their staple food is rice and, to some extent, wheat. They consume cereals and all types of pulses and use mustard oil for cooking. Vegetables, roots and tubers locally available are eaten. They consume a fair amount of fruits. They use milk sparingly but milk products are extensively consumed. Salted tea, *noon-chai*, with and without milk is extensively consumed. Alcoholic drinks are not taken. They smoke cigarette and loose tobacco by using *hookah* and *cheroot*, chew tobacco and use snuff. There has not been any significant change in their food habits but the well-to-do among them have increased the consumption of meat.

The Paras do not have any social divisions. Stratification among them may be on the basis of economic and occupational criteria. They do not have a high self-perception, neither do others have it about them.

The Paras practise endogamy at the community level. They intermarry with their cousins, irrespective of the status of blood-relations. Consanguinity of cross-cousins, father's sister's daughter and mother's brother daughter is quite common. However sororate polygyny is not practised by them.

Pre-puberty marriage even now prevails among them on a smaller scale, specially among those who live in villages. The age for marriage for girls is from 14 years onwards. Boys usually marry at 20 and above. The matrimonial alliances are negotiated by the middlemen known as *manzymyor* or by the friends or relatives. Monogamy is the most common norm of marriage. Polygamy has been discarded. There are no marriage symbols for the married women among them. Though there is no formal custom of dowry and bride-price, system of *mahr* is practised by them. *Mahr* may be paid in cash but, mostly, it is promised and payment is deferred. The rule of residence is patrilocal and divorce is permissible on grounds of mal-adjustment or cruelty. Divorce compensation is given to the wife and it is usually the husband who can seek a divorce. The children are the responsibility of the father in case of divorce. Divorced woman can remarry after the period of *iddat*. The rules regarding remarriage are stipulated under the Islamic laws.

In the urban areas, the most common family form is nuclear and, in rural areas, joint family is still common. An awareness to lead an independent life is catching up with them. Interpersonal relationships are cordial among the household members as well as with the community members. Joking relationship do not exists. Conflicts and confrontations usually does not exist among them other than where individual level pro-prietorship is concerned. They follow the Muslim law of inheritance. The male children equally share the parental property. Daughters get less share than the sons. The eldest son succeeds as the head of the family. Interfamily relations are pleasant. Disputes arising out of property or money matters are usually resolved through mutual negotiations, failing which legal measures are resorted to. Crimes and related offences are dealt with through the state's judicial system.

The Para women do not enjoy equal status with their menfolk. They do not have equal rights in the property. Women also do not play any significant role in the socio-religious functions, though they take part in other activities, especially those related to farming and handicraft. They also act as water carriers and fuel collectors for the household. In their spare time, women take to weaving wool to make blankets and pullovers. Their political participation is restricted to voting during elections.

The child can be delivered either at the would-be mother's natal house or at the house of the in-law's. Deliveries take place usually at home and very few opt for the hospitals or nursing homes. Assistance is sought from a *dai* (midwife). There are no specific post-natal restrictions. They do not have any formal christening ceremony but male children have to undergo circumcision as per the Islamic law. The first feeding of cereals *oapsoap* ceremony may or may not be observed. *Aqeeqa* ceremony is performed by them. Marital alliances are solicited through friends and relations, beside a middleman. *Nikah* is performed before marriage is solemnized and *menziraat* is performed in the night preceding the wedding. After the nupital rituals at the bridegroom's place, the bride returns to her parental house for a period of seven days. A formal messenger is sent thereafter to the bride's house with gifts and dresses to request for her return to the groom's home. *Wathal*, a return social call by the groom accompanied by a few selected friends, is a post-marriage ritual observed by these people.

The dead is given a bath and wrapped in a *kafan* (white-cloth). Thereafter, religious prayers known as *fateha-khani* are performed and then the body is taken for burial at the *mazar* or *kabristan* in a *taboot* (coffin). The fortieth day of death known as *chehallum* is observed before the *jumma-fateha*. Friday prayer is performed. Customarily, till *jumma-fateha*, close relatives of the deceased arrange food for the bereaved family. On this day tea and baked bread and cakes are served to all those who attend the prayer meeting. Except for death rites no other formal rituals are observed thereafter. Tea and baked bread is also served on the last ritual of *chehallum*.

The existing rituals have become expensive and elaborate according to the economic status of the family.

In the rural areas, they still pursue agriculture besides, their traditional occupation of stonecutting. Recent land legislations have given the ownership of land to those who were tenants. Land ownership is predominantly under individual proprietorship. Along with farming, other non-farm activities like petty trade, government and private service, home-based handicraft and trade are pursued to augment the family income. In the urban areas, they draw their sustenance from service, trade and commerce sectors. In the urban areas, they are directly linked to the market, while the same is not true in the rural areas. Their women also participate in the farm activities to supplement the household income.Women do the household chores of drawing water, collecting fuel and tending cattle. They also weave *wagoov* (straw mats) and woollen blankets. Some educated women are employed as teachers. Though child labour is used for domestic and other farm-related jobs, but is not usually marketed. Wages are mostly received in cash but, since barter system still operates in villages, it may also be in kind.

The panchayats function at the village level and their composition is heterogeneous in nature. There is no representative body exclusive for them as a separate ethnic group. In the urban areas, there is no such formal body either. Conflicts, quarrels and divorce cases may be settled through the village panchayats, failing which recourse to the law is taken. Adultery, rape and theft cases are decided under the state's legal system, though very few such cases occur among them. The panchayat does not have any power to punish or confer awards, though social boycott can be imposed. The panchayat also regulates the villages' welfare and development activities in an advisory capacity.

The Paras profess Islam as their religion and predominantly belong to the Sunni sect. They visit Hazratbal shrine, Rishi Peer, Pir Dastgir Sahib, Makhdum Sahib, Baba Rishi and Shah Hamdan. At the village and household level, affiliation to the individual *pir* prevails. Fasting during Ramzan and a pilgrimage to Mecca to perform *haj* are their main religious obligations. They observe all the Muslim festivals and participate in the local socio-religious festivities such as Nauroz, Shab-e-Meraj, the Friday following Shab-e-Meraj. Shab-e-Qadr, Jumat-ul-Vida, Urs Shah Hamdan, Urs Sheikh Nooruddin Sahib.

There are no professional craftsmen among them but, in villages, handicraft activities are carried out by them, especially during the long winter months. Their traditional craft of cutting millstones is practically forgotten by them. The oral traditions (folk songs, folklore and folk tales) pertain to religious lore and history.

They accept both cooked and uncooked food from other Muslim communities. No restriction is there to accept uncooked food from non-Muslims. They participate in all socio-religious festivals of the region. Some of them refrain from eating with the non-Muslims. Marital relations with other sections of the Muslims exist. They share well and other water sources, roads, schools and panchayat ghars with other communities, irrespective of their religious background. They share the burial grounds with other Muslims. They visit the religious shrines of *pirs* and *faqirs*, and have common cordial and non-business like relations with other people. In rural areas, a majority of them are engaged in agricultural-cum-horticultural occupations and maintain cultivator-labour relations. They receive the services of barbers, carpenter and masons.

The community is involving itself in market-oriented trade and commerce. Political awareness is also rapidly dawning on them. They have not produced entrepreneurs and creative artists. A few of them are administrators, engineers and doctors, and very few of their women are teachers and in government services.

Formal education is becoming popular and broadbased among them though boys are given preference over the girls. Boys study up to college level, while girls drop out after school level. Economic and social constraints are the reasons for dropping out.

Their attitude towards modern medicare is quite favourable but its usage is linked to its availability and cost. Family planning is catching up with them in urban areas but it has yet to make an impact on the people in rural areas. It is generally their women who get sterilized. The average family size in rural areas is seven to eight members, while in urban areas it is four to five. They have drinking water facilities within their locality. The sources of drinking water are watertaps, streams, springs and rivers.

The community has not benefited by the goverment-sponsored welfare-cum-development schemes. Cooperative societies and other public distribution facilities are available to them. Almost all the households have electricity. They use firewood and cow-dung as fuel for cooking in rural areas. Most of them own land and make use of the irrigational facilities and chemical fertilizers. Very few avail themselves of the nutrition programmes like ICDS, Anganwadis and SNP centres. A majority of them procure rations through the public distribution systems. They do not normally seek loans from the traditional moneylenders but may borrow from the shopkeepers for meeting unforeseen contingencies. A few of them also avail of the banking facilities. They do not exhibit any strong propensity to save and invest.

The Paras, as a distinct group, exhibit a soft and gentle nature with a fair amount of docility. Socio-economic compulsions of life have made them move from urban to rural areas, and vice versa, in order to secure a better life. They have totally assimilated themselves into the broad Kashmiri Muslim culture and tradition. Now they do not perceive themselves as an exclusively ethnic group, nor do they make efforts to retain their independent identity.

INDU BALA DHAR

PERNE

The Pernes or Parnas call themselves Bangali and Gad Jhir also. The people are autochthones of the region which is characterized by hot undulating plains of high humidity, thin deciduous forest cover and medium snowfall. They speak in Dogri amongst themselves and in Punjabi with others. There are no identification marks for the community. The constitutional status accorded to them is Other Backward Classes. They are non-vegetarian and eat virtually anything found in the wild, including carion. Their staple food is wheat, supplemented with rice, pulses and beans like *rajmah*. Mustard oil is the cooking medium. Tuberous vegetables such as potatoes, sweet potatoes, onion and garlic are used. Milk or milk products are used. Both sexes smoke—men smoke cigarettes and *bidi*, and women prefer *bidi*. Fruit consumption is marginal.

They are divided into four groups in order of hierarchy. These groups are Bambi, Gandhila, Khache and Ben. The hierarchy of the four subgroups is determined by the number of red flags each of them is entitled to carry to the temple of Vaishno Mata. The Bambi carry 22 flags whereas the remaining three groups carry not as many red flags as the Bambi do. They are divided into exogamous *gotras*. The community's self-perception is low whereas other communities treat them as the lowest among the various communities that live in Jammu. Endogamy is maintained at the community level. Consanguineous marriages are not allowed but cross-cousin marriages are allowed. Junior levirate is the rule but sororate is not popular though permissible. Boys marry at 22 years and girls at 19. *Sindoor*, *mangalsutra* and toe rings are the symbols of a married woman. Dowry is usually in kind, consisting of a few utensils, a cot with mattress, pillow and bedspread. The rule of residence is patrilocal, divorce is permissible on account of incompatibility and barrenness. Only the men can sue for divorce. The children are the responsibility of the father. Divorcee, widower marriage is permissible. The family is of nuclear type. Avoidance relationship is not observed and joking is prevalent. The inheritance is on the pattern of male equigeniture. Women are not entitled to inherit. The eldest male issue succeeds the father. The women collect fuel, fetch potable water and also play an active role in other economic activities. The elderly women sometimes resort to begging. They play a role in the social functions and rituals, and enjoy an equal status *vis-a-vis* men. They contribute to the family income and also control the family expenditure when their men stay away for long durations.

The child is delivered at home. Close kin are invited after seven days of delivery of a boy. The parents of the parturient mother and other close kin and members of the *biradari* (fraternity) are given a feast on the fourteenth day. The mother gives a name to the neonate and the birth pollution period ceases after 21 days. Marriage rituals such as *kurmai*, *lagan* and *phera* are performed at the bride's residence by a Brahman. The *barat* (marriage procession), consisting of the bridegroom, his parents and close kin, arrives in the evening. A Brahman priest helps in the performance of circumambulation and other marriage ceremonies. Thereafter, the bride leaves for her in-laws' house.

They used to bury the dead bodies in the past, but now the dead are cremated if enough wood is available to burn the dead body to ashes. Death pollution period ceases on the thirteenth day.

Forest is their main economic resource, besides as reported, stealing, burglary, and highway robbery, many are also engaged in liquor brewing and begging. The resources are controlled by individuals, excluding the forests which is owned by the government. The Pernes are mainly landless. The links with the regulated daily market are direct.

The mechanism of social control is ineffective. Their participation in the activities of the statutory panchayats is marginal and none of them has ever represented the community in the statutory *gram sabhas*. There is no provision for punishing the guilty or giving rewards for good deeds. Disputes regarding divorce are settled by the elders. Criminal cases are dealt with by the police and law courts. They are Hindus and Vaishno Devi is their main deity, but they worship all gods of the wider Hindu pantheon. The sacred centres for them are Raghunath and Vaishno Devi temples and Haridwar. Festivals such as Dussehra, Diwali, Lohri and Baisakhi, being socio-religiously significant, are observed.

They accept water and food (cooked and uncooked) from all the communities accepting the *churas*. Putative kinship is absent. They share the shrines and temples with other communities and have free access to water sources. Patron-client relationships exist between the female members, who earn through unfair means, and their visiting customers.

Education is deemed favourable for boys and girls but they are unable to avail of the facilities due to their poor economic conditions and the peculiar circumstances with which they are confronted. The fear of the police haunts them all the time. For any crime committed in the area, the Pernes are the first suspects. Neither girls nor boys are sent to schools. Their attitude to traditional and modern medicare is favourable but the latter is not available. They prefer a small family and the women opt for sterilization. Drinking water is not available in the locality and it is brought from the river. Opportunities of employment are lacking. Very few of them are self-employed. They listen to the radio but other media of information are lacking. Roads are not far but post offices are situated away from their locality. Wood and kerosene oil are their main fuels. They depend on the money-lenders and shopkeepers for meeting their day to day needs.

BAQAR R. RIZVI

POHUL

Pohul is a Kashmiri term used for a shepherd. The etymology of the term is not clear. One conjecture is that it has been derived from the ancient Persian term *pahlvana*, which in turn could be the distortion of the Sanskrit word *parthava*, meaning a strong-bodied urban person. Figuratively, Kashmiris use the term Pohul for a man physically strong and well-built with a tall stature.

The Pohuls are a very old community in Kashmir, perhaps much older than most of the communities found there. Since olden days, the Kashmiris generally led a pastoral life on account of natural surroundings and eco-logical conditions. So the existence of shepherds for the society was almost essential. Since the occupation continued to be carried on from one generation to the other, the term *pohul* became a part of a name in due course of time besides being an identification mark for the community. Thus we have the Aziz Pohul or Samad Pohul even if they no more continue to be the *pohul*.

The community is widely distributed over the entire rural area of Kashmir, particularly in the villages lying in the foothills having proximity to the pastures and grasslands. Since they do not live away from the villages, it is not possible to consider them living in separate habitats. They are non- migratory except for the fact that, during the summer months, they generally spend their time tending flocks in mountain pastures. The members of this community are to be found in all the districts of Kashmir province and in the hilly regions of the districts of Rajouri and Doda in Jammu region. Although their main occupation is to tend sheep, those who have become prosperous with the passage of time either through their agricultural activities or other business engagements, have given up tending sheep though they retain the name of Pohul. They speak Kashmiri which is their mother tongue and, since they are mostly illiterate, they do not use any script. They may understand Urdu to some extent but they do not speak in that language at all. Those who are literate use Arabic as the written script.

They are identified by their traditional male dress, which is a long woollen *pattu* gown called *pheran*. They seldom wear a shirt and, in the pastures and grasslands up in the mountains, they may even do away with the *salwar*. A round cotton cap is commonly worn. Footwear is almost a luxury and one made of grass is used. This is now being replaced by plastic slippers or *chappals*. The Constitution of the state has declared the Pohul as a backward community and it is now a beneficiary of that privilege. The Pohuls are totally different from the Gujjars or Bakarwals and should never be mixed up with any of these communities. In a sense, the Pohuls are the custodians of the most ancient Kashmiri pastoral cultural traditions.

The main diet of the Pohuls is cereals, vegetables, meat, milk and fruit. They are non-vegetarians but meat is seldom eaten as it is expensive. Salt tea is very common as in other Kashmiri communities. Sometimes it is taken black when milk is not available and is called *teuth*. During summer when they are with flocks of sheep on the mountain pastures, they eat bread made of cornflour with sheep or goat milk. The villagers who have entrusted their sheep to the care of the Pohuls for summer grazing on mountain pastures give victuals such as salt, tea, sugar, flour and *masala* to them. Through age-old customs, the Pohuls know the jurisdictions of their pastures. There are no encroachments in pasture grazings and no quarrels. When food is not available or has not reached them in time, they may slaughter a sheep or a goat to survive, preserving the skin to be shown to the owner. In such a case, the Pohuls generally make the excuse that the sheep has been eaten by a wild animal. The skin thus preserved is called *nyal* in Kashmiri and the practice of preserving the *nyal* has given rise to many interesting phrases, idioms and axioms in Kashmiri.

Generally, the Pohuls are not used to eating flesh but, if the need arises, they may eat mutton. Beef is generally avoided but eggs are eaten. Eating pork is forbidden by religion. Their staple food is rice, flour, cereals, vegetables and fruit. Milk and milk products are their favourites. The Pohuls do not take alcohol and their attitude towards it is that of repulsion. Milk is much liked, and the milk of a sheep or a goat recently having given birth to a lamb is preferred. It is called *khadder*. Cornflour and *moong dal* are the popular items of diet for them. During winter, beans and rice form the main food of the Pohuls and they may also eat *achar* (pickle) or a leafy vegetable called *hak*. Onions, tomatoes and potatoes are eaten frequently.

Any division in the community is on the basis of material prosperity and material status of the family. Those who tend flocks of sheep form one community without any social divisions. However, those who were traditionally Pohuls but have now acquired wealth do not like to be grouped with the flock-tending Pohuls. They mix with affluent sections of the Kashmiri Muslim society. When any Pohul family becomes prosperous, it may in due course of time drop the caste name of Pohul and suffix a more respectful title to their names such as Aziz. A Pohul may become Khwaja Abdul Aziz. This may be as it is but, for generations, the local people will continue to call them and know them and identify them by their *jati* name of Pohul. However, one who has now become prosperous and has given up tending sheep, still continues to be a respectful and elderly person of the community. He settles mutual disputes of the Pohuls and others in the village. He is the person whom the members of the community approach for advice on matrimonial relations. But there is no hierarchical order in the community. An elderly person is respected for his age, wisdom and experience. The Pohuls lend their assistance to the farmers and village folk in whatever manner possible.

The Pohuls are known to be called by their most familiar and pet names like Mahdeh for Muhammad, Suleh for Sultan, Nabeh for Nabi. Modernization has had little impact on their outlook of life. They know they are poor but do not consider themselves an inferior community. They are wary of lower communities like the wicker worker Kaneul and cotton thrasher Dhoon. Being Muslims, they have never conceived the idea that they are inferior owing to their occupation nor is their occupation looked down upon. They are considered a very useful organ of the society.

The Pohuls perform marriage according to the Muslim customs and traditions, viz., *nikah*. The grown-ups are engaged in matrimonial alliance by their parents. Child marriage is not uncommon among them though they are aware of the rules governing the age of marriage. The parents of the boy and the girl should agree on *mahr* and the date of marriage and other things. The betrothal is called *nishani* and nuptial is called *nikah* which is performed by a *mulla*. Arranged marriages are common among them. Love affairs and elopement are uncommon. The marriage is very simple. On the fixed day, the groom and his guests, whose number is settled by mutual agreement, arrive in a procession at the house of the bride where they are served the evening meal. Meat is the main dish served on this occasion.

There are no specific marriage symbols, but the bride does wear bangles of different colours, earrings of silver or gold, in some cases, and fresh clothes, shirt and *salwar*, and also a *pheran* or overdress if it is autumn. Marriages are mostly performed in autumn when the crops have been reaped and stored. Music like that of the *bhands* is also generally provided for the guests. The guests may return home at about midnight if the bride's home is nearby, but they will stay back for the night if their homes are far away. The prospective bride and bridegroom give their consent to the marriage in the presence of the guests. Then the bride leaves with the party for the house of the groom in the early hours of the day before it is dawn. The bride stays in the home of her husband for seven days, during which period, once or twice her parent's people come to enquire about her. After seven days, she goes to the house of her father and mother and may stay there for a month or so, during which period the groom may pay her occassional visits. The *mahr* (dower) is fixed. In case a husband divorces his wife, he has to pay the *mahr* amount. The bride gradually takes to the ways and manners of her in-laws and begins to do manual and physical work for the family by collecting firewood or cow-dung, or working in the field. If a divorced woman wants to remarry another person, she has to cover the restricted period of *iddat*, which is three months and ten days. A male, after having been divorced, can remarry according to his wish but he has to first provide maintenance for the children of his first wife as long as they are not able to fend for themselves.

The community follows the mixed extended family system. There is no custom of the male leaving his father's home after he is married. Usually the members of the community have a large family. The eldest of the family enjoys great respect from his juniors. There is no dominance on the part of the younger folks. Joking relations with father-in-law or mother-in-law are seldom seen. Since they do not have any large immoveable property or riches to divide, there is little scope for confrontation and conflict. Members of the family prefer to live together and the idea of living separately is not encouraged. Also there are no curbs on the movements of youngsters, which means that the prospects of conflict are reduced. The Pohuls are meek and shy, and prefer to live in natural surroundings. The rules of inheritance are generally those observed by the Sunni Muslims. The sons are equal shareholders but the daughters get the father's share called *koreh-har*. The liabilities are to be shared equally by the sons after the death of their father. After the death of a person, it is generally the eldest son who is approached by the villagers to tend their sheep. If a person has adopted a son or a daughter, the adopted heir succeeds to the property of his or her dead father. There are strong interfamily linkages. These links are primarily through matrimonial alliances. Then there are links through their occupation. It is binding that a Pohul should contract matrimonial alliance with only a Pohul family. He will not give or take a daughter to and from other families besides Pohul. Owing to the high birthrate, the incidence of mixed extended families is increasing.

If the family has a small landholding, the woman works on it along with the man. She also lends a hand in keeping the sheep. She cooks food, washes clothes, does mud-plastering of the walls of her house, rears children, takes care of them and spins wool. Her role in religious functions is that she must cook and serve. In social functions, again her role is only a passive one. She is totally ignorant of politics. Being the mother of her children, she has to exercise powers of social control. Her position is that of subservience to the husband and other male elders of the family. It is difficult to say that women of the community enjoy equal rights with men. Women have a low status and have little or no power in decision-making. They contribute to the family income by doing manual work. Women do not control the family budget, which is entirely in the hands of the males. A woman, however, does take part in the marriage parties. She may join the singing called *vanvun* or may join the *mehndi* applying function. In case of death, she may join her husband in paying condolence to the bereaved family. If it is a close relation, she may visit the bereaved family more than once.

There are no specific rituals prescribed for the pre-delivery period. However, there are certain taboos which spring from age-old traditions among the Kashmiris. These, for example, are not allowing the pregnant woman to go out in the dark, to carry heavy load, to come out to meet a stranger, to climb a tree or hew wood. These restrictions are imposed with the objective of avoiding miscarriage. When a woman conceives, close relatives come to give their greetings. When the baby is born, the first ritual is to whisper *azaan* into the child's ears. The parturient mother observes pollution for forty days. She takes a bath on the eleventh day and then, on the fortieth day, she is cleansed of pollution and returns to normal life. One post-delivery ritual is to tie a black piece of thread round the neck of the newborn baby to ward off the evil. The christening ceremony is quite simple. The *mulla* is asked to suggest a name. If the baby is struck with a common illness, the parents ask the *mulla* or *pir* to give an amulet, which is tied round the neck of the child. The first shaving of the head of a boy is accompanied by a ceremony. The parents of the young mother may give her a pair of clothes or some money on the day and, in return, they are entertained to a simple feast. Rice mixed with turmeric is cooked and distributed among the children of the neighbourhood. This is called *teher*.

Tonsuring is the first ritual of a child. It is called *zerakasi*. The second important ritual is the circumcision of the child, if it is a boy. The proper age of circumcision is after five year of age. In Kashmiri, it is called *khatnahal* or *behnawun.* The *mulla* is invited and the operation is conducted by the local barber called navid. A feast follows the ceremony. The Pohuls have a knowledge of many valuable herbs in the mountains and they keep some with them. The first feeding of the child is called *oapsoap.* It is mentioned but not observed as a specific function in the community. Now-a-days some families send their children to the local primary school, and the first day when the child goes to school is observed by distributing sweets among the school boys.

Marriage is perhaps the most important ritual in the life of a Pohul. It is performed in the house of the bride at night. It is an occasion for a grand feast, the expenditure of which is borne by the girl's parents. The groom's parents also throw a feast after the marriage has been solemnized. This is called *wathal.* The ceremony is performed at the house of the bridegroom.

When a person dies, the dead body is given a bath in warm water. Then it is wrapped in white sheet and placed in the coffin which is carried by relations and friends to the graveyard. The *gorkan* digs the grave. The body is carried on to the graveyard and all male relatives, friends and neighbours walk slowly behind the coffin and the body is slowly lowered into the grave. A slab is put over the body and it is covered with earth. The *mulla* receives a little money for *namaz-e-janaza*, the funeral prayer. There is no ancestor worship among the Pohuls, nor do they pay regular visits to the grave of the departed one. On the fourth day of the death, tea is served to the people who come to condole the bereaved family. After that there is no condolence and normal life continues. No food is cooked in the family where a death has occurred and the neighbours bring food for the bereaved family. The dead may be remembered on the days of Id, the neighbours come to console the lamenting women and again there is silence. But this is not a common feature.

Pastures, forests, land and water are the main resources of the community. They exist on pastures and grasslands where flocks of sheep graze. These resources are controlled by the community. Huge pastures are the property of the government and society. Some of the Pohuls may have few patches of land which they cultivate in the traditional manner, but these are not large enough to provide them with a substantial income. It is not a landowning community though families that have become prosperous have purchased land and consider land as their major source of income. It is mainly a landless community. The community's occupation is to tend the sheep of the farmers, peasants and village people. Each Pohul may take under his supervision as many as two thousand sheep belonging to the villagers of different villages. The flock are taken to the pastures in the upper reaches of the mountains which have been given specific names by the Pohuls themselves. The owners of the sheep have to pay them according to the number of the sheep. They have to bring his family ration as long as he tends the sheep. The normal time is about five months from May to October. Pastoralism is therefore the traditional occupation of the community of Pohuls. In winter some of them may undertake *kaneul* (wicker work) or repairing of *kangri* (earthen firepots). The Pohuls have their own sheep and this is also the major source of their livelihood. Sheering of sheep is a flourishing trade and they may get their wages in kind, namely wool. Their women spin wool in winter on indigenous *charkha* and make woollen blankets called *tsader*. Wool of light brown colour is considered valuable and any *tsader* made of it costs about Rs. 1,200 to 1,500. This may be considered a subsidiary occupation though, in practice, it is more than that. The Pohuls depend extensively on the market and make transactions in cash. Barter is not in vogue and exchange may be resorted to but very sparingly.

There are no bonded labourers in the community. The Pohuls do not generally work as labourers in the field or elsewhere. They may assist a neighbour in some work on the farm because of good relations. Landlessness is on the rise among the community because of high birth rate, leading to the fragmentation of land. There is no child labour nor is there any skilled labour among them. On the whole, the Pohuls live a very poor life. However, there have been some changes in their life after Independence. In the first place, some children are being sent to local schools where they get their elementary education. The second change is that due to the control of the goverment on pastures and grasslands for one reason or the other, the Pohuls are finding it increasingly difficult to carry on their age-old occupation. The villagers have not shown keen interest in the development of sheep and its breeding because of various reasons like the period required to breed the sheep, their vulnerability to disease and destruction, and paucity of resources to feed them. These things have forced the Pohuls to find alternative occupations. They are trying to become semi-skilled labourers for working in orchards, but on the whole life is becoming more difficult for them.

Wages of the Pohuls in each sector are decided mutually by the farmers and the Pohuls themselves. In social affairs, they are a part of the larger society deriving benefits provided to it by the government. They subject themselves to the directives of the panchayats wherever these exist but do not have their own panchayats. Rewards or punishments are decided by the law and not by any caste council.

The Pohuls are Sunni Muslims of the Hanafi sect. They observe the *shariat* laws prescribed by Islam. There are no family, clan or regional deities though they observe rituals like burning a candle in the hollow of a particular tree or distributing *teher* (yellow-coloured rice) among children. The major centres and shrines of religious importance are the tombs of the local saints, Hazratbal and Makhdum Sahib in Srinagar, Baba Rishi in Tangmarg, Baji Sạhib in Bandipore, Charar-e-Sharif near Srinagar. A *ziarat* or *astana* is often visited by them. *Pirs* are the religious specialists for them. The *pir* is invited now and then to perform certain rites or to recite the Holy Koran. Once in a year, they may present a chicken to the *pir* as a mark of respect. The *pir* gives them his blessings, amulets to the children and infants to wear on their necks or arms. The two Ids in a year are the major festivals. Then there are the festive days of local saints when people assemble at the tomb of the saint. Ramzan is the month of fasting and they observe this with due solemnity. There has not been any change in the observance of these festivals. During festivals the members of the community may buy some presents for their young children.

The Pohul have no favourite art or any specific and outstanding trait of their culture. They tend sheep to make a living. They spend most of their time in pastures on mountain recesses cut off from the rush and glamour of modern life. They have not broken the continuity of their traditional pastoral way of living. The only art which they could claim as their own is playing the flute. A Pohul is interested in telling stories and listening to legends, myth and long stories. In that art, they are almost past masters.

In all rituals, social functions and interactions, the Pohuls are connected with the other Sunni Muslim communities of Kashmir. They are as good a part of the Kashmiri society as any other community. There are absolutely no restrictions on sharing civic facilities with them. Food and water are accepted and given, and they are invited to participate in social functions. Prosperous Pohuls try to establish link with the more affluent sections of the Kashmiri Muslim society and in many cases they have succeeded. In politics, they have never formed any strong group to influence the local political trend. They cast their vote as common voters do, and are not very interested in politics. They have little say in selecting a candidate of their choice. They follow the villagers' example. The Pohuls are generally a landless community and, as such, tenant-landlord relations do not exist. However, if anyone has a little holding, he cultivates it himself. Generally, no Pohul tills the land of a landlord as that is not his occupation. Production relations do not exist nor is there any scope for employer worker relationship. In the economic sphere, he tends to be independent of these relations. Literacy rate among the Pohuls is very low. If there is a rise in literacy after Independence, it is not beyond primary or the middle class level. The Pohuls have never considered literacy or education important in life. For health and medical care, there are the government dispensaries and hospitals. But they do not eat a wholesome diet and suffer from many disabilities. In the matter of family planning, they do not take advantage of the facilities provided by the goverment. For drinking water, they depend mostly on the facility available to them in the village. Generally, water from a running stream is used. If taps are provided they make use of this water. While in pastures, they use the water of mountain streams and brooks.

There has now been a slight trend among the community to seek employment in the private concerns or goverment departments. They have been informed about the facilities of rural employment schemes and would like to benefit from them, but there appears no rush for such employment. For communication, they make use of the local transport and post offices. Where there are no roads they walk the distance, but do not keep vehicles or even horses as that is expensive. They listen to transistor for music and other programmes. Television is not common. In almost all villages of Kashmir, electricity has been supplied and the Pohuls naturally take advantage of it. But wherever there is no electricity (as in the pastures) they either light an oil lamp or burn wood to get light. For sources of fuel energy they depend on wood, cow-dung and partially, kerosene oil. Water from canals is used for irrigation purposes. Wells and tube wells do not exist. Chemical fertilizers were used sparingly but now the trend is to use them. For orchards, they use insecticides provided by the Department of Horticulture. There is no scheme of midday meals for school-going children. The Pohul children sometimes do take advantage of the mobile schools run by the state government for the Bakarwals and the Gujjars. The Pohuls also take advantage of the existing public distribution system in the state. They get rations, kerosene oil and sugar from the shops functioning under the public distribution system or from the cooperative shops; but many of them are not enlisted in the registers of the food and supplies department. Though banks have been opened in almost all big towns in the state, yet the Pohuls do not take advantage of them because of their very poor income.

It has already been said that Pohuls are trying to shift over to some other occupations as the traditional occupation is not lucrative. The sheep are tended by the villagers for obtaining wool and mutton mostly. Since wool is mostly obtained from Himachal Pradesh and other parts of the country, and woollen garments from big factories outside the state, that need is met from other sources. For mutton, the major imports are from Rajasthan and Delhi. The practice of rearing sheep is decreasing in the state and with that the occupation of the Pohuls is receiving a setback. They are getting mixed with other communities through marrying in other communities and taking to other professions.

K.N. Pandita

PUNCHI SIKH

The Sikhs of Punch maintain a separate identity *vis-a-vis* the Sikhs of Baramula (Kashmiri Sikh) and the Punjabi Sikhs. They identify themselves as Punchi Sikh. The surnames are Sudan, Sassen, Isher, Reen, Raina and Khajuria which are suffixed with their names. They are also known as Brahman Sikhs as most of them were Brahman before being converted to Sikhism. No ethnographic accounts exist but the histrical accounts about the community can be traced from Guru Gobind Singh's creation of the Khalsa Panth. It is widely believed that Guru Gobind Singh, the tenth Guru of the Sikhs and Sant Bhai Pheru Singh (1693-1768 Vikrami) came to Kashmir to preach Sikhism. They succeeded in converting a number of followers of other religions to Sikhism. In this regard, it was Bhai Punjab Singh and Bhai Rocha Singh who established Dehra Nangali Sahib in village Nangali 3 km from Punch and influenced a number of persons of other communities to convert to Sikhism. Some of the prominent preachers of Sikhism in Dera Nangli Sahib were Bhai Pheru Singh, Bhai Punjab Singh, Bhai Rocha Singh, Thakur Bhai Mela Singh, Bhai Manna Singh, Sant Bhai Mangal Singh Dutt, Mahant Ratan Singh Sudan, Mahant Rattan Singh Modi, Mahant Mohan Singh Sudan, Mahant Bachittar Singh who had undertaken a number of reformatory measures in religious, social and economic aspects of the community.

The Punchi Sikhs have migrated to their present habitat. The community perceives its distribution at inter-regional level but, outside the region, their identity gets dissolved in the common Sikh identity. They live in the Punch district of Jammu & Kashmir. The climate of this area is moderate; it is a hilly region where most of the villages are situated at more than 2,000 feet above the sea level. The humidity is high, forests are thin and the rainfall is medium. They speak in Poonchi while conversing with others. The scripts commonly used with the kin and the outsiders are Arabic and Gurmukhi. *Kesh* (hair), metallic *kara* (bangle), *kirpan* (dagger), *kangha* (comb) and *kachcha* (under garment) are the basic identity markers. The men wear turban. They are a religious and linguistic minority in Jammu & Kashmir. Wheat and maize are their staple food and consumption of rice is also very common. They consume all commonly available pulses besides *rongi* and *rajmah*. A majority of them are non-vegetarians, consuming mutton, pork and chicken. The women are mostly vegetarians. Almost all dishes are cooked in mustard oil. The men consume alcoholic drinks, which they purchase from the market. Fruits like pears and apples are consumed in plenty. Almost each household rears cows and buffaloes for milk as they are extremely fond of consuming milk and milk products. Smoking of tobacco is prohibited, but chewing of betel leaves without tobacco is permitted.

There is neither any social division nor any differention at educational, economic or social levels among them. This group's homogeneity is a direct outcome of the history of their conversion from a monolithic block of local Brahamans to Sikhism. It was, however, reported that some Khatris were also converted and were known as Khakeys whereas the Brahman coverts were called Bombay, but this differentiation has been completely given up now. The people suffixing Reen surname have lately started writing Raina.

Endogamy prevails at the community level. Exogamy prevails at *gotra* and surname levels but the latter is now on decline and intrasurname marriages pass without attracting any disapproval. Consanguineous marriages are not permissible. Junior sororate is allowed but levirate is not allowed. The age at marriage in case of boys is 18 to 25 years, and for girls 15 to 20 years. Marriages are arranged by mutual consent and negotiation. Monogamy is the rule. There are no symbols of marriage. Dowry is paid in cash and kind; the amount of dowry depends on the paying capacity of the bride's parents. The rule of residence is patrilocal. Divorce is a rare phenomenon which is discouraged by one and all. Widow's remarriage is also not encouraged, hence most of the rules regarding divorce and remarriage are not well defined.

The families are of mixed-extended type in villages, but the majority of those living in city centres have nuclear families. Avoidance exists between wife's mother and daughter's husband, son's wife and husband's father, and between younger brother's wife and husband's elder brother. Joking behaviour is noticeable between the elder sister's husband and wife's younger brother. Property is the main issue for conflicts and confrontations between the members of a family; otherwise intrafamilial relations are characterized with warmth, mutual understanding and love and respect for one another. Property is inherited equally by all the sons and the eldest son succeeds his father. The change noticed in the institution of family is the emergence of nuclear families replacing extended ones.

The women play an active role in agriculture particularly in the rural areas. They tend cattle, fetch potable water, collect fuel and fodder. They are in the forefront of all socio-religious activities and ritual performances. The degree of conformity to religion is higher among women *vis-a-vis* men. Their role in politics and social control remains marginal. On the whole, women enjoy a secondary status *vis-a-vis* men. They, however, are consulted on all family matters, be it a marriage proposal, disposal or acquisition of property or allocation of economic resources within the family. They contribute to the family income through employment and self-employment and also control family expenditure.

No rituals are observed during the pre-delivery period. The first issue is invariably delivered at the mother's natal home where she shifts a couple of months before the expected date of delivery. The birth pollution period lasts for thirteen days. On the thirteenth day, the mother and the neonate are offered *amrit* by a priest. Vegetarian meals and *karah prasad* are served to the guests. The blessed parents visit the gurdwara where the priest gives a name to the child. The birth of a male child is a special occasion for rejoicing.

The marriage involves a number of rituals such as *saha* (fixation of the date for marriage), followed by *hath bharai* (the female relations and neighbours extend a helping hand in repairs and renovation of house where the marriage ceremony is to take place) and *mani* (when sweets and bread are distributed among the kin by the respective parties). One month before the scheduled marriage, ladies assemble for a singing session every day (ladies' *sangeet)* at the bridegroom's house. This ceremony is known as *torna.* A red thread is tied on the wrist of the bride. *Gana* and a paste of mustard and flour is annointed on the body of both the bride and the bridegroom. The bride's hands are smeared with *mehndi* (myrtle). Both the bride and the bridegroom are given a bath at their respective houses. Marriage rituals are performed at the bride's residence and a marriage feast is given to the marriage party by the bride's side. The nuptials are performed at the bridegroom's place.

The death rituals are performed according to the age of the deceased. Dead bodies of children below the age of nine years are buried. The rest are cremated. In the event of death, all close relatives assemble before the funeral rituals are performed. The dead bodies of old people are wrapped in a coloured shroud whereas that of the rest are wrapped in a long white sheet of cloth. No rituals are performed near the dead body. The funeral fire is lit by the eldest male issue of the deceased. Recitation of *shabad* from *Gurbani* by the priests commences everyday at the residence of the bereaved family. The ashes are collected on the fourth day and are consigned to a holy river such as Govindwal Saheb or Kiratpur Saheb. On the seventh, tenth, thirteenth or seventeenth day of the death, *antim ardas* ritual is observed admist *akhand path* and *bhog*. All friends and relatives of the deceased are invited on this occasion and a *langar* is arranged for them. Funeral rites come to an end with the tying of *pagri* to the immediate male successor of the deceased.

Land is the main natural resource which is controlled by individual proprietorship. The community is mainly a landowing one. Agriculture is the main occupation of the people in the rural areas whereas transport is the main occupation in the cities. Their links with the market exist directly. Markets are daily and are fully regulated, all transactions are made in cash. Those who are living away from the region are engaged in the defence services. Some of them perform religious duties in the gurdwaras situated outside Punch.

The people have no mechanism of social control other than community elders who try to bring about a compromise in case parties are involved in a dispute of economic or social nature. If the intervention of the community elders does not bear fruit, the matter is referred to a court of law. Statutory panchayats plan and implement the schemes of welfare and development programmes in the villages. The guilty committing an offence against the Sikh Panth are punished by the *Panj Piaras* and the form of punishment is excommunication or any other form to be decided by them.

The Punchi Sikhs are firm believers in the teachings of the Sikh Gurus. Daily recitation of *Gurbani* is the routine form of prayers performed by every member of the community. *Japji* (morning recitation of *Bani* and *Rehras* (evening session of *Bani*) are attended daily by most of them. Sangrand and Guruparvs (birth anniversary of the various Sikh Gurus) are the festivals of socio-religious significance widely observed by all members of the community. In the nearby gurdwaras, a *langer* is arranged for all the devotees. Religious processions are also taken out on the occasion. Baisakhi and Lohri are other festivals which are celebrated with zest and fanfare. Religious specialists are from within the community who perform life-cycle rituals and inculcate religious teachings amongst the members of the community. Reformatory movements, however, have surfaced from time to time. No forms of art and craft exist but the community posseses a rich oral tradition. Folk songs are rendered by both men and women, and tales about the heroes and Gurus are popular. Percussion, wind and string instruments are used for musical rendering of semi-classcial nature. Both men and women participate in traditional dances performed on festive occasions.

The community is closely linked with other communities through commensal, socio-cultural and economic ties. During collective feasts they accept only *kachcha* food from non-Muslim communities. The same holds good for the acceptance of water. They also exchange *kachcha* food and water with other non-Muslims communities. They do not maintain commensal ties with the Muslims. They share water resources and cremation ground with other Hindu communities. They attend all regional festivals and exchange pleasantries with other communities. Places of public importance, roads, public buildings and schools are shared with other communities without any reservations. In the present setup, there are a number of scholars, doctors, engineers, politicians, members of legislative assembly and council in the community.

Education gets a high priotrity among the people and it is interesting that girls outnumber boys in seeking higher education as the boys concentrate more on family business and estates. They are well aware, and avail themselves, of the benefits from various programmes initiated by the government for the generation of self-employment. Their attitude to indigenous and modern medicare is favourable and they make use of all modern methods of family planning. Tubectomy is common among them.

Drinking water is available within the locality in urban centres but they depend on streams and springs in the rural area. They listen to the radio, watch Doordarshan but do not visit cinema due to mushrooming of cheap video parlours in the cities and villages. Dissemination of information is through political parties. Roads and post offices exist with comparatively difficult access in rural areas. They use electricity wherever available.

Firewood, cow-dung cakes and kerosene oil are used as fuel in villages whereas liquified petroleum gas is widely used as fuel in cities. Those having land depend on rain and river water for irrigation and enrich their fields with organic manures, fertilizers, and insectides. Midday meal scheme for children and Integrated Child Development Scheme are fully utilized. Fair price shops are also fully availed of. Their attitude towards saving is positive and they do not depend on the moneylenders and shopkeepers.

DEVINDER SINGH
BAQAR R. RIZVI

RATHER

The Rathers are said to be originally the community of the Rathors of Hindu history. They are basically businessmen. They also possess land in the rural areas and do cultivation. The community has no synonyms. The community is identified at the local level. In Srinagar, they are concentrated in Rather mohallah. They speak Kashmiri within the family and also with others, and use the Arabic script for writing in Urdu.

Their staple food includes *gandum* (wheat) and rice; and *moong*, *masur* and *rajmah* are the pulses they take. They are non-vegetarians and consume meat, fish, eggs and beef. Pork is prohibited by religion. The women are also non-vegetarians. *Kavdaari sag*, a leafy vegetable is consumed in large quantities. They supplement their diet with milk and milk products. Alcoholic drinks are a taboo. There is no change in their food habits.

They place themselves in the middle of the Muslim hierarchy. Marriages are usually performed within the group. Although there are no restrictions in marrying outside the community, they do not marry among the Gujari, Nanbai, Ganai and Watal. Since there are *biradari* marriages, they practise consanguinity both at parallel and cross-cousin levels. The sororate and levirate forms of marriage are also prevalent. The marriage is settled through negotiation. The usual age of marriage for boys is 25 to 27 years and for girls 18 to 20 years. Monogamy is the norm. There are no marriage symbols in the community. Dowry is prevalent among the Rathers. In dowry, usually jewellery, clothes and household articles including copper utensils are given. The parties give and take according to their status, but the expenditure incurred by the bride's parents is usually more than that by the groom's side. *Mahr* is fixed according to status. However, it varies from a minimum of Rs. 4,000 to a maximum of Rs. 40,000. *Mahr* is payable on demand but is usually condoned by the wife. In divorce cases, it is demanded by the wife. The rule of residence is patrilocal.

Divorce is permissible and may be given on grounds of adultery and maladjustment or barrenness. Divorce or *talaq* is not instant. There is no verbal *talaq* in the community. The family elders decide about the divorce. It has a social approval. A *maulvi* issues the *talaq-nama* (divorce certificate). The articles are exchanged in divorce. No compensation for divorce is given to the wife. The children become the responsibility of the father. Either party can seek divorce. The remarriages of divorcees, widows and widowers are permissible in the community. Sororate junior and levirate junior are also prevalent. In the changed circumstances of marriage, *mahr* has been increased, and divorced, widow and widower remarriages are given a liberal treatment by the community members.

The family is usually of the extended type. Nowadays, separate households within the family are also formed. Conflict and confrontation in the family are mainly on property matters. Both boys and girls have a right to inherit. The women usually do not demand their share in the property. It is distributed equally among the sons. The succession is through the eldest son. In case there is no son, the wife inherit.

Women in the community enjoy an equal status with men although they do not have decision-making powers. Women also participate in economic activities and are usually consulted on family matters and purchase of property. They do embroidery on cloth and spinning to supplement family income. They also do other household chores such as collection of fuel and drawing potable water. The women in the community attend the social functions and rituals, and participate in the religious functions.

At birth, first the *mulla* or *maulvi* whispers *azaan* in the child's left ear. On the seventh day (*satwan*), both the mother and infant are given bath and the name is given by the *maulvi*, for which he is paid in cash and kind. The midwife or *warin* is paid a sum ranging from Rs. 100 to 1,000. On the fortieth day also, a bath is given to the mother and the infant. Post-delivery pollution of forty days is observed. *Zerakasi* (headshave) is usually done when the child is one year old. This is done at the place of Rishi Sahib which is near Gulmarg. A feast is given on this occasion and four *maulvis* are also invited. They are offered food and money. *Khatna* (circumcision) is performed between one and three years of age. Earlier it was done by a *navid* (barber), but now a qualified surgeon does it for a fee. On this occasion, a feast is given.

Marriages are settled through a *manzymyor* (go-between) who may be a relative or a person belonging to a different community. The *manzymyor* gets some cash from both the parties. In the marriage rituals, first is the betrothal (*pakarlee*). In this ceremony the boy's father, accompanied by friends and relatives, visits the bride's place and gives jewellery and other presents. They are entertained at the bride's place. This ceremony is followed by *nishani* in which the bride is given jewellery, sweets and cash by the groom's relatives. *Nishani* is followed by *hazri*, in which the bride's relatives come to the groom's place and give jewellery and other presents to the persons who attend the *nishani* ceremony. Between *hazri* and *shadi*, the bride is given clothes on all the festivals. In *shadi*, *nikah* ceremony is performed by a *maulvi* or *kazi*. He gets some money for performing the ritual and also issues the *nikah-nama* (marriage certificate). The *mahr* money is also fixed by him through mutual consultations before the *nikah*. A grand feast is given by the bride's parents. At the time of marriage *vanvun* (singing) is performed by the women. They sing in praise of the bridegroom. The bride accompanies the bridegroom and comes to her in-law's place. The nuptial ceremony is performed at the bridegroom's residence. *Wathal* feast is given on the day following the marriage to which the bride's relatives are also invited. After seven days, both the bride and the bridegroom with some relatives visit the bride's parents. The groom offers *salami* to the elders and gets some cash and presents. This ceremony is known as *firsal*. A feast is also arranged on this occasion.

At the time of death, *kalma* and some verses from the Holy Koran are whispered in the ear of the dying person. The dead body is given a bath and wrapped in a *kafan* (cotton cloth). *Namaz-e-janaza* is performed in a mosque and the corpse is kept outside on the ground. The *malkhos* digs the grave and gets Rs. 50 to 60 for the service. The dead body is placed in *lahad* and the grave is closed from the left side. *Fateha* is also read on the following *Jumma* (Friday). *Fateha* is recited four times at the *kabristan* and a *pyur* (stone) indicating the name, birth and death dates is erected on the grave on this day. *Satijihum* is performed on the fortieth day, during which a *maulvi* reads *kalma* and is offered food and other articles. However, the rituals have become more expensive these days.

Land is their main natural resource and is controlled by individual proprietorship. Besides traditional occupation of business and cultivation, they are engaged in the goverment and private services. Their link with the market is functional. The local market is fully regulated and is held daily from where they purchase the items of their day to day needs.

Child labour exists and the payment is made in cash. Women and children embroider and weave shawls. The statutory panchayat, which is heterogeneous, came into existence after Independence. Its role is to plan and implement the welfare and development activities in the village.

They are *silsila* affiliated to Dastgir Sahib, Makhdum Sahib and Shah Hamdan. Their religious specialists are from other community of the Muslims. Besides imparting religious teaching, they perform the birth, marriage and death rituals for the community.

They weave shawls and embroider on cloth. This is done mainly by womenfolk and children.

The chorus singing *vanvun* is performed by the women during marriage. They also sing Kashmiri songs.

They accept and exchange water, *kachcha* and *pukka* food from all communities except the Watal (Sheikh). They intermarry with other Muslim communities. The sharing of well or water sources, burial ground and religious shrines with other communities also prevails. The modern intercommunity linkages have deepened as a result of socio-economic imperatives.

·Education receives favourable attention from both boys and girls. They study up to secondary level. The boys drop out from studies due to economic reasons which force them to look after their business affairs. The community exhibits a positive attitude towards modern medicare and make full use of it. They prefer to have as many as four or more children.

Drinking water facility is available within the locality through tap water supply. They make use of the available communication media facilities in their area. They have electricity in their houses. The fuel resources are mainly firewood, kerosene oil and LPG. Irrigation facilities are availed of but greater dependence is on rainwater. The community members use chemical fertilizers and insecticides in their fields.

Under the nutrition programme of the goverment, they get benefit of the midday meal scheme for children and also ICDS (feeding/mother infant care/immunization). The facility of food grain distribution through the fair price shops is availed of by them. Their attitude towards saving is favourable. They are not dependent on the moneylenders and shopkeepers.

A.C. SRIVASTAVA

RATTAL

The Rattals are traditionally engaged in removing carcasses from human habitations and skinning for leather. They are also engaged in weaving baskets. The Rattals are grouped along with other similarly placed Hindus of Jammu. They are better known for the type of occupation they used to pursue in the pre-Independence and immediate post-Independence era. However, with the agrarian reforms in the state, most of them have switched to new jobs and occupations. They are spread around many places in Jammu, namely Kathua, Naoshera, Udhampur, Reasi, Batote and Damana. The community perceives its distribution at the regional level within Jammu province. They claim to have had an ethnographic account, but now they have forgotten it. Most of them have been living in their present habitat for a very long time and only a few of them have migrated to other area.

They have various subtitles and surnames by which they identify themselves. These surnames are mainly Sargotra, Lakkotra, Mootan, Kath, Kulsota and Sundeh. In the present geopolitical setup, these people have been grouped with the local dominant Hindu population for census records. They live in warm and temperate climatic zones of Jammu province. Most of the Rattal settlements are located in the plains while some of them are in the hilly terrains as well. The region, on the whole, records high humidity with thin to medium forest cover at different places. The region lies in the monsoon zone. They are a Scheduled Caste. According to the 1981 census, their population was 1,646. They speak Dogri within the family and kin groups. Devanagari is the script used to correspond amongst themselves and Hindi is spoken with others.

The Rattals are predominantly non-vegetarian and eat pork, fish and eggs, but not beef, depending on their means. They consume wheat, rice and maize, and all types of pulses including beans. They take sufficient quantities of vegetables and fruit and fruit-products. Milk and milk products are also used, especially during religious festivals. The Rattals drink tea mixed with milk. Their men make frequent use of alcoholic drinks but the women abstain from drinking. Cigarette smoking is quite common among males and frequent use of cheroot is also made. Betel and tobacco chewing has also been observed among them. There has not been any significant change in their food habits but different living standards among them have resulted in variations in the quality and quantity of food intake.

The Rattals do not have any social divisions, though differentiation prevails on the basis of socio-economic standing and occupation. That is why various surnames have evolved among them. They are conscious of the *varna* system though, among themselves, they do not have any clear-cut stratification. They identify themselves more closely with the other Scheduled Caste communities of the region, that is the Chimariya, Mahasha, Saryara and Barwala. The community's self-perception is low, and so is the image they enjoy among other communities in the region. They do not practice consanguinity in the sense that marriages are not solicited either with father's sister's daughter or mother's brother's daughter. There is no restriction on sororate (junior) alliances but the same is not observed for the seniors. However, the practice of levirate (either junior or senior) is not permitted. Pre-puberty marriage was the earlier practice. Nowadays, their girls are married usually after they attain puberty. The marrying age for girls now varies between 16 and 18 years and, for boys, it is usually 22 years and above. Marital alliances are sought and negotiated by friends, relatives and family heads. Monogamy is the most prevalent form of marriage. Vermilion, *bindi*, bangles (lac and glass) are the common symbols of marriage observed among the women. Dowry is not insisted upon and has not assumed menancing proportion as observed in other Hindu communities. Dowry is paid in kind such as bedding and kitchen utensils predominantly. The rule of residence is partilocal with very few cases of uxorilocal residences (usually where a male heir does not exist within the family). Divorce is permissible after social and judicial approval. Divorce cases have been reported mainly due to maladjustment and adultery. However, very few such cases occur and the divorce rate is quite low. No divorce compensation is paid to the wife unless there is a decree from the court. Divorce proceedings can be initiated by either party, yet it is usually the husband who divorce. The children are the responsibility of both the father and mother. Rules regarding remarriage are quite flexible among these peoples as there are no specific restrictions. Widowers and divorcees of either sex can remarry with ease. Sororate (junior) is permitted but levirate of either type is not allowed. However, age for marriage for both the sexes have registered a gradual increase over a period of time. No changes are taken place in marriage symbols, dowry or *kanyadan*. The incidence of divorce is very low and rules regarding residence remain unchanged.

Joint families predominate, though there is a growing tendency towards nuclear families. Interpersonal relations are cordial among the family members. Joking relationship prevails among the affinal relatives. Avoidance relationship and joking is somewhat restrictive in nature and formal between son-in-law and mother-in-law, and also between daughter-in-law and father-in-law. Conflicts and disputes arise mainly on account of property matters and challenge to the authority of elders. The Rattals follow the rule of equigeniture but the girls do not get any share of the property nor do they ask for it. The eldest son succeeds as head of the family after the father's death. Inter-family linkages, on the whole, are cordial and pleasant. Disputes are settled through mutual negotiations, discussions and reconciliations by the friends, relatives and elders of the community. Offences and crimes are dealt with in accordance with the existing judicial system. Except for the tendency towards nuclear families no other significant changes regarding family have taken place.

The Rattal women enjoy a secondary status in comparison to their men in almost all walks of life. Though legally they are entitled to an equal share in the parental property, yet they do not get any part of it nor do they assert or press for their claim. They participate in the social functions and in religious rites. They are active partners in the economic activities of their men in agricultural operatons and animal husbandry. They collect firewood, fetch water and attend the domestic cattle. In fact the entire household chores are performed by them. Though enjoying their constitititutional right of voting, the women do not play an active role whatsoever in the regional politics. The women are a contented lot and are easily reconciled to the varying situations. They are submissive and adapt themselves quickly to the situations and the role demanded of them. Most of them are illiterate and ignorant about worldly matters.

They do not observe any pre-delivery rituals during pregnancy, though some restrictions are observed by them. Lifting of heavy objects or travelling at night by a horsecart or bus is avoided. The expectant mother is not normally allowed to open the front door of the house if a stranger comes. Deliveries take place at home with the help of an experienced midwife. However, wherever the government facilities are available in this regard, they prefer to go to the hospitals or health centres. Post-delivery pollution period is observed for twenty-one days but there are no postnatal restrictions on the mother. The boys undergo the ritual of *mundan* but *annaparshan* (the first feeding of cereals) is not observed. *Janeu*, the thread wearing ceremony is performed by them.

Marital alliances are sought and fixed by friends, relatives and community members. The marriage ceremony is a two-day affair. The first day, *mehndi-raat* is celebrated and, on the second day, the rituals of *lagan* and *jaimala* are performed around midnight. The marriage ceremonies are performed at the bride's residence. The *barat* (*janj*) leaves the bridegroom's place after sunset for the bride's residence. The bridegroom rides a mare with a sword in his hand and is accompanied by a small boy riding with him. He along with the *baratis*, who dance and sing to the tune of a bandmaster, reaches the bride's house. A poetic recitation in honour of the groom, is read by a hired person. Thereafter, *lagan* ceremonies are performed. The guests, friends and relatives are treated by both the parties on different days.

The dead body of a person given a bath and is wrapped in a white shroud. Placed on a bier it is carried to the cremation *ghat* for the final cremation. The Rattal observe 13 days' death pollution. The dead bodies of young infants normally below the age of 5 years are buried. *Shradhs* of the dead are performed. *Rasam-pagri* ritual or *uthala* is performed only after the days of pollution are over. There has not been any significant change in the life-cycle rituals of the Rattals. All the rituals have become expensive.

Land is the main resource controlled by individual proprietorship. The people have become landowners after two major land reform acts have been passed by the state government. Though the bulk of them are small and marginal farmers, yet the number of landless or casual farm workers is very small. Agriculture is the main occupation for the majority of them. As stated above, most of them used to skin the hides of dead animals (even now some of them are doing so) to make a living out of the skin trade. Some of them are working as casual labourers-cum-farm workers, especially those whose land output is not sufficient for their sustenance. Mat-weaving is another economic activity pursued by them. Running petty retail business and shopkeeping are other avenues. Some of them are employed in the state government offices and many others are working under the self-employment schemes. The Rattal families are engaged in most of the agricultural operations besides tending the livestock. Child labour is prevalent in the form of domestic labour. They receive their wages both in cash and kind. The link with market is both direct and indirect, and is based on daily to monthly cash transactions. There has been an increase in the quantum of casual and part-time agricultural workers among the Rattals.

The panchayat exists at the village level. The elected members of the panchayat are drawn from a broad spectrum of the village community and are heterogeneous in composition. These panchayats are of a statutory nature and usually monitor the development and various welfare programmes launched by the governmental agencies. The panchayat may also render services for solving disputes arising out of social or economic issues through reconciliation and negotiations between the opposite parties. The panchayat may as well issue edicts for ex-communication or boycott of a defaulter or a group of defaulting persons or even against a particular household. Adultery and problems arising out of land and water are the main causes of disputes.

The Rattals are Hindus. They worship village and regional deities. Individual affiliation to *pirs* is a common phenomenon. Their religious specialists are the Brahmans who perform the birth, marriage and death rites. The regional deities are Vaishno Devi, Raghunath, Kali and Shankar Bhagwan, and the shrines at Katra, Raghunath temple, Amarnath and Bahu Fort are visited by them. Festivals are of socio-religious nature, and they celebrate all the major Hindu festivals such as Shivratri, Janmashtami, Diwali, Holi, Rakshabandhan and Lohri.

There is no formal dance patterns prevails among them but either sex can participate in it. Local musical instruments such as *dhols* and harmonium are used. Both men and women sing folk songs which are usually based on religious or romantic themes.

They accept cooked and uncooked food from the high castes Hindus as well as from other communities which stand on equal footing in the overall social hierarchy. They accept food and exchange it with the Chimariya, Bhagats, Meghs and Ramdasiyas, but they show some restraint in accepting food and exchanging it with the Bhangis, Mahasas, Saryaras or Barwalas though it is not followed by any formal prohibition (they may even interdine with them). There is no restriction on accepting uncooked food from the non-Hindu communities. They maintain marital relations at intercommunity level within the Hindu fold. They share cremation grounds with other co-religionists. The Rattals also share schools, panchayat ghars, water sources, roads and wells with other people of the region. They visit the religious shrines of *pirs* and *faqirs*. They maintain cordial and business-like relationship with other community members. With the introduction of land reforms, they have become typical agrarian entities and, as such, maintain cultivator-labour relations. They receive the services of barbers, carpenters, and masons.

This community is in the process of adapting itself to the modern socio-economic environment. They are trying to elevate their social standing in the society. Political awareness is fast dawning on them though active participation in politics has not yet started. They have some teachers at primary school level while some are employed in the government services. Political leadership is yet to emerge from the village or block level to make an impact on the regional political scenario.

Formal education is yet to catch up with these people. They do not exhibit any keen interest or attach much importance to the education of their children. Under the present conditions, boys are given preference over girls in seeking formal education. The boys normally study up to the secondary level but girls do not pursue their studies beyond the primary level. Socio-economic compulsions are the main reasons for not taking up higher studies and there seems to be certain amount of inhibition in allowing girls to study beyond primary level.

Their attitude towards modern medicare is positive and the extent of its use depends on its availability within their settlement. Consequently, a moderate use of modern medicare along with the traditional type is the norm. They have a favourable attitude towards family planning but it has yet to become a part of their life and culture. The family size varies from five to eight members and it is generally the women who get sterilized. They have drinking water facilities within their localities and the main source is tap water and streams. The community has not significantly been benefited by the various development schemes of the government and, in certain cases, they are not even aware about them. Their main source of self-employment is agriculture, weaving and, to a small extent, petty retail trade. They listen to radio which is the main source of information. Roads and post offices exist around the Rattal settlements. They also make use of electricity for lighting purposes but use wood and cow-dung cakes as fuel. Moderate use of kerosene oil is also made by them. The sources of irrigation are mainly rainwater and canals. Farmers among them make use of organic manure besides chemical fertilizers and improved varieties of seeds. They do not avail themselves of any nutritional programmes like ICDS or midday meals. They procure essential commodities from the government-run public distribution centres. These people, being poor, do not have the capacity to save or invest. They still depend on the shopkeepers and moneylenders to meet the unforeseen contingencies by borrowing from them.

With the changes occurring in the overall socio-economic milieu in the polity, these people are in the process of snail-paced transition. Recent land reforms have helped them to become landowning farmers. They have now virtually given up their traditional occupation of skinning the dead animals which had brought them social degradition and are seeking new and honourable means of living, but they have still a long way to go.

INDU AIMA

SAIYID

The Saiyids claim that they are the progeny of the Prophet Muhammad through his daughter Saiyid-un-Nisa Fatima Zehra and her husband Saiyidna Ali Murtaza. The term Saiyed means 'chief', 'leader' or 'master'. According to Majmu'l Bihar (151) it means 'lord, king exalted, saint, merciful, meek, husband' (Hughes: 556). The synonyms are leader, Mir (master), Agha and Shah or King. Their subgroups in Kashmir are: Saadat-e-Hamadaniya (Peerzada), Mantaqi, Baihaqi, Razavi, Mosavi, Shirazi, Andrabi, and Bukhari. The community is identified at the national and transnational levels. Besides India, they are found in Pakistan, Bangladesh, Iran, Iraq and other countries of the Middle East. Their accounts exist in history and most of them were found to be true. They are immigrants to Kashmir from various places of Iran, Turkey, Afghanistan and Iraq. Historical accounts testify their immigration to Kashmir. In the state of Kashmir, they are mainly concentrated in Srinagar, Badgam, Kargil, Baramula, Anantnag and Pulwama districts where the climate is cold with low humidity, thin forests, medium rainfall, and heavy snowfall during winters. Their population according to the 1911 census was 52,463. They speak Kashmiri with the kin whereas with others they speak in Urdu and use the Arabic script. The common men do not carry any identity marker but the Shia priests wear a black turban and black tunic—the apparel that Prophet Muhammad used to wear. They are not conferred with any constitutional status.

They are non-vegetarians and eat beef. Their staple food is rice and wheat. They consume only *moth* as pulses are not very popular with them. Mustard oil is their cooking medium. They consume only non-alcoholic drinks. Milk and milk products are used in plenty. They smoke cigarettes and *jajeer*, or *hookah*. Tea and *qahwa* are their common drinks and fruits are consumed in plenty.

Social differentiation exists on the basis of territory, sect and economic status to regulate marriage alliances. One particular sect among them does not go for marriage alliance with another sect and economically well off families prefer to seek matrimonial alliances with groups at par with them. Endogamy does exist at community level. Parallel cousins are preferred but there is no restriction on marriages with cross-cousins either. Junior sororate and junior levirate are permissible but their occurrence is rare. The children are married after attaining puberty—the boys at the age of 20 to 25 years and girls at 18 to 20 years. The mates are acquired through mutual consent, negotiation, exchange and temporary marriage contract, *muta*. Monogamy is the prevailing form of marriage but polygamy is permissible. Dowry is paid in kind but it is never demanded. *Mahr* is fixed at the rate of *mahr-e-fatimi* and is paid instantly but cases of deferred payment are not uncommon. It is, however, payable on demand. The rule of residence is patrilocal. Divorce is permissible with religious approval. The reasons for divorce are adultery, maladjustment, chronic sickness, cruelty and insanity. Compensation and maintenance is paid to the wife. The children are the responsibility of the father after infancy. Widow and divorcee remarriage is permissible. Junior sororate and junior levirate are also permissible.

The families are extended as well as nuclear, the latter being the predominant type in urban areas. Avoidance and joking relationships are absent. The elders are paid due regards and intra-familial relations are cordial. No conflict and confrontations exist in intra-familial kin bonds. The paternal property is equally divided among the sons. The girls are also entitled to receive their share in paternal property, which is lesser in proportion than that of the boys. However, they never demand it. Succession is through the eldest son. The extended families are being slowly replaced by nuclear families.

The women have limited roles to perform. They are put in relative seclusion. However, they participate actively in socio-religious spheres. Some of them are in active politics. Their status is at par with their men.

The women control family expenditure. Some of them contribute to family earning by serving in various capacities such as teachers, doctors and government servants.

After a few months of pregnancy, the parturient mother is put under pre-delivery restrictions. Her movements are restricted and all efforts are made to protect her from the evil influence of malevolent spirits by wearing *taviz* which are special charms and talismans. The post-delivery pollution period is for forty days. The delivery of the child takes place in the hospital. As soon as a child is born, an elderly member of the family whispers *azaan* in the child's ears. *Aqeeqa* ceremony is performed and a goat or ram is sacrificed to mark the occasion. Male children undergo circumcision within three years of age. The marriage rituals are *nishani*, *hazri*, *nikah* and *rukhsati*. A priest delivers the *segha* of *nikah* and seeks the consent of both the bridegroom and the bride three times in succession. A feast is given by the bride's side to all the guests. All marriage ceremonies are held at the bride's place. The bridegroom's party too throws a feast called *walima*. The nuptials are performed at the husband's house. The dead are buried after the *ghusl-e-maiyat*, i.e. bathing the dead body and performance of funerary prayers called *namaz-e-janaza*. A stone slab (*pyur*) is put on the grave indicating the name and date of death of the deceased on the ritual of *chaharum* (fourth day) amidst incantation of recitation of the first *surah* of the Koran *fateha*. *Chehallum* ritual is observed in a similar manner on the fortieth day. A feast is given to the mourners on both the occasions.

The people are traditionally landless but occupations pursued by them are employment, self-employment, business, horticulture and industry. Their links with the market exist directly and all transactions are made in cash. The priests play an active role in the mechanism of social control in the absence of traditional caste panchayats. The disputes pertaining to property, familial discord and marriage are referred to them for adjudication. If their decision is not honoured, the disputes are resolved through judicial process.

The people are divided into various sect denominations such as Sunni (Hanafi), Shiite (twelvers) and Ahle-e-Hadith (Wahhabi). The Shias follow the *fatwa* decree of *alam* (*marja-e-taqleed*) the highest Shiite pontiff(s) of Iran and Iraq. It is obligatory for each Shia male adult to be in *taqleed* following of an *alam* who is the deputy of the last and living Imam al-Mahdi. The Sunnis are *silsila*-affiliated to the *pirs* and Mulsim saints but the Ahl-e-Hadith do not follow either and derive all religious guidance and inspirations from the Koran. The *mujtahids* are the religious specialists of the Shiites whereas the *maulvis* and the *pirs* are the religious specialists of Ahle-e-Hadith and Sunnis. Mecca, Karbala, Najaf, Qum, Kazmain, Koofa, Baghdad and Medina are their sacred shrines where they go far pilgrimage. The Sunnis among them undertake pilgrimage to the *astanas* of Sufi saints at Delhi, Ajmer, Roorki and Gulbarga. The specialists are from the same community who lead *namaz* prayers, supervise the conduct of life-cycle rituals, impart religious education and show the path of righteousness to the believers. They observe all the important Muslim festivals of religious significance such as Ids, Milad-ul-Nabi, Shab-e-Meraj, Shab-e-Qadr, Nauroz, Id-e-Ghadir and *urs* of the pious Muslim saints. The change of religion has not taken place in the community but sect affiliations may at times be changed. The community was involved in many socio-religious and political movements in the past such as freedom movement, Khilafat movement and Tabligh. They excel in the art of calligraphy, shawl embroidery and papier mâché. They possess a rich tradition of folklore and folktales. Music and dance other than devotional and religious in nature such as *qawwalis* and *mersia-khani* are abhorred. The women do not participate either in dance or in music but they participate in *maulood sharif, nauha* and *mersia-khani*.

The Saiyids accept water and food from all other Muslim communities. Marriages take place with the Sheikh and Mughals in contemporary situations if every effort to find out a suitable match within the community ends in a failure. The community has administrators, businessmen, scholars, creative artists, teachers, ambassadors, ministers, engineers and doctors. Political leadership has emerged even at the national level.

Education is considered favourable for both boys and girls who study up to postgraduate level. The girls often drop out due to social reasons. *Madrasa* education also plays an important role in the careers of boys and girls. They make use of both traditional and modern medicare. Their attitude towards family planning is that of aversion and no modern methods of birth control are used. Sterilization and induced abortion is considered un-Islamic. Drinking water is available through tap water supply, springs, rivulets and streams. The rural population is engaged in running small scale industries, transport agencies and contractorship. They are exposed to all the media of communication such as radio, newspapers, televisions (song and dance programmes on the television cinema are avoided). The railways do not exist but roads and post offices are situated nearby. They use electricity. Wood, kerosene oil and petroleum gas are the main fuels. Their attitude towards saving is not postive as utilization of interest on the principal is considered un-Islamic. Banking facilities, however, are used by them.

BAQAR R. RIZVI

SALARIA

The Salarias belong to the Rajput lineage. Among other groups of the Rajput living in the region of Jammu are Jamwals, Chibbs, Katoch, Sen, Biloria and Charak. They are the group of immigrants who originally inhabited the region extending from Shakargahr to Sialkot (both now in Pakistan) and also covered part of Gurdaspur in the present state of Punjab in India. After the Partition of the country, these people migrated to Gurdaspur and Pathankot in Punjab. Besides, Jammu & Kashmir, they settled in Kathua, Hirakagar and Sambha. In the historical perspective, they were stated to have been living in 200 villages prior to Aurangzeb's attempt to make the Hindus embrace Islam during the Mughal period. Consequently, almost 100 villages inhabited by the Salarias converted to Islam while the remaining 100 villages remained as Hindu. Thus, it is not surprising that a sizeable number of the Muslim Salarias are also found in the Jammu region. One of the reasons attributed is that the Muslims as an ethnic group are in majority in the state, as such, the Muslim Rajputs, especially the Chibbs and Salarias, are to be found in Jammu & Kashmir. The Salarias from the point of view of *gotra*, i.e Bhardwaj, are identified with the Pathanias and Atsis, the other two Rajput ethnic groups.

They perceive their distribution at trans-regional level. They have a very high self-perception and others also view them so. They are spread in the districts of Jammu and Kathua mostly. Their habitat records heavy to medium rainfall with dense forest cover in the upper reaches. They speak mainly Punjabi and Dogri among their own kinsmen while English and Urdu are used as the medium of communication with others. The scripts used for correspondence are mostly Devanagari, Arabic and Roman. They have a typical Punjabi style of dress which partially resembles the local Dogri pattern. In the urban areas, they wear modern dress as found in the cities all over the country.

They are essentially non-vegetarians and eat pork but not beef. Their staple food is wheat and rice. They consume all types of pulses. Mustard oil is their main cooking medium. Their men consume alcoholic drinks, besides other types of beverages. Milk and milk-products are used in abundance. Those who smoke usually smoke cigarettes and, in rural areas, *hookah*. Fruits are eaten in a moderate quantity. Social differentiation is not prevalent among them in a formal manner. However, some of the Rajput communities like the Jamwals or Katochs are considered above the rest of the ethnic groups though it does not make any qualitative difference in the socio-religious group interaction. Most of the marriages are solicited within the broader Rajput community, irrespective of their ethnic background. Marriage alliances may be sought even with other upper caste Hindus. Endogamy operates at the community level within the broad Hindu-fold. There are no restrictions on junior sororate but levirate is avoided among them. Child marriage is not performed among them now as the age for marriage for both girls and boys has considerably increased from what it was in the past. The marriage age for either sex is above 20 years. Mates are acquired through friends, relatives and the *navid* (marriage broker). Monogamy is the prevailing form of the marriage. Dowry is paid both in cash and kind. Patrilocal is the rule of residence. Divorce is permissable under the Hindu Marriage Act and, in certain cases, the Rajput Sabha may also intervene. The reasons for divorce are mainly maladjustment and insanity though, in very rare cases, the reason for divorce may be adultery. Compensation and maintenance is paid to the wife. The children are the responsibility of either of the parents.

The families are the extended type in rural areas whereas nuclear families are common in urban areas. Avoidance and joking relationships are observed among them.The elders are paid due reverence and respect. Interfamily relationships are quite firm, and cases of confrontation or conflicts are rare except for those arising out of division of ancestral property.

The parental property is shared equally by the sons, while the girl's share is deemed to have been paid in the form of dowry. The girls are, however, legally entitled to a share in the property but they do not demand it as a matter of tradition. Succession is through the eldest male issue. Extended families are being gradually phased out by nuclear families.

The women play a significant role in the overall social, economic and religious spheres of life. In the rural areas, the women participate in farm-related and other activities coupled with tending livestock. In urban areas, the women also help to augment the family income by seeking employment in the private and government offices. However, their role in day to day politics is restricted to only exercising their right to vote. A number of them are employed in white-collar jobs like teaching while others are administrators.

Pre-delivery restrictions prevail for the parturient mother. Her movements get restricted with the advancement of pregnancy. Post-delivery pollution is observed by them. *Mundan* and *janeu* ceremonies are observed for their boys. The marriage rituals are performed at the bride's house. *Barat* proceeds to the bride's residence with the bridegroom riding a mare holding a ceremonial sword and accompanied by the guests. *Lagan* ceremony is performed by encircling the sacred fire seven times by the couple with four *rakadvas* circles around the clan diety. The *barat* usually proceeds to the bride's residence after the sunset. A feast is given by both the parties.

The dead are cremated after a ceremonial bath. The body is carried to the cremation ground by the relatives and close family friends. The pyre is lit by the eldest male heir. Death pollution period is observed among them. *Rasam-pagri* is a ritual when the male members of the family wear a new headgear, either pink or rouge coloured, usually after the fourth day to mark end of the pollution. Annual *shradhs*, i.e yearly worshipping of the dead, is not practised among them. However, *chaubarsi*, i.e fourth year ritual after the demise of a person, is performed by the members of the family.

The Salarias have been essentially a rich and prosperous landowning community. In fact, in comparison to the other Rajput groups, theye held the most productive agrarian belt of Shakargarh and Sialkot region. However, after the Partition of the country, they had to be content with the farm area of Gurdaspur and Pathankot in Punjab. In the Jammu region, they had to opt for other occupational pursuits as well. They are self-employed businessmen, retail traders, government officials and a sizeable number of them are in the police and defence services. A few of them, especially their women, are in teaching and white-collar professions. Their links with the market are direct and most of the transactions are carried out in cash, though barter system also marginally prevails in rural areas. Their priests are the Hindu Brahmans of the region. These priests perform all their social and religious rites and ceremonies. The Rajput Sabha plays an active role in solving the disputes arising out of property or marriage-related problems. However, judicial recourse may also be taken if the Sabha is not able to resolve these issues.

They have an informal stratification system which appears to be more psychological rather than formal in the overall hierarchy of the Rajput community. Differentiations on account of economic, social or educational factors are not observed by them. They regularly visit their clan deities and other regional deities like Vaishno Devi, Amarnath, Sarthal Devi, Kheer Bhawani, etc. They also visit the *pirs* and *faqirs*, irrespective of their religious affiliations. The community has not undergone any major social or religious transformation. However, city life has made an impact on those who live in urban areas. They do not excel in arts or crafts. Their women have a natural talent for painting and writing prose and poetry besides being good in cloth embroidery. They possess a rich tradition of folklore and folk tales. Music and dance is quite popular among them. Both the sexes participate in it, especially on the birth and wedding ceremonies. Their clan deity is the goddess Durga. The Salarias accept and exchange food and water from all the Hindus except those who are low caste and may also refrain from the Muslims in this case. However, interdining in urban areas is a common phenomenon. Marriage alliances are mostly sought within the Rajput groups. They have a good number of administrators, engineers, doctors and lawyers but they have a special preference for the armed forces and police services. Political leadership is confined to the level of village politics. However, among the Muslim Salarias in the region, political representation is found in the Lok Sabha at the national level.

Education is favoured for both girls and boys and no special preference is exhibited for either sex in this regard. The boys study usually up to college level, while girls normally go up to high school. The pursuit of formal education is linked to economic considerations. Their attitude towards family planning is positive. They make regular use of modern medicare subject to its availability. They make use of the birth control techniques, while it is their females who generally get sterilized.

Drinking water is available through tap in urban dwellings, while in rural areas, canals and wells also supplement this requirement.

They are exposed to all the media of communication such as radio, newspaper, television and cinema. Railway facilities are available at the railway headquarters in Jammu city. They also make use of electricity, wood, kerosene oil and LPG. Their attitude towards savings and banking is positive.

ASHOK AIMA

SANGTARASH

The Sangtarashs are an artisan community of stonecutters and makers of different stone articles for generations. The term '*sangtarash*' is derived from two words *sang* and *tarash* meaning 'stone' and its 'cutting'. The history of migration of the community is not known but it is believed that their ancestors were Hindus who were converted to Islam during the Mughal period. They are placed in the Shaikh category of the Muslim and have been categorized as a Backward Class by the Jammu & Kashmir government. They are mainly concentrated around Srinagar, Pulwama, Anantnag and Badgam districts.

They inhabit the Kashmir Valley which has cold climate and hilly terrain where rainfall is medium, humidity is low, and medium to heavy snowfall during winter. The area has thin forest and surrounded by the Pir Panjal and the greater Himalayan ranges with an average altitude of five to ten thousand feet. They speak Kashmiri within the family and use Urdu and Kashmiri while communicating with others. They write in Arabic script.

There is no identification marker of the community and they wear the same attire as that of other Kashmiris—*pheran*, *pochh*, trousers and cap. The women wear *salwar*, *kurta*, *pheran* and *puts* (worn on the head). They are non-vegetarians and eat mutton, chicken, fish and eggs, but not beef which is restricted in the Valley. Eating pork is prohibited by religion.

Their staple food consist of rice, wheat, maize, pulses of gram *moong* (green-gram) *urad* (black gram), *masur* and *moth* (brown gram). Bajra, barley and millets are also consumed but not as a substitute for rice. Vegetables like cabbage, cauliflower, pumpkin, brinjal, ladies' fingers, carrot, cucumber and potato are used seasonally. Among the leafy vegetables, *hak* or *karamsag* are their favourite. Fruits are taken in plenty as they are grown locally in abundance. Mustard oil is used as the cooking medium. Seasonally available roots and tubers are also consumed by them. Bread is taken with tea in the morning and in the afternoon.

They do not consume alcohol but salty tea is popular among them. They occasionally take *qahwa* or black tea. Milk and milk products are consumed in lesser quantity owing to their scarcity. They smoke *bidis*, cigarettes, *hookah* and occasionally chew betel.

There are no social divisions in the community but occupation, economic status and educational attainment determine their social status. There is no change in their surnames. Being in the category of clean occupational castes of the Muslim community, they place themselves in the middle rank of the local social hierarchy, and other communities also recognize their rank in the hierarchy. Like the other occupational communities of the Kashmir, Sangtarashs, too include persons with different surnames such as Mir, Rishi, Dar, Sofi, Chhan, Malik, etc.

They are endogamous and prefer to marry off their daughters and sons in the same community. However, the rules of endogamy are not strictly followed. They may accept a girl or a boy from any community of the Sunni sect in case of non-availability of a suitable match in their own community, but first preference is given to cousins whether parallel or cross. The age of marriage at present is between 18 to 25 years for boys and 16 to 21 years for girls. Marriages are settled by negotiation either with the help of a common friend or a mediator called *manzymyor*.

Monogamy is the general practice though polygamy is permissible according to the *shariyat* (Islamic rules). There is no symbol of marriage of the married women. Dowry is permissible. The *mahr* money for the bride is fixed at the time of *nikah* (marriage). After marriage, the bride lives with her husband and in-laws. Divorce is permissible. The husband has the right to divorce his wife on the grounds of barrenness, adultery, maladjustment and insanity. Likewise, the wife can also seek a separation if the husband is absconding, or not bearing the expenses of his wife and children, or not having sexual contact for more than three years.

Divorce is given either orally or by a *talaq-nama* (written document). According to the Muslim law, when a marriage is dissolved by divorce, the woman is prohibited from remarrying for a specific period of time called *iddat*. If consummation of marriage has taken place and then there is a divorce, the *iddat* is for three months and ten days and, if the woman is pregnant, it is till the delivery. The purpose for fixing *iddat* period is to ascertain the legitimacy of the expected child. Cases of divorce in the community are rare. It is the duty of the father to maintain the minor children after divorce. Widow, widower and divorcee remarriages are permissible but widows are allowed to remarry only after the *iddat* period is over. It is for four months and ten days. Remarriages are performed in a simple manner.

Decrease in divorce cases, emergence of the dowry system and monogamy are the major changes which have occurred in recent years. Nuclear and mixed extended families are common among them. Interpersonal relations among the family members are amicable as due respect and regard are shown by the youngsters and elders towards each other. Avoidance exist between the daughter-in-law and father-in-law, between younger brother's wife and husband's elder brother and with outsiders and other elder relatives. *Purdah* system exists among the womenfolk. Joking relationship exists between husband's younger brother and sister-in-law and between the husband and his wife's younger sisters.

The property is divided among the daughters, sons and the widow, but the daughters get a lesser share than their brothers and the widow. The succession pattern is followed in the male line from the father to the eldest son. The breaking of joint family system and emergence of nuclear families are the recent changes.

The women have an equal status and enjoy the right of *mahr*, the amount which is fixed at the time of *nikah* by the husband. It can be claimed by the wife at any time after marriage, but it is generally demanded at the time of divorce. The women play important roles in almost all the economic activities like agriculture, collection of fuel, bringing of potable water and doing other household chores. They play a pivotal role in social and religious functions. They have the decision-making powers also and sometimes supplement the family income by involving themselves in different crafts.

The life-cycle rituals start from the pregnancy of a woman. Certain restrictions are imposed on her and she is not allowed to carry heavy loads or do strenuous work during pregnancy. Normally, the delivery takes place at home and a midwife, *warin*, from the community or a knowledgeable old woman is called to assist the parturient mother. She is paid in cash and kind. In urban areas, pregnant women are admitted in hospitals for delivery.

Immediately after birth, the neonate is given a bath and a senior male member recites *azaan* in the ears of the newborn. On the first day after birth, sweets and bread are distributed among the relatives, friends and neighbours. On the seventh day after delivery, the parturient mother first takes a bath and then the child is given a name either by the family priest or an elder. This ceremony is called *sunder* and is followed by a feast. The parturient mother is given another bath after forty days and, after this, she is allowed to perform the normal household chores. *Zerakast* is the next ceremony performed after six months when the hair of the child are shaved off by the family barber and a feast is arranged on this occasion. After this, *khatnahal* (circumcision) is performed on a male baby when he is two years old. In villages, it is done by the family barber but, in urban areas, it is done in hospitals or at the clinic of a surgeon. The ceremony is marked with a big feast.

In marriages, preference is given to the cousins. After preliminary negotiations and consent of both the parties, the father of the boy with other relatives visits the bride's house and offers some money to her and her father. This ceremony is called *gandum* (engagement). After this, the ritual of *doon-leij* is observed in which an earthen pot full of nuts and cash is presented to the father of the bridegroom by the bride's father. The ritual of *dapanbata*, or formal invitations for marriage are sent after *doon-leij. Malasbehoun* ritual is observed at the bride's place wherein the bride is not allowed to take bath and do any household work for at least three days preceeding the marriage. This is followed by the ritual of *massmechravoun* in which the hair of the bride is combed by female relatives.

The first day of the marriage is called *menziraat*, in which *mehndi* paste is applied on the hands and feet of the bride. This ceremony is followed by *yenevoul* ritual, when the father of the bridegroom sends a few copper plates containing sugar candy, sugarballs, almonds, clothes and ornaments for the bride. When the *barat* procession starts, two or three rows of women singing in chorus holding each other follow for some distance.

The *barat* procession is received at the bride's house by the womenfolk. After this, the *nikah* ceremony is observed and is presided over by the *maulvi* (priest). *Mahr* money varying from Rs. 9,000 to 21,000 is also fixed in this ceremony. When the *nikah* ceremony is over, a feast is served. At the time of departure of the bride, her female relatives follow her for some distance singing in chorus. She stays with her husband for seven days. *Wathal*, a big feast is arranged on the marriage night.

They bury their dead. First, a bath is given to the dead body by a *snangor* who is paid in cash and kind. When the relatives and friends of the deceased assemble, the dead body, wrapped in a white *kafan* (shroud) is placed in a *taboot* (coffin) and laid on the ground facing towards Mecca. A priest leads *namaz-e-janaza* prayers. Thereafter, the coffin is carried to the graveyard where a *malkhos* digs a *lahad* (grave) in which the dead body is placed and covered first with wooden planks or stone slab and then with earth. On the fourth day, relatives and friends recite the Holy Koran for the peace of the departed soul and the ceremony is repeated on the fortieth day. These are called *chaharum* and *chehallum*, respectively.

For generations, the primary occupation and source of livelihood of the community has been stonecutting and chiselling, and making different stone articles used in the construction of buildings and for grinding purposes. They prepare items such as *band*, *hamam*, *kona*, *lada*, *farsh*, *kundia*, *chakki*, *khamb* and board, which are in great demand throughout the region. Most of the families are involved in their traditional occupation and depend wholly on it as they are mainly landless. Only a few families possess some land in rural areas. A few members of the community are working in the government or private organizations.

The resources are controlled by individuals. They are directly linked with the local market, which is fully regulated, and all transactions are conducted in cash only. Bonded labour is not in existence though child labour is engaged for stone-cutting. They do not have their own traditional caste or *biradari* panchayat and disputes, except those related to business affairs, are settled either by the head of the family or some elderly person. To solve business disputes, they have their own associations in Srinagar. They are not members of the village statutory panchayat.

They are Muslim and follow the *shariat*. There are several sacred shrines and mosques which are visited by them on different occasions. Shah Hamdan, Charar-e-Sharif, Makhdum Sahib, Dastgir Sahib, Naqshband Sahib are the sacred places they visit. They have their own *pirs* who are called to perform the birth, marriage and death rites. The community observe the Muslim festivals. Urs-e-Nabi (the Prophet's birthday) known as Id-ul-Milad is celebrated on the twelfth day of Rabi-ul-Awwal. On this day, the Prophet's relic (hair) is displayed at Hazratbal shrine. Meraj-e-Alam is celebrated on the twenty-sixth of Rajab and the hair relic of the Prophet is again displayed on this occasion. Id-ul-Fitr, Id-ul-Zuha and Shab-e-Qadr are other festivals celebrated by them. Urs-e-Shah Hamdan, Urs-e-Batmaloo, Urs-e-Charar-e-Sharif, Urs-e-Makhdum Sahib, Urs-e-Pir Dastgir and Urs-e-Naqshband are celebrated by the community. All the festivals are of socio-religious and socio-economic significance.

Carving on stones and making stone articles of different sizes, shapes and designs is the traditional art and craft of the community. Besides, they are engaged in other traditional crafts of Kashmir such as shawl embroidery, wood carving, papier mâché, carpet and *namda* weaving, etc. Folk songs popular in the region are sung by the women on social occasions.

Relations between the Sangtarashs and the other Muslim communities are established through intercommunity marriages, exchange of cooked and uncooked food, sharing water resources, burial grounds and places of worship. They extend their services even to the lowest caste in the Valley like the Watals and Chamars. They accept *kachcha* and *pukka* food from all the Muslim and non-Muslim communities of the region. The services of the *pir*, *nai*, *gorkan*, *tarkhan* and *chhan* are taken on different occasions. Patron-client relationship exists in the community. At present, a few members of the community are in the government and private jobs, but most of the families continue to pursue their traditional occupation of stone cutting.

Though the attitude of the community towards formal education is favourable, yet they do not pay much attention towards women's education owing to economic and social reasons. Educational programmes of the government have not yet yielded the desired results. Rural areas being hilly, children have to walk at least 2 to 3 km to reach the nearest school. For higher education, they have to go to the cities.

They have not discarded their traditional indigenous medicare system since the facilities of modern medicare are not easily available. They always complain about non-availability of dispensaries and short supply of medicines in the rural areas. But in cities, these facilities are available. They do not have a positive attitude towards the family planning programmes. Electricity and drinking water facilities are available in their locality. Tap water, streams and springs are the sources of drinking water.

Most of the members of the community are self-employed; being involved in the traditional occupation. The media of communication are radio, television and cinema for those who live in urban areas. Cow-dung cakes, kerosene oil and firewood are used as fuel.

Those who have land in villages depend on rain water for their agricultural pursuits as proper irrigation facilities are not available. The facilities of the public distribution system through fair price shops are available and they avail themselves of these. They have a positive attitude towards savings and do not depend on the moneylenders or shopkeepers.

ANAND SARAN

SANSI

The Sansis of Jammu were traditionally engaged in petty thefts, highway robberies and illicit brewing of liquor but are now pursuing agriculture. Claiming to belong to the Rajput clan, they at some point of time were dependent on hunting and eating all types of forest animals such as cats, squirrels, vultures and horses.

They do not have any titles. However, there are various subcastes among them such as, Nandwal, Masval, Khanwal, Sandyal, Gholiya, Toliyal, Tagiyal, Nathuwal, Lodiya, Chachoo and Handariya. They are identified at the regional level. They have very scanty historical accounts which are not documented but are oral in content. The Sansis have migrated to their present habitat and keep on shifting to settle down at hospitable places. They are spread over the major parts of Jammu province, viz., Samba, Reasi, Kathua, Punch, Rajouri, Naoshera, Udhampur and Meeransahib. The community perceives its distribution at the regional as well as local level. The Sansi settlements record warm and temperate climate and are situated along mostly peripheral belts of the semi-arid plains. The region experiences high humidity with thin to dense forest cover and records medium rainfall.

They speak Dogri within the family and kin group. The language spoken with others is also Dogri and occasionally Urdu. They have no specific dress markers so as to identify themselves as a separate ethnic group. They wear dresses which are close to the Dogri and Punjabi dress pattern. The community is categorized under the backward classes category.

The Sansis are essentially non-vegetarians with vegetable consumption. Both sexes are regular non-vegetarians and eat pork, eggs, fowls, mutton and fish. Their staple food is wheat, rice and maize. The pulses they consume are *moong*, peas and beans, *moth* and *masur*. They mainly use mustard oil for cooking, though *ghee* is also used occasionally. Locally available roots and tuberous vegetables are also consumed. Tea consumption is moderate with regular use of milk and milk products. Drinking alcohol is regular among the men while it is occasional among the women. The reason for high liquor consumption is its self brewing by the majority of the Sansi households. They consume fruit occasionally. The men smoke cigarettes, tobacco and indigenous cheroot regularly. Tobacco chewing and use of snuff also prevails among them. There has not been any significant changes in their food habits, though the level and quality has improved with the living standard.

There are no social divisions among these people though they have various subcastes. They concede higher status to the Rajputs and other Hindu communities. However, among the Sansis stratification into various subcastes (essentially having different surnames) does not seem to have any significant basis except for occupation pursued by their forefathers. The economically affluent and educated among them do not interact with the other Sansis to create a new image for themselves which is socially more honourable. Consequently, an informal differentiation exist which is not so apparent. They, being of low caste, do not follow the *varna* system though they are very much conscious of it. Other communities also consider them inferior and treat them with contempt becuase of the stigma of their reputation. Their self-perception is also low.

The Sansis are an endogamous group. The exogamous surnames or titles govern their matrimonial alliances, irrespective of the regional location. As a matter of practice, alliances are not sought within the same surname. Consanguinity at the level of parallel and cross-cousins on mother's side are permitted while the same is not allowed on father's side. Sororate alliances do not prevail among them though there is no restrictions on levirate marriage. Monogamy is the prevalent form of marriage. Some cases of polygyny, however, also prevail.

Pre-puberty marriage was the earlier practice but nowadays girls are married after attaining puberty. The marriage age varies from 16 to 20 years for girls, while for boys, it is 23 years and above. Marital alliances are negotiated by their elders, friends and relatives. Marriages are solemnized under the Hindu tradition. Their married womenfolk have various symbols of marriage, i.e. vermilion, bangles (lac and glass) and nose ring being the main ones. Dowry usually consists of some dresses, kitchen utensils and ornaments according to the economic status of the bride's parents.

They follow the patrilocal rule of residence. Uxorilocal residence, however, also prevails. Divorce is permitted subject to social and judicial approval, and the proceedings may be initiated by either party in this regard. The motives of divorce are maladjustment and adultery. Compensation is given to the wife as it is the husband who generally seeks a divorce. The children are the responsibility of the father in case of divorce, and the amount of compensation may be settled mutually or through a court ruling. The rules regarding remarriage are quite flexible except that senior levirate is not permissible. Widowers and male and female divorcees can remarry.

There is a growing tendency among the Sansis to have the nuclear form of family but at present joint family system predominates. Families are vertically and horizontally extended. No restriction or avoidance prevails for any type of relationship. For both consanguineous and affinal relationship, joking is permitted among them. Conflicts and confrontations arise mainly due to property and challenge to the authority of elders, resulting in physical clashes and verbal duals. Equigeniture is the rule but females do not normally claim any share in the parental property.

The eldest son succeeds as the head of the family after the demise of the father. Interfamily relationships are cordial. Conflicts are usually settled through mutual consultations or negotiations by elders, friends and relatives. They also go to the state courts to seek remedy for the disputes arising on account of land and property. There has not been any significant changes in the rules regarding inheritance and succession. However, the number of nuclear families is increasing.

The Sansi women enjoy a secondary status compared to their men in all spheres of life. They do not enjoy equal rights to the parental property but they participate in almost all social, religious and ritual activities besides performing the household chores. At the same time, they render help in almost all agricultural operations. They collect wood, fetch water and tend the livestock and assist their men in illegal alcohol brewing. The women do not have a role in the decision-making or control of expenditure within the household. Though they enjoy voting rights as guaranteed under the Constitution, they do not play any significant role in politics. They, however, contribute to the family income. The majority of them are illiterate and ignorant of worldly events.

They do not observe any pre-delivery rituals but observe elementry restrictions during pregnancy. A woman can deliver the child either at her natal or at her husband's home as there is no formal precondition in this regard, though the former is given precedence over the latter. The majority of them deliver their babies at home with the help of an experienced midwife. The women in urban localities avail themselves of the government health centre's facilities. A forty days' post-delivery pollution period is observed among them. The christening ceremony of the child is observed without an elaborate ceremony. *Mundan* ceremony for the male child is reported among them.

Marital alliances are sought and arranged by negotiations initiated by the elders, friends and relatives. The marriage celebrations are usually one- or two-day affair. On the first day, *mehndi-raat* is celebrated, followed by wedding celebrations next day at night. Customarily, the marriage ceremony is held at the bride's residence. On the wedding night, the bridegroom accompanied by the *baratis* (guests) arrives at the bride's house where *lagan* and *jaimala* ceremonies are performed. The wedding party usually arrives at night. Drinking alcohol is quite popular and common on such occasions.

When a person dies, the dead body is given a bath, then wrapped in a white cloth and carried on a bier to the cremation ground for cremation. Forty days' death pollution is observed among them. *Rasam-pagri* or *uthala* ritual is usually performed after thirteenth day for succession of the male heir as the head of the family. *Shradh* (ancestor worship) is not performed. There has not been any major change in the life-cycle rituals of the Sansis, though the same have become more expensive and, in some cases, elaborate.

Land is their main natural and economic resource. They have now gradually become a landowning community with the resources being controlled by individual proprietorship. The men are engaged in petty trade, besides brewing illicit liquor and committing small thefts. They also work as farm labourers and unskilled workers on daily wages. A negligible number of the Sansis are employed in the government service. Settled cultivation forms the backbone of the economic activity of a majority of the Sansi families. Animal husbandry at the household level coupled with poultry farming are also catching up with these people. Child labour is not common though the same is used in domestic and non-farm activities. They receive their wages both in cash and kind. Their link with the market is direct and is based on daily to monthly transactions. There has been an increase in the number of casual and agricultural labourers among them.

The traditional village panchayats are of heterogeneous nature, though their elders do form an informal association for the overall conduct and concern for their community. The statutory panchayats are usually involved in settling disputes relating to the social problems in general. They also monitor the village and block development plans and welfare activities. In exceptional cases, the panchayats may impose social boycott or excommunicate an offender on account of theft, adultery or disputes over land and property. There is no formal system of instituting awards by the panchayats.

The Sansis claim to be Rajputs who profess Hindu religion. They worship village and regional deities. Individual affiliation to the *pirs* is a common phenomenon. Their religious specialists are the *pujaris* (Brahmans) who perform the birth, marriage and death rites. Regional deities like Vaishno Devi, Raghunath and the goddess Kali are worshipped by these people. Festivals are of socio-religious nature. All the major Hindu festivals are celebrated by them, namely, Shivratri, Janmashtami, Navratras, Diwali, Holi, Lohri, Rakshabandhan, etc.

They have oral traditions of folk songs, folklore and folk tales on which the Dogri culture exerts a strong influence. There are no experts in fine arts, music or dance among them. They do not have any expertise in art as such. Songs are sung by both men and women. There are no restrictions on either sex with regard to dancing.

They accept both cooked and uncooked food from the other Hindu and non-Hindu communities. Being a low caste community, they only accept but cannot exchange food and food items generally with the high caste Hindus. They participate in all the religious and ceremonial events of the Hindus of Jammu. They accept food and water from all communities. They do not normally maintain marital relationship with the high caste Hindus.

The community is in the process of evolving itself with a better occupational dignity. Petty trade, small businesses, retail trading and marketing of farm products are some of the activities towards which a shift has been observed. They do not have doctors, engineers or lawyers among them, but a few of them are employed by the government and some are also working in the private sector. Though they are politically conscious, they have failed to organize themselves into a collective forum. Participation in political activities is restricted at the village level. They maintain cordial and business-like relationship with people from all walks of life. They also have cultivator-labour relationship. They receive the services of barbers, carpenters and masons.

Formal education is not popular among them, though a number of the boys and girls do go to school. In fact, their attitude towards education is receptive. Preference is given to the boys for seeking education, and they usually study up to high school and then drop out on account of economic compulsions. The girls do not study beyond primary or secondary level. Formal education has yet to make a perceptible impact on the Sansis. In spite of a favourable attitude towards modern medicare, they are unable to make full use of it. They still resort to traditional methods of solving health-related problems. The average family size varies from six to eight members. The attitude towards family planning is not favourable as there seem to be no concerted efforts made by them to restrict the family size. Though they have tap water system, yet scarcity of water remains for the community.

The community has not been benefited by the various welfare and development programmes launched by the state or central government agencies. Cooperative societies help in the distribution of essential commodities through the public distribution system. Almost all the households avail themselves of electricity for lighting purposes. They use firewood and cow-dung cakes as fuel to cook their food. Most of them own land and avail themselves of irrigation facilities. Such landowners make use of the modern chemical fertilizers and improved seeds with extensive use of organic manure. None of them have taken advantage of the nutrition programmes through ICDS, Aganwadis and SNP centres. They borrow from the shopkeepers and moneylenders. Some of them also seek bank loans. They do not tend to save or invest as the concept of banking is lacking among them.

The Sansis were known for their criminal pursuits of the past. Illicit liquor brewing is still a noticeable occupation of the average household though theft-related crimes and other immoral practices seem to be gradually declining. The younger generation is more conscious and sensitive to the social stigma attached to the community. Consequently, the young generation is trying to break away from the clutches of the past by seeking a shift to respectable and socially approved avenues. They want to get rid of the heritage they inherited from their ancestors.

INDU AIMA

SANUR

The Sanurs are an artisan community who are also known as Sunar or Zargur. There are Hindu Sanurs also, who are not the original inhabitants of Kashmir and have migrated from Punjab. Sanur literally means a goldsmith or silversmith. They are experts in making gold and silver ornaments. The history and origin of the community is not known but it is believed that before the advent of Islam in the Kashmir Valley, the ancestors of this community were Hindus who were converted afterwards.

During the Mughal period, they were the chief goldsmiths in the palaces. They call themselves Sheikhs. They are widespread in most of the districts of the state but are mainly found in Srinagar district, and the Pir Panjal and greater Himalayan range.

The language of the community is Kashmiri with Arabic script. They speak in Kashmiri and Urdu with others. There is no identification marker of the community and they wear their dresses like the other Kashmiri communities. The usual dress of a man is a pair of loose drawers and long loose-fitting shirt, cap and a *pheran*. The women wear *salwar*, *kurta* and *puz*. They are non-vegetarians. Mutton, fish and some birds are consumed by them but beef is not taken as it is restricted in the Valley. Their staple food is rice and wheat. Maize is also consumed in the season. Pulses like grams, peas and *masur* are consumed by them. Mustard oil is used as the cooking medium. Alcoholic drinks are prohibited in the community as per the Islamic rules. Fruits are consumed in plenty since they are grown in the state in large quantity.

Their favourite drink is tea which is very popular not only in the community but in the entire state. Tea is consumed with salt. *Qahwa* is also occasionally consumed. Milk and milk products are not very popular in the community due to its low production in the state. Consumption of *ghee* is also low as it is considered harmful in the cold climate. However they smoke *bidis* (local cigarettes) and *hookah*.

There are no social divisions among the Sanur community but, on the basis of educational attainment, occupation and economic status, they are considered of high and low status. The community is considered in the middle rank of the local social hierarchy and are placed among the clean occupation castes of the Muslims. Others also place them in the same order. No changes in the surnames have been reported. Though the community is endogamous, the rules of endogamy are not strictly followed. They may accept girls or boys from outside the community but prefer to marry their sons and daughters within their own community. Consanguinity prevails both at cross-cousin and parallel cousin levels.

At present, marriages take place when the boys and girls attain adulthood, but, in the past, early marriages were prevalent. The age for marriage is between 18 and 25 years for both boys and girls. Marriages are settled by negotiation between the families through the services of a common friend or a mediator (*manzymyor*). Monogamy is the common form but polygyny is permissible in the community according to the *shariat*, though it is not a common practice.

There are no marriage symbols for the married women in the community. Bride price and dowry are not practiced, but, in some cases, exchange of dowry has taken place in recent times. *Mahr* is fixed at the time of *nikah* and promised for future payment. Being patrilocal, after marriage the bride goes to live with her husband and in-laws.

Divorce is permissible in the community as per the Islamic rules. A husband can divorce his wife in case of barrenness, adultery, maladjustment or insanity. Likewise, the wife can also seek separation on the grounds when the husband is absconding, does not bear the expenses of the wife and children or has not had sexual contact with wife for more than three years. A husband has more rights and privileges than the women in the matter of divorce. According to the Muslim rules, divorce may be given either orally or in writing known as *talaq-nama*. In the Muslim law, when marriage is dissolved by divorce, the woman is prohibited from remarrying for a specified period. This period is called *iddat*. If the consummation of marriage has taken place and then there is a divorce, the duration of *iddat* is for four months and ten days; if the woman is pregnant, it is until the delivery. The purpose for fixing a period of *iddat* is to ascertain the legitimacy of the expected child.

The cases of divorce are rare in the community. It is the duty of the father to maintain the children after the divorce till they are major. Widow, widower and divorcee remarriages are permissible in the community. A widow is allowed to marry when the *iddat* period is over. Remarriages are performed in a simple way. The decrease in divorce cases, emergence of a dowry and monogamy are the major changes which have come about in recent years. There are mostly nuclear families among them; but, in villages, extended families are also found. In most of the cases, a new couple establishes a new household after marriage.

Interpersonal relationship is maintained amicably among the family members. Due love and respect mark the relations existing between youngsters and elders. Avoidance relationship is maintained between the daughter-in-law and father-in-law, between younger brother's wife and husband's elder brother and with outsiders and other elderly relations. Joking relationship exists between the husband's younger brothers and sister-in-law and between the husband and his wife's younger sister.

Following the death of the head of the family, the property is divided among the sons, unmarried daughters and the widow. Daughters get lesser share than their brothers and widowed mother. The succession pattern is followed in the male line from father to the eldest son. The only change which has come about in recent years is the dissolution of the joint family system and emergence of nuclear families.

Women have a status equal to that of men. They have full rights to *mahr*, the amount which is fixed at the time of *nikah* by the bride's side. It can be claimed by the bride any time after marriage but is generally demanded at the time of divorce. Women have an important role in all the spheres of life, such as agriculture, collection of fuel, bringing potable water and other household jobs. They play a pivotal role in social and religious functions. Though they do not contribute much to the family income, they certainly help to augment it. They take part in decision-making and exercise control over the family expenditure.

During the first pregnancy, certain restrictions are imposed on the women. Delivery still takes place at home, particularly in villages. In urban areas, the services of hospitals are also utilized. A *dai* (midwife) is called to assist in the delivery and she is paid money, sweets, rice and maize according to the economic status of the family. She may be from any community. Immediately after the child's birth and first bath, a senior male member recites *azaan* into the ears of the baby. On this occasion, bread and sweets are distributed among relatives, friends and neighbours. If the delivery takes place at the girl's parents' house, sweets are sent to her in-laws' place. Her mother-in-law sends sweets, cash and clothes for the baby in return. This ceremony is called *piaw*.

On the seventh day after delivery, the parturient mother takes her first bath. On this day, the child is given a name either by the family priest or any other elderly person of the family. On this occasion, a feast is also sometimes arranged. After forty days, the woman is given another bath and then she is allowed to do all the household jobs. *Zerakasi*, in which the hair of the child is shaved, is performed after six months. It is done by the family barber. A feast is arranged on this occasion also. *Khatnahal* (circumcision) ceremony is performed on the male child when he is more than two years old by the family barber; in urban areas, it is done either in a hospital or at home by an expert surgeon. A big feast is arranged on this occasion.

Marriage is settled by negotiation and preference is always given to the cousins. If the same are not available, selection is made from outside the community. Sometimes this is done by a matchmaker called *manzymyor*. After preliminary negotiations, the father of the boy with some close relatives visit the place of the girl and offer some money to the would-be-bride and her father. It marks the *gandum* (engagement ceremony). This is followed by another ceremony called *doon-leij*. In this ceremony, an earthen pot full of nuts and cash is presented to the father of the bridegroom by the bride's father.

In the ritual of *dapanbata*, members of the family go to their relatives' houses to invite them for the marriage. *Malasbehoun* is the first ritual associated with the marriage wherein the bride is not allowed to take bath and do household jobs for at least three days before the marriage. She is fed a light meal in the belief that she would grow thinner and look more pretty. This is followed by another ritual called *massmechravoun*, in which the hair of the bride is loosened by the female relatives.

In the ritual of *menziraat* or *malamenz*, *mehndi* (myrtle) paste is applied to the hands and feet of the bride in the night before marriage. *Yenevoul* is the second day of marriage on which the father of the bridegroom sends a few copper plates containing sugar candy, sugar balls, almonds, dresses and ornaments for the bride.

When the *barat* procession starts, it is followed by two or three rows of the women singing in chorus holding each other for some distance. The *barat* procession is received at the bride's house by the women there. *Nikah* ceremony is presided over by the *maulvi* (priest). The *mahr* money which varies from Rs. 9,000 to 21,000 is also fixed during the *nikah* ceremony. When the *nikah* ceremony is over, dinner is served. When the bride leaves her parent's house after marriage, her female relatives follow her for some distance singing in chorus. The bride stays with her husband for seven days. *Wathal*, a big feast, is arranged at night by the bridegroom's father. After the marriage, the bride starts living with her husband.

The dead are buried. A bath is first given to the dead body by a professional man called *snangor*. He is paid money and given the clothes of the deceased. After the bath, the dead body is wrapped in *kafan* and is placed in a *taboot* (coffin). The *taboot* is laid on the ground facing Mecca and the priest recites prayers. Then the *taboot* is carried to the graveyard where a *lahad* (grave) is dug by a *malkhos* for which he is given money, tea and bread. The dead body is placed in the *lahad* and covered with stones and earth. On the fourth day, the priest, relatives and neighbours are called to recite the Holy Koran for the peace of the departed soul. The ceremony is repeated on the fortieth day. The two rituals are called *chaharum* and *chehallum* respectively.

The primary occupation of the community has always been the making of ornaments of gold and silver for all the communities of the state. Almost all the families of the Sanur are involved in their age-old traditional occupation. In the villages, they are involved in agriculture also but, in cities, most of the families have jewellery shops. Some members of the community are in the government or private jobs. The resources are controlled by the family or the individual. They are directly linked with the daily market which is fully regulated.

The community is still devoted to its traditional occupation and do not want to shift to other occupation as it is a profitable and clean occupation. Disputes within the community are solved either by the village headman or an elderly person of the community. Sometimes the disputes are taken to the court of law.

The community professes Islam and follow the dictum of the *shariat*. There are several sacred shrines and mosques which are visited by them on different occasions. Shah Hamdan, Charar-e-Sharif, Makhdum Sahib, Dastgir Sahib and Naqshband Sahib are some of the sacred places commonly visited by them. The community has its own *pirs* who are called to perform the birth, marriage and death rituals.

They observe the different Muslim festivals in different months. Urs Nabi, Id-ul-Milad is celebrated on the twelfth of Rabi-ul-Awwal. On this day, the Prophet's hair relic is displayed at Hazratbal shrine. Meraj-e-Alam is celebrated on the twenty-sixth of Rajab and the hair relic is again displayed at Hazratbal shrine. Meraj-e-Alam is celebrated on the twenty-sixth of Rajab and the hair relic is displayed on this day also. Id-ul-Fitr, Id-ul-Zuha and Shab-e-Qadr are the other festivals which are observed with great zeal by the community. Besides, certain festivals (*urs*) like Urs-e-Shah Hamdan, Urs-e-Batmaloo, Urs-e-Charar-e-Sharif, Urs-e-Makhdum Sahib, Urs-e-Pir Dastgir, Urs-e-Naqshband

Sahib, Urs-e-Rafimal are also celebrated in the community. Festivals observed by the community are of socio-economic and socio-religious importance. They have their own traditional art and craft of making jewellery. Weaving of *namda* and making exquisite embroidery on woollen shawls are the other crafts known to them. The women sing folk songs on various social occasions.

The members of the community maintain relations with all the Muslim and non-Muslim communities in the Valley as they are involved in the important business of making gold and silver jewellery. They are considered a clean occupational community among the Muslims. They give their services to all the communities and even to the lowest community of the Valley like the Watal and Seraj. They accept *kachcha* and *pukka* food from all the Hindu and Muslim communities but, they maintain a distance from the Watal. The services of the *pir*, *nai*, *gorkan*, *tarkhan* and other Muslim communities are taken on the occasion of childbirth, marriage and death rituals. They share water sources, burial grounds and religious shrines with others. Patron-client relationship exits in the community. Besides their traditional occupation, members of the community are in the government and non-government jobs.

Development programmes launched by the central and state governments specially for Jammu & Kashmir region have left a good impact on the Sanur community. In the villages, though the facilities of education have been provided, the results are not very satisfactory becuase the area is very remote and hilly. The community is paying attention towards education but, for better and higher education, they have to go to the cities. In the villages, children have to walk at least 2 to 5 km. to reach the nearest school.

The attitude of the community towards modern medicine is favourable but, in remote areas, the indigenous medical system is still practised. The attitude of the community towards the family planning programmes is favourable in urban areas only as they prefer fewer children now. In their locality, electricity and drinking water facilities through tap water are available but they are not fully satisfied with it. Water taps, streams and springs are the main sources of their drinking water. Being involved in agriculture and the occupation of making and selling jewellery, most of the community members are self-employed. The media of communication and entertainment used are radio, television and cinema. Cow-dung cakes, wood and kerosene oil are used as fuel resources. For agriculture, they depend upon rainwater due to non-availability of irrigation facilities. Facility of food distribution system through the fair price shops are available and they avail themselves of it. The community has a positive attitude towards saving and they are not dependent on the moneylenders or shopkeepers.

ANAND SARAN

SARYARA

The Saryaras are a small Scheduled Caste community living in the Jammu, Kathua and Udhampur districts. One of their main areas of concentration is Bahu Fort settlement across Tawi river, on a hillock, in Jammu town. About half of the community's population lives at Bahu Fort. According to the 1981 census, the total population of the Saryaras was 8,024.

They trace their origin from the followers of Bahulochan, who they say was the brother of Jambulochan. Both of them were princes or big zamindars who fought possibly for succession. The army of Bahulochan lost the battle and surrendered. With their defeat, they earned a name for themselves and came to be known as *sarhare*, that is, those who lost their heads. In due course of time, the word transformed into Saryara. The ancestors of the present Saryara community belonged, to the defeated army of Bahulochan.

At present, the Saryaras have no synonyms nor is there any title used by them. They identify themselves as Saryaras and others too identify them with the same name. They are divided into various *jatis*. These are, Basotra, Chalotra, Chhagotra, Dalotra, Dhahotra, Gotdo, Khokhar, Kragotra, Nagotra, Pagatia, Padgotra, Sagotra and Sawalia. These are exogamous divisions and no marriage within the same *jati* is permissible. There is no hierarchy among these *jatis* and all are of equal status. These divisions prevail for the purpose of regulating marriages among the Saryaras. The Saryaras also divide themselves into various *gotras*. They could identify three *gotras*, namely Bhardwaj, Kashyap and Vashishta.

The only source of information about their origin is the oral legend current in the community as narrated above.

They are distributed only in the three districts of Jammu mentioned above and nowhere else in India.

The Saryaras speak Dogri and communicate with others in the same dialect. Most of these people write either in Arabic or in Devanagari. There is nothing specific or exclusive about their dress. Men wear long *kurta* and *pyjama* and women wear *salwar*, *kurta* and a *chaddar*.

The Saryaras eat non-vegetarian food occasionally on account of their weak economic condition. They do not eat beef nor do they consume pork, but restrict themselves to the consumption of mutton, chicken and fish. Their staple food consists of wheat and rice, and pulses like gram, *urad*, *moong*, peas and beans. Mustard oil is their main cooking medium. They consume roots, tubers, milk, milk products, vegetables, fruits and smoke *bidis* and cigarettes. The men occasionally consume alcoholic drinks. The women are also non-vegetarian. The quality of food consumed has deteriorated in the wake of inflation and high cost of food articles.

The Saryaras divide themselves into various exogamous divisions of equal status called *jatis*, whose main object is to regulate marriage alliances. There has been no change of any importance as regards the clan names, title or surname of the Saryara. They recognize the *varna* system and place themselves below the Brahmans and the Rajputs, but consider themselves higher in social hierarchy than some other Scheduled Caste communities.

They feel bitter about the grant of Scheduled Caste status to them which they believe has degraded them in the eyes of other Hindu communities. They claim to be Dogra and a martial race and expect to be treated as Kshatriyas. But other communities consider them to be low caste and poor people. They are exogamous on *jati* level and do not marry in their relations from either side of the parents. Boys and girls are married on the attainment of adulthood.

Formerly, marriage at an early age was prevalent. The wife is invariably younger in age than her husband, but the age is not in any way fixed.

Marriages are negotiated with the help of a middleman known as *rewara*. It is initiated by the girl's father. Most of the marriages are settled through negotiation. At times, the boy and the girl may themselves decide.

The married women use vermilion, *bindi*, bangles, *dupatta* (coloured scarf), *chhalli* (toering) and *long* (nose-stud) as marriage symbols. Dowry is practised and is given in cash and kind, as per the economic status of the family. Dowry is mutually discussed by both the parties. Residence after marriages is patrilocal.

Divorce, though permitted, is rare. In case of acute maladjustment, efforts are made by the relatives of both to strike an understanding between the parties. Then the case is taken to the community council which also tries to bring reconciliation, failing which the council allows the divorce which is then formalized by a court of law. The compensation or return of dowry money and such other issues are settled on the financial condition of the husband. However, young children below five years may continue to live with the mother till they come of age.

Remarriage is permissible for both the sexes in case of divorcees and death of the husband or wife. Practice of junior sororate and junior levirate prevails. In the latter case, the marriage ceremony is brief and formal while, in the former, there is virtually no dowry. These marriages are also formalized by social approval and by the traditional caste council. The important changes noticed are increase in the age at marriage and the increasing importance of education in marriage negotiations.

Most of the Saryara families are nuclear, consisting of husband, wife and their children. As soon as a son is married, he establishes a separate household. Parents live with one of their sons and hence some families are extended in nature.

They observe avoidance between mother-in-law and son-in-law, and daughter-in-law and husband's elder brother. Since practice of junior sororate and junior levirate prevails, the individuals so related have a relationship of familiarity as prospective spouses. As a matter of fact, the whole Saryara community at Bahu fort, is more or less inter-related in which everyone knows everyone else or is related, prescribing to behave in a definite manner. Age is always respected and the younger persons obey elders in all situations.

It is important to note that the Saryaras, because of the legacy of a martial community, are well behaved and are a quite people, mutually helping each other. They are concerned about their fellow community members' problems and difficulties. The interfamily relations among them are defined by mutual help and cooperation.

All the sons inherit and get an equal share of their father's property. A few cases of daughters seeking their share to fathers' property were turned down by the caste council. As such, daughters do not get any share. However, they do have a right of maintenance and residence until they get married. There are but very few cases of conflict and dispute on such an issue. The eldest son succeeds his father and inherits his non-divisible assests and liabilities. In exceptional cases, any other son who maintains his parents may inherit the property.

Among the Saryara community at Bahu fort, interfamily linkages, based on actual kinship and mutual cooperation, are very close, well defined and appreciably cordial. With increasing awareness of unity, the Saryaras try to strengthen their community feelings and, in the coming years, they may come still closer to each other. One of them has won a seat in the legislative council of the state and the Saryaras look forward to a better deal as regards the privileges and amenities.

The women among the Saryaras largely remain busy in doing household chores. The education among women is extremely poor and most of them are econimically dependent on their husbands.

However, some of them who have lost their earning male member have to seek some job or go for wage labour to feed their children and maintain a household of their own. A few of them are in permanent service as peons and attendants in offices. Women do not have a right to inherit but they play an important role in the social, ritual and religious functions. Their views, suggestions and even decisions are given due respect and they play an important role in household management, regulating the family expenditure and related issues in common with the other Dogra communities of the region.

They observe restrictions in case of pregnant women, especially during advanced pregnancy. Most of the children are born at home and a woman of the same community who has acquired some experience in midwifery assists during the childbirth. Payments made for her services are neither fixed nor bargained but are made as per the consideration of the household which requires her help. It is interesting to note that such a service is promptly extended and highly valued. In recent days, some young women have taken to midwifery and nursing, and they help in childbirth. On the fifth day after the birth, the grandmother of the child brings some sweets and some special nutrient preparations for her daughter. This ritual is known as *punjap.* On the eleventh day or twenty-first day, the mother takes a bath that marks the end of pollution period and confinement. The ritual is known as *snan.* Nowadays, parents get a horoscope prepared by a Brahman and the child gets a *rashi* (sign of the zodiac) name depending on the hour, date and the position of stars at birth. During the fifth or sixth month, the child eats cereals for the first time. The ritual is known as *caridi* or *caridi carai.* It is important to note that none of these rituals are associated with any ceremonial celebration as such.

Mundan ceremony is performed in case of the male children only and this is the first major event in a boy's life. Relatives and invited community members gather and a feast is given by the parents. Girls either retain the hair at birth or may have a haircut without any ceremony.

Marriage is an important event in an individual's life and the Saryaras give due importance to it. Once a marriage is negotiated and agreed upon, the engagement ceremony takes place at the girl's place. The ceremony is known as *kurmai* (or *sagai*). Following this is the ritual of *barten* or *rumal tika* (or *tika*), when the girl's family brings gifts for the boy's parents and the occasion is celebrated with a feast hosted by the boy's parents.

In a simple ceremony known as *lagan* (or *lag*), the date for the marriage is fixed. On that fixed day, the *barat* goes to the girl's place where the actual marriage ceremony takes place. The following day, the bride accompanies the groom's party to her new home. There is another feast hosted by the groom's parents at their residence and the consummation of marriage takes place. In a day or two, the bride returns to her parents and her husband accompanies her. The following day, a second send-off known as *duphera* ceremony takes place which marks the completion of marriage.

The Saryaras claim that they utilize the service of a Brahman on the occasion of marriage, but persons of their own community who know the procedue and are recognized by the community may also officiate instead of a Brahman. Giving away the daughter ritually known as *kanyadan* takes place during the main marriage ceremony. The sacred thread, *janeu*, ceremony for a boy takes place just before the marriage. However, they are not obliged to put on *janeu* for the rest of their lives.

The Saryaras cremate their dead and share the cremation ground with other communities on the bank of river Tawi. The bones are collected after the cremation and immersed into the sacred water. A post-funeral feast is given to the relatives and invited community members which mark the end of the pollution period.

The *jati* members gather at a definite place, once a year, on the ninth day of a dark fortnight in the month of *Bhadon* (that is, the day following Krishna Janmashtami) and sacrifice goats as a token of ancestor worship known as *gungey navami*. Meat of the sacrificed goats is distributed among all the *jati* members. It is an important celebration among the Saryara community.

The Saryaras claim that in the distant past their forefathers were in the army and they are, therefore, a martial race. They have not learnt any art or craft to earn their bread and livelihood over the generations. At present, they are engaged in various economic pursuits and a major section of their population are daily wage labourers. Some of them, however, are in the government or private service holding attendant's or peon's position.

Many of the men earn their livelihood by working as daily wage labourers and painting the buildings. They have earned a name as experts in painting walls of high buildings. Some of them work as carpenters, sanitary fitters, masons, labourers and construction workers. In such a situation, their major economic resource is their own labour. They are a landless community and are dependent on others for their survival.

The Saryara community has direct links with the market and they are paid in cash. Hence, they buy their requirements from the market on cash payment. The boys start learning painting, carpentry or such other work when they are still in their teens but child labour as such is not to be found. This is mainly because of the fact that the Saryaras are not involved in agricultural or cattle herding pursuits in which children can help. This also allows the children to attend school. There is a growing awareness of the importance of education among them.

There is a traditional caste council to uphold the norms of the society. The office-bearers such as the president, vice-president, secretary and treasurer, are elected to the office by voice vote, and they continue in the office as long as they enjoy the confidence of their fellow community members. The settlement of Bahu Fort in Jammu is virtually the headquarters of the caste council, as there are area caste councils in the adjoining two districts where the Saryara live. There are no village panchayats and the Saryara panchayat also functions as the *gram* panchayat; but recently the settlement has been included in the municipal local self-government area and it has been declared as a part of ward no. 23 of Jammu city. The continuance of an effective traditional caste council among the Saryaras is an important observation since such councils have either completely broken up or have been amalgamated with other castes.

The Saryaras are Hindus and they worship all gods without any discrimination, celebrating all the Hindu festivals. In day-to-day life Kali Mata, whose shrine is within the fort, is worshipped. All the *jatis* of Saryaras have a place of importance. They gather there once every year and call this place as their *kul-devta*. They have never changed their religion and are not involved in any socio-religious movement.

They are of the opinion that there is hardly any time in their lives for leisurely activities as they are a labour class constantly worried about their future.

The Saryaras are a somewhat isolated community. They are wage labourers and have no close ties with any particular community. Intercommunity linkages which exist are circumstantial and ephemeral. Though on the face of tnis, they have no lasting ties with other communities.

They are on the road to development and progress, and some of their children attend school. Some of them even go to convent schools. They receive medical facilities at their settlement itself. They realize the importance of a small family and many of the couples use contraceptives. They use electricity, postal services, railway, road transport, banking facilities and fair price shop facilities.

B. SINGH

SEN

The Sens, a Rajput lineage of Jammu, claim to have migrated from Bengal following the invasion of Aurangzeb's army. These people fled to the mountainous belt of Kangra Valley in Himachal Pradesh to escape conversion to Islam. Thereafter, they had to flee again to the mountainous belt of district Doda in Jammu & Kashmir state, especially to Kishtwar and, to a lesser extent, to the Bhaderwah region.

In Kishtwar, they emerged as the ruling class of the region and for a considerable period they ruled this belt unchallenged. They also claim that even in Bengal they belonged to the ruling family and they claim to have come from Goud-Bengal. They perceive their distribution at the local level as an exclusive ethnic group of Bengali origin.

Having been rulers in the past, they have a very high sense of self-esteem and ego. Others also regard them so. These people are mainly concentrated in the tahsil of Kishtwar in Doda district and a few of them also live in the city of Jammu.

Being the descendants of a ruling family, the Sens are few in number. Their main habitat records very heavy snowfall with dense forest cover. They speak Kishtwari language, i.e. their native language. Besides, they also speak Dogri, Urdu and English. They mainly correspond in Arabic and Roman, quite a few even in Devnagari among their own kinsfolk as also with others.

Their dress pattern closely matches the Dogri style in the plains of the region, while in the mountainous belts of Kishtwar it is closer to the *pahari* dress. In urban areas, they wear the dress on the pattern of the modern metropolitan culture.

They are non-vegetarians and eat pork but refrain from eating beef. Their staple food is rice, maize and wheat. They consume all varieties of pulses. Mustard oil is the main medium of cooking. The men drink alcohol occasionally. They consume all varieties of beverage. Milk and milk products are used regularly. They smoke cigarettes and *hookah*. Fruits are consumed moderately.

Social differentiation is linked to the hierarchical placement of these people in the overall Rajput lineage. Being the rulers, the Sens consider themselves at the top of the group. Most of the marriages are solemnised among the Rajput community members. Endogamy operates at the community level though there is no bar in marrying with the other highcaste Hindus. Junior sororate is allowed though its occurrence is occasional.

The age for marriage for both girls and boys is now above 20 years. The mates are acquired through relatives and friends. Marriage brokers, *navaas*, also fix marriage alliances against payment. Monogamy is the prevailing form of marriage. Dowry is paid both in cash and kind. Patrilocal is the common feature of residence. Divorce is permissible with religious and judicial approval. The reasons of divorce are maladjustments, insanity and adultery.

However, divorce is very rare among them. Compensation and maintenance is paid to the wife. The children are the responsibility of either parent, depending on individual cases. Divorcee, widower and widow remarriages are permissible. Though junior sororate is allowed, levirate in any form is not practised.

The families are extended as well as nuclear in form. The nuclear type is a common phenomenon in the urban centres and has even made a dent in the typical extended rural family structure. Elders are given due regard and respect. Avoidance and joking relationships prevail. Inter-family relations are quite cordial and firm. Conflicts or confrontations occurring in intra-familial kin bonds are very rare.

The parental property is shared equally among the sons while the dowry paid at the time of marriage to girls is considered as their share of the parental property. However, girls otherwise also as a matter of tradition do not demand their share in the ancestral property. Succession is through the eldest son. The joint family system is gradually being replaced by nuclear families.

Then women play an active role in the overall socio-economic and religious activities of the community. In rural areas, their women actively pursue agriculture-related activities besides tending the livestock. In urban areas, the women make a significant contribution to the family income. They participate in socio-religious functions or ceremonies. The women play a restricted role in politics, i.e. only to the extent of casting their votes. In comparison to their men, the women are relageted to a secondary position. A sizeable number of their women in cities are employed in white-collar jobs, teaching in schools or working as administrators, and a few of them are even doctors.

Pre-delivery restrictions are reported on the parturient mother. Her movements are restricted. The post-delivery pollution period is observed by these people. Some of them also follow the twelfth day post-delivery child ceremony like Katoch known as *suraj-darshan*.

The christening ceremony is ceremonial in a token manner. *Mundan* and *janeu* ceremonies are performed for the boys.

The marriage ceremony is performed at the bride's residence. Accompanied by guests, riding on a mare and holding a ceremonial sword in hand, the groom arrives at the bride's residence to perform *lagan*. The *barat* proceeds to the bride 's residence mostly after sunset. Besides performing seven rounds around the fire known as *rakady*, some circumambulate four times round the clan deity, i.e. Goddess Kalika. A feast is given by both the parties.

The dead are cremated after a ceremonial bath. The corpse is brought to the cremation ground carried by close family relatives and friends. The male heir lights the pyre. Death pollution is reported among them. *Rasam-pagri*, wearing a saffron or pink colour headgear after the fourth day consequent to the demise of a family member marks the end of the mourning. Annual *shradhs* are not a common practice among them. However, the fourth year ceremony after death, *chaubarsi*, is observed by them.

In the rural areas, Sens are essentially a land-owning community and they would normally not seek jobs not commensurate with their royal lineage. However, in modern times, their occupational pattern exhibits entry into white-collar jobs as administrators, engineers, doctors, police and defence personnel and entrepreneurs into trade and commerce.

Their links with the market exist directly and most of their transactions are conducted in cash. In rural areas, the barter system is still prevalent in a moderate form. The priests are drawn from the Hindu Brahman community of the region. These priests conduct all their social and religious ceremonies and rites. Disputes pertaining to property, familial fueds and marriage problems may be first sorted out by the Rajput Sabha, failing which legal remedies may be sought.

These people have an unspoken stratification operating at the Rajput community level necessarily linked to the closeness with the nobility in the past. Barring this, there is no differentiation linked to economic, social or educational factors. They regularly visit their clan deities besides the ones in the state like Vaishno Devi, Amarnath, Kheer Bhawani, Sarthal Devi. They also visit *pirs* and *faqirs*, irrespective of their religious affiliations.

They seem to exhibit a natural talent for sketching, painting, writing poetry and prose and cloth embroidery. They possess a rich tradition of folklore and folk tales. Music and dance is quite popular among them but their women do not participate in public dancing.

The Sens accept food and water from other Rajput communities as well as from other high caste Hindus. Inter-dining in urban areas is quite common. Marriages as a matter of tradition and preferences are solicited among other Rajput communities barring their own. There are no restrictions in marrying other high caste Hindus. These people have doctors, engineers, lawyers, teachers administrators, entrepreneurs, scholars and people holding white-collar jobs among them. Political leadership is confined to the village level.

Pursuit of education for their boys and girls is not quite common, though it is without any sex basis. The boys usually study up to college level or even beyond, depending upon their economic conditions. The girls study at least up to the school level, beyond which economic considerations play an important role. They make frequent use of modern medicare depending upon its availability. They use birth control methods and it is mainly their woman who get sterilized. Drinking water is available through pipelines in cities, while in rural areas, streams, springs and wells supplement the water requirements. They are also employed in retail trade, business and industrial ventures.

They are exposed to all media of communication—radio, newspapers, television and cinema. The railway head is located in the Jammu city. They use electricity, wood, kerosene oil, LPG as fuels. The attitude towards savings and investments is quite positive. Though they no longer are the rulers, they still carry the grace and elegance of the nobility.

ASHOK AIMA

SETCH/SES

The Setchs are *darzi* (tailors). In Jammu, they are known as Sochi while in Kashmiri language they are called Setch which is pronounced as Ses. The word *ses* is derived from *sisen*, the Kashmiri term for needle. The history and origin of the community is not known but it is believed that, before the advent of Islam in the Valley, the ancestors of the Setchs were Hindus and were converted to Islam thereafter. During the Mughal period, they were employed in the palaces as tailors. They are distributed in all the districts of Jammu & Kashmir but their main concentration is in Srinagar.

They speak Kashmiri and use the Arabic script among themselves; while communicating with the non-Kashmiris they use Urdu and Kashmiri. They wear dresses as that of the other Kashmiris such as *pheran*, *poch* trousers and cap. The women wear *salwar*, *kurta*, *pheran* and *puz*, which is worn on the head and is made of long plain cloth. The Setchs are non-vegetarian and eat mutton, fish and chicken. They do not consume beef as it is restricted in the Valley. Rice is the staple food of the community. Maize, wheat, *bajra*, barley and millets are also eaten but not as substitutes for rice. During winter, the consumption of maize is more. Bread is consumed in the morning and in the afternoon with tea. Pulses like gram, *moong* (green gram), *urad* (black gram), *masur* and *moth* (brown gram) are consumed by them. Mustard oil is used as the cooking medium. They eat the seasonal roots and tubers. Among the vegetables, cabbage, cauliflowers, pumpkins, brinjals, ladies' fingers, carrots, cucumbers, potatoes are consumed seasonally. Among the leafy vegetables, *hak* or *karam sag* (spinach) are the favourites.

Fruits are consumed in plenty as they are grown around their habitat abundantly. Tea is their favourite drink and very popular with the people. They consume it with salt. Tea is taken with sugar also. *Qahwa* is consumed occasionally. They consume milk and milk products in lesser quantity as milk is not easily available. They smoke *bidis*, cigarettes and *hookah*, and occasionally chew betel leaves.

Social divisions do not exist but they are differentiated into higher and lower ranks on the basis of economic status, occupation and educational attainment. Like many other occupational communities of the region, the Setchs too include the persons of different other communities and surnames such as, Mir, Dar, Ganai, Wani, Butt, Sofi and Malik. They occupy middle position in the economic and social hierarchy according to their own perception. Others also put them in the same rank. They enjoy the status of a clean occupational group.

The Setchs are an endogamous group but rules of endogamy are not strictly followed. They prefer to marry their sons and daughters within the community, but if no such match available, they accept girls or boys from any other community except the Watals. Normally, marriages take place when the boys and girls attain adulthood but, in earlier days, child marriages were prevalent. At present, the age for marriage for a boy is between 18 and 25 years and for a girl between 16 and 21 years.

In most of the cases, marriages are settled through negotiations either by a common friend of the two families or sometimes by a mediator known as *manzymyor*. Monogamy is the general practice though polygyny is permitted in the community. There is no marriage symbol. Dowry exists in kind only. Money for the bride (*mahr*) is fixed at the time of marriage (*nikah*) for future payment. Being patrilocal, the bride lives with her husband and in-laws after marriage.

Divorce is permitted in the community as in the other Muslim groups. Husbands can divorce in case of barrenness, adultery, maladjustment and insanity. Likewise, the wife can also seek separation on the grounds when the husband is absconding, does not bear the expenses of wife and children, or does not have sexual relations for more than three years. According to the Muslim rules, divorce may be given either orally known as *zabani* or by written document called *talaq-nama*.

When a marriage is dissolved by divorce, the woman is prohibited from remarrying within a specified period called *iddat*. If consummation of marriage has taken place and then there is a divorce, the duration of *iddat* is for three months and ten days or, if the woman is pregnant, it is till the delivery. The purpose for fixing the period of *iddat* is to ascertain the legitimacy of the child. The cases of divorce are rare in the community. Minor children are the responsibility of the father after divorce.

Widow, widower and divorcee remarriages are permissible but a widow is not allowed to remarry before the *iddat* period is over, which is four months and ten days. Remarriages are performed in a simple manner. Decrease in divorce cases, emergence of dowry system and practice of monogamy are the major changes which have taken place in recent years. Most of the families among the Setchs are nuclear, though in rural areas extended families are also found. Normally, a newly married couple establishes a new household after marriage.

Interpersonal relationships among the family members are amicable and due love and respect is paid to youngsters and elders. Avoidance relationships exist between the daughter-in-law and in-laws, between younger brother's wife and husband's elder brother and also with the outsiders and elderly relatives. A joking relationship is maintained between the husband's younger brother and sister-in-law, and between the husband and his wife's younger sisters. Property is divided among the sons, daughters and the widow of the deceased but the daughters get less than their brothers and the widowed mother. After the death of the head of the family, it is the duty of all the brothers to arrange their sister's marriage and bear the expenses involved therein. The succession pattern is followed in the male line and runs from the father to the eldest son. The only change is the breaking up of the joint family system and emergence of nuclear families.

Women have a status equal to that of men and play an important role in all the spheres of life. They have full right on the *mahr*, the amount of which was fixed at the time of *nikah* by the husband. It can be claimed by the wife at any time after marriage, but it is generally demanded at the time of divorce. They participate actively in agriculture, collection of fuel, bringing potable water and other household jobs. They play a vital role in the social and religious functions. Though they do not contribute much to the family income, they certainly help to augment it. They have decision-making powers and exercise control over the family expenditure.

Certain rituals and restrictions are observed in case of childbirth. The women are not allowed to carry heavy loads and do strenuous work during the first pregnancy. Delivery takes place at home, particularly in villages. A midwife, *warin* or *dai*, is called to assist the parturient mother and is paid in cash and kind. She may be from any community. Immediately after birth, a bath is given to the infant and a senior family member recites *azaan* in the ears of the baby. On first birth, bread and sweets are distributed among the relatives, friends and neighbours.

If the delivery takes place at the bride's parents' house, sweets are sent to her by her in-laws. Her mother-in-law also sends sweets and clothes for the baby. The ceremony is called *piaw*. The mother takes her first bath on the seventh day and the child is given a name, either by the family priest or any elderly person of the family. The ceremony is called *sunder* and is usually followed by a feast.

After forty days, the parturient mother is given another bath and allow her to perform the normal household jobs. After the child is six months old, the hair of the child is shaved off by the family barber and a feast is arranged on this occasion. This ceremony is called *zerakasi. Khatnahal* (circumcision) of the boy is done when he is two years of age. This is done by the family barber in rural area, but, in urban areas, it is done in hospital or at home by a surgeon. A big feast is arranged to mark the occasion.

The first ritual of marriage is called *gandum*, which is the engagement. During this ceremony the father of the bridegroom with some relatives visits the bride's place and offers some money to the bride and her father. This ceremony is followed by the ritual of *doon-leij* in which an earthen pot full of nuts and money is presented to the father of the bridegroom by the bride's father. The ritual of sending marriage invitation is called *dapanbata*. Another ritual called *malasbehoun* is observed in which the bride is prohibited from taking bath and do household jobs for at least three days before the marriage. This is followed by the ritual of *massmechravoun*. On this occasion, the hair of the bride is combed by the women relatives. The first day of the marriage is called *menziraat* in which *mehndi* is applied on the hands and feet of the bride at night. The second day of marriage is called *yenevoul*. On this day, the father of the bridegroom sends a few copper plates containing sugar candy, sugar balls, almonds, clothes and ornaments for the bride.

The *barat*, i.e. the marriage procession, is sent off by two or three rows of women singing in chorus for some distance. The procession is received at the house of the bride by the women. After this, the *nikah* ceremony is observed. It is presided over by the *maulvi* (village priest). Two types of *nikah* are observed in the community. One is *nikah asaltan*, in which the bride and bridegroom are both present and a marriage contract is written with their consent in the presence of the witnesses. The other one is called *nikah vilaitan* which is performed when the bride and bridegroom are minor and the consent is given by their parents. This type of *nikah* was prevalent in the past only. *Mahr* money, which varies from Rs. 9,000 to 21,000, is also fixed at the time of *nikah*. When the ceremony is over, a feast is served. The bride goes to live with her husband. At the time of the bride's departure, her female relatives follow her for some distance singing in chorus. The bride stays with her husband for seven days. A big feast called *wathal* is arranged in the night. After marriage, the bride starts living with her husband.

In the event of death, the dead body is bathed by a *snangor*, a professional, when the relatives and friends assemble. After this the dead body is placed in a *taboot* (coffin) wrapped in *kafan* (shroud), laid on the ground facing Mecca and the priest recites the *namaz-e-janaza* prayer. Thereafter, the *taboot* is carried to the graveyard where a *lahad* (grave) is dug by the *malkhos* (gravedigger). He is paid in cash and given tea with bread to eat. The body is placed in *lahad* and covered with stones and clay. On the fourth day, the priest, relatives and neighbours recite the Holy Koran to bring peace to the departed soul. The ritual is repeated on the fortieth day also. These rituals are called *chaharum* and *chehallum*, respectively.

The traditional occupation of the community is *darzigiri* (tailoring). They either run their own shops or work on contract basis in shops owned by others. Some of them are cultivators, particularly in the rural areas. Besides this, the members of the community are also working in the government and private organizations. The entire business transaction is done in cash only. In rural areas, they are simultaneously involved in agriculture and tailoring. Resources are controlled by individuals. Persons who are engaged in agriculture have a direct link with the local market which is fully regulated. Children may be seen working. The community is still devoted to its traditional occupation and do not want to leave it.

They do not have their own traditional caste or *biradari* panchayat and disputes, if any, are settled either by the head of the family or any other old person of the community. In villages, this is done by the village headmen or the *chaudhury*. Sometimes, cases are taken to the court of law.

They profess Islam and follow its dictum the *shariat* like the other Muslim communities of the state. They visit several sacred shrines and mosques on different occasions. Shah Hamdan, Charar-e-Sharif, Makhdum Sahib, Dastgir Sahib and Naqshband Sahib are their sacred places. They have their own *pirs* who are called to perform the birth, marriage and death rites. They observe the Muslim festivals in different months. Prophet Muhammad's birthday, Urs-e-Nabi, also known as Id-ul-Milad is celebrated on the twelfth of Rabi-ul-Awwal. On this day, the Prophet's relic of hair is displayed at the Hazratbal shrine. Meraj-e-Alam is celebrated on the twenty-sixth of Rajab and the hair relic is displayed on this day also. Id-ul-Fitr, Id-ul-Zuha and Shab-e-Qadr are other festivals which are observed in the community. Besides these there are certain other occasions like Urs-e-Shah Hamdan, Urs-e-Makhdum Sahib, Urs-i-Rafimal which are also celebrated by the community. All the festivals are of socio-religious and socio-economic importance.

Tailoring is the main craft of the community. A few members of the community are involved in embroidery, wood carving, papier mâché, carpet weaving and other traditional crafts of Kashmir. *Vanvun* (folk songs) are sung on different occasions by both men and women but only the women participate in the traditional dances of Kashmir.

Tailoring being an important occupation, the members of the community maintain amicable relations with all the communities of the region and extend their services even to the lowest castes like the Watals or Chamars. The Setchs are considered a clean occupational Muslim community and all the lower and higher communities of the area accept water, *kachcha* and *pukka* food from them. They too accept food from all the communities except the Watal, whom they avoid. The services of the *Pir*, *Nai*, Gorkun, Tarkhan and other Muslim communities are required on the occasion of childbirth, marriage and death rituals. They share water sources, burial grounds, religious shrines and other places of common interest with all the other Muslim communities. Intercommunity marriages are common among them. Patron-client relationships exist in the community.

The attitude of the community towards formal education is favourable for the boys only. In rural areas, they do not pay attention towards the girls' education due to social reasons. The girls study up to the primary level only. Because of the hilly terrain, educational programmes of the government could not be successful as the children have to walk at least 2 to 3 km. in order to reach the nearest school. This is why they are unable to obtain proper education. For higher education, they have to go to the cities. Their indigenous medicare system is still in practice. Though they favour the modern system of medicare, they often complain about the non-availability of medicine in the dispensaries. They do not favour the family planning programmes but, in urban areas, people prefer to have fewer children. Drinking water facilities through tap are available in their locality but, during winters, the supply is very poor and unsatisfactory. Springs and streams are their source of drinking water. Being involved in agriculture and the tailoring business, most of the members of the community are self-employed. Radio, television and cinema are the modes of communication and entertainment for only those who live in urban areas. Cow-dung cakes, wood and kerosene oil are used as fuel resources. They mostly depend on rain and stream water due to non-availability of irrigation facilities for agriculture. They use chemical fertilizers and insecticides in their fields to get better crops. Nutritional programmes initiated by the government have been properly implemented in their area. Facilities of food distribution system through the fair price shops are available and they avail themselves of them. They have a positive attitude towards saving and are not dependent on the moneylenders or shopkeepers.

ANAND SARAN

SHAKSAZ

Shaksaz has been derived from the Kashmiri words *shak*, meaning slender branches of trees or twigs, and *saz*, meaning the act of making or craft of weaving. The Shaksaz are an artisan community of Kashmir Valley. They are concentrated in Shaksaz mohalla of Charar-e-Sharif in the district of Badgam. Apart from Charar-e-Sharif, they are also distributed sporadically in Hazratbal and in various other parts of the district of Srinagar. Neither historical nor ethnographic accounts are available regarding the origin and migration of the community.

They claim to be the original inhabitants of the region. They speak Kashmiri among themselves and with others they speak Urdu. Arabic script is commonly used by them. They are enlisted in the constitutional category of Other Backward Classes. Rice is their staple food. They are occasional non-vegetarians but do not eat beef and pork. Roots and tubers of different varieties are consumed as vegetables. Fruits are consumed moderately. Tea and milk are the common non-alcoholic beverage for them. They are habituated to drinking salty tea or *noon-chai* without sugar and *qahwa* with sugar, milk and some spices prepared in the indigenous kettle or *samawar*. They do not take alcoholic drinks. Most of the adults are in the habit of smoking tobacco in the indigenous *hookah* called *jajir*, besides *bidis* and cigarettes.

There is no social division in the community. However, in terms of experience in a specific kind of basketry and the raw materials used for the same, they can be divided into two distinct sections. Apart from their specialization in different kinds of basketry work, there is no other area of differentiation between the two sections of the community. Like most other Muslims communities of Kashmir Valley they comprise persons having surnames such as Butt, Mir, Wage, Malik, Wani, Ganai, Dar, Shah and Khạn, which are also referred to as the Krams by Walter Lawrence (1985) and in the *Census of India*, 1961. Though there is no concept of any social status or hierarchy among them and the Muslims, in general, from their own point of view, they are of middle social status. Though endogamy at the community level is preferred, marriage with any Muslim community of the Sunni sect is not prohibited. Marriages are settled through negotiation. Consanguinity is permitted at both the levels of cross-cousin and parallel-cousin. Monogamy is the common form prevailing among them. Residence after marriage is patrilocal wherein the bride comes to live with her husband and in-laws. The amount of *mahr* (dower) is generally promised at the time of *nikah* for payment in future, if and when a *talaq* or divorce is sought. It is generally the privilege of the husband to divorce through social approval. Adultery, barrenness, maladjusment and cruelty are the common reasons behind divorce. Divorce compensation is generally paid to the wife's party. The responsibility of maintenance of the minor children in divorce cases generally lies with the father. Divorcees, widows and widowers are free to remarry.

Under the Islamic dictum, a female divorcee can remarry only after the completion of *iddat* or the period of restriction, which may be at least three months or may extend till the birth of the child, in case the woman is pregnant at the time of divorce. The restriction is imposed to ascertain the legitimacy of the expected child. The *iddat* period for a widow is fixed for four months and ten days within which she cannot remarry. Both levirate and sororate at the junior level are permitted in remarriage.

Nuclear family is the predominant type followed by both vertically and laterally extended types. Interpersonal relationship within the family is guided by the principles of love and affection for the young and respect and obedience for the elders. Avoidance prevails between husband's elder brother and his younger brother's wife. Joking and friendliness prevail with elder brother's wife's younger brothers and sisters, husband's younger brothers and sisters and also with parents-in-law of sons and daughters. Following the death of head of the family, the paternal property is divided among the sons, unmarried daughters and the widow of the deceased. The unmarried daughters get a smaller share than the sons and the widowed mother. Succession follows through the male line from father to the eldest son. Apart from performing a major part of the household chores, women participate in animal husbandry, collection of fuel and bringing potable water. They also contribute to the family income and play an important role in the social and religious spheres. They participate equally and exercise their authority with men in decision-making and controlling expenditure at the family level. In view of the above mentioned roles and functions and also by virtue of their right of claim on *mahr* at the time of divorce, women in the community are treated at par with men.

No ritual is performed before the delivery of a child. Immediately after birth, the child is given a hot water bath and the recitation of *azaan* is performed by an adult male member of the family or by a priest. On the following day, the ritual of *piaw* is observed through presentation of clothes and cash by the in-laws to the mother of the newborn. *Sunder* is the ritual connected with the first bath of the mother in hot water on the seventh day after the delivery. On this occasion, a priest is invited to recite verses from the Holy Koran and a name is given to the child followed by a feast to the neighbours and relatives. The mother again takes a hot water bath on the fortieth day and becomes free to resume her normal household work.

When the child is one year old the ritual of *zerakasi* is performed to mark the shaving of head of the child. On this occasion, dinner is served to the females of the neighbourhood and relatives. After attaining two years of age, generally at the age of three to four years, a male child is ritually subjected to *khatnahal* (circumcision). The occasion is marked by a feast which is arranged for neighbours, friends and relatives. *Gandum* is the ritual per-formed in connection with finalization of a marriage proposal. On this occasion, the bridegroom's father along with some relatives visits the bride's house and pays some token money to the father of the bride towards acceptance of the marriage proposal; in return the visitors are entertained to a dinner. After about a month, the ritual of *doon-leij* is performed at the bridgeroom's place wherein the bride's father is invited for dinner. The father of the bride presents in an earthen pot, nuts and cash less than that presented by the bridegroom's father at the time of the *gandum* ritual. The bridegroom's father, however, returns the amount of cash presented to him and retains only the pot full of nuts before the bride's father departs.

The ritual of formally extending invitation to the friends and relatives for the marriage is called *dapanbata*. The marriage date is fixed with direct and mutual consent of the two parties concerned. Three days before the actual marriage ceremony the ritual of *malasbehoun* is observed at the bride's residence wherein the bride-to-be is not allowed to work or permitted to take bath, and is served with dry food during this time enabling her to become slim and look prettier. This is followed by the ritual of *massmechravoun* which involves loosening of hair plaits of the bride when her hair is combed by the female relatives and neighbours. On the marriage eve, the ritual of *menziraat* is observed wherein the hands and feet of the girl are coloured with *henna* paste by the women, who are later entertained to a dinner.

On the following morning or on the day of *nikah*, the ritual of *yenevoul* is observed in which the bridegroom's party sends presents of clothes, ornaments and footwear for the bride. The bridegroom, in the meantime, gets ready and proceeds for the bride's residence accompanied by some male relatives and friends for the *niḳah* ceremony. Both bride and bridegroom are represented by a close relative at the time of *nikah*. The marriage contract and the amount of *mahr* fixed is entered in a document called *nikah-nama* with the names and consent of six persons comprising the bride and the bridegroom, their two representatives and two witnesses. The proceedings of *nikah* are conducted by a priest (*maulvi*). The occasion is celebrated through a grand feast. On the fourth day or the day following *nikah*, a feast, called *wathal*, is given by the father of the bridegroom at his place to mark the arrival of the bride at her in-law's place.

Following the death of a person the body is given a warm water bath by the professional bather called *snangor*. The body is then wrapped in a white piece of cloth (*kafan*) from head to toe. After that the body is put in a wooden box of about 7 feet in length, called *taboot*, and covered with another piece of white cloth. At the graveyard, the dead body is placed in the grave (*lahad*) prepared by the professional grave-digger called *malkhos*. The priest leads the funeral prayers before the dead body is put in the grave keeping its head towards the north. The grave is then covered with soil. Two stones are kept at the two ends of the grave as marks of identification. Thereafter, the mourners disperse. On the following four days they offer prayer at the mosque and at the grave in memory of the deceased. On the fourth day the *snangor*, *maulvi* and *malkhos* are paid off in cash. The ritual of *chehallum* on the fortieth day marks the closure of the death rituals with a prayer and feast to the neighbours and relatives.

The Shaksaz are basically a landless community and have been depending mainly on their traditional craft of basketry. Basketry also happens to be the primary occupation and source of livelihood for most of them. Majority of them are engaged in manufacturing *kangri*, an indigenous firepot which is an indespensable domestic article of every household in the Valley. The earthen pot is procured from the *kraals* (potters) and is embedded in a frame of basketry. The beautiful basketry work for the *kangri* is made up of the *kani* or slender branches of an indigenous plant called *pohu* grown in the woods. The base of the firepot basket is made up of slender branches of a plant called *kostu*. They also use the unbreakable sheath of a plant called *lince* to make colourful designs on the firepots. They have to obtain licence for procurement of the raw materials from woods owned by the *zamindars*. Apart from the *kangri*, this section of the community also produce various types of decorative basketry work, which are in demand among the tourists. Some of those items are cigarette cases, *phuldan* or flower vases, lampshades, *darkht* or tree, *zain* (fruit), *anz* (duck), helicopter, peacock, morocco cap or *topi* and helmets, glass holder and *dadi* (gate). Other section of them manufacture mainly from the slender willow branches called *kanz* or *tili*. Some of the important articles are *kursi* (chairs), lampshades, *chandbag* or moon shaped handbaskets, fruit trays, fruit bowls, flower vase and *mazhi* (baby-swings). This typical *kanz* or willow branch basketry is reported to have been introduced in the Valley by a Briton about one hundred years back.

The basketry items produced by the men, women and children of the community are marketed through the Anjuman-e-Shaksaz, a cooperative of the craftsmen and the government emporia. Sometimes they sell the products themselves. They have direct links with the fully regulated daily local markets through cash transactions. Children below fourteen years do work to earn for the family. Landlessness has made them depend more and more on the traditional craft of basketry.

Community level disputes pertaining to adultery and disrespect for traditional norms are dealt with by the informal council of elders of the community elected by voice vote through imposition of a cash fine. Though they are aware of the modern statutory panchayat in general, they have not been benefitted by the panchayat.

They profess Islam and belong to the Sunni sect. They are followers of the dictums of Islam called *shariats*. They visit different *dargahs* or sacred shrines and *masjids* (mosques) on various socio-religious occasions. Makhdum Sahib, Shah Hamdan, Naqshband Sahib and Charar-e-Sharif are the sacred places commonly visited by them. Urs-e-Nabi or Id-ul-Milad is celebrated in connection with the birthday of Prophet Muhammed. Id-ul-Fitr, Id-ul-Zuha, Shab-e-Qadr, Urs-e-Batmallo, Urs-e-Charar-e-Sharif, Urs-e-Makhdum Sahib, Urs-e-Pir Dastgir are some of the fairs and festivals celebrated by them. Basketry is the only craft known to them which happens to be their primary occupation. Women sing folk songs on various social occasions but do not participate in dance.

Traditional linkages with the neighbouring Muslim communities prevail through exchange of food and water, marriage alliances, sharing of water sources, burial ground, and visiting the sacred shrines. Linkages with the other neighbouring communities are also established through exchange and rendering of services in various socio-religious and economic spheres. Taking part in *julus* (processions) taken out on various socio-religious occasions also helps to foster traditional linkages with various other communities of the region. Small entrepreneurs, artists, service holders and teachers of the community help perpetuate linkage with different other communities at their respective levels.

Education for boys is favoured more than that for the girls. Boys generally study up to the secondary level and at times come up to college or even up to postgraduate level. Girls, on the other hand, generally study up to primary level only. The poor economic conditions and the need to support their family are common reasons for drop-outs among the boys. Poor economic condition and other social factors are the common reasons of dropping outs among the girls. Though modern medicare system is generally used, they disfavour the idea of family planning through adoption of any indigenous or modern method. Drinking water through taps is available within the locality. Though most of them are self-employed in basketry, they do not get subsidy or loans from the government for the procurement of raw material for their craft. The Anjuman-e-Shaksaz, their own cooperative society, has been extending great help to the craftsmen. They are exposed to the mass media and communication facilities of radio, newspaper, television, cinema, roads and post-offices. The nearest railway station is, however, located far off at Jammu and many of them have not seen it till today. Information is disseminated to them through the extension agencies and political parties. Though electricity is available, its supply becomes very irregular or even stops during winter. Firewood, cow-dung cakes, charcoal and kerosene oil constitute the main fuel resources for them. No nutritional programme is made available to them. They make full use of the fair price shops for the essential ration articles like rice, sugar, wheat and kerosene oil. They favour banking system but some of them depend on the moneylenders and local shopkeepers to some extent.

B.K. Basu

SIKLIGAR

The Sikligars are a small community, living in their exclusive small hamlet known as Sikligar Dikulyan in Bhor Camp near Jammu airport.

The Sikligar believe that they migrated from Rajputana some 400 years ago, when Maharana Pratap lost the battle against the Mughals, and settled in the present surrondings. They were called Sikligar by others with whom they interacted as the craftsmen who manufacture, polish and sharpen knives and such other tools used in day-to-day life by the common folk. It is important to note that the Sikligars are found living in larger numbers in the adjoining states of Punjab and Haryana and the union territory of Chandigarh and Delhi. They also live in smaller number in different townships of western Uttar Pradesh but, in Jammu & Kashmir, they are found living only at one settlement as mentioned above.

The Sikligars of Jammu claim that there is no cultural difference of any significance between them and their brothers in Chandigarh and Delhi and they have marital relations with the Sikligars of Muzaffarnagar and Dehradun and in other towns, with whom they have regular contacts.

The Sikligars are divided into a number of territorial units on the basis of present habitat. These are not sub-groups. As mentioned above, the Sikligars of Jammu & Kashmir are a numerically large and geographically widely distributed community with one name.

The Sikligars claim that they are Rajputs and part of the martial race which fought for their leader and hero, Maharana Pratap of Mewar. Beyond that, they have no tale to narrate of their origin. They also fail to give details about how they lost their status as a Rajput caste, and ultimately accepted the status of a Scheduled Caste in the social hierarchy in some states of the country.

The Sikligars in Jammu & Kashmir live in one settlement only and having about 180 to 200 households. Geographically, Jammu may be described as a region with a warm temperate climate, hilly terrain with high humidity and forests, medium rainfall and no snowfall. The Sikligars here are town-dwellers with no land and are dependent on others for their survival.

Among themselves, the Sikligars still speak their own dialect. They talk to others in Dogri and write in Devanagari script.

Men wear a typical headgear called *pagri* (turban) and they sport a beard. However, many men of younger generation neither use *pagri* nor have a beard and have no identification mark in their dress. They are not a Scheduled Caste in the Jammu & Kashmir state as mentioned above.

They are occasional non-vegetarians. On Sundays they eat pork. Their staple diet consists of wheat and rice, and gram, *urad* and *moong*, are the pulses they eat. Mustard oil is the cooking medium. They consume roots and tubers and other vegetables. Their fruit consumption is occasional and they consume milk and milk products to a limited extent. The men take alcoholic drinks occasionally. Women take non-vegetarian food but they do not drink. They do not smoke.

They are divided into exogamous groups called *gotras*. They could mention a few *gotra* names, for example, Tale, Tangra, Talpatiya, Patna and Duborha. They claim that there were many other *gotras* as well. There have been no significant changes as regards name of the community, surnames, *gotra* and title. They claim to belong to the Rajput caste in the Hindu hierarchical order but other communities consider them as a low order community and the Sikligars are fully aware of this fact.

The Sikligars, as a community, are endogamous but their *gotras* are exogamous. Adult marriage is the norm and, in recent years, the age at marriage has further risen. Marriages are negotiated by parents with the help of a middle man, called *raware* (one who receives). The married women use vermilion, *bindi* and toe rings as marriage symbols. The Sikligar follow the Hindu marriage symbols as rigidly as the other Hindu communities.

Dowry is practised among the Sikligars and is given in cash and kind. The amount and quantity depends upon the economic status of the family. The dowry is given as a gift and there is no fixed amount for dowry. The wife moves to her husband's place after marriage as the Sikligars are patrilocal. Divorce is not permissible in the community. It was possible a few decades earlier but now the elders settle the issue and they continue to live together. In case there is a divorce, it is only with public ceremony and social approval. It occurs only because of maladjustment and there is no compensation. Either of the couple can seek a divorce and the children are the responsibility of the father. However, divorce is among the Sikligars.

Remarriage is permissible for males and females in case of widowhood as well as in case of divorce. Junior levirate and sororate are practiced by them and, in such cases, the marriage ceremony is only formal and short. The Sikligars perform *kanyadan* ritual on the occasion of marriage. There are no significant changes in marriage except that age at marriage has increased and the incidence of divorce has declined.

The Sikligars have extended families and married brothers live together as long as possible. The grown-up sons continue to live with their father and they share the same household, hearth and economic activity. The economic activity of the Sikligars requires three to four persons hence they prefer extended family to nuclear family pattern. In such households, there is a definite code of conduct is observed. Age is respected more than the actual kinship and males are regarded superior to females. Based on these principles, there are avoidance relationships and relationships of familiarity.

The married women observe *purdah* and avoid their elderly male relatives. However, they have a joking and friendly relationship with the husband's younger siblings and cousins. Likewise, there are various other relationships which can be categorized with avoidance or joking, but all these are based on the principle of respect for age and sex. Since the Sikligars are a small community living together, there are multiple relationship between any two individuals and all individuals seem to be related to each other. The situation calls for a code of conduct. The Sikligars do have an effective caste panchayat even today.

The sons inherit their father's property in equal proportions and daughters do not claim any share. A father may give in his life time a larger share to any of his sons on some consideration for which the other sons may not object. In case a man dies leaving behind unmarried daughters, his sons bear the expenses for their sisters' marriages. The eldest son usually succeeds his father and inherits the assets and liabilities. He remains responsible for his deceased father's promises and obligations.

The families living in the neighbourhood share a great deal with each other among the Sikligars, irrespective of kinship ties among them. The Sikligars exhibit solidarity and unity among themselves because of their powerful caste panchayat.

The women among the Sikligars have a lower status than that of the men. They have no right to participate in caste panchayat meetings. At the same time, they have an important role to play in social and religious functions. Once a year, all the married women gather at a place of worship on *gungey navami* and no man is allowed to accompany them to the site. The men wait for their return after worship and break their fast only when the women have returned.

The economic activity is mainly carried out by the men and women only casually help them occasionally. The men bring the material, process the same, make what they have to and then they alone go out to sell their, finished goods. As such, women do not contribute to the family income and do not have decision-making power. However, they look after the household and regulate the family expenditure. The Sikligar women are usually illiterate and they remain tied to the household only.

The Sikligars observe no rituals before a childbirth. However, during advanced pregnancy, certain restrictions are imposed on an expectant woman lest there should be any complications. After childbirth, a pollution period is observed and there are certain restrictions on the mother as regards her movements, physical labour and other household activities. Most of the deliveries take place at home and experienced elderly women help in a childbirth. In some cases, the midwife, a woman with experience, may belong to some other community. In case there are any complications during the advanced stage of pregnancy, the childbirth takes place at a hospital. The woman remains confined in the room for the first 21 days and only after the pollution period is over, she allowed to cook food. *Mundan* ceremony takes place only for male children.

The marriage ceremony is an elaborate affair with four important components: *sagai*, *mangni*, *lagan* and *barat*. Once a marriage alliance is finalized, there is an engagement ceremony which is called *sagai*. This ceremony takes place at the bride's place. Then the girl's parents and relatives approach the boy and give some gifts. This ceremony is known as *mangni*. Then the date of marriage is fixed and this ceremony is known as *lagan*. Finally, on the appopinted day, the *barat* goes to the bride's place and the actual marriage ceremony known as *kanyadan* take place there. The bride's parents give a feast on this occasion and also give dowry in cash and kind. The consummation of the marriage takes place at the bridegroom's house. Adutlt marriage is the rule.

They cremate the dead and observe a pollution period. There is post-funeral rituals in which the community members participate and the *Granth Sahib* is worshipped. There are ceremonies after the six months and a year. They believe in a religion which is a combination of the two where there is importance of *Granth Sahib* and Hindu festivals are celebrated elaborately.

At present, the Sikligars are involved in a variety of occupations to earn their livelihood. Their traditional occupation, i.e. ironsmithy, is not enough to sustain them economically. On account of mechanization, their services are largely no more required. Hence they are now doing other jobs like working as masons, or daily wage labourers, though some of them are still depending on their traditional occupation of making small metal wares. They are primarily a landless community and depend on the individual labour of their menfolk as only the male are the earning members among the Sikligars. They are an extremely backward community both economically and educationally. None of them is in the government service.

The Sikligars still have direct links with daily market and there is no bonded labour, no child labour and the payments are made in cash.

The Sikligars still have an effective traditional caste council. All adult male members of the community are members of the council and have a right to express themselves. There is a head of the council selected by a voice vote and he presides over the meetings. Other members, aged and experienced, help him and the council in deciding the cases brought to them for decision and guidance. The women stay indoors and the men usually assemble at a distance from the settlement lest they are disturbed by women and children. The traditional caste council decides each and every case and dispute of the Sikligar community in these meetings. Marital maladjustment which may lead to separation, minor thefts, disrespect for traditional norms, general welfare of the community, all are decided by this council. The council may impose a temporary social boycott on the wrong-doer and thereby compel him or her or family to conform to the societal norms.

The Sikligars are Sikhs but they worship the Hindu deities also. The life-cycle rituals are performed in the presence of *Granth Sahib* and the religious specialists who officiate on all such occasions are from some other community. The Sikligars are wise and conversant with the religious activity. They celebrate various festivals and consider these of social and religious significance. They do not actually know the importance of all these festivals but continue the tradition by religiously following them.

They are expert in metal work and claim that they can prepare anything to specifications out of iron, the craft in which they are engaged for generations. They use percussion musical instruments on certain ceremonies and festivals.

They exchange food with communities with whom they are living and, on occasions of various festivals, they celebrate together. They eat with the Rajputs Dogras and Punchi Sikhs with whom they have social interactions. They visit the religious shrines and share water sources with other communities.

The community is extremely backward in educational attainment and, hence, they do not have any modern intercommunity linkages. The boys study up to secondary level in exceptional cases and girls generally do not recieve any formal education.

The Sikligars use both modern and traditional medicare systems and do not favour family planning to any appreciable extent. Drinking water is available within the locality. They use wood and kerosene oil as fuel resources. Ration shop facilities are available. They do have savings.

The Sikligars in Jammu are poor and still cling to their traditional metalwork occupation against all odds and have an independent identity in the region.

B. SINGH

SOCHI

The Sochis are a small community of Jammu region whose traditional occupation was stitching clothes for the zamindars and maharajas. The term *sochi* is derived from *soch*, also the Sanskrit word *suchika* or needle by which clothes are stitched. According to some of them the term *sochi* is derived from *sochna* or thinking. In the olden days, the maharaja, while giving cloth to a Sochi, used to say that it should be stitched after much thinking (*soch*) hence they have been labelled as Sochis. The community has no synonyms or subgroup. Sochi is the title affixed after the names but, generally, the community hide their titles. In the past, the community was identified by their occupation of stitching clothes by needles. Others identify them by their traditional occupation. Now they have discarded their traditional occupation and are engaged in a number of other occupations.

The origin and immigration of the community is not known. Ethnographic accounts of the community do not exist. They claim themselves to be Rajputs who were degraded because of their low occupation of stitching clothes. In 1984, this community was included within the larger Rajput community by a resolution adopted by the All India Rajput Sabha in Jammu. The community is distributed in Jammu and Udhampur districts of Jammu & Kashmir state. The villages inhabited by the Sochis are situated at the foothills of the Pir Panjal range of the outer Himalayas. The altitude varies from 2,500 to 3,000' above sea level. The terrain is covered with evergreen deciduous forests. The region experiences low rainfall as it falls within the dry *kandi* belt of Jammu. The Sochis' neighbours in the villages are the Muslim Gujjars, Rajputs, Brahmans, Meghs, Mahashe and Jheevars. They live in *kachcha* houses with flat roof. They speak Dogri among themselves and Hindi, Punjabi and Urdu with outsiders. The men wear *kurta* (long shirt), *pyjama* (trousers) and white turban. The women wear *salwar*, *kameez* and *dupatta*. The community is listed as Backward in the state.

The community eats non-vegetarian food occasionally. Their staple diet consists of wheat and maize. Rice is taken occasionally. The pulses taken are gram, *urad, moong* and *masur*. Milk and milk products such as curd, cheese and *ghee* are taken by those who can afford. Tea is a favourite beverage. They smoke *bidis*, cigarettes, and chew tobacco and *pans* (betel leaves). Alcoholic drinks are taken by men. There is a change from non-vegetarian to vegetarian food due to the rising cost of non-vegetarian food items. Besides this, rice is now used more often in their daily food. Roots and tubers consumed are radish, turnip, yam, potato and carrots.

The Sochis have no social divisions. They are, however, divided into exogamous *gotras* (*jatis*). The *gotras* are similar to those of the Rajputs, such as Jamyal, Maduria, Ishchar, Jaj, Pancho and Chandak. The differentiations within the community are due to economic, occupational and educational status which regulate their marriage alliances. Sochi as a surname or title is not preferred. The community places itself in the middle rank at the regional level, but other communities consider the Sochis below the Rajputs.

The community is endogamous, but the practice is not strictly followed. There are few cases of hypergamy in the community. Marriages are negotiated by a *bicholia* (middleman) or the parents, and the boys and girls are not consulted in the matrimonial affairs. For marriage of their daughters, they first try in the nearby villages. If a suitable boy is not found, then they try at Udhampur or even Jammu. In case of death of the wife, her younger sister is the next choice for marriage with the widower. But if the husband dies, the widow cannot remarry the husband's younger brother. Elder brother's wife, *bhabhi*, is respected as mother in the community. The age at marriage for girls is between 18 and 20 years. In case of boys, the age varies from 20 to 25 years.

The employed Sochi girls get an opportunity of selecting their spouses even outside their own community. Normally, such marriages are approved by the parents. The community practise monogamy but, in case of barrenness or serious illness, a second wife is considered necessary. The symbols of married women are vermilion, bangles, *bindi*, toe ring and nose pin. The practice of giving dowry, both in cash and kind, is prevalent but it is not demanded. The dowry is paid soon after the marriage rituals. *Kanyadan* ritual is performed by a senior male relative of the girl. The Sochis follow patrilocal residence after marriage.

Divorce is permissible in the community but is generally not practised. In case of maladjustment between husband and wife, the elderly members of the community or village elders persuade them to live amicably. Some changes have been observed in the marriage rules. There is an increase in the number of inter community marriages, exchange marriages are no more in practice and there is a liberalization of rules in case of widow remarriage.

The families are generally mixed-extended, but nowadays, owing to employment opportunities and shortage of cultivable land in the villages, the families are becoming nuclear. Interpersonal relations in the family are based on love and affection. The aged parents are given due care and respect. The father is respected as the head of the family. A woman looks after the household. She has to cook the food for the family and keep the house clean. *Purdah* is observed from the father-in-law and the elder brothers of the husband. In fact, the women observe *purdah* with all the elderly persons of the village. Joking relationship exists with the wife's elder and younger sisters and younger brothers, and between grandparents and grandchildren. Avoidance relationship is found between mother-in-law and son-in-law, daughter-in-law and father-in-law, younger brother's wife and husband's elder brother. Conflicts in family usually arise from disparity of income of married sons, for which the discontented couple is made to start a separate household. Thus an extended family breaks up into a nuclear family.

The father's propety is equally divided among all the sons. Now the girls can also get a share in their father's property but they do not claim it. Succession is in the male line. In case there are no sons, then the daughter's son becomes the successor. Some changes in the family pattern have been observed. The sons after marriage want to live separately. The aged parents are left alone in the village while the sons stay in the town.

The women play an important role in the family. The men only plough the field and make arrangements for irrigation, and women do the rest from sowing of seeds to the harvesting of the crops. They milk cows, collect fuel, bring potable water and do other jobs of the household. The women are in some cases also employed as peons in the school and contribute to the family income. They have an equal status with men and their advice is sought on important family matters.

Life-cycle rituals, as observed by the community, are similar to those of the Rajputs. In case of unusual delay in conceiving, the couples visit the temples of Vaishno Devi and Baba Buwa at Jhiri in Akhnoor to seek divine blessings. For a pregnant woman, there are no antenatal rites except that they abstain from doing strenuous work in the advanced stage of pregnancy. During the eighth month of pregnancy, *reetan* ritual is celebrated when the expectant woman's mother sends her some sweets, etc. A local *dai* from the Megh helps in the delivery of the child. On the fifth day after childbirth, the *punjap* ceremony is observed when the mother and the neonate are given a bath. The period of pollution comes to a close on the thirteenth day. The priest, *pandit* or any elderly person of the house suggests a name for the child. This ceremony is called *namsanskar*. The services of a priest are availed of to determine the first alphabetical letter with which the name should begin, which he does on the basis of the horoscope (*janam kundali*) that he prepares for the child. A feast is given to the relatives and friends on this day, who in return, make payments in cash called *sagun* to the grandfather of the newborn child. On the twenty-first day, the mother is free to resume her household activities. *Annaprashan* of the child is observed at the age of five to six months. It is a simple ceremony and no feast is given. *Mundan* is observed only in case of the male child. This is observed for the child in the third, fifth or seventh year. Generally, it is observed at the village temple or at the temples of Vaishno Devi or Baba Buwa. Thread-wearing ceremony is observed at the time of marriage.

The marriages are negotiated by the parents or guardian without any middleman. If the boy gives his consent after seeing the girl, then their horoscopes are tallied. On favourable tally, negotiations are finalized and the *thaka* ceremony is celebrated in which the girl's father offers the boy a gold ring and some sweets. Afterwards the ritual of *kurmai* is celebrated in which the girl's father offers more presents to the boy besides performance of customary ritual of applying *tika* on the boy's forehead. The date of *biah* or marriage is prescribed by the *purohits* (priests) of the two families. As the date of marriage draws near, a preliminery ritual called *karie-jarija* is performed in both the families involved in the marriage. The marriage lasts for three days. The rituals that are observed in a sequence are *saint butna*, *sehrabandi* and *tambul* before the marriage procession starts. *Saint* is performed in both the houses and the boy is tied a *sehra* on this occasion. *Butna* ritual is observed both for the bride and bridegroom. *Henna* is applied only to the bride. Before the departure of *barat*, the bridegroom is seated in a room and kins and friends offer him *tambul*. The *barat* then leaves for the bride's house with the bridegroom seated on a horse and led by a band party. The rituals observed at the bride's house are *milni*, *lagan* and *kanyadan*. The *milni* ceremony takes place at the outer gate of the bride's house. The *baratis* and relatives of the bride meet each other. The *baratis* are entertained with a vegetarian dinner. The actual marriage ritual or *lagan* is performed in a *bedi* by a priest amidst chanting of vedic *mantras*. Finally, the bride and bridegroom are made to go round the sacred fire seven times called *lavan-phera*. Then *kanyadan* ritual culminates the whole affair. The bride is given a send-off along with the dowry and the *barat* returns. If it is a local marriage, the bride stays on at her in-laws for a few days after which she visits the house of her parents along with her husband. This is called *pehla phera*.

The Sochis cremate their dead. The dead bodies of children below five years are buried by the riverside. There is a common cremation ground for all the communities on the banks of the river Jhajjar. On the death of the father, the eldest son lights the funeral pyre. All the sons of the deceased get their heads shaved. On the third day, the ashes are collected and immersed in the river. On the thirteenth day, the ritual of *tehrvin* is observed. The *charji* is called to conduct the rituals for the peace of the dead man's soul. A *pagri* is offered to the person who has lit the funeral pyre by his brother-in-law. A feast is given on this day if the deceased person is an old person. *Barkhi* is observed after one year of the death. There is no change in the life-cycle rituals except that they are now abridged to save expenses; for example; marriage has become a one-day affair and exchange marriages have been given up.

Agriculture has been the major occupation of the Sochis. It continues to be their major source of livelihood. Men, women, children and the aged are found engaged in one or the other agricultural activity. In busy agricultural season, all have to contribute to get the maximum produce. Small and scattered fields, lack of irrigational facilities, steep slopes, thin soil and stone-filled land makes agriculture difficult. The Sochi villages fall in the *kandi* or dry belt of Jammu. The rainfall is minimum and, in the absence of irrigational facilities, the farmers have to depend only on the rainfall for cultivation.

The river Jhajjar flows in a deep valley and ravine land is found along its banks hence the river water cannot be used for irrigation. Cultivation is possible only by making terraces. The crops grown are *kanak* (wheat), maize, millet, *bajra*, *rongi*, *moong*, pulses, *kulthi* gram, peas, sugar cane and mustard. The Rajputs and Brahmans are the major landowners. The Sochis cultivate their land either as a sharecroppers or on wage labour. Only a few Sochis are self-cultivators but their holdings are small.

Owing to poverty and small landholdings, the community is unable to produce sufficient crops to maintain their family for the whole year. They have also lost their traditional occupation of stitching clothes. In the olden days, they used to get clothes from the zamindars and the maharaja. Needle was the only instrument for stitching clothes. Sewing machines have now replaced the needles. Besides, other communities have also taken up the job of tailoring. Now the Sochis engage themselves in other occupations such as agriculture, wage labour, *mistry* (mechanics), shopkeepers, tea-shop owners, skilled workers in a confectionary shop, motor drivers and serving in the Border Security Force. Some keep cows and sell milk. A child above fifteen years of age has to work in a tea-shop or in a grocery shop due to poverty. They have direct links with the market.

The traditional caste council does not exist in the Sochi community. Disputes, if any, are settled by the elders of the community. The statutory panchayat exists, which has a number of villages within its jurisdiction. Its main role is to plan and implement the welfare and development programmes.

The Sochis are Hindus. They worship all the gods and goddesses of the Hindu pantheon. Krishna and Radha are worshipped in almost every house. Goddess Vaishno Devi is the regional deity and her shrine is visited on the occasion of marriage, childbirth, etc. The other deities worshipped are Suggar, Kali Bir and Sidh Gauria. For fulfilment of any desire, chain made of iron, *sangal*, is offered to the deity. Nag Panchami is observed in the month of August. The region is infested with poisonous snakes, hence Nag Panchami festival is observed with great reverence. Cases of snake-bite are referred to a *debra* who cures the victim by reciting *mantras*. If there is a sudden misfortune in the family and the members are suffering from disease or have other problems, they go to the temple of Baba Buwa at Jhiri near the border of Akhnoor district and offer a *sangal*. The community gets the services of *pandit*, *purohit* and *guru*. The *pandit* (priest) performs the birth and marriage rites. The *purohit* takes some gift called *dan* and performs the death rites. The guru may belong to any community who gives *diksha* or religious teachings.

Intercommunity relations are based on mutual inter-dependence. The Sochis live in the neighbourhood of the Rajputs, Brahmans, Maharajans, Khatris, Meghs, Mahashas, Tarkhans (carpenters) and Jheevars (jheer), etc. The Rajputs and Brahmans are the major landowners and Sochis are employed as agricultural labour in their fields. The Brahmans own shops and restaurants in which the Sochi are employed for preparation of the food items.

The Sochis accept water from all the communities except the Megh and Mahasha. They exchange cooked and uncooked food with the Rajputs and Brahmans and participate on the occasion of marriage and childbirth with other communities in the village. In the sphere of connubial relations, the custom demands that the Sochi should marry within its own group. But because of a small population and non-availability of suitable matches, they try to marry their daughters among the Rajputs, Khatris and Brahmans. The Rajputs and Brahmans, however, do not aspire to get Sochi girls in marriage.

Although the community has been included within the larger Rajput community by the regional Rajput Sabha in 1984, yet the Sochis are not given an equal status by the Rajputs. The community share the water sources with other communities. They have access to all the religious shrines. They share the cremation ground with other communities. They participate in the festival of Baisakhi with other communities like the Rajputs, Brahmans, Meghs, Mahashe, and Jheevars. The Sochis work in the fields of the Rajputs and Brahmans as agricultural labourers and also as sharecroppers. As agricultural labour, they get food and Rs. 15 to 20 per day. As sharecropper, they get one-third of the production of crops.

The national highway connecting Jammu and Srinagar is available to the Sochi villages. Other roads connect Jhajjar Kotli with Dansal, the block headquarter, and with Katra. There are no entrepreneurs, scholars, engineers, doctors and administrators in the community. Political leadership has not emerged due to poverty and lack of education.

Development programmes have certainly improved the general social and economic conditions of the community. The boys and girls have facilities to study up to higher secondary level and get employment. The Tourist Complex and the Thermal Power substation at Jhajjar Kotli have attracted a few shops along the national highway. The main beneficiaries are the villagers in the neighbourhood. The villagers have some difficulty in getting potable water. Tap water is not available. The water of the river Jhajjar is used for drinking and other needs. The river flows in the deep valley while the villages are situated on high hill tops. A primary health centre is available at Dansal block at a distance of about 5 km from the villages. The hospital facilities are available at Jammu or Udhampur situated at a distance of 35 km. from Jhajjar Kotli.

The community is aware of the family welfare programmes. Generally, the men get themselves sterilized. Programmes such as IRDP, Anganwadi, social forestry, etc., have improved the general social and economic conditions of the villages. Electricity is available in the villages. The sources of domestic fuel are wood, cow-dung cakes, coal, kerosene and sawdust. Chemical fertilizers, high yielding variety of seeds and agricultural implements are available through the Block Development Office. Facilities of ration through the fair price shops is available where they buy wheat, sugar and kerosene oil.

The rural banks provide loans for purchasing milch cattle, fertilizers and small scale industsries, but the Sochi are not the beneficiaries. The community is struggling to get its rightful place among the Rajputs having lost their traditional occupation.

PARMANAND LAL

SOFI

Sofi or *sufi* is a Persian word meaning a person who wears garments made by patching together small pieces of cloth of different colours. This type of apparel was used by mendicants who lived a life of self-renunciation. In course of time, the attendants of religious preachers who rigidly followed the pattern of living of their masters were also known as Sofis. As they were held in high esteem and respected everywhere, even others who had nothing to do with any religious leader were addressed as Sofis as a mark of respect. For reasons which are not known, all the Muslim bakers in the Valley are called Sofis. The presumption is that some of their ancestors were closely associated with the religious preachers and had adopted this name.

According to Colonel Lawrence, the Sofis are the descendants of the Brahmans who embraced Islam. They adopted different occupations. The Sofis found in the southern part of Kashmir are mostly cultivators while those living in the northern part, particularly in Sopore are in business and own shops. At present, a majority of the Sofis in the Valley are bakers and are engaged in preparing and selling bread. They are also identified in the Valley by the term *kandur*.

The community is found in almost all the districts of Kashmir Valley. They are also found in the Amritsar and Ludhiana districts of Punjab. According to Colonel Lawrence, their population once extended up to Lahore and Peshawar, now in Pakistan.

The natural environment of Kashmir Valley is cold and the temperature falls below freezing point from December to March. The average height of the Valley is 1,600 metres above the sea level. The residential pattern consists of a linear cluster of houses with regular open space and with a street lined on either side by rows of houses.

In the town, a bakery shop of a Sofi is invariably found adjacent to the meat shop of a Ganai and the milk shop of a Goor. According to the 1931 census, their population was mentioned to be 11,500. They use the Arabic script for writing. They speak Kashmiri among themselves and Urdu with outsiders. They dress themselves like the other Muslims of the Valley. They are listed as an economically and educationally backward class in the state.

The community is non-vegetarian. They eat mutton but beef is taken occasionally. Their staple food consists of rice, wheat and maize. Pulses such as gram, *urad*, *moong* and *masur* are taken by the community. Mustard oil is the cooking medium. Potato, carrot, onion, garlic and radish are also consumed. *Karam hak*, a leafy vegetable, is an important item of their daily food. The people are not used to taking milk. *Noon-chai* (salty tea) is relished very much and is taken both in the morning and evening. Butter and *ghee* though available is not used in the daily food. People smoke *hookah* and cigarettes and a large majority rub their teeth with snuff.

There are no social divisions within the community. Differentiations, if any, are due to education, occupation and economic status and these factors also regulate their marriage alliances. The Sofis of Brahmanical origin are generally found among gardeners, bakers and servants. A Sofi may give his daughter in marriage to any Muslim except the Watal provided he belongs to equal status or occuption. They are considered of middle rank by other communities and they consider themselves to be under the Sheikh category.

The community practices endogamy but it is not strictly followed. Cousin marriages are preferred. In case of non-availability of a suitable match within close relatives, they select the boys from distant relations. Sororate and levirate marriages are allowed provided they are of matching age. Marriages are settled after attaining adulthood. Mates are acquired through negotiations. A common friend or relative initiate the negotiations.

In the cities, the services of the marriage negotiator *manzymyor* is obtained. When a proposed alliance is agreed upon by the concerned families, a convenient date is fixed for the formal announcement.

The women's status is inferior to their men. Women bear the major burden of domestic duties. They cook food, bring potable water and wash clothes. The wife assists her husband in his bakery. The family expenses are controlled by the husband. A woman is not allowed to carry heavy loads during the period of pregnancy. Further, visitors and even members of the family returning home late at night after a long journey are avoided by her. Women who are going to become mothers for the first time do not live for more than first five months of their pregnancy with their husbands, and spend the remaining period at their parental house. The delivery of the child generally takes place at the hands of a midwife, *dai*. She is paid a modest fee and receives gift of some sugar, rice, wheat and maize. Immediately after birth, the baby is given a bath in lukewarm water. *Azaan* is whispered into the baby's ears. On the seventh day after delivery, the woman takes her first bath with lukewarm water. Well-to-do families organize recitations of prayers by the priests who are adequately remunerated. On this day, the child is also given a name in consultation with the family priest or some learned men. On completing forty days, the woman is given a second bath. From this date onwards, she resumes her normal life. The first hair cut or *zerakasi* is done when the child attains the age of six months. The *khatanhal* (circumcision) ceremony of the male child is usually performed when the child is more than two years old. It is done by the village barber who gets paid in cash and kind. Nowadays, the operation is conducted by a surgeon.

The boys and girls do not enjoy the freedom of selecting their spouses according to their choice. The selection is the exclusive privilege of the parents or the guardians. Early marriages which were once very common have been discarded. Generally, a common friend or relative starts negotiations at the initiative of one of the parties. When the proposal receives agreement or the parties express their consent to the proposed marriage alliance, a convenient date is fixed for a formal announcement. On this day, the bridegroom's father accompanied by one or two close relatives visits the house of the bride and presents a sum ranging from Rs.11 to 121 in a cup to the host signifying the acceptance of the relationship. This ceremony is called *gandum* (engagement). A month later this is followed by the ritual of *doon-leij*. On this occasion, the bride's father accompanied by his two or three relatives calls at the house of the bridegroom. He also places equal amount of cash in the cap and supplements it with a big earthen pot full of dry walnuts.

The mates are also acquired through exchange of sisters which reduces the burden of marriage expenses on the parties concerned. Monogamy is the usual form of marriage. In case of barrenness or serious disease, a second wife is taken but only with the consent of the first wife. A few cases of polygyny also prevail in the community. No marriage is permissible unless the *mahr* (dower) and the *than* (clothes) are settled in advance. The former means a cash payment ranging from Rs. 200 to 400 and even more according to the status of the families involved, and the latter denotes jewellery worth 36 *asharfis*, a gold coin now out of circulation, or about Rs. 300. The *mahr* is paid in two instalments. In actual practice, however, no instalment is paid except in cases where a marriage is dissoved at the instance of the bridegroom. The bride, after marriage, goes to stay with her husband. A few cases of *khanadamad* (uxorilocal) have been reported in the community. This happens when there are only daughters and the father of the daughters may prefer to keep the husband of the eldest daughter as *khanadamad*.

The date of marriage is announced by the intermediary in consultation with the parties concerned. As the date of marriage draws near, several ceremonies are performed in succession. These begin with *malesbehoun*, *massmechravoun* (loosening of hair plaits of the bride), *malamenz* or applying a myrtle paste on the hands and feet of the bride, and ends with *menziraat* the night of marriage. All these rituals are performed at the house of the bride.

The second day of marriage called *yenevoul* is most important. It starts with the despatch of a number of copper plates containing sugar candy, almonds, dresses and ornaments by the groom's father for the bride. On this day, all the members of the bride's household and relations make arrangements for the reception and feast to be served in the evening to the bridegroom and the guests accompanying him.

After the arrival of the *barat*, arrangement is made for the *nikah* ceremony which is presided over by the village priest. *Nikah* can also take place much before the actual wedding. Usually, three types of *nikah* are found among the community: *nikah vakalatan* (through attorney), *nikah asaltan* (personal attendance) and *nikah vilaitan* (through guardian). The last type of *nikah* was practised in the past when early marriages were prevalent.

The bride then goes to the house of the bridegroom and stays for seven days. The day following the arrival of the bride, a feast is given by the father of the bridegroom. It is called *wathal* (thanksgiving). Sometimes, the bridegroom is invited by his in-laws where he stays for three days and this is known as *phirsal*.

Both the husband and wife are free to divorce. If the husband is not able to meet the expenses of the wife, has no sexual contact with the wife for more than three years, or is suffering from chronic sickness or insanity and resorts to physical violence, then the wife may seek separation. On the other hand, if the wife has extramarital relations, is barren or is suffering from some chronic sickness or insanity, then the husband may seek a divorce. It is usually the husband who seeks divorce. A wife seeking separation is rare. The husband seeking divorce is first persuaded by the relatives and elderly persons of the village to reconsider his decision. In case they are not successful, then both may be separated and sufficient time is given for reconciliation.

Divorce is the last resort and is sought in writing in front of the *qazi* which later on takes the form of judicial approval. The wife has to observe *iddat* for a period of one hundred days before she remarries. In case of the wife seeking *khula* (separation), she has to return the ornaments and clothes to her husband. The children are the responsibility of the husband in case of divorce. The wife can keep the children so long as they are breast-fed. Widow, widower and male or female divorcee remarriages are permissible. Sororate (junior) and levirate (senior) are possible provided the spouses are of the marriageable age. The incidence of divorce has shown an increase.

The families are normally mixed-extended type. Often a household consists of the parents and their married and unmarried children. The married sons with their children stay in separate rooms with a kitchen within a dwelling unit. Interpersonal relations within the family members are based on respect for the elders and love and affection for the young. The daughter-in-law does not observe *purdah* (seclusion) from her father-in-law. The younger brother's wife does not avoid the elder brother of her husband. Joking relations are observed within the permissible limits of kin groups.

Conflict and confrontation arise on property matters. Any attempt to put a check on the freedom of youngsters sometimes causes conflict with the elders. The father's property is divided among the sons and daughters. After the death of the father, the property is divided into three shares. The first share goes to the widow. The second share is divided equally among the sons. The third share is given to daughters. The ratio is two to one between the sons and daughters. Succession is from the father to the sons. The families are becoming nuclear due to urbanization and increase in the employment opportunities.

The body of a dead person is given a bath in warm water by the professional bather called *snangor* after which the body is wrapped in *kafan* (white sheet) and placed in the wooden *taboot* (coffin). The *taboot* is then carried to the graveyard. The grave is dug by a professional grave-digger called *malkhos*. The body is then placed in the grave and covered with earth and stone. Mourning is held on the following Friday. On the fourth day after the death, the priests, relatives and neighbours recite the Holy Koran to bring peace to the soul of the deceased. This is repeated on the fortieth day. The two rituals are called *chaharum* and *chehallum* respectively. The change observed in the life-cycle rituals is the curtailment of the rituals.

The community is landless. Even in the rural areas, the Sofis have no land for cultivation. Although it is mentioned by Fouk (1934: 368) that a major section of the Sofis inhabiting the northern part of the Kashmir Valley were cultivators, now most of them earn their livelihood from the preparation and sale of bakery products. Some of the items prepared are *tochur* (bread), *lawas* (bread prepared for the mourning), *bakerkhani*, *kulcha* and biscuits. These items are prepared in an oven and sold in the shops. Sometimes the oven and the shop are located in the same house. The owners of bakery shops engage bakers for the preparation of the products. Apart from baking bread, the members of the community also do odd jobs to supplement their income.

The traditional caste councils have become defunct. As a matter of fact, there are no caste panchayats in the villages. There are, however, statutory panchayats and multi-purpose cooperative societies to look after the interests of village communities. The statutory panchayat consists of eleven members of whom eight are elected. The other three members are nominated by the state development commissioner from a panel of names sponsored by the outgoing panchayat under the Panchayat Act. The panchayat is vested with contracts not exceeding Rs. 150 in value, recovery of movable property and damages caused by cattle trespass.

In actual effect, however, the panchayats have been confining their activities to the settlements of petty disputes among the villagers and execution of minor developmental works. The change observed is that the criminal offences are now referred to the police.

The community profess Islam, but there are also a few Hindu bakers in Tulmula who are also called Sofi. The majority of the Sofis in Kashmir are Muslims of the Sunni sect. The shrines and sacred places visited by the members of the community are Hazratbal, Shah Hamdan mosque, Jama Masjid, Ziarat Dastgir and shrine of Sheikh Zain-ud-Din, etc. The religious specialists of the community are the *pirs* and *imams.* The villagers believe in the influence of evil eye. They escape this by wearing the amulets supplied by the village priest on the arms and round the neck.

The *pir* is the spiritual guide and the *imam* leads religious prayers in the mosque. The *maulvi* performs the birth, marriage and death rites. The community observes all the Muslim festivals such as Muharram, Id-ul-Zuha, Id-ul-Milad, Rabi-ul-Awwal, Id-ul-Fitr, Shab-e-Barat.

The women spend their leisure time in knitting and embroidery. Folk songs such as *vanvun*, *wayun*, and *rouf* are sung on the occasion of marriage, betrothal and festivals.

The community's relations with the other Muslim and Hindu communities are based on mutual interdependence. In the villages, the Sofis live with other communities such as the Mir, Wani, Shah, Khadim, Baba, Bhats, Pir, Lone, Ganai, Sheikh, Tantrey, Zargar, Gilkar, Gujri, Naik, Waza, Rather, Beg and Watal. The services of the Sofis are available to all the communities on the occasion of marriages or festivals. In return, other communities participate and offer their services. There are some specific occupational relations of the Sofis with the Gujris and Ganais.

The Gujris are milk sellers and the Ganais sell mutton. It has been observed that quite often the Sofis live in the neighbourhood of the Ganais and Gujris. In the cities their shops are contiguous to each other. The Sofis accept food and water from all the communities except the Watals. Intercommunity marital exchange is possible with any Muslim community of equal status and occupation except the Watal. The community shares sources of drinking water, burrial ground, religious shrines and traditional festivals with the other Muslims. The Sofis put up stalls on festivals. The community has entrepreneurs, teachers, administrators and political leaders.

The community is aware of the development programmes. It has certainly improved its socio-economic conditions in the rural and urban areas. Earlier the boys and girls received only religious education in the mosques, *madrasas* or primary schools but now they are getting educated up to university level. English medium schools are available in the towns and parents want that their children to be taught in those schools. They have a positive attitude towards health care and modern medicine. In the olden times they depended on the local quacks, indigenous medicines and amulets, but now they visit the primary health centres and hospitals in case of illness.

For child delivery they prefer to go to the hospital. The couples now prefer two or three children and take measures for birth control. Tap water is now available in most of the villages. Some families have found employment under the IRDP. A few have received financial help from the rural banks. Radio and television are available in the urban and rural areas. A few families in Srinagar own television sets. Most of the villages are electrified. Kerosene oil, cow-dung, firewood and coal are the main sources of domestic fuel. Facilities of fair price shops are available to the villagers. Permits are also issued to their bakery shops for dealing in production and marketing of bakery products. Banking facilities are available in villages but loan facility is available only to those who have some landed property. Others depend on the moneylenders.

PARMANAND LAL

TANTREY

According to *Tarikh-e-Aqwam Kashmir*, the Tantrey a little known Muslim community of the Kashmir Valley, were the people who knew *tantar* or religious hymns. In the village survey monograph of Zachaldars, *Census of India*, 1961, Jammu & Kashmir, it has been mentioned that Sir Lawrence related the Tantreys to the Kshatriya and was of the opinion that they are great fighters. The author of *Tarikh-e-Hassan* also admits the relation of the Tantreys to the Kshatriyas and their fighting qualities. The Tantreys were very much known in the political history of Kashmir during the ancient Hindu rule. Now they have mitigated all the differences of caste and blood and have taken to the cultivation of land. They are mainly found in the districts of Badgam and Baramula of Jammu & Kashmir. They claim to be the original inhabitants of the region. They inhabit cold climate with hilly terrain and valleys experiencing medium rainfull and medium to heavy snowful during the winter months. They speak Kashmiri among themselves and with the other Kashmiris. With the non-Kashmiris, they speak Urdu. Arabic is the script commonly used by most of them. They do not belong to any constitutional category of communities.

Rice is their staple food. They are non-vegetarian and do not eat pork and beef. Various roots and tubers are consumed commonly as vegetables. Consumption of fruits among them is higher compared to that among other communities of the plains. They are fond of drinking salty tea prepared in their indigenous kettle called *samavar*. Most of them smoke the indigenous *hookah*, besides *bidis* and cigarettes.

The *krams* (clans) reported among them are Chethan, Chakpura, Aklitiura, Ramahama, Atina, Dans, Dhulipura, Lasipura, Malpura, Dausura and Gondipura. According to Sir Walter Lawrence (1895) 'The Sheikhs . . . are the descendants of Hindus, but have retained none of the caste rules of their forefathers. They have clan names known as Kram; but a man of the Tantrey *kram* may marry a girl of the same *kram*. . . .' Some hold that the *krams* known as Pandit, Kot, Bat, Aitu, Rishi, Mantu and Ganai are descended from the Brahmans, and that the Magres, Tantreys, Dars, Dangars, Rainas, Rathors, Thakurs and Naiks have sprung from a Kshatriya background. The Lon *kram* is assigned a Vaishya descent, and Damars are connected with the Shudras.

In the village survey monograph of Mattan, *Census of India*, 1961, Jammu & Kashmir, it has been mentioned 'that with the exception of a few cases the entire Hindu population of Kashmir belonged to the Brahmin caste and were broken up into numerous *gotras* which number 133. The members of each *gotra* claim to be the descendants of the *rishis* (saints) after whom *gotras* had been named. These *gotras* include various *krams* or tripple subdivisions such as Koul, Kichloo or Khar.

Differentiation does exist between the families at the levels of economic conditions and occupational pursuits, but these differentiations do not have any social implication as such. Tantrey is the only surname commonly used by them. They claim that there is no concept of any status or hierarchy among the Muslim communities in general, as is generally found among the communities of other religions.

Though they prefer marriage within their own community, marriage with the other Muslim communities of the Sunni sect is not prohibited, excepting the Watal, Najjar, Karal, Ganai and Hajjam. Consanguinity prevails both at cross-cousin and parallel-cousin levels. Adult marriages are generally settled through negotiations. Though they are permitted to marry four times under the Islamic rules, monogamy happens to be the common form of marriage.

They do not have any symbol denoting the marital status. Only the husband is permitted to divorce through oral consent or *talaq-nama*, i.e. written document of social approval. Adultery, barrenness and maladjustment are the common reasons for divorce. Divorce compensation is paid to the wife. The father is responsible for the maintenance of the children in divorce cases so long they are minors. Remarriages of divorcees, widows and widowers are permitted. Under the Islamic law, a female divorcee is permitted to remarry only after completion of the *iddat* or period of restriction which may be at least three months and ten days or may extend till the birth of the child in case the woman is pregnant at the time of divorce. The logic behind imposing the restriction is to ascertain the legitimacy of a possible child. Similarly, the period of *iddat* for a widow is fixed for four months and ten days within which she is not permitted to remarry. Both junior levirate and sororate are permitted in remarriages.

Both vertically and laterally extended families are the predominant types, followed by the nuclear family among the Tantreys. Interpersonal relationship at the family level is guided by the principle of love and affection for the young and respect and reverence for the elders. Avoidance is maintained between the daughter-in-law and father-in-law, and also between husband's elder brother and younger brother's wife. Joking relationship prevails among younger brother and sisters-in-law, elder brother's wife and also with the parents-in-law of sons and daughters. Following the death of head of the family, the property of the deceased is divided among the sons, daughters and the widow. The daughters get less than their brothers and widowed mother. Succession is followed in the male line from father to the eldest son.

As has been already mentioned, women have the right of claim on the amount of *mahr* fixed at the time of *nikah*, if and when divorce is sought. Apart from performing the household chores, the women participate in agricultural activities, animal husbandry, collection of fuel and bringing potable water. They also contribute to their family income directly and indirectly. They play an important role in the social and religious spheres of life. They do take part in the decision-making process and exercise control over the expenditure at the family level. The women enjoy status equal to that of the men in the community.

Prior to the delivery of the child, no ritual is performed in that connection. The parturient mother is not allowed to carry heavy loads. The birth of a child generally takes place at home with the help of a *dai* (midwife) who may be an elderly experienced woman of the village or neighbourhood. Sometimes, the delivery takes place in a hospital in Srinagar. The child is given the first bath immediately after delivery and then an elderly male member of the family recites *azaan* from the Koran in the ears of the child. This ritual called *piaw* is followed by distribution of bread and sweets among the relatives and friends. The ritual of *sunder* is marked by first bath of the mother on the seventh day and giving a name to the child by the family priest or an elderly member of the family, which is followed by a feast. The new mother is permitted to resume the household work after taking the second bath on the fortieth day. Tonsure, *zerakasi*, is the ritual connected with the shaving of hair of the newborn child by the family barber after six months. The occasion is marked by a feast. When a male child becomes two years old or more, the most important ritual of circumcision, *khatnahal*, is performed. The circumcision of the child is performed either by the family barber or a surgeon, followed by a feast. *Gandum* is the ritual marked for finalizing the match making through presenting some gifts and cash by the bridegroom's party to the bride's party. Similarly, *doon-leij* is the ritual observed through reciprocal gift of an earthen pot full of nuts and cash both by the bridegroom's father and the bride's father. *Dapanbata* is the ritual of formally inviting the relatives for the marriage. *Malasbehoun* is the ritual observed at the bride's residence in which the bride is not allowed to take a bath and do any household chores for at least three days preceding the marriage.

The ritual of hair dressing of the bride by her female relatives is called *massmechravoun*. *Menziraat* is the ritual of adorning the hands and feet of the bride with the dye paste of *mehndi* or *henna* two days before the marriage. *Yenevoul* is the ritual observed on the day preceding the marriage wherein the bridegroom's father sends a few copper plates containing sugar candy, sugar balls, almonds, dresses and ornaments for the bride. The ceremony of *nikah* or actual marriage is performed at the residence of the bride under the supervision of a *maulvi* or priest.

Nikah may be of two types, namely *nikah asaltan* or the actual form of *nikah* practised and *nikah vilaitan*. In *nikah asaltan*, which is a common practice, the marriage contract and the amount of *mahr* fixed are written on a *nikah-nama* or marriage document in the presence and with the consent of the bride, bridegroom and others as witnesses. *Nikah vilaitan*, on the other hand, is the type prevalent in the past when child marriages were practised. In this form of *nikah*, the parents used to give their consent for the marriage on behalf of their sons and daughters. *Nikah* is followed by the ritual of *wathal* wherein all the guests and invitees are entertained through a grand feast by the father of the bridegroom on the marriage night.

The dead are always buried. Following the death of a person, the dead body is bathed in warm water by a professional bather or *snanagor* in presence of relatives and friends of the deceased. The dead body is then wrapped up in a *kafan* which is a white piece of cloth after removing the clothes from the dead body. The *taboot* (coffin) is kept ready for placing the dead body in it. The clothes of the deceased along with some cash are given to the *snanagor* as remuneration for the services rendered by him. The coffin is carried to the graveyard where the body is lowered down into the grave or *lahad* dug out by the *malkhos* or grave-digger after *namaz-e-janaza* (funeral prayers). The *malkhos* is paid in cash along with breakfast. The coffin, after being placed in the *lahad*, is covered with stones and earth. On the fourth day friends, relatives and neighbours assemble at the residence of the deceased to attend the recitation of the Koran by the *maulvi* to mark the observation of the ritual of *chaharum*. Mourning is observed for forty days. The recitation of the Koran is organized to mark the observation of the ritual of *chehallum* on the fortieth day or completion of the pollution period.

Land has been the main natural resource of economy for them from time immemorial. Most of them possess some land. The average size of landholding generally varies from 5 to 20 *kanals* according to the local scale. The land is owned individually. Agriculture is their traditional and primary occupation. Besides this, most of them are engaged in secondary occupations of embroidery on woollen shawl known as *saznikaan*, weaving of *namda* or raw woollen spreads, working in mulberry sericulture farms and private and government services to supplement their income. The plain shawls and table cloths are collected from the wholesale dealers by the middlemen and supplied to them for *sazni* (embroidery). The men, women and children remain engaged in this work particularly during the winter months when agricultural activities are lean. Out of the total cost of embroidery work, 80 per cent of it is paid to the craftsmen and the rest 20 per cent is retained by the middlemen as their commission. The cost of embroidery varies according to its quality. Excepting shawl embroidery, they have direct link with the fully regulated daily local markets through exchange of cash. Bonded labour system does not exist among them in any form but children work to earn to supplement the income of their parents. Inadequate size of landholding have compelled many of them to depend on the secondary sources of income mentioned above.

The traditional council or panchayat does not prevail at the level of the community or the village. Problems and disputes at the community level are dealt by the informal council of elders. The council generally comprises of elderly male members of the community elected by voice vote or consent of the community members. Chieftainship does not exist among them. Though they are aware of the existence of modern statutory panchayat, they are not aware of its role and function.

They profess Islam and belong to the Sunni sect. They believe in Allah and follow the *shariat* or dicta of Islam. The community as a whole is affiliated to a *pir* whose services are required in connection with ritual performances at the family level. They visit various sacred shrines, *dargahs* and *masjids* (mosques) on different occasions. Charar-e-Sharif, Makhdum Sahib, Shah Hamdan, Dastgir Sahib and Naqshband Sahib are some of the sacred places commonly visited by them. Like most of the other Muslim communities of the region, they observe and celebrate different fairs and festivals. Urs-e-Nabi is celebrated to mark the birthday of Prophet Muhammad which is also known as Id-ul-Milad. Id-ul-Fitr, Id-ul-Zuha, Shab-e-Qadr, Urs-e-Shah Hamdan, Urs-e-Batmaloo, Urs-e-Charar-e-Sharif, Urs-Makhdum Sahib, Urs-e-Pir Dastgir and Urs-e-Naqshband are the fairs and festivals celebrated by them. There is no art or craft which is characteristic of the community. However, the weaving of *namda* and making exquisite embroidery on woollen shawls is the craft known to them, like many other communities of the valley. The women sing folk songs on various social occasions. They neither use any traditional musical instrument nor participate in traditional dances.

Traditional linkages with the neighbouring Muslim communities prevail through exchange of food, marriage alliances, sharing of water sources, burial ground, visiting the same religious shrines and rendering and exchanging service in various socio-economic spheres. Some kind of link with the other Muslim communities is established through taking part in processions (*julus*) taken out on various socio-religious occasions. In shawl embroidery work, links are established with the middlemen through a kind of patron-client relationship between them. Small entrepreneurs, government and private service holders and teachers of the community help to a great extent in establishing linkages with various communities at various levels.

Their attitude towards the education of girls is less favourable compared to that for the boys. The majority of the boys generally study up to primary level and some of them continue up to college level, and even up to post-graduate level in a few cases. The poor economic condition and the need to earn for the family are the reasons ascribed for discontinuation of their study. The girls, on the other hand, generally study up to primary level. They drop out because of poor economic conditions and for other social reasons. They have not discarded their indigenous traditional medicare sytsem altogether, but make use of it occasionally. Modern medicare is moderately used by most of them. They do not favour the adoption of any family planning method, indigenous or modern. Drinking water is available within the locality. Apart from the tap water supplied by the government, though irregularly, the perennial *chashma* or spring water coming from Sakhnaol is also used by them for drinking. Though they are not benefited through any special scheme of provision for employment, majority of them earn their livelihood through self-employment in agriculture, weaving of *namda* and shawl embroidery. They are exposed to the modern mass media facilities available in the region, namely, radio, television and cinema. Information is disseminated to them through the extension agencies and political parties. They make use of the facility of roads connecting most of the neighbouring areas. They make use of the facility of the post offices situated nearby. The nearest railway is situated 300 km. away at Jammu. Many of them have not even seen a train till today. They avail the facility of electricity. The supply of electricity is generally stopped during the winter months due to heavy snowfall. Firewood, cow-dung cakes, charcoal, kerosene oil and electricity constitute the fuel resources for them. Natural rain water and the water of the streams are the sources used for irrigation. Both organic manure, chemical fertilizers and insecticides are used by them as per their requirement. Under the ICDS programme, the children are fed with midday meals through the institution of Anganwadi. Most of them avail the facility of the fair price shops for essential food items like rice and sugar. They have favourable attitude towards the banking system but dependence on the moneylenders and local shopkeepers is also not altogether absent among them.

B.K. Basu

TARKHAN

The Tarkhans who have been pursuing their traditional occupation of carpentry are also known as Ramgarhiyas outside the region and belong to the Vishvakarma group of artisans which includes black-smiths, masons and mechanics. They perceive their identification at the national level.

The Tarkhans live in the regions which record extreme warm to temperate climate. Their habitats are in the hilly terrains and plains of Jammu province. The Tarkhan locations record high humidity and dense to thin forest cover. The region records medium rainfall.

They speak mainly Dogri within the family and the kin group though fair use of Urdu and Punjabi is also made. They use Devanagari and Arabic scripts to correspond within the family and kin group. With others, they speak Dogri and Urdu language and correspond in Arabic and Devanagari. Except for their tool box they do not have any community identification markers as their dress conforms to over all Dogri dress pattern of the Jammu region. The Tarkhans of Jammu province are spread over all the six districts, i.e. Jammu, Udhampur, Rajouri, Punch, Doda and Kathua.

These people are predominantly vegetarians. The Brahman Tarkhans abstain from eating meat while the Rajputs consume it frequently. However, their women are, by and large, vegetarians. Those among them who consume mutton, pork, fish, fowl and eggs abstain from eating beef.

Their staple food is rice and wheat with occasional use of maize. They take all types of pulses such as gram, *tur*, *urad*, peas, beans, *masur* and *moth*. They use groundnut and mustard oil as cooking medium. Recently they have started using rapeseed oil as well. They consume roots and tubers. Their men take alcoholic drinks occasionally and purchase the same from the market. Fruit consumption among them is occasional. There has been a growing tendency among them to change from vegetarian to non-vegetarian food. They take milk and milk products.

The men smoke *bidis* and cigarettes as well as loose tobacco. Chewing of betel and use of snuff also prevails among them. There has not been any significant change in their food habits though, with improved living standards, the quality of food has improved and become varied.

The Tarkhans, being a lowly placed community consisting of the Rajput, Vaishya, and Brahman elements in its fold, stand low in social status. However, differentiation of high and low among them, as part of the larger Vishvakarma section of the Hindus, is based on traditional occupation groups, like the Tarkhan, Lohar, Raj (mason) and others. Subgroups among the Tarkhans themselves are on the basis of their lineage of either the Rajput or Brahman. However, irrespective of lineage, they identify themselves more closely with the blacksmiths, masons and mechanics. They are aware of the *varna* system and predominantly belong to the Vaishya hierarchy though much later the Brahmans joined the occupation *tarkhan* because of economic compulsions. Various subcastes among them are Malhotra (Rajputs), Bhardwaj (Brahmans), Sabarwal, Gandhi, Vangotra, Debgotra, Rakhwal, Chadakh, Darmotra, Dutt, etc. Apparently there is no social differentiation among them. They consider themselves higher in status from other working, low-caste communities of the Jammu region, i.e. the Dum, Mahasha, Megh and Chmiyar. This community's self-perception is low and so is the image and status they enjoy in the eyes of the other high caste communities of the region.

They practise endogamy at the community level and within Vishvakarma fold. They do not practise consanguinity in the sense that marriages are not solicited among blood relations either on father's or mother's side. There is no restriction on sororate (junior) alliance but the same time is not allowed in case of senior sororate. However, practice of levirate of either type is not permitted. Earlier pre-puberty marriage was in vogue. The marriage age for the girls now is above 18 years and for the boys, it is from 22 years and above. Marital alliances are sought and negotiated by friends, relatives and family heads. Monogamy is the most prevalent form of marriage. Polygyny is practised in case the wife fails to bear any child. The most popular symbols of marriage are vermilion, bangles, *bindi*, finger rings, and toe rings. The practice of dowry is common among them and involves both cash and kind. The dowry comprises ornaments made of both silver and gold, furniture, bedding, utensils and dresses for both the bride and bridegroom. Cash transactions are also involved in marriages. The rule of residence is predominantly patrilocal with very few cases of uxorilocal type (usually where the father of the bride has no male heir). Divorce is sought mostly with judicial approval. Since in almost all the cases, it is the husband who seeks divorce, compensation is given to the wife. Either party can obtain the custody of the children depending upon the nature and circumstances under which separation was granted. Divorce proceedings can be initiated by any one of the two. The rules regarding remarriage are quite flexible among them as there are no specific socio-religious sanctions against this. Widowers, widows and divorcees can remarry with ease. Sororate (junior) alliance is permitted but levirate alliances of either types are not allowed. The rules regarding marriage or remarriage have not changed significantly. However, the age of marriage for both boys and girls has increased and marriages have become more elaborate and expensive. Incidence of divorce is very low and rules regarding residence remain by and large unchanged.

The family system at present is mostly of the extended or mixed-extended types (joint-family being the most common form). The preference for nuclear type of family is a very recent phenomenon emanating from the influences of urbanized independent economic life. Interpersonal relations are cordial among the household members in most of the cases. Joking relations exist among consanguineal and affinal relatives. Avoidance is observed between father-in-law and daughter-in-law as also between son-in-law and daughter-in-law and mother-in-law. Conflicts and disputes arise mainly on account of property and challenge to the authority of elders. The Tarkhans follow equigeniture and female heirs, as a matter of practice, do not normally claim any share though they are entitled to it under the law of the land. The eldest son succeeds as the head of the family after the demise of the father. Interfamily linkages in most of the cases are cordial. Disputes are usually settled through mutual negotiations and bargaining in which the relatives and friends play an important role. Offences and crimes are dealt with as per the existing judicial procedures of the state. Except for a growing tendency towards nuclear family, no other significant change has taken place in the family patterns.

The Tarkhan women have a secondary role in comparison to their men in all the spheres of life. The women participate in all the soical and religious functions and even contribute to the household income. In rural areas, women play an active role in farm and non-farm activities. They tend the domestic cattle and also attend to all the domestic chores. They collect firewood (wherever necessary) and water.

Though they enjoy voting rights, their role in active politics is insignificant. They are mostly illiterate and ignorant of the contemporary affairs in the region around them. They seem to be more reconciled to play their role as per the dictates of their men. The

Tarkhan women are yet to understand the meaning and relevance of emancipation.

They do not observe any pre-delivery rituals nor any specific type of restrictions though some sort of informal caution is observed. However, post-delivery pollution period of 21 days is observed among them. There are no postnatal restrictions on the mother nor do they have any formal ceremony for naming the child. Deliveries in rural areas are still conducted with the help of an experienced midwife but hospital and clinics are given preference. They observe the *mundan* ceremony for the boys only and exchange gifts on the occasion of *annaprashan* (first feeding of cereals) and thread wearing, *Janeu*, ceremony.

Marital alliances are sought and fixed by friends and relatives. The marriage ceremony lasts for two days. The first day, *mehndi-raat* is performed and on the night of the second day, the wedding ceremony *lagan* is performed. Customarily, the wedding ceremony is solemnized and held at the bride's residence. The bridegroom along with friends and relatives, comes in a *barat*, riding a mare and holding a ceremonial sword. The ritual of *sehra*, i.e. wearing of the ceremonial turban with recitation of song in honour of the groom is performed before the *barat* starts for the bride's place. A feast is given by both the parties on different days.

The body of a dead person is given a bath and then wrapped in a white *kafan* for carrying it to the cremation ground on a bier for the final rites. They observe eleven days death pollution period. Those who die below the age of five years are buried. Annual *shradh* is performed in the first year but not thereafter. *Rasam-pagri* or *uthala* ritual is observed after the pollution period is over.

For those who are economically well off, such rituals have become more elaborate and demonstrative but for most of them the rituals stand curtailed. They have not shown any inclination to change the life-cycle rituals.

In rural areas, land is the main natural resource for most of them. Besides carrying out their traditional occupation of carpentry, they also supplement their earnings from the land. Land is owned and controlled by individual proprietorship. As such, they are a landholding community in the rural areas but, in urban centres, they are mainly dependent on their *tarkhani* occupation.

Settled cultivation, self-employment and carpentry are their traditional occupations while business, government service and self-employment are the new occupations pursued by them. The women participate in most of the farm activities in rural areas and, in urban areas, quite a few of them are employed in the government and private sectors. Child labour is not normally hired or marketed but it exists in the form of domestic servants. They receive their wages in both cash and kind. Barter system is still prevalent among them. The link with the market is direct and also through middlemen, and transasctions are made on daily, weekly and fortnightly basis. There has been a gradual rise in the number of daily wage casual labourers and farmworkers. The mode of payment is in cash and kind, or both.

Besides having the village panchayats of a heterogeneous character, the Tarkhans have a formal carpenters association in the city of Jammu which has a membership of nearly 500. The election of the office bearers of the association is by secret ballot for electing the president, vice-president, secretary and treasurer. For the village panchayats, elections are held on the norms fixed by the government. The carpenters association renders assistance during wedding and death ceremonies by making financial contribution collected from the members of the association. The association also helps to resolve domestic and property disputes and settlement of work and payment claims. It renders punishments in the form of warning or a feast to the entire *biradari.* However, those in villages conform to the panchayat's rulings which are applicable to all, irrespective of caste or ethnic affiliations. Such panchayats monitor and plan the implementation of the welfare and developmental activities. Most common crimes and offences are adultery and disputes arising over land or water.

The Tarkhans profess Hinduism. There are also a good number of Sikh and Muslim carpenters living in Jammu region. They worship village and regional deities. Individual affiliation to a *pir* is a common phenomenon. They visit Bahu Fort, Vaishno Devi, Raghunath temple, Amarnath and Sudh Mahadev for worship. Their religious specialists are from the Brahman community who perform the birth, marriage and death rites. The festivals celebrated by them are Diwali, Shivratri, Janmashtami, Rakshabandhan and Lohri. However, all the Tarkhans celebrate Vishvakarma day, irrespective of their religious affiliation.

Their ladies do embroidery or weaving of woollen garments as a casual and part-time activity. Folk songs are sung by the community members of either sex. They are more in tune with the regional Dogri culture. They use the most common instruments of music used in the region like *dhol* (drum) and harmonium. Music is based on classical traditional pattern and songs are based on religious, social and cultural context of the Jammu region.

They accept cooked and uncooked food from the high caste Hindus as well as from those communities which stand at the same hierarchical level as themselves. They accept and exchange food and water from the Mahashas, Barwalas, Ramdasiyas, Bhagats and Meghs, but they abstain from exchanging it with the Bhangis and Chimariyas. There is no restriction in accepting uncooked food from even the non-Hindu communities.

They share water and water-sources with other communities. They share the same cremation grounds, schools and panchayat ghars, and visit the same religious places as the other Hindu communities. Though they do not have any specific role in traditional festivals and festivities, they participate in all such regional functions. They maintain patron-client and also cultivator-labourer relationship. They receive the services of the barbers, masons and mechanics.

The community is moving and evolving itself in terms with the socio-economic scenario of the region. They are trying to improve professionally, culturally and economically. Political awareness is fast catching up with them. They have entrepreneurs, businessmen, members holding white-collar jobs, administrators, doctors and engineers, and members in the defence services. Political leadership has emerged at the village and district levels only.

Formal education is favoured for both boys and girls. The boys study up to secondary and college level and drop out from further studies because of economic compulsions. The girls also study up to secondary to college level and drop out due to social and economic reasons. In both cases, restraining factors for pursuing higher education are economic compulsions and to earn and augment the household income.

Their attitude towards modern medicare is positive but the extent of its use depends upon its availability and accessibility. Consequently, the traditional medicare is also used where the modern medicare facilities are absent. Modern medicare has yet to become fully a part of their health and medical care programme. Though their attitude towards family planning is favourable, the average household size varies between five and six members. Generally, it is their women who get sterilized.

Drinking water is available within the locality. The sources for drinking water are ponds, wells and tap water. These people have been benefitted from the employment generation schemes under the Integrated Rural Development Programme and rural employment guarantee schemes in most of the cases. Their main source of self-employment has been agriculture, small-scale cottage industries and carpentry. They listen to radio and television, and visit the cinema. Roads, both metalled and *kachcha*, exist in and around their settlements. Post offices are located near their place of habitat. Most of them use electricity at their homes for lighting purposes. For cooking and heating purposes, they use firewood, cow-dung cakes, coal, kerosene oil and, to a limited extent, cooking gas.

They avail of the irrigation facilities and the main sources for it are tube wells and canals beside rainwater. Those who have their own land make use of organic manure, chemical fertilizers and insecticides. They avail of the facility of ration distribution through the fair price shops. Though their attitude towards savings is favourable, it depends upon their economic conditions.

The Tarkhans are an heterogeneous entity in the present set-up. Consequently, they have not been able to retain an exclusive ethnic character as they held in the past. Owing to chronic unemployment, people from different religions, sects and regions have taken up their occupation. Even among the local Tarkhans, occupational diversification to other sectors has been observed. As such, *tarkhani* no longer remain to be an occupation of any particular community; it is now the amalgamation of diverse socio-cultural and religious elements.

ASHOK AIMA

TELI

The Telis or Telwains are traditional oil pressers. *Tel* literally means oil and *wain* seller. Teli is an occupational name and an occupational category in Kashmir. Crushing of oil seeds is their main occupation. The history of migration and origin of the community is not known but it is believed that they were all Hindus and embraced Islam after the advent of Islam in the Valley. They place themselves in the Shaikh category of the Muslims and have been declared as one of the Other Backward Classes in Jammu & Kashmir.

They are distributed in the Pulwama, Anantnag, Baramula, Badgam and Kupwara districts of Jammu & Kashmir state but their main concentration is in Srinagar. The climate is cold. The natural vegetation is that of temperate zone and rainfall is low. The area is thickly forested and confined to the hill ranges below the snowline. The Telis speak Kashmiri language within the family and with others.

The script of the Kashmiri language is Arabic. Their dress is the same as that of the other Kashmiris—*pheren*, *pochh* (trousers), and caps. The women wear *salwar*, *kurta* and *pheran*, and *puts* which is made of two and a half yards plain cloth worn on the head.

They are non-vegetarian in their food habits. They eat mutton but beef is banned in the Valley. They do not eat pork as it is prohibited by their religion. Rice is their staple food. Wheat and maize is also consumed by them but they are not a substitute for rice. Bread is eaten with tea in the morning and afternoon. Pulses such as gram, *urad* and *masur* are consumed and mustard oil is used as the cooking medium. They consume roots and tubers, and vegetables such as cabbage, potatoes, carrot and brinjal frequently, particularly in the villages. Their favourite dish is *hak* or *karam sag* with rice.

There is no division in the community and whatever the differentiations are there, they are based on economic, occupational or educational attainments. They are considered of the middle rank in the local social hierarchy because of their occupation which is not considered respectable. Though the Telis are an endogamous group but endogamy as such is not strictly followed. They prefer to marry off their daughters and sons within their own community but, if the match is not available, they can marry in any community of the Sunni sect of equal status. They give first preference mate to the cousins. In most of the cases, marriages take place when the boys and girls are adults, although, in earlier days, they used to perform child marriages.

At present the marriage age is between 20 and 25 years for the males and females respectively. Most of the marriages are settled through negotiations, which is generally initiated by a common friend, but sometimes the services of a mediator, *manzymyor*, are sought. Though polygyny is permissible according to the Islamic rules, *shariat*, it is not common and monogamy is largely practised.

Bride price is absent but dowry exchange to some extent is prevalent. Being a patrilocal society, after marriage, the bride goes to live with her husband and in-laws. Divorce is permitted in the community as in the other Muslim communities as per the rules in the *shariat*. There are certain conditions on the basis of which separation or divorce can be carried out. If the husband is absconding, not bearing the expenses of wife and children, suffering from serious disease or has not had sexual contact with the wife for more than three years, the wife may seek separation. Likewise, a husband may divorce his wife in case of adultery, maladjustment, barrenness and insanity. According to the Muslim rules, divorce may be given either orally or by *talaq-nama* (written document). After the dissolution of marriage by divorce, the divorced woman is prohibited from remarrying within a specified time called *iddat*. If the consummation of marriage had taken place and then there is a divorce, the duration of *iddat* is for three months and ten days or until delivery if the women was pregnant. The cases of divorce, however, are rare in the community.

The women enjoy an equal status with the men. They have full rights to *mahr*, the amount which is fixed at the time of *nikah* by the husband. It can be claimed any time after marriage but is generally demanded at the time of divorce. They have important roles to play in all spheres of life. They participate in all agricultural operations except ploughing. They collect fuel, bring potable water, and do all other household chores. They play a pivotal role in the social and religious functions. Though they do not contribute much to the family income, they certainly help to augment it. They have decision-making power and exercise control over the expenditure in the family.

The life-cycle rituals start with the pregnancy of a woman. If after marriage, the women remain issueless for more than two to three years they are sent to the saints, *pirs*, and *faqirs* to invoke their blessings for bearing a child. Generally, they visit the shrine of Shah Hamdan. The woman is not allowed to carry heavy loads during the period of pregnancy. In case of first pregnancy, the woman is not allowed to live with her husband for more than the first five months of her pregnancy. Delivery generally takes place at home particularly in the village areas. A midwife, *warin*, is called for this purpose and she is given some cash, sweets, rice and maize according to the economic status of the family. The *warin* may be from any community but, generally, she is an old woman who is an expert in the job. Immediately after birth the baby is given a bath in lukewarm water. Then a senior male member recites *azaan* in the ears of the baby. On the birth of first issue, bread and sweets (sugar balls) are distributed among the relatives, friends and neighbours. If the birth has taken place at the girl's natal house, sweets are sent to her in-law's place also. In return, the mother-in-law sends bread, cash and clothes for the baby. This ceremony is called *piaw*. On the seventh day after the delivery, the mother takes her first bath. On this occasion, tea is served to the close relatives and neighbours. Some families organize prayer by the priests. On this day, the child is also given a name in consultation with the family priest or by any elder person of the family or the village. This is the christening ceremony, called *sunder*. On this occasion, sometimes a feast is also arranged.

On completion of forty days, the mother is given another bath and only then she is allowed to do all household jobs including living with her husband. *Zerakasi* is another ritual performed in the community in which the head of the child is shaved by the family barber. It is observed at the age of at least six months and, on this occasion, relatives and friends are invited to a feast. Circumcision or *khatanhal* is performed when a male child becomes two years old or more. It is obligatory and performed in all the Muslim communities of the state. The child is circumcized by the family barber in the villages but, in urban areas, it is done in hospitals or at home by a doctor. A big feast is arranged on this occasion.

After preliminary marriage negotiations and consent of both the families, the father of the bridegroom accompanied with close relatives visits the bride's place and offers to the bride's father some money and gifts for the bride. It is the ritual acceptance of the marriage proposal and this ceremony is called *gandum* (engagement). After this ceremony, another ritual is followed which is called *doon-leij*. In this ritual, an earthen pot full of nuts and cash is presented to the father of the bridegroom by the bride's father. *Dapanbata* ritual is performed when the members of the family go to their relatives to invite them for the marriage and are served with lunch. As the marriage date draws near, the bride is not allowed to take bath or do household jobs. This continues for three days and it is called *malasbehoun*.

Another ritual performed is called *massmechravoun*. On this occasion, close relatives assemble at the bride's place and women comb the hair of the bride. The first day of the marriage is called *menziraat*. In this ritual *mehndi* is applied on the hands and feet of the bride. The second day of marriage is called *yanevoul*. On this day, the father of the bridegroom sends a few copper plates containing sugar candy, sugar balls, almonds, dresses and ornaments for the bride. When the *barat* (marriage procession) starts, it is followed by a group of singing women who return after giving a send off to the *barat*. At the bride's house, the procession is received by the women singing in a chorus. The *baratis* are offered sweets and *qahwa*. After this, the *nikah* ceremony takes place. It is presided over by the *maulvi* (priest). The *nikah* in which the bride and bridegroom are present is called *asaltan*. A marriage contract is written with the consent of the bride and bridegroom in the presence of the witnesses on the occasion. *Mahr* money is also fixed during the *nikah* ceremony. In earlier days, there was another type of *nikah* called *vilaitan* or through the guardian. When the *nikah* ceremony is over, dinner is served. At the time of departure, the bride goes with her husband. The bride's female relatives follow her for some distance singing in chorus.

The bride stays with her husband for seven days. A big feast called *wathal* is given by the bridegroom's father on the marriage night. After the marriage, the bride starts living with her husband and in-laws.

In the event of death a message is sent to all the relatives and friends, and the deceased is surrounded by mourners. A bath is given to the dead body by a professional man called *snangor* for which he is paid money and given the used clothes of the deceased. After the bath, the dead body is wrapped in white cloth, *kafan*, and placed in a wooden *taboot* (coffin). The *taboot* is laid on the ground facing Mecca and the priest recites *namaz-e-janaza* prayers. The coffin is then carried to the graveyard where a *malkhos* digs a *lahad* (grave).

When the body is laid to rest, the grave is covered with clay and stones and the priest recites prayers. The *malkhos* is paid in cash and is given tea and bread on the fourth and fortieth day after the death. Mourning is held till the next Friday. On the fourth day after death, the priest, relatives and neighbours recite the Holy Koran for the peace of the departed soul. The ceremony is repeated on the fortieth day. The two rituals are called *chaharum* and *chehallum* respectively.

Crushing of oil seeds and selling oil was the primary occupation of the community. Nowadays, due to the advent of modern machines, the oil produced by machine is easily available and cheaper. The Telis therefore are concentrating on agriculture, particularly in the village areas. Some of them work as labourers in the plantations while, in urban areas, they are in the government and non-government services. Though in villages they are landowners, they are not as big as other communities. The resources are controlled by individuals or the family.

Besides agriculture and service, a few of the families have adopted other business activities, leaving their age-old traditional occupation of oil pressing. They are directly linked with the local markets which are fully regulated.

They profess Islam and follow its dicta, the *shariat.* There are several sacred shrines and mosques which are visited on different occasions by the members of the community. Shah Hamdan, Charar-e-Sharif, Makhdum Sahib, Dastgir Sahib and Naqshband Sahib are the different sacred shrines of the Muslim saints. The community has its own *pirs* and they are called to perform the birth, marriage and death rites. There are many festivals which are celebrated in the community at different times, namely Prophet Muhammad's birthday Urs-e-Nabi, also known as Id-ul-Milad. On this day, the Prophet's hair relic is displayed at the Hazratbal shrine. Meraj-e-Alam is celebrated on twenty-sixth of Rajab and the hair relic is displayed on this day also. Id-ul-Fitr, Id-ul-Zuha and Shab-e-Qadr are other festivals which are celebrated with great zeal by the community.

Besides these, there are certain days dedicated to the Muslim saints like Urs-e-Shah Hamdan, Urs-e-Batmaloo, Urs-e-Charar-e-Sharif, Urs-e-Makhdum Sahib, Urs-e-Pir Dastgir and Urs-e-Naqshband, which are attended by the Telis and other Muslim communities. The festivals of the community are of socio-religious importance. The Telis do not have any traditional art or craft of their own. A few members of the community are engaged in embroidery, wood carving, papier mâché and other crafts of Kashmir which are also practised by many other communities.

Being involved in the important business of oil production and sale, the Telis have good relations with all other Muslim and Hindu communities of Jammu & Kashmir. They are considered as a community with a clean occupation. They accept *kachcha* and *pukka* food from all the Hindu and Muslim communities except the Watals. The services of the Waza, Pir, Gorkun, Tarkhan and other Muslim communities are utilized on the occasion of birth, marriage and death ceremonies. The Telis too render their services to the various Hindu and Muslim communities. They share the water sources, burial grounds and religious shrines with the other Muslims. Patron-client relationships exist in the community. At present, the members of the community are in different government and private jobs. Families are now engaged in business and moving away from their age-old occupation of oil pressing.

The Telis have largely benefited by the diffrent development plans and programmes adopted by the government to uplift and betterment of the downtrodden. Educationally, they are still backward, particularly in the rural areas situated in remote hilly terrain where transportation and communication facilities are still difficult. Their attitude towards education of girls is less favourable and only a few of them can reach college or postgraduate level.

The attitude of the community towards modern medicare is favourable but, in remote areas, the traditional medicare system still prevails and they use it occasionally. They use the available modern medicare facilities but complain about the non-availability of necessary medicines in the government dispensaries. Now they have started taking interest in the family planning programmes and prefer to have less children.

Drinking water facilities are available in their locality. Tap water, streams and springs are the main sources of their drinking water. Being involved in agriculture, a few of them are also self employed weaving *namda*, shawls and embriodery. The mode of entertainment is radio. They do not watch television or cinema because they live in inaccessible remote areas. They use electricity for light wherever available. Cow-dung cakes, wood and kerosene oil are used as the main fuels.

Owing to non-availability of proper irrigation facilities, they depend on rain and stream water. Chemical fertilizers and insecticides are also used to boost the production of crops. Nutritional programmes of the government have not been properly implemented in the region. Facilities of food distribution through the fair price shops are availed of by the community members. The Telis have a positive attitude towards saving. Now the members of the community are not dependent on the moneylenders or shopkeepers.

ANAND SARAN

WANI

Wani is the Kashmiri term for a grocer. The members of this community run retail shops of groceries like sugar, salt, mustard oil, condiments, etc. They are also engaged in lending money to their customers under the system of *wad-dar*. The term '*wani*' may be a distorted version of Vaishyas, one of the four principal *varnas* of the Hindus who make their living by trade and commerce. Historical accounts regarding the origin and migration of the community do not exist. The 1891 census mentions the Wani titles as Kanth, Gandru, Batch, Bande, Gauna, Ganai, Dar, Pakshi, Wal, Vakil, Ashai, Shal, Kanju, etc. They are distributed in almost all the districts of Kashmir Valley. In the villages, the Wanis live with the other Hindu and Muslim communities. Sometimes a locality with predominant Wani households is named as Wani Pura. The Wanis speak Kashmiri within the family and Urdu with others.

The script of Kashmiri language is Arabic. There is no special dress to differentiate the Wanis from the other Muslims of the Valley. The men wear *pheran* or long gown, trousers and cap. The women wear *pheran* of printed cloth, *salwar*, *kameez* and a scarf over the head called *dej*.

The Wanis are non-vegetarian. They eat mutton but not pork. Beef is consumed occasionally. Rice is their staple diet. The other cereals consumed are wheat and maize. Pulses such as gram, *moong*, *urad* and *masur* are consumed occasionally. Vegetables and curd is consumed moderately. Mustard oil and animal fat are the cooking medium. Fruit consumption in the community is high. Salty tea is the main beverage and is taken generally in the afternoon. Milk and milk products are their favourite items but their consumption is low because of their rising cost. Alcoholic drinks are not taken by the community. *Hookah* is generally smoked by the aged persons. They are fond of cigarettes.

There is no social division within the community and whatever the differentiations, they are on the basis of economic, occupational and educational levels. There are Wanis associated with the lowest occupation of rearing sheep and goats and, on the other hand, there are Wanis engaged in the highest occupation like that of a *pir* or a priest. Among the Muslims of the Valley, the Wanis are considered at the middle rank of the social hierarchy. They belong both to the Shia and Sunni sects but predominantly to the latter.

Though the Wani in Kashmir region is an endogamous group, yet endogamy is not strictly followed. They prefer to marry their daughters and sons within their own title (*kram*). If a suitable match is not available, they may marry in any other *kram* of the Sheikh but of equal status or occupation. Thus it is rare that a Wani engaged in goldsmithy will marry off his daughter to a blacksmith. Similarly a Wani may give his daughter in marriage to the Ganai *kram*, and vice versa, provided both are agriculturists. The only line drawn is that one must not marry in the Saiyad families, on the one hand, nor in the families of market gardeners and menials, on the other. They give first preference to the cousins. In most of the cases, marriage takes place when the boys and girls attain adulthood. At present, the age of marriage is between 18 and 25 years for both males and females. Bachelors and unmarried girls within the community do not enjoy the freedom of spouse selection. It is the exclusive privilege of the parents or the guardians to make a selection fulfilling three conditions, namely appearance (*shaka*), wisdom (*akal*) and capacity to maintain the bride (*guzara*).

Generally a common friend starts the negotiations but sometimes it is done by a mediator (*manzymyor*). Though polygamy is permissible according to the Islamic rules (*shariat*), yet it is not practised and monogamy happens to be the common form. There are no symbols indicating marital status of a woman. Dowry was not in practice previously but it is gradually gaining ground. Being patrilocal, the bride, after marriage, goes to live with her husband and in-laws.

Divorce is permissible in the community as among the other Muslims and is practised according to the Islamic religion. If the husband is absconding, not bearing the expenses of the wife and children, suffering from serious disease or not having any sexual contact with his wife for more than three years, then the wife may divorce him. Likewise, a husband may divorce his wife in case of adultery, maladjustment, barrenness and insanity.

According to the Islamic rules, divorce may be given either orally or by written document called *talaq-nama*. According to the Muslim law, when a marriage is dissolved by divorce, the woman is prohibited from remarrying for a specified time called *iddat*. If consummation of marriage has taken place and then there is a divorce, the duration of *iddat* is three months and ten days; if the woman is pregnant, the period extends till the delivery of the child. The cases of divorce are, however, rare in the community. In case of a divorce, minor children are to be kept under the care of the father.

Widow, widower and divorcee remarriage is permissible in the community but a widow can remarry only after the *iddat* period is over. Remarriages are not performed in the manner of the regular marriage. The changes observed in the marriage rules are decrease in divorce cases, increase in monogamy and emergence of the dowry system in the community.

Families in the community are generally of two types, namely, mixed-extended and nuclear. In most of the cases, the families are nuclear due to the impact of urbanization and industrialization. Within a dwelling unit, the married brothers occupy separate rooms and kitchen. The extended families are found mostly in the villages. Interpersonal relationships are amicably established among the family members. The youngsters receive proper love and care from the elders. Avoidance relationship is maintained between the daughter-in-law and the father-in-law and between younger brother's wife and husband's elder brothers, and also with all outsiders and elder relations. *Purdah* system is observed.

Joking relationship exists between husband's younger brother and sister-in-law and between husband and his wife's younger sisters. The property is distributed equally among all the sons. The married daughters also get a share if it is provided during the lifetime of the father. After the death of head of the familly, it is the duty of all the brothers to arrange their sisters' marriage and bear the expenses. The succession pattern is followed from father to son. The major change has been breaking-up of the joint family system.

In the community, the women are considered equal to men and have certain rights. The women have full rights on *mahr* (dower), the amount which is fixed at the time of *nikah* by the husband. It can be claimed any time after marriage but generally it is demanded at the time of divorce. In the community, the women have important roles to play in all spheres of life. They participate in agricultural operations and do all the jobs except ploughing. They milch the cows, collect fuel, bring potable water and do other household jobs. Thus, through their physical labour, they contribute to family maintenance.

Several rituals, customs and ceremonies are followed on different occasions in the life cycle of the community. It starts with the pregnancy of women. If after marriage the women remain issueless for more than two to three years, they are sent to saints, *pirs* and *faqirs* to invoke their blessings. Generally, they visit the shrine of Shah Hamdan.

The pregnant women are not allowed to carry heavy loads. In case of the first pregnancy, a woman is not allowed to live with her husband for more than five months of pregnancy. In the community, delivery generally takes place at home, particularly in the villages. A *warin* (midwife) is called to help and she is paid in cash or in kind according to the economic status of the family. Immediately after birth, the baby is given a bath in lukewarm water. Then a senior male member recites *azaan* in the ears of the baby. On the occasion of the first bath, bread and *shirini* (sweets) are distributed among the relatives, friends and neighbours. The ritual is called *piaw.* On the seventh day, *sunder* ritual is observed. The woman takes her first post-delivery bath, and the child is given a name either in consultation with the family priest or by any elderly person of the family or the village. On completing forty days of the delivery, the woman is given another bath and after this she resumes her normal work. First hair-cutting ceremony, *zerakasi,* is observed at the age of six months and done by the family or village barber. On this occasion the relatives and friends are invited to a feast. The next ritual is called *khatnahal* or circumcision. This is an obligatory ritual for all the Muslims. It is performed when the child is two years old. The operation is done by a barber in rural areas but, in the cities, it is done by a surgeon. A feast is given to the relatives and friends on this occasion.

Marriage is settled by negotiation and preference is given to the cousins. If a suitable match is not available among the relations, they may select one from outside. In the community, certain marriage customs and rituals are observed as in the other Muslim communities of Jammu & Kashmir state. After mutual agreement, the father of the bridegroom together with some close relatives visits the place of the bride and offer some money to the bride and her father. It is the ritualistic acceptance of the marriage proposal called *gandum* (engagement). After this, another ritual is followed which is called *doon-leij.* In this ritual, an earthen pot filled with nuts and money is presented to the father of the bridegroom by the bride's father. *Dapanbata* ritual is performed by the relatives of the contracting parties who are invited to a feast. A prospective bride nearing her wedding day desists from taking bath or doing household work. This continues for three days and is called *malasbehoun.* Another ritual called *massmechravoun* is observed in which close relatives assemble and women comb the hair of the bride and keep on singing in chorus. It is followed by the ritual of *malamenz* in which the hands and feet of the bride are adorned with *henna* (myrtle paste).

Menziraat is an important ritual of the marriage. Dinner is served to the guests. The second day is called *yenevoul* or the day on which the bride is given away. On this day, the father of the bride makes arrangements for the reception of the *barat* and a feast. The father of the bridegroom sends a few plates filled with sugar candy, *shirini* or sugar balls, almonds, dresses and ornaments for the bride. At the house of the bride, the procession is received by the women singing in chorus. The *baratis* are offered sweets, *qahwa*, etc. The *nikah* ceremony is presided over by the village priest or *maulvi*. The *nikah* in which the bride and bridegroom are present is called *asaltan*. A marriage contract is written with the consent of the bride and the groom in the presence of two witnesses from both the sides. The amount of *mahr* is fixed during the *nikah* ceremony. One-third of the fixed *mahr* money is supposed to be paid immediately and the rest can be deferred but, generally, no *mahr* is given at the time of *nikah*. This is demanded at the time of divorce.

When the *nikah* ceremony is over, dinner is served. At the time of departure, the bride goes with her husband and the other participants of the groom's party. The bride's female relatives follow her for some distance singing in chorus. She stays with her husband for seven days. A big feast called *wathal* is given by the bridegroom. It is a thanksgiving function and is attended by the relatives and friends, including relatives of the bride. On the seventh day, the bride returns to her parents house.

The Wanis being Muslims bury their dead. A bath is given to the dead person by a professional bather called *snangor*. He is paid money and given the clothes of the deceased person. After the bath, the dead body is wrapped in *kafan* and placed in a wooden coffin called *taboot* facing Mecca and the priests recite prayer. The grave is dug by a grave-digger (*malkhos*) who is paid in cash and served with tea and bread on the fourth and fortieth day of the death. On the fourth (*chaharum*) and the fortieth (*chehallum*) day, relatives and friends gather to offer prayers for the departed soul.

Notwithstanding their traditional occupation of business, the Wanis still depend on agriculture in the villages. Some of them work as labourers in the plantations while in the urban areas they are in the government and non-government services. The main crops grown are paddy, *shali*, mustard and maize. With the subdivision of land due to the growing family size, some of the Wanis have disposed of their landed property and invested the money in business in the cities. Those having surplus land give a portion of it to other communities on rent.

They get a share of the produce which varies from one-third to one-fourth at the time of harvesting. Some members of the community own big apple orchards in the villages.

Disputes over land and matrimonial matters are solved by the elders of the community or of the village. Unresolved cases may be taken to the court of law. The Wanis have their representatives in the *gram* panchayat.

The Wanis are Muslims and follow the principles of *shariat* like the other Muslims of the state. There are several sacred shrines and mosques which are visited on different occasions by the community. Shah Hamdan, Charar-e-Sharif, Makhdum Sahib, Dastgir Sahib, Naqshband Sahib and Hazratbal shrines are their sacred places. The community has its own *pirs* and they are called to perform the birth, marriage and death rites. There are many festivals which are celebrated by the community in different months. These are Prophet Muhammad's birthday Urs-e-Nabi. On this day, the Prophet's hair relic is displayed at the Hazratbal shrine. Meraj-e-Alam is celebrated on twenty-sixth of Rajab and the holy hair relic is publicly displayed on this day also. Id-ul-Fitr, Id-ul-Zuha and Shab-e-Qadr are other festivals which are celebrated with great zeal by the community. Besides, there are certain celebrations (*urs*) like Urs-e-Shah Hamdan, Urs-e-Batmaloo, Urs-e-Charar-e-Sharif, Urs-e-Makhdum Sahib.

Some members of the community are involved in embroidery, wood carving, papier mgchÈ work and carpet weaving.

Being involved in business and trade, the Wanis maintain good relations with all other occupational communities. They are considered a clean occu-pational community. They accept food and water from all the Hindu and Muslim communities except the Watals. The services of artisans and craftsmen are availed of. The Wanis too render their services to other higher and lower castes of the Hindus and Muslims. They share the water resources and religious shrines with the other Muslims. Patron-client relationship exists in the community. At present the members of the community are in different government and private jobs. Some of them hold important administrative positions while a few run big business in towns particularly in Srinagar.

The Wanis have been benefited by the different development plans and programmes undertaken by the government. The Wanis in urban areas are ahead of their community members in rural areas. For higher education they have to go to the cities. The facilities of primary health centres are available in villages near the block headquarters while remote areas still depend on indigenous medicines. Health-care facilities are provided under the ICDS programmes. Health visitors also advise the villagers on sanitation. But open latrines and poor drainage in the villages pose health hazards. The community's interest in family planning programmes is catching up and preference is given to small family. In villages, drinking water facilities are available through tap. In this connection, the UNICEF has provided clean drinking water to many villages. Under the IRDP stipends are given to the boys and girls of poor families for vocational training in tailoring, carpet weaving and carpentry.

Most of the villages are electrified. Facilities of Dehati Ellaquai Banks are available to the villages, which have certainly improved the general economic conditions of the rural community. The community uses cow-dung, firewood, leaves and twigs and kerosene oil as fuel in the villages. Irrigation facilities through canals are available. The community uses chemical fertilizers and pesticides in agriculture. The improved variety of milch cows such as Holstein and Frisians have been provided to the people in the villages. This has made quantitative improvement in milk yield. The facilities of food distribution system through the ration shops prevails.

PARMANAND LAL

WATAL

The Watal, Batal, Battal and Batul are the people who carry a broomstick. A *gotra* of the similar title is found among the Kashmiri Pandits as well, but they have been kept out of the purview of this paper as they do not form a community. Lawrence (1895) and Sharma (1983) are of the opinion that the Watal are inhabitants of an earlier period than the Aryans. They had all the manners and appearance of the gypsies. Because of their indiscriminate consumption of any food, they were looked down upon by the Hindus and Muslims.

The Watals consider themselves as a localized community, their population being confined to the Valley. The Valley is surrounded by the Pir Panjal and Zanskar ranges of the Himalayas. The resplendent lakes, Wular and Dal, vast glaciers and thick forests consisting of pine and *deodar* and the stately chinar tree have turned the Valley into a paradise on earth. The humidity is low and rainfall is medium.

The Watals speak to each other in Kashmiri whereas the language of conversation with the outsiders is Urdu. The literate Watals write in Arabic script. They have been declared as a Scheduled Caste in Jammu & Kashmir. According to the *Census of India* (1981) their population was only 88.

The Watals are non-vegetarians and eat eggs, mutton and fish. Like the other Kashmiri Muslims, the Watals refrain from consuming beef. Their staple diet consists of rice and green vegetables. Mutton is cooked and consumed on festive occasions. Kashmir is famous for its apples, pears and cherries, and the Watals too enjoy the nature's bounty when markets are flooded with fruits. The rural Watals keep sheep and goats as milch animals, sometimes the comparatively better-off families keep cows for milk but, in the urban area, keeping animals poses a problem, hence their milk intake has reduced considerably. Alcoholic drinks are prohibited for the Muslims but some Watals of the lower rungs of the class hierarchy consume liquor with the general disapproval of the family, kin and neighbourhood. Alcoholism is more noticeable in the urban surroundings where liquor is easily available and may be consumed away from the place of residence.

There appears to be a considerable improvement in their food habits due to easy availability of food grains from the fair price shops and the rising income as a result of the governmental reforms in wage policy.

The Watals resent if they are called so, as they treat the term as an abuse. Instead they prefer to call themselves as Sheikh, Seraj or Ganai. They are broadly divided in the following categories: (1) the Seraj are cobblers by profession, and manufacture, repair and polish shoes; (2) the Schupriya Watal are manufacturers of *schup* (winnowing fans) with reed, thong and hide which are in great demand in the rural hinterland; (3) the Khumb Watal occupy the lowest rung of the hierarchy and work as scavengers, as well as skin the carcasses of dead animals and process, refine and tan the skin.

Their profession compels them to live at the periphery of a village. Although they are Muslims, their entry is banned within the precincts of a mosque or a shrine as they are still suspected to be carrion eaters. Those who have left the habit have improved their social identity and face less social disadvantage within the overall Muslim society in Kashmir.

The basis of class differentiation is the occupation that is followed by each of their segments, which operate in matrimonial alliances. The Watal, though Muslim, are endogamous as the concept of *izzat* (family honour) keeps the other Muslim communities of Kashmir away from forging matrimonial alliances with them. Their failure to merge with the larger Kashmiri Muslim entity has embittered them to such an extent that they feel isolated and deprived both socially and culturally.

'We are like dropped leaves of a tree being swept away by the wind to unknown directions. We have no shelter over our heads, successive governments have done so much for the poor but we still remain deprived of the benefits', complained a Watal from Batwara (Srinagar). The Kashmiris in general feel that the Watals are facing socio-economic disabilities, and there is an imperative need to do something substantial for their upliftment.

Pollution, commensality, sanctified group hierarchy and spatial differentiation hardly determine the Watal marriage rules but the occupation followed by them is a prime consideration behind the group endogamy. Within the community, marriage with a bad character is forbidden. Other prohibited set of kin for matrimony are the siblings, foster mother's children, and the non-Muslims. A boy is considered marriageable at the age of fifteen years and a girl at fourteen.

Negotiated marriages are the general rule. Negotiations for marriage are initiated by a mediator (*khusra*). Elopements were frequent in the past but now the parents of the eloping couple disown them from being their children (*prathak-nama*). The disowned individuals do not easily find shelter within the community.

The *mahr* (dower) is payable to the bride by the bridegroom at the time of *nikah* (contract) or later. But in case of divorce, the husband is bound to pay the dower. The Watals have minimum *mahr* of Rs. 2,200 but a bigger amount may be determined by the bride's parents keeping in view the personal qualities of the bride and the status of the family she belongs to. *Daaj* (dowry) is given to the bride by her parents both in cash and kind. The current minimum rate of dowry is Rs.2,000. In case of divorce, the husband is not only liable to pay the dower but also one seventh part of his movable and immovable property to his divorced wife.

Verbal divorce is considered unfair and obsolete as many such momentary outbursts of uttering the term *talaq* (divorce) thrice were later denied by the repentant husband. Nonetheless, such a pronouncement renders the conjugal bonds annulled and creates a tremendous psychological strain in the minds of the couple. Now a person willing to divorce his spouse approaches the *pir* (priest) who, in return, obtains the consent of the two. Thereafter, the agreement is written on a stamped paper and duly endorsed by a court notary.

A woman willing to seek separation from her husband will have to forgo her claim of dower. A woman can remarry three months and ten days after divorce. For a widow the *iddat* (period of abstinence) is four months ten days after which she can remarry. A married woman goes to live in her husband's parental house after marriage. The marriage symbol is a nose stud.

The economic condition of the community is reflected in their system of marriage, e.g. the amount of *mahr* has gone up from Rs. 900 to Rs. 2,200 in the last forty years. The boys have become more assertive in the choice of their spouse due to their economic independence from the parents. The marriageable girls on the other side have also become very cautious in the choice of their life partners. There is an emerging trend among the prospective spouses to meet each other before marriage. Such occasional and clandestine meetings are ignored but frequent meetings of the two are disapproved.

Laterally and vertically, extended families are common among them but those living in urban areas have a tendency to establish nuclear families. Intra-family relations are characterized by love and affection but conflicts within a family cannot be ruled out due to continuously rising stress and strains of urbanization. The time has come when parents feel that they should not treat their children as subservients but as friends.

Joking relationships exist between one's elder brother's wife and wife's younger sister or husband's younger brother. The sons have no right on their father's property during the latter's lifetime. Thereafter, they are entitled to inherit two-thirds of the deceased father's property. The line of succession runs patrilineally. The daughters inherit one-third from the father's property.

The manifestations of interfamily linkages are discernible in the life-cycle rituals, exchange and economic help among themselves. There is a growing trend to establish nuclear families. The small famlily norm is also making inroads among the Watals. The socio-economic dependence of children on their parents is also on the decline causing a slow erosion of parental authority.

The Watal women, *Watlanis*, were exceedingly beautiful but poor and various rulers and petty chiefs exploited them by keeping them as dancing girls. Now the status of the Watal women has undergone a change since the Watals have discarded most of their old habits and are slowly inching nearer to the larger body of the Kashmiri Muslim population. The women have become more assertive about their rights on the property of their husband and of the deceased father. In order to maintain pleasant relations with their male siblings, they invariably forgo their rights on parental property in favour of their brothers but their right on the deceased husband's property, the right of maintenance, the spreading network of communication and educational facilities have helped them to enlarge their world view.

A Watal woman is still a traditional housewife. Keeping the house and hearth warm during the severe winters is the job of the woman who walks 3 to 4 km everyday in order to collect chinar leaves, weeds from lake and rivers, small twigs, and head loads of firewood. In other spheres of economic activity, she helps her parents before marriage, and the husband thereafter in self-employed activities like skinning of dead animals, and manufacturing of winnowing fans.

The first issue is born in the natal house of the parturient mother. The elderly ladies or the *warin* (village midwife) help during birth. The parturient mother is served with a concoction of herbs for eight days, thereafter she is permitted to eat rice and mutton curry for the next seven days only once a day. Thereafter, she may take her normal diet. After a child is born, the neonate is given a bath with a warm water touched by a red hot iron bar. The parturient mother takes a bath on the seventh day and the purificatory bath is given to her after forty days which makes her free from pollution to resume her normal duties and household chores.

The first shaving of hair, *zerakasi* is done by the *navid* (barber) within a year from the birth. The name of the new born is suggested by a *pir* (priest) or any other pious man of the village. Circumcision of the boy is done when he is two years old. The services of a *jarrah* (native surgeon) are employed for the purpose. *Naak-chembeen* (piercing of girl's nose) and *kaan-chembeen* (piercing ears) is done by the elderly ladies without any ceremony.

Nikah is the main marriage ceremony in which consent of the bridegroom and the bride is obtained for the marriage. Thereafter amidst incarnation of the Holy Koranic verses, the two are declared as husband and wife. *Nikah* is performed at the natal house of the bride. *Nikah-nama*, a marriage deed, duly signed by the representatives and witnesses from the two sides is ratified by a court of law. The bride accompanies her husband immediately after the feast that follows *nikah*. She returns to her parents after seven days and stays as long as her husband or his representative does not come to escort her back to her in-laws house. Exchange of gifts takes place on such visits.

When a person dies, the body is given a bath by the members of the Malla community. The coffin is prepared and the grave is dug by the same people. After the ritual of *ghusl-e-janaza* (purificatory bath), prayers known as *namaaz-e-janaza* are recited for the deceased. All those present on the occasion throw a handful of earth in the grave after the body is lowered for final rest. After three days, the kin and neighbours assemble in the house of the bereaved family to recite verses from the Holy Koran in order to bring *sawaab* (merit) to the departed soul. Third-day ritual is known as *chaharum*. A similar ritual is repeated after forty days and is called *chehallum* with a wider participation of the kin. Economic stringencies have made the life-cycle rituals less elaborate and individualistic in approach than what they used to be in the past.

The Watals are a landless community. However, the nearby forests, streams and lakes supplement their economic needs marginally. As stated in the beginning, the main occupation of the community living in the cities is to work in the local municipalities, notified areas and cantonment boards. In the rural areas the Watals serve as sweepers and scavengers for the farmers and zamindars for a petty sum of Rs. 12 to 15 per month from each household they serve. The self-employed earn slightly more, that too in the cities, but their earnings again are irregular, especially during the prolonged winters when the tourist traffic to the Valley comes to a standstill.

Winters are rigorous for the employed Watals whose services are used, for removing the accumulated snow from the roads, lanes, bylanes and gutters. Those employed by the Srinagar Cantonment Board are the highest paid, getting a monthly salary ranging from Rs. 300 to 475. Neverthleless, a major portion of their income is spent on housing and food.

In terms of capital, their assets consist of a few kitchen utensils made of clay or aluminium, scanty clothes and rooms sans any item of furniture. Possession of bicycles and radio sets by a very few present a grim contrast between the elite and the layman of the community.

Children from the age of ten may be seen squatting on the pavements of Srinagar with their shoe-shining outfit doing brisk business in the tourist season. The Watals never had a viable means of subsistence barring a few who work for the government and semi-government agencies. A few of them have started running cobbler's shops but the replacement of skin with cheap plastics has caused a substantial setback to their income.

Disputes arising out of the breach of customary laws are brought to the notice of the village *nambardar*. If the latter fails to resolve the differences, the disputes are taken to the court of law.

The Watals belong to the Sunni sect of Islam but the degree of the people's conformity to the basic Islamic tenets remains peripheral. A few of them have been reported to have visited the tombs of Khwaja Nizamuddin in Delhi, Khwaja Moinuddin Chishti in Ajmer and Khawaja Salim Chishti in Agra. These pilgrim centres have helped the Watal pilgrims to evolve a better degree of conformity to the Islamic tenets. In the village, the *pir* (priest) inculates in them an awareness to be clean Muslims. He also acts as a religious guide during the performance of the life-cycle rituals. The festivals observed are Id-ul-Fitr, Id-e-Qurban, Id-e-Milad-ul-Nabi and Gyarhawin Sharif.

It has been observed that a number of occupational groups serve the Watals and the Watals too serve a number of communities, the government and semi-government agencies. Being Muslims, no commensal taboos are observed *vis-a-vis* other Muslim communities but, on the social scene, the elite Muslim communities keep a distance from them. The Watals share with other communities the places of worship, water resources, roads and schools.

Development has little meaning for the Watals who still remain illiterate, unemployed, isolated and the weakest segment of the Kashmiri society. Only two matriculates were reported from Batwara and both were unemployed.

In spite of their constitutional status, the Watals have been denied the facilities made available to the Scheduled Castes. Various schemes on rural land and urban housing have not so far helped the Watal build houses for themselves. Srinagar Cantonment Board has, however, provided a few dwellings to their Watal employees. The nearby streams are the only source of drinking water. Electricity is consumed for lighting purpose only.

The network of roads and communication has not helped in occupational diversification. The benefits accrued from the development planning have percolated down only to a limited section of the community living in urban agglomerates.

BAQAR R. RIZVI

WAZA

Waza literally means a 'cook' in Kashmiri language. The Wazas are well known as experts in cooking during marriages and other social functions. It is an occupational category of the Muslims and is quite distinct from the other Muslim communities on the basis of their profession. The history and origin of the community is not known but it is believed that, before the advent of Islam in the Kashmir Valley, the ancestors of the Waza were Hindus and were converted to Islam thereafter.

During the Mughal period, they were the chief cooks in the palaces. They place themselves in the Sheikh category of the Muslims and take pride in their profession. They are found in Srinagar, Baramula, Anantnag, Pulwama, Badgam and Kupwara districts of Jammu & Kashmir but are mainly concentrated in Srinagar district, which is surrounded by the Pir Panjal and greater Himalayan ranges.

The climate is cold, natural vegetation is temperate and rainfall is low. The area is thinly forested and confined to the hill ranges below the snow-line. Their population figure is not available. The language of the Wazas is Kashmiri using Arabic script. They speak Kashmiri among themselves and Urdu with others. There is no identification mark of the community but at the time of cooking food, they wear a white apron called *safed posh* and a white cap. Otherwise, they dress like the other Kashmiris such as *pheran*, *pochh*, trousers and cap. The women wear *salwar*, *kurta*, *pheren and puts* (which is worn on head and is made of long plain cloth). They are non-vegetarian. They eat mutton, fish and chicken. Beef is not consumed. Rice is their staple food. Wheat, maize, bajra, barley and millets are also consumed but not as a substitute for rice. During winters, maize is consumed in large quantities. Bread is consumed in the morning and noon time with tea. Among the pulses gram, *moong* (green gram), *urad* (black gram), *masur* and brown gram (*moth*) are consumed. Mustard oil is used as the cooking medium. The community consumes roots and tubers also. Vegetables like cabbage, cauliflower, pumpkin, brinjals, ladies' finger, carrot, cucumber, potato, etc., are used seasonally. Among the leafy vegetables, *hak* or *karam sag* (spinach) are a favourite. Fruits are consumed in plenty. Tea is their favourite drink and is very popular in the community, like in other communities of Kashmir. They consume it with salt. The tea which is taken with sugar is called *qahwa* and occasionally consumed. Milk and milk products are consumed by the community in lesser quantities due to its non-availability. Consumption of clarified butter (*ghee*), is low as it is considered harmful in the cold climate. Consumption of alcoholic drinks and pork is religiously prohibited. They smoke *bidis*, cigarettes and *hookah*.

On the basis of economic status, occupation and educational attainment, they place themselves in the high or low ranks. No changes have been reported in their surnames. The Wazas are placed in the middle rank in the local social hierarchy and are considered to pursue a clean occupation.

They are an endogamous group but rules of endogamy are not strictly followed. Though they prefer to marry their sons and daughter within the community, in case of non-availability of a suitable match, they may accept girls from any community of the Sunni sect of Muslims.

In the selection of girl, first preference is given to the cousins. If there is no such marriageable girl available, then they select a girl from outside their community. Nowadays, marriages take place when the boys and girls are adults, but in the past early marriages were prevalent. The age at marriage is between 18 and 25 years for both the boys and girls. Most of the marriages are settled by negotiations. Generally, a common friend starts the negotiation between the families but sometimes it is done by a mediator (*manzymyor*).

Monogamy is the general practice. Polygyny, though permissible in the community according to the *shariat* (Islamlic rules), is not reported in the community. There is no symbol of marriage. Dowry is permissible in the community. *Mahr* for the bride is fixed at the time of marriage. After marriage, the bride goes to live with her husband and in-laws. Divorce is permissible in the community as in the other Muslim groups. Only the husband can divorce due to barrenness, adultery, maladjustment and insanity. Likewise, the wife can also seek separation if the husband is absconding or unable to bear the expenses of his wife and children or is not having sexual contact with his wife for more than three years.

In the community, a husband enjoys more rights and privileges than a wife in the matter of divorce. According to the Muslim rules, divorce may be given either orally or in writing known as *talaq-nama*. In the Muslim law, when a marriage is dissolved by divorce, the woman is prohibited from remarrying within the specified period of *iddat*. If there is a divorce after consummation of marriage, then the duration of *iddat* is for three months and ten days or, if the woman is pregnant, it is until the delivery. The purpose for fixing a period of *iddat* is to ascertain the legitimacy of a possible child and also to bring about a reconciliation between the husband and wife. The cases of divorce are rare in the community. It is the responsibility of the father to maintain the children after divorce when they are minor. Widow, widower and divorcee remarriages are permissible in the community. Widows are allowed to remarry after the *iddat* period is over. Remarriages are performed in a simple way. Decrease in divorce, emergence of dowry system and monogamy are the major changes which have taken place in recent years.

Among the Wazas, there are mostly nuclear families though extended families are found mostly in rural areas. In most of the cases, the new couple establishes a new house after marriage. Interpersonal relationships are amicable among the family members. Due love and respect are paid to youngsters and elders. Avoidance relationship is maintained between the daughter-in-law and parents-in-law, and between younger brother's wife and husband's elder brother; likewise with outsiders and elderly relatives. Joking relationship prevails between husband's younger brother and elder brother's wife and between elder sister's husband and wife's younger sisters.

The property is divided among the sons, daughters and the widow. The daughters get a share less than that of their brothers and widowed mother. Succession is followed in the male line from father to the eldest son. The only change which has come about is the breaking up of joint family system and the emergence of nuclear families. In the community, women have equal status with men. They have full right to *mahr*, the amount which was fixed at the time of *nikah* by the husband. It can be claimed by the wife at any time after marriage but generally it is demanded at the time of divorce.

The women play an important role in all spheres of life like agriculture, collection of fuel, bringing potable water and doing other household jobs. They have pivotal role in the social and religious functions. Though they do not contribute much to the family income, they certainly help to supplement it. They have decision-making powers and exercise control over the expenditure in the family.

During the first pregnancy, the woman is not allowed to carry heavy load and do household work. They do not live with their husbands for more than the first five months of their pregnancy. The delivery takes place at home, particularly in rural areas. A *warin* (midwife) is called to assist the parturient mother and is paid in cash and kind (such as sweets, rice and maize) according to the economic status of the family. She may be from any community. Generally, they are old women who are expert and have knowledge in this regard. Immediately after birth a warm water bath is given to the child and a senior male member recites *azaan* in the ears of the baby.

On the first birth, bread and sweets are distributed among the relatives, friends and neighbours. If the delivery takes place at her parents' house, sweets are sent to her in-laws. Her mother in-law also sends sweets, cash and clothes for the baby in return. This ceremony is called *piaw*. On the seventh day after delivery, the mother of the baby takes her first bath. On this day, the child is given a name either by the family priest or any elderly person of the family. The ceremony is called *sunder*. It is usually followed by a feast.

After forty days the parturient mother is given another bath and then she is allowed to perform normal household jobs. *Zerakasi* is performed after six months when the hair of the child are shaved by the family barber. A feast is also arranged on this occasion. Circumcision (*khatnahal*) is the next ceremony observed when the male child is more than two years. It is performed by the family barber but in urban areas it is done in a hospital or at home by an expert doctor. A big feast is arranged on this occasion.

The marriages are settled by negotiation and preference is given to the cousins. If it is not possible, selection is made from outside the community. Sometime, a *manzymyor* (matchmaker) negotiates the marriage between the families. After preliminary negotiations and mutual consent, the father of the boy with some relatives visits the place of the bride and offers some money to the bride and her father. This marks the *gandum* (engagement) ceremony.

After this ceremony, *doon-leij* ritual is performed in which the father of the bride sends an earthern pot full with nuts and some cash for the father of the bridegroom. *Doon-leij* is followed by *dapanbata* ritual in which members of the family go to their relatives for extending invitation for the marriage. In the house of bride, *malasbehoun* ritual is observed, wherein the bride is not allowed to take bath and do household jobs for at least three days before the marriage.

Another ceremony called *massmechravoun* is observed in which the hair of the bride is combed by the female relatives. The first day of the marriage is called *menziraat*. In the night, *mehndi* (myrtle paste) is applied on the hands and feet of the bride. The second day of the marriage is called *yenevoul*. On this day, the father of the bridegroom sends few copper plates containing sugar candy, sugar balls, almonds, clothes and ornaments for the bride. When the *barat* procession starts it is followed by two or three rows of women singing in chorus holding each other for some distance. At the house of the bride, the marriage procession is received by the women singing in chorus in the same manner.

After this, *nikah* ceremony is observed. It is presided over by the village priest (*maulvi*). There are two types of *nikah—nikah asaltan* and *nikah vilaitan*. In *nikah asaltan*, both the bride and the bridegroom are present and a marriage contract is written with their consent in the presence of some witnesses. *Mahr* money is also fixed in the *nikah* ceremony which varies from Rs. 9,000 to 21,000. *Nikah vilaitan* is performed when the boy and girl are minor. This type of marriages was prevalent in the past. In this *nikah*, the parents used to give their consent on behalf of the bride and the bridegroom. When the *nikah* ceremony is over, a feast is given. At the time of departure when the bride goes with her husband, the bride's female relatives follow her for some distance singing in chorus. The bride stays with her husband for seven days. A big feast is arranged on the marriage night called *wathal*. After marriage, the bride starts living with her husband.

After the death of a person, the relatives and friends of the deceased assemble and a bath is given to the dead body by a professional man called *snangor*. He is paid money and given clothes of the deceased. After bath, the dead body is wrapped in *kafan* (white cloth) and placed in a (coffin) *taboot*. The *taboot* is laid on the ground facing Mecca and the priest recites *namaz-e-janaza* prayers. Thereafter the *taboot* is carried to the graveyard where a grave called *lahad* is dug by a digger (*malkhos*) who is paid money and given tea with bread. The dead body is placed in the *lahad* and covered with stones and earth. On the fourth day after death, the priest, relatives and neighbours recite verses from the Holy Koran for the peace of the departed soul. The ceremony is repeated on the fortieth day. These rituals are called *chaharum* and *chehallum*, respectively. There has been no change in these customs except their curtailment.

The primary occupation of the community is to cook food for all the Muslim and non-Muslim communities on different occasions such as marriage, child birth, death and in other big feasts. Almost all the families of the Waza community are engaged in their traditional occupation of cooking. They are specialized in cooking Kashmiri dishes such as *methi*, *kabab*, *khain*, *dhani*, *rishta*, *choru*, *yakhni*, *roganjosh*, *palawa*, *gustaba*, *phirini* and *halwa*.

In rural areas, they are engaged in agriculture also. Only a few members of the community are in the government or private jobs. Economic resources are controlled either by the family or by individuals. They are directly linked with the local market which is fully regulated. The community is still devoted to its traditional occupation and do not want to leave it because it is profitable.

Disputes in the family are settled either by the head of the family or other elders and relatives. In villages, this is done by the village headmen. Sometimes their disputes are taken to the court of law.

They believe in Islam and follow its dicta, i.e. *shariat*. There are several sacred shrines and mosques which are visited by them on different occasions. Shah Hamdan, Charar-e-Sharif, Makhdum Sahib, Dastgir Sahib, Naqshband Sahib are their sacred pilgrimage centres. The community has its own *pirs* who are engaged to perform the birth, marriage and death rites. They observe all the Muslim festivals, namely Urs-e-Nabi (Prophet Muhammad's birthday) also known as Id-ul-Milad celebrated on twelfth of Rabi-ul-Awwal. On this day, the Prophet's hair relic is displayed at the Hazratbal shrine. Meraj-e-Alam is celebrated on the twenty-sixth day of Rajab and the hair relic is displayed on this day also. Id-ul-Fitr, Id-ul-Zuha, Shab-e-Qadr are other festivals which are celebrated with great zeal by the members of the community. Besides, there are certain festivals like Urs-e-Shah Hamdan, Urs-e-Batmaloo, Urs-e-Charar-e-Sharif, Urs-e-Makhdum Sahib, Urs-e-Pir Dastgir, Urs-e-Naqshband, Urs-e-Rafimal which are also celebrated by the Waza community.

The festivals of the community are of socio-religious importance. A few members of the community are involved in embroidery work, wood carving, papier mgchÈ and other traditional crafts of Kashmir. The women sing folk songs on various social occasions.

Being involved in the important occupation of cooking, the community maintains its relations with all the Muslim and non-Muslim communities. The Wazas extend their services even to the lowest castes of the valley like the Watals and Serajs. They accept *kachcha* and *pukka* food from all the Hindus and Muslims but to some extent try to maintain a distance with the Watals. The services of the *pirs*, Navids, Gorkan, Tarkhan and other Muslim communities are taken on the occasions of childbirth, marriage and death rituals. They share water sources, burial grounds and religious shrines with the other Muslims. Patron-client relationship exists in the community. At present, the members of this community are employed in different govern-ment and non-government services. They are still involved in their traditional occupation.

The development programmes of the government have left appreciable impact on the community. Their attitude towards the education of girls is less favourable than that towards the boys. Though in the rural areas they are still backward in education, in urban areas they are paying more attention towards education. In villages the educational programmes of the government could not be successful as the schools are far away. That is why they are unable to respond for proper education. For higher education, they have to go to the cities.

The attitude of the community towards the modern medicare is favourable but their indigenous traditional medicare system is still practised in remote areas. The attitude of the community towards family planning programmes is also favourable as they now prefer to have less children. Electricity and drinking water facilities are available in their locality. Tap water, streams and springs are their main sources of drinking water. Being involved in agriculture and cooking, most members of the community are self-employed. The media of communication and entertainment used are radio, television and cinema for those who live in urban areas. Cow-dung cakes, wood and kerosene oil are used as fuels for cooking.

In villages, they mostly depend on rain and stream water due to non-availability of irrigation facilities for agriculture. The facilities of public distribution system through the fair price shops are available and the community avails of them. The community has a positive attitude towards saving and they are not dependent on the money-lenders or shopkeepers.

ANAND SARAN

APPENDIX

A Note on Castes and Caste Names in the Kashmir Valley

1. Caste in Kashmir

As is common in all societies and communities in the Indian subcontinent, caste names have been adopted and maintained by the inhabitants of the Kashmir Valley too, irrespective of their differences in religion and culture. In actuality, caste names in Kashmir have a long history. These names were adopted in the ancient period when the Kashmiris were Hindus. Subsequently, the total conversion of Kashmiris (first, from Hinduism to Buddhism, and second, from Buddhism and Hinduism to Islam) in the medieval period did not affect this practice. Now, these caste names have become a part of cultural heredity, an important dimension of social structure, and an inseparable aspect of social life.

2. List of Caste Names

This list of caste names in Kashmir have been compiled by me in the last four years. In fact, an effort was made to trace and identify every caste name which is used by the people living in the Valley of Kashmir. The structure, function and other aspects of caste in Kashmir differs from the Hindu caste system. Caste in the Kashmiri context essentially refers to an occupational community, a family title, a social caste category, and a *biradari* or *quam.*

3. Nature of Caste

The caste system, in the traditional sense of the term, does not exist in the Kashmir Valley. But, at the same time, caste exists in Kashmir and plays a definite role in the Kashmiri society. In fact, it is peculiar in terms of structure and function. These castes neither fit in the traditional hierarchical caste system nor do they reflect any aspect of Islamic egalitarianism. In actuality, it refers to three types of social categories which are as follows:

(i) *Biradari*: a family or clan title which reflects social, cultural, and economic status;
(ii) *Quam*: an occupational community which emerged on the basis of similarities in occupations; and
(iii) *Zaat*: a social group which is culturally determined and an arrangement of the groups in a set hierarchy.

It may not be out of place to mention here that there exists no outcaste in the Kashmir Valley.

4. Origin of Caste

The origins of caste names among the Muslims in Kashmir are different. Most of these caste names have been inherited from the pre-Islamic Hindu society and have been kept intact even after the conversion. These varying origins may be explained as follows:

(i) Sayyid origin: The Sayyid caste names such as Qadri, Fazili, Chisti, Andarabi and Naqashbandi reveal their descent from the Prophet of Islam directly or indirectly.
(ii) Alien origin: Some caste names such as Khan, Geelani, Panjabi, Pathan and Durrani reveal their alien descent. The members of these caste groups have migrated to Kashmir in the medieval times and have settled here permanantly.
(iii) Occupational origin: A lot of occupational communities in the Kashmir Valley have adopted the caste names from their occupations such as Najar, Sofi, Dhobi, Misger and Tarkhan.
(iv) Nickname origin: Many caste names in Kashmir have been adopted because these were used as nicknames for certain individuals, families and clans such as Teng, Chottu, Lalmot and Chela.
(v) Origin from birds: Significant number of caste names in Kashmir have been taken from the local birds such as Tota, Kaw, Braer, Batkhoo and Gagroo.
(iv) Animal origin: Several caste names in Kashmir have been adopted from the names of local animals such as Dand, Chopan, Khar, Panj.

5. *Features of Caste*

(i) Hierarchy: The castes in the Kashmir Valley have been related to a set status depending upon the descent, origin, occupation, economic and social status. Thus the castes may be arranged hierarchically in terms of their position in the broader society, some at the top, some at the bottom, and the rest in between.

(ii) Endogamy: The practice of endogamy is still a dominant practice. However, the implications of change and development have made it less effective. Consequently, it has lost its primacy. Thus the practice of exogamy is increasing fast.

(iii) Occupational specialization: Traditionally, castes in Kashmir were related to particular occupations. However, a radical change has occurred in this regard because of economic, social, and political developments in the state after 1947. Now the castes may not be necessarily related to particular occupations.

(iv) Ideology: There exists no theoretical, cultural and religious justification of caste system in Kashmir. While the emphasis on Hinduism leads to the legitimacy of the caste system, the emphasis on Islam delegitimizes the caste system in any form. So, the problems related to purity and pollution do not exist in the Kashmiri society.

6. *The Kashmiri Pandits*

The castes among Hindus in Kashmir, called the Kashmiri Pandits (KPs), exist in the ideal form, though certain crucial changes have occurred. The KP castes belong to different *varnas* such as Brahmans and Shudras. They practise many features of the Hindu caste system such as endogamy, purity and pollution, hierarchy and occupational specialization. However, as a result of the implications of change, especially the impact of the Kashmiri Muslims in the previous few decades, the KPs have undergone significant degree of change in the caste practices. Consequently, while many urban Pandits have opted for business career, the rural Pandits have adopted agriculture as their sole occupation, working by themselves on the land. This was not the case in the past.

7. *Change in the Caste*

Last but not least, is the dimension of caste related to change and mobility. In the broader context of the implications of change and development, a significant number of non-Sayyid castes have adopted the Sayyid caste titles. According to an unofficial estimate, there are about 30 to 45 per cent Sayyids who have adopted these titles in the recent past. Now, it is very difficult to differentiate between the real and the fictitious Sayyid in the Valley. While this phenomenon may be characterized as part of the broader process of Islamization, this may also be considered a process of Sayyidization, which is more like the process of Sanskritization.

8. Caste Names

Aali, Aazim, Aba, Adalti, Adhami, Afaq, Aga, Agha, Agoo, Ahangar, Ahrar, Aima, Akhoon, Akmali, Alai, Alim Allaie, Allakaband, Alvi, Ambardar, Amiq, Amla, Anand, Andaleeb, Andarabi, Anim, Ansari, Anungo, Arikash, Arm, Arosa, Ashai, Asmi, Atri, Attaf, Auaue, Auluck, Awan, Azad.

Bara, Babu, Baccha, Bacha, Badam, Badana, Bader, Badgami, Badha, Badoo, Badri, Badyari, Bafanda, Bafroo, Bagal, Bagati, Bagaw, Bagdadi, Bagloo, Bagwan, Bahaqi, Bahar, Baig, Bajad, Bajaw, Bajwa, Bakaya, Bakh-Roo, Bakkal, Bakshi, Baktoo, Bala, Baldev, Bali, Belkhi, Balkhi, Balla, Balloo, Baltee, Balti, Bamsunt, Bamzia, Band, Bandar, Bandari, Banday, Bandroo, Bangi, Bangru, Banihali, Banka, Bansal, Bantoo, Bapari, Bapada, Barangaroo, Barwa, Basmati, Basu, Bataphalu, Bath, Batieb, Batkhoo, Batkoo, Batloo, Batoo, Batra, Batruqu, Batti, Battiv, Bawani, Bayroo, Bazaz, Bazari, Bedebe, Beg, Bhan, Bhandari, Bhar, Bhat, Bhatia, Bhawan, Bhuni, Bhuru, Bichoo, Bihaqi, Bijli, Billa, Billo, Bindri, Bindroo, Bira, Bisati, Bishtoo, Biyu, Boblie, Boda, Bodha, Bogra, Bohadur, Bossa, Boza, Bradi, Braro, Braru, Breth, Broca, Buchh, Buchoo, Budoo, Burdoo, Budshah, Bhroo, Bukhari, Bukhtv, Bulaki, Buland, Bulbul, Bulla, Bungri, Bungriee, Bungroo, Buni, Burbuz, Buth, Buthar, Butt, Buwa, Byaroo.

Cada, Cadroo, Cano, Chabral, Chabuk, Chacha, Chache, Chadhu, Chadoo, Chadroo, Chaghat, Chaira, Chak, Chakan, Chaku, Chaladoo, Chalak, Chalk, Chalkoo, Chaloo, Chan, Chandra, Chandru, Changal, Chanla, Channa, Chansaz, Chapri, Chapu, Charag, Charngu, Charloo, Charoo, Chashoo, Chashool, Chat, Chatoo, Chatyany, Chaurasia, Chebsi, Chechak, Chekoo, Chela, Chenga, Chersoo, Chatoo, Chnotu, Chib, Chibber, Chiken, Chillo, Chillum, Chinna, Chisti, Chitra, Choku, Chondhri, Chonka, Chonkoo, Chooh, Choor, Choora, Chopan, Choran, Chothai, Chowdhry, Chowoo, Chrungu, Chula, Chutoo, Clay.

Dabla/Dubla, Dabloo, Daenposh, Daftari, Daga, Dahal, Daimi,

Daing, Dalal, Dand, Dander, Dandoo, Dangar, Dangloo, Dangola, Dangoo, Dangroo, Dar, Dareel, Darez, Darial, Dariah, Darma, Darsaroo, Darwash, Darwesh, Darzi, Dass, Dassu, Datloo, Dawan, Dawrki, Dedmari, Deen, Dehqani, Dembi, Dev, Dewa, Dewanani, Dewani, Dharbari, Dhawan, Dhir, Dhobi, Digoodijg, Diju, Dilnanz, Dilwari, Diya, Dodeja, Dohond, Doka, Dolwal, Dongala, Doom, Door, Doshab, Dotiwala, Dout, Drabi, Draboo, Drangry, Duda, Dug, Dugloo, Dukroo, Dullu, Dunarki, Dunoo, Durani, Duru, Dutta.

Eachkoti

Factoo, Fafoo, Famboo, Famoda, Faqir, Farash, Farid, Faridie, Farooqi, Fata, Fatay, Fatehkhan, Fateing, Fazili, Fehrist, Fote-Dar, Frier.

Gabroo, Gadar, Gadda, Gaddu, Gadoo, Gadroo, Gaduari, Gadwali, Gaegoo, Gagar, Gagloo, Gagroo, Galikrapa, Gallani, Gama, Gami, Gamir, Ganani, Ganauaa, Ganderbali, Gangoo, Ganhar, Ganie, Ganjoo, Garuali, Gas, Gashroo, Gassi, Gatoo, Gazi, Guri, Geelani, Geer, Gernail, Ghai, Ghasi, Ghazi, Ghughtoo, Gigo, Gigu, Gilkar, Giloo, Gira, Girn, Goble, Gochkoo, Gochoo, Goiree, Gojri, Gojwari, Goni, Goona, Goosani, Gopi, Gora, Goroo, Gortoo, Goru, Gowhar, Gugtor, Gugoo, Guhnoo, Guknoo, Gul, Gulab, Gundroo, Gupkari, Gura, Gurkari, Gurku, Gurloo, Gurnt, Gurop, Gusoo, Gutoo.

Haak, Hafiz, Hagroo, Hailkhani, Haja, Hajam, Haji, Hajni, Haiku, Hak, Hakachar, Hakak, Hakani, Hakeem, Hakhoo, Hakim, Hakju, Hakroo, Haksar, Halvie, Halwaai, Handani, Hangal, Hant, Hapa, Hara, Hargoo, Haroo, Haroon, Haroor, Hasha, Hashia, Hastiwal, Hatam, Hawabaz, Hazar, Hazari, Hella, Hofan, Hojewah, Honga, Howash, Hudowalo, Hukhu, Hundoo, Hura, Hurra, Hyderi.

Illahi, Imam, Ithadi, Itoo.

Jad, Jaggia, Jajia, Jala, Jalali, Jaloo, Jamie, Jan, Janbaz, Janda, Jandgoro, Jangeva, Janwari, Jarabi, Jasid, Jathoo, Jatkay, Jatta, Jattu, Jawaid, Jawansher, Jeelani, Jet, Jeth, Jhampoo, Jhat, Jinsi, Jogi, Jota, Jotshi, Juisi, Jukara, Juneja.

Kaahroo, Kachkar, Kada, Kadalabuyu, Kadhari, Kadla, Kadoo, Kahue, Kakhshgir, Kakpori, Kala, Kalim, Kalpush, Kalu, Kalwal, Kambay, Kandar, Kandoo, Kangoo, Kant, Kanthjoo, Karawani, Karihalu, Karnel, Kashgari, Kashkari, Kashu, Kat, Katai, Kathroo, Kathsho, Katjoo, Katshoo, Katsru, Keena, Keloo, Kem, Kemdar, Keni, Kera, Khachoo, Khaibri, Khaki, Khanakata, Khankashi, Khanyari, Khari, Khashu, Khatana, Khatayee, Khateeb, Khaumush, Khawaja, Kheshu, Khod, Khoja, Khoru, Khride, Khurdi, Kichhu, Kissu, Kockru, Koheem, Kokru, Kondie, Konkoo, Kotar, Kothdar, Kozeer, Kucha, Kukroo, Kulkatloo, Kumar, Kundiji, Kundroo, Kushkhan, Kutty, Kyani.

Labroo, Lachka, Laherwal, Lahori, Lakra, Lal, Lala, Lalee, Lali, Lalla, Lalye, Lamba, Lange, Langer, Langoo, Lanker, Lankroo, Lara, Larah, Latoo, Laway, Laya, Lidi, Lidoo, Ligaroo, Lizzye, Lodi, Lolu, Lone, Loolu, Lovedari, Lueli.

Maala, Madni, Mahaldar, Majhanji, Majhu, Makai, Makaya, Makya, Maldaya, Mallah, Malya, Manda, Manroo, Mansoor, Margoob, Masala, Matass, Mathai, Mava, Mirab, Mistri, Miydo, Mizada, Mochi, Moharkan, Mohind, Mohju, Monga, Mori, Mudi, Mugloo, Mukhtari, Mundoo, Mungroo, Muntazir, Mushvi.

Naazir, Nadatie, Nadif, Nadroo, Nagain, Nagami, Nagari, Nagash, Nagoo, Nahamoo, Nahir, Nahvi, Naik, Naika, Naikoo, Naiyma, Najar, Naji, Najmi, Naka, Nalband, Namak, Namtejali, Nanda, Nangnoo, Nangroo, Nanvaiy, Naqashbandi, Naqashi, Naqati, Naqeed, Naqib, Naqshi, Narchoor, Nari, Narwari, Nasri, Nasti, Nath, Nathu, Navas, Nawaz, Nawchoo, Naz, Nazera, Naziki, Nehru, Neyak, Nida, Nika, Nilla, Niyaz, Niyazi, Nizami, Nokh, Noori, Nowsheri.

Oberia, Ogra, Oja, Oontoo, Order.

Pache, Pachegaroo, Packhliwal, Padi, Paddar, Padeer, Padora, Padroo, Padwal, Pah, Pahalwan, Pahloo, Pajnoo, Pajwari, Pakchiwal, Pakhtoon, Pal, Pala, Palav, Palla, Paloo, Pampori, Pandani, Pandit, Pandita, Pandow, Panht, Panjra, Pant, Panzoo, Paray, Parbati, Pardesh, Parikala, Parimoo, Parimu, Parra, Partaz, Pasha, Paswal, Paswan, Patar, Pathan, Patigaroo, Patikoo, Patnaik, Patloo, Pattoo, Paul, Payer, Pedhar, Peerzada, Pehloo, Perienjee, Peshin, Phalgaroo, Phalvi, Phamboo, Piala, Pinchoo, Pir, Pishen, Pishoo, Pohla, Posh, Posha, Poswal, Puju, Punjabi, Puri, Purzger, Put, Putra, Putu.

Qadeemi, Qadiri, Qamri, Qandhari, Qari, Qasba, Qasmi, Qazi, Quanoon, Qureshi, Qurpal.

Radoo, Rafiqi, Rafiz, Rafoogar, Rah, Raina, Raja, Rajpuri, Rambal, Ramshoo, Ranga, Rangateng, Rangrez, Rangroo, Ranjoor, Ranwali, Rather, Rathore, Ratta, Rattanpuri, Raua, Raval, Rawal, Rawandah, Rawloo, Raz, Razdan, Razvi, Reeiq, Regoo, Rehani, Rehbar, Reheza, Renco, Renoo, Renzoo, Reshi, Revoo, Rey, Ringshawl, Rizavi, Rizmi, Roshoo, Ronga, Roshenger, Roshi, Ruffalie, Rungnoo.

9. Sources of Caste Names

The list of caste names in the Kashmir Valley has been prepared from diverse and largescale primary sources. These include the following sources:

- Revenue records of J&K Government (1990 onwards)

- Telephone directories of J&K (1988 onwards)
- Local telephone directories of different offices, agencies and organizations.
- University and JK Board Gazettes
- University, college and school admission lists and other records.
- Other government records.
- Local newspapers in Urdu and English
- *Srinagar Times* (Srinagar)
- *Aftab* (Srinagar)
- *Alsafa* (Srinagar)
- *Nidai* Mushriq (Srinagar)
- *Afaaq* (Srinagar)
- *Chattan* (Srinagar)
- *Kashmir Times* (Jammu)
- *Greater Kashmir* (Srinagar)
- Books, papers and articles on Kashmir.

BASHIR AHMAD DABLA

A BIO-ANTHROPOLOGICAL PROFILE

The state of Jammu & Kashmir has three distinct physiographic regions with diverse ethnic elements. The Ladakh region is primarily dominated by the populations of Mongoloid stock. In the hilly tracts of Pir Panjal up to Punjab plains, the Dogras are predominant, followed by the semi-nomadic Gujjars and Gaddis, who are mainly concentrated in Punch and Udhampur districts. In between, the Kashmir Valley is dominated by the Muslims and Pandits.

A detailed anthropometric investigation was conducted by Anthropological Survey of India as part of All India Anthropometric Survey (AIAS) from April to June 1967 (Haq, Bhowmik and Basu, 1989). It covered seven districts and collected data on five populations, namely, Kashmiri Brahmans, Chamars, Mahasas, Muslims and Rajputs. No population from Ladakh region was covered. The survey found that the people of Jammu & Kashmir are on an average below medium in stature (163.88 cms.). They have long and narrow head (mean cephalic index 77.45), long nose (mean nasal index 67.05) and long face (mean total facial index 88.89). The findings are supplemented as per Martin's classification. It is found that 25 per cent of the population is below the medium stature, followed by short (22.16 per cent) and medium (20.13 per cent) statured individuals. Only 15 per cent of the population studied are tall. Long and narrow head (*dolichocephaly*) is found in 55 per cent of the population. Broadhead (*brachycephaly*) is rare (3.57 per cent). Around 58 per cent of them have long nose. Likewise, long face (33.76 per cent) and very long face (21.02 per cent) is a common feature among the population of Jammu & Kashmir (Singh, Bhalla and Kaul, 1994).

The All India Bio-Anthropological Survey (AIBAS) covered five nodal locations in Jammu & Kashmir state (Ghosh, 1988). Demographic data revealed that on an average, the state have 114 males per 100 females. The population of Jammu & Kashmir lives predominantly (52 per cent) in small households (1-5 individuals per house), whereas large households (11+ members) are rare (2 per cent). There are more illiterates among females (69.54 per cent) than males (50.18 per cent). Among the literate, only 9.23 per cent of males and 4.51 per cent of females are educated up to the level of matriculation and above. Relatively less females (46.00 per cent) are unmarried in comparison to males (59.30 per cent). But occurrence of divorced and widowed individuals is more among females (6.24 per cent) than males (3.67 per cent) (Singh, Bhalla and Kaul, 1994).

A number of reports besides AIAS are available on morphological features of Jammu & Kashmir population. The populations of Ladakh, which are generally Mongoloid, have been mainly studied by Eickstedt (1927). Communities like the Balti, Bod, Changpa and Ladakhi are on an average below medium stature (162.58 cms), have round head (CI 76.32) and medium nose (NI 70.79). The Kashmiri Pandits, studied by Chakladar (1921), Raychoudhuri (1961) and Kaul (1971), are below medium to medium in stature, have long and narrow head, long nose and face.

In dermatoglyphics, Bansal (1968) reported greater incidence of whorls (56.00 per cent) than loops (42.00 per cent) in Ladakhi populations. But Pandit of Kashmir Valley show the loops (48.52 per cent) preponderate over whorls (45.51 per cent) (Kumbanani, 1963; Arora, 1976-7). Among the Muslims, incidence of loops and whorls range from 43 to 52 per cent and 45 to 54 per cent respectively (Arora, 1976-77; Tyagi et al., 1977; Sen, 1968 and Gupta, 1976). Pattern intensity index varies from 14, recorded among the Muslims, to 16 found in the Mongoloid population. Colour blindness has been recorded in 7 per cent of the individuals of Dogra community (Bhalla et al., 1980; and Sharma and Bhalla, 1980, and the Pandits (Delhi Univ., 1958). Bala (1978) reported low incidence of colour blindness among the Muslim females (1.33 per cent) but high in Muslim males (10.66 per cent).

The incidence of taster genet (PTC) has been reported low frequency in Ladakhi population (23.79 per cent) (Bhalla, 1972) as compared to other populations, such as the Dogra (61.62-62.96 per cent) (Bhalla et al., 1980), the Pandits (51.53-55.14 per cent) and the Muslim (51.10-59.57 per cent) (Tyagi et al. (unpublished, and Chandhoke, 1976).

ABH secretion system has been studied among the Muslims, Pandits and the Dogras only. The frequency of non-secretor gene(s) ranges from 42.22 per cent, recorded among the Pandits (Bhattacharjee, 1966), to 60.19 per cent among the Dogra Brahmin (Bhalla, et al., 1980). Incidence of G6PD deficiency is low and ranges from 4 per cent, found among the Pandit females, to 6 per cent among the Sunni Muslims (Bala and Seth, 1978).

Around 30 studies are available on ABO blood group system on different communities of the state. Invariably the occurrence of B gene

(21-31 per cent) is greater than A gene (14-25 per cent) in all the communities. The frequencies of O gene is generally above 50 per cent, ranging from 51 per cent among the Brahmans of Srinagar (Chatterjee, 1963) to 60 per cent among the Ladakhi populations (Kaur et al., 1977). Interestingly, the frequency of A gene is greater among the Muslims (15-51 per cent) (Bansal, 1967; Bhattacharjee, 1966; Grover 1976-7; Gupta and Singhal, 1989) than other communities (14-25 per cent).

The frequency of M gene is generally above 70 per cent in the populations of Jammu & Kashmir with a range variation of 70-83 per cent. Bhattacharjee (1966, 1967, 1968) observed low frequency of MS (14 per cent) and NS (8 per cent) genes in Ladakhi population as compared to that of the Pandits (MS-22 per cent, NS 11 per cent) and Muslims (MS-24 per cent; NS-13 per cent).

The prevalence of r haplotype (Rh system) is generally low among the Ladakhis (11 per cent) than the Kashmiris (16-28 per cent). However, Bhalla et al. (1980) reported low incidence of r haplotype among the Dogra Brahman (9 per cent) in contrast to the Dogra Rajput (16 per cent). Unpublished report of Tyagi and others observed low incidence of r haplotype among the Muslims (3 per cent) which is at variance with that reported by Bhattacharjee (1966) among the Ladakhi Muslims (18 per cent) (Kaur, 1979) or the Brahmans of Srinagar (Grover, 1976-7). The Muslims have relatively high d gene frequency (22 per cent).

Very limited information is available on serum proteins or Biochemical variants in Jammu & Kashmir. Kaur (1979) has studied serum proteins of the Ladakhi Buddhists and Muslims. She found the incidence of different genes as follows: Hp^1 (27 per cent), Tf^c (98 per cent), Tf^b (1.10 per cent), GC^1 (76 per cent). Tf^d (0.70 per cent) is also found in the Ladakhi population. Another study by Chahal (1989) reported biochemical variants of the Sunni Muslims. The incidence of different genes among the Muslims is P^a (30 per cent), P^c (1.20 per cent), PGM^1 (63 per cent), ESD^2 (26 per cent), GLO^1 (30 per cent), AK^2 (6.20 per cent), ADA^1 (89 per cent). $PGM_1{}^7$ is also found in low frequency (0.60 per cent) among them.

V. KAUL
N.K. BAGCHI

REFERENCES

Arora, Harish Chandra, 'A report on the finger dermatoglyphics of Kashmiri Pandits and Kashmiri Muslims', M.Sc. thesis (unpublished), Anthropology Department, University of Delhi, 1976-7.

Bala, S. and S. Seth, 'Glucose-6-phosphate dehydogenase deficiency among Kashmiri Pandits and Muslims of Srinagar', *Indian Journal of Physical Anthro-pology and Human Genetics*, 4(2), 1978, pp. 117-22.

Bansal, I.J.S., 'A study of ABO blood groups of people of Ladakh', *American Journal of Physical Anthropology*, 27, 1967, pp. 211-12.

———, 'Palmar dermatoglyphics of the groups of the Buddhist Ladakhi', *Journal of the Indian Anthropological Society*, 2, 1967, pp. 145-51.

———, 'Fingerball configurations of the Ladakhis', Proceedings of International Symposium on Dermatoglyphics, in P.C. Biswas and A. Sharma (eds.), Delhi, 1968.

Bhalla, V., 'Variations in taste threshold for PTC in populations of Tibet and Ladakh', *Human Heridity*, 22, 1972, pp. 453-8.

Bhalla, V., K. Bhatia, L. Sharma and N. Dutta, 'Genetic Polymorphism in Cis-Himalayan populations, IV: Allele frequencies at six loci in the Dogras of Tawi Valley (Jammu & Kashmir)', *Journal of the Indian Anthropological Society*, 15, 1980, pp. 85-9.

Bhattarcharjee, P.N., 'Distributions of the blood groups (A_1, A_2, BO, MNSs, Rh) and the secretor factor among the Muslims and the Pandits of Kashmir', *Zeitschriff fur Morphologie and Anthropologie*, 58(1), 1966, pp. 86-94.

———, 'The blood groups (A_1, A_2, BO, MNSs & Rh) of the Ladakhis', *Acta Geneticae et Statistica Medica*, 18, 1967, pp. 78-83.

———, 'Further study of Tibetan blood groups', *Journal of the Indian Anthropological Society*, 3, 1968, pp. 57-66.

Chahal, S.M.S., B.K. Sandhu and A. Mahajan, 'Bio-chemical variation in the Sunni Muslims of Pulwama district, Jammu & Kashmir, *Human Heredity*, 39, 1989, pp. 113-15.

Chakladar, H.C., 'Translation of the first outlines of a Systematic Anthropology of Asia', by V. Gluffrida-Ruggeri, Anthropological papers. University of Calcutta, No. 6, Revised edition of No. 5, 1921.

Chandhoke, Bharati, 'Taste sensitivity to PTC among Pandits and Muslims of Srinagar, Kashmir', M.Sc. thesis (unpublished), Anthropology Department, University of Delhi, 1976-77.

Chatterjee, 1963 c.f. P.P. Majumdar and J. Roy, 'Distribution of ABO blood groups in the Indian Subcontinent: A cluster analytic approach', *Current Anthropology*, 23(5), 1982, pp. 539-53.

Delhi University, 1958, c.f. V. Bhalla, 'Blood group distribution pertaining to ABO, MNSs and Rh-Hr systems in the Indian subcontinent (An ethnogeographical variation)', *Anthropologie* (Brno), 4, 1966, pp. 67-86.

Dutta, R.N. and S. Sen, 'A study of Australian Antigen, cold antibodies and ABO blood group frequencies in Ladakhis', *Indian Journal of Medical Research*, 63, 1975, pp. 1635-40.

Eickstedt, E. Von, 'The races and types of the western and central Himalayas', *Man in India*, 6, 1926, pp. 237-76.

Ghosh, G.C., 'All India Bio-Anthropological Survey', Calcutta: *Anthropological Survey of India*, 1988.

Grover, Saroj Kumar, 'A study of A_1, A_2, BO blood groups and Rh factor among Kashmiri Muslim and Kashmiri Brahmin of Srinagar (J&K)', M.Sc. thesis (unpublished), Anthropology Department, University of Delhi, 1976-7.

Gupta, Nutan, 'A study of the palmer dermatoglyphics of the Brahmans and Muslims of Srinagar (J&K)', M.Sc. thesis (unpublished), Anthropology Department, University of Delhi, 1976-7.

Gupta, P. and P. Singhal, 'Distribution of ABO and Rh blood groups among Muslims of Haripari village in Pulwama district (Srinagar)', *Man in India*, 67(3), 1989, pp. 278-84.

Haq, Faizul, D.C. Bhowmik and Arabinda Basu, All India Anthropometric Survey, North Zone, Basic Anthropometric data, Jammu & Kashmir, Vol. 6, Calcutta: Anthropological Survey of India, 1989.

Kashyap, L.K., 'The ABO blood groups in four endogamous caste groups of Jammu', *The Anthropologist*, 23(1-2), 1976, pp. 55-60.

Kaul, S.S., 'Physical growth and development (human): A study based on Kashmiri Pandit school going boys in Srinagar, Kashmir', Ph.D. thesis (unpublished), Chandigarh, Punjab University, 1971.

Kaur, S., 'Biochemical and genetic studies on some Indian population', Ph.D. thesis (unpublished), Patiala, Punjabi University, 1979.

Kumbanani, H.K., 'Finger dermatoglyphic study of Pandits of Kashmir', *The Anthropologist*, 10(1 & 2), 1963, pp. 21-8.

Negi, R.S., 'Population dynamics of central and western Himalayas', Seminar, Human Variation in India, Calcutta: Anthropological Survey of India, 1977.

Raychaudhuri, T.C., 'The Pandit and Mohammedan of Kashmir: An anthropometric study', *Eastern Anthropologist*, 14(1), 1961, pp. 84-93.

Sen, D.K., 'Dermatoglyphics of palm and fingerballs of Kashmiri Muslims', pp. 215-27, in Proceedings volume of *International Symposium on Dermatoglyphics*, ed. P.C. Biswas and A. Sharma, Delhi: University of Delhi, 1968.

Sharma, I. and V. Bhalla, 'PTC taste sensitivity and colour blindness deficiency in the Dogras of Tavi valley (J&K)', *Indian Journal of Physical Anthropology and Human Genetics*, 7(1), 1981, pp. 7-51.

Singh, K.S., V. Bhalla and V. Kaul, 'The Biological Variation in Indian populations', *People of India*, National Series, Vol. X, Delhi: Oxford University Press, 1994.

Tyagi, D., R.S. Negi, B.R. Bhatnagar and B.N. Sahay, 'Finger dermato-glyphics of Pandits and Muslims of Kashmir', paper presented at the Seminar on Human Variations in India, Calcutta: Anthro-pological Survey of India, 27 June and 2 July 1977.

GLOSSARY

aak: to disown
aalam: high pontiff of the Shia Muslims
aalu: potato
aat gath: gifts brought by the bride to the bridegroom's house
aathwan: pre-delivery ritual performed during the eighth month of pregnancy
achar: pickles
achkan: tunic/a type of coat
adh-barkhi: death rituals performed half-yearly
agamat: prayers whispered in the left ear of a male baby
agha: master, a synonym used for the saiyid.
ahaadis: plural of *hadis* (tradition)
ahimsa: non-violence
ahoi: a festival
ahuti: offering
akak: wisdom
akapawn: ornaments fastened to hair plaits
akha: akshay teej (a festival)/formal request for acceptance of marriage proposal
akhand path: recitation of the *Guru Granth Sahib* without a break
akhun: locally trained priests
al: lineage group
alim: scholar
Allah: Almighty God
amama: white turban worn by the priests
ambal: a sour sauce
amchi: Ladakhi medicine man
amrit: sacred water
amrud: guava
anardana: pomegranate seeds
anderli bed: marriage rituals performed inside the house
anganwadi: nursery school
angia: blouse
anjuman: associations/councils
annaprashan sanskar: food-giving ceremony of a newborn child
antasanskaras: death rites
antimdan: alms offered by the dying for the last time
antyeshti: funeral rites, cremation
anuloma: hypergamy (giving daughters in marriage to higher castes)
anz: duck
apchup: ritual of first feeding of cereals to a child

aqiqa/aqeeqa: tonsure ceremony
ardh-marg shradh: ritual performed on the way to cremation ground
argha: marking of a tuft of hair at the back of the head
arghwani: beautiful red-coloured flowers and fruits of a plant known as *arghwan* (*arbora judae*)
arhats: Jain monks
arthi: bier
arti: worshipping with sacred lamp
arwi/arbi: a type of vegetable
asalatan: marriage contract made through personal presence of the couple and the witnesses
asharfis: gold coins
astana: sacred shrine
asthi: ashes of burnt bones
athuar: ribbon hanging from the earrings signifying marriage symbol
atta: flour
atthai: eight sacred days observed by the Jains
aulias: sacred specialists
avtars: incarnations
azaan/azan: call for *namaz*/prayers/whispering of the verses of Holy Koran in the ears of a child for the first time
bab: father-like
babool: a species of acacia plant (*acuria arabica*)
bada: senior
bada din: Id
bahnoi: sister's husband
baisak: sitting mats
baisakhi: festival performed on the last day of the month of Baisakh
bajra: millet
bakar khani: a special type of bread
bakhstan: marriage by negotiation
bakhtum: acceptance of marriage proposal
bakriwale: goat herders/shepherds
bakshis: tips
balakru: a nose ornament
bali: ritual of animal sacrifice
baltah buhnana: a death ritual of breaking earthen pots on the way to the crematorium
balu and nath: nose ring
band: fastening/an article of stone
banda: a type of vegetable
band-gobhi: cabbage
bangri: bangles
bania: grocer
bans: lamenting on the departed soul with repetitive gloomy rhymes; groups/divisions which have a common ancestor

baoli: stepped well/natural spring
baordah: Id
baqmo: bride
baqpa: bridegroom
baqship: marriage by exchange
bar: ballad
barah: twelve/death rituals performed on the twelfth day
barat: bridegroom's party
barati: members of the bridegroom's party
bardhana: departure
bare-adalat: the council of elders
bargad: banyan tree
barkhi: first anniversary of death
bartan or *rumal tika* or *tikka* ceremony: a marriage ritual of bringing gifts for the groom by the bride's party
batai: sharecropping
batnal: a premarriage ritual in which the marrying partners are annointed with herbal paste
batta: rice/religious performance
batta-satta: marriage by exchange within certain number of families
bawa: priest of shiv temple
bawanja: fifty-two
bawe-dijar: sacred place where the idols of clan deities are kept
beah/biah: marriage
bedi: altar for marriage
begar: forced labour
belcha: spade/an agricultural implement
besar: nose ring; a marriage symbol among Dogri women
bhabhi/bharjai: brother's wife
bhag: cash received by a daughter from her parents at the time of marriage
bhagat: devotee
bhajan: devotional songs
bhakti: devotion
bhala: good
bhand daekher: insincere blessings
bhangra: a typical Punjabi folk dance
bhangur: a sweet made of jaggery
bhao: style, motive
bhatta: cooked rice
bhikhus: a section of the Jains who live on alms
bhut-pret: ghost
bicholia: middleman for settling marriage
bichue: toe ring
bidai: send-off ritual of the bride alongwith bridegroom's party
bidi: indigenous cigeratte
bi-donrus: death rituals performed on the third day

bindi: coloured round mark on the forehead of married women
biradari: community
biryani: a special dish of fried rice and meat
bishan patey: songs sung during marriage
bodi or *choti:* a small tuft of hair kept on the back of head as a ritual
bokal haak: special vegetable dish given to women after delivery
bokhari: earthen fire-pot for heating room
boojh: to tell/perceive
bosti-yoni: ritual bath taken by the mother on the seventh day after delivery.
brit: offerings in return of the services received from the Brahmans
bua: father's sister
bura: bad
butna: a type of herbal paste
cha/chai: tea
chaab: lunch hosted in connection with reception of the bride.
chabutara: raised platform in the courtyard
chadar: sheet of thick cloth
chadar dalna: a type of junior levirate marriage wherein the widow ritually offers a shawl to her deceased husband's younger brother
chaharum: ritual observed on the following four days after death
chajiyon: ritual performed on the fortieth day after death
chak: a preparation of *nadru* (lotus stem)
chakki: wheels of stone used for grinding flour
chalima: rituals performed on the fortieth day marking the end of birth pollution
chaliswan: death rituals observed on the fortieth day
challi: toe rings
chalu: a loose type of dress
chana: gram
chandla vrata: a ritual observed by the young Gujarati Brahmans of twelve to sixteen years wherein they apply saffron marks on the forehead of five married ladies
chang: beer made of barley
chapati: unleavened bread
chappal: a casual footwear
char: four/grand feast given to relatives
chariban/chaubarkhi/chaubari: death rituals performed in the fourth year
charkha: spinning wheel
charpai: cot
charton: locally-made woollen or leather boots
chashma: spring
chaudhury: head of the caste council
chaugan: horse polo
chauk: a gold ornament
chauki: wooden stool/cot
chautra charhna: ritual entry of the mother in the kitchen after the childbirth

cheepa: people of other community
cheera: minor external surgery
chehallum/chelum: ritual of reciting verses from the Holy Koran on the fortieth day of death
chela: pupil with occult and supernatural power
cheroot: indigenous smoking pipe
Chhamachhri: the holiest day of the Jains on the eighth of the month of *Bhadon*
chhanda: holy verses recited by the bridegroom
chhat: ceiling/roof
chhatti: a ritual observed on the sixth day of childbirth
chhena: milk product/cheese
chileshtie: invited guests
chhinna: boycott
chhiton da sahar: town famous for printed cloth
chhota: junior
chil: eagle
chilam: indigenous earthen smoking pipe
chilla: death rituals performed on the fortieth day
chimana: a death ritual
chimeh: ritual feast given to the lineage members by the groom's father two days before marriage
chimta: a musical instrument
chinana: a funeral rite
chinar: majestic tree native to Kashmir Valley (*platanus orientalis*)
choga: gown worn as an overdress
choksikdu kehes: joint family
chola: long loose piece of white cloth used as cover/tunic
chole: white gram
chomo: Buddhist nun
chotkang: a prayer room
chumkoo: boiled buttermilk
chunari: a thin sheet of cloth used by women for covering the upper part of the body
chunda-vand: a rule of inheritance in which co-wives receive equal portion of the deceased husband's property
chura: bangles/dry powdered cheese
churail: evil spirits/ghosts
churan: a pounded mixture of sugar and bread
churidar pyjama/suthan: tight *pyjama* with wrinkles.
churma: typical mixture of flour, sugar and *ghee* given to the parturient women
chuspur: religious brotherhood
chutai: indigenous food item prepared by mixing barley flour with mutton
daan: giving alms
dadi: wooden doors

dadmoj: the woman who accompanies the bride to her husband's house after marriage
dado: father's father
dah-samskar: funeral rites/cremation
dai: midwife
daj/dahej: dowry; person expert in branding horses
dak: musical drum
dal: pulse
dalmash: a pre-marriage ritual
dan-punn: pious deed of giving alms
dapanbata: ritual invitation of relatives in marriage
daphera: rituals signifying end of marriage
dareshas: a temple shaped wooden structure that contains framed photos of lord Krishna and Radha
dargah: sacred shrine of the Muslims
darzigiri: tailoring
dastar: turban
dastarkhwan: a sheet of cloth spread out for feasts
daswan: death rituals on the tenth day after death
da-tsang: birth rituals performed after one month of delivery
datso: marriage mediator
debra: specialists caring for snakes-bites
dehjore: typical golden hanging earring used by married Kashmiri women
dehries: sacred earthen mound recognized as the abode of deities
dey: scarf
deodor/deodar: Himalayan cedar (*cidrus deodara*)
der: husband's younger brother
desi: locally made
desi chai: locally made tea
desi ghee: locally clarified butter
desi sharab: locally distilled alcoholic liquor
devar/dewar: husband's younger brother
devis: deities/goddess
dhaba: wayside eating place
dhai: two-and-a-half
dhai/dhay/warin: midwife
dhamas: subgroups
dhambael: a type of folk dance performed by the Dhamali Faqirs
dhap: musical drum
dharam-bhai: putative brother
dharam-karam: pious deed
dharam-punn: marriage by negotiation without the involvement of dowry
dharamshastras: sacred texts
dheri: measurement of equal share of property
dhobi anjuman: traditional caste council of the Dhobis
dhol/dholak/dholki: musical drum

dhoti: loin cloth
dhunuche: pre-delivery ritual on completion of seventh month of pregnancy
diramfiti: typical dish of yeast bread
diwan: the official post of commander
diya-batti-dene: ritual of showing lighted earthen oil lamp to the dying persons
doab: the area surrounded by two rivers
dodh: milk
dogra pahnawa: Dogra apparel
dogra dham: community feast
dogra ghatna: a type of tight trouser
dohri: a type of exchange marriage that exists within certain families and clans
doli: palanquin
doman: a musical drum
done: leaf cups
donn: form of fine or punishment
doon-leij: ritual presentation of an earthen pitcher filled with nuts and some cash by the bride's father to the bridegroom's father
door: earrings
dooreh-hor: ear pendants regarded as marriage symbol of women
dreyu: flour of a wild grain
dropran: a special type of bread which can be divided into two parts
dua: verses/prayers
duggar: Dogri speaking area
dugri: of the lower hills
dulij: one-sided musical drum
dun: a birth ritual
dupatta: scarf
dur: earring symbolizing marital status
durpo: radish
ekahri: a type of marriage wherein wives are taken from certain clans but do not give their daughters to them in marriage
ethna-e-ashari: a sub-sect of Islam believing in twelve Imams
fakir/faqir: one who lives on alms
falahar/phalahar: remaining on the diet of fruit
farsh: stone slabs used for flooring
fasal-ka-sadqa: offering of thanksgiving
fateha/fateh/fateha-khani: recitation of the first *surah* of the Koran for the deceased person
fatwa: a religious decree
ferozi: azure coloured
fiqah: training in Islamic jurisprudence and logic
fiqah-e-jafaria: the code of conduct laid down by the Eighth Imam, Imam Jafar-e-Sadiq
firini/firni: a special sweet dish
firoza: safoon/scarf worn on the head by ladies

firsal: ritual feast at the bride's place on the seventh day after marriage
gachha: a social division among the Jains
gaddi: school of thought
gallen: Carpet made of wool and silk.
gana: red thread tied on the wrist of the bride
gandian: a ritual performed before seven days of marriage
gandum: wheat/a ritual signifying marriage engagement
Ganesh bana: worshipping Lord Ganesh
Ganga-jal: sacred water of the river Ganga
gangni: a type of millet
ganz: skin
ganzum: the *maqpa* form of widow remarriage wherein the new husband takes over the inherited property of her deceased husband
gaona: return visit of the husband after marriage to take his bride back to his house
garat: stone grinding machine
garnme: church elders' council
garu: the type of songs sung by the men during the start of sowing crops
gatti: lineage
geil: curves in bodhi
geluqpa: yellow appron
ghar: house
ghar aehun: a post-marriage ritual wherein the bride's parents and relatives attend a feast at the groom's place by giving money and rice as gift
ghar baithana: widow remarriage
gharpet: the system in which the man goes to live with his in-laws after marriage
ghat: hill/cremation ground
ghee: clarified butter
gheri: marriage songs
ghori: ritual riding on a mare by the bridegroom on his way to the bride's house for marriage
ghusl: bath
ghusl-e-niffas: purificatory bath of the mother on the fortieth day after child birth
ghusl-e-maiyat: ritual bath given to the corpse before burial
giddi: a cloth wrapped around the body by women
goba: head of village elder's committee
gobhi: cauliflower
gojal: a mixture of wheat and barley
gompa: Buddhist monastery
goncha: long coat/gown
gora: same as *garu*
goratt: stone mill for grinding corn
gorkan/gorkun: professional grave digger
gooji: chestnut

got: a social division analogous to clan
gotra: exogamous group analogous to clan
graha: position of stars/planets in the horoscope
gram panchayat: village council
grim: naked barley
guhllara: fried sweetened rice powder
gujara: wife
gulmeth: ritual of giving presents to the bridegroom by his relatives and friends
guncha: wollen cloak
gungey navami: annual date of ancestor worship
gur: jaggery
gurgur: churner fitted with a piston
gurgur-cha: salty tea
guru: teacher
gusal/gussal/ghusl: bath
gushtaba/gostaba: a special Kashmiri dish made of minced meat balls
guzara: maintenance
gyuts: blood relatives/agnates
haazri: ritual of presentation of gifts to the groom's party who witness the *nishani* ceremony in a marriage
haj: pilgrimage to Mecca and Madina by the Muslim
hajamat: shaving and trimming of hair
haji: one who returned from Haj pilgrimage
hak: green leafy vegetable
hal or *dhamal:* meditative dance of animal
halal: slaughtering of animal in the Islamic way
haldi: turmeric
halpa: marriage mediator
halwa: a kind of sweet dish
hamam: bathroom
hatya: murder
havan: worship of sacred fire
havanphere: ritual of circumbulating the sacred fire seven times by the bride and the bridegroom in a marriage
hay-zalun: a death ritual performed after the cremation wherein the family members circumambulate the fire made by accumulating dry grass outside the cremation ground
hena/henna: myrtle paste
hookah/huka/huḳka: hubble bubble
hoontch: period of birth pollution
hookahpani chhekna: excommunication
hund: spinach
Id-e-Milad: a festival to mark the birth anniversary of Prophet Muhammạd on the twelfth of Rabi-ul-Awwal (a Muslim month)
Id-ul-Fitr: religious festival

Id-ul-Zuha: religious festival
iddat: specified time of restriction
imam: leader
ishnen mizaan: feast hosted by the groom's party in honour of the bride's relation
izzat: honour
jaal: weaver
jad: ritual of *mundan* ceremony/tonsuring
jadoo: magic
jadua-jarhian: witchcraft, sorcery, black magic
jaj/jajeer: hubble-bubble
jajmans/yajmans: patrons/clients
janam kundali/patri: horoscope
janaza: bier/corpse
jandian: ritual of *mundan* ceremony/tonsure
janeu/janijoora/juneo: sacred thread
jang: thigh
janj/janni: bridegroom's party
japuji: morning session of recitation of *Guru Granth Sahib*
jarhian: herbs with occult power
jarrah: local surgeon
jashan: elaborate dramatic performance
jati: caste, community
jatkarm: a birth ritual
jatra and jarhian khedana: a typical occult dance
jenaza: same as *janaza*
jeth: husband's elder brother
jhaari: indigenous smoking pipe
jhatka: slaughtering according to the Hindu way
Jheeri: Dogra Jheer woman
jhikli: lower region/plains
jhumke: a type of earring of the ladies
ji: the conqueror
jibchoo: same as *chehallum*
jija: elder sister's husband
jinnat: genii of Suratul Jinn, Chapter LXXII (Koran)
jirgah/jirgha: tribal/court comprising clan heads
jog-havan: offerings to holy fire
jogini: ghosts
jora: typical shoes of hillmen
jowar: millet
julus: procession
jumma-fateha: Friday prayer
jumma: Friday
jut pang: spinning wheel.
juyana: enlightenment

kabergah: a typical Kashmiri meat dish.
kabristan: burial ground
kachalu: a tuberous vegetable
kachcha house: huts made of clay and mud
kachcha: uncooked food
kachha: undergarment
kachchi lassi: beverage of milk mixed with water
kafan: shroud; a piece of cloth to cover a dead body
kagaz banane ke paise: service charges for preparing written docu-ments
kagazi: superior quality of nuts
kal: era
kala chana: black gram
kalash: earthen pitcher/urn
kalhon: big landowner
kalima/kalma: the Muslim creed, 'La illahailallah, Mohammadun Rasul Allah'.
Kali mata: goddess Kali
kaliya: a meat dish
kameez/kamiz: shirt
kamzat: labour class
kan chembeen: ritual ear-piercing ceremony for the girls
kanak: wheat
kandal: a type of locally manufactured earthen pot
kandi: hilly dry and undulating plains
kangani: a type of millet
kanghi: comb
kangiri/kangri: portable earthen fire pot, brazier
kanjak: divine
kantha: necklace
kanvaj: big earrings
kanyadan: ritual of giving away the daughter to the bridegroom in marriage among the Hindus
kanz: slender willow branches used in basketry
kaodaari sag: a leafy vegetable
kapar chadar: white cloth-sheet kept on shoulders
kapda uthana: removal of cloth from the dead body
kar: white
kar mukar: death ritual performed on the tenth day
kara: bangle of iron or steel worn by the Sikh men
karah: a sweet dish of dry nuts boiled in sweetened milk
karakul: a cap made of karakul sheep skin
karam sag: a local leafy vegetable
karewa: upland
karhai poojan: a marriage ritual among the Gujarati Brahmans
karhi: a dish made of curd and flour of gram
karie-jarija: a preliminary ritual of marriage
karma: action/activities

karmai/kudmai/kurmai: marriage betrothal/engagement of the girl
kartik poornima: fifteenth day of full moon in the month of *Kartik*
kasaba: head gear
kash: marriage
katha: story/legend
katlam: a bakery item
katori: cup/a small metal bowl
kazi: Muslim priest
kesari: orange colour
kesh: hair
khabar: a post-marriage ritual wherein the relatives of the bride go to meet and enquire about her with presentation of sweets during her first seven day's stay at in-laws' place
khachepa: term of reference of Ladakhis for the Kashmiris
khachi: flour of parched *grim.*
khadder: milk of a sheep or goat which has recently given birth to a lamb/kid
khaddi: loom
khadi: cotton cloth made in handloom
khaini: tobacco leaves mixed with lime
khamb: stone pillar
khan: a title
khanadamad: person living in his in-law's house after marriage
khandan: lineage/family
khandar: marriage
khan dress: loose *salwar* and long *kurta* as that worn by the Pathans
khang: nuclear family
khangoo: joint polyandrous family set-up
khangso: feast hosted by the bride's party for the bridegroom'a party
kharh: long grass
kharore: a variety of meat dish
khatak: scarf of white silk cloth
khatm-e-sharif: complete recitation of the Holy Koran
khatna/khatnahal/khatnal: circumcision
khazana: treasure/treasury
khenus: barber's kit
khes: bedspread
khewa/qahwa/kahwa: a typical black tea with saffron and almond
khichi amavas: the first day celebration of ensuing winter
khichri: rice cooked with pulses
khidmatgars: caretakers, servants
khidui: wooden windows
khir/kheer: a sweet delicious dish of rice and milk
khooni: slayers
khuftan: temporary secret marriage contract
khula: seeking divorce by the wife

khulaq: flour of parched grain seasoned with butter and eaten with meat or vegetables
khule-sagan: the day of commencement of activities of marriage
khum: a levy paid by the Baltis to the Shia Muslims
khusra: eunuchs acting as mediators in marriage
kiang: wild asses or wild horses.
kikar or *jandi:* a kind of tree (*acacia arabica*)
konthalgur: procession of horses
korha: a food item made of ground almonds, coconut, ginger, resins and sugar cooked in *ghee* and milk
kona: stone articles made by the *Sangtrash*
koran: religious text of the Muslims
korankhani: recitation of Koran
koreh-har: daughter's share of paternal property
korma: a delicious dish of meat
kothedar: wholesale supplier
kram: title/section or family appellation
kripan: dagger
kriya-karam: death rituals performed on the last day of the pollution period
kuhls: artificial aqueduct
kuichih: same as *kulcha*
kul: family tree/clan/lineage
kul-devi: clan goddess
kul-devta: clan god
kulah-i-namad: person wearing felt
kulcha: a type of bread
kumba-pach: the fortnight in early autumn marked for ancestor worship and *shradh*
kumhars: potters
kunba: family
kurksar: a marriage ritual of the Gujarati Brahmans
kursi: chair
kurta: loose long shirt
kusha: grass
kushak: reincarnated Lama
kuteer: hut/cottage
laf-tsang: purification of the house
lagan: date of marriage
lahad: grave
lahri wadan: weeping and recalling the good qualities of the deceased
lahwas/lawas/lawaseh: bread of wheat flour prepared in a *tandoor*
lakdi dena: arranging firewood for funeral
lal chura: red bangles
lalvakh: devotional songs of famous Kashmiri poetess Lalded
lamboo dena: a death ritual
lamkhan: cobbler

langanj: the ritual observed after one month of cremation
langar: a community feast arranged for the devotees where food is served free of cost
langari: cook
langdeh: corporate labour system
larango: a typical style of music
lassi: liquified curd/a common beverage
lath bharai: extending help in renovating the house for marriage ceremony
lay: raw wool
lej: earthen cooking pot
lipton-cha: tea prepared by adding sugar
lohar: blacksmith
lokachar: common marriage rituals performed by the family members
lungi: loin cloth
mad: alcoholic liquor
madra: a liquid food preparation of dry fruits
madrasa: school for religious teachings for the Muslims
mah: a type of pulse (*phaseoius radiatus*)
Mahabharata: the great Indian epic written by the Rishi Ved Vyas
mahatma: a noble person
mahr: dower
mahr-e-muwajjil: deferred payment of *mahr*
mahr-e-Fatimi: *mahr* paid to Fatima, the Prophet Muhammad's daughter
mahr-e-muajjal: *mahr* in which instant payment is made
majlis: assembly
makki: maize
maklawa/muklawa: ritual of home taking of the bride
makpa/maqpa: marriage by service in which the husband goes to stay at his wife's residence.
malamenz: a pre-marriage ritual to adorn the hands and feet of the bride with *henna* paste
malasbehoun: a ritual in which the bride is prohibited from taking bath and doing household jobs for three days before marriage
mal-e-sadaat: a portion of the *khums* levy given to the deserving Saiyid
malkhos: gravedigger/sexton
mall: reservation of the boy for marriage
mama: maternal uncle
manakfarchin: a special variety of cap
mandap: marriage *pandal*
mangalsutra: most auspicious pendant worn by women as a marriage symbol
mangnee or kori mangeh gantha: first betrothal
mangrik: farmers of middle rank
mani: a marriage ritual of distribution of sweets and bread among the kins
mantra: Hindu religious verses
mansar devta: religious shrines
manzhi: baby swing

manzymyor: a go between middleman for marriage negotiation
maodil: a variety of coarse millet
margs: meadow
marja-e-taqleed: alam—the highest pontiff of Iraq/Iran
marsia: dirge/a funeral song or hymn
masala: spices
mash ki dal: pulse of blackbeans (*rox burghi*)
masik: monthly death ritual
masik dan: monthly donation
masjid: mosque
masoor/masur: a kind of pulse (lentil)
massmechravoun: a marriage ritual of loosening of hair plaits of the bride
matamsara: an enclosed building where Moharram rituals are performed/ mourning house
maulvi: religious teacher
mazar: sacred shrine of the Muslim
mechravoun: same as *massmechravoun*
meg: reward
mehndi: henna
mehndi-raat: ritual of applying myrtle paste to the bride and bridegroom on the day preceding marriage
melan chulam: a type of boycott in which exchange of fire and water with the person is stopped
menzidul: pot of *henna*
menziraat: rituals performed on the preceeding day of marriage
mersia-khani: religious songs
milani: ritual introduction of the members of the bride's and groom's party with each other through exchanging garlands
mistri: masion
mitha bhatt: sweetened rice
mitti: earth/soil
miungma: turnip
mog-mog: a favourite Buddhist food of wheat flour and minced meat balls
mohalla: locality
mome: close friends
momo: mother's brother
moondan: ritual of tonsure
moong: green gram (*phaseolus mungo*)
moong dal: pulse of green gram
mog-mog: a favourite Buddhist food of wheat flour and minced meat balls
moth/mothi: brown gram (*phaseolus aconitifolius*)
mudaw: back wounds of horses
muhurat: auspicious date and time or moment
mujawar: caretaker
mujtahid: learned priest
mukat: crown/decorated headgear

mundri: marriage ritual of presenting fingerring to the bride by the groom's party
mundri: gold ring
mungi: green gram
muta/mutah: a temporary marriage contract among the Muslims
nadru: lotus stalk
nag: cobra
nagara: a type of musical drum
nahi an al munkir: path of righteousness
nai: barber
naib-sadar: vice-president
naint: silver bangles
naintian: gold earring of men
najand: reciprocal help
najarida rupea dena: ritual of giving money to the dying person by all the family members, except the daughters and sisters
nal: a horseshoe
nalas: rituals
nam: varieties of baked bread
namaz: Muslim prayer
namaz-e-janaza: prayers for the deceased at the time of burial
nambardar: headman
namda: woollen felt
nampey: barley
namsanskar: naming ceremony
nanad: husband's sister
nang-chang: a term synonymous to household
nangpa: people of one's own community
nanoia: sister-in-law's husband
naqqash: designer
nath: nose ring
natta brata: religious feasts
nauha: lamentation
nauratra/navratra: the nine days of worship during which they abstain from non-vegetarian food
nav: boat
navid: barber
navrog puja: worship of trees
nazari: thanksgiving
neondra: ritual of inviting the relatives
nifaas: purificatory bath on the fortieth day of the childbirth
nikah: marriage contract
nikah asaltan: written marriage contract with the consent of both the bride and the bridegroom
nikah-e-daimi: lasting marriage contract
nikah-e-inqatai: breakable marriage contract

nikah khani: the ceremony of marriage contract
nikah vilaitan: verbal contact of marriage by the parents on behalf of their minor daughter
nirvana: death ritual performed for the deceased for attainment of salvation
nishani: carrying presentation by the groom's party for the bride to her place/ betrothal
nom-chonru: name giving
noonchai: salty tea
noshyoni: ritual of purificatory bath taken by the mother on the seventh day after childbirth
nritya: dance
nyopa: a representative of the bridegroom
oapsoap: first feeding of cereals to a child
ogun: room
othala: death rituals performed at the end of the mourning period
pa: people
padha: priest
pagri: turban
pagri ceremony: death ritual of putting turban on the head of the deceased's eldest son on the thirteenth day
pag-vand: the rule of inheritance by the offspring of the same wife
paintra: grassring
pairi pouna: salutation by touching the feet
pajeba (payal): anklet
pakarlee: first betrothal
pasham/pashmina: a superior quality of wool
pat: wooden plank
pathwar: death ritual performed on the fifteenth day after death
patri: horoscope
pattale/patal: leaf plates
pattoo/pattu: a type of hand-made coarse cloth
payur/puyur/pyur: merorial stone slab installed on the graves
peera: small wooden stool
peokien di dar: as *kar mukar*
perak: cap worn by Buddhist ladies
pharsak: servicing husband or additional husband.
phasphuns: a brotherhood pool for rendering their mutual services at the time of birth, marriage and death
phera: home taking of bride
pheran: loosely fitted male dress of the Kashmiris
pheras: marriage ritual of circumambulating the sacred fire by the bride and the groom
phirsal: a marriage ritual of inviting the bridegrom by his in-laws to stay at their place for three days
phoa: death ritual performed by the Lama
phool-gobhi: cauliflower

phud: generation
phul: ashes of the cremated dead body
phul chunna: ritual collection of ashes and bones of the deceased after the cremation
phuldan: flower vase
phumanian: a style of dance
piaj: onion
piaw: a birth ritual in which the blessed mother is presented with new clothes and some money by her in-laws.
pinda: morsel of food offered to the departed soul as a death ritual
piri-muridi: followers of a particular *pir*
pirs: saints, holymen
pitra-paksha: ritual of ancestor worship
pohu: an indigenous plant grown in the woods
pohul: shepherd
poori: puffed small bread of wheat flour fried in *ghee* or oil
posh: white cloth piece carried on shoulder by men
potch: white turban
pugg: a death ritual of putting a turban on the head of the eldest male member of the family
puja: worship
pujari: priest of temple
pukka: cooked food
pulao: fried rice
punn: to earn blessing by giving alms
punjali: yoke
punjap: birth ritual of purificatory bath on the third and fifth day after the childbirth
purdah: veil/avoidance
purohit: Hindu priest
qahwa: sweet and black tea offered to distinguished guests
qawwali: a typical style of song
qazi: priest of the Muslims
quam: a social division, that traces its descent from a common male ancestor or from the place of his origin
rabab: a string instrument played for light music
radaq: tonsuring ceremony
rafoogiri: darning
raj: principality
rajma/rajmah: a kind of bean, pulse
rakaide: a marriage ritual of going round a berry tree by the bride and the groom
rakas tauma: staple food with pulses, vegetable, oil, *ghee*, sweet, etc.
ralchang: ritual of tonsure of a child
ramzan: a holy month of Muslim calender
rangrez: dyers

ranthoq-pa: miller
raphera: marks of marriage ceremony
rapshit: barren woman
rarho: same as *beah* or *biah*
rasam-pagri: death ritual performed to mark the completion of pollution period
rashi: configuration of planets
rasta rokna: a ritual of marriage wherein the groom's sisters jokingly prevent entry of the couple at the door of the house for some cash
rathehaap: marriage ritual of entry of the couple at the house of the bridegroom
raungi: millet
ravara: middleman/marriage negotiator
raware: the receiver
reboos: conical yak skin tents of the Champas of Ladakh.
reet/ritan: tradition/custom
rikanum: occupational groups
rishi: saint
ritan: the antenatal restrictions
rogan josh: a delicious Kashmiri dish of meat
ronanq kudpa chhas: a ritual for obtaining formal divorce from the deceased husband by cutting the black thread tied to both of them
rongi: a type of pulse
roth-khaber: post-marriage ritual wherein the bride's parents send gifts to the groom's parents before calling on the family
roti: baked unleavened bread of wheat flour
rouf: typical style of Kashmiri poetry
rukhsat/rukhsati: ritual of formally bidding farewell to her parents, friends, and kin by the bride on her way to in-law's house
rurhi: home-made liquor
saagzaar: kitchen garden
saal: annual death rituals
saant/shanti yajna: rituals performed to bring peace to ancestral spirits on the ultimate day of marriage
saat salona: a special food item consumed in marriage feast
sabha: council
sadr-e-anjuman: president of the association
sadri: dress
safed posh: white apron
sagai/sagan: ritual confirmation of marriage engagement and fixation of the date of marriage
saget: a group comprising farmers and artisans
sahukars: moneylenders/financers
saiyum: death ritual performed on the third day with the recitation of the Koran

sajarali: clan diety
sajra: genealogy
sakhi: putative relation of friendship among the ladies
sala: wife's brother
salami: a section among the Dogra/a post-marriage ritual in which the groom visits his in-law's house to offer salute to the elders for which he is remunarated in cash
salehar: wife's brother's wife
salgam: turnip
sali: wife's sister
salwar: loosely fitted trouser worn by ladies
samajik: social
samavar: typical indgenous kettle
sambat: Hindu calendar system
samman: honour/facilitation
sandh: a marriage ritual of conducting *yajna* to pacify the evil effects of the planets
sang: stone/birth ritual of giving purificatory bath to the child by the Lama immediately after birth and again after one month
sangal: chain made of iron
sangeet: music
sanskar: Hindu ritual/customs
sant: ascetic
santi yajna: prayer for peace through conducting *yajna*
shanti: peace
sapenda: group of agnates
saptapadi: marriage ritual of circumambulating the sacred fire seven times by the bride and the groom
sarak turmash: carrot
saran-ka-sag: a type of leafy vegetable
sarpanch: headman of the panchayat
sarf: holy bath
satijihum: death ritual performed on the fifteenth and fortieth day in which the *pir* recite *fateha* from the Koran
sati samadhis: sacred shrines where virtuous women sacrificed their lives in the pyres of their husbands
sattoo: parched grain flour
satwa: birth ritual of purificatory bath on the seventh day
savarna: belonging to the same status category
sawaab: merit
saz: act of craftsmanship
seddha: cobra
segha: Ladakhi version for the *nikah* verses
sehra: turban in marital attire
sehrabandi: ritual of putting turban on the head of the bridegroom
sesrih gogjih: boiled turnips

sewain: a sweet dish
shabdeb: marriage by exchange
shabd-karna: lamenting loudly by men and women of the berieved family for the departed soul
Shab-e-Qadr: a Muslim festival
shadi: marriage
shagan /shagoon: same as *sagai/ sagan*
shahnai: wind musical instrument
shak: slender branches of trees or twigs
shakal: feature
shakarkandi: sweet potato
shakhsi: autocratic
shakten: shirt/trousers
shakti: power, strength
shali: paddy
shamiana: canopy
shamshanghat: the place of cremation
shanma: peas
shanti: leaves of spinach
shanti havan: worshipping sacred fire for invoking peace
sharah/shariat: Muslim code of conduct.
sharbat: a soft drink
shastric: according to Hindu doctrines
shastric mantras: verses from the Hindu religious texts
sherak: belt around the waist
shikar: meat/game animal
shikara: small boat of Kashmir
shilararti: clan deity
shinkhan: carpenter
shipkun: mason
shira: a syrupy sweet of flour, sugar and *ghee*
shirini: sugar candy
shirmal: a baked food item
shishnadeva: deity with of two phallic symbols
shoke: mourning
shradh: Hindu death rituals performed on the tenth day
shulmet: same as halal
shus: sharecropping
sidha: raw edibles/uncooked food articles
sigak: ritual observed after one year of the death
siku: steamed balls of fried flour of wheat or gram
silsila: affiliation to the *pir* among Shia Muslims
sindoor: vermilion
singhara: water chestnut.
siri: mill
sirki: a type of bamboo mat

sirto: long cap
sisen: needle
sithnian: songs full of mock abuse sung to greet the groom's party during marriage
settanian/sithanis: humorous joyful folk songs sung during marriage
siyan: Brahman cook
sizak: rituals of death anniversary
skiu: an item of food
skootak: aristocracy
skus-khoyangches: courtship and clandestine marriage
skuth-kherches: clandestine marriage
slum: feast hosted in honour of the groom by his in-laws
snan: bath
snangor/snangoru: professional men who give bath to the dead bodies
sochna: to think
sofi: bakers
sog: mourning
sohag: husband
sohagan: married woman
sonder/sunder: a ritual of purification performed on the seventh day after the child birth
sotrey: post-delivery pollution
sran: birth
susnikam: shawl embroidery
storma: the prayer that protects the couple from evil spirits
stridhan: woman's property
stuti: singing in praise
sue: needle
suhagan: same as *sohagan*
suhag chinha: symbol of married women
sukla paksh ashtami: eighth day of moonlit nights of the lunar month
sulma: plaited skirt worn by married women
sum: thick blanket of ice
sundkhand/sundh: indigenous medicinal diet for the mother to regain strength after the delivery
sunnat: acts of Prophet Mohammad
surah: chapter of the Holy Koran
suraj-darshan: sun sighting
surna: musical flute
surney: long musical flute
surya-vanshi: belonging to the clan of Sun worshippers
sutak/sootak: period of birth pollution
suthan: tight fitted Dogra *pyjama*
sutra: birth ritual performed on the eleventh day/ritual of naming the baby on the thirteenth day
swan-khan: same as *biah* or *beah*

swaran: high class Dogras
swell veyas: ritual of capturing the bride for marriage/marriage by capture
taaviz: amulets
tabaq: plates
tabla: a percussion musical instrument
tabligh: act of preaching
taboodh/taboot: coffin
tagair: wash basin
tahmad/tehmad: loincloth
tahriri: initiation of divorce by the husband in writing
taka: ritual of confirmation of marriage fixation
takbir: ritual of whispering of *azaan* in the left ear of a newborn baby by a *mulla*
talak-nama/talaq-nama: written document of divorce
talaq: divorce
tam: death ritual performed on the tenth day through tonsuring of all the agnates
tamol/tambul: a ritual of marriage wherein the relatives present gifts of cloth and money to the groom before proceeding for the bride's house for the marriage
tamra: copper
tankha: the typical style of Buddhist miniature paintings
taqeed: follower
taq-kuk: marriage engagement
taqskan: weavers
tarang: headgear of women
tarar: a type of vegetable
tarash: cutting/shaping
tarkhan: carpenter
tel: a pre-marriage ritual in which mustard oil is applied on the hair of both the bride and the bridegroom
terahi: death rituals performed on the thirteenth day
teuth: salted tea without milk
thaka/theka: acceptance of the marriage proposal confirmed by presenting gifts by the bride's party
thakpendh: resting place on the way to the crematorium
than: cloth/sacred place
thazan: marriage feast hosted by the bride's party after the *nikah* ceremony
thukpa/thuqppa: steamed noodles seasoned with mutton and vegetables
thuksang: divorce compensation
tika/takka: marriage ritual of marking the forehead of the groom with red colour with presentation of gifts/betrothal
tilak: marking on the forehead
tili: same as *kanz*
tirth: pilgrimage centres of the Hindus
tochur: a type of bread

tonga: horse driven cart
toor: metallic bowl
traem: a big round tray
tram: copper
trehari: system of exchaning daughters in marriage between three groups of families in triangular fashion
tresh: a death ritual of offering water by the son daily throughout first year of death of the parents
trom: common place
tsader: woollen blanket
tsampa: roasted barley flour
tulsi: *ocimumem sanctum* plant (basil)
tunda: net knitted with cotton thread
tunib: vein
tupi: cap
tur/toor: a type of pulse
turen: rituals of death anniversary
turumba: a type of locally grown millet
ulema: the learned Muslim priest
umbal: a delicious dish served at a marriage feast
und-khand: food consisting of dry fruits
upanayan: sacred thread-wearing ceremony
urad: a kind of pulse
urs: congregations
Urs-e-Nabi: birthday of Prophet Muhammad
uthala: same as *rasam-pagri*
vaharvoor: annual death rituals
Vaishno Devi: a pilgrimage centre of the Hindus
vakil: lawyer
vanshavali: genealogy
vanvun: typical dance and songs of marriage
vapul-sag: a kind of leafy vegetable
varmal: marriage ritual of exchange of garlands between the bride and the groom
varna: the four-tier Hindu caste system
vathal/wathal: the feast hosted at the groom's house in reception of the bride
vedi: altar for conducting marriage rituals
vedic: according to the Vedas
vehervar: name of the feast hosted on the first death anniversary
vezar: *pyjama*
vikshu: person initiated to live on alms
vilaitan nikah: same as *nikah vilaitan*
vivah-sanskar: marriage rituals
vrat: religious fasting
wakalatan: judicial marriage contract

wakil: representatives of both spouses at the time of divorce
walima: marriage feast hosted by the groom's party
wanawun/ wanchwon: marriage songs sung in praise of the bride/same as *vanvun*
wani: grocer
warin: midwife
wathal: a reception feast given at the bridegroom's place after marriage
wayun: folk songs sung during marriage
waza: cooks
wazwan: lavish marriage dinner hosted by the bride's parents
yag: marriage ritual performed by the priest on behalf of the bride's father
yajnopavit: sacred thread
yakhni: a variety of mutton dish
yenevoul: marriage rituals of the second day
yeng bodpa: same as in *mangriks/*social division among the farmers
yoni: sacred thread
zabani: verbal initiation of divorce by the husband
zabiha: same as shulmet/Islamic way of slaughtering animals
zain: fruit basket
zamindar: landlord
zarj: money
zarju: death rituals observed on the forty-ninth day
zataq: horoscope
zen: women
zerakasi: tonsure ceremony among the Muslim
ziarat: the relics of holymen or the festival to perpetuate the memory of good saints
zitsik: feast given to the mourning family members for a death in the family

BIBLIOGRAPHY

Abul Fazl, *Ain-i-Akbari*, Calcutta: Bibliotheca Indica, 1872-73, English translation, Vol. I by Blochmann, Calcutta, 1927; Vols II and III by H.S. Jarret, Calcutta, 1868-94.

———, *Akbarnama* (3 vols), English translation by Henry Beveridge, Calcutta, 1897-1939.

Ahluwalia, Major H.P.S., *Hermit Kingdom Ladakh*, New Delhi: Himalayan Books, 1987.

Angeli, Mam, 'Hanjis of Dal Lake, Origin and Demographic Characteristics', pp. 142-57, *Geography of J. & K.*, Srinagar: Kashmir University.

Anon., *Tarikh-e-Jammu* (Urdu), Srinagar: Government Research Department Library.

Atkinson, Edwin T., *The Himalayan Districts of the North Western Provinces of India*, 5 vols (rpt 1981, New Delhi: Cosmo Publications under the title *The Himalaya Gazetteers*).

Badauni, Abdul Qadir, *Muntakhab-ut-Tawarikh*, Calcutta: Bibliotheca Indica, 1865-9; English translation, 3 vols by Ranking, Lowe and Haig, Calcutta, 1884-1925.

Baloria, Thakur Kahan Singh, *Tarikh-e-Rajputana-Mulk-e-Punjab*, Jammu: Govt. Press, 1930.

———, *Tarikh-i-Rajgan-i-Jammu-wa-Kashmir*, Part I, Lahore: Prakash Steam Press; Part II, Lahore: Diwan Printing Press, 1986.

Bamzai, Anand Kaul, *The Kashmir Pandit*, Calcutta: Thackers Spink & Co., 1924.

———, *Geography of Jammu and Kashmir State*, 1st edn 1913; 2nd revd edn 1925, Calcutta: Thackers Spink & Co. (Updated and Introduction by P.N.K. Bamzai, New Delhi: Light & Life Publishers, 1925.)

———, *Archaeological Remains in Kashmir*, Lahore: Mercantile Press, 1935.

Bamzai, Prithvi Nath Kaul, *A History of Kashmir: Political, Social and Cultural*, New Delhi: Metropolitan Book Company Pvt. Ltd., 1962.

Banerjee, B.G., 'The Bajigar', in *Child Development and Socialization*, New Delhi: Deep and Deep Publications, 1987.

Bates, Charles Euison, *A Gazetteer of Kashmir and the Adjacent Districts of Kishtwar, Badrawar, Jammu, Naoshera, Punch and the Valley of the Kishen Ganga*, New Delhi: Light & Life Publishers, rpt 1980.

Bellow, H.W., *An Inquiry of Ethnography of Afghanistan*, London, 1891.

———, *Races of Afghanistan*, London, 1880.

———; *Kashmir and Kashghar*, London, 1875.

Bodfour, Edward, *The Encyclopaedia of India*, Eastern and Southern Asia, Vol. I, 1967.

Benvatol, G., *Through the Heart of Asia, Over the Pamirs to India*, 2 vols, London, 1889.

Buck, Major C.H., *Faiths, Fairs and Festivals of India*, New Delhi: Asian Publication Service, rpt 1977.

Campbell, George, *The Afghan Frontier*, London, 1879.

Campbell, Jeffrey Young, 'Ladakh', in *India*, edited by Israel and Bikram Grewal, Singapore: APA, 1983.

Census of India, 1881, Punjab (Report), New Delhi: Govt. of India Publication.

———, *Punjab Castes*, New Delhi: B.R. Publishing Corporation, rpt 1974.

———, 1901, Vol. XXIII, Part I, Kashmir (Report), Lahore.

———, 1921, Vol. XXII, Part I, Kashmir (Report), Lahore.

———, 1931, *Report on Jammu and Kashmir State*, Calcutta.

———, 1931, *Jammu and Kashmir State*, Vol. XXIV, Part I, rpt, Jammu: Ranbir Govt. Press, 1933.

———, 1961, Vol. VI, Part VI, No. 1, *Jammu and Kashmir*, New Delhi: Publication Div., Govt. of India, 1961.

———, 1961, *Village Survey Monograph of Aishmugam*, New Delhi: Publication Div., Govt. of India, 1961.

———, 1971, *Report on Jammu and Kashmir State*, New Delhi: Publication Div., Govt. of India, 1971.

———, 1981, *Report on Jammu and Kashmir State*, New Delhi: Publication Div., Govt. of India, 1981.

———, 1981, *Primary Census Abstract, Jammu & Kashmir*, New Delhi Publication Div., Govt. of India, 1981.

Charak, S.D.S., *Gulabnama*, annotated English translation from the Persian text by Diwan Kirpa Ram, New Delhi: Light & Life Publishers, 1977.

———, (ed.), *Introduction to the History and Culture of the Dogras*, Pathankot: Ajaya Prakashan, 1977.

———, *A Short History of Jammu Raj*, Pathankot: Ajay Prakashan, 1971.

Chib, Sukh Dev Singh, *The Beautiful India, Jammu and Kashmir*, New Delhi: Light & Life Publishers, 1977.

Cunningham, Col. W.B., *Dogras*, Calcutta, 1932.

Cunningham, Alexander, *Ladakh: Physical Statistical and Historical*, with notices of the surrounding countries, New Delhi: Sagar Publications, rpt. 1970.

Das, Narsingh, *Tarikh-i-Dogra Desh* (Urdu), Jammu: Chand Publishing House, 1967.

Dass, Bhagwan, *Bajigars of Punjab: A Case Study in Patiala District* (mimeo), 1978.

Dawson, John, *Classical Dictionary of Hindu Mythology and Religion*, New Delhi: Manu Publishers, 1978.

Deb, P.C., *Bajigars of Punjab: A Socio-Economic Study*, New Delhi: Mittal Publications, 1987.

Deet, Bhai Jai Singh, *Poonch Ate Punjabi Sahit* (Punjabi), Punch: Panjabi Sahit Sabha, 1979.

Deekhia, Harnam Singh, *Paharan Vich Sukhi Jeevan* (Punjabi), Amritsar: New Age Book Centre, 1983.

Department of Sociology, Kashmir University/UNICEF India Country Office/

District Administration Programme, Budgaon, *Gender Discrimination in the Kashmir Valley* (A Study of two districts), 1996.

Department of Sociology, University of Kashmir (compiled by)/UNICEF India Country Office, New Delhi and Government of Jammu & Kashmir, National Seminar on *Gender Discrimination in the Kashmir Valley, Recommedations*, 1997.

Diddamari, Mohammad Azam, *Tarikh-i-Azami*, Lahore: Muhammadi Press, AH 1303; Urdu translation under *Tarikh-i-Kashmir Azami* by Munshi Ashraf Ali, Delhi: Delhi Madrassa, 1846.

District Statistical Agency, *Socio-Economic Indicator, District Leh*, Leh, 1983.

Diwan, Kriparam, *Gulzar-i-Kashmir*, Lahore, 1870.

———, *Gulabnama*, Jammu, 1875.

Drew, F., *The Jammu and Kashmir Territories, 1875*, New Delhi: Cosmo Publications, rpt 1976.

Dughlat, Mirza Haidar, *Tarikh-i-Rashidi*, English translation by E.Denison Ross with Introduction by E.N. Elias, London, 1895.

Dutt, Yogesh Chandra, *The Kings of Kashmir—2nd Series; A translation of the Sanskrit work Rajatarangini of Kalhana Pandita, Jonarajshrivara, and of Prajyabhatta and Shuka*, New Delhi: Gyan Publishing House, 1986 (original translation published in 1879 and 1887).

Earl of Dunmore, 1893, *The Pamirs* (2 vols), London, 1893, New Delhi: Oriental Publisher, rpt, 1971.

Ferishta, *Tarikh-i-Ferishta* (*History of the Rise of the Muhammadan Power in India till 1612*) 12, translated by J. Briggs, Calcutta, 1808-10.

Fouq, Munshi Muhammad Din, *Mukamal Tarikh-i-Kashmir* (Urdu), Lahore, 1910.

———, *Tarikh-i-Kashmir*, Lahore: Zafar Brothers, 1912.

———, *Mashahir-i-Kashmir*, Lahore, 1930.

———, *Tarikh-i-Aqwam-i-Kashmir* (Urdu), Lahore, 1934.

Francke, A.H., *A History of Ladakh*, New Delhi: Sumit Publication, 1981.

Galwan, Ghulam Rasool, *The Saheb's Servant*, London: Cambridge University Press, 1923.

Ganesh Das Badhera, *Rajdarshinis* (Persian): History of the Rajas of Jammu, copies of the manuscript are in Victoria and Albert Museum, and India Office Library, London. Srinagar: S.P.S. Museum.

Garbe, R., '*Yogis*', in *Encyclopedia of Religion and Ethics*, Vol. 12, Edinburgh: T. and T. Clark, 1980.

Govt. of India, *Gazetteer of Kashmir and Ladakh*, Calcutta: The Superintendent Govt. Printing Press; New Delhi: Vivek Publishing House, rpt 1980.

Griffin, Sir Jepel and C.F. Massey, *Chief and Families of Nat in the Punjab*, Lahore, 1909.

Gulam Hussain, Sayyid, *Siyar-ul-Mutkharin*, Kanpur: Newal Kishore Press, 1897.

Gupta, N.S. and N.C. Prabhakar, *Socio-Economic Development of Jammu and Kashmir*, Jammu: Jay Kay Book House, 1988.

Hashmatullah, Khan Lakhnavi Moulvi, *Tarikh-i-Jammu wa Riyasat-hai-Maftuha-i-Maharaja Gulab Singh*, Lucknow: Tegh Bahadur Press, 1939.

Hassan, Mohibul, *Kashmir under Sultans*, Calcutta: Iran Society, 1959.

Hassan, Tazkir-i-Awalia, *Kashmir*, Srinagar: Noor Mohammad and Sons, translation by Molvi Abdul Kadir Spori, 1960.

Heber, A.R. and M.H. Heber, *Himalayan Tibet and Ladakh*, New Delhi: ESS Publications, 1978.

Hedin Swen, *Trans Himalaya*, London: Mac Millan & Co., 1913.

Herodotus, *History*, Oxford, 1913-14.

Hindu Marriage Act 1955.

Hughes, Thomas Patrick, *Dictionary of Islam*, New Delhi: Cosmo Publications, 1977.

Iqbal, S.M. and K.L. Nirash (eds), *The Culture of Kashmir*, New Delhi: Marwah Publications, 1978.

Jahangir, Emperor, *Tuzuk-i-Jahangiri*, 2 vols, English translation by A. Rogers and H. Beveridge, London, 1909-14.

John Bray, 'A History of Moravian Church in India', *The Himalayan Mission*, 1985.

Joldan, F., *Harvest Festival of Buddhist & Dards of Ladakh*, Srinagar: Kapoor Bros., 1985.

Jonaraja, Pandit, *Rajatarangini*, Calcutta and Bombay editions, 1835 and 1875; English trans. by J.C. Dutt under the title of *The Kings of Kashmir*, Vol. III, Calcutta, 1935; Delhi: Gyan Publishing House, rpt 1986.

Joshi, Manoj, 'The Mori Massage : Silver Lining in Kashmir's Cloud', *The Times of India*, New Delhi, 10 June 2002.

———, 'Vision Kashmir : Towards an Autonomy of the Mind', *The Times of India*, New Delhi, 28 October 2002.

Kalhana, Pandit, *Rajatarangini*, see Stein.

Kaul, Arun, 'Kesar : The Cultural Geography of Kashmir', in Geeti Sen and Ashis Banerjee (eds), *The Human Landscape*, New Delhi: Orient Longman and India International Centre, 2001.

Khajuria, Hardev Singh, *The Panjabi Lok Sahit*, Amritsar: New Age Centre, 1987.

Khan, Jamal Ahmad, 'Kashmiriat : An Ethos in Peril', *The Times of India*, New Delhi, 26 June 2001.

Khan, Mohammad, *History of Kashmir 1847-1947*, Srinagar: Amir, 1958.

Khan, M. Ishaq, *Kashmir's Tansition to Islam: The Role of Muslim Rishis*; New Delhi: Manohar, 1997.

Khemendra, Pandit, *Lokaprakasa*, English translation of some extracts by Dr. A. Weber, Indische Studien XVIII, 1898.

———, *Dasavatara Carita*, edited by Durga Prasad and N.S.P. Parab, Bombay, 1891.

———, *Desopadesa, Narmamala*, edited by Madhusudan Kaul, Poona: Kashmir Series of Texts and Studies, 1923.

———, *Samayamatraka*, edited by Durga Prasad and N.S.P. Parab, Bombay, 1925.

Kilam, Jia Lal, *A History of Kashmiri Pandits*, Srinagar: Gandhi Memorial College, rpt 1955.

Knight, E.F., *Where Three Empires Meet*, London, 1895.

Kumari, Ved (Dr.), *Nilamata Purana,* translation, Vol.1, Srinagar: Jammu and Kashmir Academy of Culture, 1968.

Lawrence, W.R., *The Valley of Kashmir*, Srinagar: Kesar Publishers, rpt 1967, London: Oxford University Press, 1895.

———, *Provincial Gazetteer of Kashmir and Jammu*, New Delhi: Rima Publishing House, rpt 1985.

———, *The India We Served*, London: Cassell & Co. Ltd., 1928.

Lidhoo, M.L., *Kashmir Tribals*, Srinagar: Minakshi Publishers, 1987.

Madan, T.N., *Family and Kinship: A Study of Pandits of Rural Kashmir*, Bombay: Asia Publishing House, 1965.

———, 'Religious Ideology in a Plural Society: The Muslim and Hindu of Kashmir', in *Contribution to Indian Sociology*, New Series, No. VI, 1973.

———, 'The Social Construction of Cultural Identities in Rural Kashmir', in T.N. Madan (ed), *Muslim Communities of South Asia: Culture, Society and Power*, New Delhi: Manohar, 1995.

———, 'Meaning of Kashmiriyat: Cultural Means and Political Ends', *The Times of India*, 4 June 1994.

Maiti, S., 'Ethnography: Structure and Process among the Bakarwals', Dehradun: Anthropological Survey of India, 1982 (unpublished).

Mann, R.S., *The Ladakhi: A Study in Ethnography and Change*, Calcutta: Anthropological Survey of India, 1986.

Manzoor, Fazili, *Kashmir Government and Politics*, Srinagar: Gulshan Publishers, 1982.

McKim Marriot, 'Little Community in an Indigenous Civilisation', *Village India,* edited by Mckim Marriot, Chicago: Chicago University Press, 1955.

Miskin, Haji Mohi-ud-Din, *Tarikh-i-Kabir-i-Kashmir*, Amritsar, AH 1322.

Moorcroft, William and G. Trebeck, *Travels in the Himalayan Province of Hindustan and the Punjab, Ladakh and Kashmir*, 2 vols. (1819-35), illustrated and edited by H.H. Wilson, London: John Murray, 1841.

Moulvi, Hasan Shah, *Tarikh-i-Hasan*, 4 vols, Srinagar: Research Library, Urdu translation of Vol. III (Political) by Moulvi Mohammad Ibrahim, Srinagar.

Munshi, Ganeshlal, *Siyahat-i-Kashmir*, March-June 1846; English translation by Vidyasagar Suri (The Punjab Govt. Record Office Publication), Simla, 1955.

Nabha, Kahan Singh, *Mahan Kosh*, Patiala: Bhasha Vibhag, 1981.

Narain, A.K., *The Indo-Greeks*, Delhi : Oxford University Press, rpt 1980.

Nizam-ud-Din, Ahmad, *Tabaqat-i-Akbari*, 3 vols, Calcutta: Bibliotheca Indica, 1927-36, Lucknow edn,1920.

Pamdhe, M.K., *Bonded Labour in India*, Calcutta: Indian Book Exchange, 1976.

Pandita, K.N., *A Chronicle of Mediaeval Kashmir*, Calcutta, 1984.

———, *Ladakh: Life and Culture*, Srinagar: Centre of Central Asian Studies, University of Kashmir, 1986.

Panini, *Ashtadhyayi.*

Parmer, R.K., *A History of Sikh Rule in Kashmir (1819-46)*, Srinagar, 1977.

Pathik, Jyoteeshwar, *Cultural Heritage of the Dogras*, New Delhi : Light & Life Publishers, 1980.

Przyluski, J., 1890, *Ancient People of the Punjab: The Audumbaras and the Salavas*, New Delhi: Sagar Publications, rpt 1971.

Punjabi, Riyaz, 'Kashmiriyat : The Mystique of an Ethnicity, *India International Centre Quarterly*, Vol. 17, No. 2, 1990, pp. 101-16.

Puri, Balraj, 'Major Identities of Jammu and Kashmir State', *India International Centre Quarterly*, Vol. 1, No. 28, 2001, pp. 69-79.

———, 'Kashmiriyat: The Vitality of Kashmiri Identities' (mimeo).

Raina, A.N., *Geography of Jammu and Kashmir*, New Delhi: National Book Trust, 1971.

Raza, Moonis, et al., *The Valley of Kashmir: A Geographical Interpretation*, New Delhi: Vikas Publishing House, 1978.

Regional Autonomy Committee Report, Jammu, 13 April 1999.

Rizvi, Janet, *Ladakh: Crossroads of High Asia*, New Delhi: Oxford University Press, 1983.

Rose, H.A. (compiled), *A Glossary of the Tribes and Castes of the Punjab and N.W. Frontier Province*, Based on the *Census Report for the Punjab 1883*, by Sir Denzil Ibbetson and the *Census Report for the Punjab 1892*, by Sir Edward Maclagan, New Delhi: Amar Prakashan, rpt 1980.

Russell, R.V. and Hiralal, *The Tribes and Castes of the Central Province of India*; Vol. IV, New Delhi: Cosmo Publications, 1975.

Sanyal, Shanta, *The Boats and Boatsman of Kashmir*, New Delhi: Sagar Publications, 1979.

Sarkar, R., V. Sarkar and M.K. Raha, 'The Gujjars and Their Society', in P.K. Misra and K.C. Malhotra (eds), *Nomads in India*, Calcutta: Anthropological Survey of India, 1982.

Shali, S.L., *Kashmir: History and Archaeology through the Ages*, New Delhi, 1993.

Shant, Tara Singh, *Sant Rattan Mala* (Punjabi), Jammu: Gurmat Sahit Prakashan, Digiana Ashram, 1973.

Sharma, D.C., *Kashmir Under Sikhs*, New Delhi: Seema Publication, 1983.

Sherring, M.A., *Hindu Tribes and Castes*, Vol. I, New Delhi: Cosmo Publications, rpt 1974.

Singh, Budh (Giani), *Gunjhe Hue Punch*, Lahore: Kirpa Singh Press, 1984.

Soodan, Bhupender Singh, *Poonch Di Lokdhara* (Punjabi), Amritsar: Ravi Sahit Prakashan, 1986.

Spian, James W., *The Pathan Border Land*, London, 1763.

Srivara, Pandit, *Rajatarangini* (Sanskrit), English translation by Y.C. Dutt as *The Kings of Kashmir*, Vol. III, Calcutta, 1935.

Stein, M.A., *Kalhan's Rajtarangini* (Eng. tr.), 2 vols, London: West Minister, 1900; rpt, New Delhi: Motilal, 1962.

Sufi, G.M.D., *Kashmir, Being a History of Kashmir from the Earliest Times to our own*, 2 vols, Lahore: University of Lahore, 1948-9; rpt, New Delhi, Light & Life Publishers, 1974.

———, *Kashmir*, New Delhi: Light & Life Publishers, Vols I and II, 1974.

———, *Islamic Culture in Kashmir*, New Delhi, 1979.

Sufi, Mohi-ud-Din, *Jammu wa Kashmir maen Urdu Suhafat*, Srinagar, 1973.

Sumi, Tokan, D. Oki Kassato and Hassnain Fida M., *Ladakh: The Moonland*, New Delhi: Light & Life Publishers, 1975.

Urban Environmental Engineering Department, Govt. of Jammu & Kashmir. Project Report on Integral Development of Dal Lake, Srinagar, 1982.

Vigne, G.T., *Travels in Kashmir*, Ladakh, Iskardo, Countries Adjoining the Mountain-Courses of the Indus and the Himalaya, North of the Punjab, 2 vols, London: Henry Colburn, 1842.

Vogel, J. Ph. and J. Hutchison, *History of Punjab Hill States*, Calcutta: Govt. Press, 1934.

Wahid, Siddiq, 'Ladakh: Political Convergence and Human Geography', in Geeti Sen and Ashis Banerjee (eds), *The Human Landscape*, New Delhi: Orient Longman and India International Centre, 2001.

JAMMU AND KAŞHMIR
COMMUNITIES STUDIED
UNDER PEOPLE OF INDIA PROJECT

INDEX

Region	Sl. No. of Communities Studied
Jammu	9 Barwala, 10 Basith, 11 Batwal, 14 Bhagat, 16 Bhat (Muslim), 17 Bhojru, 23 Charak, 24 Charji, 27 Chib, 28 Chibali, 29 Chhimba/Chimbe, 31 Chuhra/Chuhre, 37 Dholwala, 38 Dhyar, 39 Dogra, 40 Dogra Brahman, 41 Dogra Jheer, 42 Dogra Muslim, 44 Domal, 45 Dosali, 46 Dum, 47 Gaddi, 52 Gardi, 55 Gujarati Brahman, 57 Gumar, 59 Jain, 60 Jangam, 61 Jaral, 62 Jat, 63 Jogi, 65 Katoch, 67 Khatri, 72 Mahajan, 74 Manhas, 76 Megh, 77 Mochi/Chamar, 78 Mohyal Brahman, 81 Mughal, 82 Nagvanshi, 89 Perne, 91 Punchi Sikh, 93 Rattal, 95 Salaria, 97 Sansi, 99 Saryara, 100 Sen, 103 Sikligar, 104 Sochi, 107 Tarkhan
Kashmir	1 Afghan, 3 Baba, 4 Bafanda, 5 Bajigar, 8 Banduk Khar, 13 Beg, 15 Bhand, 19 Bomba, 20 Botraja, 25 Cheintz, 26 Chhan, 30 Chopan, 32 Dandel, 33 Dar, 34 Desil, 35 Dhamali Faqir/Faqir, 36 Dhobi, 48 Galwan, 49 Ganai, 50 Ganz, 53 Gorkan, 54 Gujjar, 56 Gujri, 58 Hanji, 64 Kashmiri Pandit, 66 Kavoj, 68 Kraal, 69 Kul Faqir/Faqir, 70 Lohar, 71 Lone, 73 Malik, 75 Manjygur, 83 Nalband, 84 Namdagur, 85 Naqqash, 86 Navid/Hajjam, 87 Panyach, 88 Para, 90 Pohul, 92 Rather, 94 Saiyid, 96 Sangtarash, 98 Sanur, 101 Setch/Ses, 102 Shaksaz, 105 Sofi, 106 Tantrey, 108 Teli, 109 Wani, 110 Watal, 111 Waza
Ladakh	2 Argon, 6 Bakarwal, 7 Balti, 12 Beda, 18 Bodh, 21 Broqpa, 22 Champa, 43 Dokhpa, 51 Gara, 79 Mon, 80 Moravian

Not to scale

By D.S. Hooda

JAMMU AND KASHMIR –
ECO-CULTURAL ZONES

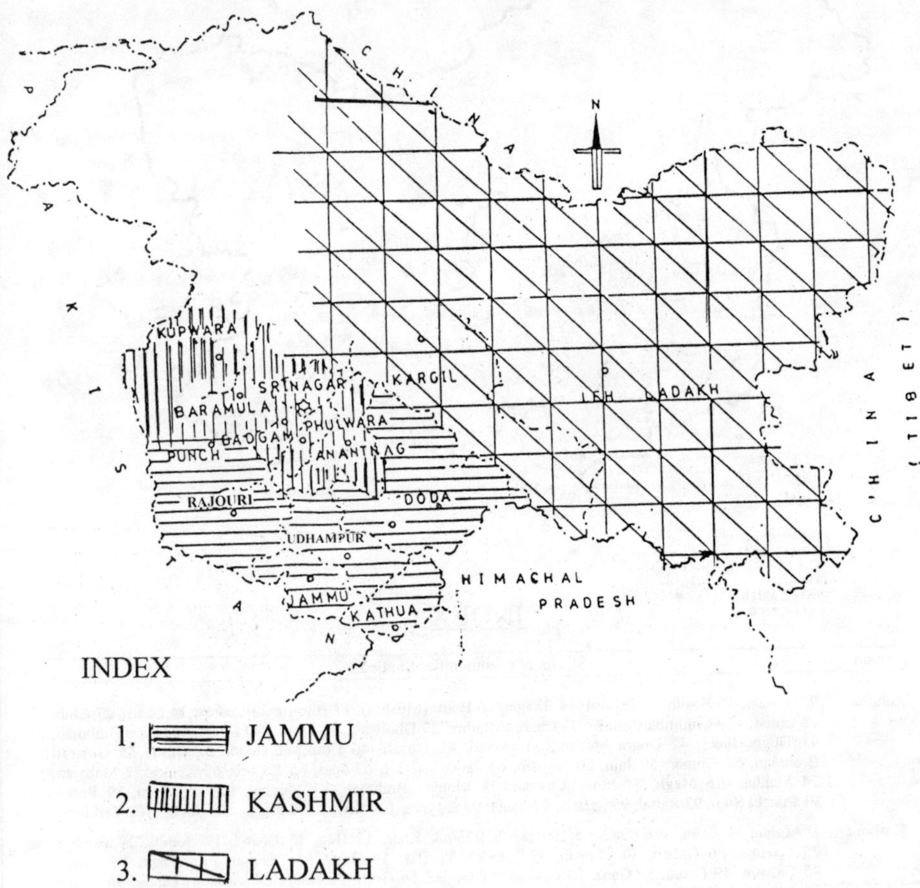

INDEX

1. JAMMU
2. KASHMIR
3. LADAKH

Not to scale

By D.S. HOODA

INDEX